Time Out
New York

Penguin Books

PENGUIN BOOKS

Published by the Penguin Group
Penguin Books Ltd, 27 Wrights Lane, London W8 5TZ, England
Penguin Books USA Inc., 375 Hudson Street, New York, New York 10014, USA
Penguin Books Australia Ltd, Ringwood, Victoria, Australia
Penguin Books Canada Ltd, 10 Alcorn Avenue, Toronto, Ontario, Canada M4V 3B2
Penguin Books (NZ) Ltd, 182-190 Wairau Road, Auckland 10, New Zealand

Penguin Books Ltd, Registered Offices: Harmondsworth, Middlesex, England

First published 1990
Second edition 1992
Third edition 1994
Fourth edition 1996
Fifth edition 1997
Sixth edition 1998
Seventh edition 1999
10 9 8 7 6 5 4 3 2 1

Copyright © Time Out Group Ltd, 1990, 1992, 1994, 1996, 1997, 1998, 1999
All rights reserved

Color reprographics by Precise Litho, 34–35 Great Sutton Street, London EC1
Mono reprographics printed and bound by William Clowes Ltd, Beccles, Suffolk NR34 9QE

*View finder: Sightseeing in New York happens everywhere—**Annex Antiques & Flea
Market** shoppers can't miss the **Empire State Building** while searching for bargain items.*

Edited and designed by

Time Out New York Guides
627 Broadway, seventh floor
New York, NY 10012
Tel: 212-539-4444
Fax:212-253-1174
E-mail: guides@timeoutny.com

Editor Shawn Dahl
Art Director Erin Wade
Assistant Editor Anna Kirtiklis
Editorial Intern Jennifer O'Keefe
Copy Editors Ann Abel, Paschal Fowlkes, Ian Landau, James Lochart, Karen Petroski, Gretchen Sidu
Index Robert Warren; Carrie Smith

With

Time Out New York
E-mail: letters@timeoutny.com
Internet: www.timeoutny.com

President/Editor-in-Chief Cyndi Stivers
Executive Editor Joe Angio
Art Director Ron de la Peña
Production Director Ayad Sinawi **Systems Manager** Shambo Pfaff **Production Manager** Carl Kelsch
Digital Operator Ryan Dunlavey

Publisher Alison Tocci
Advertising Manager Roger Gonzalez **Senior Advertising Account Managers** Dan Kenefick, Jim Lally, Anne Perton
Advertising Account Managers Matthew Bianciniello, Janine Brier, Julie Fisher, Ridwana Lloyd-Bey,
Aisling McDonagh, Lauren Miller, Tony Monteleone
North American Guides Ad Director Liz Howell
Advertising Production Manager Andy Gersten **Advertising Production Coordinator** Aja Harris
Financial Director Daniel P. Reilly

For

Time Out Guides Ltd
Universal House
251 Tottenham Court Road
London W1P 0AB
Tel: 44(0)171 813 3000
Fax:44(0)171 813 6001
E-mail: guides@timeout.com
Internet: www.timeout.com

Editorial Director Peter Fiennes
Art Director John Oakey
Group Advertising Director Lesley Gill **Sales Director** Mark Phillips

Publisher Tony Elliott **Managing Director** Mike Hardwick **Financial Director** Kevin Ellis
Marketing Director Gillian Auld **General Manager** Nichola Coulthard **Production Manager** Mark Lamond

Features in this guide were written and researched by

Welcome to New York Shawn Dahl **History** Robert Kolker **Architecture** Shawn Dahl **New York by Season** Greg Emmanuel
Downtown, Midtown Ian Landau **Uptown** Lambeth Hochwald **Outer Boroughs** Margaret Daly **Accommodations** Anna Kirtiklis,
Jennifer O'Keefe **Shopping & Services** Milena Damjanov, Kristina Richards **Restaurants, Cafés & Bars** Adam Rapoport, Salma
Abdelnour **Art Galleries** Alex Neel **Books & Poetry** Anna Kirtiklis, Jennifer O'Keefe **Cabaret & Comedy** Greg Emmanuel, H. Scott
Jolley **Clubs** Adam Goldstone **Dance** Gia Kourlas **Film & TV** Nicole Keeter **Gay & Lesbian** Erik Jackson **Kids' Stuff** Barbara
Aria **Museums** Greg Emmanuel, Alex Neel **Music** Gail O'Hara, Rob Kemp, K. Leander Williams, Smith Galtney, Susan Jackson
Sports & Fitness Brett Martin, Jennifer O'Keefe **Theater** Erik Jackson **Trips Out of Town** Emily Stone **Directory** Anna Kirtiklis

Photographs by Alys Tomlinson

Additional photographs courtesy of Macy's, 9; Joseph Barna/Heritage of Pride, 10 (top); Richard L. Cummings for Outsider
Art Fair 13 (top), Jefferson Siebert/Washington Square Music Festival, 13 (bottom); Steve Rossi/Agence, 14; Frank DeSisto,
15; Detroit Publishing Company/Library of Congress, 17, 18, 22, 24; Associated Press/Jeffrey Pattit, 25; Joseph Reyes/Office
of the Mayor, 27; Natural History Museum, 30; Vicky Donner/NYC Parks and Recreation, 36; Pierpont Morgan Library, 59; Dan
Perdue/Carnegie Hall, 64; David Heald/Solomon R. Guggenheim Museum, 67; Royalton, 95; Habitat, 96; Bouley Bakery, 171;
Magdalena Caris, 187; Lombard Freid Fine Arts, 191; Apex Art, 197; Nancy Compton/92nd Street Y, 202; Casey Cronin/NYPL
Center for Humanities, 203; Amanda Green, 204; A. Maroule, 205; Yola Monakhov, 209; Robert Whitman/Pilobolus Dance
Theater, 217; Danielle Freedman/New York City Ballet, 218; Joseph Barna/Heritage of Pride, 229; Wildlife Conservation
Society, 241; A. A. Murphy/Metropolitan Museum of Art, 243 (bottom); Museum of American Folk Art, 244; Japan Society, 245;
John Berens/Isamu Noguchi Museum, 246; Fashion Institute of Technology, 250; Museum for African Art, 252; Josef
Astor/EOS Orchestra, 266; Stephanie Berger/Lincoln Center for the Performing Arts, 269; Peter Serling, 270; New York
Yankees, 273; Bowlmor, 278; Joan Marcus/Disney, 283, 286; Atlantic City Convention & Visitors Authority, 291; Howe
Caverns, 295; John Hill/Historic Hudson Valley, 299; Photodisc, 329.

Maps by JS Graphics, Hill View Cottage, 17 Beadles Lane, Old Oxted, Surrey RH8 9JG; maps on pages 343–346 reproduced
by kind permission of the Metropolitan Transportation Authority.

Contents

*Battery charge: Energize yourself at the riverside environs of **Battery Park**.*

About the Guide

The *Time Out New York Guide* is one of an expanding series of city guides that includes *London, Paris, Amsterdam, Rome, Prague, Vienna, Tokyo, Boston, San Francisco, Los Angeles, Miami* and *Washington, D.C.* This seventh edition of the *Time Out New York Guide* has been thoroughly updated by the staff of the weekly *Time Out New York* magazine. *TONY* has been "the obsessive guide to impulsive entertainment" for all inhabitants of the city (and a few passers-by) for four years. Our writers aim to provide you with all the information you'll need to take on the world's most exciting city—and win. Some chapters have been rewritten from scratch, all have been thoroughly revised and new features have been added. Along with a series of color maps of Manhattan and other areas, a New York City Subway map covering all five boroughs has also been included.

CHECKED AND CORRECT

We've tried to make this book as useful as possible. Addresses, telephone numbers, transportation tips, opening times, admission prices and credit card information are all included in our listings. We've given up-to-date details on facilities, services and events, all checked and correct at press time. However, owners and managers can—and often do—change their policies. It's always best to call and check the when, where and how much.

The prices we've listed should be treated as guidelines, not gospel. Fluctuating exchange rates and inflation can cause prices, especially in stores and restaurants, to change overnight. If you find things altered beyond recognition, ask why—and then write to let us know. We aim to give the best and most up-to-date advice, so we always appreciate feedback.

CREDIT CARDS

The following abbreviations have been used for credit cards in the listings throughout the guide: **AmEx**, American Express; **DC**, Diners' Club; **Disc**, Discover; **JCB**, JCB Credit Cards; **MC**, Mastercard (Access); **V**, Visa (Barclaycard). Nearly all shops, restaurants and attractions accept United States–dollar traveler's checks issued by a major financial institution (such as American Express).

There's an online version of this guide, together with weekly events listings for New York and other international cities at www.timeout.com.

TELEPHONE NUMBERS

All telephone numbers in this guide are written as dialed from the United States. As of October 1, 1999, all New York City telephone numbers require 11 digits (1 + area code + local number) for dialing, even if you're calling from the same area code. The area codes for Manhattan are 212 and 646; Brooklyn, Queens, Staten Island and the Bronx are 718 and 347; generally (but not always) 917 is reserved for cellular phones and pagers. Numbers preceded by 800, 877 and 888 are free of charge when dialed anywhere in the U.S. When numbers are listed as letters (e.g. 800-AIR-RIDE) for easy recall, dial the corresponding numbers on the telephone keypad.

THINGS YOU SHOULD KNOW

While navigating through this guide and the city, there are a few facts you should know. Throughout the book, we have bold-faced information (place or restaurant names, for example) that is particularly important or referred to elsewhere in the guide. New York City law requires that all facilities constructed after 1987 provide complete disabled access, including restrooms and entrances/exits. In 1990, the American Disabilities Act made the same requirements federal law. In the wake of this legislation, many owners of older buildings have voluntarily added disabled-access features. Due to the widespread compliance, we have not specifically noted the availability of disabled facilities in our listings. However, it's a good idea to call ahead and check. (For additional information on disabled access, *see chapter* **Directory**.)

The 1995 NYC Smoke-Free Air Act makes it illegal to smoke in virtually all public places, including subways, movie theaters and most restaurants—even if there isn't a no-smoking sign displayed. Exceptions are bars and restaurants with fewer than 35 indoor seats, although large restaurants can have separate regulated smoking areas. Smokers can be fined at least $100 for a violation, so be sure to ask before you light up.

YOU TELL US

The information we give is based on the editorial judgment of our writers. No organization has been included because it has advertised in our publications. We hope you enjoy the *Time Out New York Guide*, but please let us know if you don't. We welcome tips for places that you think we should include in future editions as well as criticism of our choices. There's a reader's report card at the back of this book.

Heart attack: Make your presents felt with a genuine I♥NY gift.

Welcome to New York

Welcome to New York

Take a deep breath and get ready for an adventure of a lifetime—New York City packs an awful lot into a little space

On a bright day, the towers of New York glisten in the distance like some lost city of legend. If you didn't peer down at them from your plane, you'll catch glimpses of them on your way in from the airport. When you finally reach the river crossings and get your first close-up look at the island of Manhattan—a slender capsule of land covered by inconceivable tons of steel, glass and concrete—the sight is invariably breathtaking.

On your first day out, you might wend your way up from the skyscraper canyons of Wall Street (where the nearby Staten Island Ferry and the World Trade Center offer stunning views) to Chinatown or Little Italy for lunch. Then head west to do some Soho shopping or cross East Houston Street to search for some East Village spunk. A few blocks west from there brings you to the classic bohemia of Greenwich Village and, farther up, the gallery district of Chelsea. If your feet can stand to keep walking, it's just minutes to the hubbub of Times Square. If you've gone this far, you might as well keep trekking north so you can cool it in the great expanse of Central Park. And this is only Manhattan; you still have four more boroughs to explore. Believe it or not, an excursion like this can be done in one day! But

*Free expression: Who needs canvas? **Graffiti** artists show their stuff on any surface.*

*Between a rock and a wet place: A river runs through Brooklyn's **Prospect Park**.*

unless you're feeling superhuman, don't try to cover more than three neighborhoods per day.

A NEW YORK MINUTE

Within these pages, you'll find a plethora of places, information and tips that will help you plan your trip. If you've got only a New York minute, quickly turn to the chapter **Key Sights** to make up your hit list. For a more in-depth feel of city life, take one of the sightseeing excursions in the section **New York by Neighborhood**. And in case you dozed off in school, you can brush up on your names and dates by reading the **History** chapter (there's a cheat sheet, too; *see* **Those were the days**, *page 20*).

New York offers more—and a wider range of—entertainment and cultural activities than almost anywhere on Earth. On any given day, you can start by checking out the latest exhibit in one of the city's world-class museums or galleries. Follow that by hearing a renowned author reading from his or her latest work at an independent bookstore. After lunch, enjoy one of the numerous (especially in summer) free classical music recitals. Cineasts will find a vast array of films—blockbusters, foreign classics or edgy indies—playing in the scores of theaters and film societies. Evening? Take your pick: The world's best in dance, rock, jazz, opera, cabaret and comedy occupy New York's stages every night of the week. And if you're still not tired, you can dance till dawn in the city's after-hours clubs.

*Pet project: Dog fanciers gather in Greenwich Village's **Washington Square Park**.*

A New York trip provides more information and stimulation per second than a vacation anywhere else. Don't be put off by that velocity, though. Underneath the surface roughness, New York is genuinely welcoming. Although it was founded as a trading post, New York's predominant commodity has always been people—especially the "tired, poor, huddled masses" lured by the Statue of Liberty and fired with the drive to begin their lives anew.

Orientation express

To learn your way around, hit the road, Jack—on foot, that is

As New Yorkers will tell you, the best way to master Manhattan is on foot. The island is small (13.4 miles [21.5 km] long by 2.3 miles [3.7 km] wide and, above 14th Street, logically laid out in a grid, which makes getting lost almost impossible. The avenues run north to south and are numbered from east to west (Lexington, Park and Madison are wedged between Third and Fifth). Beginning with 1st Street, just north of Houston (*HOW-stun*) Street, numbered streets run perpendicular to the avenues, with Fifth Avenue acting as the dividing line between East and West. On cross streets, the lower the building number, the closer it is to this equator. The major oddity is Broadway, an old Indian trail that runs north to south, then cuts diagonally downtown from the West to the East Side. Downtown streets are more confusing, since they were built before the grid pattern was established (*see* **Maps**, *page 329 for help*).

Those seeking a faster pace can run, bike or inline skate, assuming they have the confidence and experience needed. To rent or buy a set of wheels, *see chapters* **Shopping & Services** *and* **Sports & Fitness**. **Transportation Alternatives** (212-628-3311), an organization that promotes city cycling and safe streets, is an excellent source of information.

If you do find yourself lost, don't be put off by New Yorkers' (often justified) reputation for gruffness; it's okay to ask for directions. The trick is to deliver your question within earshot of at least two people. One of them may be completely wrong, but the inevitable debate (sometimes involving the entire bus, subway car or street corner) will ensure that the issue is hammered out sufficiently for you to know where to go. The arguments sparked by your innocent inquiry may well continue long after you've left.

IMPORTS, EXPORTS...

The first Europeans arrived here 400 years ago to hunt and trade fur. New York today is a world gumbo like never before. In a city where half of the residents are either immigrants or the children of immigrants, ethnic communities thrive. Current trends show increasing arrivals from the Far East, the Indian subcontinent and Eastern Europe. South-Asian Americans—from India, Pakistan and Bangladesh—are among the most visible and industrious immigrants. New York's Chinese population long ago spilled over the boundaries of its traditional enclave in lower Manhattan and now includes satellite Chinatowns in Brooklyn and Queens. And since the collapse of Communism, Russian immigrants have settled in Brooklyn's Brighton Beach.

Newcomers don't just arrive from overseas. The city continues to attract a relentless stream of disaffected refugees from middle America: kids from the heartland blinded by the sheer excess and possibility of the place. Lower Manhattan, especially, teems with young hopefuls and trendoids. One prototypical success story is Beck Hanson, who hopped off a bus from sunny Southern California, made a beeline for the dark, dank Lower East Side, dropped his last name and emerged a short time later as a multiplatinum-selling musician. All it took was two turntables and a microphone.

Recently, more sophisticated technology has lured other would-be stars to New York's "Silicon Alley": young cutting-edge cyberheads who hope to make their mark on the digital frontier. As the longtime center of American banking, law, publishing, fashion, advertising and art, New York continues to draw the best and brightest in each of those fields, too.

TOWN WITHOUT PITY

For all the gravy at the top, New York still has more unemployed people than any other Ameri-

So good they named it twice

The sobriquets for this town range from Gotham to Fun City

"The Naked City," "the City that never sleeps," "Babylon on the Hudson"—New York, New York (for city and state) has been named many more times than twice.

The first name, **Mannahatta**, or Manhattan, was given to the sheltered, hilly island by its original tenants, the Munsee Indians. Centuries later, Brooklyn-born poet Walt Whitman praised the name: " 'Mannahatta, the place encircled by many swift tides and sparkling waters.' How fit a name for America's great democratic island city!"

When the first Dutch settlers arrived in 1624, the name became **New Amsterdam**, in honor of the Netherlands capital. The settlement wasn't called **New York** until August 1664, when four British warships were welcomed into town and Captain Richard Nicolls signified British rule by honoring Charles II's brother, the Duke of York.

Besides its official appellations, New York has had many names in fact, fiction and fantasy. **Gotham**, its comic-book alter ego (the city Batman inhabits), is a name taken from a village near Nottingham famous for its insane residents (Gotham actually means "goat town"). Washington Irving coined the nickname in 1807 in a satirical story. Irving noticed, as many have since, that New Yorkers work hard to preserve an impressive level of madness.

The satire is subtle, since the original Gothamites were only feigning insanity in order to avoid King John's taxation.

The **Big Apple**, meaning "the pinnacle," was a phrase popularized around the 1920s. It was used by actors and musicians (especially jazz folk) to signify that performing in New York represented the height of success as well as monetary fortunes. In 1971, the nickname was given a boost when the city began using it to market itself to tourists, replacing the less successful 1960s campaign that christened New York **Fun City** (a moniker that was the subject of much derision).

Metropolis, alluding to the city of the future, was the title of Fritz Lang's 1926 film of the same name about a fascistic society that exploited its workers (against a backdrop of skyscrapers and flying cars). Metropolis was also used for Superman's hometown, a thinly veiled version of New York.

In the real future, as suburban communities sprawl over the naked countryside and the notion of a city center is killed by telecommuting, New Yorkers could find themselves living in a gigantic conurbation extending from Boston to Washington, D.C. William Gibson, who coined the term "cyberspace," has written about this scenario, giving New York surely the last name it will need—**the Sprawl**.

They'll take Manhattan: **Staten Island Ferry** *commuters sail across the harbor.*

can city, an inflation rate among the nation's highest and one of the lowest overall job-creation rates. In the midst of the boom, the income of middle-class New Yorkers who work outside banking and finance has barely kept pace with inflation—and a dizzying real-estate market.

The current mayor, Rudolph Giuliani, has presided over an astounding economic recovery: Tourism figures are higher than ever; crime is lower than anyone could have imagined; high-profile parts of town such as Soho and Times Square are noticeably cleaner; and increased film, theater and TV production has showcased New York's comeback to the nation and the world. His take-charge attitude hasn't won him friends everywhere, though.

Police relations with minority communities have soured in the wake of several highly publicized incidents of excessive force. Every year seems to bring a new high-profile accusation of brutality. In 1997, the vicious attack on Haitian immigrant Abner Louima shocked the nation; the primary accused officer, Justin A. Volpe, pleaded guilty during the 1999 trial to sexually assaulting Louima in the station house while he was under arrest. In February 1999, four white police officers from the city's special Street Crime Unit shot unarmed West African immigrant Amadou Diallo 41 times—and the grand jury voted to indict the officers.

THE BIG PICTURE

No other city could sustain such great highs and lows. Your visit here provides a full spectrum of possibilities—a chance to ride the subways and see Wall Street profiteers rubbing shoulders with welfare mothers. At the end of the day, however, everyone's equal. Stars of stage and screen wear sweatpants to the corner deli, just as your average schmo does, and no one seems to notice.

Some may feel that New York breeds anonymity—that you're just one more face in the crowd. Yet, that cloak of invisibility is ultimately liberating. Because you're an unknown, you're free to reinvent yourself. New Yorkers do it all the time: Just ask Josephine Esther Mentzer (Estée Lauder), Ralph Lifshitz (Ralph Lauren) or Allan Konigsberg (Woody Allen)—each of whom arrived to Manhattan from the outer boroughs to seek fame and fortune. The sense of possibility may be this amazing city's greatest appeal: After all, if you can make it here, you can make it anywhere.

New York by Season

Gotham's lineup of parades, festivals and other events will keep you busy and entertained at any time of year

As each season turns, one of New York's multiple personalities emerges. Winter's holiday parties and slushy traffic jams melt into the flowers and in-line skates of spring. Summer is hot, sweaty and slower, with garden restaurants, outdoor concerts and neighborhood fairs (not to mention air-conditioning) providing welcome relief from the sizzling streets. The pace picks up again in the fall, when New Yorkers enjoy the last of the sun's long rays and the beginning of the opera, dance and music seasons.

The festivals, parades and events listed below are held regularly. The New York Convention & Visitors Bureau has lots of details on seasonal events, including newer and smaller happenings that may not be described here. For more information on related events and locations, *see section* **Arts & Entertainment**. For other sources of entertainment news such as websites, *see chapter* **Directory A–Z**. All the sports seasons are detailed in the chapter **Sports & Fitness**; summer music events in the chapter **Music**; film festivals in **Film & TV**. Don't forget to confirm that an event is happening before you set out.

Spring

Whitney Biennial
Whitney Museum of American Art, 945 Madison Ave at 75th St (212-570-3600). Subway: 6 to 77th St. Late March–early June.
Every two years, the Whitney showcases what it deems to be the most important American art, generating much controversy in the process. The next show is in 2000.

St. Patrick's Day Parade
Fifth Ave between 44th and 86th Sts (212-484-1222) www.nycvisit.com. Mar 17.
New York becomes a sea of green for the annual Irish-American day of days, starting at 11am with the parade up Fifth Avenue and extending late into the night in bars all over the city.

Ringling Bros. and Barnum & Bailey Circus
Madison Square Garden, Seventh Ave at 32nd St (212-465-6741). Subway: A, C, E, 1, 2, 3, 9 to 34th St–Penn Station. Late March–early May.
The Barnum & Bailey half of this famous three-ring circus annexed the line "the Greatest Show on Earth" back in its

early days in New York City. Don't miss the free midnight parade of animals through the Queens-Midtown Tunnel and along 34th Street that traditionally opens and closes the show's run.

Easter Parade
Fifth Ave between 49th and 57th Sts (212-484-1222) www.nycvisit.com. Easter Sunday.
The annual Easter Parade kicks off at 11am. Try to get a spot around St. Patrick's Cathedral, which is the best viewing platform—but get there early.

New York Antiquarian Book Fair
Park Avenue Armory, Park Ave between 66th and 67th Sts (212-777-5218). Subway: 6 to 68th St. April.
More than 170 international booksellers exhibit rare books, maps, manuscripts and more.

New York International Auto Show
Jacob Javits Convention Center, Eleventh Ave between 34th and 39th Sts, main entrance at 36th St (800-282-3336). Subway: A, C, E to 34th St–Penn Station. April.
Each year, cars from the past, present and future are on display during this annual rite of spring.

New York City Ballet Spring Season
New York State Theater, 20 Lincoln Center Plaza, 65th St at Columbus Ave (212-870-5570). Subway: 1, 9 to 66th St–Lincoln Ctr. Late April–June.
The NYCB's spring season usually features a new ballet, in addition to repertory classics by Balanchine and Robbins, among others.

Bike New York: The Great Five Boro Bike Tour
Starts at Battery Park, finishes on Staten Island (212-932-0778). Early May.
Every year, thousands of cyclists take over the city for a 42-mile (68km) bike ride through the five boroughs. You'll feel like you're in the Tour de France—sort of.

You Gotta Have Park
Parks throughout the city (212-360-3456). May.
This is an annual celebration of New York's public spaces, with free events in the major parks of all five boroughs. It heralds the start of a busy schedule of concerts and other events in green places throughout the city.

Ninth Avenue International Food Festival
Ninth Ave between 37th and 57th Sts (212-581-7029). Subway: A, C, E, to 34th St–Penn Station. Mid-May.
A glorious mile of gluttony. Hundreds of stalls serve every type of food. Fabulously fattening.

I am the egg man: Humpty Dumpty floats by in **Macy's Thanksgiving Day Parade**.

*Witty, pretty and gay: Out-and-proud spectators watch the **Gay and Lesbian Pride Parade**.*

*Concrete jungle: Animals head across town for the **Ringling Bros. and Barnum & Bailey Circus**.*

Fleet Week
Sea, Air & Space Museum, USS Intrepid, Pier 86, 46th St at the Hudson River (212-245-2533, recorded info 212-245-0072). Subway: A, C, E to 42nd St–Penn Station. End of May.
The U.S. Navy visits New York, along with ships from other countries—with a sail past the Statue of Liberty, maneuvers, parachute drops, air displays and various ceremonies. During the week, you can visit some of the ships at Pier 86.

Lower East Side Festival of the Arts
Theater for the New City, 155 First Ave at 10th St (212-245-1109). Subway: L to First Ave, 6 to Astor Pl. Final weekend of May.
This annual arts festival and outdoor carnival celebrates the neighborhood that helped spawn the Beats, Method acting and Pop Art. It draws performances by more than 20 theatrical troupes and appearances by local celebrities.

Summer

Toyota Comedy Festival
Various locations (800-798-6968). Early to mid-June.
Hundreds of America's funniest men and women perform at 30 venues around the city. The information line operates from May to mid-June only.

Puerto Rican Day Parade
Fifth Ave between 44th and 86th Sts (212-484-1222, 718-401-0404) First Sun in June.
Featuring colorful floats and marching bands, this parade has become one of the city's busiest street celebrations.

Central Park SummerStage
Rumsey Playfield, Central Park at 72nd St (212-360-2777). Subway: 6 to 77th St. June–August.
Enjoy free weekend afternoon concerts featuring top international performers and a wide variety of music; there are a few benefit shows for which admission is charged. Some years, dance and spoken-word events are offered on weekday nights as well.

Metropolitan Opera Parks Concerts
Various locations (212-362-6000). June.
The Metropolitan Opera presents two different operas at open-air evening concerts in Central Park and other parks throughout the five boroughs and New Jersey. The performances are free. To get a good seat, you need to arrive hours early and be prepared to squabble.

Museum Mile Festival
Fifth Ave between 82nd and 104th Sts (212-606-2296). Second Tue in June.
Nine of New York's major museums hold an open-house festival. Crowds are attracted not only by the free admission but also by the highbrow street entertainment.

Gay and Lesbian Pride Parade
From Columbus Circle, along Fifth Ave to Christopher St (212-807-7433). Late June.
Every year, New York's gay and lesbian community parades through the streets of midtown to Greenwich Village to commemorate the Stonewall uprising of 1969. The celebrations have expanded into a full week, and in addition to a packed club schedule, there is an open-air dance party on the West Side piers. The event draws thousands of visitors to the city.

New York Jazz Festival
Various locations (212-219-3006). Early June.
More than 300 acts in ten different venues—including the Knitting Factory, one of the festival's sponsors—offer all kinds of jazz performances, from mainstream to acid, in this two-week festival. Note: The festival adopts the name

of its major corporate sponsor each year (in 1998, it was the Texaco Jazz Festival), so call to find out what it is currently being called.

Midsummer Night Swing
Lincoln Center Plaza, Broadway between 64th and 65th Sts (212-875-5766). Subway: 1, 9 to 66th St–Lincoln Ctr. Late June–July.
This popular outdoor series offers dancing under the stars Tuesday through Saturday evenings beside picturesque Lincoln Center. Each night is devoted to a different style, ranging from swing and salsa to tango and even square dancing. If you have two left feet, not to worry—evening performances are proceeded by free dance lessons.

New York Shakespeare Festival
Delacorte Theater, Central Park at 81st St (212-539-8750, 212-539-8500). Subway: B, C to 81st St; 6 to 77th St. Late June–late August.
The Shakespeare Festival is one of the highlights of a Manhattan summer, with big-name stars pulling on their tights for a whack at the Bard. There are two plays each year (one Shakespeare, one American classic), and tickets are free.

JVC Jazz Festival
Various locations (212-501-1390). Mid- to late June.
The direct descendant of the original Newport Jazz Festival, the first event of its kind ever held in the U.S., the JVC bash has become a New York institution, with concerts in most of the city's major venues and some smaller ones as well.

Bryant Park Free Summer Season
Sixth Ave at 42nd St (212-922-9393). Subway: B, D, F, Q, N, R, S, 1, 2, 3, 9, 7 to 42nd St. June–August.
This reclaimed park, a lunch time oasis for midtown's office population, is the site of a packed season of free classical music, jazz, dance and film. Best of all are the Monday-night open-air movies.

Mermaid Parade
From Steeplechase Park to Boardwalk at 8th St, Coney Island, Brooklyn (718-372-5159). Subway: B, D, F to Stillwell Ave. Saturday before summer solstice.
If your taste runs to the wild and free, don't miss Coney Island's annual showcase of bizarreness, consisting of elaborate floats, paraders dressed as sea creatures, kiddie beauty contests and other über-kitschy celebrations to kick off the summer.

Washington Square Music Festival
W 4th St at La Guardia Pl (212-431-1088). Subway: A, C, E, B, D, F, Q to W 4th St–Washington Sq. Tuesdays at 8pm in July and August.
This open-air concert season, featuring mainly chamber music, has been running in Greenwich Village for years.

Macy's Fireworks Display
East River (212-494-4495). Jul 4 at 9:15pm.
The highlight of Independence Day is this spectacular fireworks display. The FDR Drive between 14th and 51st Streets is the best viewing spot; it's closed to traffic for a few hours as $1 million worth of flashes light up the night. Another display is launched from the South Street Seaport.

New York Philharmonic Concerts
Various locations (212-875-5709). Late July–early August.
The New York Philharmonic presents a varied program, from Mozart to Weber, in many of New York's larger parks. The bugs are just part of the deal.

New York Renaissance Faire
Sterling Forest, Tuxedo, NY (914-351-5171). Travel: George Washington Bridge to Rte 4 West, then Rte 17 North to Exit 15A to Rte 17A; buses also available from Manhattan. Early August–late September.

U.S. holidays

A roster of red-letter days

Although most banks and government offices close on these major U.S. holidays (except Election Day), stores and restaurants are often open. If you are planning a trip around a holiday, be sure to call ahead to find out if there are special hours on these days.

New Year's Day January 1

Martin Luther King Jr. Day third Monday in January

Presidents' Day third Monday in February

Memorial Day last Monday in May

Independence Day July 4

Labor Day first Monday in September

Columbus Day second Monday in October

Election Day first Tuesday after first Monday in November

Veterans' Day November 11

Thanksgiving fourth Thursday in November

Christmas Day December 25

For those who prefer wild knights to those wild nights—the Ren Faire is *the* event. More than 500 costumed daredevils, artisans, horseback-riding jousters, live chess players and mud-pit enthusiasts liven up this annual festival.

Thursday Night Concert Series
Main Stage, South Street Seaport, South St at Fulton St (212-732-7678). Subway: J, M, R, 2, 3, 4, 5 to Fulton St. Memorial Day–Labor Day.
Free outdoor concerts—of all types of music—are held throughout the summer at the South Street Seaport. *See chapter **Downtown** for more information on the seaport.*

Summergarden
Museum of Modern Art, 11 W 53rd St between Fifth and Sixth Aves (212-708-9400). Subway: E, F to Fifth Ave. July–August.
Free classical concerts, organized with the Juilliard School, are presented in the museum's sculpture garden.

Celebrate Brooklyn! Performing Arts Festival
Prospect Park Bandshell, 9th St at Prospect Park West, Park Slope, Brooklyn (718-855-7882). Subway: F to Seventh Ave. July–August.
Nine weeks of free outdoor events—music, dance, film and theater—are presented in Brooklyn's answer to Central Park.

Mostly Mozart
Avery Fisher Hall, Lincoln Center, 65th St at Columbus Ave (212-875-5399). Subway: 1, 9 to 66 St–Lincoln Ctr. Late July–August.
For more than a quarter-century, the Mostly Mozart festival has mounted an intensive four-week schedule of performances of Mozart's work. There are also lectures and other side attractions.

Harlem Week
Throughout Harlem (212-862-8477). Subway: C, 2, 3 to 116th St. Early to mid-August.
The largest black and Latino festival in the world features music, film, dance, fashion, exhibitions and sports. The highlight is the street festival on Fifth Avenue between 125th and 135th Streets, which includes an international carnival of arts, entertainment and great food. Don't miss the jazz, gospel and R&B performances.

Hong Kong Dragon Boat Festival
The Lake at Flushing Meadows–Corona Park, Queens (718-539-8974). Subway: 7 to Main St–Flushing. Mid-August.
In this colorful event, teams from the New York area race traditional dragon boats—39-foot teakwood crafts with dragon heads at the bow and tails at the stern—in an effort to find a local champion.

U.S. Open
USTA National Tennis Center, Flushing, Queens (info and tickets 718-760-6200). Subway: 7 to Willets Point–Shea Stadium. Late August–early September.
The final Grand Slam event of the year, the U.S. Open is also one of the most entertaining tournaments on the international tennis circuit. Tickets are hard to come by, however.

Greenwich Village Jazz Festival
Throughout Greenwich Village (212-929-5149). Late August.
This ten-day festival brings together most of the Village's many jazz clubs and includes lectures and films. It culminates in a free concert in Washington Square Park.

West Indian Day Carnival
Eastern Pkwy from Utica Ave to Grand Army Plaza, Brooklyn (718-625-1515). Subway: 3, 4 to Utica Ave; 2 to Eastern Pkwy–Brooklyn Museum. Labor Day weekend.
This loud and energetic festival of Caribbean culture, with a parade of flamboyantly costumed marchers, offers a children's parade on Saturday and an even bigger celebration on Labor Day.

Richmond County Fair
Historic Richmond Town, 441 Clarke Ave between Richmond and Arthur Kill Rds, Staten Island (718-351-1611). Travel: Staten Island Ferry, then S74 bus. Labor Day.
This is an authentic county fair, just like in rural America, with arts and crafts and extra-large produce and strange agricultural competitions.

Wigstock
Pier 54 between 12th and 13th Sts (800-494-8497). Subway: L, to Eighth Ave; A, C, E, to 14th St. Labor Day weekend.
This event is a celebration of drag, glamour and artificial hair. Anyone who can muster some foundation and lipstick dresses up as a woman, and real girls had better be extra fierce to cope with the competition. Having outgrown its origins in the East Village's Tompkins Square Park, Wigstock has made its new home at Pier 54, on the Hudson River near the West Village.

*Outsider chance: Art lovers gamble on "naive" works at the popular **Outsider Art Fair**.*

*Orchestral maneuvers in the park: **Music festivals** play outside during the summer months.*

Fall

Feast of San Gennaro
Mulberry St from Houston to Worth Sts (212-484-1222)
www.nycvisit.com. Subway: J, M, N, R, Z, 6 to Canal St.
Third week in September.
Celebrations for the feast of the patron saint of Naples last
ten days, from noon to midnight daily, with fairground
booths, stalls and plenty of Italian food and wine.

Downtown Arts Festival
Various Soho locations (212-243-5050). Mid-September.
The former Soho Arts Festival has expanded from a September block party to a mammoth event of art exhibitions,
gallery tours and critical forums, as well as performance-art
happenings, experimental video shows and good old-fashioned readings.

Broadway on Broadway
43rd St at Broadway (212-768-1560). Subway: N, R, S,
1, 2, 3, 9, 7 to 42nd St–Times Sq. Mid-September.
For one day at least, Broadway is remarkably affordable, as
the season's newest productions offer a sneak (free!) peek at
their latest work right in the middle of Times Square.

Brooklyn BeerFest
Outside the Brooklyn Brewery, N 11th St between Berry
St and Wythe Ave, Williamsburg, Brooklyn (718-486-
7422). Subway: L to Bedford Ave. Mid-September.
Taste more than 100 beers from around the world at this
annual ale festival set outside the home of NYC's best local
brew. Industry insiders will be around to highlight the finer
points of hops and barley.

Atlantic Antic
Brooklyn Heights, Brooklyn (718-875-8993).
Subway: N, R to Court St; 2, 3, 4, 5 to Borough Hall.
Last Sun in September.
This multicultural street fair on Brooklyn's Atlantic Avenue
features live entertainment and waterfront art exhibitions.

New York Film Festival
Alice Tully Hall, Lincoln Center, 65th St and
Columbus Ave (212-875-5610). Subway: 1, 9 to 66th
St–Lincoln Ctr. Late September–early October.
One of the film world's most prestigious events, the festival
is a showcase for major directors from around the world.
Many U.S. and world premieres are on the schedule.

New York City Opera Season
New York State Theater, Lincoln Center, 65th
St and Columbus Ave (212-870-5570). Subway: 1, 9
to 66th St–Lincoln Ctr. September–November,
February–April.
Popular and classical operas, more daring but lesser-known
work and the occasional musical comedy all find a home here.

Columbus Day Parade
Fifth Ave between 44th and 86th Sts (212-484-1222)
www.nycvisit.com. Columbus Day.
To celebrate the first recorded sighting of America by Europeans, the whole country gets an Italian flavored holiday
(though not always a day off from work)—and the inevitable
parade up Fifth Avenue.

Halloween Parade
Starts from Broome to Spring Sts, up Sixth Ave to 23rd
St (475-3333, ext. 7787). Oct. 31, 7pm.
Anyone can participate in this parade (and about 25,000 do
every year); just wear a costume and line up at the beginning
of the route about an hour before with the rest of the fascinating characters.

New York City Marathon
Starts at the Staten Island side of the Verrazano-
Narrows Bridge (212-860-4455). Last Sun in October or
first Sun in November at 10:40am.
A crowd of 35,000 runners covers all five boroughs over a
26.2-mile (42km) course. The race finishes at Tavern on the
Green, in Central Park at West 67th Street.

Joggernauts: 35,000 runners race through the boroughs in the **New York City Marathon**.

Macy's Thanksgiving Day Parade

From Central Park West at 79th St to Macy's, Broadway at 34th St (212-494-4495). Thanksgiving Day at 9am.
Bring the kids to this one: It features enormous inflated cartoon-character balloons, elaborate floats and Santa Claus, who makes his way to Macy's department store, where he'll spend the next month in Santaland. Also, you can't miss the popular Inflation Eve—watch the big balloons take shape on 81st Street the night before.

Winter

The Nutcracker Suite

New York State Theater, Lincoln Center, 65th St at Columbus Ave (212-870-5570). Subway: 1, 9 to 66th St–Lincoln Ctr. November–December.
The New York City Ballet's performance of this famous work, assisted by students from the School of American Ballet, has become a much-loved Christmas tradition. *See chapter* **Dance.**

Christmas Tree Lighting Ceremony

Rockefeller Center, Fifth Ave between 49th and 50th Sts (212-484-1222) www.nycvisit.com. Subway: B, D, F, Q to 47–50th Sts–Rockefeller Ctr. Early December.
The giant tree in front of the GE Building is festooned with five miles of lights. The tree, the skaters on the rink in the sunken plaza and the shimmering statue of Prometheus make this the most enchanting Christmas spot in New York.

Messiah Sing-In

National Chorale Council (212-333-5333). Mid-December.
Around Christmas—usually a week before—21 conductors lead huge audiences (sometimes 3,000-strong) in a rehearsal and a performance of Handel's *Messiah.* You don't need any experience, and you can buy the score on-site. Location changes from year to year, so call for date, time and place.

Christmas Spectacular

Radio City Music Hall, 1260 Sixth Ave at 50th St (212-632-4000). Subway: B, D, F, Q to 47th–50th Sts–Rockefeller Ctr. November–early January.
This famous long-running show features the fabulous high-kicking Rockettes in a series of tableaux and musical numbers that exhaust the thematic possibilities of Christmas.

New Year's Eve Fireworks

Central Park (212-360-3456). Dec 31.
The best viewing points for a night of pyrotechnics are Central Park at 72nd Street, Tavern on the Green (Central Park West at 67th Street) and Fifth Avenue at 90th Street. The fun and festivities, including hot cider and food, start at 11:30pm.

New Year's Eve Ball Drop

Times Square (212-768-1560). Subway: N, R, S, 1, 2, 3, 9, 7 to 42nd St–Times Sq. Dec 31.
A traditional New York year ends and begins in Times Square, where a glittering ball encrusted with lights is hoisted above the crowd and dropped at midnight. A recent ball overhaul means the sphere now sports 180 75-watt bulbs and some 12,000 rhinestones. If teeming hordes of drunken revelers turn you on, by all means go. The surrounding streets are packed by 9pm.

Chinese New Year

Around Mott St, Chinatown (212-484-1222) www.nycvisit.com. Subway: J, M, Z, N, R, 6 to Canal St. First day of the full moon between Jan 21 and Feb 19.
The Chinese population of New York celebrates the new year in style, with dragon parades, performers and delicious food throughout Chinatown. Private fireworks have now been banned, so the celebrations don't have the bang they used to.

Navy zeal: Sailors wash ashore by the hundreds during **Fleet Week** *in late May.*

Winter Antiques Show

Seventh Regiment Armory, Park Ave at 67th St (718-292-7392). Subway: 6 to 68th St. Mid-January.
This is the most prestigious of New York's antiques fairs, with an eclectic selection of items ranging from ancient to Art Nouveau. The show's vast American collections come from all over the country. Sales benefit the East Side House Settlement.

Outsider Art Fair

The Puck Building, 295 Lafayette St at Houston St (212-777-5218). Subway: B, D, F, Q, N, R to Broadway–Lafayette St; 6 to Bleecker St. Late January.
A highlight of the annual art calendar, this three-day extravaganza draws crowds of buyers and browsers from all over the world. Its 35 dealers exhibit outsider, self-taught or visionary art in all media, at prices that range from $500 to $350,000. Have a ball.

Empire State Building Run-Up

350 Fifth Ave at 34th St (212-860-4455). Subway: B, D, F, Q, N, R to 34th St–Herald Sq. Early February.
The race starts in the lobby; runners speed up the 1,575 steps to the 86th floor. The average winning time is an astonishing 12 minutes.

The Art Show

Seventh Regiment Armory, Park Ave at 67th St (212-766-9200). Subway: 6 to 68th St. Late February.
Begun in 1988 and sponsored by the Art Dealers Association of America, this is the big daddy of New York art fairs. Exhibitors offer paintings, prints and sculptures dating from the 17th century to the present. Proceeds go to the Henry Street Settlement, a Lower East Side social-service agency.

History

In a nutshell, here's how New York City evolved from a sleepy settlement to a modern metropolis

THE PROSPECTORS

Before Manhattan ever lured wide-eyed visitors with awesome skyscrapers and street-corner spectacles—in fact, long before it was even called Manhattan—this lush, forested region offered the finest natural harbor on the East Coast. The island itself was well protected from the elements and provided access along a vast river to the agriculturally rich area to the west—in short, it was the greatest trading post Mother Nature ever provided. New York became a natural destination for immigrants seeking their fortunes. At every turn in the region's history, the buzzword was *commerce.*

The first starry-eyed European to get a glimpse of the island was not Christopher Columbus but Giovanni da Verrazano, a Florentine sailing under the French flag and searching for the fabled Northwest Passage to China. In 1524, he took refuge from a storm in what is now New York Harbor; later, he took a small boat into the Upper Bay, where he was greeted by the local Native Americans. Today, Verrazano is remembered by the graceful bridge that links Brooklyn and Staten Island and bears his name.

It would be 85 years before the next European arrived. Henry Hudson, who was employed by the Dutch East India Company, was also looking for the Northwest Passage. He sailed up the river later named for him as far as Fort Orange (today the state capital, Albany). Hudson's logbook relates that he encountered "friendly and polite people who had an abundance of provisions, skins, and furs of martens and foxes, and many other commodities, such as birds and fruit, even white and red grapes, and they traded amicably with the peoples."

LET'S MAKE A DEAL

In 1613, four years after Hudson's journey, a trading post—the beginning of a Dutch settlement—was established at Fort Orange. In 1621, Holland granted the Dutch West India Company a long-term trade and governing monopoly over New Netherland (and elsewhere). Soon the first Dutch settlers, about 30 families, arrived to the area. By 1626, when the first director general (or governor), Peter Minuit, took power, 300 Europeans lived on the tip of a certain 13-mile-long island called Manhatta.

In an exchange now known as the best real-estate bargain in human history, Minuit gave a Munsee Indian chief a few trinkets and blankets and got him to sign an incomprehensible document. Minuit then assumed the deal was sealed; the Dutch had bought themselves all of Manhattan Island. Of course, like all of the best real-estate deals, this one was a bit of a scam: The Native Americans had very different ideas about property and could not conceive of owning land, let alone in perpetuity.

It also turned out to be a shakedown. Once the Europeans had moved in, they wouldn't budge. The Dutch settlement tried to tax native hunters and keep them from owning firearms, and enforced harsh penalties for petty crimes. It was only a matter of time before a bloody war between the Dutch and the Native Americans broke out in the 1640s. It lasted two and a half years. Guess who won?

Europeans allowed little trace of New York's original inhabitants to remain, apart from various Munsee place names, such as Canarsie (grassy place), Rockaway (sandy place), Maspeth (bad water place) and Matinecock (at the lookout point).

PEG-LEG PETE

After the colonists massacred more than 100 Indians in 1643, the Dutch West India Company hired Peter Stuyvesant to keep the peace. Stuyvesant's right leg had been shattered by a cannonball—hence his nickname, Peg-Leg Pete. He ordered a defensive ditch and wall to be built along the northern end of New Amsterdam (today's Wall Street), and the muddy streets were paved with cobblestones. A commercial infrastructure was established (banks, brokers' offices, wharves), and chandlers and taverns soon lined the booming waterfront. Manhattan's capitalist culture was born.

And so was its first locally administered government. Stuyvesant founded a municipal assembly, and he encouraged the education of the colony's children. In his 17 years as governor, the settlement doubled in size. The town grew more cosmopolitan, including English, French, Portuguese and Scandinavian settlers and the area's first African slaves. Both English and Dutch were spoken.

But old Peg-Leg was a little too authoritarian. His intolerance of Jewish refugees and Quaker

*Water world: The **Brooklyn Bridge** looms above the **South Street Seaport** in 1901.*

leader John Bowne provoked scoldings from his bosses at the Dutch West India Company, and forced Stuyvesant to make the new settlement a haven for religious freedom.

THE BRITISH ARE COMING

Perhaps the Dutch West India Company tried to expand its colony too quickly. By 1661, less than four decades after the Dutch had settled the place, New Amsterdam was nearly bankrupt. When four British warships sailed into the harbor one day in August 1664, the population abandoned the fortifications Stuyvesant had built and welcomed Captain Richard Nicolls and his crew. New Amsterdam was renamed after the British king's brother, the Duke of York.

By 1700, New York's population had reached about 20,000. The colony was a big moneymaker for the British, but it was hardly what you would call a stable concern. In 1683, to cut administrative costs, the British had tried to consolidate New York, New Jersey and New England into a single dominion. The colonies rebelled, and after 21 months of battle, ten men were hanged for treason. In the 1730s, John Peter Zenger's *New-York Weekly Journal* provoked gasps by accusing British Governor William Cosby's administration of corruption. Zenger's trial on libel charges resulted in a landmark decision: The newspaper publisher was acquitted because, as his lawyer argued, the truth cannot be libelous.

The Zenger verdict sowed the seeds for the First Amendment to the Constitution, which established the principle of freedom of the press. This was just the beginning of trouble for the British.

REVOLUTION—AND THE BATTLE FOR NEW YORK

In British-run outposts in Virginia, Philadelphia and Boston, great thinkers such as Thomas Jefferson, Benjamin Franklin and John Adams spread the ideals of fair and democratic government. The merchants of New York, meanwhile, felt the pinch from their British bosses, who imposed more and higher taxes on their colonial possessions in order to pay off debts accumulated in colonial wars against France.

When independence was declared on July 4, 1776, New York was too important for the British to give up—both because of its economic importance and because of its strategic position on the Hudson River. That summer, British commander Lord Howe sailed 200 ships into New York Harbor and occupied the town. New Yorkers vented their fury by toppling a gilded equestrian statue of George III that stood on Bowling Green.

The war's first major battle took place on Long Island and in Brooklyn (then called King's County). It was a complete disaster for the Americans, led by George Washington, who retreated to New Jersey. (While preparing his army, Washington slept at what is now called the Morris-Jumel Mansion in the Bronx; *see chapter* **Architecture**.) On September 11, 1776, Benjamin Franklin met Lord Howe in Staten Island's Billop Manor House (now known as the Conference House), but he refused Howe's offer to make all colonists full-fledged British subjects. "America cannot return to the domination of Great Britain," said Franklin, demanding independence.

Life in occupied New York was pretty grim. The town was overrun with British soldiers and loyalists fleeing the American army. Fires destroyed much of the city, and many of the inhabitants died of starvation. When the Crown finally surrendered in 1783, bitter British forces

in New York greased the city's flagpole in an attempt to make it harder for the revolutionaries to raise the banner of the new republic.

But the war was won. On December 4, Washington joined his officers for an emotional farewell dinner at Fraunces Tavern on Pearl Street (now the Fraunces Tavern Museum; *see chapter* **Downtown**), where the general declared his retirement. Yet he was not to evade public life: On April 23, 1789, in the Old Federal Hall (on the same site as the present one, on Wall Street), he took the oath of office as the first president of the United States of America, and New York became the capital city.

THE FIRST U.S. CAPITAL

Before the revolution, a young New Yorker named Alexander Hamilton was studying at King's College (now Columbia University) and hobnobbing with colonial high society. Hamilton had married into a powerful merchant family after serving under Washington in the war. He took advantage of New York's newfound status as the nation's capital to push for the founding of the nation's first bank in 1784—much to the horror of Thomas Jefferson, who wanted the United States to have a simple, agrarian economy.

Night light: **Coney Island**'s *Luna Park amused millions until fire destroyed it in 1944.*

By the time the nation's capital was moved, at Jefferson's insistence, to a new city built on mosquito-infested swampland next door to Virginia, Hamilton (who became the first U.S. Treasury Secretary) had already secured New York's control over the new nation's money. The city's business boomed, merchants grew richer, and the port prospered. Thanks to its financial clout, New York didn't need to be the political capital.

CROWD CONTROL

By 1800, more than 60,000 people lived in what is now lower Manhattan. Rents were high, and housing demands were great, although development had been spotty. The government decided the city needed a more orderly way of selling and developing land. A group of city officials, called the Commissioners, came up with the solution: the famous "grid" street system of 1811. It ignored all the existing roads—with the exception of Broadway, which ran the length of Manhattan Island, following an old Indian trail—and organized New York into a rectangular grid wide, numbered avenues running north to south and streets running river to river. Commenting on the vast area thus earmarked for the city, it was observed: "It may be a subject of merriment that the Commissioners have provided space for a greater population than is collected at any spot on this side of China."

When the 362-mile Erie Canal opened in 1825—linking New York to the Midwest via the Hudson and the Great Lakes—the port city became even more vital to the young country. Along with the new railroads, this trade route facilitated the making of many fortunes, and New York's merchants and traders flourished.

THE ABOLITIONISTS

Today, lower Manhattan's African-American Burial Ground near City Hall preserves the chilling memory of a time when New York was second only to Charleston, South Carolina, as a slave-trade port. As late as the 1700s, such prominent local families as the Van Cortlandts and Beekmans increased their fortunes by dealing in human beings.

But as northern commercial cities relied less and less on manual labor, dependence on slavery waned—and the abolition movement bloomed. In 1827, when New York State abolished slavery, the city celebrated with two days of fireworks and parades. As the states in the South remained defiant, the abolition movement grew stronger in Boston and New York.

In New York, the cause was kept alive in the columns of Horace Greeley's *Tribune* newspaper and in the sermons of Henry Ward Beecher, pastor of the Plymouth Church of the Pilgrims on Orange Street in Brooklyn. The minister brother of Harriet Beecher Stowe (who wrote *Uncle Tom's Cabin*) once shocked his congregation by auctioning a slave from his pulpit and using the proceeds to buy her freedom.

NEW YORK AND U.S. CIVIL WAR

Preservation of the Union was the hot issue of the presidential campaign of 1860. Abraham Lincoln wavered in his position on slavery—until one fateful trip to New York that year, when he addressed a meeting in the Great Hall of the Cooper Union (the first American school open to all, regardless of race, religion or gender). In his speech, Lincoln declared, "Neither let us be slandered from our duty by false accusations against us, nor frightened from it by menaces of destruction to the government nor at dungeons to ourselves. Let us have faith that right makes might, and in that faith let us, to the end, dare to do our duty as we understand it."

The newly formed Republican Party moved to make Lincoln its presidential candidate. The Southern states promptly seceded from the Union and became the Confederate States of America. The Civil War had begun.

THERE'S A RIOT GOING ON

When Lincoln started a military draft in 1863, the streets of New York erupted in three days of rioting. Although New York sided with the Union against the Confederacy, there was considerable sympathy for the South, particularly among poor Irish and German immigrants, who feared that freed slaves would compete with them for work.

For three days, New York raged. African-Americans were assaulted in the streets; Horace Greeley's office was attacked twice; Brooks Brothers was looted. When all was said and done, 100 were dead and 1,000 injured. The violence came to an end only when Union troops returning from victory at Gettysburg subdued the city. The Draft Riots remain the worst single uprising in American history—beyond Watts, beyond Crown Heights, beyond Rodney King.

But apart from those three days in 1863, New York emerged from the Civil War unscathed. It had not seen any actual fighting—and it had prospered as the financial center of the North. As the city thrived, immigration thrived, and so did New York's upper-class captains of industry.

HIGH FINANCE

Jay Gould made enormous profits during the Civil War by having the outcome of military engagements secretly cabled to him and trading on the results before they became public knowledge. Jim Fisk, together with Gould, seduced Cornelius Vanderbilt into buying vast quantities of Erie Railroad bonds before the bottom dropped out of the market. (Vanderbilt had the resources to sit out the crisis and the grace to call Gould "the smartest man in America.") Vanderbilt, Andrew Carnegie and banker J.P. Morgan consolidated their fortunes by controlling the railroads. And John D. Rockefeller made his money in oil, owning, by 1879, 95 percent of the refineries in the United States.

All of these men—each in his own way representing a 19th-century blend of capitalist genius and robber baron—erected glorious mansions in New York. Their homes now house some of the city's art collections, and their legacies are as apparent on Wall Street as they are along Fifth Avenue. Swindles, panics and frequent market collapses were cyclical in the late 19th century, but New York's millionaires weathered the crises, built major cultural institutions and virtually created high society.

The 1800s saw the birth of the Metropolitan Museum of Art (now the largest art museum in the western world), the Astor Library (now the Public Theater), the American Museum of Natural History, the New York Historical Society and the Metropolitan Opera. Carnegie gave Carnegie Hall to New York, even though the devoted Pittsburgher never really mingled much much among New York's rich (his Fifth Avenue mansion is now the Cooper-Hewitt National Design Museum). When the New York Public Library was built in 1895, Carnegie offered $52 million to establish

Those were the days

Bone up with this timeline of key events in New York history

1524 Giovanni da Verrazano is the first European to visit what is now Manhattan.
1609 Henry Hudson sails into the New York harbor.
1624 The colony of New Amsterdam is founded, and the first settlers arrive.
1626 Peter Minuit, the first governor, arrives and "buys" Manhattan from the Indians. New Amsterdam has a population of 300.
1643 Peter Stuyvesant is made governor.
1661 The Dutch colony nearly goes bankrupt.
1662 John Bowne's struggle wins the people of New Amsterdam the right to religious freedom.
1664 The British invade. New Amsterdam is renamed New York.
1733 John Peter Zenger's *New-York Weekly Journal,* establishes the right to free speech.
1754 King's College (which will become Columbia University) is founded.
1776 The Declaration of Independence is adopted. The Revolutionary War rages; the British occupy New York.
1783 The defeated British army leaves New York.
1785–90 New York serves as the new nation's capital.
1811 The Commissioners' Plan envisages the geographical grid system that prescribes how the city ought to grow.
1812–14 America fights another war with Britain. New York is isolated from international trade.
1837 Financial panic ruins all but three city banks.
1843 Immigrants flood into the city.
1851 *The New York Times* is first published.
1857 Frederick Law Olmsted and Calvert Vaux lay out Central Park.
1859 Cooper Union, the first American school open to all, regardless of race, religion or gender, is established.
1860 Abraham Lincoln is elected president.
1861 The Civil War erupts.
1863 Conscription causes riots in New York.
1865 The Union (the North) wins, and slavery is ended.
1870 The Metropolitan Museum of Art is founded.
1872 Organized labor strikes for an eight-hour day.
1883 The Brooklyn Bridge is completed.
1886 The Statue of Liberty is unveiled.
1890 Photojournalist Jacob Riis publishes *How the Other Half Lives,* spurring new housing regulations.
1895 The New York Public Library is founded.

1898 New York City—comprising Manhattan, Brooklyn, Queens, Staten Island and the Bronx—is incorporated, creating the world's second-largest city.
1902 The Fuller Building (later known as the Flatiron), is built, becoming the world's first skyscraper.
1907 Metered taxicabs are introduced.
1911 The Triangle Shirtwaist factory fire sparks the introduction of workplace safety regulations.
1917 America enters WWI.
1920 Women win the right to vote. Prohibition bans alcohol.
1929 The Wall Street stock market crash on October 29 plunges the nation into the Great Depression. The Museum of Modern Art opens nine days later.
1930s Roosevelt's New Deal funds massive public-works schemes. The Empire State Building, the Chrysler Building and Rockefeller Center are built.
1939 Corona Park, Queens, hosts the World's Fair.
1941 America enters WWII.
1946 The United Nations is established in New York.
1947 The Brooklyn Dodgers' Jackie Robinson breaks the color barrier in major league baseball.
1959 The Guggenheim Museum opens.
1962 Lincoln Center opens.
1977 There is a 25-hour citywide power blackout (some say it caused a spike in the birth rate nine months later).
1968 A student sit-in shuts down Columbia University.
1970 The World Trade Center is built.
1975 The city goes bankrupt.
1978 Mayor Ed Koch presides over an economic turnaround.
1987 The other Wall Street crash.
1990 David Dinkins is the city's first black mayor.
1991 The city's budget deficit hits a record high.
1993 Terrorists attempt to blow up the World Trade Center. Rudolph Giuliani becomes the city's first Republican mayor in 28 years.
1997 A new wave of immigration peaks. The Dow Jones average tops 7,000. The murder rate hits a 30-year low. Disney arrives on 42nd Street.
1998 New York City falls to 37th on the list of most dangerous urban centers.
1999 The Dow hits 10,000. Unarmed immigrant Amadou Diallo is shot at 41 times by police. First Lady Hillary Rodham Clinton mulls over a run for U.S. Senate from New York.

branch libraries. The nucleus of the library consists of the combined collections of John Jacob Astor, Samuel Jones Tilden and James Lenox.

MAJOR CAPITAL IMPROVEMENTS

The wealthy also started moving uptown. By 1850, the mansions along Fifth Avenue had indoor plumbing, central heating and a reliable water supply—secured by the 1842 construction of the Croton Reservoir system. In 1857, Frederick Law Olmsted and Calvert Vaux welcomed crowds to Central Park, the nation's first landscaped public green space. A daring combination of formal gardens and vast, rolling hills, the park remains the city's great civilizing force, offsetting the oppressive grid and bringing an oasis of sanity into the heart of the city.

Nineteenth-century New York also witnessed some of America's industrial marvels. In 1807, Robert Fulton started the world's first steamboat service on Cortlandt Street. Samuel Morse founded his telegraph company in the 1840s. By the 1860s, Isaac Merritt Singer was producing 13,000 sewing machines a year here. In the late 1800s, Thomas Edison lived in New York (and New Jersey) where he formed the world's first electric company, which still carries his name, Consolidated Edison; in 1882, 800 new street lamps turned New York into the city that never sleeps.

Another extraordinary achievement of the time was the Brooklyn Bridge (1869–83). When it was built, it was the longest suspension bridge in the world and the first to use steel cable. Designed by John A. Roebling (who died in an on-site accident before construction began) and completed by his son, Washington, the bridge opened up the independent city of Brooklyn—and helped pave the way for its merger with New York.

POLITICAL MACHINATIONS

The 1898 consolidation of all five boroughs into the City of New York assured New York's 20th-century transition into a crucial world-class force—it became the planet's second-largest city (only London was bigger). But this happened only after several false starts. Local bosses wouldn't give up their power, and most of the town had been mired in corruption. William M. "Boss" Tweed, the young leader of a Democratic Party faction called Tammany Hall (named after a famous Indian chief), turned city government into a lucrative operation. As commissioner of public works, he collected large payoffs from companies receiving city contracts. Tweed and his ring are estimated to have misappropriated $160 million during the construction of the Tweed Courthouse (52 Chambers Street), among other projects. They distributed enough of that money in political bribes to keep a lot of influential mouths shut.

The likes of Boss Tweed ultimately ran up against Theodore Roosevelt, a different kind of New York big shot. Roosevelt drew his power not so much from his wealth and class as from the sheer force of his personality (and his ability to work the media). As a state assemblyman in the 1880s, Roosevelt turned the town on its ear, accusing even respected capitalist Jay Gould of corrupting a judge. And as president of the city's police board in the 1890s, he made friends with news reporters and led a temperance movement—two things that could never be pulled off simultaneously today. (*See chapter* **Midtown** for information on the museum re-creating Roosevelt's childhood home.)

COMPANY

"Give me your tired, your poor, your huddled masses yearning to breathe free," entreats Emma Lazarus's "The New Colossus," inscribed at the base of Frédéric Auguste Bartholdi's 1886 Statue of Liberty—one of the first sights seen by newcomers to the U.S. as they approached by sea.

The first great waves of immigration to America started well before the Civil War; the twin ports of welcome were Boston and New York. German liberals were fleeing their failed 1848 revolution, and an influx of Irish surged after the 1843 potato famine. In the 1880s, large numbers of immigrants from the old Russian empire—Ukrainians, Poles, Romanians and Lithuanians, many of them Jews—arrived alongside southern Italians. Chinese laborers, who had been brought to America to do backbreaking work on the railroads in California, moved east to New York in droves.

From 1855 to 1890, the immigration center at Castle Clinton in Battery Park processed eight million people. The Ellis Island center, built in 1892, served the same purpose for roughly the same length of time and handled twice that number. With the introduction of a quota system in 1921, the flood slowed; Ellis Island was closed in 1932.

HOW THE OTHER HALF LIVES

New immigrants usually ended up in the grim, crowded tenements of the Lower East Side. By 1879, the first of a series of housing laws was passed to improve conditions for the poor. In 1890, writer and photographer Jacob Riis published his *How the Other Half Lives,* an exposé of sweatshops and squalor in the ghetto; the uptown populace was horrified. In 1886, New York had established its first settlement house for the underprivileged at 146 Forsyth Street. The settlement-house movement and the temperance drive dominated New York's philanthropic circles through the Depression.

The frenetic growth of the city's industries created appalling health and safety conditions. Child labor was common. "Nearly any hour on the East Side of New York City you can see them—pallid boy or spindling girl—their faces dulled, their backs bent under a heavy load of garments piled

*What's my line? New York City's **tenement housing** was notoriously overcrowded.*

*Dig it: Submersion of **Grand Central**'s rails enabled Park Avenue to become a tony address.*

on head and shoulders, the muscles of the whole frame in a long strain," wrote poet Edwin Markham in 1907. As early as 1872, 100,000 workers went on strike for three months until they won the right to an eight-hour workday.

But it took the horror of the 1911 fire at the Triangle Shirtwaist factory on Washington Place in Greenwich Village, which killed 146 workers, to stir politicians into action. More than 50 health and safety measures were passed by the state legislature within months of the fire.

THE SUBWAY

If, while staring at a subway map, you wonder why there is no easy connection between such natural depots as Grand Central and Penn Station, it is because the terminals were at one time run by different private rail companies. The original names of the subways—the IRT (Interborough Rapid Transit), BMT (Brooklyn-Manhattan Transit Corporation) and IND (Independent Subway System)—are still preserved in old subway signage. Many lifelong New Yorkers still use these names to refer to various routes.

The 714-mile subway system, an astounding network of civic arteries that currently serves 3.9 million passengers a day, became this century's largest single factor in the growth of the city. The first of the three companies started excavation in 1900, but by the 1940s, the system had been consolidated and had become very much as it is today—except, of course, for the 1990s replacement of the stately, substantial, classic token with the sleek, institutional MetroCard.

The subway also holds a unique place in the city's imagination: It offers the perfect metaphor for New Yorkers' fast, crowded lives lived among strangers. Most famously, the Duke Ellington Band's signature song, written by Billy Strayhorn, implored its listeners to "Take the 'A' Train," noting, "that's the quickest way to get to Harlem." Subway culture permeates New York life. Tin Pan Alley's songwriters composed such popular ditties as "Rapid Transit Gallop" and "The Subway Glide," and new words and phrases like *rush hour* entered the language.

NEW YORK STORIES

Since the 19th century, New York has consistently sprouted its own artistic and literary movements. Following the seminal figures of New York letters—people like satirist Washington Irving and Gothic storyteller Edgar Allan Poe, a transplanted Southerner—were Brooklyn poet Walt Whitman and novelists Edith Wharton and Mark Twain. Wharton became an astute critic of old New York society; her most memorable novels, among them *The Age of Innocence*, are detailed renderings of New York life at the turn of the century. Samuel Clemens (a.k.a. Mark Twain) moved

in and out of New York (mostly Greenwich Village) during his most prolific period, when he published *The Adventures of Tom Sawyer, Life on the Mississippi* and *Huckleberry Finn*.

By the turn of the century, New York's social conscience was evident in its literature. Lincoln Steffens (the political muckraker), Stephen Crane (*Maggie, a Girl of the Streets*), Theodore Dreiser (*Sister Carrie*) and O. Henry all captured the city's pathos with style and fervor.

THE JAZZ AGE

Once World War I had thrust America onto center stage as a world power, New York benefited from wartime commerce. The Roaring Twenties brought looser morals (women voting and dancing the Charleston!) at the same time that the reactionary Prohibition provoked a bootleg-liquor culture. Speakeasies fueled the general Jazz Age wildness and made many a gangster's fortune. Even Mayor Jimmie Walker went nightclubbing at a casino located in Central Park.

At Harlem's Cotton Club, Lena Horne, Josephine Baker and Duke Ellington played for white audiences enjoying what poet Langston Hughes called "that Negro vogue." On Broadway, the Barrymore family—Ethel, John and Lionel (Drew's forebears)—were treading the boards between movies. Over at the New Amsterdam Theater on West 42nd Street, the high-kicking Ziegfeld Follies dancers were opening for such entertainers as W.C. Fields, Fanny Brice and Marion Davies.

New York also saw the birth of the film industry: D.W. Griffith's early films were shot in Manhattan and the Marx Brothers made movies in Astoria. In 1926, hundreds of thousands of New Yorkers flooded the streets to mourn the death of matinee idol Rudolph Valentino.

RADIO DAYS

After the 1929 crash, when Americans stopped going out and turned to their radios for entertainment, New York became the airwaves' talent pool. Unemployed vaudeville players such as George Burns and Gracie Allen became stars, as did Jack Benny and Fred Allen. The careers of artists as disparate as Bing Crosby and Arturo Toscanini were launched on New York radio. Italian immigrant Enrico Caruso became one of the first worldwide recording stars here. The Deco masterpiece Radio City Music Hall became the industry's great Depression-era palace.

And as theatrical productions were tailored for the airwaves, some of the most acclaimed stage directors made their names in radio. In 1938, Orson Welles and John Houseman, who both had already shaken up Harlem with an all-African-American stage version of *Macbeth*, shocked America with their radio adaptation of H.G. Wells's *War of the Worlds*.

LA GUARDIA, FDR AND THE POWER BROKER

The first skyscrapers (including the Woolworth Building) were erected at the turn of the century, but the 1920s saw a second boom in buildings: The Chrysler and Empire State Buildings and Rockefeller Center were all built by the 1930s. Art Deco design dominated these projects (*see chapter* **Architecture**).

In 1932, with the Depression in full swing, the city elected a stocky, short-tempered young congressman, Fiorello La Guardia, as mayor. Boosted by former New York Governor Franklin D. Roosevelt's election as president, La Guardia imposed austerity programs that, surprisingly, won wide support. FDR's New Deal, meanwhile, re-employed the jobless on public-works programs and allocated federal funds to roads, housing and parks.

Enter Robert Moses, the city's master builder. As the head of a complex web of governmental authorities and commissions, Moses employed thousands of New Yorkers to build huge parks (including Long Island's Jones Beach) and recreation centers for the masses; he also mowed down entire neighborhoods to construct bridges (including the Verrazano-Narrows) and expressways that invited urban sprawl. No one since Dutch colonizer Peter Minuit had left a greater stamp on the city. Before his influence faded in the 1960s, Moses erected such indelible New York landmarks as Lincoln Center, Shea Stadium and the Flushing World's Fair Grounds.

BUILDING BETTER ARTISTS

The Federal Works Progress Administration (WPA) also made money available to New York's actors, writers, artists and musicians. And as the Nazis terrorized the intelligentsia in Europe, the city became the favored refuge. Architects Ludwig Mies van der Rohe and Walter Gropius (the former director of the influential Bauhaus school of design) and composer Arnold Schoenberg were among those who moved to New York from Germany, along with many visual artists.

Arshile Gorky, Piet Mondrian, Hans Hofmann and Willem de Kooning were among the painters welcomed by the fledgling Museum of Modern Art, founded in 1929 by three collectors. By the '50s, MoMA had fully embraced a generation of painters known as the New York school. Critics such as Clement Greenberg hailed Abstract Expressionism as the next step in painting. Jackson Pollock, Lee Krasner, Willem and Elaine de Kooning, Robert Motherwell and Mark Rothko

*Lofty aspirations: In the 1930s, the Art Deco **Chrysler Building** rose gloriously above its neighbors along 42nd Street.*

*Where have you gone? **Joe DiMaggio**'s name now graces the West Side Highway.*

became the stars of a gallery scene that, for the first time, topped that of Paris.

When a young man named Andrew Warhola decided to leave Pittsburgh to become an artist, it was no surprise that he chose to come to New York. Dropping the last letter of his name, Warhol used commercial silk-screening techniques to fuse the city's ad culture and art world until the two could barely be distinguished. At the peak of the 1960s Pop Art movement, some critics argued that painting had reached its final destination in New York.

MEDIA CENTRAL

The 1920s literary scene was dominated by Ernest Hemingway and his friend F. Scott Fitzgerald, whose *The Great Gatsby* portrayed a dark side of the 1920s. They worked with editor Maxwell Perkins at Scribner's publishing house, along with Thomas Wolfe, who constructed enormous semi-autobiographical mosaics of small-town life. The city's days as a publishing mecca arrived: Such literary luminaries as Dorothy Parker, Robert Benchley, George S. Kaufman and Alexander Woollcott gathered regularly at the famous Round Table at the Algonquin Hotel (*see chapters* **Accommodations** *and* **Books & Poetry**). Royals of stage and screen like Douglas Fairbanks, Tallulah Bankhead and various Marx Brothers would show up to pay their respects. Much of the modern New York concept of sophistication and wit took shape in the alcoholic banter of this glamorous clan.

By World War II, the city's socialist scene—divided over the support some showed for Stalin—inspired the work of a generation of intellectuals, including Norman Podhoretz, Irving Howe, Lionel and Diana Trilling, and William F. Buckley Jr. At the same time, a counterculture sprang up: Jack Kerouac and Allen Ginsberg attended Columbia in the '40s, giving rise to the Beats of the '50s. Throughout the century, Greenwich Village was the lab for alternative culture, from '20s Bolshevism to the '60s New York School of poets (John Ashbery and Kenneth Koch among them).

ENCORES AND HOME RUNS

In the theater, George and Ira Gershwin, Irving Berlin, Cole Porter, Richard Rodgers and Oscar Hammerstein II codified and modified the Broadway musical, adding plots and characters to the traditional follies format. Eugene O'Neill revolutionized American drama in the '20s, only to have it revolutionized again by Tennessee Williams a generation later. By mid-century, the Group Theater had fully imported Stanislavski acting techniques to America, launching the careers of Actors Studio founder Lee Strasberg, director Elia Kazan and the young stage actor Marlon Brando.

Theater—especially on Broadway—became big business in New York. The Shubert brothers started a national 100-theater empire here in the 1910s. In mid-century, David Merrick pushed such modern musicals as *Gypsy*. By the '60s, Joseph Papp's Public Theater was bringing Shakespeare to the masses with free performances in Central Park that continue today.

Meanwhile, in the outer boroughs, baseball was providing as much excitement as the stage. Along the way, New York became America's baseball heart. The unbeatable Yankees—Babe Ruth, Lou Gehrig, Joe DiMaggio and later Mickey Mantle—provided as much excitement as any Broadway show. Jackie Robinson integrated baseball in Brooklyn in 1947; when the Dodgers left town a decade later, the borough was devastated.

THE INTERNATIONAL CITY

The affluence of the 1950s also allowed many families to head for the suburbs: Towns sprang up around new highways, and roughly a million children and grandchildren of European immigrants—mostly Irish, Italian and Jewish—moved there. Their places in the city were taken by a new wave of immigrants—one million Puerto Ricans and African-Americans, most of the latter relocating from the South.

At this same time, the United Nations, the international organization supporting global peace and security, established its headquarters overlooking

*NYPD blues: The city's **police** has had to deal with some blows to its image as New York's finest.*

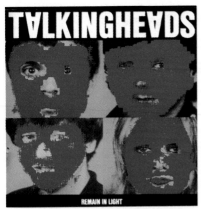

*Punk prophets: Before **Talking Heads** hit the big time, they were CBGB regulars.*

the East River in Manhattan on land donated by John D. Rockefeller (*see chapter* **Architecture**).

By the mid-'60s, poverty, prejudice and an increase in street crime had cast a shadow of fear across the city. Many white New Yorkers in working- and middle-class neighborhoods grew disenchanted with the city and its ability to provide safe streets or effective schools and fled to the suburbs in large numbers. To make matters worse, by 1975 the city was all but bankrupt. With a growing population on welfare and a declining tax base, the city resorted to heavy municipal borrowing.

Culturally, New York remained a mecca for music and nightlife. The Brill Building gave Carole King, Neil Diamond and Burt Bacharach their starts, and Bob Dylan rose to fame in the Village. In the '70s, CBGB, on the Bowery, launched Blondie, the Ramones and Talking Heads, while midtown's Studio 54 blended disco, drugs and Hollywood glamour into a potent, if short-lived, cocktail.

BOOM AND BUST

New York climbed out of its fiscal crisis under Mayor Edward I. Koch, a one-time liberal from Greenwich Village who wrangled state and federal help to ride the 1980s boom in construction and finance. The '80s and early '90s were the best and worst of times for New York: A new art scene and booming Wall Street takeover culture brought money back downtown. New neighborhoods such as the East Village, Soho and Tribeca blossomed. But the AIDS and crack epidemics hit the city hard, as did racial politics. David Dinkins became New York's first African-American mayor in 1989. His tenure, however, was marred by racial tensions—incidents in Crown Heights, Brooklyn, and Washington Heights polarized the people of those neighborhoods as well as the entire city.

Dinkins was succeeded in 1994 by Rudolph Giuliani, a tough Italian-American lawyer who entered the political limelight as a fearless federal prosecutor. Crime rates plunged in the late '90s, thanks in part to the mayor's relentless crackdown on petty crime. While racism and, perhaps most acutely, police brutality remain troublesome in New York, the continued growth of cultural and high-tech industries combined with 1960s-level crime figures have brightened New York's reputation.

TOWARD THE MILLENNIUM

The problems facing the mayor of New York are like those of any other city, only magnified. AIDS and homelessness persist, as well as extremes of wealth and poverty. But at the same time, New York is rebuilding: You'll see scaffolding and construction everywhere you turn. Locals and visitors—tourists, business executives and conventions—pour into dozens of new restaurants and stores. Times Square is now a family-friendly playground, and new residential towers are on the way on the East and West Sides (both courtesy of Donald Trump). Uptown, a federal Empowerment Zone has brought a long-awaited building boom to Harlem. Even parts of the South Bronx, a war zone in the '70s, are middle-class homesteads today.

New York remains a city of pioneers. Recent arrivals from Asia, Latin America, the Caribbean and the former Soviet Union make up a foreign-born population of more than two million. The flow of humanity gives the place energy. After all this time, the New York City remains a modern invention, surviving in style.

*Crime fighter: **Mayor Rudolph Guiliani**'s get-tough tactics reduced NYC's crime rate.*

Architecture

When the expansion of a city is limited by its island location, the only way to go is up

O. Henry once said of New York, "It'll be a great place if they finish it." In fact, it is the constant construction that has made the city an architectural wonderland. Here are a few highlights of New York's architectural styles, including the year construction was completed. Anyone with a strong interest in the architecture of the city might want to visit the Urban Center, home to both the Municipal Art Society and the Architectural League (*see chapter* **Museums**). Other chapters to help you plan your architecture sightseeing: **Tour New York**, **Further Reading**, and the **New York by Neighborhood** section.

Dutch Colonial

The style based on New York's first European settlers (1626–64) generally features wood-frame buildings with tile roofs, stepped gables and stone stoops.

Pieter Claesen Wyckoff House Museum
Circa 1652. 5902 Clarendon Rd at Ralph Ave, East Flatbush, Brooklyn (718-629-5400). Travel: 2, 5 to Newkirk Ave, then B7, B8 or B78 bus to Clarendon Rd. Times vary; call for details.
Possibly the oldest building in New York State, Pieter Claesen Wyckoff's farmhouse was built on land bought in 1636 from the Canarsie Indians.

Bowne House
1661. 37-01 Bowne St between 37th and 38th Aves, Flushing, Queens (718-359-0528). Subway: 7 to Main St–Flushing. Tue, Sat, Sun 2:30–4:30pm. $2.
Nine generations of the family descended from John Bowne—a fighter for religious freedom—lived here until it was turned into a museum in 1945. Only part of the house is original.

Dyckman Farmhouse Museum
Circa 1785. See chapter **Uptown**.
Though this home was rebuilt in the 18th century, it is based on the earlier structure's style.

British influence

Much building went on while the British controlled the city (1664–1783), though little of it remains; however, the Georgian style favored at the time can be seen in these structures:

Historic Richmond Town
Circa 1670–1860. See chapter **Outer Boroughs**.
Several buildings of various styles were moved here from across Staten Island and restored.

Morris-Jumel Mansion
1765. See chapter **Uptown**.
This Palladianesque mansion was built for a British colonel.

Van Cortlandt House Museum
1748. Van Cortlandt Park, Broadway at 242nd St, Riverdale, Bronx (718-543-3344). Subway: 1, 9 to 242nd St–Van Cortlandt Park. Tue–Fri 10am–3pm; Sat, Sun 11am–4pm. $2, under 12 free. No credit cards.
This two-and-a-half-story stone manor house features classic Georgian touches: It's almost square, with dormer windows poking out of the top floor. The interior retains most of the period's architectural features as well.

The Federal period

As a new country, the United States developed its own version of the Georgian style, called Federal, which was favored in the city through the late 1800s. In addition, the residences seen all over the city—tenements and brownstones—were built by the thousands during this period.

City Hall
1803–12. City Hall Park between Broadway and Park Row (Mayor's office: 212-788-3000). Subway: J, M, Z to Chambers St; 2, 3 to Park Pl; 4, 5, 6 to City Hall. Mon–Fri 10am–4pm. Free.
The Mayor's headquarters is a neoclassical specimen that combines the Federal style with French Renaissance influences. The interior is pure American Georgian.

Charlton-King-Vandam Historic District
Circa 1820s. 9–43 and 20–42 Charlton St, 11–49 and 16–54 King St, 9–29 Vandam St, 43–51 MacDougal St. Subway: 1, 9 to Houston St.
In addition to having the largest concentration of Federal-style houses in New York, this area includes fine examples of Greek Revival, Italianate and late-19th-century domestic architecture.

Beaux Arts

Probably the best known (and loved) era of New York architecture came with the Gilded Age of the early 1900s. With the destruction of the original Pennsylvania Station (designed by the city's most important architectural firm, McKim, Mead & White) in 1965, only 54 years after it was built, the city's Landmarks Preservation Commission was instituted. However, many beautiful buildings remain.

New York Public Library
1902–1911. See chapters **Midtown** *and* **Museums**.
The epitome of Beaux Arts. Designed by the firm Carrère & Hastings, which also designed the **Frick** mansion (now a museum) and **Grand Army Plaza** in Manhattan.

*Eero dynamic: Eero Saarinen's **TWA Terminal** soars among mere airplanes and jetways.*

General Post Office
*1913. See chapter **Directory**.*
McKim, Mead & White designed the General Post Office to complement the original Penn Station. Other evidence of the firm's taste for the French and Italian Renaissance: the **Municipal Building** (circa 1914, Centre St at Chambers St), the **University Club** (circa 1899, 1 W 54th St at Fifth Ave), the **Metropolitan Club** (circa 1894, 1 E 60th St at Fifth Ave) and **Pierpont Morgan Library** (*see chapter **Museums***).

Grand Central Terminal
*1913. See chapter **Midtown**.*
Warren & Wetmore designed the majestic soaring (and now restored) Grand Central Terminal, as well as the ornate building behind it—the **Helmsley Building** (circa 1929, 230 Park Ave between 45th and 46th Sts).

Cast iron

New technology allowed buildings to be constructed quickly from cheap precast materials (*see* **Soho** *in chapter **Downtown***).

Haughwout Building
1857. 488–492 Broadway at Broome St. Subway: J, M, Z, N, R, 6 to Canal St.
Located in Soho, this "Parthenon of cast-iron architecture" is so called for its elegant proportions and beautiful detail. Other fine cast-iron examples include the **Cary Building** (105–107 Chambers St at Church St); **72–76 Greene Street**, known as "the King of Greene Street"; and **28–30 Greene Street**, "the Queen." There are a great many larger buildings in the district known as Ladies' Mile (Broadway between Union and Madison Squares).

85 Leonard St
*1860–61. See chapter **Downtown**.*
This is the only extant structure known to have been designed by James Bogardus, the self-described "inventor of cast-iron buildings."

Skyscrapers

They're what New York is famous for: the tallest buildings in the world (well, many of them were at some point). For further exploration, visit the Skyscraper Museum (*see chapter **Museums***).

Flatiron Building
1902. 175 Fifth Ave between 22nd and 23rd Sts. Subway: N, R to 23rd St.
The Flatiron was one of the earliest buildings to use an interior steel cage for support. Its exterior echoes the traditional Beaux Arts facades of its time.

Woolworth Building
1913. 233 Broadway between Park Pl and Barclay St. Subway: N, R to City Hall; 2, 3 to Park Place.
Architect Cass Gilbert designed this monument of wealth as a kind of Gothic cathedral, complete with gargoyles. It was the world's tallest until the Chrysler Building came along.

The Chrysler Building
1930. 405 Lexington Ave at 42nd St. Subway: S, 4, 5, 6, 7 to 42nd St–Grand Central.
At 1,046 feet, this was the tallest skyscraper in the world (it was built in a race against 40 Wall St) until the Empire State Building was finished. *See chapter **Midtown**.*

The Empire State Building
*1931. See chapter **Midtown**.*
A 102-story Art Deco tower of limestone and granite with thin vertical strips of nickel that glint when they catch the sun, the Empire State was the work of William F. Lamb, who was told to "make it big." Built in only 18 months, it soon became the world's favorite building, as well as its tallest. Other important Art Deco works include **Rockefeller Center** (*see chapter **Midtown***), the monochrome tower of the **Fuller Building** (1929, 45 E 57th St at Madison Ave) and the twin copper crowns of the **Waldorf-Astoria Hotel** (1931, 301 Park Ave between 49th and 50th Sts). Raymond Hood's **News Build-**

*Sphere and now: The **Rose Center for Earth and Space** will be NYC's millennial star.*

ing (1930, 220 E 42nd St between Second and Third Aves) is a soaring skyscraper of white brick piers with black and reddish-brown spandrels (as seen in the *Superman* films).

McGraw-Hill
Circa 1931. 330 W 42nd St between Eighth and Ninth Aves. Subway: A, C, E to 42nd St–Port Authority.
Architect Raymond Hood didn't intend to build a modern structure, but in the end his design—with shimmering blue-green terra-cotta and ribbons of double-hung windows—is a perfect blend of Art Deco and International styles. The "jolly green giant" has recently been cleaned and repaired.

Glass boxes

After the Art Deco era of skyscraper construction (and once the Depression ended), a Modernist and International style emerged.

United Nations Secretariat
*1950. See chapter **Midtown**.*
The main building of the U.N. is a perfectly proportioned single rectangle (its face is designed to the "golden ratio" of the Greeks), and the design incorporates New York's first walls made entirely of glass.

Lever House
1952. 390 Park Ave between 53rd and 54th Sts. Subway: E, F to Lexington Ave; 6 to 51st St.
Designed by the firm Skidmore, Owings & Merrill, this narrow steel and greenish glass skyscraper rises out of its broad mezzanine lobby, which seemingly floats above the street, supported by columns set back from the perimeter.

Seagram Building
1958. 375 Park Ave between 52nd and 53rd Sts. Subway: E, F to Lexington Ave; 6 to 51st St.
Ludwig Mies van der Rohe designed this bronze and bronze glass office tower with Philip Johnson. With its 38 stories occupying only 52 percent of the site, the plaza gratifyingly stretches out to the broad boulevard of Park Avenue.

Other postwar standouts

Solomon R. Guggenheim Museum
*1952. See chapter **Museums**.*

As his crowning achievement, America's most celebrated architect, Frank Lloyd Wright, designed a conical museum that's wondrous inside and out.

TWA Terminal A
*1962. John F. Kennedy International Airport, Terminal A. See chapter **Directory**.*
Controversial for years after the terminal's opening but now landmarked, Eero Saarinen's design is, according to the *AIA Guide to New York*, "soaring, sinuous, surreal and…well worth a visit."

World Trade Center
*1972–73. 1 and 2 World Trade Center between Church and West Sts and Liberty and Vesey Sts. See chapter **Downtown**.*
At 1,350 feet tall, the 110-story twin towers of 1 and 2 World Trade Center dominate the lower Manhattan skyline. In addition, a plaza, a hotel, an underground mall and five other office buildings make up the center's complex.

Citicorp Center
1978. 599 Lexington Ave between 53rd and 54th Sts. Subway: E, F to Lexington Ave; 6 to 51st St.
Constructed of aluminum and glass, Citicorp Center added a unique silhouette to Manhattan's skyline with its angled roofline. The building's tower hovers over huge pillars centered between the corners of the base.

Sony Building
1984. 550 Madison Ave between 55th and 56th Sts. Subway: E, F to Fifth Ave.
With this building, Philip Johnson (a former proponent of the International style) changed the face of architecture in New York from Modern glass to Postmodern stone. He designed this pink granite office tower (notorious for its ornamental "Chippendale" top) for AT&T. In 1991, when Sony moved in, it had the public plaza redesigned and enclosed.

The new millennium

The newest architectural wonder in New York is also an engineering feat. The **Rose Center for Earth and Space** at the Museum of Natural History features a six-story glass cube containing an 87-foot metal sphere perforated with 5.5 million holes and supported by six tapered steel legs with a spiraling entrance ramp. It will house the new Hayden Planetarium as well as other exhibits.

As for the future: The most publicized skyscraper looming on the horizon is Donald Trump's proposed "tallest residential building in the world"—a 70-story behemoth to rise just down the street from the U.N. In response, the city has proposed closing a zoning-law loophole that allows developers to build extra floors in exchange for constructing public plazas—most of which are dark, dreary places, unwelcoming even on the brightest summer days.

While other cities around the world—most notably Bilbao, Spain, with its Frank Gehry–designed Guggenheim Museum—have recently won praise for their striking new buildings, New York City has lagged behind. If the prosperity of the late '90s continues, New York may soon see cornerstones laid for some exciting new designs in Columbus Circle, Times Square, the Brooklyn waterfront and the current railyards of Manhattan's West 30s.

*Station identification: The ornate **Astor Place** subway entrance is an East Village landmark.*

New York by Neighborhood

Key Sights

If you just gotta get to the top of Miss Liberty—no matter what we have to say—or want to know what's not to miss, these are it

**American Museum
of Natural History**
Central Park West at 79th St (212-769-5000, recorded information 212-769-5100). Subway: B, C to 81st St. See page 244 for more information.

**Bronx Zoo/Wildlife
Conservation Society**
Bronx River Pkwy at Fordham Rd, Bronx (718-367-1010). Subway: 2, 5 to Bronx Park East. See page 90 for more information.

Brooklyn Botanic Garden
1000 Washington Ave between Eastern Pkwy and Empire Blvd, Prospect Park, Brooklyn (718-623-7200). Subway: 2, 3 to Eastern Pkwy–Brooklyn Museum. See page 85 for more information.

Brooklyn Bridge
Subway: 4, 5, 6 to City Hall–Brooklyn Bridge. See page 85 for more information.

Central Park
59th St to 110th St between Fifth Ave and Central Park West. (212-360-3456). See pages 70–71 for more information.

Chinatown
Subway: J, M, Z, N, R to Canal St. See page 47–48 for more information.

**Coney Island Sideshows by
the Seashore/Coney Island USA**
1208 Surf Ave at W 12th St, Coney Island, Brooklyn (718-372-5159). Subway: B, D, F, N to Stillwell Ave–Coney Island. See page 85 for more information.

Empire State Building
350 Fifth Ave at 34th St (212-736-3100). Subway: B, D, F, Q, N, R to 34th St–Herald Sq. See pages 29 and 64 for more information.

Metropolitan Museum of Art
1000 Fifth Ave at 82nd St (212-535-7710). Subway: 4, 5, 6 to 86th St. See pages 245 for more information.

New York Botanical Garden
200th St at Southern Blvd, Bronx (718-817-8705). Subway: B, D, 4 to Bedford Pk Blvd, then Bx26 bus. See page 90–91 for more information.

**New York Public Library/
Center for the Humanities**
Fifth Ave at 42nd St (212-869-8089). Subway: B, D, F, Q to 42nd St; 7 to Fifth Ave. See pages 60–61 and 253 for more information.

Rockefeller Center
48th–51st Sts between Fifth and Sixth Aves (212-632-3975). Subway: B, D, F, Q to 47–50th Sts–Rockefeller Ctr. See page 64 for more information

South Street Seaport
Water St to the East River, between John St and Peck Slip (212-SEA-PORT, 212-732-7678). Subway: J, M, Z, 2, 3, 4, 5 to Fulton St. See page 46 for more information.

Staten Island Ferry
South St at the foot of Whitehall St (718-727-2508). Subway: 1, 9 to South Ferry; 4, 5 to Bowling Green. See page 36 for more information.

**Statue of Liberty
and Ellis Island Immigration Museum**
Liberty Island and Ellis Island (212-363-3200, ferry information 212-264-5755). Travel: 4, 5 to Bowling Green, then ferry from Battery Park to Liberty Island and Ellis Island. See page 251 for more information.

Times Square
Broadway at W 42nd St. Subway: N, R, S, 1, 2, 3, 9, 7 to 42nd St–Times Sq. See pages 61–62 for more information.

World Trade Center
West St between Liberty and Vesey Sts (212-323-2340, groups 212-323-2350). Subway: C, E to World Trade Ctr; N, R, 1, 9 to Cortlandt St. See pages 30 and 46 for more information.

*Do we stay or do we go? **Ellis Island** was the first stop to NYC for thousands of people.*

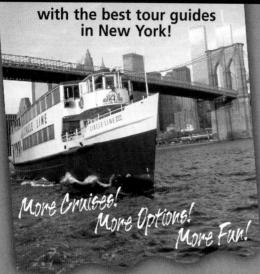

Tour New York

**Okay, you're never going to see it, live it and be it in one week—
but one sure way to get NYC-savvy in a limited time is with a tour**

The diverse masterpiece that is New York City offers an equally varied assortment of tours to show off its many faces. Gaze at the towering silver spires by boat, glide through the Central Park greens by bicycle, experience the thrills and frustrations of a midtown traffic jam by bus, or explore the nooks and crannies of a Chinese apothecary on foot. It's your choice—through a telescope, microscope or kaleidoscope—New York will meet and amaze you at every level.

By bicycle

Central Park Bicycle Tours
Tours meet outside 2 Columbus Circle, 59th St and Broadway (212-541-8759). Subway: A, C, B, D, 1, 9 to 59th St–Columbus Circle. 10am, 1pm and 4pm. $30, under 15 $20. Includes bicycle rental fee.
This leisurely two-hour bicycle tour visits the John Lennon memorial at Strawberry Fields, the Belvedere Castle, the Shakespeare Garden and many other Central Park sights. There are plenty of opportunities to rest when the guide stops to talk and

when the tour breaks for refreshments. Call in advance to reserve either the English- or Spanish-language tour.

By boat

Bateaux New York
Pier 62, Chelsea Piers, 23rd St at the West Side Hwy (212-352-2022; fax 212-352-1367) www.bateauxnewyork. com. Subway: C, E to 23rd St. Dinner cruise 7–10pm, $74.75–$91.50; brunch cruise Sat, Sun noon–2pm, $45.75.
Eat a meal while traveling in a glass-covered vessel view ing the Manhattan skyline. The à la carte menu was created by the same chef as Veritas (*see chapter* **Restaurants**). After dinner, you can shake it to Broadway, jazz and blues tunes on a hardwood dance floor.

Chelsea Screamer
Pier 62, Chelsea Piers, 23rd St and the Hudson River (212-924-6262). Subway: C, E to 23rd St. Mon–Fri approximately one tour every two hours; Sat, Sun one tour per hour. $15, under 12 $8. Reservations not required, call for exact cruising times.
This narrated speedboat cruise takes you past the Statue of Liberty, Ellis Island, the *Intrepid*, the Brooklyn Bridge and, of course, Manhattan's skyscrapers. However, this is not for

*Pedal to the mettle: Take a spin and test your strength with **Central Park Bicycle Tours**.*

*It's a plane? It's Superman? No, it's birdwatching with the **Urban Park Rangers**.*

the mild-mannered tourist—the bright yellow-and-blue boats really do "scream" along in the river.

Circle Line
Pier 83, 42nd St at West Side Hwy (212-563-3200) www.seaportliberty.com. Subway: A, C, E to 42nd St–Port Authority. Three-hour trip $22, seniors $18, under 12 $12; two-hour trip $18, seniors $16, under 12 $10.
From April to November, Circle Line operates a three-hour trip that circumnavigates Manhattan, one of the cheapest and best ways to get a glimpse of the whole city. From June to August, there's also a two-hour "harbor lights" cruise in the evening.

The Petrel
North Cove Marina, Battery Park City (212-825-1976). Subway: C, E to the World Trade Center; 1, 9 to Cortlandt St. Call for charter rates.
A 70-foot yawl designed by Sparkman and Stephens, the Petrel is built of teak and mahogany. It was launched in 1938 as a racing yacht, and the owners still pride themselves on using a sail as much as possible. This is a New York favorite, so you'll need to book two weeks in advance. The Petrel sails between May and November.

Seaport Liberty Cruises
Pier 16, South Street Seaport, Water St to the East River, between John St and Peck Slip (212-630-8888) www.seaportliberty.com. Subway: A, C to Broadway–Nassau; J, M, Z, 2, 3, 4, 5 to Fulton St. One-hour cruise $12, seniors $10, children $6; speedboat $15, children $10.
One-hour cruises and two-hour evening music cruises are offered on a large sightseeing boat. Thirty-minute trips on a speedboat called the *Beast* are also available.

Staten Island Ferry
South St at the foot of Whitehall St (718-727-2508). Subway: 1, 9 to South Ferry; 4, 5 to Bowling Green. Free.
The poor man's Circle Line is actually just as much fun, provided you bring the one you love. No-cost (and unguided) panoramas of Manhattan and the Statue of Liberty turn a

trip on this commuter barge into a romantic sojourn when the sun goes down. When you get to Staten Island, it may not be as scenic, but it has a nice personality. Boats depart South Ferry at Battery Park every half hour, 24 hours a day.

Bus tours

Gray Line
Port Authority Bus Terminal, Eighth Ave at 42nd St, and the Times Square Visitors Center, Broadway between 46th and 47th Sts (212-397-2600). Subway: A, C, E, N, R, 1, 2, 3, 9 to 42nd St. 7:45am–8pm, $22–$55. AmEx, Disc, JCB, MC, V.
Gray Line offers more than 20 bus tours around the city, from a basic two-hour ride to the monster nine-hour "Manhattan Comprehensive," which includes lunch. The firm also runs Central Park trolley tours; call for info.

Hassidic Tours
Tour bus departs from 42nd St and Fifth Ave (800-838-8687) www.jewishtours.com. Subway: B, D, F, Q to 42nd St; 7 to Fifth Ave. Sun 9:30am–1:30pm. $36. Reservations required.
New York City is home to a large Hassidic Jewish community. Guided by Hassidic Jews, these tours introduce their life to the general population. You will travel to Brooklyn to visit a synagogue, witness a Torah scroll being written, have lunch at a kosher deli and explore a Hassidic library. The tours include some walking and there's time to shop for Jewish gifts and delectables.

New York Apple Tours
800-876-9868. Tours begin at New York Apple Tours' Visitors Information Center (Eighth Ave at 53rd St), Rockefeller Center (Fifth Ave at 50th St), the Plaza Hotel (Fifth Ave at 59th St) and Times Square (Seventh Ave at 42nd St). Starting at 9am, buses continuously follow a 65-stop route. $25–$78. AmEx, DC, Disc, JCB, MC, V.
Take a guided tour uptown or downtown, or combine the two for a daylong ride around Manhattan in open-top, red-and-yellow double-deckers. Once you have a ticket, you can get on and off at any point along the route. (On the combined tour, you can spread this over two days.) Buses are frequent enough to make this practical. The company also offers a "Harlem Gospel Express" itinerary, a trip that makes stops in Brooklyn and expeditions by bus and helicopter.

By helicopter

Liberty Helicopter Tours
VIP Heliport, West Side Hwy at 30th St (212-967-6464, recorded info 212-465-8905). Subway: A, C, E to 34th St–Penn Station. 9am–9pm. $46–$159. AmEx, MC, V.
The Liberty copters are larger than most, which makes the ride fairly smooth. There are between 10 and 40 rides a day, depending on the weather. Reservations are unnecessary, and several tours are offered. Even the shortest ride is long enough to get a good close-up view of the Statue of Liberty, Ellis Island and the Twin Towers.

By foot—walking and other tours

For more information on various walking tours of New York—covering historic neighborhoods, celebrity sites, ethnic cuisines, architectural

*Taking liberty: Get up close to the **Statue of Liberty**, and soon you'll carry a torch for her.*

themes and more—consult the Around Town section of *Time Out New York* or Sunday's *New York Times*.

Adventures on a Shoestring
(212-265-2663) Sat, Sun. $5. Call for current tours, meeting locations, times and reservations.
Its motto is "Exploring the world within our reach…within our means," and founder Howard Goldberg is undyingly faithful to "real" New York and to the tour's $5 price tag (which hasn't gone up in 30 years). Tours like "Ethnic East Village," "Hell's Kitchen Hike" and "Haunted Greenwich Village" explore New York, neighborhood by charming neighborhood. The 90-minute tours often finish with a group lunch and useful handouts.

Big Apple Greeter
1 Centre St at Chambers St, 20th floor (212-669-2896; fax 212-669-3685). Subway: 4, 5, 6 to Brooklyn Bridge–City Hall. Mon–Fri 9:30am–5pm; recorded information at other times.
If you don't feel like letting one of the many tour companies herd you along the New York-by-numbers trail, or if you'd simply prefer to have a knowledgeable and enthusiastic friend to accompany you as you discover the city, put in a call to Big Apple Greeter. Since 1992, this immensely successful program has been introducing visitors to one of 600 carefully chosen volunteer "greeters" and giving them a chance to see New York beyond the well-trodden tourist traps. Go visit Vinny's mom in Bensonhurst, have Renata show you around the hidden treasures of Polish Greenpoint, or let Carmine take you to the parks in the South Bronx where hip-hop was invented. The service is completely free, though donations are welcome, and it also can be tailored to visitors with disabilities. Write, call or fax the office to find yourself a New York friend.

Big Onion Walking Tours
212-439-1090; www.bigonion.com. Tours are scheduled every weekend and holiday. Most are $10, students and seniors $8.
This business, started by Columbia University doctoral candidates in history, puts together astoundingly informative tours of New York's historic districts and ethnic neighborhoods. Private tours are also available.

Chinatown Walking Tours
212-561-1575. Daily tours. $15. Call for times and meeting locations.
On these tours, chef Eleanor Toy gives you an insider's look at the Chinatown marketplace, with visits to Chinese bakeries, a ginseng tea parlor, an apothecary and food emporium, tofu-and-noodle shops and much more. Toy takes you inside each store and introduces you to a vast array of Asian ingredients–you'll even get to taste a few. You also receive a complimentary set of chopsticks.

Foods of New York Walking and Tasting Tours
Tour meets on Seventh Ave South at Bleecker St (732-636-4650) www.citysearch.com/nyc/food. Subway: 1, 9 to Christopher St–Sheridan Sq. Daily 11:30am–1:30pm. $20 (all food included). Reservations required.
These entertaining tours, which started in April 1999, take the mystery out of where to eat in New York. Your food-savvy tour guide walks you through some of the most famous eating establishments and specialty food shops in Greenwich Village and Soho, like Rocco's Bakery, Joe's Pizza and the restaurant row of Cornelia St. Be sure to go

*See level: Get an eyeful of Manhattan's downtown skyline from the **Staten Island Ferry**.*

with an empty stomach; you'll sample at least seven different foods along the way.

Grand Central and 34th Street Partnerships

212-818-1777.

These neighborhood business organizations offer free tours of their districts such as a grand tour of midtown including Grand Central Terminal. There is also a monthly tour of the remnants of the demolished Pennsylvania Station (call 212-868-0521 for info).

Harlem Spirituals

690 Eighth Ave between 43rd and 44th Sts (212-391-0900) www.harlemspiritual.com. Subway: A, C, E to 42nd St–Port Authority. Mon–Sat 8am–7pm; book at least one day ahead. $15–$75. AmEx, MC, V.

Sunday-morning gospel tours take in Sugar Hill, Hamilton Grange and the Morris-Jumel Mansion, as well as a service at a Baptist church. Gospel tours (Sun, Wed and Fri) skip by the Schomburg Institute for Research into Black Culture and visit a Baptist church choir. Visit cabarets on the evening "Soul Food and Jazz" tours (Mon, Thu, Sat). Thursday "Historical" tours include lunch.

Heritage Trails New York

Federal Hall National Memorial, 26 Wall St between Broad and William Sts (212-269-1500). Subway: 4, 5 to Wall St. Mon–Fri 9am–5pm. Guidebooks $5, guided tour fee varies (call for details).

The red, blue, orange and green dots of paint that mark four and a half miles of lower Manhattan sidewalk make up this detailed self-guided tour, which highlights some of the neighborhood's tougher-to-find tourist attractions, such as the Vietnam War Veterans Memorial and the Seamen's Church Institute. The guidebook is essential and is available from the office. Heritage Trails also offers tours of the Federal Reserve and the Stock Exchange (*see chapter* **Downtown**).

Joyce Gold History Tours of New York

212-242-5762; fax 212-242-6374; www.nyctours.com. Sat, Sun 1pm. Call for current tours and meeting locations. $12.

Joyce Gold, a history professor at New York University and a Manhattan expert, has been conducting these informative two- to three-hour weekend tours for more than 15 years. Her talks focus on neighborhood evolutions and cultural movements, and she can customize walks to address the special interests of any group.

Lauren's Walking Tours

718-204-5133; fax 718-204-5283; pager 917-823-1177; www.LoneDaughter.com. Sun 10am–2pm; Fri, Mon 8pm–midnight. $15–$40.

The "Sunday Harlem Gospel" tour explores the sights and sounds of Harlem including Malcolm X Boulevard, the Apollo Theater, Strivers Row, Sylvia's and a gospel service at the First Corinthian Baptist Church. The new "Harlem Jazz Evenings" tour introduces the Harlem jazz era over dinner and finishes at a jazz club.

Mainly Manhattan Tours

212-755-6199. Sat noon, Sun 1pm. $10.

Anita Baron, a born-and-bred New Yorker and former Big Apple Greeter, conducts two tours every weekend. "West Side Story" includes Lincoln Center, Hotel des Artistes, the Dakota and Zabar's food market. "Greenwich Village: New York's Left Bank" visits the homes of famous literary residents Mark Twain, Edith Wharton and e. e. cummings. Call for information on more tours, dates and times.

Municipal Art Society Tours

457 Madison Ave between 50th and 51st Sts (212-935-3960) www.mas.org. Subway: E, F to Fifth Ave; 6 to 51st St. Mon–Wed, Fri, Sat 11am–5pm. $10–$18.

The society organizes some very informative tours, including hikes around Harlem, the Upper West Side, Greenwich Village and Brooklyn Heights. It also offers a free tour of Grand Central Terminal on Wednesdays at 12:30pm.

New York City Cultural Walking Tours

212-979-2388; www.nycwalk.com. Private tours $25/hr for four persons or more, $15/hr for three persons or fewer. Public tours Thu 10am. $10.

Alfred Pommer's tours explore New York's neighborhoods—such as Murray Hill, Gramercy Park, Soho and Little Italy—through history, architecture, pictures and stories. Private tours can be scheduled for your convenience. Call for meeting locations of public tours.

New York Curmudgeon Tours

212-629-8813; fax 212-594-4346. Sat, Sun 10am. $10. Call for meeting locations.

Bill Walters, a seasoned theater professional, guides these tours past many of New York's famous Broadway theaters, classic movie locations and sites from television's golden era—from Times Square to the Ed Sullivan Theater. He combines an insider's personal experience with historical tidbits to bring the famed New York City entertainment scene to life.

Radical Walking Tours

212-492-0069. Two weekend tours a month at 1pm. $10. Call for dates and meeting locations. No reservations required.

Bruce Kayton's tours emphasize left-wing history and include tales of Yippie leader Abbie Hoffman, Bob Dylan's folkie days, Margaret Sanger and the birth control movement, and the Black Panthers.

Street Smarts N.Y.

212-969-8262. Sat, Sun 2–4pm and 6–8pm. $10. Call for meeting locations. No reservations required.

Claiming New York has a thriving ghost population, these tours visit several bars, streets and hotels rumored to accommodate the supernatural. Other, unhaunted, tours include a gaslight-era pub crawl and "glorious" Gramercy Park.

Talk-a-Walk

30 Waterside Plaza, New York, NY 10010 (212-686-0356; fax 212-689-3538).

This mail-order service offers a choice of five 85-minute audiocassette tours ($9.95 each). Each contains directions and commentary for a walk lasting two to four hours. You can fax your address to the number above to receive a three-page catalog.

Tours with the 92nd Street Y

1395 Lexington Ave at 92nd St (212-996-1100) www.92ndsty.org. Subway: 4, 5, 6 to 86th St. Call for schedule. Prices vary.

The Y offers an impressive array of walking tours, day trips and weekend excursions, including everything from "Allen Ginsberg's New York" to "Maple Tapping and Herbal Lunch, Native American–Style." Walking tours are usually on Sundays.

Urban Park Rangers

212-360-2774 (9am–5pm). Places and times vary. Free.

A service of the Parks Department (888-NY-PARKS; www.nycparks.org), the Rangers organize pleasant free walks and talks in all city parks. Subjects and activities covered include fishing, wildlife, bird watching and Native American history. *Time Out New York* lists tour locations and schedules each week.

World Trade C.
Wall Street
Empire State Building

Downtown

Wall Street power brokers, Soho fashionistas, East Village punks and immigrants of every stripe make lower Manhattan come alive

Since New York City grew northward from the area now known as Battery Park, the richest and most diverse concentration of places and people is located below 14th Street. Here the crooked streets (most of which have names, not numbers) are made for walking. Lose yourself for hours wandering from the architectural wonderland of the Financial District and Civic Center, through the trendy art-lined streets of Soho and the vivid ethnic enclaves of the Lower East Side, to the punk's-not-dead spirit of the East Village and the café society of Greenwich Village.

Battery Park

The southern tip of Manhattan is where you are most conscious of being on an island. The Atlantic breeze blows in over New York Harbor, along the same route taken by the hope-filled millions who arrived here by sea: past the golden torch of the **Statue of Liberty**, over the immigration and quarantine center of **Ellis Island** (now a splendid museum) and on to the statue-lined promenade of **Battery Park**. Today, instead of overcrowded steamships, the harbor is filled in summer with daredevils on Jet-Skis jumping the wakes left by sailboats and motorboats. Seagulls perch on the promenade railing, barking at fishermen, whose lines might snag a shad or a striped bass (although state health department officials don't recommend eating these fish more than once a month). The promenade is also a stage for numerous performers, who entertain the lines of people waiting for the ferry to whisk them to the Statue of Liberty and Ellis Island. The park frequently plays host to international touring events such as the Cirque du Soleil (*see chapter* **Kids' Stuff**). Free outdoor music is often a summer-evening feature here as well. **Castle Clinton**, inside the park, was built during the Napoleonic wars to defend the city against the British, who had just been thrown out. The castle has been a theater and an aquarium, and now it's a National Parks visitors' center with historical displays. Buy your tickets for the Statue of Liberty and Ellis Island here.

Whether or not you join the crowds of tourists heading for the Statue of Liberty, you can go

Take the long view: Catch a glimpse of the **Statue of Liberty** from **Battery Park**.

around the shore to the east and catch the famous and free **Staten Island Ferry** for a surprisingly romantic ride offering an unparalleled view of the downtown skyline and, of course, a fine glimpse of Miss Liberty (*see chapter* **Tour New York**). The historic terminal was destroyed by fire in 1991, and its replacement has not yet been built. But next door is the beautiful **Battery Maritime Building** (11 South Street), terminal for the many ferry services between Manhattan and Brooklyn in the years before the Brooklyn Bridge was built. The restaurant **American Park at the Battery** (212-809-5508) also sits at the eastern end of the Battery Park promenade, and although its surf-and-turf menu is rather expensive, its outdoor patio overlooking the harbor is a prime spot to sip a cocktail. To the west is the restored **Pier A** (22 Battery Place), the last Victorian pier shed in Manhattan, now home to fine-dining establishments and historic vessels.

North of Battery Park is the triangle of **Bowling Green**, the city's oldest extant park and home to the beautiful Beaux Arts **U.S. Custom House** (built in 1907), which is now the fascinating **National Museum of the American Indian**. Nearby is sculptor Arturo DiModica's dynamic bronze bull representing the snorting power of Wall Street, as well as the **Shrine of Elizabeth Ann Seton**, a strange curved building in the Federal style dedicated to the first American-born saint. Also nearby is the **Fraunces Tavern Museum**, a restoration of the alehouse where George Washington celebrated his victory against the British. It is now a museum of revolutionary New York and a restaurant (*see chapters* **Architecture** *and* **Museums**).

The Statue of Liberty & Ellis Island Immigration Museum

212-363-3200; www.nps.gov/stli. Reached via the Statue of Liberty Ferry, departing every half hour from Gangway 5 in Battery Park at the southern tip of Manhattan. Subway: 1, 9 to South Ferry; 4, 5 to Bowling Green. 9am–5pm. $7, seniors $6, ages 3–17 $3, under 3 free. Tickets purchased at Castle Clinton.

"A big girl who is obviously going to have a baby. The Birth of a Nation, I suppose," wrote wartime wit James Agate about the Statue of Liberty. Get up close to this most symbolic New York structure by visiting the island it stands on. Frédéric Auguste Bartholdi's statue was a gift from the people of France (the framework—which can be seen only if you go inside the statue—was designed by Gustave Eiffel), but it took the Americans years to collect enough money to give Liberty her pedestal. The statue stands 111 feet 6 inches toe-to-crown; there can be an excruciating wait to climb the 154 steps to the observation deck. Go early, of course. Or spend your time on Ellis Island, walking through the restored buildings dedicated to the millions of immigrants who passed through here, and pondering the ghostly personal belongings that hundreds of people left behind in their hurry to become part of a new nation. It's an arresting and moving museum (*see chapter* **Museums**).

Shrine of Elizabeth Ann Seton

7 State St between Pearl and Whitehall Sts (212-269-6865). Subway: N, R to Whitehall St. Noon–6pm. Free.

Wall Street

Since the city's earliest days as a fur-trading post, wheeling and dealing has been New York's prime pastime and commerce the backbone of its prosperity. Wall Street (or just "the Street," if you want to sound like a local) is the thoroughfare synonymous with the world's greatest capitalist gambling den.

Wall Street itself is actually less than a mile long; it took its name from a small wooden defen-

*Column what you will: The former **Merchants Exchange** is now a Cipriani restaurant.*

sive wall the Dutch built in 1653 to mark the northern limit of New Amsterdam. In the days before telecommunications, financial institutions established their headquarters here to be near the action. This was where corporate America made its first audacious architectural assertions; there are many great buildings here built by grand old banks and businesses.

Notable ones include the old **Merchants Exchange** at 55 Wall Street (now Cipriani's Downtown), with its huge Ionic columns, giant doors and, inside, a rotunda that holds 3,000; the **Equitable Building** (120 Broadway), whose greedy use of vertical space helped inspire the zoning laws governing skyscrapers (stand across the street from the building to get a decent view); and 40 Wall Street (now owned by real-estate tycoon Donald Trump), which in 1929 went head to head with the Chrysler Building in a battle for the mantle of "world's tallest building." At the western end of Wall Street is the Gothic spire of **Trinity Church**, once the island's tallest structure but now dwarfed by skyscrapers. Stop in and see brokers praying the market stays hot, or stroll through the adjacent cemetery, where cracked and faded tombstones mark the final resting places of dozens of past city dwellers, including signers of the Declaration of Independence and the U.S. Constitution.

A block east is the **Federal Hall National Memorial**, a Greek Revival shrine to American inaugural history—sort of. This is the spot where Washington was sworn in as the country's first president on April 30, 1789. The original building was demolished in 1812.

Across the street is the **New York Stock Exchange**. The visitors' center here is excellent for educating the clueless about the workings of financial trading and lets you look out over the trading floor in action. (For a sense of Wall Street's influence through the years, check out the **Museum of American Financial History**). The exchange is all computerized these days, so except for crashes and panics, it's none too exciting as a spectator sport (for the "Buy! Buy! Buy!" action you've seen in the movies, you want the far more frenzied **Commodities Exchange**; *see* **World Trade Center and Battery Park City**, *page 44*). Far more fun is just people watching on the street outside the Exchange—an endless pageant of power, with besuited brokers marching up and down Broad Street, glowing with the confidence instilled by the recent unprecedented bull market.

The **Federal Reserve Bank**, a block north on Liberty Street, is an imposing Florentine Renaissance–style building. It holds 40 percent of the world's gold (you saw Jeremy Irons clean it out in *Die Hard 3*) in a vault housed on the bedrock of Manhattan island, five stories below street level.

*Power hungry: Lunchtime at the **Exchange**.*

As you'd expect, the Wall Street area is fairly deserted after the end of the business day. But there is something relaxing about the empty streets during off hours, and a stroll through the area, especially on weekends, can be a pleasant alternative to seeing it in full hustle-and-bustle mode. Otherwise, the time to see it is around midday, when the suits emerge for their hurried lunches. Join them in stopping for a burger at the ultimate **McDonald's** (160 Broadway). By some quirk of individualism, it boasts uniformed doormen, a stock ticker, a special dessert menu and a Liberace-style pianist.

Federal Hall National Memorial

26 Wall St at Nassau St (212-825-6888). Subway: 2, 3 to Wall St. Mon–Fri 9am–5pm. Free.

Federal Reserve Bank

33 Liberty St between William and Nassau Sts (212-720-6130) www.ny.frb.org. Subway: 2, 3 to Wall St. By appointment only. Free.
The free one-hour tours through the bank must be arranged at least one month in advance; tickets are sent by mail.

Museum of American Financial History

28 Broadway at Bowling Green Park (212-908-4110). Tue–Sat 10am–4pm. Free.
This tiny museum is located on the ground floor of the Standard & Poor's building.

New York Stock Exchange

20 Broad St at Wall St (212-656-5168). Subway: J, M, Z to Broad St; 2, 3, 4, 5 to Wall St. Mon–Fri 9am–4:30pm. Free.
A gallery overlooks the trading floor, and there are lots of multimedia exhibits.

Trinity Church Museum

Broadway at Wall St (212-602-0872). Subway: N, R to Rector St; 4, 5 to Wall St. Mon–Fri 9–11:45am, 1–3:45pm; Sat 10am–3:45pm; Sun 1–3:45pm; closed during concerts. Free.
The small museum inside features exhibits on the history of the church and its place in New York history.

World Trade Center and Battery Park City

The area along lower Manhattan's west coast contains grand developments that combine vast amounts of office space with new public plazas, restaurants and shopping areas. There have been concerted efforts to inject a little cultural life into these spaces, and plenty of street performers work the area in summer months, though the general atmosphere is defined by the schedule of the working day.

Completed in 1976, the **World Trade Center** is actually seven buildings, though to most visitors it means the famous twin towers, which look like two huge silver sticks of butter floating above the downtown skyline. Tower 2 contains the famous observation deck; on good days you can walk outside and spare a thought for the crazies who have suction-climbed the walls, parachuted off the top floor or walked a tightrope between the two towers. It's the city's tallest structure and for a short time in the '70s (until Chicago's Sears Tower was completed) also held the world height record. Fine dining in the clouds is available at Windows on the World and Wild Blue, or you can medicate your vertigo with a drink at the **Greatest Bar on Earth** (*see chapter* **Cafés & Bars**). Back in the lobby, you can marvel at the dated '70s decor of the Trade Center, including a rather scruffy wool and hemp tapestry by Spanish artist Joan Miró, or pick up some cheap tickets to a Broadway show at the **TKTS outlet** in the mezzanine plaza (*see chapter* **Music**).

Below the Trade Center complex is a massive underground mall with 123 shops. Large chains such as the Gap, Banana Republic, the Limited and Borders are here, along with hair salons, cosmetics stores and tons of inexpensive eating establishments. The great free floor show that is the **Commodities Exchange** is at 4 World Trade Center. Across Church Street between Dey and Cortlandt Streets is **Century 21**, a huge store that sells designer clothes at sometimes massive discounts (*see chapter* **Shopping & Services**). Covered pedestrian bridges over West Street lead to the **World Financial Center** and the rest of **Battery Park City**, a 92-acre project built on earth dug up when the World Trade Center's foundations were built. The World Financial Center, completed in 1988, is the ultimate expression of the city-within-a-city concept. Crowned by Cesar Pelli's four elegant postmodern office towers, it contains an upscale retail area, a marina where water taxis to New Jersey dock and a series of plazas with terraced restaurants. The stunning, vaulted, glass-roofed **Winter Garden**, with its indoor palm trees, has become a popular venue for concerts and other entertainment, most of which are free (*see chapter* **Music**).

The most impressive part of Battery Park City, however, is the esplanade and park running north and south from the Financial Center along the Hudson River. In addition to offering spectacular, romantic views of the sunset behind **Colgate Center** (look for the huge Colgate sign/clock) and Jersey City, New Jersey, across the river, the esplanade is a paradise for joggers, in-line skaters and bikers—although just walking it is plenty fun, too. The northern end of the park (officially called **Nelson A. Rockefeller Park**) features the large North Lawn, which becomes a surrogate beach in summer, with sunbathers, kite flyers and soccer players all jostling for a patch of grass. Basketball and handball courts, concrete tables with chess and backgammon boards painted on them, and playgrounds and swings round out the recreational options available on the esplanade. Tennis courts and baseball fields are also available, just off West Street at Murray Street to the north and Warren Street to the south. The park ends at Chambers Street but links up with the piers to the north that are slowly being claimed for public use and will eventually become the Hudson River Park. The southern end of the park links Battery Park City with Battery Park. Here you'll find the inventively designed **South Cove** area, **Robert F. Wagner Jr. Park** (with an observation deck that offers fabulous views of the harbor and the Verrazano Narrows Bridge) and New York City's Holocaust museum—the **Museum of Jewish Heritage**. The entire park area is littered with fine art, most notably Tom Otterness's whimsical sculptural installation *The Real World* behind the North Lawn. The park also hosts outdoor cultural events throughout the warmer months.

The residential area of Battery Park City houses, among others, wealthy Wall Streeters whose high rents go to subsidizing public housing elsewhere in the city. Because this area is cut off from the rest of the city and because it's so new (some buildings are still under construction), the distinctiveness that makes New York so charming is lost here; Battery Park City feels like a gated community that could be in almost any American city.

Commodities Exchange

4 World Trade Center, ninth floor (212-748-1006). Subway: C, E to World Trade Ctr; N, R, 1, 9 to Cortlandt St. Mon–Fri 10:30am–3pm. Free.
The Stock Exchange has lost much of its drama in these days of computerized trading; not so the Commodities Exchange.

Splendor in the glass: **World Trade Center** *Tower 1 looms over the airy* **Winter Garden**.

Here you can still see manic figures in color-coded blazers scream and shout at each other as they buy and sell gold, pork bellies and orange juice. There are three tours a day—at 11am, 1pm and 3pm; book two weeks in advance.

Lower Manhattan Cultural Council
212-432-0900.
This group offers information on cultural events happening in and around this part of Manhattan.

World Financial Center & Winter Garden
West St to the Hudson River, Vesey St to Albany St (212-945-0505). Subway: N, R, 1, 9 to Cortlandt St. Free.
Phone for information about the many free arts events.

World Trade Center *morning*
West St between Liberty and Vesey Sts (212-323-2340, groups 212-323-2350). Subway: C, E to World Trade Ctr; N, R, 1, 9 to Cortlandt St. Observation deck in World Trade Center 2 open 9:30am–9:30pm, rooftop promenade open, weather permitting. $12.50, students $10.75, seniors $9.50, children 6–12 $6.25, under 6 free. MC, V.
The WTC's rooftop promenade is the world's highest open-air observation platform. Even from the bottom looking up, the view is enough to make your head spin. Ascend to the 110th floor, and you'll really feel the vertigo. The scariest thing is that there's another tower of equal size only a stone's throw away. First thing in the morning is the best time to avoid the line, which can take up to an hour.

Rock me, Amadeus: The **Woolworth Building** *is called the "Mozart of skyscrapers."*

The Seaport

While New York's importance as a port has diminished, the city's fortune rolled in on the salt water that crashes around its natural harbor. The city was perfectly placed for trade with Europe—with goods from middle America arriving via the Erie Canal and Hudson River. And because New York was the point of entry for millions of immigrants, its character was formed primarily by the waves of humanity that arrived at its docks.

The **South Street Seaport** is where you'll best see this seafaring heritage. Redeveloped in the mid-1980s, the Seaport is an area of reclaimed and renovated buildings converted to shops, restaurants, bars and a museum. It's not an area that New Yorkers often visit, though it is rich in history. The shopping area of Pier 17 is little more than a picturesque tourist trap of a mall by day and a postwork yuppie watering hole by night, but the other piers are crowded with antique vessels. The Seaport Museum—detailing New York's maritime history—is fascinating (*see chapter* **Museums**). The Seaport's public spaces are a favorite with street performers; there are outdoor concerts in the summer. The Fulton Market building (with gourmet food stalls and seafood restaurants that spill out onto the cobbled streets in summer) is a great place for slurping oysters as you watch people stroll by. The surrounding streets are filled with upscale brand-name shops such as J. Crew and Abercrombie & Fitch. If you enter the Seaport area from Water Street, the first thing you'll notice is the whitewashed **Titanic Memorial Light-**

house, originally erected the year after the great ship went down and moved to its current location in 1976. The area offers fine views of the **Brooklyn Bridge** (*see chapter* **Outer Boroughs**) and plenty of restored 19th-century buildings, including **Schermerhorn Row** (2–18 Fulton St), constructed on landfill in 1812. The smell on South Street is a clear sign that the **Fulton Fish Market**, America's largest, is here too, though the fish are delivered by land and the market lives under the constant threat of relocation. If you wish to continue with the salt-water theme, Pier 16 is where to find the tour boats of **Seaport Liberty Cruises** (*see chapter* **Tour New York**).

Fulton Fish Market
South St at Fulton St (212-669-9416). Subway: J, M, Z, 2, 3, 4, 5 to Fulton St. Midnight–9am. Tours Apr–Oct on first and third Thu of the month, 6am. $10, reservations required. AmEx, MC, V.

South Street Seaport
Water St to the East River, between John St and Peck Slip (for info about shops and special events, call 212-SEA-PORT, 212-732-7678). Subway: J, M, Z, 2, 3, 4, 5 to Fulton St.

Civic Center

The business of running New York takes place among the many grand buildings of the **Civic Center**. Originally, this was the city's focal point, and when **City Hall** was built in 1812, its architects were so confident the city would grow no farther north they didn't bother to put any marble on its northern side (*see chapter* **Architecture**). The building, a beautiful blend of Georgian formality, Federal detailing and French Renaissance influences, sits in its own patch of green: **City Hall Park**. It was in this park, in 1776, that the Declaration of Independence was read to Washington's army. For years, the steps of City Hall and the park have been the site of press conferences and political protests. Under New York City's current mayor, Rudolph Giuliani, the steps have been closed to such activity, although civil libertarians have vowed to defy the ban. The much larger **Municipal Building**, which faces City Hall and reflects it architecturally, is home to the overspill of civic offices, including the marriage bureau, which can churn out newlyweds at remarkable speed. **Park Row**, east of the park and now host to an array of cafés and stereo shops, once held the offices of 19 daily papers and was known as Newspaper Row. It was also the site of Phineas T. Barnum's sensationalist American Museum, which burned down in 1865.

Facing the park from the west is Cass Gilbert's famous **Woolworth Building**, a vertically elongated Gothic cathedral of an office building that has been called "the Mozart of Skyscrapers" (*see chapter* **Architecture**). Its beautifully detailed lobby is open to the public during working hours. Two blocks down Broadway is **St. Paul's Chapel** (1766), an oasis of peace modeled on London's St. Martin-in-the-Fields, and one of the few buildings left from the century of British rule. The houses of crime and punishment are also located in the Civic Center, around Foley Square—once a pond and later the site of one of the city's most notorious slums, Little Five Points. Here you'll find the **New York County Courthouse** (60 Centre Street), a hexagonal neoclassical building with a beautiful interior rotunda featuring a mural called *Law Through the Ages*. Next door is the **United States Courthouse** (40 Centre Street), a golden, pyramid-topped tower above a Corinthian temple. Back next to City Hall is the old New York County Courthouse, more popularly known as the **Tweed Courthouse**, a symbol of the runaway corruption of mid-19th-century city government. Boss Tweed, leader of the political strong-arm faction Tammany Hall, pocketed $10 million of the building's huge $14-million cost (remember, this was at the end of the 19th century). You can't spend that much and fail to get a beautiful building, however. Its Italianate detailing may be symbolic of immense greed, but it is of the highest quality. The **Criminal Courts Building**, at 100 Centre Street, is by far the most intimidating of them all. Great slabs of granite give it an awesome presence, emphasized by the huge judgmental towers guarding the entrance. This Kafkaesque home of justice has been known since its creation as "the Tombs," a reference not only to its architecture but to the deathly conditions of the city jail it once contained.

All of these courts are open to the public weekdays from 9am to 5pm, though only some of the courtrooms allow visitors. Your best bet for a little courtroom drama is the Criminal Courts, where if you can't slip into a trial, you can at least observe the hallways full of seedy-looking lawyers and the criminals they are representing. Or, for a twist on predinner theater, check out Night Court (Sun–Thu 6pm–1:30am; Fri–Sat 6–9pm).

A major archaeological site, the **African Burial Ground** is located on Duane Street between Broadway and Lafayette Street. The ground is a remnant of a five-and-a-half-acre cemetery, closed in 1794, where 20,000 African men, women and children were buried. The site was unearthed during construction of a federal office building in 1991 and was designated a National Historic Landmark.

St. Paul's Chapel

211 Broadway between Fulton and Vesey Sts (212-602-0874). Subway: A, C, J, M, Z, 2, 3, 4, 5 to Fulton St–Broadway Nassau. Sun–Fri 9am–3pm.

Chinatown

Chinatown used to be the largest Chinese community in the western hemisphere, but in recent years many of the area's residents have moved to other Chinese enclaves in Brooklyn and Queens or other cities. Still, Manhattan's Chinatown remains large, and the neighborhood is a bracing change from the sanitized Chinatowns in San Francisco and London. More than 150,000 Chinese live in its many tenements and high-rise buildings, and many of them work in this concentrated and very self-sufficient area. New immigrants arrive daily, and some residents almost never leave. On its busy streets—which get even wilder during the Chinese New Year festivities in January or February, and around the 4th of July, when it is the city's source of (illegal) fireworks—little English is spoken. The posters in shop windows advertising Chinese movies highlight the area's cultural cohesion.

Food is everywhere. The markets on **Canal Street** sell some of the best fish, fruit and vegetables in the city. There are countless restaurants— Mott Street, from Worth Street right up to Kenmare Street, is lined with Cantonese and Szechuan places, as is East Broadway—and you can buy wonderful snacks from street stalls, such as bags of little sweet egg pancakes. Worth a visit, too, is the **Chinatown Ice Cream Factory** (65 Bayard Street between Mott and Elizabeth Streets), whose flavor options run from red bean to green tea. Canal Street is also (in)famous as a source of blank cassette tapes and counterfeit designer items, including fake Rolexes and the cheapest "brand-name" running shoes. It's a bargain-hunter's paradise. Push past the doors of any of the area's gift shops and you'll be rewarded with all manner of unique, inexpensive one-of-a-kind Chinese imported goods, from teacups and good-luck charms to kitschy pop-culture paraphernalia. One of the best shops is the bilevel **Pearl River Mart** at the corner of Canal Street and Broadway, which is filled with import-

*Sole on ice: Fresh fish is one of the many culinary treats to catch while seeing **Chinatown.***

ed food, dresses, traditional musical instruments and videos (*see chapter* **Shopping & Services**).

A statue of Confucius marks **Confucius Plaza** at the corner of Bowery and Division Streets. On Bayard Street is the **Wall of Democracy**, where political writings about events in Beijing are posted. On weekends, **Columbus Park** at Bayard and Mulberry Streets is the hangout of choice for elderly men and women wishing to get in a game of mahjongg, while younger folks practice martial arts (*see* **Park places**, *page 50*). Immediately upon entering the open doors of the **Eastern States Buddhist Temple of America**, you'll notice the glitter of hundreds of Buddhas and the smell of incense. Another much larger Buddhist temple, **Mahayana Temple Buddhist Association**, is near the entrance to the Manhattan Bridge.

For a different taste of Chinatown culture, there's the noisy **Chinatown Fair** (8 Mott Street), an amusement arcade that until January 1998 featured a live chicken in a glass box that played tic-tac-toe against patrons. Another strange sight is the Fair's **Chinese Museum**, a place of such mystery that it is virtually impossible to gain entry—"only groups of eight," they say. (It is supposed to contain the dragon used in the New Year festival.) Another cultural institution is the **Music Palace Movie Theater**, at 93 Bowery at Hester Street, featuring strictly Chinese films with English subtitles. Finally, although gentrification has not really invaded Chinatown, the **Double Happiness** bar, at 173 Mott Street between Broome and Grand Streets, is a trendy watering hole for Gen Xers with a Chinese decorative touch (*see chapter* **Cafés & Bars**).

Moving east, Chinatown stretches across the lower end of **Sara Delano Roosevelt Park**, where youths engage in spirited games of basketball and handball. City officials closed a market of tin-roofed food stalls in the park in 1998, and political activists continue to agitate for it to be reopened. Across Forsythe Street, Chinatown runs through what is more commonly called the Lower East Side. This area has fewer restaurants and shops than the western end.

Chinatown Fair
8 Mott St at Canal St. Subway: J, M, Z, N, R, 6 to Canal St.

Eastern States Buddhist Temple of America
64B Mott St between Canal and Bayard Sts (212-966-6229). Subway: N, R, 4, 5, 6 to Canal St. 9am–7pm.

Mahayana Temple Buddhist Association
133 Canal St, No. 33 (212-925-8787). Subway: J, M, Z, 6 to Canal St; B, D, Q to Grand St. 8am–6pm.

Lower East Side

The Lower East Side tells the story of New York's immigrants: the cycle of one generation making good and moving to the suburbs, leaving space for the next wave of hopefuls. It is busy and densely populated, a patchwork of strong ethnic communities, great for dining and exploration. Today, Lower East Side residents are largely Asian or Hispanic, though the area is more famous for its earlier settlers, most notably Jews from Eastern Europe. It was here that mass tenement housing was built to accommodate the 19th-century influx of immigrants (including many Irish, German,

Polish and Hungarian families). Unsanitary, overcrowded buildings forced the introduction of building codes. To appreciate the conditions in which the mass of immigrants lived, take a look at the **Lower East Side Tenement Museum** (*see chapter* **Museums**).

Between 1870 and 1920, hundreds of synagogues and religious schools were established here. Yiddish newspapers were published, and associations for social reform and cultural studies flourished, along with vaudeville and Yiddish theaters. (The Marx Brothers, Jimmy Durante, George and Ira Gershwin, and Eddie Cantor were just a few of the entertainers who lived in the area.) Now, however, only 10 to 15 percent of the population is Jewish; the **Eldridge Street Synagogue** finds it hard to round up the ten adult males required to conduct a service.

The area today is characterized by its large Hispanic—Puerto Rican and Dominican—population, which began to move here after World War II. *Bodegas,* or corner groceries, abound, with their brightly colored awnings. There are many restaurants serving Puerto Rican dishes of rice and beans with fried plantains, pork chops and chicken. In the summer, the streets throb with the sounds of salsa and merengue as the residents hang out, slurping ices, drinking beer and playing dominoes.

Beginning in the 1980s, what could be described as the latest immigrants started to move to the area: young artists, musicians and other rebels, attracted by the area's high drama and low rents. The bars, boutiques and music clubs that cater to this crowd initially sprouted on Ludlow Street, an East Village extension. Now they're spreading like dandelions to the surrounding streets. Stanton and Orchard Streets, in particular, are filling in with clubs and restaurants such as **Arlene Grocery** and **Baby Jupiter**. Other outposts are **Tonic**, on Norfolk Street, which is owned by the avant-garde jazz musician John Zorn, and the **Bowery Ballroom**, a club on Delancey Street between Bowery and Chrystie Street (*see chapters* **Bars & Cafés** *and* **Music**). Recently, many small boutiques have opened alongside the clubs—or within them, in the case of the Incommunicado bookstore inside Tonic (*see* **The joy of Essex**, *pages 128–29*).

The Lower East Side has always been a haven for political radicals, and this tradition lives on at **ABC No Rio**, a squat at 156 Rivington Street between Clinton and Suffolk Streets that also houses a gallery and performance space.

Orchard Street below Stanton is the heart of the **Orchard Street Bargain District**, a row of shops selling uninteresting but utilitarian goods such as luggage, sportswear, hats and T-shirts. Some remnants of the neighborhood's Jewish traditions remain. The shabby **Sammy's Roumanian** is only for those with strong stomachs—hearty servings of Eastern European fare are served with a jug of chicken fat and

a bottle of vodka—but it's one of the most famous of the Lower East Side eateries. If you prefer "lighter" food, **Katz's Deli** sells some of the best pastrami in New York, and the orgasms are pretty good, too, if Meg Ryan's performance in *When Harry Met Sally…* is any indication (the scene was filmed there). **Ratner's**, a kosher dairy restaurant, is a New York institution that also perfectly illustrates the collision between old and new Lower East Side: Its back room, **Lansky Lounge**, is a swinging club named for the infamous mobster Meyer Lansky, a former area resident. **Guss' Pickles** at 35 Essex Street between Hester and Grand is another Lower East Side landmark.

Eldridge Street Synagogue
12 Eldridge St between Canal and Division Sts (212-219-0888). Subway: F to East Broadway. Sun 11am–4pm. Tours Tue, Thu.
This beautifully decorated (and now restored) building was the pride of the Jewish congregation that once filled it. Tours are at 11:30am and 2:30pm on Tuesdays and Thursdays.

First Shearith Israel Graveyard
55–57 St. James Pl between Oliver and James Sts. Subway: B, D, Q to Grand St.
The burial ground of the oldest Jewish community in the United States—Spanish and Portuguese Jews who escaped the Inquisition—contains gravestones dating from 1683.

Israel Israelowitz Tours
718-951-7072.
Call for details of guided tours of the Lower East Side, boat tours of Jewish New York and lecture programs.

Sammy's Roumanian
157 Chrystie St at Delancey St (212-673-0330). Subway: B, D, Q to Grand St. Mon–Fri 3pm–10pm, Sat–Sun 3pm–11pm.
The place to go for authentic Jewish soul food and spirits.

Shapiro's Winery
126 Rivington St between Essex and Norfolk Sts (212-674-4404). Subway: F to Delancey St; J, M, Z to Essex St. Tours on the hour, Sun 11am–4pm. $1.
Shapiro's has been making kosher wine ("so thick you can cut it with a knife") since 1899. The wine tours include tastings.

Little Italy

Another neighborhood that has undergone tremendous change in the past several decades is Little Italy—once a vivid pocket of ethnicity, with all the sights and sounds of the mother country. It's getting smaller, though, as Chinatown encroaches and Italian families flee to the suburbs. These days the neighborhood hardly resembles the insular community portrayed in films such as Martin Scorsese's *Mean Streets*. All that's really left of the Italian community that has existed here since the mid-19th century are the cafés and restaurants on Mulberry Street, between Canal and East Houston Streets, and short sections of cross streets. But a strong ethnic pride remains. Limoloads of Italians parade in from Queens and Brooklyn to show their love for the old neighborhood during the Feast of San Gennaro each September

Park places

The grass is just as green in the parks below 14th Street

No city in America has more urban parkland than New York. And while uptown's Central Park tends to hog the spotlight, scores of other smaller parks exist. In addition to containing the city's oldest park, Bowling Green (at the beginning of Broadway), downtown is particularly blessed with its unique open spaces. All parks are open from dawn to dusk. For recorded info on events, call 888-NY-PARKS. Here are some of the more notable green spots to enjoy:

Battery Park

Between State St and the Hudson River and Battery Pl. Subway: 1, 9 to South Ferry; 4, 5 to Bowling Green.
As you walk through its canyons of concrete, steel and glass, it's easy to forget that the island of Manhattan is a mere stone's throw away from the Atlantic Ocean. Luckily, getting in touch with the city's saltwater side is as easy as a trip to the esplanade at Battery Park. The park actually looks out on New York Harbor, not the ocean proper (which is beyond the Verrazano Narrows Bridge in the distance), but the seagulls and the folks fishing for bluefish and striped bass are sure signs of its proximity. The harbor itself is gorgeous, and simply sitting on a bench and staring out at the Statue of Liberty, Ellis Island, Staten Island and all the boats bobbing on the water is one of the most peaceful experiences you can find in the entire city.

North River Park

Along the Hudson River between the World Financial Center and Chambers St. Subway: 1, 2, 3, 9 to Park Pl; A, C, E, to World Trade Ctr.

One of the city's newest parks, North River Park abuts the lower Hudson River on the city's west side. Long and narrow, it's a recreational dream, with basketball and handball courts, concrete tables painted with checkerboards, and ultramodern playground equipment. A large field at the northern end is a favorite spot for soccer players, Frisbee throwers and kite flyers, while the narrow esplanade along the river is a runner's and in-line skater's paradise. An additional advantage of the park is that because it's a bit of a hike from the subway, it tends to be fairly uncrowded.

City Hall Park

Between Broadway and Park Row and Chambers St. Subway: J, M, Z to Chambers St; 2, 3 to Park Pl; 4, 5, 6, to Brooklyn Bridge–City Hall.
At the time of this writing, City Hall Park was undergoing a major renovation to restore it to its 19th-century magnificence. The elegant City Hall at the northern end of the park contains the mayor's office and the legislative chambers of the City Council, and is thus ringed with news vans waiting for the mayor to appear. The city often uses the park for official celebrations, but it's also the prime location for protests, and on any given day you're likely to see somebody in the park protesting something. Of course, the pretty landscaping and abundant benches also make it a popular lunchtime spot for area office workers.

Washington Market Park

Between Greenwich and West Sts and Chambers and Duane Sts. Subway: 1, 9 to Chambers St.
Named for a huge 19th-century food market that used to be nearby, this small, family-oriented Tribeca park is teeming with neighborhood kids and their well-to-do par-

*Big game hunting: Chess players battle in the open air in **Washington Square Park**.*

ents. There's a country feel to it, thanks to the pretty gazebo at the southern end of its oblong green and the community-tended garden plots at its northern edge.

Seward Park

Essex St between Hester St and Straus Sq.
Subway: F to East Broadway.
Tall pin oaks and an abundance of basketball courts can't hide the fact that Seward Park is a bit tattered. Located in an area that was once one of the worst slums in America, the neighborhood around this Lower East Side park is a little better off today, and the park is filled on weekends with teens, mostly Asian, playing basketball.

Columbus Park

Between Bayard and Mosco Sts and Mulberry and Baxter Sts. Subway: J, M, Z, N, R, 6 to Canal St.
This Chinatown neighborhood park is jam-packed on weekend mornings with elderly men playing mah-jongg, while over in the fenced-in, paved play area, people practice martial arts.

Sara Delano Roosevelt Park

Between Houston and Canal Sts and Chrystie and Forsyth Sts. Subway: B, D, Q to Grand St; F to Second Ave.
Only a block wide but eight blocks long, Sara Delano Roosevelt Park (named for Franklin's mother), cuts through the heart of the Lower East Side. Chinatown abuts the southern end of the park, and here crowds of teens play basketball and handball, and slide around on skateboards and in-line skates. The middle section of the park contains abandoned, paved playing fields that show the signs of years of neglect. At the northern end, which borders the East Village, basketball rules. Here, pickup games can be very competitive.

Tompkins Square Park

Between 7th and 10th Sts and Aves A and B. Subway: 6 to Astor Pl.
The community park of the East Village, Tompkins Square is one of the most lively places in the entire city. Here, drum circles, Latin musicians, acoustic guitar–wielding hippie types, punk squatters, dogs, the neighborhood's yuppie residents and the homeless mix and mingle and sit on the grass under huge old trees. In summer, the park's southern end is often the site of musical performances, while the north is the province of basketball, hockey and handball enthusiasts.

Washington Square Park

Between Waverly Pl and W 4th St and MacDougal St and Washington Sq East. Subway: A, C, E, B, D, F, Q to W 4th St–Washington Sq.
Located smack in the middle of bustling Greenwich Village, Washington Square Park is probably the most famous park below 14th Street. The arch at its northern edge, dedicated to George Washington, and the large fountain in its center give it a European feel. Its central location ensures that it's packed with all manner of downtown types. Where once drug dealers plied their trade on every corner, now musicians ring the park's middle section, and street performers work around (and even *in*) the fountain. The southwest corner is home to a community of diehard chess players, and in summer evenings concerts and guerrilla theater are common. Area residents, NYU students and teachers jog the perimeter. But the best thing to do here is find somewhere to park yourself, and indulge in the best people-watching just about anywhere on earth.

(*see chapter* **New York by Season**). In summer, Italian films are shown outside in the De Salvio Playground at Spring and Mulberry Streets.

Naturally, Little Italy is caught up in the lore of the American Mafia, and there are a few sights related to this aspect of the community. Celebrity don John Gotti ran much of his operation from a social club at 247 Mulberry Street (between Prince and Spring Streets); in a twist of fate that sums up the changes happening in the neighborhood, it is now an upscale boutique. Mob figure Joey Gallo was shot to death in 1972 while eating with his family at **Umberto's Clamhouse**, which has relocated around the corner (to 386 Broome Street at Mulberry Street). The Italian eateries here are mostly pricey, ostentatious grill and pasta houses that cater to tourists. Still, it's worth your while to enjoy a dessert and coffee at one of the many small cafés lining the streets (*see chapters* **Restaurants** *and* **Cafés & Bars**). For a drink, head straight to **Mare Chiaro**, at 176 Mulberry Street between Kenmare and Grand Streets, a dive that was once a favorite haunt of Frank Sinatra's back in the day and is now a destination for young revelers.

As you'd expect, the neighborhood is home to great food stores (specializing in strong cheeses, excellent wines, spicy meats, freshly made pasta and the like). For that truly unique gift, **Forzano Italian Imports**, at 128 Mulberry Street, is the best place in New York for papal souvenirs, ghastly Italian pop music and soccer memorabilia. Two buildings of note here are **Old St. Patrick's Cathedral** (260–264 Prince Street at Mulberry Street), which was once the premier Catholic church of New York but was demoted when the Fifth Avenue cathedral was consecrated, and the former **Police Headquarters Building**, (240 Centre Street between Grand and Broome Streets), which was converted into much sought-after co-op apartments in 1988. The very hip northern end of the neighborhood, which lies just to the east of Soho, is now known as Nolita. Especially on Mott and Elizabeth Streets between Houston and Prince Streets, an array of small shops sell kitschy art and gifts. The area also has some good restaurants and funky boutiques (*see chapters* **Restaurants** *and* **Shopping & Services**).

Soho

Soho is designer New York, in every sense. Walk around its cobbled streets, among the elegant cast-iron buildings, boutiques and bistros, and you'll find yourself sharing the sidewalks with the beautiful people of young, moneyed, fashionable NYC. The bars and cafés are full of these trendsetters, while the shop windows display the work of the latest arrivals in the world of fashion. The area's art galleries, though still plentiful, have been vacating their converted lofts to move to cheaper (and now cutting-edge) neighborhoods like Dumbo in Brooklyn and far west Chelsea (*see chapter* **Art Galleries**).

Soho (south of Houston Street) was earmarked for destruction during the 1960s, but the area was saved by the many artists who inhabited its (then) low-rent former warehouse spaces. They protested the demolition of these beautiful buildings, whose cast-iron frames prefigured the technology of the skyscraper (*see chapter* **Architecture**). Two examples of cast-iron architecture at its best are **109 Prince Street** at the corner of Greene Street, which now houses a Replay clothing store, and **95 Greene Street**. As loft living became fashionable and the buildings were renovated for residential use, the landlords were quick to sniff gentrification's increased profits. Several upscale hotels, including the Mercer and the Soho Grand, have opened in the area, and the names on the shop windows read like a who's who of fashion: Calvin Klein, Louis Vuitton, Vivienne Tam, Vivienne Westwood, agnès b., Anna Sui and Helmut Lang are just a few of the designers who have opened boutiques (*see chapter* **Shopping & Services**). Surprisingly, plenty of sweatshops remain here, especially near Canal Street—though, increasingly, the buildings house such businesses as graphics studios, magazines and record labels. There has also been a noticeable invasion over the past few years by large chain stores: Starbucks, Old Navy, Pottery Barn, J. Crew and Banana Republic have all put down roots, prompting locals to mutter darkly about the "malling of Soho." For an increasing number of more singular shops, head for the area dubbed Nolita, which borders Soho, Little Italy and the East Village, or for the Lower East Side (*see* **The joy of Essex**, *pages 128–29*).

West Broadway, the main thoroughfare of Soho, is lined with the chain stores, pricey shops and art galleries. On the weekend, French, German and Italian are as likely to be heard as English, due to the huge number of European tourists attracted by the fine shopping. Four blocks east, on Broadway, the **Guggenheim Museum** has a branch that exhibits both temporary collections and selections from the museum's permanent collection. In addition, Broadway has a collection of other galleries specializing in lesser-known artists. The **New Museum of Contemporary Art** and the **Alternative Museum** often exhibit controversial works; the neighboring **Museum of African Art** is also worth a look. Just off Broadway on Spring Street is the **Fire Museum**, a small building housing a collection of gleaming antique engines dating back to the 1700s (*see chapters* **Museums** *and* **Art Galleries**).

West of West Broadway, tenement- and townhouse-lined streets contain remnants of the Italian community that dominated this area. Elderly men and women walk along Sullivan Street up to the **Shrine Church of St. Anthony of Padua**, which was founded by the Franciscan Friars in 1866. The church also supports a convent and rectory nearby.

Some businesses that predate Soho's gentrification are still thriving, including **Joe's Dairy** at 156 Sullivan Street, **Pino's Prime Meats** at 149 Sullivan Street and **Vesuvio Bakery** at 160 Prince Street.

Tribeca

Tribeca (triangle below Canal Street) today is a textbook example of the process of gentrification in lower Manhattan. It's very much as Soho was 15 or 20 years ago: Some parts are deserted and abandoned—the cobbles dusty and untrodden and the cast-iron architecture chipped and unpainted—and other pockets throb with arriviste energy. Unlike Soho in its early days, however, the rich and famous have been the pioneers here: John F. Kennedy Jr., Harvey Keitel, MTV Chairman Tom Freston and many other local and national celebrities all live in the area. In particular, this is the hot spot for new restaurants, including Nobu, Layla, Zeppole and Bouley Bakery (*see chapter* **Restaurants**). A number of bars have established themselves as well, especially near the corner of North Moore Street and West Broadway, and clubs such as the Knitting Factory are expanding the cultural offerings (*see chapters* **Cafés & Bars** *and* **Music**). The buildings here are generally larger than those in Soho and, particularly near the river, are mostly warehouses. However, there is some fine smaller-scale cast-iron architecture along White Street and the parallel thoroughfares (*see chapter* **Architecture**), including **85 Leonard Street**, the only remaining cast-iron building attributable to James Bogardus, the developer of the cast-iron building method. Harrison Street is home to a row of well-preserved Federal-style townhouses. As in Soho, art is a prominent industry here, and there are several galleries representing the more cutting-edge (read: hit-or-miss) side of things. Salons, furniture stores, spas and other businesses that cater to the upscale residents of the neighborhood have followed the galleries.

Tribeca is also the unofficial headquarters of New York's film industry. Robert De Niro's **Tribeca Film Center** houses screening rooms and production offices at 375 Greenwich Street, in the old Martinson Coffee Building. Nearby, at 99 Hudson Street, are the Queens-bred brothers Bob and Harvey Weinstein and the main offices of their company, Miramax. The **Screening Room**, at 54 Varick Street at the corner of Laight Street, shows art-house films in an upstairs theater and serves gourmet food in its elegant dining room. Another collision between film and food is the **Tribeca Grill**, partly owned by De Niro and housed on the ground floor of his Greenwich Street film center.

West Village

Most of the West Village, roughly the area between Seventh Avenue and the river, is filled with quaint

*Book 'em: This former civil and criminal court now houses the **Jefferson Market Library**.*

tree-lined streets of historic townhouses. It was historically a middle-class neighborhood, but today many of the city's media power elite live here; they fill its bistros and bars, many on Bleecker Street and Hudson Street, the area's main thoroughfares. The northwest corner of this area is known as the **Meatpacking District**, which explains the many businesses advertising QUALITY VEAL and other meats. In recent years, clubs have taken advantage of the large spaces available here, and now partyers share the empty nighttime streets with transsexual prostitutes. Restaurants have moved in as well: **Florent**, a 24-hour French diner at 69 Gansevoort Street between Greenwich and Washington Streets, has been here for years and is always crowded.

Farther south and west of Hudson Street are cobblestone streets of immense charm. At Bethune and Washington Streets is Westbeth, a block-long old building formerly owned by Bell Telephone (it's where the vacuum tube and the transistor were invented) that in 1965 was converted to lofts for artists. Around the corner on Bank Street is the **Westbeth Theatre Center Music Hall**, which often has fine rock shows (*see chapter* **Music**). (A new development of luxury condos along Washington Street has sparked claims that the neighborhood's charm is slowly diminishing.) On Hudson Street between Perry and 11th Streets is the famous **White Horse Tavern**, where poet Dylan Thomas spent the better part of the 1940s. Earlier in the century, writers like John Steinbeck and John Dos Passos passed the time at **Chumley's**, a Prohibition-era speakeasy, still unmarked

at 86 Bedford Street (*see chapter* **Cafés & Bars**). On and just off Seventh Avenue South are numerous jazz and cabaret clubs, including the **Village Vanguard, Small's, Arthur's Tavern** and **Marie's Crisis Cafe** (*see chapter* **Music**).

The West Village is also a renowned gay area, with many famous bars, including the **Stonewall** on Christopher Street. Orignally the Stonewall Inn, this bar was the scene of the 1969 Stonewall Rebellion, which marked the birth of the gay liberation movement. There are as many same-sex couples strolling along Christopher Street as straight ones, and plenty of shops, bars and restaurants that are out and proud (*see chapter* **Gay & Lesbian**).

Greenwich Village

The middle section of "the Village" has been the scene of some serious hanging out throughout its history. Stretching from 14th Street down to Houston Street, and from Broadway west to Seventh Avenue South, leafy streets with townhouses, theaters, coffeehouses, and tiny bars and clubs have witnessed and inspired bohemian lifestyles for almost a century. It's a place for idle wandering, for people-watching from sidewalk cafés, for candlelit dining in secret restaurants, or for hopping between bars and cabaret venues. The Village gets overcrowded in summer, and it has lost some of its quaintness as the retail center of lower Broadway has spread west, but much of what attracted creative types to New York still exists. The jazz generation lives on in smoky clubs (*see chapter* **Music**). Sip a fresh roast in honor of the Beats—Jack Kerouac, Allen Ginsberg and their ilk—as you sit in the coffee shops they frequented. Kerouac's favorite was **Le Figaro Café**, at the corner of MacDougal and Bleecker Streets.

The hippies, who tuned out in **Washington Square**, are still there in spirit, and often in person: The park hums with musicians and street artists. (The once-ubiquitous pot dealers have largely become victims of strict policing.) Chess hustlers and students from **New York University** join in, along with today's new generation of hangers-out: hip-hop kids who drive down in their booming jeeps and Generation Y skaters/ravers who clatter around the fountain and the base of the arch (a miniature Arc de Triomphe built in 1892 in honor of George Washington).

The Village first became fashionable in the 1830s, when elegant townhouses were built around Washington Square. Most of these are now owned by NYU; the university dominates this section of the Village, and many of the large apartment complexes on or near the square serve as dormitories. Literary figures including Henry James, Mark Twain and Edith Wharton lived on or near the square, and Herman Melville wrote *Moby-Dick* in a house on the northern reaches of the Village. In 1870, this growing artistic community founded the **Salmagundi Club**, America's oldest artists' club, which is still extant, just above Washington Square on Fifth Avenue. And although it has moved from its original location at the corner of 8th Street, the **Cedar Tavern** on University Place between 11th and 12th Streets was where the leading figures of Abstract Expressionism discussed how best to throw paint: Jackson Pollock, Franz Kline and Larry Rivers drank there in the 1950s.

Eighth Street, now a long procession of punky boutiques, shoe shops, piercing parlors and cheap jewelry vendors, was the closest New York got to San Francisco's Haight Street; Jimi Hendrix's Electric Lady Sound Studios are still here at No. 52. Once the stomping grounds of Beat poets and hipster jazz musicians, the area around Bleecker Street between La Guardia Place and Sixth Avenue is now a dingy stretch of poster shops, cheap ethnic restaurants and a number of music venues that showcase local talent and cover bands for the college crowd. The famed Village Gate jazz club used to be at the corner of Thompson and Bleecker Streets; it is now a CVS pharmacy.

In the triangle formed by 10th Street, Sixth Avenue and Greenwich Avenue, you'll see the neo-Gothic Victorian **Jefferson Market Courthouse**; once voted America's fifth most beautiful building, it's now a library. Across the street is **Balducci's** (*see chapter* **Shopping & Services**), one of the finest food stores in the city, and down Sixth Avenue at 4th Street you stumble on "the Cage," outdoor basketball courts where you can witness hot hoops action (*see chapter* **Sports & Fitness**).

Jefferson Market Courthouse
425 Sixth Ave between 9th and 10th Sts (212-243-4334). Subway: F to 14th St. Library open Mon, Thu 10am–6pm; Tue, Fri noon–6pm; Wed noon–8pm; Sat 10am–5pm. Free.

Salmagundi Club
47 Fifth Ave at 12th St (212-255-7740). Subway: L, N, R, 4, 5, 6 to 14th St–Union Sq. Open for exhibitions only; phone for details. Free.
Now the home of a series of artistic and historical societies, the club's fine 19th-century interior is worth a look.

East Village

Far scruffier than its western counterpart, the East Village has a long history as a countercultural mecca. Originally considered part of the Lower East Side, the neighborhood first took off in the 1960s, when throngs of writers, artists and musicians moved in and turned it into ground zero for the '60s cultural revolution. Many famous clubs and coffeehouses were established, including the Fillmore East rock club on Second Avenue between 6th and 7th Streets (now demolished), and the Dom, where the Velvet Underground was a regular headliner, at 23 St. Marks Place (now a community center). In the '70s, the neighborhood took a dive as drugs and crime became prevalent—facts that didn't stop many artists and punk rockers from continuing to live here. In the early '80s, area galleries were among the first to display the work of hot young artists Jean-Michel Basquiat and Keith Haring.

Today, the area east of Broadway between 14th and Houston Streets is no longer quite so cutting-edge, though remnants of its spirited past live on. Here you'll find an amiable population of punks, yuppies, hippies, homeboys, homeless and trustafarians—would-be bohos who live off trust funds. This motley crew has crowded into the area's tenements—along with older residents, mostly survivors from various waves of immigration—and provides the area with funky, cheap clothes stores (check for quality before forking over any cash), record shops, bargain restaurants, grungy bars and punky clubs.

St. Marks Place (essentially East 8th Street between Lafayette Street and Avenue A), lined with bars squeezed into tiny basements and restaurants overflowing onto the sidewalks, is the main drag (in more ways than one). It's packed until the wee hours with crowds browsing for bargains in T-shirt boutiques, comic-book shops, record stores and bookshops. The more interesting places are to the east, and you'll find cafés and great little shops of all kinds on or around Avenue A between 6th and 10th Streets. Since tattooing became legal in New York City in 1997 (it had been banned in 1961), a number of parlors have opened up, including the now famous **Fun City** parlor, at 94 St. Marks Place

*Kickin': Vintage finds in the **East Village**.*

between First Avenue and Avenue A, whose awning advertises CAPPUCCINO AND TATTOO.

Astor Place, with its revolving cube sculpture, is always swarming with young skateboarders. It is also the site of Peter Cooper's **Cooper Union**, the city's first free educational institute, opened in 1859; it's now a design and engineering school. Astor Place marked the boundary between the ghettos to the east and some of the city's most fashionable homes, such as **Colonnade Row**, on Lafayette Street. Facing these was the distinguished Astor Public Library, now the **Joseph Papp Public Theater**, a haven for first-run American plays and home of the **New York Shakespeare Festival** (*see chapter* **Theater**) as well as a trendy new nightspot called **Joe's Pub**. In the '60s, Papp rescued the library from demolition and got it declared a landmark.

East of Lafayette Street on the Bowery are numerous missionary organizations that cater to the downtrodden who, for better or worse, still make the Bowery the Bowery. In recent years, a few restaurants have also established themselves here. At 315 Bowery is the hallowed **CBGB** club ("Country, Blue-Grass, Blues"), the birthplace of American punk. CB's still packs in guitar bands, both new and used (*see chapter* **Music**). Many other local bars and clubs successfully apply the formula of cheap beer and loud music, including the **Continental**, **Brownies** and the **Mercury Lounge**.

East 7th Street is a Ukrainian stronghold; the focal point is the Byzantine-looking **St. George's Ukrainian Catholic Church**, built in 1977 but looking at least a century older. Across the street there is often a long line of beefy fraternity types

waiting to enter **McSorley's Old Ale House**, the oldest pub in the city (or so it claims); it still serves just one kind of beer—its own brew (*see chapter* **Cafés & Bars**).

On East 6th Street, between First and Second Avenues, is **Little India** (one of several in New York). Here, roughly two dozen Indian restaurants sit side by side, the long-running rumor being that they all share a single kitchen. And if you're wondering about the inordinate number of fat men on Harleys on East 3rd Street between First and Second Avenues, it's because the New York chapter of Hell's Angels is headquartered here.

Toward the East River are Avenues A through D, an area known as **Alphabet City**. Its largely Hispanic population (Avenue C is known as "Loisaida Ave," the phonetic spelling of "Lower East Side" when pronounced with a Spanish accent) is slowly being overtaken by an influx of young counterculture arrivals. Two interesting churches on East 4th Street are Spanish-colonial style: **San Isidero Y San Leandro**, at No. 345 between Avenues C and D, and **Iglesia Pentecostal Camino A Damasco**, at No. 289 between Avenues B and C. The neighborhood's long romance with heroin continues (rocker Scott Weiland was busted here in 1998 during a sweep of housing projects on Avenue D); consequently, venturing much farther east than Avenue B can be dodgy at night. Alphabet City is not without its attractions, though: The **Nuyorican Poets Cafe** (*see chapter* **Books & Poetry**), a focus for the recent resurgence of espresso-drinking beatniks, is famous for its "slams," in which performance poets do battle before a score-keeping audience. **Tompkins Square Park** (7th to 10th Streets between Avenues A and B), now well maintained and landscaped, has historically been the focus for political dissent and rioting (*see* **Park places**, *pages 50–51*). The latest uprising was in 1991, after the controversial decision to evict the park's squatters and renovate it to suit the taste of the area's increasingly affluent residents. Political dissent lives on at **Blackout Books**, an anarchist bookshop at 50 Avenue B between 3rd and 4th Streets. North of Tompkins Square, around First Avenue and 11th Street, are remnants of earlier communities: good Italian cheese shops, Polish restaurants, discount fabric shops and two great Italian patisseries. Visit **De Roberti's** (176 First Avenue) for delicious cakes and **Veniero's** (342 11th St) for wonderful minipastries and butter biscuits.

St. Mark's in-the-Bowery
131 E 10th St at Second Ave (212-674-6377). Subway: 6 to Astor Pl. Mon–Fri 10am–6pm.
St. Mark's was built in 1799 on the site of Peter Stuyvesant's farm. Stuyvesant, one of New York's first governors, is buried here, along with many of his descendants. The church is now home to several arts groups (it was the church in *The Group* where the wedding and funeral took place). Call for details of the performances here.

Midtown

Commuters and tourists crowd the gridlocked streets by day and come out to see the bright lights of Broadway at night

Midtown, roughly 14th to 59th Streets, is the city's engine room, powered by the hundreds of thousands of commuters who pour in each day. By day, the area is all business. Garment manufacturers have long called the area on and around Seventh ("Fashion") Avenue home. The rest is occupied by towering office buildings, many headquarters to huge international companies. It's also where you'll find most of the city's large hotels (and the hordes of tourists and traveling execs who occupy them), the department stores and classy retailers of Fifth Avenue and Rockefeller Center, and major landmarks such as the Empire State Building, St. Patrick's Cathedral and Carnegie Hall. By night, life centers on the neon glitz of the newly rehabilitated Times Square. Locals and visitors converge here to see Broadway shows and movies, to eat in the numerous restaurants or to do some late-night shopping for music and home electronics.

Flatiron District

The Flatiron District is clearly on the edge of downtown—both in its cultural style and in its newfound identity as a hotbed of new-media businesses. As Broadway cuts diagonally through Manhattan, it inspires a public square wherever it intersects an avenue. Two such places, Union Square at 14th Street and Madison Square at 23rd, once marked the limits of a ritzy 19th-century shopping district known as **Ladies' Mile**. Extending along Broadway and west to Sixth Avenue, this collection of huge retail palaces (Macy's first store was on Sixth between 13th and 14th Streets) attracted the "carriage trade"—wealthy ladies buying the latest fashions and household goods from all over the world. By the time World War I began, most of the department stores had moved farther north, and all that was left of the glamorous shops were the proud cast-iron facades of the buildings that had housed them. Today, the area has reclaimed much of its glamour as a shopping destination. The city's best sporting-goods store, **Paragon**, is at the corner of 18th Street and Broadway, and the upscale home-design store **ABC Carpet and Home** is in a beautiful old building at the corner of 19th Street and Broadway. Paul Smith and Emporio Armani showcase their wares on Fifth, while on Sixth large chain stores such as Old Navy and Bed, Bath & Beyond have moved in (*see chapter* **Shopping & Services**).

Union Square is named after neither the Union of the Civil War nor the lively labor rallies that once took place here, but simply for the union of Broadway and Bowery Lane (now Fourth Avenue). From the 1920s until the early 1960s, it had a reputation as a political hot spot, a favorite location for rabble-rousing oratory. These days, the gentrified square is home to the **Union Square Greenmarket**—an excellent farmers' market that is open several days a week. The streets leading from it are chock-full of restaurants, including one of the city's best: **Union Square Cafe**. The park is also a popular meeting place. In the summer months, a large outdoor café beckons alfresco diners, while packs of skateboarders practice their wild-style stunts on the steps and railings of the square's southern edge. West of the recently opened **Virgin Megastore** and 14-screen movieplex, 14th Street is a downmarket retail bonanza offering cheap clothes and electronics (*see chapter* **Shopping & Services**).

The Renaissance palazzo **Flatiron Building**—originally named the Fuller Building after its first owners—is famous for its triangular shape and as the world's first steel-frame skyscraper (*see chapter* **Architecture**). It stands just south of Madison Square at the intersection of 23rd Street, Broadway and Fifth Avenue, and gives its name to the surrounding streets, an area dotted with boutiques, bookshops, and photo studios and labs, not to mention wandering models. Since the early '90s, however, many Internet-related companies have moved into lofts in the buildings lining Broadway and Fifth Avenue—hence the area's nickname, **Silicon Alley**.

Madison Square (23rd Street to 26th Street between Fifth Avenue and Madison Avenue) is rich in history. It was the site of P.T. Barnum's Hippodrome, and the original Madison Square Garden, as well as the scene of prize fights, one famous society murder and lavish entertainment. These are now gone, and after years of neglect, the once scruffy, statue-filled park is finally getting a facelift (*see* **Park places**, *pages 50–51*). The area bordering the park's east side is also up and coming. For years it was notable only for the presence of such imposing buildings as the gold-topped **Metropolitan Life Insurance Company**, the **New York Life Insurance Company** and the **Appellate Court**, but two new upscale restaurants, **11 Madison Park** and **Tabla**, have injected a shot of chic into this once-staid area (*see chapter* **Restaurants**).

*Vegas on the Hudson: Bright, colorful neon gleams in the once gritty **Times Square**.*

Union Square Greenmarket

North end of Union Square, 17th St between Park Ave South and Broadway (212-477-3220). Subway: L, N, R, 4, 5, 6 to 14th St–Union Sq. Mon, Wed, Fri, Sat 7am–6pm.

Gramercy Park

Gramercy Park, at the bottom of Lexington Avenue between 20th and 21st Streets, must be entered with a key, something possessed only by those who live in the beautiful townhouses and apartment buildings that surround it—or who stay at the **Gramercy Park Hotel** (*see chapter* **Accommodations**). (Anyone, however, can enjoy the tranquillity of the neighboring district, between Third and Park Avenues.) Gramercy Park was developed in the 1830s, copying the concept of a London square. **The Players**, at 16 Gramercy Park, is housed in a building bought by Edwin Booth, brother of Abraham Lincoln's assassin, John Wilkes Booth, and the foremost actor of his day. Booth had it remodeled as a club for theater professionals. (Winston Churchill and Mark Twain were also members.) At No. 15 is the **National Arts Club**, whose members have often donated impressive works in lieu of annual dues. Its bar houses perhaps the only original Tiffany stained-glass ceiling left in New York City.

Irving Place, leading south from the park to 14th Street, is named after Washington Irving, who didn't actually live on this street (his nephew did). It does have a literary past, though: **Pete's Tavern**, which insists that it (not McSorley's) is the oldest bar in town (*see chapter* **Cafés & Bars**), was where New York wit O. Henry wrote "The Gift of the Magi." Near the corner of 15th Street is **Irving Plaza**, a popular midsize rock venue that hosts many big-name acts (*see chapter* **Music**).

East of Irving Place, at the corner of 17th Street and Park Avenue South, is the last headquarters of the once all-powerful Tammany Hall political organization. Built in 1929, the building now houses the **Union Square Theater** and the **New York Film Academy**.

West of Gramercy Park is the **Theodore Roosevelt Birthplace**, now a small museum. To the east is the **Police Academy Museum**, where you can see hundreds of guns, including one of Al Capone's, and exhibitions describing famous cases and gruesome murders. The low, fortresslike **69th Regiment Armory** (Lexington Avenue at 25th Street), now used by the New York National Guard, was the site of the sensational 1913 Armory Show, which introduced Americans to the modern forms of Cubism, Fauvism, the precocious Marcel Duchamp and other artistic outrages.

National Arts Club

15 Gramercy Park South between Park Ave South and Irving Pl (212-475-3424). Subway: 6 to 23rd St. Open for exhibitions only.

Police Academy Museum

235 E 20th St between Second and Third Aves (212-477-9753). Subway: 6 to 23rd St. Mon–Fri 9am–2pm. Free.

Theodore Roosevelt Birthplace

28 E 20th St between Broadway and Park Ave South (212-260-1616). Subway: 6 to 23rd St. Wed–Sun 9am–5pm. $2, children free. No credit cards.
The popular president's birthplace was demolished in 1916 but has since been fully reconstructed, complete with period furniture and a trophy room.

Kips Bay and Murray Hill

Running from 23rd to 42nd Streets between Park Avenue (and Park Avenue South) and the East

River, this area is dominated by two things: large apartment buildings and hospitals. The southern portion, known as **Kips Bay** (after Jacobus Kip, whose 17th-century farm used to occupy the area), is populated mainly by young professionals. Third Avenue is the main thoroughfare, and it's dotted with ethnic restaurants representing a surprising variety of mainly Eastern cuisines, including Afghan, Turkish and Tibetan. One exception to the otherwise sleepy tone of the neighborhood is the **Rodeo Bar**, on Third Avenue and 28th Street, a Texas-style restaurant and roadhouse that offers live roots music (*see chapter* **Music**). Lexington Avenue between 27th and 30th Streets is called **Curry Hill** due to the swath of Indian restaurants and groceries offering cheap food, spices and imported goods (*see chapter* **Restaurants**). Other than a recently developed complex with a multiplex movie theater, a bookstore and several large chain stores on Second Avenue at 30th Street, Second Avenue is primarily home to a collection of pubs and small, undistinguished restaurants. First Avenue is hospital row; **New York University Medical Center**, the city-run **Bellevue Hospital** and the city's Chief Medical Examiner's office are all here.

Between 30th and 40th Streets is **Murray Hill**. Townhouses of the rich and powerful were once clustered here around Park and Madison Avenues. While it's still a fashionable neighborhood, only a few streets retain the elegance that once made it such a tony address. **Sniffen Court**, at 150–158 East 36th Street, is an unspoiled row of carriage houses, within spitting distance of the Queens-Midtown Tunnel's ceaseless traffic.

The charming Italianate **Pierpont Morgan Library**, on Madison Avenue between 36th and 37th Streets, is the reason most visitors are drawn to the area. Two elegant buildings, linked by a glass cloister, house the silver and copper collections, manuscripts, books and prints owned by the famous banker, mostly gathered during his travels in Europe (*see chapter* **Museums**).

Chelsea

Chelsea is the region between 14th and 30th Streets west of Sixth Avenue. It is populated mostly by young professionals and has become a hub of New York gay life (*see chapter* **Gay & Lesbian**). You'll find all the trappings of an urban residential neighborhood on the upswing: countless stores (some dull) and a generous number of bars and fine restaurants. (Most cluster on Eighth Avenue.) Chelsea's western warehouse district, currently housing some large dance clubs, is being developed for residential use. Pioneering galleries, like the **Dia Center for the Arts** at the west end of 22nd Street, have dragged the art crowd westward, and the whole area has become a thriving gallery district (*see* **West Chelsea** *in chapter* **Art Galleries**).

Cushman Row (406–418 West 20th Street) in the **Chelsea Historic District** is a good example of how Chelsea looked when it was developed in the mid-1800s—a grandeur that was destroyed 30

*Petal pushers: Fresh food, flowers and more abound at the **Union Square Greenmarket**.*

*Catch a wave: the **Morgan**'s Garden Court.*

and mimes…well, do whatever mimes do. Farther toward the river on 19th Street is the **Kitchen**, the experimental arts center with a penchant for video (*see chapters* **Dance**, **Film & TV**, *and* **Theater**).

When you reach the Hudson River, you'll see the piers, derelict fingers raking the water. These were originally the terminals for the world's grand ocean liners (the *Titanic* was scheduled to dock here). Most are in a state of disrepair, though development has transformed the four between 17th and 23rd Streets into a dramatic-looking sports center and TV studio complex called **Chelsea Piers** (*see* **No pier pressure here**, *page 274*). After you've hit some of the art galleries, keep heading west along 22nd Street to watch a peaceful sunset while lounging on one of the pier's park benches.

Chelsea Historic District
Between Ninth and Tenth Aves from 20th to 22nd Sts.
Subway: A, C, E to 14th St; L to Eighth Ave.

General Theological Seminary
175 Ninth Ave between 20th and 21st Sts (212-243-5150). Subway: A, C, E, to 14th St; L to Eighth Ave. Mon–Fri noon–3pm, Sat 11am–3pm. Free.
You can walk through the grounds of the seminary (when open) or take a guided tour in summer (call for details).

Herald Square and the Garment District

Seventh Avenue in the 30s boasts a slightly more memorable moniker: Fashion Avenue. Streets here are gridlocked permanently by delivery trucks. The surrounding area is the **Garment District**, where midtown office buildings mingle with the buzzing activity of a huge manufacturing industry that's been centered here for a century. Shabby clothing and fabric stores line the streets (especially 38th and 39th), and there are intriguing shops selling exclusively lace, buttons or Lycra swimsuits. Most are wholesale only, but some sell to the public. At Seventh Avenue and 25th Street is the **Fashion Institute of Technology**, a state university where aspiring Calvin Kleins and Norma Kamalis (both former students) dream up the fashions of tomorrow. FIT's gallery features excellent exhibitions open to the public (*see chapter* **Museums**).

Macy's will most definitely sell things to you, though you can usually find the same items cheaper elsewhere. Plunked at the corner of Broadway and 34th Street, and stretching all the way to Seventh Avenue, Macy's still impresses as the biggest department store in the world (*see chapter* **Shopping & Services**). **Manhattan Mall**, down a block, is a phenomenally ugly building, a kind of neon-and-chrome Jell-O mold. This is American mall shopping at its best, though, and most of the big chain stores have outlets here. This retail wonderland's home, **Herald Square**, is named after a long-gone newspaper. The lower part is known as **Greeley Square**, after the owner of the *Herald*'s

years later when the noisy elevated railways came to steal the sunlight and dominate the area. Just north, occupying the entire block between Ninth and Tenth Avenues and 20th and 21st Streets, is the **General Theological Seminary**; its garden is a sublime retreat. Over on Tenth Avenue, the flashing lights of the **Empire Diner** (a 1929 chrome Art Deco beauty) attract pre- and post-clubbers. In recent years, the Diner has been joined by a number of other hip eating establishments, including the taxi garage–turned–hot spot **Lot 61** (*see chapters* **Restaurants** *and* **Cafés & Bars**).

Sixth Avenue around 27th Street can seem like a tropical forest at times—the pavement overflows with the palm leaves, decorative grasses and colorful blooms of Chelsea's **flower district**. The garment industry has a presence here as well, as it spills west and south from its Seventh Avenue center farther north. Sixth Avenue in the mid-20s is also full of antiques showrooms, which sell everything from old posters to classic furniture, and excellent flea markets operate year-round on weekends in empty parking lots on 24th, 25th and 26th Streets (*see chapter* **Shopping & Services**).

On 23rd Street, between Seventh and Eighth Avenues, is the **Chelsea Hotel**, where many famous people checked in—some of whom never checked out, like Sid Vicious's girlfriend Nancy Spungen. It's worth a peek for its weird artwork and ghoulish guests (*see chapter* **Accommodations**). On Eighth Avenue, you'll find the **Joyce**, a stunning renovated Art Moderne cinema that's a mecca for dance lovers, and on 19th Street, the wonderful **Bessie Schönberg Theater**, where poets recite

Putting the stars back in the sky

Some of New York's famous public spaces get a makeover

Never content to just leave things the way they are, New York has always undergone constant change. While this approach to life certainly has its ups (this is a town where raw ambition and creativity are encouraged), it also has its downs, such as when magnificent buildings and other public spaces are destroyed in the name of progress. Excellent examples of this ongoing trade-off can be seen up close in midtown, where recent renovations of Grand Central Terminal and the New York Public Library's main reading room have been universally hailed, and where the more controversial transformation of Times Square continues.

Described by *New York Times* architectural critic Herbert Muschamp as "the palace of all train stations," Grand Central Terminal was pretty damn impressive *before* it was renovated. Behind its Beaux Arts facade is a huge concourse with a soaring ceiling, underneath which thousands of busy people rush to catch commuter trains. For years, the ceiling was a grimy, smudged brown, but now its constellations are clearly visible in a bright shade of green, thanks to a massive renovation completed in autumn 1998. Other marvelous touches include the addition of a new staircase on the eastern side of the concourse that matches the one on the west side and provides access to a balcony above, and the uncovering of the walkways that lead to the terminal's lower level. Many restaurants have been added, including Michael Jordan's Steak House on the western balcony, and more are soon to come. Gourmet food stalls now line the hallways jutting off the main concourse. The terminal is bright again, and as sunlight streams into the epic space, all who travel through it feel a sense of grandeur.

Just two blocks west, at the main branch of the New York Public Library, is an equally impressive display of the city's capability at both preserving and updating its architectural heritage. The main reading room, on the library's top floor, reopened in autumn 1998 after a $15-million renovation. The attention to detail that the renovators lavished on the room boggles the mind: Leaf blowers were used to clean the sunken-paneled

No longer terminal: **Grand Central**'s *main concourse thrives after its renovation.*

ceiling; the 18 bronze chandeliers were polished and outfitted with 1,620 new lightbulbs; the 22-foot-long tables were completely refinished, as were the tables' matching oak chairs; and finally, most of the tables were outfitted with bronze plates containing hookups for laptop computers, making the beautiful old room ready for the future. The only problem with the renovation is that it's so marvelous to look at, people may have a hard time staying focused on their reading.

Just a little farther west is Times Square—the "Crossroads of the World." The recent change of the square—from a seedy den of pornographic moviehouses, video stores and strip clubs to a family-friendly entertainment mecca—has met with less than universal praise. The change began in earnest in 1990, when the city condemned most of the properties along 42nd Street between Seventh and Eighth Avenues (a.k.a. "the Deuce"). Then the city changed its zoning laws, specifically to make it harder for adult-entertainment establishments to continue operating legally. But Times Square's XXX days were officially numbered when the Walt Disney Company moved in and renovated the historic New Amsterdam Theatre, currently home to the musical *The Lion King*. More corporations have relocated to the area, making the few remaining sex shops look increasingly out of place. The result of all these changes is that Times Square is undeniably safer and less grimy than it was ten years ago. But the process has also obliterated an entire subculture of endlessly entertaining and fascinating sleaze, making people question if the city is becoming more and more culturally homogenized.

Debates over New York's public spaces are destined to continue, and as they do, some New Yorkers will inevitably be upset about the changes that occur. But these people would be wise to remember that, in time, whatever changes are made now may someday be undone by yet more changes.

Grand Central Terminal

42nd to 44th Sts between Vanderbilt and Lexington Aves. Subway: S, 4, 5, 6, 7 to 42nd St–Grand Central.

New York Public Library

42nd St at Fifth Ave (212-930-0830). Subway: B, D, F, Q, to 42nd St; 4, 5, 6, 7 to 42nd St–Grand Central. Mon, Thu, Fri, Sat 10am–6pm; Tue, Wed 11am–7:30pm. Some sections closed Mondays.

Times Square

42nd St at Broadway. Times Square Visitor's Center, 1560 Broadway between 46th and 47th Sts (212-768-1560). Subway: N, R, S, 1, 2, 3, 9, 7 to 42nd St–Grand Central.

rival, the *Tribune,* a paper for which Karl Marx wrote a regular column. *Life* magazine was based around the corner on 31st Street, and its cherubic mascot can still be seen over the entrance of what is now the **Herald Square Hotel**. East of Greeley Square, mostly on 32nd Street, is a bustling district of Korean shops and restaurants that offer authentic, inexpensive cuisine.

The giant doughnut of a building one block west is the famous sports and entertainment arena **Madison Square Garden** (*see chapter* **Sports & Fitness**). It occupies the site of the old Pennsylvania Station—the McKim, Mead & White architectural masterpiece that was inexplicably destroyed by 1960s planners, an act that brought about the creation of the Landmarks Preservation Commission. The railroad terminal is now underground, its name shortened to **Penn Station**, as if in shame (although it is the busiest station in the country, serving some 600,000 people daily). Thankfully, the **General Post Office**, designed by the same prolific firm, still stands across the street, an enormous Beaux Arts colonnade occupying two city blocks along Eighth Avenue (*see chapter* **Directory**). Built in 1913, the post office's design complemented the station's. In an amazing turn of events, plans are now in the works to move Penn Station into this building, hopefully beginning in 2001.

Herald Square

Junction of Broadway and Sixth Ave at 34th St. Subway: B, D, F, Q, N, R to 34th St–Herald Sq.

Broadway and Times Square

The night is illuminated not by the moon and stars but by acres of glaring neon. An enormous television screen high above makes the place feel like some giant's brashly lit living room. Waves of people flood the streets as the blockbuster theaters disgorge their audiences. This bustling core of entertainment and tourism is often called "the Crossroads of the World," and there are few places that represent the collective power and noisy optimism of New York as well as **Times Square**.

Originally called Long Acre Square, Times Square was renamed after *The New York Times* moved to the site in the early 1900s, announcing its arrival with a spectacular New Year's Eve fireworks display. Around its building, 1 Times Square, the *Times* erected the world's first moving sign, where the paper posted election returns in 1928. The paper has now moved to 43rd Street (the old Times building is vacant except for the Warner Bros. store on the ground floor), but the sign (a new, improved one) and New Year's Eve celebration remain (featuring a new ball encrusted with lights for the year 2000). Times Square is really just an elongated intersection, where Broadway crosses Seventh Avenue. That's why the **Theater**

Step back in time: **Macy's** *wooden escalators evoke the golden age of department stores.*

District is known as Broadway. It's home to 30 or so grand stages used for dramatic productions, plus probably 30 more that are movie theaters, nightclubs or just empty—the latter due to the much-ballyhooed cleanup of Times Square's once-famous sex trade. With an eye on the millennial celebrations, a major state development plan to attract hotels and family entertainment has virtually (some say regrettably) wiped out the cinematic lowlife that once dominated **42nd Street** west of Sixth Avenue. The sex industry is still here, but the few remaining video supermarkets now sell kung fu films next to skin flicks (thanks to a city ordinance that requires 40 percent of their stock to be nonpornographic), and the live peep shows of yore are virtually nonexistent. To see how much things have changed, stop by **Show World** (Eighth Avenue between 42nd and 43rd Streets), a former porn emporium that now sells tourist trinkets and hosts a short (nonporno) film series. Theme restaurants, brew pubs and Hollywood studio stores are the hallmarks of the new Times Square. Mickey Mouse's squeaky-clean influence has gone a long way toward sanitizing the place.

The streets west of Seventh Avenue are home to dozens of eating establishments catering primarily to theatergoers. West 46th Street between Eighth and Ninth Avenues—**Restaurant Row**—has an almost unbroken string of them.

As you'd expect, the office buildings in the area are full of entertainment companies: recording studios, theatrical management companies, record labels, screening rooms and so on. **The Brill Build-** ing, 1619 Broadway at 49th Street, has the richest history, having long been the headquarters of music publishers and arrangers. The strip it's on is known as **Tin Pan Alley** (though the original Tin Pan Alley was West 28th Street). Such luminaries as Cole Porter, George Gershwin, Rodgers and Hart, Lieber and Stoller, and Phil Spector produced their hits here. Visiting rock royalty and aspiring musicians drool over the selection of new and vintage guitars and countless other instruments in a string of shops on 48th Street, just off Seventh Avenue. At the southern end of the square is the headquarters of **MTV** (44th Street and Broadway), which often sends camera crews into the streets to tape various segments (*see chapter* **Film & TV**). In warmer months, crowds of screeching teens congregate under the windows of the network's second-floor studio, hoping for a wave from visiting celebrities inside.

Across the street from MTV, at **4 Times Square**, is the swanky new glass home of magazine-publishing giant Condé Nast—the first office tower to be built in Manhattan since the late-'80s recession. During construction, the building suffered several major mishaps, killing one woman and closing the area for several days. On the positive side, the structure's skin features tiny cells to capture sunlight and will generate some of the energy needed for the building's day-to-day operations.

The great landmark on Broadway just south of Central Park is **Carnegie Hall** (*see chapter* **Music**). Nearby is the ever-popular **Carnegie Deli**, one of the city's most famous sandwich shops (*see chapter* **Restaurants**).

Nightlife in the square is dominated by the theaters and theme restaurants; however, for a genuinely quirky experience, check out the **Siberia Bar**, a vodka lover's paradise that occupies a hole in the wall in the 50th Street station of the downtown 1 and 9 subway.

West of Times Square, past the curious steel spiral of the Port Authority Bus Terminal on Eighth Avenue and the knotted entrance to the Lincoln Tunnel, is an area known as **Hell's Kitchen**. During the 19th century, an impoverished Irish community lived here, amid gangs and crime. Following the Irish were Greeks, Puerto Ricans, Dominicans and other ethnic groups. It remained rough and tumble (providing the backdrop for the popular musical *West Side Story*), and in an effort to attract the forces of gentrification, the neighborhood was renamed Clinton, after **De Witt Clinton Park** on Eleventh Avenue between 52nd and 54th Streets. Today, crime has receded, and Clinton's pretty, tree-lined streets and neat red brick apartment houses are filled with a diverse group of black and Hispanic old-timers, actors and theater professionals.

Ninth Avenue is the main street of the area, and in recent years many new, inexpensive restaurants and bars catering to a young crowd have opened. There's also a little Cuban district around Tenth Avenue in the mid-40s, but otherwise Tenth is a little desolate.

On 50th Street between Eighth and Ninth Avenues is **Worldwide Plaza**, a massive commercial and residential development. It contains **CO Worldwide Encore**, a cinematic treasure. This second-run movie theater charges only $3.50 per ticket (*see chapter* **Film & TV**).

South of 42nd Street, the main attraction is the **Jacob K. Javits Convention Center**, on Eleventh Avenue between 34th and 39th Streets; this enormous structure hosts conventions and trade shows. Finally, along the Hudson River piers, you'll find the **Circle Line** terminal on Pier 83, at 42nd Street (*see chapter* **Tour New York**). At the end of 46th Street is the aircraft carrier *Intrepid* and the **Sea, Air and Space Museum** it contains (*see chapter* **Museums**).

Fifth Avenue

This majestic thoroughfare is New York's Main Street, the route of the city's many parades and marches. It runs through a region of chic department stores and past some of the city's most famous buildings and public spaces.

The **Empire State Building** is at 34th Street (*see chapter* **Architecture**). Although it's visible from much of the city (and lit up at night in various colors, according to the season or holiday), only at the corner of 34th and Fifth can you marvel at its height from top to bottom. In 1931, it was the champ: the world's tallest building at 1,250 feet (1,472, or 448 meters, including the transmitter). It's still arguably the best of Manhattan's heights. Why? Location, location, location: The observatory is in the dead center of midtown and offers brilliant views in every direction, putting you right in the center of the world's most complex jigsaw puzzle. After a 1997 shooting incident, airport-style metal detectors were installed, but the building is still impossibly romantic, so don't forget to pack a loved one for the ascent to the 102nd floor.

Impassive stone lions guard the steps of the **New York Public Library** at 41st Street, a ten-minute walk north. This beautiful Beaux Arts building provides an astonishing escape from the noise outside (*see* **Putting the stars back in the sky**, *pages 60–61*). Behind the library is **Bryant Park**, an elegant lawn often filled with lunching office workers and home to a dizzying schedule of excellent free entertainment (*see chapters* **Music** *and* **Film & TV**).

On 44th Street between Fifth and Sixth Avenues is the famous **Algonquin Hotel**, where scathing wit Dorothy Parker held court at Alexander Woollcott's Round Table (*see chapter* **Accommodations**). The city's diamond trade is conducted along the 47th Street strip known as **Diamond Row**. In front of glittering window displays you'll see Orthodox Jewish traders, precious gems in their pockets, doing business in the street. Near here (231 East 47th Street, but since demolished) was where **Andy Warhol's Factory** enjoyed most of its 15 minutes of fame.

Walk off Fifth Avenue into **Rockefeller Center** (48th to 51st Streets), and you'll understand why this masterful use of public space is so lavishly praised. As you stroll down the Channel Gardens, the stately Art Deco **GE Building** gradually appears over you. The sunken plaza in the middle of the Center is the site of the famous ice-skating rink in winter (above it sits the equally renowned Rockefeller Center Christmas tree) and a restaurant in summer. Gathered around the plaza's perimeter are the lower blocks of the **International Building** and its companions. The NBC television network's glass-walled ground-level studio (home of its *Today* program) at the southwest corner draws a crowd weekday mornings. Over on Sixth Avenue are the stark towers of Rockefeller Center's secondary phase, as well as **Radio City Music Hall**, the world's largest cinema when it was built in 1932.

Across Fifth Avenue from Rockefeller Center's sweeping lines is **St. Patrick's Cathedral**, a beautiful Gothic Revival structure and the largest Catholic cathedral in the U.S.

In the 1920s, 52nd Street was "Swing Street," a row of speakeasies and jazz clubs. All that's left is the '21' Club (at No. 21), now a power-lunch spot (*see chapter* **Restaurants**). This street also contains the **Museum of Television & Radio**. The **Museum of**

Modern Art is on 53rd Street, as is the **American Craft Museum** (*see chapter* **Museums**).

The blocks of Fifth Avenue between Rockefeller Center and Central Park house expensive retail palaces selling everything from Rolex watches to gourmet chocolate. Along the stretch between **Saks Fifth Avenue** (50th Street) and **Bergdorf Goodman** (58th Street), the rents are some of the highest in the world, and you'll find such names as Cartier, Chanel, Gucci and Tiffany (*see chapter* **Shopping & Services**). Recently, however, some upstart neighbors have joined them, including the big movie-studio merchandising outlets of Warner Bros. and Disney, as well as the National Basketball Association's official store. The pinnacle of this malling trend is **Trump Tower**, Donald's ostentatious, soaring chrome spire, with its pink marble interior.

Fifth Avenue is crowned by **Grand Army Plaza**, at 59th Street. A statue of General Sherman presides over a public space, with the elegant chateau of the **Plaza Hotel** to the west (one of the ritziest places in town since Edwardian times) and the **General Motors Building**—with the famous FAO Schwarz toy store at ground level—to the east.

Empire State Building

350 Fifth Ave at 34th St (212-736-3100). Subway: B, D, F, Q, N, R to 34th St–Herald Sq. Observatories open 9:30am–midnight; last tickets sold at 11:25pm. $6, seniors and children under 12 $3. No credit cards.
Visit it before seeing anything else to get the lay of the land. Expect to wait in line at the second stage (86th floor), where another elevator takes you to the giddy heights of floor 102.

*Practice makes perfect: Only the cream of the crop perform at **Carnegie Hall**.*

If you're a fan of virtual-reality rides, the Empire State houses two amusing big-screen flight simulators (though both are useless as actual tours): *New York Skyride* (10am–10pm; $11.50, children and seniors $9.50) and *Transporter: Movies You Ride* (9am–11pm; $8.50–$14.50, children $6.50–$10.50).

NBC

30 Rockefeller Plaza (212-664-7174). Subway: B, D, F, Q to 47–50th Sts–Rockefeller Ctr. NBC tours are Mon–Sat 9:30am–4:30pm. $8.25.
Look through the *Today* show's studio window with the hordes of gazing tourists at 49th St and wrap up a Fifth Avenue shopping spree at the underground Rockefeller Plaza mall (renovations should be complete in 2000).

Radio City Music Hall

50th St and Sixth Ave (212-632-4041). Subway: B, D, F, Q to 47–50th Sts–Rockefeller Ctr. Tours Mon–Sat 10am–5pm, Sun 11am–5pm. $12, children $6.

Rockefeller Center

48th St to 51st St between Fifth and Sixth Aves (212-632-3975). Subway: B, D, F, Q to 47–50th Sts–Rockefeller Ctr. Free.
Self-guided tours are available at the GE Building, 30 Rockefeller Plaza (the north-south street between Fifth and Sixth Aves).

St. Patrick's Cathedral

Fifth Ave between 50th and 51st St (212-753-2261). Subway: E, F to Fifth Ave; B, D, F, Q to 47–50th Sts–Rockefeller Ctr. Free. Tours given Mon–Fri 9–11am and 1:30–4:30pm. Call for date and time of next tour.

Midtown East

Sometimes on New Year's Eve you can waltz in the great hall of **Grand Central Terminal**, just as the enchanted commuters did in *The Fisher King*. This beautiful and recently renovated Beaux Arts station (*see* **Putting the stars back in the sky,** *pages 60–61*) is surely the city's most spectacular point of arrival (though the constellations of the winter zodiac that adorn the ceiling of the main concourse are backward). Thanks to the renovation, the terminal is now filled with places to grab a quick bite to eat, as well as some fancier restaurants, including Michael Jordan's eponymous steak house and the vaulted-ceilinged Oyster Bar in the terminal's lower level (*see chapter* **Restaurants**). The station stands at the junction of 42nd Street and Park Avenue, the latter rising on a cast-iron bridge and literally running around the terminal.

East 42nd Street also offers much architectural distinction, including the spectacular hall of the **Bowery Savings Bank** (at No. 110) and the Art Deco detail of the **Chanin Building** (No. 122). Built in 1930, the sparkling chrome **Chrysler Building** (at the corner of Lexington Avenue) pays homage to the automobile. Architect William van Alen outfitted the base of the main tower with brickwork cars, complete with chrome hubcaps and radiator caps enlarged to vast proportions and projected out over the edge as gargoyles. The building's needle-sharp stainless-steel spire was added

Speakeasy, memory: '21' now serves high-class burger fare for high-rolling deal makers.

to the original plans so that it would be taller than 40 Wall Street, which was under construction at the same time. The **News Building** (No. 220), another Art Deco gem, was immortalized in the *Superman* films and still houses a giant globe in its lobby, although its namesake, the *Daily News* tabloid newspaper, no longer has offices here.

The street ends at **Tudor City**, a pioneering 1925 residential development that's a high-rise version of Hampton Court in England. North of here is an area called **Turtle Bay**, though you won't see too many turtles in the East River today. This is dominated by the **United Nations** and its famous glass-walled Secretariat building. Although you don't need your passport, you are leaving U.S. soil when you enter the UN complex—this is an international zone. Optimistic peacemongering sculptures dot the grounds, and the **Peace Gardens** along the East River bloom with delicate roses. Threatening that peace, however, is a plan by Donald Trump to build the world's tallest residential building just a few blocks north of the UN, on First Avenue. Several high-powered area residents have formed a coalition to stop him.

Rising behind Grand Central, the **Met Life** (formerly Pan Am) building was once the world's largest office tower. Its most celebrated tenants are the peregrine falcons that nest on the roof, living on a diet of pigeons they kill in midair. Next to the Met Life tower is the **Helmsley Building**. Built by Warren & Wetmore, the architects of Grand Central, its glittering gold detail presents a fitting punctuation to the vista south down Park Avenue.

On Park Avenue itself, amid the solid blocks of international corporate headquarters, is the **Waldorf-Astoria Hotel** (*see chapter* **Accommodations**). The famed hotel was originally located on Fifth Avenue but was demolished in 1929 to make way for the Empire State Building and has been located here since 1931. Ninety-minute tours are given (contact the concierge at 212-872-4790). Many of the city's most famous revolutionary International Style office buildings are located here as well (*see chapter* **Architecture**). Built in 1952, **Lever House**, at 390 Park Avenue between 53rd and 54th Streets, was the first glass box on Park. The **Seagram Building**, 375 Park Avenue between 52nd and 53rd Streets, designed by Ludwig Mies van der Rohe and others and completed in 1958, is a stunning bronze and glass structure that also contains the Philip Johnson–designed (and landmarked) **Four Seasons** restaurant (*see chapter* **Restaurants**). The **IBM Building**, at 56th Street and Madison, boasts one of the city's finest atrium lobbies; across the street is Johnson's **Sony Building**, with its distinctive postmodern Chippendale crown. Inside you'll find Sony's public arcade and **Wonder Technology Lab**, offering hands-on displays of innovative technology (*see chapter* **Kids' Stuff**).

United Nations Headquarters

First Ave at 46th St (212-963-7713). Subway: S, 4, 5, 6, 7 to 42nd St–Grand Central. 9:15am–4:45pm. Free. Guided tours every half-hour. $7.50, children under 5 not permitted.

Uptown

Downtown may have the fun and the funk, but uptown has the cash and the Culture, with a capital C (not to mention Central Park)

Central Park is one of the biggest draws for both uptown visitors and those who live nearby. The park's glorious green space, which is bigger than the nation of Monaco, will always dominate Manhattan life between 59th and 110th Streets (*see* **Heaven central**, *pages 70–71*). The neighborhoods on either side are quite different. The east is rich and respectable, full of old-guard fashion boutiques and museums; the west is more intellectual, revolving around the academia of Columbia University to the north and the music and performance of Lincoln Center to the south. For more information on many of the sites mentioned in this section, *see chapter* **Museums**.

Upper East Side

Once Frederick Law Olmsted and Calvert Vaux had wrought the wondrous Central Park out of swampland, New York society felt ready to move north. By the mid-1800s, the rich had built mansions along Fifth Avenue, and by the beginning of the 20th century, the super-rich had warmed to the (at first outrageous) idea of living in apartment buildings, provided they were near the park. Many grand examples of these were built along Park Avenue and the cross streets between Park and Fifth Avenues.

The Upper East Side, especially the avenues hugging the east side of Central Park, is all about the greed and gold of New York high society. The residents of the mansions, townhouses and luxury apartment buildings of Fifth, Madison and Park Avenues between 59th and 96th Streets include elderly ladies who lunch as well as young trust-funders who spend their (ample) spare change in Madison Avenue's chichi boutiques; the rich heads of corporations take advantage of tax write-offs to fund cultural institutions here. The results of these philanthropic gestures of the past 100 years are the art collections, museums and cultural institutes attracting most visitors to the area referred to as **Museum Mile**.

Museum Mile is actually a promotional organization rather than a geographical description, but since most of the member museums line Fifth Avenue, it is an apt name. The **Metropolitan Museum of Art**, set just inside Central Park on Fifth between 80th and 84th Streets, is the grandest of them all. A sunset drink in the Met's rooftop

sculpture garden is a chance to check out not only Central Park's vistas but also the city's singles scene in action. Walking north from the steps of the Met, you reach the stunning spiral design of Frank Lloyd Wright's **Guggenheim Museum** at 88th Street; the **National Academy of Design** at 89th; the **Cooper-Hewitt Museum**, the Smithsonian Institution's design collection set in Andrew Carnegie's mansion, at 91st; the **Jewish Museum** at 92nd; and, at 94th, the **International Center of Photography**, which displays everything from late-19th-century photography to contemporary works.

The brick fortress facade at 94th Street and Madison Avenue is what's left of the old **Squadron A Armory**. Just off Fifth Avenue at 97th Street are the onion domes and rich ornamentation of the **Russian Orthodox Cathedral of St. Nicholas**. A little farther north are two excellent (and seldom crowded) collections: the **Museum of the City of New York** and **El Museo del Barrio**, at 103rd and 104th Streets, respectively.

There's another clump of museums in the 70s: The **Frick Collection**, the art-filled mansion and former home of industrialist Henry Clay Frick, faces the park at 70th Street. A few blocks south is the **Society of Illustrators**. At Madison and 75th Street is the **Whitney Museum of American Art**, home of the often controversial Whitney Biennial.

The wealth concentrated in this area has also been used to found societies promoting interest in the languages and cultures of foreign lands. Rockefeller's **Asia Society** is on Park Avenue at 70th Street. Nearby are the **China Institute in America** and the **Americas Society**, dedicated to the nations of South and Central America. On Fifth Avenue is the **Ukrainian Institute** (at 79th), the **German Cultural Center** (at 83rd) and the **YIVO Institute for Jewish Research** (at 86th), which focuses on the history of Eastern European Jews.

Since the 1950s, **Madison Avenue** has symbolized the advertising industry (even though only a couple of agencies have actually had offices on the street). Now it's synonymous with ultra-expensive shopping; don't even think about buying here

Wright angle: Here's a bird's-eye view of Frank Lloyd Wright's curvy **Guggenheim.**

unless you have serious loot. The world's best couturiers—Yves Saint Laurent, Givenchy, Missoni, Geoffrey Beene, Giorgio Armani, et al.—all have pricey boutiques here. Thriftier shoppers might prefer to head to **Bloomingdale's**, that frantic, glitzy supermarket of fashion (*see chapter* **Shopping & Services**). Commercial art galleries abound here too, including the Knoedler Gallery and Hirschl & Adler Modern (*see chapter* **Art Galleries**). Established artists such as Robert Rauschenberg and Frank Stella prefer to show here rather than downtown in Soho's circus. And, for a quick bite during your Madison Avenue stroll, stop in at **E.A.T. Cafe** on Madison between 80th and 81st Streets, an airy take-out-food emporium with an adjoining restaurant serving owner Eli Zabar's signature breads and a selection of salads that would make any dieter swoon. An egg-salad sandwich may go for $10, but that's a small price to pay to watch Madison Avenue's fanciest in action.

At 66th Street and Park Avenue is the **Seventh Regiment Armory**, the interiors of which were designed by Louis Comfort Tiffany, assisted by a young Stanford White. It now houses the Winter Antiques show, among other events.

From Lexington Avenue to the East River, the aura is less grand, although this area's history is still glamorous. The **Abigail Adams Smith Museum** (61st Street near First Avenue) is a lovely old coach house dating from 1799 that is now operated as a museum by the Colonial Dames of America. It was once part of a farm owned by the daughter and son-in-law of John Adams, the second American president. For an evening of laughs nearby, check out **Chicago City Limits** (First Avenue at 61st Street), New York's longest-running improvisational comedy venue, which offers nightly improv shows and even a Sunday matinee (*see chapter* **Cabaret & Comedy**). Kim Novak, Montgomery Clift, Tallulah Bankhead and Eleanor Roosevelt all lived a little bit farther west, in the tree-lined streets of three- and four-story brownstones known as the **Treadwell Farm Historic District**, on 61st and 62nd Streets between Second and Third Avenues.

The central building of **Rockefeller University**—from 64th to 68th Streets, on a bluff overlooking FDR Drive—is listed as a national historic landmark. Its Founder's Hall dates from 1906, five years after the medical research institute was established. Look out for the President's House and the domed Caspary Auditorium. The next few blocks of York Avenue are dominated by medical institutions, including the New York Hospital/Cornell Medical Center, into which the city's oldest hospital was incorporated.

Rockefeller University

1230 York Ave between 63rd and 68th Sts (212-327-8000). Subway: 6 to 68th St.
Founder's Hall is open to groups by appointment only.

Seventh Regiment Armory

643 Park Ave at 66th St (212-452-3067). Subway: 6 to 68th St. Open by appointment only.

Society of Illustrators

128 E 63rd St between Park and Lexington Aves (212-838-2560). Subway: S to 63rd St; 6 to 68th St. Tue 10am–8pm; Wed–Fri 10am–5pm; Sat noon–4pm. Free.
Exhibitions focusing on illustration are held regularly.

Yorkville

The east and northeast parts of the Upper East Side are residential, mostly yuppie-filled neighborhoods. There are any number of restaurants and bars here, including the rip-roaring **Elaine's** (*see chapter* **Restaurants**) and **Penang** (1596 Second Avenue at 83rd Street), which first opened in Queens and has since sprouted multiple Malaysian restaurants in Manhattan. There are tons of cozy neighborhood Italian and Chinese restaurants, and 86th Street, the main thoroughfare, is lined with all the chain stores you could need, from Barnes & Noble to HMV.

The area extending from the 70s to 96th Street east of Lexington Avenue has been known historically as **Yorkville**. This predominantly German stronghold was once a quaint little hamlet on the banks of the river. In the last decades of the 19th century, East 86th Street became the Hauptstrasse, filled with German restaurants, beer gardens and pastry, grocery, butcher and clothing shops. When World War II broke out, tensions developed. Nazis and anti-Nazis clashed in the streets, and a Nazi newspaper was published here. While the German influence is much less noticeable today, the European legacy includes **Schaller & Weber** (Second Avenue between 85th and 86th Streets), a homey grocery that has been selling 75 different varieties of German sausage and cold cuts since it opened in 1937. Two other must-sees: **Elk Candy Company** (1628 Second Avenue between 84th and 85th Streets), which recently moved to a brand-new shop but still sells 60 kinds of delectable marzipan candies, and **Kramer's**, a German bakery known for its *spekulatius,* or spicy gingerbread (1643 Second Avenue between 85th and 86th Streets).

Although the famous comedy club **Catch a Rising Star**, where Robin Williams started out, has moved to West 28th Street, you can still have a good laugh at the **Comic Strip**—where Eddie Murphy kicked off his career—on Second Avenue near 81st Street (*see chapter* **Cabaret & Comedy**).

On East End Avenue at 86th Street is the **Henderson Place Historic District**, where 24 handsome Queen Anne row houses, commissioned by fur dealer John C. Henderson, still stand, their turrets, double stoops and slate roofs intact; the block still looks much as it did in 1882. Across the street is **Gracie Mansion**, New

Candyland: Soothe your sweet tooth with 60 kinds of marzipan at the **Elk Candy Company**.

York's official mayoral residence since 1942 and the only Federal-style mansion in Manhattan still used as a home. The house is the focal point of **Carl Schurz Park**, named in honor of a German immigrant, senator and newspaper editor. The park is remarkable for its tranquillity and offers spectacular views of the fast-moving East River. Its long promenade, the John H. Finley Walk, is one of the most beautiful spots in the city (especially in the early morning and at dusk). During the Revolutionary War, Washington built a battery on this strategic site.

The **92nd Street Y** (Lexington Avenue at 92nd Street) offers the most extensive walking tour program in town, as well as concert series, lectures and special events (*see chapters* **Tour New York** *and* **Books & Poetry**). While you're in the neighborhood, be sure to walk by the private wood-frame home at 160 East 92nd Street (between Lexington and Third Avenues). Built in the mid-1800s, the house has retained its ancient shutters and Corinthian-columned front porch. The founders of *The New Republic* housed their staff here in the early 1900s, and jewelry designer Jean Schlumberger lived in the house for three decades before his death in 1987.

Gracie Mansion

Carl Schurz Park, 88th St at East End Ave (212-570-4751). Subway: 4, 5, 6 to 86th St. Open by appointment only.
The tour (call for details) takes you through the mayor's living room, a guest suite and smaller bedrooms.

Roosevelt Island

Roosevelt Island, a submarine-shaped East River isle, was called Minnehanonck ("island place") by the Indians who sold it to the Dutch (the buyers made a vast creative leap and renamed it Hog's Island). The Dutch farmed it, as did Englishman Robert Blackwell, who moved there in 1686; the island later came to be known as Blackwell's Island. His old clapboard farmhouse is in **Blackwell Park**, adjacent to Main Street (the one and only commercial street, on which you can find several restaurants). In the 1800s, a lunatic asylum, a smallpox hospital, prisons and workhouses were built on what was by that point known as Welfare Island. On the southern tip are the weathered neo-Gothic ruins of **Smallpox Hospital** and the burned-out shell of **City Hospital**. The **Octagon Tower**, at the island's northern end, is the remaining core of the former New York City Lunatic Asylum. Charles Dickens visited during

Heaven central

When you need a bucolic break, veg out in Central Park

New Yorkers like their relaxation to be as intense as possible, and for this there is Central Park: the compressed, urban version of Eden, and perhaps the only thing that keeps New Yorkers from going stir-crazy. This 843-acre expanse of greenery, set in the center of Manhattan, is home to a small city's worth of activities (some 15 million people visit the park every year) and has many distinct regions, each with its own atmosphere and purpose.

As natural as it may seem, the vast park is as prefab as Manhattan's street grid; everything except the prehistoric rock is man-made. Journalist and landscaper Frederick Law Olmsted and architect Calvert Vaux worked for 20 years to create their masterpiece. It was long believed that the land on which the park was built had been nothing more than a swamp when construction began in 1840, but it's now clear that a settlement of some 600 free blacks and Irish and German immigrants occupied an area known as Seneca Village, located in what would be the West 80s.

Anywhere you go in the park, watch out for joggers, cyclists and in-line skaters speeding their way to new aerobic highs. The Byzantine

Bethesda Fountain and Terrace, at the center of the 72nd Street Transverse Road, is the park's most popular meeting place, and the fountain is especially appreciated in the summer by **Mall**, site of an impromptu roller-disco rink (with not-to-be-missed costumes and acrobatics), in-line skating paths, volleyball courts and ample spots for sunbathing.

To the east, on a mound behind the Naumburg Bandshell, is the site of the **Central Park SummerStage** and its impressive series of free concerts and spoken-word performances (*see chapter* **Music**). To the west is the **Sheep Meadow**—yes, sheep actually grazed there as recently as the 1930s. You may see kites, Frisbees or soccer balls zoom past, but most people are here to work on their tans. If you get hungry, repair to glitzy **Tavern on the Green** (*see chapter* **Restaurants**), or wolf down a hot dog at the adjacent snack bar.

West of Bethesda Terrace, near the 72nd Street entrance, is peaceful **Strawberry Fields**. This is where John Lennon, who lived and died nearby, is remembered. You can rent a boat or

Beau bridge: **Central Park** *is also NYC's favorite summer tanning salon.*

gondola at the **Loeb Boathouse** on the **Lake**, crossed by the elegant **Bow Bridge**. For sailing on a smaller scale, head east to the **Conservatory Water**, where model sailboats race. The **Ramble** is a wild area known for bird-watching by day and anonymous, mostly gay, rendezvous at night (not the safest place to be).

Farther uptown is **Belvedere Castle**, with the **Henry Luce Nature Observatory**; the **Delacorte Theater**, where the New York Shakespeare Festival mounts plays during the summer; and the restored **Great Lawn**, where concerts and other events are held. The **Reservoir**, above 86th Street, is named in honor of Jacqueline Kennedy Onassis, who used to jog around it. North of the sports fields and tennis courts, the park is mostly wild and wooded. Highlights include **Harlem Meer** at the northeastern corner and the beautiful formal **Conservatory Garden** (Fifth Ave at 105th St). *See chapter* **Kids' Stuff** *for fun things to do with children in the park.*

Central Park Zoo/Wildlife Center
See chapter **Kids' Stuff.**

Charles A. Dana Discovery Center
Enter at Fifth Ave at 110th St (212-860-1370). Subway: 6 to 110th St. Tue–Sun 10am–5pm. Free.
Stop in for weekend family workshops, outdoor performances on the plaza and cultural exhibits in the gallery.

The Dairy
Mid-park at 64th St (212-794-6565). Mid-Apr–mid-Oct Tue–Sun 11am–5pm; mid-Oct–mid-Apr Tue–Sun 11am–4pm. Free.
This information center for Central Park contains an interactive exhibition and a six-minute video on the history of the park.

Department of Parks & Recreation
888-NY-PARKS or 212-360-2774.

Henry Luce Nature Observatory
Belvedere Castle, mid-park at 79th St (212-772-0210). Subway: B, C to 81st St; 6 to 77th St. Apr 1–Sept 1 Tue–Sun 10am–5pm; Sept 2–Mar 31 Tue–Sun 10am–4pm. Free.
Ranger-led walks—a great way to learn to bird—start at the Castle and head into the Ramble every Sunday at 9am.

Loeb Boathouse
The Lake, near Fifth Ave and E 74th St (212-517-4723). Subway: 6 to 77th St. May 1–Nov 1 Mon–Fri noon–4pm; Sat, Sun 11am–4pm. $10 per hour plus $30 deposit; $30 per half-hour for chauffeured gondola only at night. No credit cards.
Rent a rowboat, ride a gondola or grab a more formal lunch at the café, which offers a full menu, including its signature seafood salad.

Urban Park Rangers
212-360-2774. 9am–5pm.

Wollman Memorial Rink
See chapter **Sports & Fitness.**

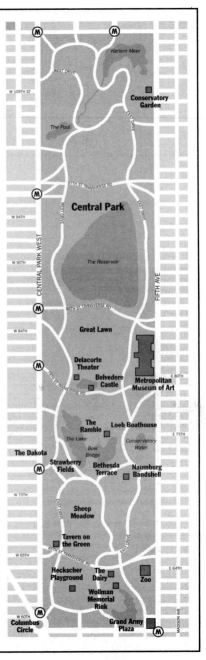

*Say cheese: Upper West Siders never go hungry with **Zabar's** bounty in the neighborhood.*

the 1840s and was disturbed by its "lounging, list-less, madhouse air." In an early feat of investiga-tive journalism, reporter Nellie Bly feigned insanity and had herself committed to the asylum for ten days in 1887, then wrote a shocking exposé of the conditions in this "human rat trap."

Roosevelt Island has been a perfectly sane res-idential community since the state began planning its development in 1971 (people began moving into apartments in 1975-76). Although the island is accessible by road from Queens, the red cable cars (or trams) that cross the East River from Manhat-tan offer some of the very best vistas of the city (embark at Second Avenue and 60th Street). You can also take the S train for a less scenic, but faster, ride. When you arrive, you'll have to ride three escalators up the equivalent of ten stories to get out of the subway stop, one of the deepest in the metropolitan area.

A new pier faces Manhattan, and picturesque picnic spots are scattered about the island. **Octa-gon Park** has tennis courts, gardens and an eco-logical park. The riverfront promenades afford fabulous panoramas of the skyline and the East River, but the tram remains the biggest attraction: You've seen it in a host of films, including, most recently, *City Slickers*. Wander down the **Medita-tion Steps** for river views, or take one of the river-

side walks around the island. The latest addition to Roosevelt Island's attractions is the **Sculpture Center**, at Motorgate Plaza, the island's unusual transportation complex. Here, large outdoor works are displayed, and many of the pieces are inspired by features of the island.

Roosevelt Island Operating Corporation
591 Main St (212-832-4540). Mon–Fri 9am–5pm.
Call for details of events and free maps of the island.

Upper West Side

The Upper West Side is a fairly affluent residential area packed with movie theaters, bars and restau-rants that's also home to dozens of reclusive celebri-ties, including Jerry Seinfeld, a proud West Sider who just bought a multimillion-dollar apartment overlooking Central Park. Historically, its residents have been thought of as serious, intellectual and politically liberal. European immigrants were attracted here in the late 19th century by the build-ing boom sparked by Central Park, as well as by Columbia University's new site to the north.

The start of the Upper West Side is **Columbus Circle**—a rare rotary in a city of right angles—where Broadway meets 59th Street, Eighth Avenue, Central Park South and Central Park West. Columbus Circle can be confusing if you're behind the wheel, although new signage is making it a bit easier to navigate. To the south, across from the 700-ton statue of Christopher Columbus, is an odd building that once housed the NYC Convention and Visitors Bureau (2 Columbus Circle). West of the circle is the **New York Coliseum**. This venue is in flux. Apart from a few one-shot events, it has been largely out of business since the Javits Convention Center (*see chapter* **Midtown**) opened in 1986; development deals have been in the works since then. Donald Trump already has his imprint on the north side of the circle with his megapricey **Trump International Hotel and Tower**, which features the acclaimed restaurant **Jean Georges** (1 Central Park West). On Broadway at 68th Street, the 12-screen (plus a huge 3-D-capable IMAX facility) **Sony Lincoln Square Cinema** is an example of a multiplex done right—just be sure to arrive early for your film of choice, since it's a popular theater that attracts visitors from all over the city (*see chapter* **Film & TV**).

It's not unusual to see folks striding around this area in evening dress; that's because they're going to **Lincoln Center**, a complex of concert halls and auditoriums that's the heart of classical music in the city. Its buildings are linked by sweeping public plazas and populated by sensitive-looking musical types or, in the summer, mostly amateur dancers who gather in the plaza to dance alfresco for Midsummer Night Swing (*see* **Classical & Opera** *in chapter* **Music**).

From Lincoln Center Plaza, you can see a small-scale replica of the Statue of Liberty atop a building on West 64th Street. Across the street, at 2 Lincoln Square, is the small but fascinating **Museum of American Folk Art**.

It took longer for the West Side to become a fashionable residential area than it did Fifth Avenue, but once the park was built, Central Park West promptly filled up with luxury apartment buildings. After well-off New Yorkers had adjusted to the idea of living in "French flats," as they called them, apartment living became almost desirable.

The Art Deco building at 55 Central Park West is best remembered for its role in *Ghostbusters*. On 72nd Street is the **Dakota**, most famous these days as the building outside which John Lennon was murdered. It was one of New York's first great apartment buildings and the one that accelerated the drift to the west. (Skeptical New Yorkers commented that it was so far away from the center of town that it might as well be in the Dakotas.) Yoko Ono and other famous residents can be seen popping in and out. The massive, twin-towered **San Remo** at 74th Street dates from 1930 and is such an exclusive address that even Madonna had to settle for the waiting list and ended up buying an apartment farther south on Central Park West.

The **New York Historical Society**, the oldest museum in the city, is at 77th Street. Across the street, the **American Museum of Natural History** attracts visitors with its IMAX theater (which shows Oscar-winning documentary nature films) and permanent rain forest exhibit, as well as such standbys as stuffed and mounted creatures, dinosaur skeletons and ethnological collections (*see chapter* **Museums**). By early 2000, the museum will complete the $210-million **Rose Center for Earth and Space**, which will include the retooled Hayden Planetarium, housed in an 87-foot sphere that appears to float in a glass cube.

Columbus and Amsterdam, the next avenues west from Central Park West, experienced a renaissance when Lincoln Center was built in the '60s. The neighborhood has long been gentrified and is now full of restaurants, gourmet food shops and boutiques, though a few of the old inhabitants and shops remain. A popular Sunday outing is still the Columbus Avenue stroll, which usually starts at the **Flea Market** (77th and Columbus) (*see chapter* **Shopping & Services**) and continues either up or down Columbus. If you head south, be sure to stop at **Pug Bros. Popcorn** (265 Columbus Avenue between 72nd and 73rd Sts) for a bag of crispy caramel corn handmade in old-fashioned copper kettles, and for an iced cappuccino in the back garden at **Café La Fortuna** (69 W 71st Street between Columbus and Central Park West), a neighborhood favorite for more than 70 years.

On Broadway, the **72nd Street subway station** is notable for its Art Nouveau entrance, and notorious for its crowded, narrow platforms. It's on Sherman Square, named after the general. The opposite triangle, at the intersection of 73rd and Broadway (where a Saturday market has become a favorite among locals shopping for produce and flowers), is **Verdi Square**. It's a fitting name: Along with Arturo Toscanini and Igor Stravinsky, Enrico Caruso lived in the nearby **Ansonia Hotel** (Broadway between 73rd and 74th Streets) and kept other inhabitants entertained and awake with renditions of his favorite arias. The Ansonia, a vast Beaux Arts apartment building with exquisite detailing, was also the location for *Single White Female*. Bette Midler got her break at the **Continental Baths**, a gay spa and cabaret that occupied the bottom few floors in the 1970s. This was also where star DJs Frankie Knuckles and Larry Levan first honed their skills.

The **Beacon Theater** on Broadway (at 75th Street) was once a fabulous movie palace and is now a concert venue. The phenomenal interior is a designated landmark. Across the street are **Fairway** and **Citarella**, two gourmet markets vying for shoppers. Fairway is known citywide for its bountiful and reasonably priced produce, and Citarella is renowned for its seafood and meat departments. A few blocks north are the **Children's Museum** of Manhattan; **H&H Bagels**, the city's largest provider of this New York staple; the enormous **Zabar's** (Broadway between 80th and 81st Sts), supplier of more than 250 types of cheese, hand-sliced smoked fish, prepared foods and more (*see chapter* **Shopping–and–Services**); and the nearby **Barney Greengrass the Sturgeon King** (541 Amsterdam Avenue between 86th and 87th Sts), an old-time cafeteria-style restaurant with a to-die-for smoked salmon–and–bagel platter.

Just off Broadway, on the north side of 94th Street, is the 1920s **Pomander Walk**, a quaint mews of townhouses built around a courtyard. Sadly, it's about to be overshadowed by a new high-rise going up atop **Symphony Space** (*see chapter* **Music**), which features repertory film series and eclectic musical programs, including the famous Wall-to-Wall concerts. Nearby is the **Claremont Riding Academy** (*see chapter* **Sports & Fitness**), where you can rent horses to ride in Central Park or just watch the horses trot around the smallest corral you've ever seen.

Riverside Park lies between Riverside Drive and the banks of the Hudson River, from 72nd to 145th Streets. Once as fashionable an address as Park Avenue and similarly lined with opulent private houses, Riverside Drive was largely rebuilt in the 1930s with luxury apartment buildings. The park is a welcome stretch of undulating riverbank. You may see luxury yachts berthed at the little **79th Street Boat Basin**, along with a few houseboats and a little cafe in the adjacent park (open in the summer). Farther north, above the park at 89th Street and Riverside Drive, the **Soldiers' and Sailors' Monument** is a memorial to the Civil War dead.

Soldiers' and Sailors' Monument
Riverside Dr at 89th St. Subway: 1, 9 to 86th St.
The 1902 monument was designed by French sculptor Paul DuBoy and architects Charles and Arthur Stoughton.

Harlem

Harlem's reputation as a dangerous place is greatly exaggerated. Certainly, some parts are quite run-down, and if you're white, be prepared to stand out in the crowd. But a daytime visit to the attractions should pose no problems for anyone, and Harlem's as important a historic area as any.

Harlem's elegant stone buildings reverberate with the history of black America's struggle for equality. Its institutions and streets are christened with the names of great liberators, teachers and orators, and there are constant reminders of proud Afrocentric culture, from Francophone Africans selling trinkets to Jeeps booming out the latest hip-hop street politics.

Harlem was originally composed of country estates, but when the subways arrived at the turn of the century, the area was developed for middle-class New Yorkers. When the bourgeoisie failed to fill the grandiose townhouses, speculators reluctantly rented them out to African-Americans. The area's population doubled during the 1920s and '30s, a growth that coincided with the cultural explosion known as the Harlem Renaissance. The poets, writers, artists and musicians living in this bohemian republic helped usher in the Jazz Age.

Harlem's soundtrack is now provided by the rap and reggae of the younger generation, as well as by the salsa and merengue of the Cubans and Dominicans who have moved in among the older black community. They have added to the Hispanic population of **Spanish Harlem**, or El Barrio ("the neighborhood"), the section east of Fifth Avenue and above 96th Street. Treat your senses to the colorful fruits, vegetables, spices and meats at **La Marqueta** on Park Avenue between 110th and 116th Streets, or smell the flowers in Central Park's **Conservatory Garden** at Fifth Avenue and 105th Street. **El Museo del Barrio**, Spanish Harlem's community museum, is on Fifth Avenue at 104th Street (*see chapter* **Museums**).

The **Graffiti Hall of Fame**, at 106th Street between Park and Madison Avenues, is actually just a schoolyard, but here you'll see the large-scale work of "old-school" graffiti writers—you may even bump into someone completing a piece. There are also several *casitas,* Puerto Rican "little houses," which function as communal hangouts and create a slice of island life amid the high-rises. Two of them can be found on the way from the 103rd Street subway station to El Museo del Barrio: one on a vacant lot on 103rd Street between Park and Lexington Avenues, the other around the corner on Lexington between 103rd and 104th Streets.

At 116th Street and Lenox Avenue is **Masjid Malcolm Shabazz**, the silver-domed mosque of the late Malcolm X's ministry. Opposite this is the market where the street vendors who once lined 125th Street now hawk T-shirts, tapes and purportedly African souvenirs. **Sisters Cuisine** (1931 Madison Avenue at 123rd Street) balances Guyanese food with such Caribbean favorites as Jamaican jerk chicken and curried goat. Just north is the **Lenox Lounge**, where Malcolm X's early career as a hustler began. Farther north is **Sylvia's** (328 Lenox Avenue at 138th Street), known for its gospel brunch, and at 138th Street is the **Abyssinian Baptist Church**, containing a small museum dedicated to Adam Clayton Powell Jr., the first black member of New York's City Council and Harlem's congressman from the 1940s through the 1960s. Just below 125th Street, on Fifth Avenue, lies **Marcus Garvey Park** (previously Mt. Morris Park), Harlem's only patch of green. It's located at the center of a historic district of elegant brownstones, some of the more beautiful of which are open to the public several

*Longing for lox? Find some of New York's best at **Barney Greengrass.***

*Imagine: John Lennon fans leave flowers in his beloved **Central Park.***

times a year. Call the Mt. Morris Park Community Association (212-369-4241) for details.

The **Studio Museum in Harlem** (*see chapter* **Museums**) presents exhibitions focusing on the area and its artists, while the **Schomburg Center for Research in Black Culture** (*see* **Black pride**, *page 77*), part of the New York Public Library system, is the largest research collection devoted to African-American culture.

Harlem's main commercial drag is 125th Street, and the **Apollo Theatre** (located between Adam Clayton Powell Jr. and Frederick Douglass Boulevards) is its focus. For four decades after it began presenting live shows in the 1930s, the Apollo was the world's most celebrated venue for black music. It's had its ups and downs since then, but the Apollo continues to present live music, mostly hip-hop and R&B, as well as tapings of the television program *Showtime at the Apollo* (*see chapter* **Music**). The Theresa Towers office complex, at 125th Street and Adam Clayton Powell Jr. Boulevard, was formerly the **Hotel Theresa**. Fidel Castro stayed here during a 1960 visit to the United Nations, and his visitors included Nikita Khrushchev and Gamal Abdel Nasser.

The area between 125th and 155th Streets west of St. Nicholas Avenue is known as **Hamilton Heights**, after Alexander Hamilton, who had a farm here at Hamilton Grange. The Federal-style home, designed by the same architect who designed Gracie Mansion and City Hall, may be moved to nearby **St. Nicholas Park** by 2002. This is the gentrified part of Harlem, where you'll find the neo-Gothic City College, the northern outpost of the City University of New York. On the City College campus, check out the **Croton Gatehouse** at Convent Avenue at 135th Street. In the 1880s, the Gatehouse played an important role in bringing water from the Croton Reservoir to New York City.

While you're in the area, tour **Strivers' Row** (Adam Clayton Powell Jr. Boulevard between 138th and 139th Streets), a strip of magnificent row houses developed in 1891 by David H. King (who also constructed the first Madison Square Garden). In the 1920s, such prominent members of the black community as Eubie Blake and W.C. Handy lived in the neo-Georgian houses here, and you can still see signs on the gates that read WALK YOUR HORSES.

Stop afterward for a bite at **Londel's Supper Club** (2620 Frederick Douglass Boulevard between 139th and 140th Streets), owned by Londel Davis, a police officer–turned–restaurateur who serves some of the best blackened catfish in town. Or try **the Sugar Shack** (2611 Frederick Douglass Blvd at 139th Street), which offers a tasty chicken-and-waffles combo and open-mike poetry on Wednesday evenings. The area hops at night, especially at the legendary **St. Nick's Pub** (located farther west, at 773 St. Nicholas Avenue and 149th Street), which provides purists with old-school live jazz and jam sessions late into every night except Tuesday.

Knock on wood: **Sylvan Terrace** is lined with historic wood-frame homes.

Continuing north, on Broadway at 155th Street, you'll also find **Audubon Terrace**, a double cluster of Beaux Arts buildings containing an unusual group of museums: the **Hispanic Society of America**, the **American Numismatic Society** and the **American Academy of Arts and Letters** (*see chapter* **Museums**), all part of artist John James Audubon's former estate.

Abyssinian Baptist Church
132 W 138th St between Seventh and Lenox Aves (212-862-7474). Subway: B, C to 135th St–St. Nicholas Ave; 2, 3 to Lenox Ave. Mon–Fri 9am–5pm.
The church is under renovation until sometime in 2000.

Hamilton Grange
Convent Ave at 142nd St (212-283-5154). Subway: A, C, B, D, 1, 9 to 145th St. Fri–Sun 11am–4pm.

Morningside Heights

The area sandwiched between Morningside Park and the Hudson River from 110th to 125th Streets is **Morningside Heights**, a region dominated by **Columbia University**. One of the oldest universities in the U.S., Columbia was chartered in 1754 as King's College (the name changed after U.S. independence). It moved to its current location in 1897. Thanks to its large student presence and that of its sister school, **Barnard College**, the surrounding area has an academic feel, with bookshops and cafés along Broadway and quiet, leafy streets toward the west overlooking Riverside Park.

Miss Mamie's Spoonbread Too (366 W 110th Street at Columbus Avenue) is the place for gumbo and banana pudding, as well as live piano and Saturday sing-alongs. **Nacho Mama's** (2893 Broadway between 112th and 113th Streets) is loved for its burritos; **Tom's Restaurant** (2880 Broadway at 112th Street), made famous because the *Seinfeld* gang practically lived there, packs them in for brunch; and the **West End** (2911 Broadway between 113th and 114th Sts) is notable for its $4 pitchers and the fact that this was the hangout for many a Beat poet. For dessert, follow your nose to **Mondel Chocolates** (2913 Broadway at 114th Street), sating students' sweet teeth since 1944.

The neighborhood has two immense houses of worship, the **Cathedral of St. John the Divine** (the largest in the U.S.) and **Riverside Church**, built with Rockefeller money and containing the world's largest carillon. Ride to the top of the 21-story steel-frame tower for views across the Hudson. Look down on **Grant's Tomb** in Riverside Park (at 122nd Street), burial site of Ulysses S. Grant, the victorious Civil War general and U.S. president.

The hammering and chiseling at the Cathedral of St. John the Divine will continue well into the next century. Construction began in 1892 in Romanesque style, was stopped for a Gothic Revival redesign in 1911 and didn't begin again

Black pride
The rich history of Harlem lives on at the Schomburg Center

Those interested in the social and cultural history of African-Americans in New York should visit the **Schomburg Center for Research in Black Culture**, located in the heart of Harlem on the site of one of the Speakers' Corners established by Marcus Garvey's Back to Africa movement (*see chapter* **Museums**).

The Center features an extensive research collection, and at least two exhibitions are on display at all times, reflecting the range and depth of African-American achievement in the arts, literature and politics. Photographs and other archival materials chart the singular successes of actors from Paul Robeson to Denzel Washington. Audio and visual recordings commemorate the outstanding talents of black musicians and singers from Bessie Smith to Tina Turner. Recorded speeches and publications explore the political messages and social impact of leaders like Marcus Garvey, the Black Panthers and Jesse Jackson.

Houston Cornwill's *Rivers,* an elaborate artwork of multicolored terrazzo with brass inlay, is on permanent display. The piece occupies the entire floor of the entrance to the Langston Hughes Auditorium. Based on Hughes's poem "The Negro Speaks of Rivers," the work traces the flow of the world's great rivers as if they were part of an astrological chart, with one ocean in the middle. The poet's words appear in brass.

The research collections are open to the public as part of the New York Public Library system; tours can be made by appointment.

Schomburg Center for Research in Black Culture
515 Malcolm X Blvd at 135th St (212-491-2200) www.nypl.org/research/sc/sc.html. Subway: 2, 3 to 135th St. Mon–Wed noon–8pm, Thu–Sat 10am–6pm, Sun 1pm–5pm. Free.

until 1941. Then, after another pause for fund-raising, work resumed in earnest this past decade. When the towers and great crossing are completed, this will be one of the world's largest churches and the closest thing New York will have to the grandeur of Paris's Notre Dame. In addition to Sunday services, the cathedral also hosts concerts, tours and, on occasion, funerals of the rich and famous. In season, be sure to check out the cathedral's rose and herb gardens.

Out in Inwood

Hike back in time to Manhattan's original landscape

In 1626 (as the legend goes), Peter Minuit offered goods worth 60 guilders (about $24) to the Munsee Indians for the purchase of a strip of land called Manahatta, a hilly, mostly wooded place surrounded by rivers and notched with marshy inlets, the flowing streams rich with beavers and fish. Some believe this transaction took place in what we now call Manhattan's northern tip: Inwood Hill Park. This 196-acre refuge contains the last remnant of primeval forest in Manhattan. Largely due to the efforts of landscape architect Frederick Law Olmsted, the area was not leveled in the 1800s—the house-size, glacier-carved boulders were probably a factor, too. Today, with a little imagination and a sporty attitude, you can hike through this mossy forest and see a bit of the beautiful land the Munsees unwisely sold.

Inwood Hill Park
Entrance on 207th St and Seaman Ave (212-360-8111). Subway: A, 1, 9 to 207th St.

At the **Hungarian Pastry Shop** (1030 Amsterdam Avenue between 110th and 111th Streets) right across the street, academic types arrive with books, laptops and notes, and work feverishly over a cup of coffee (free refills) and croissants. Still others flirt, sketch and chat away the day in this European-style coffeehouse. Next door is **V&T Pizzeria** (1024 Amsterdam Avenue), where the pizza remains some of the best in the city. After hours, students and locals head to the **1020** bar (1020 Amsterdam Avenue at 110th Street) and **Soha** (as in "South of Harlem," 988 Amsterdam Avenue near 109th Street), a funkily decorated club offering live jazz without a cover or minimum.

Cathedral of St. John the Divine
Amsterdam Ave at 112th St (212-662-2133). Subway: 1, 9 to 110th St. 7am–5pm.

Columbia University
Between Broadway and Amsterdam Ave and 114th to 120th Sts (212-854-1754). Enter Barnard College at Broadway, just north of 116th St (212-854-5262). Subway: 1, 9 to 116th St.

General Grant National Memorial
Riverside Dr at 122nd St (212-666-1640). Subway: 1, 9 to 125th St. 9am–5pm. Free.
The Memorial is more commonly known as Grant's Tomb because Ulysses S. Grant is buried here with his wife, Julia. The surrounding mosaic benches were designed in the 1960s by young community residents.

Riverside Church
Riverside Dr at 122nd St (212-870-6700). Subway: 1, 9 to 125th St. 9am–4pm.

Washington Heights

The area from 155th Street to the northern tip of Manhattan is called Washington Heights. Here the island shrinks in width, and the parks on either side culminate in the wilderness and forest of **Inwood Hill Park** (*see* **Out in Inwood**, *left*). **High Bridge** (Amsterdam Avenue at 177th Street) will give you an idea of how old New York got its water supply. This aqueduct carried water across the Harlem River from the Croton Reservoir in Westchester County to Manhattan. The central piers were replaced in the 1920s to allow large ships to pass underneath.

The main building of **Yeshiva University** (186th Street at Amsterdam Avenue) is one of the strangest in New York, a Byzantine orange-brick structure decorated with turrets and minarets. Equally surprising is the **Cloisters**, at the northern edge of flower-filled Fort Tryon Park. A reconstructed monastery incorporating several original medieval cloisters that the Rockefellers shipped over from Europe, it might have been custom-designed for romantic picnics. In fact, it houses the Metropolitan Museum's medieval collections—illuminated manuscripts, priceless tapestries and sculpture. It also offers some of the most incredible views of the New Jersey Palisades and the Hudson River (*see chapter* **Museums**).

The neighborhood also has two significant American historic sites. **Morris-Jumel Mansion** (Edgecombe Avenue at 160th Street) was where George Washington planned for the battle of Harlem Heights in 1776, after the British colonel Roger Morris moved out. The handsome 18th-century Palladian villa also has some fantastic views. (A quick walk across **Jumel Terrace** is **Sylvan Terrace**, between 160th and 162nd Streets, which has the largest number of old wooden houses in Manhattan.) **Dyckman House**, a Dutch farmhouse with a high-shouldered gambrel roof and flared eaves, built around 1783, is the oldest surviving home in Manhattan and something of a lonely sight on busy Broadway (at 204th Street). In 1915, when the house was threatened with demolition, the Dyckman family's descendants purchased it and filled it with heirlooms (*see chapter* **Architecture**).

Dyckman Farmhouse Museum
4881 Broadway at 204th St (212-304-9422). Subway: A to Dyckman St. Tue–Sun 11am–4pm. Free.

Morris-Jumel Mansion
1765 Jumel Terrace (which runs from Edgecombe Ave to St. Nicholas Ave) between 160th and 162nd Sts (212-923-8008). Subway: A, C to 163rd St. Wed–Sun 10am–4pm. $3. No credit cards.

The Outer Boroughs

Over the river or through the tunnel, out of Manhattan you go—to explore historic sites, verdant parks and tasty ethnic restaurants

The population of New York City—counting all five boroughs—hovers around 7 million, and fewer than 2 million of those people live in Manhattan. But the population of Manhattan swells to around 10 million during the day. So if you feel you're spending too much time looking at the back of the head of the person in front of you in line at the Empire State Building, the Statue of Liberty or the TKTS booth, or if you've had enough of the crowded stores, escape the crowds by hopping on the train or the boat and going where most New Yorkers live.

The four "outer boroughs" of NYC—Brooklyn, the Bronx, Queens and Staten Island—developed at a slower pace and on a smaller scale than Manhattan. Here, you'll find good food, interesting archi-tecture, splendid views, and places to bike and walk, and you'll get a taste of how people make living in the city work (and working in the city livable).

Brooklyn

Even though Manhattan is not connected to it by land, the best way to get to Brooklyn is to walk 1,595.5 feet across its namesake bridge. The 1883 completion of the **Brooklyn Bridge** changed Brooklyn from a spacious suburb that still con-tained areas of farmland to a bustling city. Stroll or bike across on the pedestrian walkway at the center of the bridge for spectacular views of lower Manhattan, the Statue of Liberty and New York Harbor as it opens at the Verrazano Narrows

*High-wire act: Enter Manhattan—or Brooklyn—in grand style via the **Brooklyn Bridge**.*

Bridge. Northward, you'll see a series of bridges linking Manhattan to other parts of Brooklyn and Queens and the jewel-like tops of the Empire State and Chrysler Buildings. The bridge itself is an exciting piece of engineering and architecture. As you walk along the path, you'll see plaques detailing the story of its construction.

The **Anchorage** of the bridge, a cathedral-like structure with ceilings up to four stories high, holds up the Brooklyn side (the Manhattan side has one too, but it's not open to visitors). It's open in the summer for art exhibits and concerts (*see chapter* **Music**), and it's a great place to cool off after a brisk walk across the bridge on a hot, steamy day.

South of the bridge is the **Brooklyn Heights Esplanade**, a pedestrians-only perch overlooking the East River that runs from Cranberry Street to Remsen Street. This walkway offers spectacular views of Manhattan and the bridges. The main entrance is at the foot of Montague Street, but the esplanade is also accessible from Remsen and Cranberry Streets. Benches are plentiful; it's a good place to sit and observe other tourists, lunching locals and skating kids. Stroll through Brooklyn Heights to see well-preserved Federal-style and Greek Revival brownstones. Middagh, Cranberry, Willow, Orange, Pineapple and Montague are some of the prettiest streets. Restaurants are plentiful on Montague Street. Also in the Heights, on Orange Street, is the imposing **Plymouth Church of the Pilgrims**, founded by famous abolitionist Henry Ward Beecher.

Brooklyn was incorporated into New York City in 1898; the remains of its days as a separate municipality still exist in the somewhat fragmented downtown. **Borough Hall** (209 Joralemon Street at Fulton Street), built in 1851, is at the center. Its renovation in the early 1990s was awarded the top prize for a public restoration project by the Municipal Art Society. Borough Hall is linked to the **Supreme Court** by a vast plaza where farmers from the tristate area sell fresh produce on Fridays and Saturdays. Nearby is the massive **General Post Office** (271–301 Fulton Street).

The primary business district is across the way in the recently built Metrotech Center. There is a commons providing a shady place to rest between Metrotech and Polytechnic University, the second oldest science and engineering school in the country. At the easternmost edge of the commons is **Wunsch Student Center** (311 Bridge Street). Long before it became part of the Poly campus, the 1846 Greek Revival structure was the home of the Bridge Street African Wesleyan Methodist Church, which met there until the congregation moved to Bedford-Stuyvesant in 1938.

Farther east, at the very edge of downtown, is the **Brooklyn Academy of Music** (locals call it "BAM"). This is a venue where theater, music

and performance art that is so new it's too hot for Manhattan can find a space in one of the city's oldest theaters. The Brooklyn Philharmonic is the orchestra in residence, and the Next Wave Festival draws audiences from all over the metropolitan area for its contemporary and emerging-artists programs (*see chapters* **Dance, Music, Theater** *and* **New York by Season**).

Brooklyn boasts many all-day diversions. A good place to start is the **Brooklyn Museum of Art**, originally planned to be the largest museum in the world. Although it was never finished, it's still enormous and contains more than one and a half million artifacts (*see chapter* **Museums**). The **Brooklyn Botanic Garden**, right next door, has one of the world's largest collections of bonsai trees. In the spring, the Cherry Blossom Esplanade dazzles visitors with trees in full bloom; the Cranford Rose Garden is at its best in June. Year-round plant lovers can stroll the gardens as well as the indoor, climate-controlled Steinhardt Pavilion.

Brooklyn's 526-acre heart of green, **Prospect Park**, is just south of the museum and the garden. Although it's smaller than Central Park, it's also calmer and more rural—a wonderful place to bird-watch or rent a pedal-boat from the boathouse. Frederick Law Olmsted and Calvert Vaux (designers of Central Park) wanted Prospect Park to be enjoyed on horseback. While it is possible to rent horses at nearby **Kensington Stables**, biking is the next best thing (*see chapter* **Sports & Fitness**). Pedal alongside in-line skaters and runners, past Frisbee-catching dogs and picnicking families scattered in the park's meadows. At the southern and eastern ends of the park, West Indian drummers and bands set up on the hottest days of the summer; feel free to join a circle of dancers. You might even be offered an ice-cold sorrel. Children of all ages enjoy riding the hand-carved horses, goats and lions on the park's carousel. In the summer, a series of outdoor concerts and events are scheduled for the Celebrate Brooklyn festival (*see chapter* **New York by Season**).

You can easily bicycle all through Brooklyn, in fact. Leave the park and get onto the bike path on Ocean Parkway, a wonderful roadway that cuts through the center of Brooklyn. You'll see old men playing chess and even older women gathered to share neighborhood news. You can take the parkway all the way to Coney Island, or cut across to Shore Road on 59th Street and ride along the East River as it opens onto the harbor.

Another great diversion is a tour through Victorian **Flatbush**, just south of Prospect Park. The homes are extravagant, and no two are alike (the turn-of-the-century developer wouldn't allow it). In early spring, the Flatbush Development Corporation sponsors a house tour that lets you into mansions that were inhabited by the city's elite,

*Bklyn, 5BR, EIK: Huh? Get five bedrooms with an eat-in kitchen in a **Brooklyn brownstone**.*

including reporter Nellie Bly, silent-film star Mary Pickford and the philanthropist Guggenheims.

Coney Island (which is not an actual island) is a destination in itself. It was once home to the most extravagant amusement park in the world; its distinguishing symbol is an abandoned ride, the 250-foot Parachute Jump. In the 1920s and '30s, a series of apocalyptic fires destroyed the wooden structures of the various competing funfairs here. Nowadays, despite a thriving collection of rides, sideshows and other spangly things, the greatest attraction is the air of decayed grandeur. Grab a **Nathan's Famous** hot dog (1310 Surf Avenue at Stillwell Avenue), get a gander at the gruesome **Coney Island Sideshows by the Seashore**, take a spin on the Cyclone at Astroland and walk out to the beach or stroll along the boardwalk, perhaps as far as the **Aquarium for Wildlife Conservation** (*see chapter* **Kids' Stuff**), where you can marvel at the famous beluga whales.

Coney Island is a gathering place for teenagers, senior citizens and oddball improvisational performers. It is becoming more precious as Times Square and Greenwich Village give way to the gentrifying forces of the Gap and Disney. On any given day—winter or summer—you can find a show: Perhaps it's the Puerto Rican man who does a passionate salsa dance to recorded music with a

blow-up doll or the guy who calls himself Lizard Man because he parades around with a foot-long lizard perched on his head.

Coney Island also hosts Deno's Wonder Wheel Park and Astroland. The Cyclone, a 72-year-old wooden roller coaster, is the park's top attraction. The ride lasts only 90 seconds, but the initial drop is nearly straight down, and the dozen or so cars clatter along the 3,000 feet of track at 60 miles per hour. It is rated as one of the top ten roller-coaster experiences in the world.

To truly experience Brooklyn, focus on its neighborhoods and the people who live in them. More than 90 ethnic groups permeate city life with the colors of their homelands. **Fort Greene**, near downtown, is Brooklyn's bohemian center, with an increasingly multiethnic population of successful creative types: Spike Lee, Chris Rock, Rosie Perez and Branford Marsalis have all called this neighborhood home. At the **Concord Baptist Church of Christ**, you can experience some old-time religion alongside one of the largest black congregations in the U.S. The fabulous gospel music here will convince you that the devil doesn't have dibs on all the best tunes.

Bedford-Stuyvesant, just east of Fort Greene, is predominantly African-American. Stroll the streets anytime to see the stately brownstones, or join the Brownstoners of Bedford-Stuyvesant House Tour to get a more intimate view.

On the border between Bed-Stuy and Crown Heights is tiny **Weeksville**, a row of four houses that were once a part of the larger Weeksville community, the first free black settlement in New York. One of the houses is now a museum that includes a pair of leg irons as a grim reminder of bleaker days.

Crown Heights and **Flatbush** are primarily West Indian. Calypso and soca music blast from windows and doors. Every block has at least one carry-out place where you can get spicy jerk chicken or meat patties. Try **Sybil's** (2210 Church Avenue at Flatbush Avenue, 718-469-9049), a brightly lit cafeteria-style restaurant that serves the gamut of Caribbean food, all made in the vast kitchen in the rear. Service is friendly, and the staff will help you choose between the *escabèche* and the *ackee*. The best day to be in the neighborhood is Labor Day in September. The entire area spends a good part of the year preparing for the Carnival-style West Indian Day Parade (*see chapter* **New York by Season**). More than two million gather to watch the dazzling revelers make their way up Eastern Parkway to the thumping Caribbean beat.

Carroll Gardens is a quiet, charming Little Italy. Although it's fun just to walk through **Carroll Park**, where grandmothers watch kids run about and the old men play bocce, it's even better to stroll **Court Street** and stop in the shops for a taste of Italy. Tuck a prosciutto loaf from the

A view from the bridge

Homesteading artists bring a bit of bohemia to blue-collar Brooklyn

Since rents for Manhattan loft spaces are beyond the reach of all but a lucky few, the active machine of artistic creation has packed its paint and clay and moved across the river to the post-industrial neighborhood of Williamsburg, Brooklyn. While the artists' migration began well over a decade ago, only in recent years has gentrification followed: Cool restaurants, hipster cafés and trendy bars, mostly clustered around Bedford Avenue's subway stop on the L line, all serve the new bohemian population.

The young artistic colonists are settling amid one of New York's more curious multiculti amalgams. To the south, Broadway divides a noisy, vibrant Hispanic neighborhood from a quiet, ordered community of Hasidic Jews. Williamsburg's northern half is shared by Polish and Italian blue-collar residents, who originally worked the East River docks. Manufacturing still occurs here, but the old factory buildings are increasingly being converted into lofts and studios. Not surprisingly, the neighborhood also houses several art galleries, and on some weekends area artists hold group exhibitions in their studios or organize sprawling, almost carnival-style street fairs. Check the free neighborhood weekly, *Waterfront Week,* for details.

Art

Flipside

84 Withers St between Leonard and Lorimer Sts, third floor (718-389-7108). Subway: L to Lorimer St. Sun 1–6pm.
Visit this off-the-beaten-path gallery to sample home-grown Williamsburg art created by local, though not necessarily native, artists.

Momenta

72 Berry St between North 9th and North 10th Sts (718-218-8058). Subway: L to Bedford Ave. Fri–Mon noon–6pm.
The most professional and imaginative organization in the area, Momenta presents strong solo and group exhibitions by an exhilarating mix of emerging artists. Catch their work before it's snapped up by Manhattan dealers.

Food for thought: **Pierogi 2000** *serves up a nourishing diet of avant-garde art.*

Pierogi 2000

167 N 9th St between Bedford and Driggs Aves,
Williamsburg (718-599-2144). Subway: L to Bedford
Ave. Sept–Jun Mon, Sat, Sun noon–6pm and by
appointment.
Monthly openings at this artist-run gallery feature work
by emerging and midcareer Brooklyn artists and tend
to attract the whole neighborhood, which shows up as
much for the free drinks and pierogi as for the art. At
the Flat File, you can peruse an impressive collection of
drawings, prints and photos by local artists that sell for
under $200.

Williamsburg Art
& Historical Center

135 Broadway at Bedford Ave (718-486-7372).
Subway: L to Bedford Ave.; J, M, Z to Marcy Ave.
Sat, Sun noon–6pm; Mon by appointment.
At the foot of the Williamsburg Bridge sits this art
center, built to acknowledge the presence of more than
3,000 artists and performers living in the neighborhood.
Housed in a four-story 1867 building, it includes an art
gallery and a theater.

Food

Amarin Café

617 Manhattan Ave between Driggs and Nassau
Aves (718-349-2788). Subway: G to Nassau Ave.
Mon–Thu 11am–10:30pm; Fri, Sat 11am–11pm;
Sun 11:30am–10:30pm. No credit cards.
Amarin's sign outside—MODERN THAI CUISINE—explains
some of the more incongruous offerings on an otherwise
traditional menu.

Diner

85 Broadway at Berry St (718-486-3077).
As if Williamsburg weren't hip enough, this 72-year-old
dining car gives you one more reason to bail on Manhattan (*see chapter* **Restaurants**).

Kasia's

146 Bedford Ave at North 9th St
(718-387-8780). Subway: L to Bedford Ave. Mon–
Fri 6am–9pm. AmEx, MC, V.
Greasy Polish diner food, including pierogi and apple
sauce, are served amid '50s-era institutional decor.

L Café

189 Bedford Ave at North 7th St (718-388-6792).
Subway: L to Bedford Ave. Daily 8:30am–midnight;
kitchen closes at 11pm. No credit cards.
Schmooze with local artists and less motivated types in
this smoky coffeehouse, which now has a full kitchen.

Napoli Bakery

619 Metropolitan Ave between Leonard and
Lorimer Sts (718-384-6945). Subway: L to Lorimer
St. Mon–Sat 7am–7pm. No credit cards.
This 60-year-old bakery designates its Italian-style
breads only by size and shape (small or large, rounds or
loaves)—and they are all delicious.

Oznot's Dish

79 Berry St at North 9th St (718-599-6596).
Subway: L to Bedford Ave. Mon–Fri 11am–midnight;
Sat, Sun 10am–midnight. No credit cards.
Eat your way through the Middle East and Mediterranean
with seafood and vegetarian dishes from North Africa,
Greece, Italy, Turkey and more.

Peter Luger

178 Broadway between Driggs and Bedford Aves
(718-387-7400).
Awaken your inner carnivore at this New York institution
(*see chapter* **Restaurants**).

Plan-Eat Thailand

184 Bedford Ave between North 6th and North 7th Sts
(718-599-5758). Subway: L to Bedford Ave. Mon–Sat
11:30am–11:30pm, Sun 1–11pm. No credit cards.
One of the first neighborhood arrivals, this tiny Thai joint
offers large (and tasty) portions for small money.

Seasons

556 Driggs Ave at North 7th St (718-384-9695).
Subway: L to Bedford Ave. Sun, Tue–Thu 6–10:30pm;
Fri, Sat 6pm–11:30pm. AmEx, MC, V.
This charming little bistro serves American food influ-
enced by Italian and French peasant fare at way-below-
Manhattan prices.

Teddy's

96 Berry St at North 8th St (718-384-9787).
Subway: L to Bedford Ave. Sun–Thu 11am–midnight;
Fri, Sat 11am–2am. MC, V.
Relax with a pint and enjoy simple pub fare alongside
artists and firemen at this well preserved bar/restaurant.

Shopping

Beacon's Closet

110 Bedford Ave at North 11th St (718-486-0816).
Subway: L to Bedford Ave. Sun, Tue–Fri noon–9pm; Sat,
Sun 11am–8pm. AmEx, Disc, MC, V.
Vintage clothes, books and music are the highlights here.

Domsey's Warehouse

431 Kent Ave between South 8th and South 9th Sts
(718-384-6000).
Ground zero of the New York thrift-store experience (*see*
chapter **Shopping & Services**).

Earwax Records and CDs

204 Bedford Ave between North 5th and North 6th Sts
(718-218-9608). Subway: L to Bedford Ave. Mon–Sat
noon–8pm, Sun noon–6pm. Amex, MC, V.
A good thing about starving artists is that they usually have
great used records and CDs to sell; here's where to buy them.

Main Drag Music

207 Bedford Ave between North 5th and North 6th Sts
(718-388-6365). Subway: L to Bedford Ave. Tue–Fri
noon–9pm; Sat, Sun noon–6pm. MC, V.
A good thing about struggling musicians is they often
have vintage and used musical equipment to sell.

Spacial Etc.

149 North 6th St at Bedford Ave (718-782-5919).
Subway: L to Bedford Ave. Mon–Sun 9am–6pm.
AmEx, MC, V.
Spacial Etc. is home to Brooklyn Handknit, the makers of
funky knit hats and scarves that sell for twice the price at
Barneys. They also stock beautiful handmade porcelain
vases by the local designers Klein/Reid.

Ugly Luggage

214 Bedford Ave between North 5th and North 6th Sts
(718-384-0724). Subway: L to Bedford Ave.
Afternoons. Hours vary, call ahead. AmEx, MC, V.
Don't look for those roll-along suitcases here! Plenty of
used clothes, furniture and collectibles are available.

*Keep it wheel: **Coney Island**'s amusement park attracts New Yorkers of all stripes.*

*Prominent promenade: **Prospect Park** is Brooklyn's favorite nearby getaway.*

Caputo Bakery (329 Court Street between Sacket and Union Streets) under your arm, pick up freshly made buffalo mozzarella at **Caputo's Fine Foods** (460 Court Street between 3rd and 4th Streets), grab an aged sopressato from **Esposito and Sons** (357 Court Street between President and Union Streets) and settle down in the park. There are also several wonderful restaurants to choose from, **Marco Polo** (345 Court Street at Union Street, 718-852-5015) being top among them.

Brighton Beach is known as "Little Odessa" because of its large population of Russian immigrants—you'll feel as if you've landed somewhere in Eastern Europe. If you get an irresistible yen for caviar, vodka and smoked sausages, this is the place to come. You can wander the aisles of **M&I International** (249 Brighton Beach Avenue between 1st and 2nd Streets), a huge Russian deli and grocery, or make a reservation to spend a drunken evening at one of the local nightclubs. Dress is formal, food and vodka plentiful, and dancing goes on until the wee hours.

Brooklyn has the largest population of observant Jews outside Israel, and to get a better understanding of their rituals and beliefs, you can go to the heart of that community in **Borough Park**. Take a Hasidic Discovery tour (*see chapter* **Tour New York**) or just wander the streets grazing on the great food. On Fridays before sundown, the streets are at a fever pitch just before the Sabbath (Shabbes) begins; on Saturdays, the neighborhood appears abandoned, so plan accordingly.

Arabs have made part of **Atlantic Avenue** their own, on the border between Brooklyn Heights and Cobble Hill. The epicenter is most certainly **Sahadi Importing Company** (187–189 Atlantic Avenue between Court and Clinton Streets), which carries every Mediterranean delicacy. But stop in at any of the restaurants along the strip and you'll be treated to a savory souvenir of your trip to Brooklyn.

Aquarium for Wildlife Conservation
Surf Ave at W 8th St (718-265-FISH). Subway: D, F to W 8th St. 10am–6pm. $8.75, children and seniors $4.50.

Brooklyn Botanic Garden
1000 Washington Ave between Eastern Pkwy and Empire Blvd (718-623-7200). Subway: 2, 3 to Eastern Pkwy–Brooklyn Museum. Oct–Mar Tue–Fri 8am–4:30pm; Sat, Sun, holidays 10am–4:30pm. Apr–Sept Tue–Fri 8am–6pm; Sat, Sun, 10am–6pm. $3, students and seniors $1.50, children under 16 free. Sat 10am–noon, Tue free. No credit cards.

Brooklyn Bridge
Subway: 4, 5, 6 to Brooklyn Bridge–City Hall; A, C to High St.
New York has many bridges, but none is as beautiful or famous as the Brooklyn Bridge. The twin Gothic arches of its towers offer a grand gateway no matter which way you are heading. The span took more than 600 men some 16 years to build; when completed in 1883, it was the world's largest suspension bridge and the first to be constructed of steel. Engineer John A. Roebling was one of 20 men who died on the project—before construction even started. His son stayed on the job until he was struck by caisson disease (the bends) and then supervised construction, with the help of his wife, from the window of his Brooklyn apartment. "All that trouble just to get to Brooklyn!" was the vaudevillian quip of the time. The walkway is great for an afternoon stroll; for incredible views, take the A or C train to High Street, and walk back to Manhattan.

Brooklyn Heights Esplanade
On the East River between Remsen and Orange Sts. Subway: 2, 3 to Clark St, then walk down Clark toward the river.

Brooklyn Information and Culture
718-855-7882.
This organization, also known as BRIC, provides information about Brooklyn. To get a quarterly calendar of Brooklyn events, *Meet Me in Brooklyn*, dial extension 6, then extension 51. The Brooklyn Tourism Council is at extension 53.

Concord Baptist Church of Christ
833 Marcy Ave between Putnam and Madison Aves (718-622-1818). Subway: A, C to Nostrand Ave. Call for times of services.

Coney Island Sideshows by the Seashore/Coney Island USA
1208 Surf Ave at W 12th St (718-372-5159) www.coneyisland.com. Subway: B, D, F, N to Stillwell Ave–Coney Island.

Prospect Park
Flatbush Ave at Grand Army Plaza (events hot line 718-965-8999; Leffert's Homestead 718-965-6505; zoo 718-399-7339). Subway: 2, 3 to Grand Army Plaza. Carousel at Flatbush Ave and Empire Blvd (718-282-7789). Subway: D, Q to Prospect Park.

Weeksville Society Hunterfly Road Houses
1968–1708 Bergen St between Rochester and Buffalo Aves (718-756-5250). Subway: A, C to Utica Ave.

Queens

Queens is called the Borough of Homes. No other borough has as many single-family homes, and nearly every building boom in this century was led by developers in Queens. On a drive through Queens neighborhoods, you'll see almost every style of American housing, from single-family detached, townhouse and condominium to duplex and bungalow.

The quantity of available, affordable housing has made Queens a mecca for immigrants—a third of Queens residents are foreign-born. The borough was also a manufacturing capital for the city, and though New York no longer supports much heavy industry, what little remains is mostly in Queens. Much of the borough's unused industrial space has been converted into artists' lofts.

Queens developed as a series of small towns whose names remain as neighborhood appellations, including Forest Hills, Flushing, Bayside and Kew Gardens. Residents will say that they are from Flushing rather than Queens, for instance, and use the town name as a postal designation.

Let me tell you Astoria

A day trip on the N train takes you from Steinway pianos to souvlaki

Known for its outstanding Greek and Eastern European restaurants and markets, this sprawling Queens neighborhood has long been a destination for shopping and dining. There's some sightseeing to be done, too. Long before Hollywood was movieland, there was Astoria. W.C. Fields, Rudolph Valentino, Gloria Swanson and the Marx Brothers all made films at Kaufman Astoria movie studios, which opened in 1917. Filming still goes on; the Children's Television Workshop—producers of *Sesame Street*—and the Lifetime Network are based here, as is the **American Museum of the Moving Image**. Nearby (but not open to the public) is **Broadway Studios**, a gutted old theater where the AMC network's television show about radio's early days, *Remember WENN*, is filmed. The **Steinway** piano factory is located at the northernmost end of Astoria. Call ahead for a free two-hour tour of the plant to see how some of the best pianos in the world are still mostly hand-crafted. Of course, you'll find plenty of places to eat Greek; the neighborhood has been attracting Greek immigrants since the 1920s. You can try any of the restaurants along 31st Street, or pick up some bread, feta and olives for a picnic.

American Museum of the Moving Image
35th Ave at 36th St (718-784-0077). Subway: G, R to Steinway St.
In addition to the exhibits, classic films are shown on a regular basis (*see chapters* **Film & TV** *and* **Museums**).

Elias Corner for Fish
24-02 31st St at 24th Ave (718-932-1510).
Simple, good Greek seafood (*see chapter* **Restaurants**).

Steinway Piano Factory
Steinway Pl between 19th Ave and 38th St (718-721-2600). Subway: N to Ditmars Blvd. Tours by appointment only. Free.

Tony's Souvlaki
28-44 31st St between Newtown and 30th St (718-728-3638). Subway: N to Broadway. 11–1am. Average main course: $9. Amex, MC, V.

Uncle George's Greek Tavern
34-19 Broadway at 34th St (718-626-0593). Subway: N to Broadway. 24 hours. Average main course: $8. No credit cards.

*Tickling the ivories: Pianos are made the old-fashioned way at the **Steinway Factory**.*

Because of its patchwork development, Queens is difficult to navigate. Manhattan has a fairly strict grid, and the other boroughs have patterns to them, but Queens is a maze. Arm yourself with a good map and be prepared to enjoy wherever the roads take you.

So who are these people who made Queens their home? Well, Louis Armstrong, for one. Satchmo lived at 34-56 107th Street in Corona. The house, which will hold the **Louis Armstrong Archives**, is being renovated and will be open to the public in 2000. The jazz great is one of almost 100 jazz musicians from the 1930s, '40s and '50s who lived in Queens. Those who were from the South found the space and green they were accustomed to, and for others, like Count Basie, Fats Waller and Ella Fitzgerald, Queens offered a quiet, dignified retreat in a house with a yard and a driveway—the American Dream (Milt Hinton still lives here). **Flushing Town Hall** sponsors a jazz tour with a history of the area and the artists' migration. You can take a guided tour or pick up a map there and make your own pilgrimage.

As Queens has attracted immigrants from around the world, they have made the borough their own. The signs of many stores on **Main Street** in **Flushing** are in Chinese to cater to the dominant population. In **Jackson Heights**, the overwhelming aroma is of curry and other spices used by the local Indian residents. Come to these neighborhoods to see how these people have made their own mark on the culture—and to eat.

The 7 train, which becomes elevated in Queens, is also known as the International Express, because just about every stop in Queens takes you into a different ethnic community. Stop at 74th Street–Broadway in Jackson Heights, and you'll be struck by the glittering red, blue and green saris and jewels worn by many residents, not to mention the fresh fruits displayed by grocers along the street. Check out the **Sari Palace** at 37-07 74th Street for Indian clothing and jewelry. Get mehndi, the intricate henna design usually painted on the hands and arms of brides, at the **Gulzar Beauty Salon** at 74-01 Roosevelt Avenue or the **Menka Beauty Salon** at 37-56 74th Street. Spend hours going through the menu at **Shaheen** at 72-09 Broadway, **Jackson Diner** at 37-03 74th Street, **Delhi Palace** at 37-33 74th Street, or **Shaheen's Palace** at 73-10 37th Street.

Elmhurst is just down the pike at the 82nd Street–Jackson Heights or 90th Street–Elmhurst Avenue stop. Here, you'll find Mexicans from Oaxaca, Puebla and Guerrero, who flooded the area in the late 1980s. Colombians and Ecuadoreans are also beginning to create a presence. For a great place to eat, try **Amancer Rancheros** at 85-09 Roosevelt Avenue or **Taco Mexico** at 88-12 Roosevelt Avenue. To make a full day, call the **Queens Council on the Arts** to find out when festivals or parades are happening.

Flushing is the place that newly arrived Asian immigrants have made their home and where most of Queens's historic houses are located. Main Street in Flushing (the last stop on the 7 train) is dotted with Chinese and Korean restaurants and food stores. Street vendors sell Toho, a creamy tofu custard with honey and rosewater syrup.

The **Friends' Meeting House**, built in 1694 by religious protester John Bowne, is still used as a Quaker meeting place, making it the oldest house of worship in continuous use in the United States. Next door is **Kingsland House**, a mid-18th-century farmhouse that is also the headquarters of the Queens Historical Society. You can also visit **Bowne House**, which dates back to 1661 (*see chapter* **Architecture**).

Long Island City, the area closest to Manhattan, is home to **P.S. 1**, a former public school converted into a gallery and studio space (*see chapter* **Museums**). The nonprofit studio space attracts artists from around the world with open workshops, multimedia galleries, several large permanent works and controversial, censor-taunting exhibitions. Nearby, in a striking riverside location, the **Socrates Sculpture Garden** contains large-scale sculptures by both well- and lesser-known artists, and hosts occasional concerts and video presentations. Just down the road is the **Noguchi Museum**, Isamu Noguchi's great self-designed sculpture studios, where more than 300 of his works are displayed in 12 galleries (*see chapter* **Museums**).

The heart of Queens is **Flushing Meadows–Corona Park**, a huge complex that contains **Shea Stadium**, home of the New York Mets, and the **United States National Tennis Center**, where the U.S. Open is held every August (*see chapter* **Sports & Fitness**). The 1939 and 1964 World's Fairs were held in Corona Park (then known as Flushing Meadow Park), and some incredible half-derelict structures and the huge stainless-steel Unisphere globe built for the fairs are still standing. Preservationists are working to make sure that the remaining structures are spared the wrecker's ball. Outside the curved concrete structure of the **New York Hall of Science**, you can marvel at cast-off pieces of space rockets. Have a look at the ghostly amphitheater overlooking the boating lake, too. A leftover 1939 World's Fair pavilion is the home of the **Queens Museum**, where the main attraction is a 1:12,000 scale model of New York City made for the 1964 fair (*see chapters* **Museums** *and* **Kids' Stuff**).

Today, **Corona Park** is the scene of weekend picnics and some hotly contested soccer matches between teams of European- and South American-born locals, not to mention the annual Dragon Boat Races. You can rent bikes in the summer.

Enjoy more open space at the **Queens County Farm Museum** in the edge-of-borough **Floral Park** neighborhood. The farm dates back to 1772 and features exhibits on the city's agricultural history. Near Kennedy Airport are the tidal wetlands of the **Jamaica Bay Wildlife Refuge**, home to a large population of birds, plants and animals. Waterfowl flock here during the autumn. Bring your binoculars and spot both birds and planes. Nearby **Kennedy Airport** is itself a sight to behold. Terminal 5, the TWA terminal, is landmarked. Its curvy, modern structure was designed by architect Eero Saarinen.

One of the best bargains in New York City is a day at **Aqueduct** race track, which is a major part of the thoroughbred racing season. Seats range from $1 to $3 (no kidding!), compared with $50 to $80 at other tracks. The Wood Memorial, run in April, is the major precursor to the Kentucky Derby. In 1985, Aqueduct hosted the prestigious Breeder's Cup, and the winners have included Secretariat and Cigar (*see* chapter **Sports & Fitness**).

Corona Park
Between Northern Blvd and Roosevelt Ave. Subway: 7 to Willets Pt–Shea Stadium.

Flushing Town Hall
137-35 Northern Blvd (718-463-7700). Subway: 7 to Main St–Flushing. Mon–Fri 10am–5pm; Sat, Sun noon–5pm.

Jamaica Bay Wildlife Refuge
Cross Bay Blvd at Broad Channel (718-318-4340). Subway: A to Broad Channel. 8:30am–5pm. Free.
The wildlife refuge is part of a local network of important ecological sites administered by the National Parks Service. Guided walks, lectures and all sorts of nature-centered activities are offered.

Louis Armstrong Archives
Queens College, 6530 Kissena Blvd between Melbourne and Reeves Aves (718-997-5411). Travel: E, F to Parsons Blvd, then Q25 bus to Queens College.

Queens Council on the Arts
79-01 Park Ln South, Woodhaven (718-647-3377; info 718-291-ARTS). Subway: J to 85th St–Forest Pkwy. Mon–Fri 9am–4:30pm.
This organization provides exhaustive details, updated daily, on all cultural events in the borough.

Queens County Farm Museum
73-50 Little Neck Pkwy, Floral Park (718-347-3276). Travel: E, F to Kew Gardens, then Q46 bus to Little Neck Pkwy. 9am–5pm (farmhouse and museum galleries Sat, Sun noon–5pm). Voluntary donation.

Socrates Sculpture Park
Broadway at Vernon Blvd, Long Island City (718-956-1819). Subway: N to Broadway. 10am–sunset. Free.
The setting, a vacant postindustrial lot by the river, is inspiring. Some of the pieces, like the Sound Observatory, are engagingly interactive.

Friends' Meeting House
137-16 Northern Blvd between Main and Union Sts, Flushing (718-358-9636). Subway: 7 to Main St–Flushing. By appointment only.

Kingsland House/Queens Historical Society/Weeping Beech Park
143-35 37th Ave at Parsons Blvd, Flushing (718-939-0647). Subway: 7 to Main St–Flushing. Tue, Sat, Sun 2:30–4:30pm. $2, $1 concessions. No credit cards.
Built in 1785 by a wealthy Quaker, the house was moved to a site beside Bowne House. The Queens Historical Society now uses it for exhibitions detailing local history. Staffers can give you more information about the borough's historical sites.

The Bronx

The Bronx is so named because it once belonged to the family of Jonas Bronck, a Swede from the Netherlands who built his farm here in 1636. (People would say, "Let's go over to the Broncks'.") As Manhattan's rich were moving into baronial apartment palaces on Fifth Avenue alongside Central Park, a similar metamorphosis took place here. As a result, the Bronx contains some of the city's most important cultural landmarks, including the Bronx Zoo, the New York Botanical Garden and Yankee Stadium.

Grand Concourse, a continuation of Madison Avenue, is the Bronx's main thoroughfare. It was built up in the 1920s and is now lined with grand Art Deco apartment buildings. The architecture was influenced by the two World's Fair Expositions in Paris, especially the 1925 show, which first unveiled Art Deco designs. You'll see gorgeous mosaics, decorative terra cotta, etched glass and ironwork adorning the buildings along the street. It's worthwhile to walk around the area and even sneak a peek in a lobby or two. **The Bronx General Post Office** at 558 Grand Concourse, for example, is easy to pass by. The exterior is dull, but inside are wonderful murals painted by Ben Shahn as part of a WPA project in the 1930s.

Halfway up Grand Concourse, just south of Fordham Road, the rotunda of the **Hall of Fame of Great Americans** comes into view. This wonderful colonnade honors scholars, politicians, thinkers, educators and other great Americans. The colonnade and nearby buildings were all built by Stanford White (of McKim, Mead & White) for New York University's uptown campus and now house Bronx Community College. Several blocks north, at East Kingsbridge Road and Grand Concourse, is the small clapboard house where **Edgar Allan Poe** lived for a year until his sickly young wife died.

Near the foot of the concourse, at 161st Street, is **Yankee Stadium** (*see* chapter **Sports & Fitness**). Team owner George Steinbrenner has threatened to move to New Jersey, while Mayor Rudolph Giuliani is making a pitch to relocate the Bronx Bombers to Manhattan. No need to worry—both plans have drawn only a Bronx cheer. Tours can be arranged through the Yankee office. You'll see the clubhouse, the dugout and the famous right-field fence, built low enough so that Babe

*It's academic: Take a stroll through **Fordham University**'s campus, a Bronx institution.*

Ruth could set his home-run records. The best way to get to the stadium is by boat: New York Waterways will carry you to the game and back aboard the *Yankee Clipper*. The trip includes spectacular views of the city's skyline.

Riverdale is perhaps the most beautiful neighborhood in the city. It sits atop a hill overlooking the Hudson, and its huge, rambling homes on narrow, winding streets have offered privacy to the famous and the obscure. Perhaps the most famous home, **Wave Hill**, is open to the public. Originally a Victorian country estate where exotic plants were cultivated, it has been occupied by such illustrious tenants as William Thackeray, Theodore Roosevelt, Mark Twain and Arturo Toscanini. The gardens are now a small, idyllic park overlooking the Hudson River. Concerts are presented during the summer.

For a completely different view of life in the Bronx, go to **Parkchester** and **Co-op City**. In its time, each was the largest housing complex ever built. Parkchester, located in the East Bronx between East Tremont Avenue, Purdy Street, McGraw Avenue and White Plains Road, came first. Completed in the early 1940s, it was the first city-within-a-city. It has easy subway access to Manhattan and loads of shops and movie theaters. It really works, too, mainly because the designers included lots of pedestrian pathways and landscaping. In contrast, the bigger and newer Co-op City, located in the North Bronx just east of the Hutchinson River Parkway, has malls, parks and schools, but no real community center. Both are extraordinary examples of American urban planning.

There are many colleges and universities in the Bronx, but **Fordham University**, a Jesuit institution founded in 1841, is the central academic institution. Its small, Gothic-style campus is a wonderful, shady place for a walk—and you can stick around for a rousing game of college basketball.

In nearby **Belmont**, a mostly Italian-American neighborhood, the houses are small and plain, but the main street, **Arthur Avenue**, is lively and inviting (except on Sunday, when the neighborhood is dead). The avenue is lined with shops offering every kind of Italian gastronomic delicacy. Stop in the **New York City Retail Market**, a European-style market built in the 1940s by Mayor Fiorello La Guardia to get the pushcarts off the street but still provide a place for immigrant merchants to work. Inside is **Mike's Delicatessen**, where handsome Italian men ply you with compliments and push parmesan. The cappuccino is better than anything you'll find at Starbucks, and the restaurants offer great fare at reasonable prices (*see* **You want a quickie?**, *page 180*).

Belmont is a perfect place to end up after visiting the **New York Botanical Garden** and the **Bronx Zoo**. The Botanical Garden is a lush, gorgeous place to wander and rest—for a whole day! Its collection of plants is one of the best in the world. Visit the newly renovated Enid A. Haupt Conservatory, originally built in 1902.

*Arthurian legend: Get fresh in the Bronx at Little Italy's **Arthur Avenue** market.*

The zoo was built in 1899 and was then considered rambling and spacious. It's still the largest urban zoo in the U.S., but now it seems a little cramped, compared with more modern zoos like San Diego's. Still, it's fun to wander along the banks of the Bronx River and see the animals. The best part is the World of Darkness, which creates instant day or night so visitors can really see what goes on with nocturnal and cave-dwelling animals.

The Bronx is a great parks borough. Watching a game of cricket in **Van Cortlandt Park** at Broadway and 249th Street will do a lot to dispel the rough-and-tumble image of "da Bronx." The **Van Cortlandt Mansion**, a fine example of pre-Revolutionary Georgian architecture, sits amid this vast expanse of green and has been open to the public since 1897. It was built by Frederick Van Cortlandt in 1748 as the homestead of his wheat plantation (*see chapter* **Architecture**).

Much farther to the northeast, facing Long Island Sound, is **Pelham Bay Park**, which offers all sorts of diversions, including the man-made shoreline of **Orchard Beach**. Inside the park is **Bartow-Pell Mansion**, a Federal manor set amid romantic formal gardens.

Perhaps the most uncharacteristic part of the Bronx is **City Island**, on Long Island Sound. Settled in 1685, it was originally a prosperous shipbuilding center with a busy fishing industry. Back when New York was first being developed, this tiny piece of real estate (only a mile and a half long and half a mile wide) was a serious competitor for Manhattan's prestige. Now, it offers New Yorkers

a slice of New England–style maritime recreation—it's packed with marinas, seafood restaurants and nautically themed bars.

The majority of the Bronx's population these days is Hispanic. The palace at the center of Bronx nightlife is **Jimmy's Bronx Café** (*see chapter* **Restaurants**). Jimmy Rodriguez opened the club five years ago in an old car dealership off the Major Deegan Expressway at Fordham Road. The cuisine is Caribbean seafood, but dancing is what has made it a hit.

Bartow-Pell Mansion
895 Shore Rd at Pelham Bay Park (718-885-1461). Travel: 6 to Pelham Bay Park, then one-mile walk or cab ride. Wed, Sat, Sun noon–4pm. $2.50, $1.25 concessions, under 12 free.
The International Garden Club has administered this 1836 mansion since 1914; the grounds include formal gardens, a fountain and a 19th-century carriage house and stable.

Bronx County Historical Society Museum
Valentine-Varian House, 3266 Bainbridge Ave between Van Cortlandt Ave and 208th St (718-881-8900). Subway: D to 205th St. Mon–Fri by appointment only; Sat 10am–4pm; Sun 1–5pm. $2.
This 1758 fieldstone farmhouse is a fine example of the pre-Revolutionary Federal style.

Bronx Zoo/Wildlife Conservation Society
Bronx River Pkwy at Fordham Rd (718-367-1010) www.wcs.org Subway 2, 5 to Bronx Park East. Mon–Fri 10am–5pm; Sat–Sun 10am–5:30pm. $7.75 adults, $4 children under 12 and seniors. Wed free. No credit cards.
The pythons slither around a lush, indoor tropical rain forest. The ponds are brimming with crocodiles. The elusive snow leopard wanders around the mountaintops of the Himalayan Highlands. More than 30 species of the rodentia family coexist in the Mouse House. Birds, giraffes, lions and reptiles abound. There's a new Congo Gorilla Forest exhibit. And apes mercilessly mimic anyone who catches their eye. The zoo is home to more than 4,000 creatures. Although it covers 265 acres, it's not too hard on the feet; there's a choice of trams, monorails and express trains.

City Island
Travel: 6 to Pelham Bay Park, then Bx21 bus to City Island. Call the City Island Chamber of Commerce (718-885-9100) for information about events and activities.

Edgar Allan Poe Cottage
Grand Concourse at East Kingsbridge Rd (718-881-8900). Subway: B, D, 4 to Kingsbridge Rd. Sat 10am–4pm, Sun 1–5pm. $2.
The cottage in Fordham Village where Poe once lived has been moved across the street and turned into a charming museum dedicated to his life.

North Wind Undersea Institute
610 City Island Ave, City Island (718-885-0701). Travel: 6 to Pelham Bay Park, then Bx29 bus to City Island. Mon–Fri noon–4pm, Sat noon–5pm. $3, $2 concessions. No credit cards.
Among the attractions at this charming old maritime folk museum are whale bones, old diving gear and a 100-year-old tugboat.

New York Botanical Garden
200th St at Southern Blvd, Bronx (718-817-8705). Subway: B, D, 4 to Bedford Park Blvd, then Bx26 bus.

Apr–Oct Tue–Sun and Monday holidays 10am–6pm; Nov–Mar Tue–Sun 10am–4pm. $3, students and seniors $1.50, children $1, under 2 free. Wed 10am–6pm, Sat 10am–noon free. Ask about Garden Passport, which includes grounds and adventure garden admission. No credit cards.

Across the street from the zoo, you'll find a complex of grand glass houses set among 250 acres of lush greenery, including a large stretch of virgin forest along the Bronx River.

Pelham Bay Park
718-430-1890. Subway: 6 to Pelham Bay Park.

Wave Hill
675 W 52nd St at Independence Ave (718-549-2055). Travel: Metro-North train from Grand Central Terminal to Riverdale. Tue, Thu–Sun 9am–5:30pm; Wed 9:30am–dusk. $4, $2 concessions, no admission charge Tue. No credit cards.

Wave Hill, with its formal European gardens, is now a venue for concerts, educational programs and exhibitions, including a permanent sculpture garden featuring works by Henry Moore, Alexander Calder and Willem de Kooning.

Corpus Christi Monastery
1230 Lafayette Ave at Baretto St, Hunts Point (718-328-6996).Subway: 6 to Hunts Point.

Visit on Sunday morning for Mass or in the afternoon, when the cloistered Dominican nuns sing the office. Both services are music-filled, and the 1890 church is lighted mostly by candles, exposing a mosaic floor and austere walls.

Staten Island

Staten Island may be part of New York City, but it's fair to say that the borough has a love-hate relationship with the rest of the city—with the emphasis on hate. A move to secede from the city was approved by a healthy margin a few Election Days ago, and while they didn't actually break away, Islanders continue to argue that City Hall takes their taxes to pay for its own problems and gives them nothing in return but garbage. (The famous landfill at Fresh Kills is one of the world's largest man-made structures.) Driving through its tree-lined suburbs and admiring its open spaces and expansive parks, you can see why the generally well-to-do inhabitants of this borough are so eager to keep themselves separate from the pressing urban concerns of the rest of New York City.

Because of its strategic location, Staten Island was one of the first places in America to be settled. Giovanni da Verrazano discovered the Narrows—the body of water separating the island from Brooklyn—in 1524, and his name graces the bridge that connects the two boroughs today. (At 4,260 feet, or 1,311 meters, it's the world's second longest suspension bridge.) Henry Hudson christened the island "Staaten Eylandt" in 1609. In 1687, the Duke of York sponsored a sailing competition, with Staten Island as the prize. The Manhattan representatives won the race, and since then it has been governed from New York.

You reach the island from Manhattan by the Staten Island Ferry. The ride from Battery Park in lower Manhattan is free (*see chapter* **Tour New York**). You pass close to the **Statue of Liberty** before sailing into the St. George ferry terminal.

The **Snug Harbor Cultural Center** was originally a maritime hospital and home for retired sailors. It comprises 28 buildings—grand examples of various periods of American architecture—in an 80-acre park. Sailors lived here until 1960, and the city took over the site in 1976, converting it into a cultural center with exhibitions and arts events. Near the lighthouse at the island's highest point is the **Jacques Marchais Center of Tibetan Art**, a collection of art and cultural treasures from the Far East with an emphasis on all aspects of Tibetan prayer, meditation and healing. Its Buddhist temple is one of New York's more tranquil places.

Historic Richmond Town is a spacious collection of 29 restored buildings, some dating back to the 17th century. Many of the buildings have been moved here from elsewhere on the island. There's a courthouse, a general store, a bakery and a butcher shop, as well as private homes. During the Revolutionary War, Billop House (now **Conference House**) was where an unsuccessful peace conference took place between the Americans, led by Benjamin Franklin and John Adams, and England's Lord Howe. The building has been turned into a museum. Combine your visit here with a trip to nearby Tottenville Beach.

Conference House (Billop House)
7455 Hylan Blvd, Tottenville (718-984-2086). Travel: Staten Island Ferry, then S78 bus to Hylan Blvd at Craig Ave. Mar–Nov Wed–Sun 1–4pm. $2, $1 concessions.

John Adams recalled that for the attempted peace conference at Billop House, Lord Howe had "prepared a large handsome room" and made it "not only wholesome but romantically elegant." Built circa 1680, this is the earliest manor house in New York City, and it has been restored to its former magnificence.

Historic Richmond Town
1441 Clarke Ave between Arthur Kill and Richmond Rds, Richmond Town (718-351-1611). Travel: Staten Island Ferry, then S74 bus. Wed–Sun 1–5pm. $5, seniors and students $2.50, under 6 free. No credit cards.

Fourteen of the houses are open to the public, including Lake-Tysen House, a wooden farmhouse built in about 1740 in the Dutch Colonial style for a French Huguenot. Voorlezer's House is the oldest surviving elementary school in America. Actors in 18th-century garb lurk in the doorways; crafts workshops are never far away. It's as if you've left the city far behind.

Snug Harbor Cultural Center
1000 Richmond Terrace (718-448-2500). Travel: Staten Island Ferry, then Snug Harbor trolley or S40 bus. 8am–5pm. Tours Sat, Sun 2pm. $2 suggested donation.

Exhibitions of painting, sculpture and photography are held in the Newhouse Center. The Staten Island Botanical Garden is here, with tropical plants, orchids and a butterfly house. Opera, chamber groups and jazz musicians play in the Veterans' Memorial Hall. The Art Lab offers classes, and there's also a children's museum.

Staten Island Chamber of Commerce
130 Bay St (718-727-1900).

Call for details of cultural events and travel directions on Staten Island.

Fill 'er up: You can get everything you need 24-seven in New York City.

New York Necessities

Accommodations

Where to catch some ZZZs in the city that never sleeps

Thanks to plummeting crime rates and the Cinderella-like transformation of Times Square from peep-show paradise into Disneyfied family-entertainment capital, New York is back on the map as a safe and vibrant city to visit. If you're planning a trip, however, all the Big Apple polishing can be a mixed blessing. It seems everybody's heading to Gotham these days, which means hotels are full to overflowing and, unless you plan far enough ahead, you may find no room at the inn. Hotel occupancy hit an all-time high of 85.5 percent in 1997, and average room rates topped $200 for the first time ever, according to recent statistics. With the U.S. economy going strong, there's no end in sight to the domestic travel boom. Not surprisingly, the biggest push is for hotels under $100 a night—a rare commodity in NYC. Although many new hotels are opening and old ones revamping, the room crunch won't ease anytime soon.

So what's a traveler to do? If you're not one of the fortunate few who has a friend with a hide-a-bed, book well ahead. And always ask about special deals, weekend rates, family discounts and other bargains. It usually pays to shop around.

Consider checking with the reservation agencies listed here; many book blocks of rooms in advance and can offer deals even when everyone else swears the city is completely sold out. Another option: Bed-and-breakfasts, once the domain of quaint New England villages, are now catching on in New York. Several services offer thousands of hosted and unhosted apartments.

For some other accommodation listings, *see* chapter **Gay & Lesbian**.

One more caveat: Even though room taxes were rolled back to 13.25 percent a few years ago, they can still cause sticker shock for the uninitiated. Brace yourself for a $2-per-night occupancy tax, and ask in advance about unadvertised costs—like phone charges, minibars and faxes—or you might not find out about them till you check out.

For more information, contact the Hotel Association of New York City, 437 Madison Ave, New York, NY 10022 (212-754-6700; www.hanyc.org), or call the New York Convention and Visitors Bureau (800-VISIT-NYC) to ask for a copy of its accommodations booklet.

Telephone tip: The 800 numbers listed here can only be called toll-free from within the U.S.

HOTEL RESERVATION AGENCIES

These companies book blocks of rooms in advance and thus can offer reduced rates. Discounts cover most price ranges, from economy upward; some agencies claim savings of up to 65 percent, although around 20 percent is more likely. If you already know where you'd like to stay, it's worth calling a few agencies before booking, in case the hotel is on their list. If you're simply looking for the best deal, mention the part of town you'd like to stay in and the approximate rate you're willing to pay, and see what's available. The following agencies work with selected hotels in New York and are free of charge. A few require payment by credit card or personal check ahead of time, but most let you pay directly at the hotel.

Accommodations Express
801 Asbury Ave, sixth floor, Ocean City, NJ 08226 (609-391-2100, 800-444-7666) www.accommodationsxpress.com.

Central Reservations Service
9010 SW 137th Ave, #116, Miami, FL 33186 (305-408-6100, 800-950-0232; fax 305-408-6111) www.reservation-services.com.

Hotel Reservations Network
8140 Walnut Hill Lane, suite 203, Dallas, TX 75231 (800-964-6835) www.180096hotel.com.

Express Reservations
3825 Iris Ave, Boulder, CO 80301 (303-440-8481, 800-356-1123) www.express-res.com.

Quikbook
381 Park Ave South, New York, NY 10016 (212-779-ROOM, 800-789-9887; fax 212-779-6120) www.quikbook.com.

Deluxe

The Carlyle Hotel
35 E 76th St between Park and Madison Aves (212-744-1600, 800-227-5737; fax 212-717-4682). Subway: 6 to 77th St. Single/double $350–$595, suite $600–$2,500. AmEx, DC, MC, V.
The sumptuous Carlyle is one of New York's most luxurious hotels, featuring whirlpools in almost every bathroom. Since it opened in 1930, the hotel has attracted famous guests—especially those who want privacy. Service is so discreet that two members of the Beatles stayed here after the group split without either knowing about the other. The Cafe Carlyle, a cozy cabaret with low lighting, rose-velvet banquettes and pastel murals, is a perpetual draw for its live musical acts, including Eartha Kitt, Dixie Carter, Woody Allen on Mondays and the gravel-voiced Bobby Short, a consistent crowd pleaser now in his 30th year there.

*Shipshape: The rooms at Ian Schrager's **Royalton** are as elegant as a luxury liner.*

*Habitual elegance: Once a women's residence, the **Habitat Hotel** is sophisticated and cheap.*

Across the hall is Bemelmans Bar, named for Ludwig Bemelmans, the children's author who created Madeline; it's lined with charming murals he painted in 1947, when he lived at the hotel.
Hotel services *Air-conditioning. Baby-sitting. Bar. Beauty salon. Cable TV. Conference facilities. Currency exchange. Fax. Fitness center. Laundry. Multilingual staff. Restaurant.* **Room services** *Cable TV. Fax. Hair dryer. Minibar. Radio. Refrigerator. Room service. Safe. VCR.*

Four Seasons Hotel

57 E 57th St between Park and Madison Aves (212-758-5700, 800-332-3442; fax 212-758-5711) www.fourseasons.com. Subway: N, R to Lexington Ave; 4, 5, 6 to 59th St. Single from $515, double from $555, suite from $1,050. AmEx, DC, JCB, MC, V.
Renowned architect I.M. Pei's sharp geometric design (in neutral cream and honey tones) is sleek and ultramodern, befitting this favorite haven of media moguls and entertainment execs. The Art Deco–style rooms are among the largest in the city, with bathrooms made from Florentine marble and tubs that fill in just 60 seconds. Views of Manhattan from the higher floors are superb. Guests can unwind at Fifty Seven Fifty Seven, the hotel's ultrachic piano bar, where power brokers and gossipmongers gather nightly.
Hotel services *Air-conditioning. Baby-sitting. Bar. Conference facilities. Currency exchange. Disabled access. Fax. Fitness center and spa. Laundry. Multilingual staff. Parking. Restaurants.* **Room services** *Cable TV. Fax. Hair dryer. Minibar. Radio. Refrigerator. Room service. Safe. VCR.*

Millennium Hilton

55 Church St between Fulton and Dey Sts (212-693-2001, 800-HILTON; fax 212-571-2316) www.hilton.com. Subway: N, R, 1, 9 to Cortlandt St. Single $455, double $505, suite $550–$2,000. AmEx, DC, Disc, JCB, MC, V.
This 58-story black-glass skyscraper, located next to the World Trade Center and a stone's throw from Wall Street, draws a large corporate clientele. Lower Manhattan's four-star hotel features fax machines in each room and high-tech facilities, not to mention a rooftop swimming pool and solarium overlooking St. Paul's Church. The upper floors have splendid views of New York Harbor and the Brooklyn Bridge.
Hotel services *Air-conditioning. Bar. Concierge. Conference facilities. Currency exchange. Disabled access. Fax. Fitness center. Laundry. Multilingual staff. Parking. Restaurant.* **Room services** *Cable TV. Fax. Hair dryer. Minibar. Radio. Refrigerator. Room service. Safe. VCR.*

The New York Palace

455 Madison Ave at 50th St (212-888-7000, 800-697-2522; fax 212-303-6000) www.newyork palace.com. Subway: E, F to Fifth Ave. Single/double from $475, tower room from $600, suite from $900. AmEx, DC, Disc, JCB, MC, V.
Every inch of the luxurious New York Palace was renovated in 1998. It now has an elegantly refurbished lobby and new room decor, ranging from traditional to Art Deco, as well as revamped fitness and meeting centers. The main hotel—once the Villard Houses, a cluster of mansions designed by Stanford White—is the new home of Sirio Mac-

cioni's acclaimed Le Cirque 2000, and the decor is something to see: Pre-Raphaelite murals combined with a circus motif. It's nearly impossible to get into, but worth the effort.
Hotel services *Air-conditioning. Bar. Business center. Conference facilities. Concierge. Disabled access. Fax. Fitness center. Laundry. Multilingual staff. Nonsmoking floors. Parking. Restaurant.* **Room services** *Cable TV. Dual-line phones. Fax. Hair dryer. Iron. Minibar. Modem line. Radio. Refrigerator. Room service. Safe. VCR.*

The Pierre Hotel

2 E 61st St at Fifth Ave (212-838-8000, 800-PIERRE4; fax 212-826-0319) www.fourseasons.com. Subway: N, R to Fifth Ave. Single from $325, double from $395, suite from $475. AmEx, DC, JCB, MC, V.
Once Salvador Dalí's favorite hotel, the Pierre has been seducing guests since 1929 with its superb service and discreet, elegant atmosphere. The rooms may be out of your price range, but you can always take afternoon tea in the magnificent rotunda. Front rooms overlook Central Park, and some of Madison Avenue's most famous stores are a block away.
Hotel services *Air-conditioning. Baby-sitting. Bar. Beauty salon. Business center. Concierge. Conference facilities. Currency exchange. Fax. Fitness center. In-room exercise equipment on request. Laundry. Modem line. Notary public. Parking. Restaurant. Theater desk. Valet packing/unpacking.* **Room services** *Cable TV. Hair dryer. Minibar. Modem line. Radio. Refrigerator on request. Room service. Safe. VCR and fax on request.*

The Plaza Hotel

768 Fifth Ave at 59th St (212-759-3000, 800-759-3000; fax 212-759-3167) www.fairmont.com. Subway: N, R to Fifth Ave. Single/double $335–$800, suite $800–$15,000. AmEx, Disc, DC, JCB, MC, V.
Perfectly located for a shopping spree, the famous Plaza Hotel is just a few minutes' walk from Fifth Avenue's most exclusive stores. It's also across the street from Central Park, with breathtaking views from the high-floor rooms facing 59th Street. Although Ivana Trump no longer runs the place, her signature touches remain. The rooms and suites, renowned for their Baroque splendor, have been freshly renovated. The famous Palm Court has a delightful Tiffany ceiling; the Edwardian Room is currently closed for a makeover by designer du jour Adam Tihany. In the meantime, stop in at Istana, a new Mediterranean restaurant featuring a tapas afternoon tea, more than 30 types of olives and a sherry menu. A Plaza spa is also in the works.
Hotel services *Air-conditioning. Bar. Beauty salon. Conference facilities. Fax. Fitness center. Laundry. Multilingual staff. Parking. Restaurant.* **Room services** *Cable TV. Hair dryer. Minibar. Modem line. Radio. Room service. Safe. VCR on request. Voice mail.*

Trump International Hotel and Tower

1 Central Park West at Columbus Circle (212-299-1000; fax 212-299-1150). Subway: A, C, B, D, 1, 9 to 59th St–Columbus Circle. Suite $475–$1,500 (call for weekend rates). AmEx, Disc, DC, MC, V.
The Donald's striking glass-and-steel skyscraper towers over Columbus Circle, just steps from Central Park. Inside the year-old hotel, all is subdued elegance—from the small marble lobby to the 168 suites equipped with fax machines, Jacuzzis and floor-to-ceiling windows. Each guest is assigned a personal assistant to cater to his or her whims, and a chef will come to your room to cook on request. Better yet, head downstairs to Jean Georges, the newest restaurant from four-star chef Jean-Georges Vongerichten, of Jo Jo and Vong fame.
Hotel services *Air-conditioning. Bar. Cellular phones. Conference facilities. Fitness center. Personal attaché service. Restaurant.* **Room services** *Cable TV. CD player. Computer on request. Fax. Hair dryer. Kitchenette. Minibar. Modem line. Refrigerator. Room service. Telescope. VCR.*

The Waldorf-Astoria

301 Park Ave at 50th St (212-355-3000, 800-924-3673; fax 212-872-7272) www.hilton.com. Subway: E, F to Lexington Ave; 6 to 51st St. Single $255–$475, double $335–$375, suite $375–$1,700. AmEx, DC, Disc, JCB, MC, V.
The famous Waldorf salad made its debut in 1931 at the grand opening of what was then the world's largest hotel. Ever since, the Waldorf has been associated with New York's high society (former guests include Princess Grace, Cary Grant, Sophia Loren and a long list of U.S. presidents). This year, the grande dame of New York hotels wraps up a $60 million renovation that will restore the main lobby to its original Art Deco grandeur. The Peacock Alley restaurant's new French chef has drawn rave reviews, and the erstwhile coffee shop, Oscar's, is now a stylish American bistro.
Hotel services *Air-conditioning. Bar. Beauty salon. Concierge. Conference facilities. Fax. Fitness center with steam rooms. Iron. Laundry. Multilingual staff. Parking. Restaurant.* **Room services** *Cable TV. Fax in tower rooms. Hair dryer. Minibar. Radio. Room service.*

Stylish

The Mercer

147 Mercer St at Prince St. (212-966-6060). Subway: N, R to Prince St. Single from $350, double from $375, suite $925–$2,000. AmEx, DC, MC, V.
When entrepreneur Andre Balazs bought the site for the Mercer hotel, scenesters waited years for its doors to open. Balazs finally unveiled his 75-room gem in 1998. Its location in the dead center of Soho gives it a leg up on its closest competitor, the two-year-old SoHo Grand. The lobby offers a hint of the understated chic you'll find in the rooms: Each features techno amenities, an oversize bathroom and furniture made of exotic African woods.
Hotel services *Air-conditioning. Complimentary access to David Barton Gym. Lobby book and magazine library. Private business cards and stationery. Private meeting rooms. Restaurant and Bar. Video and CD library.* **Room services** *Cable TV. VCR. Cassette and CD player. Modem/fax. Three two-line telephones. Minibar. Safe. Fireplace. Room service.*

Morgans

237 Madison Ave between 37th and 38th Sts (212-686-0300, 800-334-3408; fax 212-779-8352). Subway: S, 4, 5, 6, 7 to 42nd St–Grand Central. Single $280–$305, double $285–$375, suite $375–$400. AmEx, Disc, DC, JCB, MC, V.
This cozy, understated hotel was the first non-nightclub venture by Studio 54 impresarios Ian Schrager and Steve Rubell. It's named in honor of J.P. Morgan, whose nearby library was converted into a museum (the Pierpont Morgan Library) in 1924. The cavelike Morgans Bar remains a favorite late-night haunt of models and other trendy types, and the restaurant, Asia de Cuba, serves spicy Chino-Latino cuisine.
Hotel services *Air-conditioning. Baby-sitting. Bar and café. Concierge. Conference facilities. Continental breakfast. Fax. Conference center and spa. Laundry. Multilingual staff. Restaurant.* **Room services** *Cable TV. CD player on request. Hair dryer. Laptop on request. Minibar. Modem line. Refrigerator. Room service. VCR on request.*

On the Ave

2178 Broadway at 77th St (212-362-1100; fax 212-787-9521) www.stayinny.com. Subway: 1, 9 to 79th St. Single/double $125–$245, penthouse suite $280–$350. AmEx, DC, Disc, JCB, MC, V.
The new On the Ave hotel brings some sorely needed style to the Upper West Side's stodgy hotel scene. Its most winning attractions are the canopied "floating beds" and the

Get a group

These hotels have a similiar vibe, just different locations

In addition to some of the national chains like Sheraton and Howard Johnsons, New York has a few pleasing hotel groups that operate several locations in Manhattan.

THE EMPIRE HOTEL GROUP

See listings below for phone numbers; www.newyorkhotel.com. AmEx, DC, Disc, JCB, MC, V.
The Empire Hotel Group accommodations range from the most basic with shared bathrooms to plush and full-service; however, they still manage to maintain a consistently low price range for their budget-minded, predominantly European clientele. You'll find archaic-looking bathroom facilities at the lower-priced end, but they're still functional. Call hotels or check the website for individual services.
Hotel services, all hotels *Air-conditioning.* **Hotel services, some hotels** *Bar. Coffee shop. Concierge. Conference center. Continental breakfast. Convenience store. Gift shop. Fitness center. Kitchenettes. Laundry. Parking. Restaurant. Safe. Swimming pool. Tour desk.* **Room services, all hotels** *Cable TV.* **Room services, some hotels** *Hair dryer. Iron and ironing board. Microwave. Modem line. Radio. Refrigerator. Roomservice. Voice mail.*

The Lucerne

201 W 79th St between Broadway and Amsterdam Ave (212-875-1000, 800-492-8122; fax 212-721-1179). Subway: 1, 9 to 79th St. Single $150–$200, double $160–$210, suite $180–$450.

The Carnegie

229 W 58th St between Broadway and Seventh Ave (212-245-4000; fax 212-245-6199). Subway: N, R to Seventh Ave; A, C, B, D, 1, 9 to 59th St–Columbus Circle. Suite $159–$300.

Belvedere Hotel

319 W 48th St between Eighth and Ninth Aves (212-245-7000; fax 212-265-7778) Subway: A, C, E, 1, 9 to 50th St; N, R to 49th St. Suite $140–$240.

Travel Inn

515 W 42nd St between Tenth and Eleventh Aves (212-695-7171; 800-869-4630; fax 212-967-5025). Subway: A, C, E to 42nd St Port–Authority. Double $140–$200 (add $10 per extra person).

Hotel Newton

2528 Broadway between 94th and 95th Sts (212-678-6500, 800-643-5553; fax 212-678-6758). Subway: 1, 2, 3, 9 to 96th St. Double $85–$140 (add $10 per extra person).

Hotel Riverside

350 W 88th St between West End Ave and Riverside Dr (212-724-6100; fax 212-873-5808). Subway: 1, 9 to 86th St. Single/double with shared bath $100, single/ double with private bath $130 (add $10 per extra person).

Americana Inn

69 W 38th St between Fifth and Sixth Aves (212-840-2019; fax 212-840-1830). Subway: B, D, F,

Q, N, R to 34th St–Herald Sq. Single $85, double $85–$95, triple $105 (add $10 per extra person).

FITZPATRICK HOTELS

800-367-7701; fax 212-308-5166; www.fitzpatrickhotels.com. Single $295, double $325, suite $365–$395. AmEx, DC, Disc, MC, V.
You can't miss the fact that these family-run East Siders are New York's only Irish-owned lodgings: There are kelly-green carpets with a Book of Kells pattern in the lobbies. The hotel restaurants serve rashers, bangers, soda bread (what else?) and high tea. Just don't plan to go on St. Patrick's Day; you'll never get in.
Hotel services: *Air-conditioning. Bar. Fax. Laundry. Restaurant.* **Room services** *Cable TV. Complimentary coffee and tea. Iron. Room service.*

Fitzpatrick Grand Central Hotel

141 E 44th St between Lexington and Third Aves (212-351-6800; fax: 212-949-8969). Subway: S, 4, 5, 6, 7 to 42nd St–Grand Central.

Fitzpatrick Manhattan Hotel

687 Lexington Ave between 55th and 56th Sts (212-355-0100, 800-367-7701; fax 212-308-5166). Subway: E, F, N, R to Lexington Ave; 6 to 59th St.

MANHATTAN EAST SUITE HOTELS

800-637-8483; www.mesuite.com. Rates $179–$275. AmEx, DC, MC, V.
Manhattan's largest all-suite hotel group, these ten hotels are family-owned and charming. They offer the services of larger hotels along with small-town hospitality and reasonable rates. Some guests stay here especially for the kitchenettes located in the suites.
Hotel services, all hotels *Air-conditioning. Coin-operated laundry. Complimentary coffee and tea. Fax. Grocery shopping service. Monthly rates. Nonsmoking floors. Valet service.* **Hotel services, some hotels** *Concierge. Fitness center. Meeting/banquet rooms. Restaurant. Secretarial services. Sauna. Terrace suites. Valet parking.* **Room services, all hotels** *Cable TV. Hair dryers. Iron and board. Modem line. Room service. Voice mail.* **Room services, some hotels** *Safe.*

Beekman Tower

3 Mitchell Place, E 49th St at First Ave (212-355-7300; fax 212-753-9366). Subway: E, F to Lexington Ave; 6 to 51st St.

Dumont Plaza

150 E 34th St between Lexington and Third Aves (212-481-7600; fax 212-889-8856). Subway: 6 to 33rd St.

Eastgate Tower

222 E 39th St between Second and Third Aves (212-687-8000; fax 212-490-2634). Subway: S, 4, 5, 6, 7 to 42nd St–Grand Central.

Lyden Gardens

215 E 64th St between Second and Third Aves (212-355-1230; fax 212-758-7858). Subway: N, R to Lexington Ave; 4, 5, 6 to 59th St.

Lyden House

*320 E 53rd St between First and Second Aves
(212-888-6070; fax 212-935-7690). Subway: E, F
to Lexington Ave; 6 to 51st St.*

Plaza Fifty

*155 E 50th St between Lexington and Third Aves
(212-751-5710; fax 212-753-1468). Subway: E, F
to Lexington Ave; 6 to 51st St.*

Shelburne Murray Hill

*303 Lexington Ave at 37th St (212-689-5200;
fax 212-779-7068). Subway: S, 4, 5, 6, 7 to 42nd
St–Grand Central.*

Southgate Tower

*371 Seventh Ave at 31st St (212-563-1800; fax 212
643-8028). Subway: 1, 2, 3, 9 to 34th St–Penn Station.*

Surrey Hotel

*20 E 76th St between Fifth and Madison Aves (212-
288-3700; fax: 212-628-1549). Subway: 6 to 77th St*

UNIQUE HOTELS

*See listings below for phone numbers;
www.uniquehotels.com AmEx, MC, V.*
These small, stylish hotels, popular with the fashion
industry, offer some unique complimentary treats; the
espresso and cappuccino flow freely all day, and some
hotels have afternoon tea. All provide a healthy continental breakfast and a free dessert buffet every
evening. The cedar closets and down comforters are
another draw. Some may find the minimalist decor
sparse and somber.
Hotel services, all hotels *Air-conditioning.
Continental breakfast. Multilingual staff. Video and
CD library.* **Hotel services, some hotels** *Bar.
Complimentary passes to fitness center. Fax.
Laundry. Parking. Restaurant.* **Room services, all
hotels:** *Cable TV. CD player. Hair dryer. VCR.*
Room services, some hotels *Radio.
Refrigerator. Room service. Safe.*

Franklin Hotel

*164 E 87th St between Third and Lexington Aves
(212-369-1000, 800-600-8787; fax 212-369-8000).
Subway: 4, 5, 6 to 86th St. $199–$245 ($10 off
Internet bookings).*

Hotel Wales

*1295 Madison Ave at 92nd St (212-876-6000,
800-428-5252; fax 212-860-7000). Subway: 6 to
96th St. Single/double from $209, suite $339–$389.*

Mansfield

*12 W 44th St between Fifth and Sixth Aves
(212-944-6050, 800-255-5167; fax 212-764-4477).
Subway: B, D, F, Q to 42nd St; 7 to Fifth Ave.
Standard $209, deluxe $209-$229, double $249,
one-bedroom suite $269.*

The Roger Williams Hotel

*131 Madison Ave at 31st St (212-448-7000, 888-
448-7788; fax 212-448-7007). Subway: N, R, 6 to
28th St. Single/double $245–$305, suite from $425.
AmEx, DC, MC, V.*

Shoreham Hotel

*33 W 55th St between Fifth and Sixth Aves
(212-247-6700, 800-553-3347; fax
212-765-9741). Subway: B, Q to 57th St; E, F to
Fifth Ave. Standard $255–$295, suite $349–$375.*

slick, industrial-style bathroom sinks. Original artwork and
innovative touches, such as individual breakfast trays that
can double as laptop desks, help to warm the minimal decor.
On the Ave houses neither a bar nor a restaurant, so patrons
must be prepared to venture into the surrounding Lincoln
Center environs for food, drink and entertainment.
Hotel services *Air-conditioning. Conference facilities.
Concierge. Disabled access.* **Room services** *Cable TV. Hair
dryer. Iron. Modem line. Room service. Voice mail.*

Paramount

*235 W 46th St between Broadway and Eighth Ave (212-
764-5500, 800-225-7474; fax 212-575-4892). Subway:
N, R to 49th St. Single $145–$295, double $260–$320,
suite $475–$675. AmEx, DC, Disc, JCB, MC, V.*
Designed by Philippe Starck and owned by Ian Schrager, the
Paramount, like the Royalton (*see below*), is chic almost beyond
belief. The cavernous, windowless lobby was inspired by the
great transatlantic liners. A "weather mirror" near the elevator on each floor gives the daily forecast, and Vermeer's *Lace-
maker* is silk-screened on the headboard of each bed. (There's
also a Dean & DeLuca shop and an espresso bar.) The hotel
has just been renovated, but one thing hasn't changed: The
Whiskey Bar is still a good place for model spotting.
Hotel services *Air-conditioning. Bar. Business center.
Conference facilities. Currency exchange. Fax. Fitness
center. Laundry. Multilingual staff. Nonsmoking floors.
Restaurants.* **Room services** *Cable TV. Minibar. Modem
line. Room service. VCR.*

Royalton

*44 W 44th St between Fifth and Sixth Aves
(212-869-4400, 800-635-9013; fax 212-869-8965).
Subway: B, D, F, Q to 42nd St; 7 to Fifth Ave. Standard
$305–$355, superior $340–$400, deluxe $390–$440.
AmEx, DC, MC, V.*
Like the Paramount (*see above*), Ian Schrager's Royalton was
designed by Philippe Starck, whose style makes for soothing
hotel rooms. Waitresses in satin minidresses serve fashionable young things in the vaultlike lobby, and the restaurant
(called 44) has some of the most sought-after lunch tables in
town (keep an eye out for Condé Nast editors). The rooms feature sleek slate fireplaces and marvelous round bathtubs. Discounted weekend rates are often available.
Hotel services *Air-conditioning. Bar. Conference
facilities. Currency exchange. Fax. Fitness center. Laundry.
Multilingual staff. Parking. Restaurant.* **Room services**
*Cable TV. Minibar. Modem line. Radio. Room service.
VCR. Video library.*

SoHo Grand Hotel

*310 West Broadway between Grand and Canal Sts
(212-965-3000, 800-965-3000; fax 212-965-3200)
www.sohogrand.com. Subway: A, C, E, 1, 9 to Canal St.
Single $334–$434, double $354–$534, suite from
$1,099. AmEx, DC, MC, V.*
When it welcomed its first guests in 1996, this was Soho's
first hotel to open since the 1800s. The unusual design pays
homage to both Soho's contemporary artistic community
and to the area's past as a manufacturing district. Architecturally, it's one of the city's most striking hotels. A dramatic bottle glass–and–cast iron stairway leads up from street
level to the elegant lobby and reception desk, where a mon-
umental clock presides. Rooms are decorated in soothing
grays and beiges, with nonfat munchies in the minibar and
photos from local galleries on the walls. Both the Grand Bar
and the Canal House restaurant are worth a visit. If you're
feeling lonely, request a pet goldfish to keep in your room
during your stay.
Hotel services *Air-conditioning. Bar. Business services.
Conference facilities. Concierge. Fax. Fitness center.
Laundry. Restaurant.* **Room services** *Cable TV. CD
player on request. Minibar. Modem line. Room service.
Voice mail.*

The Time

*224 W 49th St between Broadway and Eighth Ave
(212-246-5252, 877-846-3692) www.timehotel.com.
Subway: C, E, 1, 9 to 50th St; N,R to 49th St. Single/
double from $275, suite $400–$1,100. AmEx, DC, Disc,
JCB, MC, V.*

Designer Adam D. Tihany says of this stylish new addition
to the Times Square panorama, "The idea is to truly experience a color—to see it, feel it, taste it, smell it and live it."
This experience includes guest rooms entirely furnished in
the primary color of your choice, including artfully placed
food of that color as well as a color-inspired scent and reading material. Sound like too much? You can always chill out
in the hotel's neutral and subdued public spaces, or at Jean-
Louis Palladin's New York–debut restaurant, Palladin. Make
sure to bring a color choice and your sense of humor.
Hotel services *Air-conditioning. Concierge. Currency
exchange. Fitness center. Gift shop. Laundry. Nonsmoking
rooms. Restaurant. Screening room. Shopping services.*
Room services *Cable and Web TV. Fax/copy/printer.
Hair dryer. Iron. Minibar. Modem line. Radio. Room
service. Safe. VCR. Video rental. Voice mail.*

W Hotel

*541 Lexington Ave at 49th St (212-755-1200,
877-W-HOTELS) www.whotels.com. Subway: 6 to 51st St.
Single/double $199–$565, suite $489–$1,100. AmEx,
DC, Disc, JCB, MC, V.*

Designed for the sophisticated executive and leisure traveler, the W Hotel offers every convenience. Rooms are both
sharp and soothing, with oversize desks, chaise lounges and
luxurious feather beds. If the atmosphere isn't enough to calm
frayed nerves, there's craniosacral message at the alternative
Away Spa, or organic teas at Heartbeat, the hotel's health-
conscious restaurant. Expect the same suavity from W's
newly renovated sister hotels, the Court and the Tuscany.
Hotel services *Air-conditioning. Baby-sitting. Bar.
Business services. Conference facilities. Concierge.
Continental breakfast. Disabled access. Fax. Fitness center
and spa. Laundry. Nonsmoking rooms. Parking.
Restaurant. Multilingual staff.* **Room services** *Cable TV.
Fax. Hair dryer. Minibar. Modem line. Radio/CD player.
Refrigerator. Room service. Safe. VCR.*
Other locations: *The Court, 130 East 39th St (212-
685-1100; fax 212-889-0287). The Tuscany, 120 East
39th St (212-686-1600; fax 212-779-7822).*

First-class

Algonquin

*59 W 44th St between Fifth and Sixth Aves
(212-840-6800, 800-555-8000; fax 212-944-1419)
www.camberleyhotels.com. Subway: B, D, F, Q to 42nd St;
7 to Fifth Ave. Single/double $259–$379, suite
$309–$419. AmEx, DC, Disc, JCB, MC, V.*

Arguably New York's most famous literary landmark, this
was the place where Dorothy Parker, James Thurber and
other literary lights of the 1920s and '30s gathered at the Oak
Room's legendary Round Table to gossip and match wits. The
newly refurbished rooms are on the small side but cheerful
and charming, and the hallways now feature *New Yorker*–cartoon wallpaper. Don't miss Matilda, the house cat, who has
her own miniature suite and four-poster bed in a corner of
the redone lobby. On Sunday and Monday evenings, there are
readings by local playwrights and authors—or you may prefer to head straight to the cozy Blue Bar.
Hotel services *Air-conditioning. Baby-sitting. Bar.
Conference facilities. Currency exchange. Disabled access.
Fax. 24-hour fitness center. Laundry. Multilingual staff.
Nonsmoking floors. Restaurant.* **Room services** *Cable
TV. Hair dryer. Radio. Refrigerator in suites and on
request. Room service. Safe. VCR on request. Voice mail.*

Barbizon Hotel

*140 E 63rd St at Lexington Ave (212-838-5700,
800-223-1020; fax 212-888-4271). Subway: N, R to
Lexington Ave; 4, 5, 6 to 59th St. Single $250–$275,
double $270–$295, suite from $475. AmEx, DC,
Disc, MC, V.*

The Barbizon was originally a hotel for emancipated women
(whose parents could feel confident that their daughters were
safe in its care). During its years as a women-only residence,
guests included Grace Kelly, Ali McGraw and Candice
Bergen, and the rules stated that men could be entertained
only in the lounge. The hotel recently completed a $40-mil-
lion renovation, which included adding a branch of the local
Equinox health club (free for guests) with an Olympic-size
pool and full spa. Children under 12 stay free if sharing a
room with their parents.
Hotel services *Air-conditioning. CD library. Currency
exchange. Disabled access. Fax. Fitness center. Laundry.
Multilingual staff.* **Room services** *Cable TV. CD player.
Fax. Hair dryer. Laptop. Minibar. Modem line.
Refrigerator. Safe.Voice mail.*

The Benjamin

*125 East 50th St at Lexington Ave (212-715-2500,
888-4-BENJAMIN; fax 212-715-2525)
www.thebenjamin.com. Subway: E, V to Lexington Ave;
6 to 51st St. Superior from $320, deluxe from $350, suite
$420–$775. AmEx, DC, Disc, JCB, MC, V.*

Now occupying Emory Roth's famous city landmark the
Hotel Beverly (which Georgia O'Keeffe used to paint from
her apartment across the street), the Benjamin has restored
its historic heritage while modernizing into a fully-equipped
executive suite hotel with a high-tech communications system. The recent refurbishment has restored Roth's original
details. In addition, the noted chef Larry Forgione moved his
popular restaurant An American Place to the hotel (the
kitchen is also providing the room service).
Hotel services *Business services. Concierge. Conference
facilities. Fitness center and spa. Laundry. Restaurant.*
Room services *Cable and Web TV. CD/cassette player.
Fax/printer/copier. Hair dryer. Kitchenette. Minibar.
Modem line. Radio. Room service. Safe. VCR. Voice mail.*

Hotel Elysée

*60 E 54th St between Park and Madison Aves
(212-753-1066; fax 212-980-9278)
members.aol.com/elysee99. Subway: E, F to Lexington
Ave; 6 to 51st St. Single/double $295–$325, suite
$375–$525. AmEx, DC, JCB, MC, V.*

This is a charming and discreet hotel with attentive service. The quarters feature antique furniture and Italian-
marble bathrooms; some of the rooms also have colored-
glass conservatories and roof terraces. It's popular with
publishers, so don't be surprised if you see a famous author
enjoying the complimentary afternoon tea in the club room.
You can also eat in the whimsically decorated Monkey Bar
next door. Rates include continental breakfast and evening
wine and hors d'oeuvres. The Elysée has been restored to
its original 1930s look and displays photographs showing
the likes of Joan Crawford and Marlene Dietrich gathered
around the piano.
Hotel services *Air-conditioning. Baby-sitting. Bar.
Conference facilities. Disabled access. Fax. Laundry.
Library. Multilingual staff. Valet parking.* **Room
services** *Cable TV. Hair dryer. Minibar. Modem line.
Radio. Refrigerator. Room service. TV. VCR. Voice mail.*

The Iroquois

*49 W 44th St betweem Fifth and Sixth Aves
(212-840-308, 800-332-7220; fax 212-398-1754)
www.slh.com. Subway: B, D, F, Q to 42nd St; 7 to Fifth
Ave. Single/double $295–$375, suite $450–$925.
AmEx, DC, JCB, MC, V.*

Taking advantage of the Times Square makeover that banished all traces of prerevival seediness, the Iroquois, once a budget hostelry, has morphed into a full-service luxury hotel—guess the investors smell money in the neighborhood. A mahogany-paneled library, marble-lined bathrooms and a lobby furnished in polished stone are just a part of the $13-million renovation that did away with an archaic barbershop and a photographer's studio. The famous Algonquin sits directly across the way, but the only similarity is the Native American name.

Hotel services *Air-conditioning. Bar. Conference facilities. Continental breakfast. Disabled access. Fitness center and spa. Library. Nonsmoking rooms and floors. Parking. Restaurant. Multilingual staff.* **Room services** *Cable T.V. CD player. Hair dryer. Iron. Modem line. Radio. Room service. Safe. VCR.*

The Kitano
66 Park Ave at 38th St (212-885-7000, 800-548-2666, fax 212-885-7100) www.kitano.com. Subway: 4, 5,

Name your fantasy
Some say you are where you sleep. These are the best hotels for…

ASPIRING WRITERS
History practically seeps from the walls of the **Algonquin**, a literary landmark where Dorothy Parker, James Thurber and other famous wits once gathered. Even the wallpaper is peppered with *New Yorker* cartoons. Or try the **Chelsea Hotel**, where Mark Twain, Thomas Wolfe and other novelists spent their more down-at-the-heels years. If you end up with writer's block, at least you can follow in Dylan Thomas's footsteps and stumble down to a nearby watering hole in the West Village to drown your sorrows.

BUDGET-MINDED BROADWAY FANS
Broadway Inn and the **Hotel Casablanca**, just off Broadway, are two of the Theater District's few truly affordable options.

FOOD FANATICS
Who says hotel dining can't be fabulous? The **New York Palace**'s Le Cirque 2000 and **Trump International Hotel and Tower**'s Jean Georges rank among the top restaurants on every gourmet's list. The **Waldorf-Astoria**'s Peacock Alley chef has also been drawing praise.

HISTORY LOVERS
The **Roosevelt Hotel** is where Guy Lombardo broadcast "Auld Lang Syne" on many a New Year's Eve. Another good bet: the **Waldorf-Astoria**, a society favorite for decades, where the lost-and-found department has turned up such items as Sophia Loren's eyeglasses, Cary Grant's X-rays and Matt Dillon's barbells.

KILLER VIEWS
The **Millennium Hilton** offers unparalleled vistas of New York Harbor and the Brooklyn Bridge from the upper floors. If you're not lucky enough to land a room with a view, just head to the rooftop pool. The elegant **Four Seasons Hotel** on 57th Street also offers breathtaking views from its upper floors.

ART BUFFS
The restored **Hotel Wales** is an historic charmer and an easy stroll from Museum Mile on upper Fifth Avenue. The **Mark** is also popular, thanks to its proximity to major museums like the Met, the Whitney and the Guggenheim. If you'd rather stay downtown, try the **SoHo Grand Hotel**, a stone's throw from New York's trendiest art galleries.

MUSIC AFICIONADOS
The **Carlyle**'s Cafe Carlyle is where Woody Allen plays jazz on Monday nights, Eartha Kitt and Dixie Carter are frequent performers, and gravel-voiced crooner Bobby Short is in his 30th year. You can also hang out in Bemelmans Bar across the lobby and enjoy live piano music for free. Classical-music fans won't want to miss the **Empire**, across the street from the operas and symphonies of Lincoln Center.

ROCK & ROLLERS
The eccentric **Hotel 17**, where Madonna and David Bowie have done photo shoots, is home to many up-and-coming rockers. The revamped **Star Hotel** also lays claim to Madonna's fame. At the **Washington Square Hotel**, you can retrace the steps of Bob Dylan and Joan Baez, both of whom stayed here and played for pennies in nearby Washington Square Park before hitting it big.

SHOPAHOLICS
Strategically placed for a visit to Fifth and Madison Avenues' finest stores, the **Plaza Hotel** is perfect for a shopping spree. And if you're a parent, F.A.O. Schwarz is just across the street.

SPORTS FANS
The **Southgate Tower Hotel** is nothing special, but it's directly across the street from Madison Square Garden and close to all the bars offering pregame drink and dinner specials.

6, 7, S to 42nd St–Grand Central. Superior $345, deluxe $360–$450, suite $550–$1,400. AmEx, DC, Disc, JCB, MC, V.
The Kitano has a serene Japanese aesthetic—warm mood lighting, mahogany paneling, polished stone floors, even complimentary green tea. It is also home to Japanese restaurant Nadaman Hakubai and an authentic tatami suite. The views of surrounding Murray Hill are stunning, and there are two large terraces for functions and parties. The Kitano is popular with businesspeople, but those who like to shake that office feeling after a long day may have a hard time here—the sleek decor and neutral colors feel a bit like an office (albeit a nice one).
Hotel services *Air-conditioning. Bar. Concierge. Conference facilities. Gallery. Gift shop. Access to New York Sports Club. Limousine service to Wall St. Restaurant.* **Room services** *Cable TV. Hair dryer. Heated towel rack. Japanese tea cups and green tea. Minibar. Modem line. Voice mail.*

The Mark

25 E 77th St between Fifth and Madison Aves (212-744-4300, 800-843-6275; fax 212-744-2749) www.themarkhotel.com. Subway: 6 to 77th St. Single $390–$420, double $420–$450, suite $600–$2,200. AmEx, DC, MC, V.
Towering potted palms and arched mirrors line the entranceway to this cheerful European-style Upper East Sider. The marble lobby, decorated with 18th-century Piranesi prints and magnums of Veuve-Clicquot, is usually bustling with dressy international guests and white-gloved bellmen. Especially popular are Mark's Bar, a clubby hideaway with lots of dark green furnishings and polished wood, and the more elegant Mark's Restaurant.
Hotel services *Air-conditioning. Bar. Conference facilities. Fax. Fitness center. Lounge. Multilingual staff. Restaurant.* **Room services** *Cable TV. Fax. Hair dryer. Kitchenette. Modem line. Room service. VCR.*

The Michelangelo

152 W 51st St between Sixth and Seventh Aves (212-765-1900, 800-237-0990; fax 212-581-7618) www.michelangelohotel.com. Subway: B, D, E to Seventh Ave; N, R to 49th St; 1, 9 to 50th St. Single/double $325–$395, suite $475–$1,300. AmEx, DC, Disc, JCB, MC, V.
Posh and very European, this charming little haven in the Theater District welcomes guests with a cozy lobby full of peach marble, oil paintings, giant potted palms and over-stuffed couches in rose and salmon tones. The 178 sizable rooms are decorated in styles ranging from French country to Art Deco; each room includes two TVs (one in the bathroom), a fax machine, a terry-cloth robe and a giant tub. Complimentary breakfast includes espresso, cappuccino and Italian pastries.
Hotel services *Air-conditioning. Bar. Business center. Conference facilities. 24-hour fitness center. Multilingual staff. Limousine service to Wall St (Mon–Fri). Laundry.* **Room services** *Cable TV. CD player on request. Complimentary shoe shine and newspaper. Fax/printer/copier. Minibar. Modem line. Radio. Room service. Voice mail.*

Roger Smith

501 Lexington Ave between 47th and 48th Sts (212-755-1400, 800-445-0277; fax 212-319-9130). Subway: E, F to Lexington Ave; 6 to 51st St. Single/double $240–$260, suite $295–$400. AmEx, DC, JCB, MC, V.
The hotel is owned by sculptor and painter James Knowles, and some of his work decorates the lobby. The large rooms are individually furnished, the staff is helpful and there's a library of videocassettes for those who want to stay in for the night. It's popular with touring bands, and there's often live jazz in the restaurant.

Hotel services *Air-conditioning. Baby-sitting. Bar. Conference facilities. Disabled access. Fax. Laundry. Multilingual staff. Restaurant. Valet parking.* **Room services** *Cable TV. Coffeemaker. Hair dryer on request. Iron. Modem line. Radio. Refrigerator. Room service. VCR. Voice mail.*

The Warwick

65 W 54th St at Sixth Ave (212-247-2700; fax 212-957-8915) www.warwickhotels.com. Subway: B, Q to 57th St. Single $197–$279, double $255–$295, suite $500–$1,200. AmEx, DC, JCB, MC, V.
Built by William Randolph Hearst and patronized by Elvis and the Beatles in the 1950s and '60s, the Warwick is still polished and gleaming. It was once an apartment building, and the rooms are exceptionally large by midtown standards. Ask for a view of Sixth Avenue (double glazing keeps out the noise). The top-floor suite was once the home of Cary Grant.
Hotel services *Air-conditioning. Baby-sitting. Bar. Conference facilities. Currency exchange. Disabled access. Drugstore. Fax. Fitness center. Laundry. Men's clothing store. Multilingual staff. Parking. Restaurant. Theater desk.* **Room services** *Cable TV. Hair dryer. Minibar. Modem line. Radio. Refrigerator. Room service. Safe. VCR. Voice mail.*

Boutiques

The Gorham New York

136 W 55th St between Sixth and Seventh Aves (212-245-1800, 800-735-0710; fax 212-582-8332) www.gorhamhotel.com. Subway: B, Q, N, R to 57th St; B, D, E to Seventh Ave. Single/double $205–$440, suite $235–$475. AmEx, DC, JCB, MC, V.
The 120-room Gorham, opposite the City Center theater, has clocks over the front desk showing the hour everywhere from Paris to Tokyo. The lobby's marble floors, maple walls and slightly worn oriental carpets contribute to the rather European ambience. Rooms, though not luxurious, have been recently redecorated in a contemporary style. The kitchenettes in each are a definite plus for families.
Hotel services *Air-conditioning. Baby-sitting. Bar. Luxury car service. Conference facilities. Disabled access. Fax. Fitness center. Laundry. Multilingual staff. Parking. Restaurant.* **Room services** *Cable TV. Hair dryer. Kitchenette with coffeemaker, tea and coffee. Minibar. Nintendo. Modem line. Radio. Refrigerator. Room service. Safe. VCR on request.*

Hotel Casablanca

147 W 43rd St between Sixth Ave and Broadway (212-869-1212, 888-9-CASABLANCA; fax 212-391-7585) www.casablancahotel.com. Subway: N, R, S, 1, 2, 3, 9, 7 to 42nd St–Times Sq; B, D, F, Q to 42nd St. Single from $245, double from $265, suite from $375. AmEx, DC, JCB, MC, V.
This is a cozy 48-room hotel in the Theater District with a cheerful Moroccan-style lobby. Rick's Café (get it?) is on the second floor, serving free wine and cheese on weeknights. A rooftop bar is set to open in the summer of 2000.
Hotel services *Air-conditioning. Conference facilities. Cybercafé. Disabled access. Fax. Laundry. Multilingual staff. Restaurant.* **Room services** *Cable TV. Radio.*

The Inn at Irving Place

56 Irving Pl between 17th and 18th Sts (212-533-4600, 800-685-1447; fax 212-533-4611) www.innatirving.com. Subway: L, N, R, 4, 5, 6 to 14th St–Union Sq. Rates $295–$450. AmEx, DC, MC, V.
For a bit of Victorian charm, book a room at this 19th-century townhouse near Gramercy Park. With only a dozen rooms, it's one of Manhattan's smallest inns and one of its most romantic. Instead of a front desk, there's a parlor with

a blazing fireplace and an antique cart serving punch and sherry. Some rooms are quite small, but each has a fireplace and a four-poster bed. The Madame Wollenska suite has a pretty window seat. Rates include continental breakfast. **Hotel services** *Air-conditioning. Bar. Restaurant. Room service. Safe. Tearoom.* **Room services** *Cable TV. CD player. Hair dryer. Minibar. Modem line. VCR.*

The Lowell Hotel

28 E 63rd St between Park and Madison Aves (212-838-1400; fax 212-319-4230) lowelhtl@aol.com. Subway: N, R to Lexington Ave; 4, 5, 6 to 59th St. Single $345, double from $445, suite $545–$1,295. AmEx, DC, Disc, MC, V.
Renovated in 1997, the Lowell is a small, charming hotel in a landmark Art Deco building. Rooms boast Scandinavian comforters, Chinese porcelain and marble baths; there are even wood-burning fireplaces in the suites. The gym suite has lodged the likes of Madonna, Arnold Schwarzenegger and Michelle Pfeiffer.
Hotel services *Air-conditioning. Baby-sitting. Bar. Currency exchange. Fitness center. Laundry. Multilingual staff. Restaurant.* **Room services** *Cable TV. Fax. Hair dryer. Minibar. Modem line. Radio. Refrigerator. Room service. VCR.*

Comfortable

Best Western Manhattan

17 W 32nd St between Broadway and Fifth Ave (212-736-1600, 800-567-7720; fax 212-563-4007). Subway: B, D, F, Q, N, R to 34th St–Herald Sq. Single/double $99–$399, suites $159–$500. AmEx, DC, Disc, MC, V.
This is a good-value hotel with a stylish Beaux Arts facade, a black-and-grey marble lobby and rooms inspired by different neighborhoods—choose between a floral Central Park look and a trendy Soho motif. The hotel is just a few blocks from Macy's and the Empire State Building, but the block is a bit seedy. Intrepid travelers will enjoy exploring the Korean shops lining 32nd Street; first-timers might want to opt for a more mainstream locale. Tullio's, an Italian restaurant next door, is open 24 hours and provides room service for guests.
Hotel services *Air-conditioning. Beauty salon. Business center. Conference facilities. Disabled access. Fax. Fitness center. Multilingual staff. Valet parking.* **Room services** *Cable TV. Hair dryer in most rooms. Iron. Minibar in most rooms. Modem line. Nintendo. Voice mail.*

Comfort Inn Manhattan

42 W 35th St between Fifth and Sixth Aves (212-947-0200, 800-228-5150; fax 212-594-3047) www.hotelchoice.com. Subway: B, D, F, Q, N, R to 34th St–Herald Sq. Single/double $129–$349. AmEx, DC, Disc, MC, V.
This small family-oriented hotel, around the corner from Macy's and the Empire State Building, underwent a $4.5-million renovation several years ago. Alex at the front desk is a hoot. A hotel fixture for more than a decade, he loves collecting bizarre English place names, so come prepared if you can. Rates include a continental breakfast.
Hotel services *Air-conditioning. Continental breakfast. Fax. Multilingual staff.* **Room services** *Cable TV. Hair dryer. Radio. Refrigerator, microwave and coffeemaker on request. Safe. Voice mail.*

The Empire Hotel

44 W 63rd St at Broadway (212-265-7400, 888-822-3555; fax 212-245-3382). Subway: A, C, B, D, 1, 9 to 59th St–Columbus Circle. Single/double
$180–$300, suite $300–$650. AmEx, DC, Disc, JCB, MC, V.
This hotel is perfectly located opposite Lincoln Center and next door to the eccentrically stylish Iridium bar. The lobby is surprisingly baronial, with wood paneling and velvet drapes. The rooms are small—some almost closet-size—but tasteful, with plenty of chintz and floral prints.
Hotel services *Air-conditioning. Bar. Conference facilities. Currency exchange. Disabled access. Fax. Multilingual staff. Restaurant. Theater/tour ticket desk. Valet parking.* **Room services** *Cable TV. Hair dryer. Minibar. Radio. Refrigerator on request. Room service. Two-line phones. VCR, CD and cassette player.*

Excelsior Hotel

45 W 81st St between Columbus Ave and Central Park West (212-362-9200, 800-368-4575; fax 212-721-2994). Subway: B, C to 81st St; 1, 9 to 79th St. Single/double $149–$209, suite $189–$269. AmEx, DC, Disc, MC, V.
On the Upper West Side, where hotels are scarce, the Excelsior offers a prime location just steps from Central Park and across the street from the American Museum of Natural History. The rooms are newly renovated but still affordable.
Hotel services *Air-conditioning. Coffee shop. Conference facilities. Continental breakfast. Fax. Fitness center. Library.* **Room services** *Cable TV. Modem line. Radio. Room service from coffee shop. Voice mail.*

Gramercy Park Hotel

2 Lexington Ave at 21st St (212-475-4320, 800-221-4083; fax 212-505-0535). Subway: 6 to 23rd St. Single $155, double $170, suite from $200. AmEx, DC, Disc, JCB, MC, V.
This hotel is in a surprisingly quiet location adjoining the small green oasis of Gramercy Park. Guests vary from business travelers to rock stars. There are no nonsmoking rooms.
Hotel services *Air-conditioning. Bar. Beauty salon. Conference facilities. Disabled access. Fax. Laundry. Multilingual staff. Newsstand/theater-ticket office. Parking. Restaurant.* **Room services** *Refrigerator. Radio. Room service.*

Hotel Beacon

2130 Broadway between 74th and 75th Sts (212-787-1100, 800-572-4969; fax 212-787-8119). Subway: 1, 2, 3, 9 to 72nd St. Single $165, double $155–$195, suite $225–$275. AmEx, DC, MC, V.
If you're looking for a break from the throngs of tourists clogging Times Square—or if you want to see how Gothamites really live—consider the Beacon. It's in a desirable residential neighborhood and only a short walk from Central Park, Lincoln Center and the famous Zabar's food market. The hotel has a cheerful black-and-white marble lobby and friendly staff. The hallways are a bit drab, and rooms vary in decor, but they are all clean and spacious. Since the Beacon is the tallest building in the area, its windows let in light and offer views of the neighborhood (unlike many other hotels).
Hotel services *Air-conditioning. Coffee shop. Fax. Laundry (self-service). Nonsmoking rooms. 24-hour valet dry cleaning.* **Room services** *Cable TV. Coffeemaker. Hair dryer. Kitchenette. Radio. Refrigerator. Voice mail.*

Hotel Metro

45 W 35th St between Fifth and Sixth Aves (212-947-2500, 800-356-3870; fax 212-279-1310) www.hotelmetronyc.com. Subway: B, D, F, Q, N, R to 34th St–Herald Sq. Single/double $165–$250, suite from $250. AmEx, DC, MC, V.
It's not posh by any stretch of the imagination, but the Metro has good service and a convenient location near the Empire State Building. The lobby has a charming retro feel, though the halls are army-chic, with olive-drab doors and greenish-gray carpets. Rooms are small but neat and clean, and the

roof terrace offers splendid views. The Metro Grill in the lobby specializes in Mediterranean and Italian food.
Hotel services *Air-conditioning. Continental breakfast. Fax. Fitness center. Laundry. Multilingual staff. Rooftop terrace.* **Room services** *Cable TV. Coffeemaker. Hair dryer. Kitchenette. Radio. Voice mail.*

Hotel Wellington
871 Seventh Ave at 55th St (212-247-3900, 800-652-1212; fax 212-581-1719) www.wellington hotel.com. Subway: B, D, E to Seventh Ave; N, R to 57th St. Single/double $145–$210, suite from $195, quad $185–$230. AmEx, DC, JCB, MC, V.
This hotel has some charming old-fashioned touches, like a gold-domed ceiling with a chandelier, though it's a tad frayed around the edges. Still, it's close to Central Park, Broadway and the Museum of Modern Art. There's a diner, a steak house and a Greek restaurant next door.
Hotel services *Air-conditioning. Bar. Beauty salon. Conference facilities. Disabled access. Fax. Laundry. Multilingual staff. Parking. Restaurant. Ticket service.* **Room services** *Cable TV. Refrigerator in some rooms. Room service.*

Howard Johnson
429 Park Ave South between 29th and 30th Sts (212-532-4860, 800-258-4290; fax 212-545-9727) www.bestnyhotels.com. Subway: N, R, 6 to 28th St. Single $105–$199, double $115–$249, suite $149–$449. AmEx, DC, Disc, JCB, MC, V.
Popular with Europeans, this recently renovated hotel has good-value suites and a noteworthy staff. There's a small breakfast bar that doubles as a cocktail lounge in the evenings. It's enough to make you forget you're at the less fashionable end of Park Avenue.
Hotel services *Air-conditioning. Baby-sitting. Bar. Fax. Laundry. Multilingual staff.* **Room services** *Cable TV. Coffeemaker. Hair dryer. Minibar. Radio. Room service for breakfast.*

Lexington Hotel
511 Lexington Ave at 48th St (212-755-4400, 800-448-4471; fax 212-751-4091). Subway: E, F to Lexington Ave; 6 to 51st St. Single/double $185, suite $275–$575. AmEx, DC, Disc, MC, V.
The Lexington, which is close to both Grand Central Terminal and the United Nations, is popular with business travelers. The lobby has a marble floor and rosewood pillars; 20 of the 27 floors have been renovated. There are two restaurants: Vuli, serving Italian cuisine, and the Chinese J. Sung Dynasty.
Hotel services *Air-conditioning. Baby-sitting. Bar. Business center. Coffee shop. Conference facilities. Currency exchange. Dance club. Disabled access. Exercise room. Fax. Laundry. Multilingual staff. Restaurants.* **Room services** *Cable TV. Hair dryer. Radio on request. Refrigerator. Room service. Safe.*

The Mayflower Hotel
15 Central Park West at 61st St (212-265-0060, 800-223-4164; fax 212-265-5098) www.mayflower hotel.com. Subway: A, C, B, D, 1, 9 to 59th St–Columbus Circle. Single $165–$205, double $180–$220, suite $215–$295. AmEx, DC, MC, V.
This haven for musicians faces Central Park and is just a few blocks from Lincoln Center. You can't argue with the spectacular park views from the front rooms, though the decor is getting a bit drab, and the hotel now has stiff competition from its new neighbor, the Trump International. The Conservatory, on the first floor, is still a nice spot for a light breakfast.
Hotel services *Air-conditioning. Baby-sitting. Bar. Conference facilities. Fax. Fitness center. Laundry. Multilingual staff. Parking. Restaurant.* **Room services** *Cable TV. Hair dryer. Modem line. Radio. Refrigerator. Room service. VCR on request. Voice mail.*

Off-Soho Suites Hotel
11 Rivington St between Chrystie St and Bowery (212-979-9808, 800-633-7646; fax 212-979-9801) www.offsoho.com. Subway: B, D, Q to Grand St; F to Second Ave. Suite with shared bathroom $179–$189. AmEx, MC, V.
Off-Soho is an excellent value for suite accommodations, but the Lower East Side location might not suit everyone. If you're into clubbing, bars and the Soho scene, this spot is perfect—but take a cab back at night. All suites are roomy, clean and bright, with fully equipped kitchens and polished wooden floors. There's a café on the ground floor.
Hotel services *Air-conditioning. Café. Disabled access. Fax. Fitness room. Laundry. Multilingual staff. Parking.* **Room services** *Hair dryer. Microwave. Refrigerator. Room service. TV.*

Quality Hotel and Suites Midtown
59 W 46th St between Fifth and Sixth Aves (212-719-2300, 800-848-0020; fax 212-790-2760) www.hotelchoice.com. Subway: B, D, F, Q to 50th Sts–Rockefeller Ctr. Single $149, double from $159, suite from $179. AmEx, DC, MC, V.
Somehow, this convenient Theater District hotel, built in 1902 and recently refurbished, has hung on to its old-time prices.
Hotel services *Air-conditioning. Barbershop. Beauty salon. 24-hour business center. Conference facilities. Fax. 24-hour fitness center. Multilingual staff.* **Room services** *Cable TV. Coffeemaker. Hair dryer. Safe. Iron. Radio.*

Quality Hotel Fifth Avenue
3 E 40th St between Fifth and Madison Aves (212-447-1500, 800-228-5151; fax 212-213-0972) www.hotelchoice.com. Subway: B, D, F, Q to 42nd St; 7 to Fifth Ave. Single/double $179–$250. AmEx, DC, Disc, JCB, MC, V.
The rooms here are newly renovated and a good value. Ask for rooms number three to six (the higher the floor, the better) for a street view with more light; back rooms are darker and look directly into offices. The Quality is a stone's throw from the New York Public Library, Bryant Park and Lord & Taylor. Ask about corporate and weekend rates.
Hotel services *Air-conditioning. Business services. Complimentary newspaper. Disabled access. Fax. Multilingual staff. Nonsmoking rooms. Restaurant.* **Room services** *Cable TV. Coffeemaker. Iron. Modem line. Radio. Room service.*

Ramada Milford Plaza Hotel
270 W 45th St with entrance on Eighth Ave (212-869-3600, 800-2RAMADA; fax 212-944-8357) www.ramada.com. Subway: A, C, E, N, R, S, 1, 2, 3, 9, 7 to 42nd St. Single $149–$179, double $164–$195. AmEx, Disc, JCB, MC, V.
The dismal shopping-mall lobby, with its fluorescent lighting and lack of decor, makes this enormous Theater District hotel anything but welcoming. Still, as the ads used to say, it is in the center of it all, close to the Broadway shows and Restaurant Row. There's very visible 24-hour security, and thanks to an influx of new upscale coffeehouses and shops, this stretch of Eighth Avenue is much more visitor-friendly than it was in past years. Recently added: an international-telephone room.
Hotel services *Air-conditioning. Concierge. Disabled access. Fax. Fitness center. Laundry. Multilingual staff. Parking. Restaurant. Tour/transportation desk.* **Room services** *Cable TV. Radio.*

The Roosevelt Hotel
45 E 45th St at Madison Ave (212-661-9600, 888-TEDDY-NY) www.theroosevelthotel.com. Subway: S, 4, 5, 6, 7 to 42nd St–Grand Central. Single/double $169–$289, suite $350–$1,800. AmEx, DC, MC, V.
After a two-year, $65-million makeover, this historic charmer is back and better than ever. Built in 1924, the 1,033-room hotel

*Alpha wave: Sit back, relax and let the cool vibe at the **W Hotel** envelop you.*

was a haven for celebs and socialites in the Golden Age (it's where Guy Lombardo first broadcast "Auld Lang Syne" on New Year's Eve). Nostalgic grandeur lives on in the bustling lobby, with 27-foot fluted columns, lots of marble, huge sprays of fresh flowers—and, often, large groups of teen tourists on class trips. The Palm Room serves afternoon tea under a brilliant blue-sky mural; the Madison Club Cigar Bar serves cocktails in a clubby setting with stained-glass windows.
Hotel services *Air-conditioning. Bar. Business services. Conference facilities. Concierge. Fax. Health club. Laundry. Restaurant. Valet. Valet parking.* **Room services** *Cable TV. Modem line. Room service. Voice mail.*

Less than $150

Broadway Inn
264 W 46th St at Eighth Ave (212-997-9200, 800-826-6300; fax 212-768-2807) www.broadway inn.com. Subway: A, C, E to 42nd St–Port Authority. Single $85, double $115–$170, suite $195. AmEx, DC, Disc, MC, V.
In contrast to Times Square's megahotels (many of which have prices to match), this inn (a renovated single-room-occupancy) feels small and personal—think Off Broadway rather than Broadway. The lobby, though small, has exposed-brick walls, ceiling fans, shelves loaded with books you can borrow and a hospitable front-desk staff. The 40 guest rooms are a bit spartan but are new, clean and fairly priced for the district. Be warned: The stairs are steep, and the inn has no elevator. Rates include continental breakfast.
Hotel services *Air-conditioning. Multilingual staff.* **Room services** *Cable TV.*

Cosmopolitan
95 West Broadway at Chambers St (212-566-1900, 888-895-9400; fax 212-566-6909) www.cosmohotel.com.
Subway: A, C, E, 1, 9 to Chambers St. Single $99, double $129. AmEx, MC, V.
It's not luxurious by anyone's standards, but after years as a down-at-the-heels rooming house, this recently renovated little hotel does have rock-bottom rates and a primo location in the trendy Tribeca area, an easy walk to Chinatown, Little Italy, the South Street Seaport and Soho.
Hotel services *Air-conditioning. Discount parking.* **Room services** *Cable TV. Modem line.*

The Gershwin Hotel
7 E 27th St between Fifth and Madison Aves (212-545-8000; fax 212-684-5546) www.homenet. com/gershwin. Subway: N, R, 6 to 28th St. $27 per person in four- to eight-bed dorms, $89–$139 for one to three people in private rooms ($12 more Thu–Sat). MC, V.
The bohemian Gershwin offers extremely reasonable accommodations just off Fifth Avenue. It's popular with young student types who don't demand much from their lodgings. While the lobby pays homage to Pop Art, with Lichtenstein and Warhol works, the rooms are spartan. When booking be very specific and reconfirm.
Hotel services *Bars. Fax. Lockers. Multilingual staff. Public telephones. Restaurant. Roof garden. Transportation desk.* **Room services** *Modem line. TV in private rooms. Voice mail.*

Habitat Hotel
130 E 57th St at Lexington Ave (212-753-8841, 800-255-0482; fax 212-829-9605) www.stayinny.com. Subway: N, R to Lexington Ave; 4, 5, 6 to 59th St. Single with shared bath $90, double with shared bath $99, single/double with private bath $130. AmEx, DC, MC, V.
The brand-new Habitat Hotel has had some well-publicized trouble taking over all the rooms of what had become a dilapidated women's residence (a few tenants still legally remain). The result of the $20-million overhaul is a fresh-looking

*Native comfort: The **Iroquois**'s recent renovation provides all the amenities of home.*

"sophisticated budget" hotel with an urban feel. Each room has its own sink and mirror, and black-and-white photos of the city grace the walls. Rooms can get tight when you pull out the trundle (which makes a double) and the shared bathrooms are minuscule, but overall the Habitat makes an ideal resting place for group and budget travelers.
Hotel services *Air-conditioning. Bar. Continental breakfast. Library. Nonsmoking rooms.* **Room services** *Cable TV. Hair dryer. Modem line. Voice mail.*

The Herald Square Hotel

19 W 31st St between Fifth Ave and Broadway (212-279-4017, 800-643-9208; fax 212-643-9208) www.heraldsquarehotel.com. Subway: B, D, F, Q, N, R to 34th St–Herald Sq. Single with shared bath $55, with private bath $80; double $110–$125; triple $140; quad $150. AmEx, Disc, JCB, MC, V.
Herald Square was the original *Life* magazine building, and it retains its charming cherub-adorned entrance. All rooms were recently renovated, and most have private bathrooms; corridors are lined with framed *Life* illustrations. It's near Macy's and the Empire State Building, and it's a good deal, so book well in advance. There are discounts for students.
Hotel services *Air-conditioning. Fax. Multilingual staff.* **Room services** *Cable TV. Radio. Safe.*

Hotel Edison

228 W 47th St at Broadway (212-840-5000, 800-637-7070; fax 212-596-6850) www.edison hotelnyc.com. Subway: N, R to 49th St; 1, 9 to 50th St. Single $125, double $145–$170 ($10 for each extra person up to four in a room), suite $145–$215. AmEx, DC, Disc, JCB, MC, V.
After its full renovation, the Edison looks decidedly spruced-up. The large, high-ceilinged Art Deco lobby is particularly colorful, and even the green marble–lined corridors look good. Rooms are standard, but theater lovers won't find a more convenient location. The coffee shop just off the lobby is a longtime favorite of Broadway gypsies.

Hotel services *Air-conditioning. Bar. Beauty salon. Currency exchange. Disabled access. Dry cleaning. Guest fax. Laundry. Multilingual staff. Parking. Restaurants. Travel/tour desk.* **Room services** *Cable TV. Hair dryer on request. Radio.*

Hotel Grand Union

34 E 32nd St between Park and Madison Aves (212-683-5890; fax 212-689-7397). Subway: 6 to 33rd St. Double $126, triple $143, quad $174 (all tax included). AmEx, Disc, MC, V.
There is certainly nothing fancy about the Hotel Grand Union, but you do find spacious rooms and clean, private bathrooms for the same price that similar hotels would charge for shared bathrooms. Many of the rooms have been renovated and in the busy seasons they quickly fill with European and Japanese tourists, so reserve at least a month in advance. A helpful staff will book tours for you and provide helpful New York advice.
Hotel services *Air-conditioning. Coffee shop. Gift shop. Hospitality desk. Multilingual staff.* **Room services** *Cable TV. Modem line. Refrigerator. Voice mail.*

Larchmont Hotel

27 W 11th St between Fifth and Sixth Aves (212-989-9333; fax 212-989-9496). Subway: F to 14th St; L to Sixth Ave. Single $70–$80, double $90–$109. AmEx, DC, Disc, MC, V.
This attractive, affordable newcomer is housed in a renovated 1910 Beaux Arts building on a quiet side street. Guests enter through a hallway adjacent to the lobby, making the place feel more like a private apartment building. Some rooms are small, but all are cheerful and clean. Each is equipped with a washbasin, a robe and slippers, although none has a private bath. Rates include continental breakfast.
Hotel services *Air-conditioning. Fax. Multilingual staff.* **Room services** *Cable TV. Hair dryer.*

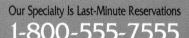

Hostel takeover: A coffee bar and jazz lounge are just some of the perks at **Jazz on the Park**.

Malibu Studios Hotel

*2688 Broadway at 103rd St (212-222-2954,
800-647-2227; fax 212-678-6842) www.malibuhotelnyc.
com. Subway: 1, 9 to 103rd St. Single with shared bath
$49–$79, with private bath from $79, double with shared
bath $49–$79, with private bath from $109. Cash or
traveler's checks only.*
Rooms are neat and clean, and the Malibu has some surprising amenities—even chocolates on check-in. Free passes to local nightclubs are often available. Far from the
traditional tourist sights, this Upper West Sider offers visitors a chance to live like a local in the primarily residential
neighborhood near Riverside Park and not far from Columbia University. The neighborhood is generally safe, but it can
get a bit dicey after dark.
Hotel services *Air-conditioning. Concierge. Fax.
Nonsmoking rooms.* **Room services** *Cable TV. Clock
radio. Iron.*

Murray Hill Inn

*143 E 30th St between Third and Lexington Aves
(212-683-6900, 888-996-6376; fax 212-545-0103)
www.murrayhillinn.com. Subway: 6 to 28th St. Single
from $65, double from $85, triple/quad from $105.
Cash or traveler's checks only.*
Tucked away on a quiet, tree-lined street in midtown within
walking distance of the Empire State Building and Grand
Central Terminal, this fairly new 50-room inn offers good
value for the price. Rooms are basic, but neat and clean. And
if a room doesn't have a private bath, it does have a sink.
Hotel services *Air-conditioning. Concierge. Fax. Message
center. Multilingual staff.* **Room services** *Cable TV.*
Other locations: *The Amsterdam Inn, 340 Amsterdam
Ave at 76th St (212-579-7500; fax 212-579-6127)
www.amsterdaminn.com. Subway: 1, 9 to 72nd St; B, C
to 72nd St.*

Pickwick Arms

*230 E 51st St between Second and Third Aves
(212-355-0300; fax 212-755-5029). Subway: E, F to
Lexington Ave; 6 to 51st St. Single with shared bath $65,
with semiprivate bath $75, with private bath $95, double
from $120. AmEx, DC, MC, V.*
The rooms may be small at the Pickwick Arms, but they
are clean. And although it's in a reasonably quiet district,
it's still near restaurants, movie theaters, Radio City Music
Hall and the United Nations. Most of the rooms have private bathrooms, but some share an adjoining bathroom,
while others share a bathroom down the hall.
Hotel services *Air-conditioning. Coffee shop. Fax.
Multilingual staff.* **Room services** *Radio. Room service.
TV. Voice mail.*

Riverside Towers Hotel

*80 Riverside Dr at 80th St (212-877-5200, 800-724-3136;
fax 212-873-1400). Subway: 1, 9 to 79th St. Single $85,
double $90, suite $100–$120. AmEx, DC, Disc, JCB, MC, V.*
The Riverside has a good price for the Upper West Side and
is the only hotel in Manhattan located on the Hudson River.
The views are fine, but accommodations are basic: This is
strictly a place to sleep. The wonderful Zabar's market is up
the street on Broadway.
Hotel services *Air-conditioning. Fax. Laundry.
Multilingual staff.* **Room services** *Hair dryer on
request. Refrigerator. TV.*

Washington Square Hotel

*103 Waverly Pl between Fifth and Sixth Aves
(212-777-9515, 800-222-0418; fax 212-979-8373)
www.wshotel.com. Subway: A,C, E, B, D, F, Q to W 4th
St–Washington Sq. Single $116, double $136, quad
$167. AmEx, MC, V.*
Location, not luxury, is the key here. Bob Dylan and Joan
Baez lived in this Greenwich Village hotel when they were
street musicians singing for change in nearby Washington
Square Park. Rooms are no-frills, and hallways are so narrow that you practically open your door into the room opposite. Rates include breakfast and Tuesday-night Jazz at C3
(the bistro next door).

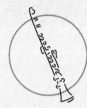

*Nights of the Round Table: You provide the wit these days at the **Algonquin**.*

Hotel services *Air-conditioning. Baby-sitting. Bar. Coffee shop. Conference facilities. Discounted tours of Washington Square Park. Fax. Fitness center. Multilingual staff. Restaurant.* **Room services** *Hair dryer on request.*

The Wolcott Hotel

4 W 31st St between Broadway and Fifth Ave (212-268-2900; fax 212-563-0096) www.wolcott.com. Subway: B, D, F, Q, N, R to 34th St–Herald Sq. Single/double with shared bath $80–$120, with private bath $99–$245, suite $130–$350. AmEx, JCB, MC, V.
The ornate gilded lobby belies as a surprise in this Garment District hotel. Rooms are small but inexpensive.
Hotel services *Air-conditioning. Fax. Laundry. Multilingual staff.* **Room services** *Cable TV.*

Wyndham Hotel

42 W 58th St between Fifth and Sixth Aves (212-753-3500, 800-257-1111; fax 212-754-5638). Subway: N, R to Fifth Ave; B, Q to 57th St. Single $125–$140, double $140–$155, suite $185–$365. AmEx, DC, MC, V.
Popular with actors and directors, the Wyndham has generous-sized rooms and suites with walk-in closets. The decor is a little worn, but homey. This is a good midtown location—you can walk to the Museum of Modern Art, Fifth Avenue shopping and many of the Broadway theaters—and it's low-priced, so book well ahead.
Hotel services *Air-conditioning. Bar. Disabled access. Fax. Multilingual staff. Restaurant.* **Room services** *Cable TV. Hair dryer on request. Radio.*

Hostels

Banana Bungalow

250 W 77th St at Broadway (212-769-2441; fax 212-877-5733). www.bananabungalow.com;

NYres@bananabungalow.com. Subway: 1, 9 to 79th St. $23–$24 per person, $5 refundable deposit. MC, V.
Palm trees and Astroturf set the tropical scene atop the roof of the Banana Bungalow, where weary travelers escape the city to sunbathe and socialize. Located in the Hotel Belleclaire on the Upper West Side, this bungalow offers the standard hostel experience along with some excellent perks: low-cost city tours, parties, bar outings and the rooftop sundeck with excellent views of the city. Make sure to reserve your bunk as soon as possible—they fill up weeks in advance.
Hotel services *City tours. Internet access. Kitchen facilities. Movies nightly. Multilingual staff. Rooftop common room. TV room.*

Chelsea Center

313 W 29th St between Eighth and Ninth Aves (212-643-0214; fax 212-473-3945) chelcenter@aol.com. Subway: A, C, E to 34th St–Penn Station. $23 per person in dorm, including linen. No credit cards.
This is a small, welcoming hostel with clean bathrooms and a patio garden in the back. It has the feel of a shared student house. Since there's a limited number of beds in each dorm, book at least a week in advance. There's no curfew, and the price includes continental breakfast.
Hotel services *All rooms nonsmoking. Fax. Garden patio. Kitchen facilities. Multilingual staff. TV room.*

Hosteling International New York

891 Amsterdam Ave at 103rd St (212-932-2300; fax 212-932-2574) www.hostelling.com. Subway: 1, 9 to 103rd St. $22 per person in dorm sleeping 10–12 people, $23 in dorm sleeping 6–8, $25 in room sleeping 4, $3 extra for nonmembers; family room $75, private room with bath $100. JCB, MC, V.
This 500-bed hostel was formerly a residence for elderly women. It was recently renovated to include a new coffee bar with CD jukebox. Rooms are basic but clean, the staff is friendly, and there's a garden in the back. Off-season rates (November to April) are lower.

Dive right in!

If you prefer quirks to consistency, consider these oddball oases

These colorful classics are really off the beaten track. What you won't find: complimentary shoe shines or chocolate mints on the pillow. What you will find: loads of atmosphere, interesting characters and a one-of-a-kind experience. Just keep an open mind, and think of the stories you'll have to tell the folks back home.

Carlton Arms Hotel

160 E 25th St at Third Ave (212-679-0680). Subway: 6 to 23rd St. Single with shared bath $57–$63, with private bath $68–$75, double with shared bath $73–$80, $84–$92 with private bath; triples $90–$111; quads $95–$117. MC, V.
The Carlton Arms is a cheerful and basic budget hotel popular with Europeans. The corridors are brightly decorated with murals of the city; each room has been painted by a different artist. The artwork is hit-and-miss, but fun. Check out the funky new top-floor bathroom with walls covered in toys, tickets, sunglasses and other tchotchkes. Discounts are offered for students and overseas guests.
Hotel services *Café. Multilingual staff. Telephone in lobby.* **Room services** *Hair dryer on request.*

Chelsea Hotel

222 W 23rd St between Seventh and Eighth Aves (212-243-3700; fax 212-675-5531) www.chelseahotel.com. Subway: C, E, 1, 9 to 23rd St. Single from $125, double from $160, studio $175, suite from $300. AmEx, JCB, MC, V.
The Chelsea has a reputation to uphold. Built in 1884, the famous red-brick building oozes history. In 1912, *Titanic* survivors stayed here for a few days; other for-

mer residents include the likes of Dylan Thomas, Mark Twain, Thomas Wolfe, O. Henry and Brendan Behan. No evidence remains of the hotel's most infamous association: the murder of Nancy Spungen by Sid Vicious of the Sex Pistols. Although there's a decided air of seediness, the Chelsea has atmosphere. The lobby doubles as an art gallery, showing work by past and present guests, and rooms are large, with high ceilings. Most, but not all, have a private bathroom. A basement café is in the works.
Hotel services *Air-conditioning. Fax. Multilingual staff. Valet parking.* **Room services** *Cable TV. Kitchenettes and refrigerators in some rooms. Safe. TV.*

Hotel 17

225 E 17th St between Second and Third Aves (212-475-2845; fax 212-677-8178) www.citysearch.com_nyc_hotel17. Subway: N, R, 4, 5, 6 to 14th St–Union Sq; L to Third Ave. Single $75, double $90–$149, triple $200, weekly rates from $487. No credit cards.
This is the ultimate dive hotel and one of the hippest places to stay if you're an artist, musician or model. Everyone on the underground circuit knows the place. Madonna posed here for a magazine shoot, and Woody Allen used the hotel in *Manhattan Murder Mystery.* The decor is classic shabby chic, with labyrinthine hallways leading to high-ceilinged rooms filled with a hodgepodge of discarded dressers, gorgeous old fireplaces, velvet curtains and 1950s wallpaper. Don't be put off by the permanent "no vacancy" sign.
Hotel services *Air-conditioning in some rooms. Fax. Laundry. Roof terrace. Tourist and nightclub information.* **Room services** *Cable TV in some rooms. Hair dryer on request.*

Hotel services *Air-conditioning. All rooms nonsmoking. Café. Cafeteria. Conference facilities. Fax. Garden. Laundry. Lockers. Multilingual staff. Shuttles. Travel bureau. TV lounge and game room.*

International House

500 Riverside Dr at 125th St (212-316-6300, in summer 212-316-8436; fax 212-316-1827). Subway: 1, 9 to 125th St. Single $100, double/suite $125. MC, V.
This hostel is in a peaceful location, surrounded by college buildings and overlooking the small but well-tended Sakura Park. There's a subsidized cafeteria with main dishes around $3 and a delightful living room and terrace overlooking the park. Only the suites have private bathrooms. Summer is by far the best time to book, since during the academic year, International House is filled with foreign graduate students and visiting scholars. Summer single rates drop as low as $45. Be warned that though the area immediately around Columbia University is generally safe, you might not want to stroll far after dark if you don't know the neighborhood.
Hotel services *Air-conditioning in suites. Bar. Cafeteria. Conference facilities. Fax. Game room. Gymnasium. Laundry. Multilingual staff. TV room.*

Jazz on the Park Hostel

36 W 106th St between Central Park West and Manhattan Ave (212-932-1600; fax 212-932-1700)

www.jazzhostel.com. Subway: B, C to 103rd St. 4- to 14-bed rooms $25–$35. MC, V.
This new hostel has a great location next to Central Park, and not only does it have live jazz, but the manager's name is Jazz—and he's congenial. He also has some revealing info on the spooky mansion next door and its sordid past. Jazz on the Park is certainly more than just a place to stay—with its coffee bar, jazz lounge and rooftop terraces, it threatens to keep hostelers entertained even before they've exploited the city. Be sure to book in advance.
Hotel services *Bike and in-line skate rental (summer only). Café. Complimentary breakfast. Internet access. Linen. Organized outings and activities. Private lockers. Sundry shop.*

The Star Hotel

300 W 30th St at Eighth Ave (212-244-7827, 877-827-NYNY; fax 212-279-9018) Subway: A, C, E to 34th St–Penn Station. Dorm and private rooms with shared bathroom from $25. MC, V.
It's gone from a hot-sheets hotel to a hostel and the Star Hotel certainly has a right to its name, considering this was one of Madonna's first New York homes in its red-light days. Her room is small and dismal with a less-than-stunning view of Madison Square Garden, but you can spend the night in it for a mere $25. An aspect of seediness still pervades this refurbished old dive, now under new management, but it's all a part

of the experience. A roof deck, brick-lined dorm and common room make this one of the best steals in the city for hostelers and starstruck wanderers.

Hotel services *Bicycle and in-line skate rental.* **Common room.** *Internet access. Kitchenette. Rooftop deck.* **Room services** *Linen.*

YMCA (Vanderbilt)

224 E 47th St between Second and Third Aves (212-756-9600; fax 212-752-0210) www.ymca.com. Subway: S, 4, 5, 6, 7 to 42nd St–Grand Central. Single $65, double $78, suite $125. AmEx, MC, V.

This cheerful, standard YMCA was completely renovated in 1992. The more expensive rooms have sinks, but none are very large; the beds barely fit in some rooms. Book well in advance by writing to the reservations department and including a deposit for one night's rent. There are about 377 rooms, but only the executive suites have private baths.

Hotel services *Air-conditioning. Conference facilities. Disabled access. Fax. Gift shop. Laundry. Left luggage room. Multilingual staff. Restaurant. Sports and fitness facilities.* **Room services** *All rooms nonsmoking. Cable TV. Radio. Refrigerator on request. Room service.*

YMCA (West Side)

5 W 63rd St between Central Park West and Broadway (212-875-4100; fax 212-875-1334) www.ymca.com. Subway: A, C, B, D, 1, 9 to 59th St–Columbus Circle. Single $65, with bath $95, double $75, with bath $105. AmEx, MC, V.

A large, echoing building close to Central Park and Lincoln Center, this Y has rooms that are simple and clean. Book well in advance. A deposit is required to hold a reservation. Most of the 540 rooms have shared bathrooms.

Hotel services *Air-conditioning. Cafeteria. Disabled access. Fax. Laundry. Multilingual staff. Sports and fitness facilities.* **Room services** *Cable TV.*

YMHA (de Hirsch Residence at the 92nd St Y)

1395 Lexington Ave at 92nd St (212-415-5650, 800-858-4692; fax 212-415-5578). Subway: 6 to 96th St. For stays less than two months single occupancy $75 nightly, double occupancy $48 nightly per person; for stays longer than two months with shared bath $835 montly , double occupancy $580–$690 monthly. AmEx, MC, V.

The Young Men's Hebrew Association is rather like its Christian counterpart, the YMCA, in that to stay there you don't have to be young, male or—in this case—Jewish. The dorm-style rooms are spacious and clean, with two desks and plenty of closet space. There are kitchen and dining facilities on each floor. The YMHA is good for tours, lectures and classes, and the Upper East Side location is a bonus.

Hotel services *Air-conditioning. Disabled access. Fitness center. Laundry. Library. Multilingual staff. TV lounge.* **Room services** *Refrigerator on request.*

Bed-and-breakfast

New York's bed-and-breakfast scene is deceptively large. There are thousands of beds available, but since there isn't a central B-and-B organization, rooms may be hard to find. Many of the rooms are unhosted, and breakfast is usually continental (if it exists at all). The main difference from a hotel is the more personal ambience. Prices are not necessarily low, but B-and-Bs are a good way to feel less like a tourist and more like a New Yorker. Sales tax of 8.25 percent is added on hosted bed-and-breakfast rooms, but not on unhosted

apartments if you're staying for more than seven days. It's always a good idea to ask about decor, location and amenities when booking and, if safety is a concern, whether the building has a 24-hour doorman. One caveat: Last-minute changes can be costly; some agencies charge guests for a night's stay if they cancel reservations less than 10 days before arriving.

More B-and-Bs are listed in the chapter **Gay & Lesbian**—and they all welcome those from the straight world, too.

At Home in New York

P.O. Box 407, New York, NY 10185 (212-956-3125), private number, please call Mon–Fri 10am–5pm, 800-692-4262; fax 212-247-3294) athomeny@erols.com. Hosted single $45–$90, hosted double $70–$125, unhosted studio $80–$400. MC, V.

This agency has reasonably priced accommodations in about 300 properties; most of them are in Manhattan, a few in Brooklyn. The minimum stay is two nights.

Bed and Breakfast (and Books)

35 W 92nd St, Apt 2C, New York, NY 10025 (212-865-8740 phone and fax, please call Mon–Fri 10am–5pm). Hosted single $60–$100, hosted double $80–$110, unhosted studio $110–$150, unhosted two-bedroom apartment from $200. No credit cards (though AmEx, DC, Disc, MC, V can be used to guarantee rooms).

Several hosts in this organization are literary types, hence the bookish title. There are 40 hosted and unhosted rooms.

Bed and Breakfast in Manhattan

P.O. Box 533, New York, NY 10150 (212-472-2528; fax 212-988-9818). Hosted $90–$110, unhosted from $130. No credit cards.

Each of this organization's 100 or so properties has been personally inspected by the owner, who also helps travelers select a bed-and-breakfast in the neighborhood best suited to their interests.

City Lights Bed and Breakfast

P.O. Box 20355, Cherokee Station, New York, NY 10021 (212-737-7049; fax 212-535-2755). Hosted single/double with private or shared bath$80–$130, unhosted single/double $130–$300, monthly hosted $1,000–$1,500, unhosted $1,900–$3,500. DC, MC, V.

This helpful agency lists 300 to 400 properties in Manhattan and Brooklyn. A two-night minimum stay and a 25-percent deposit are required.

New World Bed and Breakfast

150 Fifth Ave, Suite 711, New York, NY 10011 (212-675-5600; fax 212-675-6366). Hosted single $85, hosted double $90, unhosted studio from $110, unhosted one-bedroom apartment from $130. AmEx, DC, MC, V.

Accommodations can be arranged in most Manhattan neighborhoods. Hosted apartments include continental breakfast. There are reduced rates for monthly stays. Larger apartments are also available.

West Village Reservations

425 W 13th St (212-614-3034; fax 212-674-3393) westvillagebb.com. Room $90–$135, studio apartment $125–$145, larger apartment from $225.

This reservation service has locations all over Manhattan. The B-and-B rooms are priced according to room size, number of guests and whether the bathroom is adjacent to the room (i.e. private) or shared with other guests. Hosts provide neighborhood information and continental breakfast. All apartments are private and completely furnished.

Shopping & Services

If you can't find it somewhere in New York, it probably doesn't exist

People may say they come to New York for the museums and the cultural highs, but deep down they're really here for the shopping. After all, New York *is* the shopping capital of the world. Some come for the city's plethora of gargantuan department stores, others for the high fashion and still others for cheap Levi's and good deals on electronics. Regardless of your agenda, as you're making your way through the myriad options, it helps to think like a New Yorker. If an object catches your eye, keep in mind that you don't have to buy it. Simply put it on hold and come back when the time is right. Or if you do what many locals do—buy the item to possibly return it later—be sure to check store policy, because some will only give credit toward a new purchase. So, on your mark, get set, spend!

TACTICAL SPENDING

A few decades ago, upper Fifth Avenue was the only place to shop. Today, at least a half-dozen major shopping neighborhoods beckon, each with its own allure.

Starting at the southern tip of Manhattan, the Winter Garden at the **World Financial Center** is one of the few indoor shopping centers (in Manhattan, no one calls them malls) on the island: It contains tall palm trees and is flanked by a wide variety of boutiques and cafés.

Shopping becomes more serious as you head north, to the cast-iron landmarked buildings of **Soho**. Lately, a herd of chains such as Banana Republic and Victoria's Secret have joined big-name designers like Miu Miu and Helmut Lang (so much so that vanguard labels such as Comme des Garçons, which moved to the area a decade ago, have relocated, along with many art galleries, to **West Chelsea**). If you wish to avoid crowds, head to **Nolita**, the neighborhood east of Soho that is currently ground zero for hip up-and-coming designers. For fake Rolexes and Prada bags, as well as the best DJ mix tapes, **Canal Street**'s market

Feet first: Hipsters head to one of three **Tootsi Plohound** shops for the latest footwear.

stalls hawk heaping piles of counterfeit designer wares, electronics, sports shoes and T-shirts. And in **Chinatown**, along Mott and Mulberry Streets, you can pick up slippers, parasols and lanterns.

The **Lower East Side** is still bargain-hunting territory, although fun-lovin' shops and bars are sprouting in this neighborhood as well (*see* **The joy of Essex**, *page 128*). Many of the old shops close early Fridays and all day Saturdays for the Jewish Sabbath. Still, don't miss Orchard Street between Houston and Delancey Streets, where you'll find leather goods, luggage, designer clothes, belts, shoes and yards of fabric. The **East Village** has more trendy boutiques, along with an abundance of secondhand shops. Check out East 9th and 7th Streets for clothes, furnishings and young designers.

Head west to **Greenwich Village**, and the streets become progressively prettier and more winding. As in the East Village, shops here stay open late and are especially good for jazz records, rare books and vintage clothing—and don't forget the unmissable food shop, Balducci's.

Another cluster of designer boutiques and chains can be found on Fifth Avenue and Broadway between 14th and 23rd Streets, also known as the **Flatiron District**. Here's where to head for Paul Smith's stylish menswear and the countrified home furnishings of ABC Carpet & Home.

But it's the midtown stretch of **Fifth Avenue** where you'll find the city's famed department stores—Lord & Taylor, Saks Fifth Avenue, Bergdorf Goodman—along with their fantastic window displays. Despite the encroaching theme emporiums, such as Niketown and the Warner Bros. store, this area is also famous for tony jewelers such as Tiffany, Cartier and Bulgari (although the Diamond District, on 47th Street between Fifth and Sixth Avenues, is where plebes buy their rocks). **Madison Avenue** is the place for expensive top designers: Calvin Klein, Dolce & Gabbana, Ralph Lauren, et al. It's also great for window shopping and celebrity spotting.

Although the **Upper West Side** is primarily a residential pocket for the city's yuppies, the neighborhood boasts another mall-like stretch of stores. Of all the shopping destinations, this one is least likely to surprise. Chain stores, including Club Monaco and the Gap, have sunk their roots deep. Still, if you're looking for an unexpected retail haven, proceed north to **125th Street** in **Harlem**, where you can lunch at Sylvia's and shop for hip-hop clothing.

SHOP TILL YOU DROP

New Yorkers are the smartest kind of shoppers: They wait for end-of-season discounts, shop at discount emporiums such as Daffy's and Century 21, and sneak off to sample sales during lunch hour. Consider the calendar as you shop: Department stores usually hold sales at the end of seasons;

August and February seem to be the best months. The post-Christmas reductions tend to occur earlier in December than they used to, but most shopkeepers think all holidays (Fourth of July, Easter, Labor Day, etc.) are a good reason for a sale.

Designers' sample sales are some of the best sources of low-priced chic clothes. For information about what's happening where, see either *Time Out New York*'s Check Out section or the weekly "Sales & Bargains" column in *New York* magazine. You can also try getting hold of the *S&B Report* (available from 108 E 38th St, suite 2000, New York, NY 10016; 212-683-7612); or call the SSS Sample Sales hotline (212-947-8748). These are also sources for details of appliance, furniture and other types of sales.

Downtown shops stay open an hour or two later than those uptown (they open later in the morning, too). Thursday, however, is the universal—though unofficial—shopping-after-work night; most stores are open till 7pm, if not later. At some of the larger and more tourist-oriented places, you can avoid paying the 8.25-percent city sales tax if you arrange to have your purchase shipped outside New York State. Or you can schedule your visit to coincide with the now semiannual no-tax week (typically the first week in September and the third week in January), when the New York City government temporarily exempts shoppers from paying sales tax on clothing and shoe purchases less than $500 (there are plans to eventually lift the tax permanently).

Keep in mind that certain stores listed below have multiple locations. If a shop has more than two branches, we suggest that readers check the business pages in the phone book for other addresses.

Department stores

For other clothing stores *see* **Fashion**, *page 122*.

Barneys New York
660 Madison Ave at 61st St (212-826-8900). Subway: N, R to Fifth Ave; 4, 5, 6 to 59th St. Mon–Fri 10am–8pm; Sat 10am–7pm; Sun noon–6pm. AmEx, MC, V.
All the top designers, as well as a decent selection of lesser-known labels, are represented at this haven for New York style. There are also hip home furnishings and fancy children's clothes, and the Christmas windows are usually the best in town. Every August and March, the store hosts the Barneys Warehouse Sale (call for locations), which is highly recommended if you're in town. Alterations on regularly priced items are free.

Bergdorf Goodman
754 Fifth Ave at 58th St (212-753-7300). Subway: E, F, N, R to Fifth Ave. Mon–Wed, Fri 10am–7pm; Thu 10am–8pm; Sat 10am–6pm. AmEx, JCB, MC, V.
While Barneys shoots for a young, trendy crowd, Bergdorf is dedicated to an elegant, understated one—with lots of money to spare. As department stores go, it's one of the best for clothes and accessory shopping, being intimate on a large scale. In addition to selling all the major American and European designers, Bergdorf has a number of exclusive lines. The men's store is across the street.

Bloomingdale's

1000 Third Ave at 59th St (212-355-5900). Subway: N, R to Lexington Ave; 4, 5, 6 to 59th St. Mon, Tue 10am–8:30pm; Wed–Fri 10am–10pm; Sat 10am–7pm; Sun 11am–7pm. AmEx, MC, V.

This gigantic, glitzy department store has everything you could ever want. The ground floor features designer handbags, scarves, hosiery, makeup and jewelry, and upstairs you'll find linens, two floors of shoes, designer names and a variety of cheaper goods. The sale racks are always worth a look.

Felissimo

10 W 56th St at Fifth Ave (212-956-4438). Subway: B, Q to 57th St. Mon–Wed, Fri, Sat 10am–6pm; Thu 10am–8pm. AmEx, JCB, MC, V.

This five-story townhouse—recently renovated—is a Japanese-owned, eco-hip speciality store that stocks a collection of covetable items for the heart and home. Choose from jewelry, furnishings, clothing and collectibles. Assistance is available in nine languages.

Henri Bendel

712 Fifth Ave at 56th St (212-247-1100). Subway: E, F, N, R to Fifth Ave; 4, 5, 6 to 59th St. Mon–Wed, Fri, Sat 10am–7pm; Thu 10am–8pm; Sun noon–6pm. AmEx, DC, Disc, JCB, MC, V.

Bendel is a sweet-smelling sliver of heaven. Its lavish quarters resemble a plush townhouse—there are elevators, but it's nicer to mount the elegant, winding staircase. The first floor features a slew of makeup lines, including some lesser-known ones such as Awake and BeneFit. Prices are comparable with those in other upscale stores, but somehow things look more desirable here. It must be those darling bags in the store's signature brown-and-white-stripe.

Lord & Taylor

424 Fifth Ave between 38th and 39th Sts (212-391-3344). Subway: B, D, F, Q to 42nd St; 7 to Fifth Ave. Mon, Tue, Sat 10am–7pm; Wed–Fri 10am–8:30pm; Sun 11am–7pm. AmEx, Disc, MC, V.

Lord & Taylor is a conservative, rather old-fashioned department store, the kind where you go to buy sensible underwear—and not much else. It was here that the Fifth Avenue tradition of dramatic Christmas window displays began.

Macy's

151 W 34th St between Broadway and Seventh Ave (212-695-4400). Subway: B, D, F, Q, N, R, 1, 2, 3, 9 to 34th St. Mon–Sat 10am–8:30pm; Sun 11am–7pm. AmEx, MC, V.

Macy's doesn't have the cheapest or the hippest merchandise in New York, but it's still worth the trip. Macy's calls itself the biggest department store in the world—it occupies an entire city block. You'll find everything from designer labels to cheap, colorful knockoffs, a pet shop, a fish market, the Metropolitan Museum gift shop and a juice bar. Beware the aggressive perfume sprayers, and resign yourself to getting hopelessly lost. The store has its own concierge service (212-560-3827) to help you maximize your shopping potential.

Saks Fifth Avenue

611 Fifth Ave between 49th and 50th Sts (212-753-4000). Subway: B, D, F, Q to 47–50th Sts–Rockefeller Ctr; E, F to Fifth Ave. Mon–Wed, Fri 10am–7pm; Thu 10am–8pm; Sat 10am–6:30pm; Sun noon–6pm. AmEx, CB, DC, Disc, JCB, MC, V.

Saks is the classic upscale American department store. It features all the big names (and some of the better lesser-known ones), an excellent menswear department, two standout shoe departments, fine household linens, a large kids' section and good service. The ground floor is packed with accessories and has a stylish beauty area where personal consultations and makeovers are available. Upstairs, you'll find a well-chosen selection of designer labels.

Takashimaya

693 Fifth Ave between 54th and 55th Sts (212-350-0100). Subway: E, F to Fifth Ave. Mon–Sat 10am–7pm. AmEx, DC, Disc, JCB, MC, V.

The New York branch of this Japanese department store opened in April 1993 and has been giving traditional Fifth Avenue retailers a run for their money ever since. The five-story palace mixes Eastern and Western aesthetics and extravagance. The first two floors offer 4,500 square feet (419 square meters) of art gallery space and a men's and women's signature collection, as well as Japanese makeup and exotic plants; the top floor is dedicated to designer accessories.

Books

New York has no shortage of sources for books, both new and used. Many shops have no problem mailing your selections overseas (if the books are shipped out of state, you don't pay sales tax, which usually works out about the same as mailing charges). Many bookstores feature readings by prominent authors (check the Book listings in *Time Out New York* for weekly schedules). Don't overlook the smaller landmark stores, however, which continue to provide meticulous service. For A Different Light Bookstore & Café and the Oscar Wilde Memorial Bookshop, *see chapter* **Gay & Lesbian**.

General

Barnes & Noble

105 Fifth Ave at 18th St (212-675-5500). Subway: L, N, R, 4, 5, 6 to 14th St–Union Sq. Mon–Fri 9:30am–7:45pm; Sat 9:30am–6:15pm; Sun 11am–5:45pm. AmEx, DC, Disc, MC, V.

The world's largest bookstore and the flagship of this bustling chain is a good source of recent hardcovers at discount prices. The record, tape and CD department has one of the largest classical-music selections in the city, as well as videos, and there are also children's books, toys and an enormous number of secondhand paperbacks, including play scripts. One of B&N's many branches, the megastore at 2289 Broadway (at 82nd St, 212-362-8835), carries some 1,500 magazines and newspapers and features a children's theater, a reading area and gift-wrapping service. Check the phone book for other locations.

Borders Books & Music

461 Park Ave at 57th St (212-980-6785). Subway: N, R to Lexington Ave; 4, 5, 6 to 59th St. Mon–Fri 9am–10pm; Sat 10am–8pm; Sun 11am–8pm. AmEx, Disc, MC, V.

Borders seems folksier than Barnes & Noble; there's an extensive selection of music and videos, and even if you're searching for an obscure book, a staff member is usually able to come across a copy.

Other location: *5 World Trade Center between Church and Vesey Sts (212-839-8049).*

Gotham Book Mart

41 W 47th St at Sixth Ave (212-719-4448). Subway: B, D, F, Q to 47–50th Sts–Rockefeller Ctr. Mon–Fri 9:30am–6:30pm; Sat 9:30am–6pm. AmEx, MC, V.

"Wise men fish here" is Gotham's motto—and they most certainly do. This is a delightful haven for out-of-print titles, first editions and rare books. Opened by Frances Steloff in the '20s, Gotham was one of the leaders in the fight against censorship, stocking banned books by James Joyce, D.H. Lawrence and Henry Miller. Upstairs is a gallery showing works on literary themes. It's dusty and wonderful.

Candid camera: Stock up on books by famous shutterbugs at *A Photographers Place*.

Gryphon Book Shop
2246 Broadway between 80th and 81st Sts (212-362-0706). Subway: 1, 9 to 79th St. 10am–midnight. MC, V.
Gryphon specializes in poetry and fiction and also stocks rock records. It's a good source for secondhand and rare books on theater, film, music and drama.

Shakespeare & Co.
716 Broadway at Washington Pl (212-529-1330). Subway: N, R to 8th St–NYU; 6 to Astor Pl. Mon–Thu, Sun 10am–11pm; Fri, Sat 10am–midnight. AmEx, MC, V.
This bookshop has no real connection to the famous Hemingway haunt in Paris, except in spirit. Real service is the raison d'être here; the major qualification for staff is that they must be college graduates—i.e., readers. Not only will they order anything you covet, they'll probably have heard of it, too. Check the phone book for other locations.

St. Mark's Bookshop
31 Third Ave between St. Marks Pl and 9th St (212-260-7853). Subway: 6 to Astor Pl. Mon–Sat 10am–midnight; Sun 11am–midnight. AmEx, Disc, MC, V.
This late-night East Village literary and political bookshop stocks works on cultural criticism and feminism as well as university and small-press publications. Newspapers and more than 800 periodicals are available; it's an excellent source for magazines and literary journals.

Strand Book Store
828 Broadway at 12th St (212-473-1489). Subway: L, N, R, 4, 5, 6 to 14th St–Union Sq. Mon–Sat 9:30am–10:30pm; Sun 11am–10:30pm; AmEx, Disc, MC, V.
In the '50s, there were 40 or 50 antiquarian booksellers along Broadway between Astor Place and 14th Street. The Strand is the only one left; it is also reputedly the largest secondhand bookshop in the U.S. Most—including a large but unpredictable selection of best-sellers—are sold for half the published price or less.
Other location: *95 Fulton St between William and Gold Sts (212-732-6070).*

Tompkins Square Books & Records
111 E 7th St between Ave A and First Ave (212-979-8958). Subway: F to Second Ave; L to First Ave; 6 to Astor Pl. Mon–Fri 5pm–midnight; Sat, Sun noon–midnight. No credit cards.
It's hard to leave this cozy secondhand book and record shop without a paperback or two. There's also a vintage record collection complete with a record player; you're always welcome to audition your selections in the shop.

Tower Books
383 Lafayette St at 4th St (212-228-5100). Subway: B, D, F, Q to Broadway–Lafayette St; 6 to Bleecker St. 9am–midnight. AmEx, Disc, MC, V.
Tower isn't limited to just CDs; Tower Books is a decent stop for literature, travel books, photography titles and paperbacks. It has also turned into the best spot for obscure newspapers, the strangest of fanzines and international magazines. Browsing isn't deterred. For **Tower Records**, *see page 148*.

Unoppressive Non-Imperialist Bargain Books
34 Carmine St between Bleecker and Houston Sts (212-229-0079). Subway: 1, 9 to Houston St. Mon–Thu 11am–10pm; Fri, Sat 11am–midnight; Sun noon–10pm. AmEx, DC, Disc, MC, V.
Probably the smallest bargain bookstore around, it features all-new books sold for no more than half the cover price and usually less than one third. Unoppressive buys the returns that the big chains send back to publishers, so some copies are a bit dog-eared. Expect great finds in art, photo, music and film coffee-table books as well as some "highbrow" fiction and literature.

Specialist

Biography Bookshop
400 Bleecker St at 11th St (212-807-8655). Subway: A, C, E to 14th St; L to Eighth Ave. Mon–Thu

11am–9pm; Fri 11am–10pm; Sat 11am–11pm; Sun 11am–7pm. AmEx, MC, V.
Proof, if proof were needed, that biography is of wide interest: This whole store is devoted to it (new titles only).

Complete Traveler Bookstore
199 Madison Ave at 35th St (212-685-9007). Subway: 6 to 33rd St. Mon–Fri 9am–7pm; Sat 10am–6pm; Sun 11am–5pm. AmEx, DC, Disc, MC, V.
Travel books and maps of all descriptions, covering New York City, the U.S. and the world.

Drama Bookshop
723 Seventh Ave at 48th St (212-944-0595). Subway: C, E, 1, 9 to 50th St; N, R to 49th St. Mon, Tue, Thu, Fri 9:30am–7pm; Wed 9:30am–8pm; Sat 10:30am–5:30pm; Sun noon–5pm. AmEx, MC, V.
Everything a theater lover could desire, including plays and biographies.

Forbidden Planet
840 Broadway at 13th St (212-473-1576). Subway: L, N, R, 4, 5, 6 to 14th St–Union Sq. Mon–Sat 10am–10pm; Sun 10am–8:30pm. AmEx, Disc, MC, V.
Devotees of science fiction and fantasy won't be able to resist Forbidden Planet's vast selection of comics, featuring vintage and new titles from around the world. There are also stacks of classic books and magazines, and even a pricey toy section.

Murder Ink
2486 Broadway between 92nd and 93rd Sts (212-362-8905). Subway: 1, 2, 3, 9 to 96th St. Mon–Sat 10am–7:30pm, Sun 11am–6pm. AmEx, MC, V.
If you're in need of a killer title, this is your best bet. Murder Ink's enormous stock ranges from William Faulkner's The Unvanquished to the complete works of Jim Thompson, along with books on how to write mysteries and The Mystery Reader's Walking Guide: New York.

Mysterious Book Shop
129 W 56th St between Sixth and Seventh Aves (212-765-0900). Subway: B, D, E to Seventh Ave; N, R to 57th St. Mon–Sat 11am–7pm. AmEx, DC, MC, V.
More than 20,000 new and secondhand mystery and murder titles. There's a free rare book–finding service.

A Photographers Place
133 Mercer St between Prince and Spring Sts (212-431-9358). Subway: C, E to Spring St; N, R to Prince St. Mon–Sat 11am–8pm; Sun noon–6pm. AmEx, Disc, MC, V.
For those who like to look at pictures, this place stock books on all subjects by the world's best photographers; how-to manuals can be found here, too.

See Hear
59 E 7th St between First and Second Aves (212-505-9781). Subway: F to Second Ave; L to First Ave; 6 to Astor Pl. Noon–8pm. MC, V.
This shop has moved back to its original nook on 7th Street. A haven for fanzines, music books, comics and assorted subcultural texts, See Hear is an ideal place to lose an afternoon.

Village Comics
214 Sullivan St between 3rd and Bleecker Sts (212-777-2770). Subway: A, C, E, B, D, F, Q to W 4th St–Washington Sq. Mon, Tue 10am–7:30pm; Wed–Sat 10am–8:30pm; Sun 11am–7pm. AmEx, Disc, MC, V.
Comics are big business: Shop here for complete sets, missing back issues of Marvel or underground comics, and new releases. There's a free mail-order service. The Science Fiction Shop (940 Third Ave at 56th St; 212-759-6255) is run by the same company.

Cameras and electronics

The Flatiron electronics area (14th to 23rd Street between Broadway and Sixth Avenue) offers some great bargains. Rapid turnover (we hope) is what allows shopkeepers to price items such as Walkmans, CD players and computers so low. Know exactly what you want before venturing inside: If you look lost, you will certainly be given a hard sell. When buying a major item, check newspaper ads for price guidelines (start with the inserts in the Sunday *New York Times*). If you're brave, you can get small pieces such as Walkmans even cheaper in the questionable establishments along Canal Street, but don't expect a warranty. Another reason to go to a more reputable place is to get reliable (and essential) advice about compatibility in whatever country you want to use the equipment in. For video and TV rental, *see* **Video,** *page 154.*

B&H Photo
420 Ninth Ave between 33rd and 34th Sts (212-444-5040). Subway: A, C, E to 34th St–Penn Station. Mon–Thu 9am–7pm; Fri 9am–2pm; Sun 10am–5pm. AmEx, Disc, MC, V.
If you can deal with odd hours (it's also closed on all Jewish holidays), long lines and a bit of a schlepp, B&H is the ultimate one-stop shop for all your photographic, video and audio needs. This is the only place for an up-and-coming professional photographer without an expense account.

Harvey
2 W 45th St between Fifth and Sixth Aves (212-575-5000). Subway: B, D, F, Q to 42nd St. Mon–Wed, Fri 9:30am–6pm; Thu 9:30am–8pm; Sat 10am–6pm; Sun noon–5pm. AmEx, MC, V.
Harvey offers a chain-store feel without the lousy warranties and mass-market stereo components. There are lots of high-end products, but plenty of reality-based items, too.
Other location: *888 Broadway at 19th St (212-228-5354).*

J&R Music & Computer World
33 Park Row between Beekman and Ann Sts (212-732-8600). Subway: 4, 5, 6 to Brooklyn Bridge–City Hall; J, M, Z to Chambers St; 2, 3 to Park Pl. Mon–Wed, Fri, Sat 9am–7pm; Thu 9am–7:30pm; Sun 10:30am–6:30pm. AmEx, Disc, MC, V.
Everything for home entertainment is here at discount prices: CD players, hi-fi equipment, Walkmans and tapes.

The Wiz
726 Broadway between Washington and Waverly Pls (212-677-4111). Subway: N, R to 8th St–NYU; 6 to Astor Pl. Mon–Fri 10am–9:30pm; Sat 9am–9:30pm; Sun 11am–7pm. AmEx, Disc, MC, V.
With the Wiz's claim that it will match or beat any advertised price on electronic equipment, even the illegal importers on Canal Street have a hard time keeping up. Check the phone book for other locations.

Photo processing

Photo-developing services can be found on just about any city block. Most drugstores (Rite Aid and CVS, for example) and megastores such as Kmart offer the service, but best results should be expected from those who develop on the premises.

Harvey's One Hour Photo

698 Third Ave between 43rd and 44th Sts (212-682-5045). Subway: 4, 5, 6, 7 to 42nd St–Grand Central. Mon–Fri 8am–6pm. AmEx, MC, V.
Color film can be developed in 60 minutes; slides and black-and-white film require 24 hours.

Showbran Photo

1347 Broadway at 36th St (212-947-9151). Subway: B, D, F, Q, N, R to 34th St. Mon–Fri 7:30am–6:30pm. AmEx, Disc, MC, V.
Passport and visa photos are taken and developed while you wait. Showbran also offers other developing and printing services. Check the phone book for other locations.

Spectra Photo

510 La Guardia Pl between Bleecker and Houston Sts (212-979-1100). Subway: 6 to Bleecker St. Mon–Fri 9am–7pm; Sat noon–5pm. AmEx, MC, V.
Drop off your film—color or black-and-white—before noon, and Spectra will turn it around by 6pm the same day (artsy white borders and print on matte paper at no extra charge). Their film selection rocks (i.e., it includes every Polaroid film imaginable). Check the phone book for other listings.

Cross-dressing

Miss Vera's Finishing School for Boys Who Want to Be Girls

85 Eighth Ave between 14th and 15th Sts (212-242-6449). Subway: A, C, E to 14th St; L to Eighth Ave. No credit cards.
Feeling feminine but don't have the plumbing to match? Private classes begin at $550 and are taught by Veronica Vera and her faculty. All-day sessions begin at $1,125; a weekend on the town with Vera and the girls starts at $3,250. Consult the back pages of *The Village Voice* and the *New York Press* for similar services. There are even "telephone classes" available, via Miss Vera's 900 line.

Dry cleaners

Meurice Garment Care

31 University Pl between 8th and 9th Sts (212-475-2778). Subway: N, R to 8th St–NYU. Mon–Fri 7:30am–7pm; Sat 7:30am–5pm. AmEx, MC, V.
Don't be fooled by the old-fashioned washboards adorning the walls. Laundry is serious business here. The company's roster of high-profile clients includes Armani and Prada, and the company handles all kinds of delicate stain removal and other repair jobs.
Other location: *245 E 57th St between Second and Third Aves (212-759-9057).*

Midnight Express Cleaners

Call 212-921-0111 or 800-999-8985. Mon–Fri 8am–8pm; Sat 9am–1pm. AmEx, MC, V.
Telephone Midnight Express, and your laundry will be picked up anywhere below 96th Street within 10 or 15 minutes and returned to you the next day. It costs $6.95 for a man's suit to be cleaned, including pickup and delivery. There are various minimum charges, depending on your location.

Eco-friendly

Planet Hemp

423 Broome St between Crosby and Lafayette Sts (212-965-0500). Subway: 6 to Spring St. Sun–Thu noon–6pm; Fri, Sat noon–7pm. AmEx, Disc, MC, V.

The hemp rage lives on at this shop, which sells men's and women's sportswear, bed linens, paper goods and body products. There are even shoes made from hemp and "terra-gard," a leather substitute.

Terra Verde

120 Wooster St between Prince and Spring Sts (212-925-4533). Subway: N, R to Prince St. Mon–Sat 11am–7pm; Sun noon–6pm. AmEx, MC, V.
Manhattan's first eco-market combines art and activism. Architect William McDonough renovated this Soho space using nontoxic building materials and formaldehyde-free paint. Get your chemical-free linens, natural soaps and solar radios here.

Eyewear emporiums

Alain Mikli Optique

880 Madison Ave between 71st and 72nd Sts (212-472-6085). Subway: 6 to 68th St–Hunter College. Mon–Sat 10am–6:30pm. AmEx, Disc, MC, V.
French frames for the bold and beautiful are available from this 11-year-old Madison Avenue outlet.

Myoptics

123 Prince St between Greene and Wooster Sts (212-598-9306). Subway: N, R to Prince St. Mon–Sat 11am–7pm; Sun noon–6pm. AmEx, Disc, MC, V.
Plastics are hot at Soho's Myoptics; look for styles by Matsuda, Oliver Peoples, l.a. Eyeworks and Paul Smith. Check the phone book for other locations.

Selima Optique

59 Wooster St between Spring and Broome Sts (212-343-9490). Subway: C, E to Spring St. Mon–Sat 11am–7pm; Sun noon–7pm. AmEx, DC, JCB, MC, V.
Selima Salaun's wear-if-you-dare frames are popular with famous four-eye faces such as Sean Lennon and Lenny Kravitz (both of whom have frames named for them). She also stocks Alain Mikli, Matsuda, Face a Face and others.

Sol Moscot Opticians

118 Orchard St at Delancey St (212-477-3796). Subway: J, M, Z to Essex St; F to Delancey St. 9am–5:30pm. AmEx, DC, Disc, MC, V.
At this 80-year-old family-run optical emporium, expect to find all the big-name designer frames found at the pricier uptown boutiques for at least 20 percent off. Sol Moscot also carries vintage varieties starting at $29. Check the phone book for other locations.

Zeitlin Optik

40 E 52nd St between Madison and Park Aves (212-319-5166). Subway: E, F to Fifth Ave. Mon–Fri 10am–6pm, Sat 10am–5pm. AmEx, MC, V.
At Mark Zeitlin's 11-year-old boutique, you'll find not-so-recognizable brands from around the world: Mikko, Eight 8 and Blaze, from Japan; Binocle and Morucci, from France; and Marwitz, from Germany. Don't see what you want? Zeitlin will whip you up a custom pair.

Fashion

Uptown's big guns

Burberry

9 E 57th St between Fifth and Madison Aves (212-371-5010). Subway: N, R to Fifth Ave. Mon–Fri 9:30am–7pm; Sat 9:30am–6pm; Sun noon–6pm. AmEx, CB, DC, Disc, JCB, MC, V.
Classic Burberry's gone hip. Wave goodbye to the trench coat every commuter owns and say hello to doggie coats in

the company's signature plaid as well as a stunning new women's collection.

Calvin Klein

654 Madison Ave at 60th St (212-292-9000). Subway: N, R to Lexington Ave; 4, 5, 6 to 59th St. Mon–Wed, Fri, Sat 10am–6pm; Thu 10am–8pm; Sun noon–6pm. AmEx, Disc, MC, V.
This minimalist flagship store opened in 1995 and is tout Calvin, from the couture lines and footwear to housewares.

Celine

51 E 57th St between Madison and Park Aves (212-486-9700). Subway: N, R to Fifth Ave. Mon–Sat 10am–6pm. AmEx, DC, Disc, JCB, MC, V.
American designer Michael Kors recently took over this traditional French house, dramatically revitalizing the entire line and making it a more casual but equally luxurious collection.

Chanel

15 E 57th St between Fifth and Madison Aves (212-355-5050). Subway: E, F, N, R to Fifth Ave; 4, 5, 6 to 59th St. Mon–Wed, Fri 10am–6:30pm; Thu 10am–7pm; Sat 10am–6pm. AmEx, DC, JCB, MC, V.
The spirit of Mademoiselle Chanel lives on at this opulent store. There's even the Chanel Suite, a Baroque salon modeled after the divine Coco's private apartment on the Rue Cambon in Paris.

Christian Dior

703 Fifth Ave at 55th St (212-223-4646). Subway: E, F to Fifth Ave. Mon–Wed, Fri, Sat 10am–6pm; Thu 10am–7pm; Sun 11am–5pm. AmEx, JCB, MC, V.
Like Alexander McQueen at Givenchy, John Galliano has breathed new life into formerly predictable designs. This elegant boutique carries the famous French line.

Dolce & Gabbana

825 Madison Ave between 68th and 69th Sts (212-249-4100). Subway: 6 to 68th St–Hunter College. Mon–Wed, Fri, Sat 10am–6pm; Thu 10am–7pm. AmEx, JCB, MC, V.
Italian Dolce & Gabanna is the label of choice for pretty young things such as Christina Ricci and Gwyneth Paltrow. For a price, why not make it yours?

Emporio Armani

601 Madison Ave between 57th and 58th Sts (212-317-0800). Subway: N, R to Lexington Ave; 4, 5, 6 to 59th St. Mon–Fri 10am–8pm; Sat 10am–7pm; Sun noon–6pm. AmEx, DC, JCB, MC, V.
The postmodern decor serves as a stark backdrop for top Armani designs. The store also houses the chic Armani Café.
Other location: *110 Fifth Ave at 16th St (212-727-3240).*

Gianni Versace

647 Fifth Ave between 51st and 52nd Sts (212-317-0224). Subway: E, F to Fifth Ave. Mon–Sat 10am–6:30pm. AmEx, DC, MC, V.
Housed in the former Vanderbilt mansion, this is one of the largest (28,000 square feet) boutiques in New York City. Go and stare longingly at the mosaics, even if you can't afford to buy the clothes.
Other location: *815 Madison Ave between 68th and 69th Sts (212-744-6868).*

Giorgio Armani

760 Madison Ave at 65th St (212-988-9191). Subway: 6 to 68th St–Hunter College. Mon–Wed, Fri, Sat 10am–6pm; Thu 10am–7pm. AmEx, MC, V.
This enormous boutique features all three Armani collections: the signature Borgonuovo—tailored suits, evening wear and a bridal line—as well as the Classico and Le Collezioni.

Givenchy

954 Madison Ave at 75th St (212-772-1040). Subway: 6 to 77th St. Mon–Sat 10am–6pm. AmEx, DC, MC, V.
With the talented English designer Alexander McQueen holding the scissors, the styles are no longer quite as understated as when Hubert de Givenchy created Audrey Hepburn's to-die-for ensembles.

Gucci

685 Fifth Ave at 54th St (212-826-2600). Subway: E, F to Fifth Ave. Mon–Wed, Fri 10am–6:30pm; Thu, Sat 10am–7pm; Sun noon–6pm. AmEx, DC, JCB, MC, V.
When Tom Ford revitalized Gucci a few years back, he made the old-lady label hip again. Its slinky, Halston-inspired duds are still extremely popular. Pants start at $400, and there are always plenty of logo belts, key chains and sunglasses to choose from.

Issey Miyake

992 Madison Ave between 77th and 78th Sts (212-439-7822). Subway: 6 to 77th St. Mon–Fri 10am–6pm; Sat 11am–6pm; Sun noon–5pm. AmEx, MC, V.
This minimalist store houses Issey Miyake's breathtaking women's and men's collections and accessories.

Moschino

803 Madison Ave between 67th and 68th Sts (212-639-9600). Subway: 6 to 68th St–Hunter College. Mon–Sat 10am–6pm. AmEx, MC, V.
Expensive and irreverent clothes for men and women. And you can always pick up a pencil kit for $5. Really.

Polo/Ralph Lauren

867 Madison Ave at 72nd St (212-606-2100). Subway: 6 to 68th St–Hunter College. Mon–Wed, Fri, Sat 10am–6pm; Thu 10am–8pm. AmEx, DC, Disc, JCB, MC, V.
Ralph Lauren spent $14 million turning the old Rhinelander mansion into an Ivy League superstore, filled with Oriental rugs, English paintings, riding whips, leather chairs, old mahogany and fresh flowers. The homeboys, skaters and other young blades who've adopted Ralphie's togs for a season or two head straight to **Polo Sport** across the street at 888 Madison Ave (212-434-8000).

Prada

841 Madison Ave at 70th St (212-327-4200). Subway: 6 to 68th St–Hunter College. Mon–Wed, Fri, Sat 10am–6pm; Thu 10am–7pm. AmEx, MC, V.
Prada remains the label of choice for New York's fashion set (yes, you still have to put your name on a waiting list to buy the latest shoe styles). If you're only interested in the accessories, skip the crowds at the two larger stores and stop by the small 57th Street location. If you're downtown, see if the new branch has opened next to the Soho Guggenheim.
Other locations: *724 Fifth Ave between 56th and 57th Sts (212-664-0010); 45 E 57th St between Park and Madison Aves (212-308-2332).*

Shanghai Tang

655 Madison Ave at 61st St (212-888-0111). Subway: N, R to Fifth Ave; 4, 5, 6 to 59th St. Mon–Sat 10:15am–7pm; Sun noon–6pm. AmEx, Disc, MC, V.
This is the first Hong Kong department store to grace New York. Owner David Tang worships color, so expect lots of it. Along with silk Chinese dresses and jackets, there are housewares, including lamps constructed from Chinese lanterns.

TSE

827 Madison Ave at 69th St (212-472-7790). Subway: 6 to 68th St–Hunter College. Mon–Wed, Fri, Sat 10am–6pm; Thu 10am–7pm. AmEx, MC, V.
Stop by not only for the most fab cashmere knits but for the überhip styles by house designer Hussein Chalayan.

Valentino

747 Madison Ave at 65th St (212-772-6969).
Subway: 6 to 68th St–Hunter College. Mon–Sat
10am–6pm. AmEx, MC, V.
Celebrities and New York ladies who lunch just adore
Valentino. Can you be as elegant as Sharon Stone? Only if
you have enough money, honey.

Yves Saint Laurent

855–859 Madison Ave between 70th and 71st Sts
(212-988-3821). Subway: 6 to 68th St–Hunter College.
Mon–Sat 10am–6pm. AmEx, DC, JCB, MC, V.
Saint Laurent's fashions are a bit old-lady chic, but his
clothes are still glamorous enough to be sought-after.

Downtown heavies

agnès b.

116 Prince St between Wooster and Greene Sts
(212-925-4649). Subway: N, R to Prince St. 11am–
7pm. AmEx, MC, V.
Simple designs for women (stores carry accessories and
makeup, too). If only the timeless styles could withstand
wear and tear a bit longer.
Other locations: *1063 Madison Ave between 80th and*
81st Sts (212-570-9333); 13 E 16th St between Union Sq
West and Fifth Ave (212-741-2585).

Anna Sui

113 Greene St between Spring and Prince Sts
(212-941-8406). Subway: C, E to Spring St. Mon–Sat
11:30am–7pm; Sun noon–6pm. AmEx, DC, JCB, MC, V.
Judging from her frequent sweeps of thrift stores in the East
Village and flea markets throughout the city, Anna Sui's
ideas come from the past. Her clothes, displayed in
a lilac-and-black-decorated boutique, are popular with funky
rich kids. Her just-launched makeup line will be, too.

APC

131 Mercer St between Prince and Spring Sts
(212-966-9685). Subway N, R to Prince St. Mon–Sat
11am–7pm; Sun noon–6pm. AmEx, JCB, MC, V.
APC is France's answer to the Gap. Here, you'll find basic
essentials in muted colors and minimal styling in a stunning
store designed by Julian Schnabel. The French part is evident in the prices, which tend to be on the high side.

Atsuro Tayama

120 Wooster St between Prince and Spring Sts
(212-334-6002). Subway: N, R to Prince St; C, E to
Spring St. Mon–Sat 11am–7pm; Sun noon–6pm.
AmEx, MC, V.
Former Yohji Yamamoto assistant designer Atsuro Tayama
has been creating his own looks since 1982. Choose from
asymmetrical modern dresses, sheer shirts and billowy skirts.

Betsey Johnson

138 Wooster St between Prince and Spring Sts
(212-995-5048). Subway: N, R to Prince St. Mon–Sat
11am–7pm; Sun noon–7pm. AmEx, MC, V.
When the Betsey Johnson flagship opened on Wooster Street,
her tiny Thompson Street store closed. But the larger store
has room not only for her mid-priced collection but for her
signature collection, Ultra, as well. In a departure from the
hot pink color that covers the walls of her other shops, sunshine yellow livens up this boutique. Check the phone book
for other locations.

Comme des Garçons

520 W 22nd St between Tenth and Eleventh Aves
(212-604-9200). Subway: C, E to 23rd St. Tue–Sat
11am–7pm; Sun noon–6pm. AmEx, MC, V.

This breathtaking store is devoted to Rei Kawakubo's architecturally constructed, quintessentially Japanese designs for
men and women. It's no surprise that the boutique is found
in the new art mecca of Chelsea: Kawakubo's clothing is
hung like art, and the space gives every nearby gallery a run
for its money.

Costume National

108 Wooster St between Prince and Spring Sts
(212-431-1530). Subway: C, E to Spring St; N, R
to Prince St. Mon–Sat 11am–7pm; Sun noon–6pm.
AmEx, MC, V.
This minimalist but not plain collection features Italian fashions designed by Ennio Capasa, who collaborated with architect Cosimo Antoci on the look of this 3,000-square-foot space.

Cynthia Rowley

112 Wooster St between Prince and Spring Sts
(212-334-1144). Subway: C, E to Spring St; N, R
to Prince St. Mon–Sat 11am–7pm; Sun noon–
6pm. AmEx, MC, V.
Rowley's ultrafemme dresses, pants, shirts and accessories
are all housed in this bright, youthful boutique. Last fall she
expanded into menswear, which is also on display here.

D&G

434 West Broadway between Prince and Spring Sts
(212-965-8000). Subway: N, R to Prince St. Mon–Sat
11am–7pm; Sun noon–6pm. AmEx, MC, V.
While most of Milan's heavies still prefer the Upper East
Side, some are choosing Soho as the home for their more
youthful, less pricey lines. Domenico Dolce and Stefano
Gabbana opened this posh shop two years ago. Custom-
mixed music—house, disco and opera—plays as gals and
guys shop for jeans, suits, collection dresses, shoes and
signature black bags.

Daryl K

21 Bond St at Lafayette St (212-777-0713). Subway:
B, D, F, Q to Broadway–Lafayette St; 6 to Bleecker St.
Mon–Sat 11am–7pm; Sun noon–6pm. AmEx, MC, V.
Daryl Kerrigan's clothing attracts rock & rollers with vinyl
pants, colored cords, hip-hugger bootlegs and graffiti-
inspired Ts. Her much anticipated menswear collection, Fir,
will hit stores fall '99. The East 6th Street locale is where last
season's goods end up, often at half price.
Other location: *208 E 6th St between Bowery and*
Second Ave (212-475-1255).

Helmut Lang

80 Greene St between Spring and Broome Sts
(212-925-7214). Subway: C, E to Spring St; N, R to
Prince St. Mon–Sat 11am–7pm; Sun noon–6pm.
AmEx, MC, V.
This 3,000-square-foot store houses Austrian designer Hel-
mut Lang's sexy suits and dresses. The casual Helmut Lang
Jeans line, which features denim pants, killer jean jackets
and sweaters, is also available.

Jill Stuart

100 Greene St between Prince and Spring Sts
(212-343-2300). Subway: N, R to Prince St. Mon–Sat
11am–7pm; Sun noon–6pm. AmEx, MC, V.
Jill Stuart's first free-standing American boutique features
her young, modern women's wear (including shoes and
handbags), as well as supersweet children's clothes.

Louis Vuitton

114–116 Greene St between Prince and Spring Sts
(212-274-9090). Subway: N, R to Prince St. Mon–
Fri 11am–7pm; Sun noon–5pm. AmEx, Disc, DC,
JCB, MC, V.
When French luxury-goods company Louis Vuitton hired
American Marc Jacobs as artistic director, everyone knew

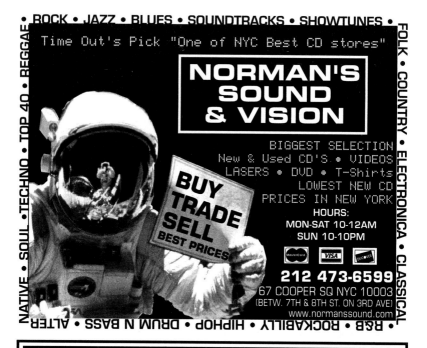

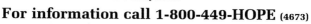

the bourgie monogrammed luggage and accessories were in for a spin. Now, they're revamped in powder blue and baby pink; at the Soho outpost, a full range of men's and women's ready-to-wear collections is also on display.

Other location: *49 E 57th between Park and Madison Aves (212-371-6111).*

Lucien Pellat-Finet
226 Elizabeth St between Prince and Houston Sts (212-343-7033). Subway: N, R to Prince St; 6 to Spring St. Mon–Sat 11am–6pm. AmEx, JCB, MC, V.
Parisian Lucien Pellat-Finet settled on an 800-square-foot space to house his lusted-after cashmere collection. The basic collection includes crewnecks, T-shirts, V-necks and cardies for men and women.

Marc Jacobs
163 Mercer St between Houston and Prince Sts (212-343-1490). Subway: N, R to Prince St. Mon–Sat 11am–7pm; Sun noon–6pm. AmEx, MC, V.
Marc Jacobs's first Manhattan boutique, housed in a former art gallery, is long and narrow, with white walls and distant ceilings. The impeccable designs displayed here include Jacobs's collections of both men's and women's ready-to-wear, accessories and shoes.

Miu Miu
100 Prince St between Mercer and Greene Sts (212-334-5156). Subway: N, R to Prince St. Mon–Sat 11am–7pm; Sun noon–6pm. AmEx, MC, V.
This is the first home for Miuccia Prada's secondary line, Miu Miu. Secondary, yes; cheap, no. Still, $225 for the season's most coveted shoes isn't *that* bad.

Philosophy di Alberta Ferretti
452 West Broadway between Houston and Prince Sts (212-460-5500). Subway: C, E to Spring St. Mon–Sat 11am–7pm; Sun noon–6pm. AmEx, MC, V.
This four-level store features mother-of-pearl-colored walls and cascading water, elements that echo the layering, translucence and craft in Ferretti's collection of delicate women's wear.

Pleats Please
128 Wooster St at Prince St (212-226-3600). Subway: N, R to Prince St. Mon–Sat 11am–7pm; Sun 11am–6pm. AmEx, MC, V.
New Yorkers can't seem to get enough of Japanese designer Issey Miyake's mid-priced line of pleated clothing: The accordion-like pants, skirts and dresses are featherweight, machine-washable *and* wrinkle-proof.

Prada Sport
116 Wooster St between Prince and Spring Sts (212-925-2221). Subway: C, E to Spring St. Mon–Sat 11am–7pm; Sun noon–6pm. AmEx, DC, JCB, MC, V.
Prada's new sportswear collection—a line of waterproof and windproof garments that look as good on the sidewalk as they do on the slopes—moved into the former Comme des Garçons space, keeping the same sleek vibe.

René Lezard
417 West Broadway between Prince and Spring Sts (212-274-0700). Subway: N, R to Prince St; C, E to Spring St. Mon–Sat 11am–7pm; Sun noon–6pm. AmEx, JCB, MC, V.
This store, the former home of Mary Boone's Soho gallery, is now filled with Lezard's luxe Italian designs.

Tocca
161 Mercer St between Prince and Houston Sts (212-343-3912). Subway: N, R to Prince St. Mon–Sat 11am–7pm; Sun noon–6pm. AmEx, MC, V.
What girl doesn't melt at the sight of Tocca's window? Colorful dresses and separates are housed in this gorgeous

cerulean boutique. There are children's and home lines previously only available in the Tokyo store.

Todd Oldham
123 Wooster St between Spring and Prince Sts (212-219-3531). Subway: C, E to Spring St; N, R to Prince St. Mon–Sat 11am–7pm; Sun noon–6pm. AmEx, MC, V.
This colorful boutique houses Todd Oldham's imaginative fashions, including the cutesy Jeans line.

Vivienne Tam
99 Greene St between Prince and Spring Sts (212-966-2398). Subway: N, R to Prince St. Mon–Fri 11am–7pm; Sat 11:30am–7:30pm; Sun noon–7pm. AmEx, MC, V.
Vivienne Tam's first U.S. boutique, with its oxblood walls and massive Chinese character cut out of a partition (it means "double happiness"), is decidedly exotic. Offering long, transparent dresses with mandarin collars, flowy skirts and sheer knit sweaters, the Canton-born Tam has that special something for your feminine side.

Vivienne Westwood
71 Greene St between Spring and Broome Sts (212-334-5200). Subway: C, E to Spring St. Mon–Sat 11am–7pm; Sun noon–6pm. AmEx, DC, JCB, MC, V.
Finally, Vivienne Westwood has set up shop in New York. Known for her experimental draping, Savile Row–style tailoring and impeccable construction, Westwood has been setting fashion trends since 1971. This location doubles as her showroom; all five labels can be found here.

Yohji Yamamoto
103 Grand St at Broadway (212-966-9066). Subway: J, M, Z, N, R, 6 to Canal St. Mon–Sat 11am–7pm; Sun noon–6pm. AmEx, DC, MC, V.
Yohji Yamamoto's flagship store is a huge, lofty space filled with well-cut designs.

Young & restless

A Détacher
262 Mott St between Houston and Prince Sts (212-625-3380). Subway: 6 to Spring St. Tue–Sun noon–7pm. MC, V.
A Détacher is designer Mona Kowalska's placid boutique, featuring her own line of "minimalist but constructed" women's clothing and designer knickknacks.

Bond 07
7 Bond St between Broadway and Lafayette Sts (212-677-8487). Subway: B, D, F, Q to Broadway–Lafayette St; 6 to Bleecker St. Mon–Sat 11am–7pm; Sun noon–7pm. AmEx, MC, V.
Selima Salaun, of Le Corset and Selima Optique fame, has branched out from undies and eyewear, this time offering a carefully edited selection of clothing, accessories and vintage 20th-century French furniture.

Built by Wendy and Cake
7 Centre Market Pl between Broome and Grand Sts (212-925-6538). Subway: 6 to Spring St. Noon–7pm. MC, V.
Wendy Mullin and Sara Koziowski, the women behind these two seminal labels, have joined forces to open a store and work space on the fringe of Chinatown.

Calypso on Broome
424 Broome St between Crosby and Lafayette Sts (212-274-0449). Subway: 6 to Spring St. Mon–Sat 11am–7pm; Sun noon–6pm. AmEx, MC, V.
While customers can still shop at the original Calypso, this new location (which is about four times the size) features more upscale merchandise (less resort wear) and totally different vendors. Stop by either shop for gorgeous slip dresses, suits, sweaters and scarves, many from unknown French designers.

The joy of Essex

…and Ludlow and Stanton, in the newly groovy Lower East Side

In New York City, *downtown* has always been synonymous with *cool*. But as below–14th Street neighborhoods such as Soho—and more recently Nolita—have been co-opted by the mainstream, so hipsters' search for undiscovered stomping grounds has moved farther east and south.

Rivington view: **Patch** culls the latest styles from up-and-coming designers.

The Lower East Side is one neighborhood they've recently moved into. Once the crowded home to thousands of European immigrants (and more recently a destination for bargain shoppers searching for cheap leather jackets, fabrics and luggage), the area is now rife with pretty young things and would-be rebels without causes. Bars such as Max Fish and boutiques such as TG-170 were the first to bring cachet to the neighborhood's formerly drug-ridden streets. But in the last few years, more and more businesses have followed suit. The result is a district that still feels slightly unpolished but offers a wide variety of unique fashion, housewares and eats.

As you head east on Houston Street, the first street you'll stumble over is Eldridge. This small block features bOb, a small joint that's more of a miniclub than a bar, and **Vinnie's Tampon Case Factory Store** (245 Eldridge Street; 212-228-CASE). Make sure to stock up on Vinnie Angel's artful canvas tampon pouches and cool magnets for your girlfriends. On Allen Street, the next stop on your shopping grid, visit graffiti artist **A. Charles**'s store (188 Allen Street; 212-777-9029) for all sorts of spray-painted Ts and other streetwear.

Once you reach Orchard Street, you're nearing the neighborhood's commercial hub. Amid the slowly disappearing leather shops and luggage outlets, there's **Xuly Bët** (189 Orchard Street; 212-982-5437), which sells the eponymous Parisian deconstructivist clothing line—not for the meek. On the same block look for **Timtoum** (179 Orchard Street; 212-780-0456), a club-oriented clothing and record store, and **Eduardo** (181 Orchard Street; 212-477-5459), a trendy two-year-old antiques-restoration business. And don't miss **Cherry** (185 Orchard Street; 212-358-7131), which specializes in vintage clothing from the '20s through the '80s; much of the clothing is "dead stock," complete with original tags. Newest on the block is **Oxygene Colectif** (188 Orchard Street; 212-995-8497), a jewelry store worth checking out. Probably the most captivating of the lot is **DDC Lab** (180 Orchard Street; 212-375-1647); this airy newcomer specializes in items you can't get anywhere else in New York, such as a pair of Nike sneakers commemorating Hong Kong's transfer to Chinese rule.

Move on to Ludlow Street, and you've reached the epicenter of cool. Before you enter you may want to grab a hot dog or a pastrami sandwich at the venerable Jewish eatery Katz's Deli. But if you're in a rush, make a beeline for **TG-170** (170 Ludlow Street; 212-995-8660). Every girl worth her Miu Mius comes here for the latest dresses and separates from the leading downtown designers. Down the block is **Las Venus** (153 Ludlow Street; 212-982-0608), a vintage furniture store chock-full of groovy couches, lamps, turntables and even clothing.

At the intersection of Orchard and Stanton Streets are three great shops (and one great place to get take-out margaritas): One of the area's pioneers, **Mary Adams** (159 Ludlow Street; 212-473-0237) makes beautifully girly versions of the old-fashioned party dress, favoring silks, satins, velvets and cottons. Across the way is **Min Lee** (105 Stanton Street; 212-375-0304), a store featuring Lee's pretty raw-silk shirts and dresses as well as accessories by a host of young designers. **Nova USA** (100 Stanton Street; 212-228-6844) is the last to have moved to this intersection. Tony Melillo sells his casual menswear collection here, including his super-popular judo pants and other basics in fleece, wool crepe and cotton twill.

Just around the corner are two more worthwhile stops: **MIKS** (100 Stanton Street; 212-505-1982) brings an Asian vibe to the 'hood. The shop features imported Japanese sneakers and accessories as well as one of the four owners' clothing lines. Next door is **Lucky Wang** (100 Stanton Street; 212-353-2850), a wacky boutique filled with all things tinsel, including rugs, hooded jackets and eyeglass cases. Before you head even farther east, there's one more destination: **Yu** (151 Ludlow Street; 212-979-9370) is a designer consignment store that carries clothing by such avant-garde labels as Issey Miyake and Comme des Garçons.

You'll find a final cluster of shops once you cross Essex Street. Occupying a former beauty-supply store, **Patch** (155 Rivington Street; 212-533-9995) sells clothes, accessories and gifts by mostly undiscovered designers. Around the corner is **Duh** (102 Suffolk Street; 212-253-1158), a handbag store featuring the sweet designs of owner Etsuko Kizawa.

If you're more interested in sprucing up your home, check out **Have a Seat** (37 Clinton Street; 212-353-9550), which specializes in chic mid-century design (there's an excellent selection of chairs, lamps and housewares).

Other location: *Calypso St. Barths, 280 Mott St between Houston and Prince Sts (212-965-0990).*

Canal Jean
504 Broadway between Spring and Broome Sts (212-226-1130). Subway: N, R to Prince St; 6 to Spring St. Mon–Thu, Sun 10am–8pm; Fri, Sat 10:30am–9pm; Sun 11am–9pm. AmEx, DC, MC, V.
Browse the vast acreage of jeans, T-shirts and other basics, plus new (e.g., French Connection) and vintage clothing and accessories, socks, bags and fun jewelry. Canal's prices are definitely worth the trip.

Catherine
468 Broome St at Greene St (212-925-6765). Subway: N, R to Prince St. Mon–Wed 11am–7pm; Thu–Sat 11am–8pm; Sun noon–8pm. AmEx, MC, V.
If chain stores take over the universe, take refuge at Catherine. The colorful store showcases everything from tile-topped cocktail tables and vintage glass vases to beaded silk pillows and chocolate. Oh, did we mention the breathtaking fashions of owner-designer Catherine Malandrino?

Diesel
770 Lexington Ave at 60th St (212-308-0055). Subway: N, R to Lexington Ave; 4, 5, 6 to 59th St. Mon–Sat 10am–8pm; Sun noon–6pm. AmEx, DC, Disc, JCB, MC, V.
This 14,000-square-foot emporium will quench any denim craving you might have. In addition to jeans and stylish vinyl clothing and accessories, there are also shoes, under- and outerwear, and refreshments of the coffee variety.

Dressing Room
49 Prince St between Lafayette and Mulberry Sts (212-431-6658). Subway: N, R to Prince St. Mon–Sat 1–7pm; Sun 1–6pm. AmEx, MC, V.
The Dressing Room, one of Nolita's first clothing boutiques, set the rest of the 'hood in motion. It carries girly goodies, from frilly panties and feather necklaces to nylon skirts and denim duds.

Frida's Closet
296 Smith St between Union and Sackett Sts, Carroll Gardens, Brooklyn (718-855-0311). Subway: F to Carroll St. Tue–Fri 1–8pm; Sat, Sun 11am–6pm. MC, V.
Thick fuchsia ropes hang from a bright red ceiling, holding two racks of urban garments by designer-owner Sandra Paez. Inspired by daring Mexican surrealist painter Frida Kahlo, Paez brings the sensibilities of her own Mexican heritage to her work; skirts, tops and pants in floral patterns and velvet ribbons lend her designs flair.

Hedra Prue
281 Mott St between Houston and Prince Sts (212-529-7324). Subway: B, D, F, Q to Broadway–Lafayette St. Mon–Sat 11am–7pm; Sun noon–7pm. AmEx, MC, V.
A trip to Nolita isn't complete unless you check out the wares at Hedra Prue. This shop stocks downtown's latest and greatest young designers and accessories.

Hotel Venus
382 West Broadway between Broome and Spring Sts (212-966-4066). Subway: A, C to Spring St. Mon–Sun noon–8pm. AmEx, JCB, MC, V.
Patricia Field's new store features a Japanese-animation influence; the decor is more mod and the staff more serious and dressed-up than at her 8th Street boutique (see below). Along with clothing, Hotel Venus stocks platforms, stationery, barrettes, wallets, blow-up furniture and lots of bags.

Jade

*240 Mulberry St between Houston and Prince Sts
(212-925-6544). Subway: B, D, F, Q to Broadway–
Lafayette St. Mon–Sat 11am–7pm; Sun noon–6pm.
AmEx, DC, MC, V.*
Christiane Celle snatched up property in überhip Nolita
long before it was hot; first she opened Calypso (*see* **Calypso on Broome** *above*), then Jade. Here, she sells mainly
Chinese-influenced clothing.

Jussara

*125 Greene St between Houston and Prince Sts
(212-353-5050). Subway: N, R to Prince St. Mon–Sat
11am–7:30p;, Sun noon–7pm. AmEx, MC, V.*
Of Korean descent, Jussara Lee was raised in Brazil, which
explains a lot about this shop's decor as well as her style:
romantic modernism. One side is decorated with slanted
roofs constructed from terra-cotta shingles, a tall balcony, a
stone fountain and benches; the other side features tweed
and velvet jackets, coats and dresses.

Intermix

*125 Fifth Ave between 19th and 20th Sts
(212-533-9720). Subway: N, R to 23rd St. Mon–Sat
11am–8pm; Sun noon–6pm. AmEx, Disc, JCB, MC, V.*
Intermix is a Flatiron district fave; the buyers have amazing
taste. Designers carried here include Plein Sud, Kostum,
Catherine and Bloom.

Louie

*68 Thompson St between Spring and Broome Sts
(212-274-1599). Subway: C, E to Spring St. Tue–Sat
noon–7pm; Sun noon–6pm. AmEx, MC, V.*
At Laura Pedone's boutique, Louie, every design is an original. It's also the launching pad for young, unknown clothiers.

Malia Mills

*199 Mulberry St between Spring and Kenmare Sts
(212-625-2311). Subway: 6 to Spring St. Noon–7pm.
AmEx, MC, V.*
Ever since one of her designs made it onto the cover of *Sports
Illustrated*'s swimsuit issue two years ago, Malia Mills's
swimwear has become a staple for those who spend their
New Year's on St. Barth's.

Nylonsquid

*222 Lafayette St between Spring and Broome Sts
(212-334-6554). Subway: 6 to Spring St. Sun–Thu
noon–7pm; Fri, Sat noon–8pm. AmEx, MC, V.*
Nylonsquid gives new meaning to Cool Britannia. London-based sneaker and clothing distributors Mick Hoyle and John
Chatters originally wanted to open a showroom but opted
instead for a retail space that doubles as one.

Olive & Bette's

*252 Columbus Ave between 71st and 72nd Sts
(579-2178). Subway: 1, 2, 3, 9 to 72nd St. Mon–Sat
10am–7pm; Sun 11am–6pm. AmEx, MC, V.*
Olive & Bette's, the store that for three years succeeded in
getting even the most uptown/crosstown-phobic girls to
trot over to its West Side store, did it again last fall when
an East Side outpost opened. These shops have it all:
underwear, outerwear, jewelry and even itsy-bitsy decals
for your nails.
Other location: *1070 Madison Ave between 80th and
81st Sts (212-717-9655).*

P.A.K.

*229 Mott St between Prince and Spring Sts
(212-226-5167). Subway: 6 to Spring St. Tue–Sat
noon–7:30pm; Sun 1–6pm. AmEx, MC, V.*
This is minimalist women's clothing designed by owner
Corey Pak (hence the name).

Patricia Field

*10 E 8th St at Fifth Ave (212-254-1699). Subway:
N, R to 8th St–NYU. Mon–Sat noon–8pm; Sun 1–7pm.
AmEx, Disc, MC, V.*
Field is brilliant at working club and street fashion. Her store,
with its ambisexual staff, has an eclectic mix of original
jewelry, makeup, on-the-edge club gear and East Village
design. There's always something new, the clothing is gorgeous and durable, and the wigs are the best in town. See
also Hotel Venus above.

Phare

*252 Elizabeth St between Houston and Prince Sts
(212-625-0406). Subway: B, D, F, Q to Broadway–
Lafayette St. Tue–Sat noon–7pm; Sun noon–6pm.
AmEx, MC, V.*
This Nolita-based, model-owned store epitomizes the neighborhood: The clothes are desirable, elegant, whimsical and
a touch trendy.

Product

*71 Mercer St between Broome and Spring Sts
(212-274-1494). Subway: N, R to Prince St; C, E to
Spring St. Mon–Sat 11am–7pm; Sun noon–6pm.
AmEx, MC, V.*
Product is a hip clothier for women that features wonderful
stretchy fabrics, sleek lines and frivolous accessories. Expect
very good-looking clothes that aren't as expensive as those at
APC, which is just up the block. Sales are frenzied and frequent.

Red Tape Rebecca Danenberg

*333 E 9th St between First and Second Aves
(212-529-8483). Subway: 6 to Astor Pl. Noon–8pm.
AmEx, MC, V.*
Rebecca Danenberg's signature collection sells at Barneys
and Bloomies, but her lower-priced basics are sold only at
her East Village store.

Scoop

*532 Broadway between Prince and Spring Sts
(212-925-2886). Subway: N, R to Prince St. Mon–Sat
11am–8pm; Sun 11am–7pm. AmEx, MC, V.*
Scoop is the ultimate young fashion editor's closet. Clothing
from Tocca, Daryl K, Susan Lazar, Katayone Adeli and plenty more is arranged by hue, not label.
Other location: *275 Third Ave between 73rd and
74th Sts (212-535-5577).*

Stacia New York

*267 Smith St at DeGraw St, Carroll Gardens, Brooklyn
(718-237-0078). Subway: F, G to Carroll St. Mon–Sat
11:30am–8pm; Sun 11:30am–6:30pm. AmEx, MC, V.*
A former J. Crew fabric sourcer and Cynthia Rowley's right-hand gal, Stacy Johnson has created a collection of colorful,
flirty dresses, skirts and sweaters should make her the new
Tocca for the fashion flock.

Steven Alan

*60 Wooster St between Spring and Broome Sts
(212-334-6354). Subway: C, E to Spring St. 11am–
7pm. AmEx, MC, V.*
Steven Alan's stock is coveted by hip girls in all neighborhoods. The Soho store is a good place to scout fashion's next
big things; the East Village branch is a mix of seasonless staples and season-old (translation: discounted) clothing.
Other location: *330 E 11th St between First and
Second Aves (212-982-2881).*

TG-170

*170 Ludlow St between Houston and Stanton Sts
(212-995-8660). Subway: F to Second Ave. Noon–8pm.
AmEx, MC, V.*
Terry Gillis has an eye for emerging designers: She was the
first to carry Rebecca Danenberg, Pixie Yates and Built by

*We're jammin: Shop alfresco for homemade jellies at the **Union Square Greenmarket**.*

Wendy. Gillis also has her own line—called TG-170, of course—consisting of simple separates in unusual fabrics.

Tracy Feith
209 Mulberry St between Spring and Kenmare Sts (212-334-3097). Subway: 6 to Spring St. 11am–7pm. AmEx, MC, V.
Tracy Feith, known for his darling dresses, recently relocated to a larger, 1,500-square-foot shop. The additional space hasn't gone to waste: Feith fans will find not only the primary women's line, but also the Raj collection (a seasonless, ultracolorful line inspired by the fabrics of India), a men's line and kid's clothes.

Trash & Vaudeville
4 St. Marks Pl between Second and Third Aves (212-982-3590). Subway: 6 to Astor Pl. Mon–Fri noon–8pm; Sat 11:30am–9pm; Sun 1–7:30pm. AmEx, MC, V.
This punk staple has two floors of fashion, accessories and shoes: stretchy tube dresses, leathers, snakeskin boots, collar tips and jewelry.

Wang
219 Mott St between Prince and Spring Sts (212-941-6134). Subway: 6 to Spring St. Tue–Sun noon–7pm. AmEx, MC, V.
Wang, a boutique owned by sisters Sally and Jennifer Wang, carries simple, chic clothes.

Zero
225 Mott St between Prince and Spring Sts (212-925-3849). Subway: 6 to Spring St. Tue–Sat 12:30–7:30pm; Sun 12:30–6pm. AmEx, MC, V.
This shop, ground zero for downtown hipsters, sells offbeat clothing, much of it based on simple geometric shapes.

Streetwear

Active Wearhouse
514 Broadway between Spring and Broome Sts (212-965-2284). Subway: N, R to Prince St. Mon–Sat 9am–9pm; Sun 10am–8pm. AmEx, Disc, JCB, MC, V.

Active Wearhouse has become *the* place to pick up the latest in footwear from Adidas, New Balance, Nike, Saucony and others. The store also sells clothing; the North Face section is especially strong. Active's sister shop Transit stocks the same in its subway-themed store.
Other location: *Transit, 665 Broadway between Bond and Bleecker Sts (212-358-8726).*

Memes
3 Great Jones St between Broadway and Lafayette St (212-420-9955). Subway: B, D, F, Q to Broadway–Lafayette St; 6 to Bleecker St. Noon–8pm. AmEx, MC, V.
Tetsuo Hashimoto believes it takes more than a Kangol hat and a pair of Adidas to establish street cred. His shop, Memes, offers refined men's streetwear, more fitted than most but by no means uptight.

Phat Farm
129 Prince St between West Broadway and Wooster St (212-533-7428). Subway: C, E to Spring St. Mon–Sat 11am–7pm; Sun 11am–6pm. AmEx, MC, V.
This store showcases Def Jam records impresario Russell Simmons's classy and conservative take on hip-hop couture: phunky-phresh oversize and baggy clothing. For gals, there's the Baby Phat line.

Recon
237 Eldridge St between Houston and Stanton Sts (212-614-8502). Subway: F to Second Ave. Tue–Sun noon–7pm. AmEx, MC, V.
This joint venture of famed graffiti artists Stash, Futura and Bleu opened in 1998 offering graf junkies a chance to wear the work of their favorite artists. In addition to clothes, Recon carries accessories like backpacks and dop kits with plenty of places to stow the requisite Recon gadgets (key chains, Swiss Army knives, Zippo lighters).

SSUR
219A Mulberry St between Prince and Spring Sts (212-431-3152). Subway: 6 to Spring St. Mon–Fri noon–7pm; Sat noon–7:30pm; Sun 1–6pm. AmEx, MC, V.

DIESEL®

FOR SUCCESSFUL LIVING

Number 96

WHERE
In a series of Diesel "How to..."
guides to SUCCESSFUL LIVING.

INFO
Call Diesel headquarters
212-755-9200   www.diesel.com

770 LEXINGTON AVE @ 60TH STREET   212 308 0055

Designer Russ Karablin's gallery-turned-shop, SSUR (*Russ* spelled backward) combines military-surplus antichic with streetwear style.

Stüssy
104 Prince St between Mercer and Greene Sts (212-274-8855). Subway: N, R to Prince St. Mon–Thu noon–7pm; Fri, Sat 11am–7pm; Sun noon–6pm. AmEx, MC, V.
Check out the fine hats, T-shirts and other skatesome/surfy West Coast gear that Sean Stüssy is famous for.

Supreme
274 Lafayette St between Houston and Prince Sts (212-966-7799). Subway: N, R to Prince St. Mon–Sat 11:30am–7pm, Sun noon–6pm. AmEx, MC, V.
Sunshine lights up the racks and shelves of the latest skatewear, mostly from East Coast brands like Independent, Zoo York, Chocolate and the shop's own line. Of course, there are decks and the necessary skate accessories, too.

Triple Five Soul
290 Lafayette St between Houston and Prince Sts (212-431-2404). Subway: B, D, F, Q to Broadway–Lafayette St. 11am–7:30pm. AmEx, MC, V.
"Jungle boogie" is the phrase that first comes to mind at this urban-meets-rainforest-themed shop. The bamboo bike in the window is from Vietnam, but the clothing and accessories inside are from New York designers. 555 Soul also offers curvier versions of its menswear for the ladies.

Union
172 Spring St between West Broadway and Thompson St (212-226-8493). Subway: C, E to Spring St. Mon–Sat 11am–7pm; Sun noon–7pm. AmEx, MC, V.
Can't make it to London? The folks at Union have brought the city to you. The store is the exclusive dealer of Duffer St. George, the famed streetwear sold at the British shop of the same name. Union also sells Maharishi, 68 and Brothers, and the Union label.

X-Large
267 Lafayette St between Prince and Spring Sts (212-334-4480). Subway: N, R to Prince St. Noon–7pm. AmEx, Disc, MC, V.
New Yorkers were thrilled when X-Large graduated from its closet-size shop on Avenue A and moved into these sleek digs. Now girls can get the Mini label at the same time and place their boys are getting their X-Large duds.

Strictly for men

Although chic department stores such as Barneys New York and Bergdorf Goodman have enormous men's sections (Bergdorf's is even housed in a separate building across the street from the main store), it's not always easy or comfortable for guys to search for new duds (*see **Department stores**, page 118*). At many fashion boutiques, the men's collections are either limited or tucked away in the back. The following shops offer stylish clothing for men only. Here, it's the ladies who will find themselves waiting on the couch outside the dressing room.

agnès b. homme
79 Greene St between Spring and Broome Sts (212-431-4339). Subway: N, R to Prince St. Mon–Sat 11am–7pm; Sun noon–6pm. AmEx, DC, MC, V.
The films of Jean-Luc Godard and his contemporaries are clearly a primary inspiration for agnès b's designs. Men's

Tunnel of love: ***Comme des Garçons'*** new Chelsea shop was once a taxi garage.

basics include the classic snap-front knit cardigan and navy-blue-and-white striped long-sleeved T-shirts that will make you feel like Picasso in his studio.

Paul Smith
108 Fifth Ave between 15th and 16th Sts (212-627-9770). Subway: L, N, R, 4, 5, 6 to 14th Street–Union Sq. Mon–Wed, Fri, Sat 11am–7pm; Thu 11am–8pm; Sun noon–6pm. AmEx, Disc, MC, V.
Stop by Paul Smith for the relaxed-English-gentleman look. These designs are exemplary in their combination of elegance, quality and wit. Accessories are also available.

Sean
132 Thompson St between Houston and Prince Sts (212-598-5980). Subway: C, E to Spring St; N, R to Prince St. Mon–Thu, Sat 11am–8pm; Fri 11am–9pm; Sun noon–7pm. AmEx, MC, V.
A former director of marketing at Scholastic (the textbook publisher), Sean Cassidy (don't laugh) discovered French designer Pierre Emile Lafaurie during visits to Paris; he fell in love with Lafaurie's men's suits, cotton shirts and corduroy jackets. Now Sean devotes his shop to Lafaurie's designs.
Other location: *224 Columbus Ave between 70th and 71st Sts (212-769-1489).*

Seize sur Vingt
243 Elizabeth St between Houston and Prince Sts (212-343-0476). Subway: N, R to Prince St. Tue–Sun noon–7pm. AmEx, M, V.
This charming boutique offers a selection of menswear that falls somewhere between suits and jeans. Men's shirts come in vibrant colors and are made with impeccable details:

mother-of-pearl buttons and square, short collars designed to look good with the top button open.

Ted Baker London

107 Grand St at Mercer St (212-343-8989).
Subway: C, E to Spring St. Mon–Wed 11:30am–7pm;
Thu 11:30am–7:30pm; Fri, Sat noon–7:30pm; Sun
noon–6:30pm. AmEx, DC, MC, V.
The Brits behind this label present a modern, restrained line of men's clothing whose focus is short- and long-sleeved shirts in bright colors. Customers should not overlook the rest of the collection, which has been popular in England for over a decade.

Thomas Pink

520 Madison Ave at 53rd St (212-838-1928).
Subway: E, F to Fifth Ave. Mon–Fri 10am–7pm; Thu
10am–8pm; Sat 10am–6pm; Sun 11am–5pm. AmEx,
DC, JCB, MC, V.
This shirt shop opened on London's Jermyn Street 20 years ago. Although the younger American shop looks tony and British, it's modern and user-friendly. Pink's shirts are offered in bold, dynamic colors intended to be paired with more conservative suits.

Children's clothes

Baby Gap and Gap Kids

Baby Gap, 1037 Lexington Ave at 74th St
(212-327-2614). Subway: 6 to 68th St–Hunter College.
Mon–Sat 10am–7:30pm; Sun 11am–6pm. AmEx,
Disc, MC, V.
Gap sure knows how to hit a nerve. Even those repulsed by mass-produced Gapwear swoon at the sight of a pair of tiny blue jeans or a miniature V-neck sweater. Gap Kids also features adult clothing. Check the phone book for other locations.

Bu & the Duck

106 Franklin St between West Broadway and
Church St (212-431-9226). Subway: 1, 9 to Franklin St.
Mon–Sat 10am–7pm. AmEx, Disc, MC, V.
Owner Susan Lane-Camacho draws her inspiration in part from the past—specifically, the 1930s. The result is charmingly unique clothing and a well-chosen, whimsical selection of children's antiques.

Calypso Enfants

284 Mulberry St between Houston and Prince Sts
(212-965-8910). Subway: B, D, F, Q to Broadway–
Lafayette St; 6 to Bleecker St. Mon–Sat 11am–7pm;
Sun noon–6pm. AmEx, MC, V.
Fans of Calypso—and its utterly desirable women's clothing, bags and accessories—positively adore this children's store. There's the same French influence here: Items such as a wool coat look as if they leapt from the pages of *Madeline*.

Hoyt & Bond

248 Smith St between Douglass and DeGraw Sts,
Carroll Gardens, Brooklyn (718-488-8283). Subway:
F, G to Carroll St. Tue–Thu 10am–6pm; Fri, Sat
10am–7pm; Sun 11am–6pm. MC, V.
Hipsters with kids need places to shop, too. Designer Elizabeth Beer's new store features both her line of children's clothing (A-line skirts, color-saturated ponchos, kiddie cowboy hats) and women's pieces (chic angora and wool kerchiefs and mittens).

Lilliput

265 Lafayette St between Prince and Spring Sts
(212-965-9567). Subway: B, D, F, Q to Broadway–
Lafayette St; N, R to Prince St; 6 to Spring St. Mon, Sun
noon–6pm; Tue–Sat 11am–7pm. AmEx, DC, MC, V.
This hip source for kids and babies sells secondhand as well as new clothing.

Little O

1 Bleecker St between Bowery and Mott St
(212-673-0858). Subway: 6 to Bleecker St. Tue–Sat
12:30–7:30pm; Sun 1–7pm. MC, V.
Model/mom Debbie Deitering has dug to the bottom of vintage bins to provide hipster parents with a chic alternative to cookie-cutter, crayon-colored choices when they shop for their tots. Items at the store span decades.

Shoofly Q

465 Amsterdam Ave at 83rd St (212-580-4390).
Subway: B, C, 1, 9 to 86th St. Mon–Sat 11am–7pm;
Sun noon–6pm. AmEx, MC, V.
Boaters, caps, fleece-lined boots, suspenders, gloves and shoes are to be found among the Flintstones-style furniture, tree trunks and animal-footprint decor.
Other location: *42 Hudson St between Duane and*
Thomas Sts (212-406-3270).

Space Kiddets

46 E 21st St between Park Ave South and Broadway
(212-420-9878). Subway: 6 to 23rd St. Mon, Tue, Fri
10:30am–6pm; Wed, Thu 10:30am–7pm; Sat 10:30am–
5:30pm. AmEx, MC, V.
This shop strives for a unique combination: clothing that is hip, practical, comfortable and fun for kids. There's always a range of one-of-a-kind items (including some furniture and toys) created by tiny, artsy companies, as well as secondhand clothes (it's *the* place for 1950s cowboy outfits).

Clothing Rental

See **Weddings/Formalwear** *page 155.*

Just Once

292 Fifth Ave between 30th and 31st Sts
(212-465-0960). Subway: 6 to 28th St. By appointment
only. AmEx, MC, V.
This bridal service stocks a wide selection of expensive gowns—Vera Wang and Carolina Herrera are among the labels—for sale or rental (rentals range from $300 to $800).

One Night Out and Mom's Night Out

147 E 72nd St between Lexington and Third Aves
(212-988-1122). Subway: 6 to 68th St–Hunter College.
Mon–Wed, Fri 10:30am–6pm; Thu 10:30am–8pm;
Sat, Sun 11am–5pm. AmEx, D, MC, V.
One Night Out rents brand-new evening wear to uptown socialites and downtown girls trying to pass for the same. Across the hall, Mom's Night Out provides the same service to expectant mothers for $195 to $225.

Zeller Tuxedos

201 E 56th St at Third Ave, second floor
(212-355-0707). Subway: 4, 5, 6 to 59th St; N, R to
Lexington Ave. Mon–Fri 9am–6:30pm; Sat 10am–
5pm. AmEx, MC, V.
Armani, Ungaro and Valentino tuxes are available for—horrors!—those who didn't think to pack theirs. Check the phone book for other locations.

Discount fashion

For outlet malls, like Woodbury Commons in upstate New York, *see chapter* **Trips Out of Town**.

Century 21 Department Store

22 Cortlandt St at Broadway (212-227-9092).
Subway: N, R, 1, 9 to Cortlandt St. Mon–Wed 7:45am–
7:30pm; Thu 7:45am–8:30pm; Fri 7:45am–8pm; Sat
10am–7:30pm; Sun 11am–6pm. AmEx, Disc, MC, V.

Some discerning shoppers report finding clothes by Romeo Gigli and Donna Karan here, but you have to visit every ten days or so to get such bargains. Rack upon rack is heavy with discounted designer and name-brand fashions. Housewares and appliances are also sold cheap, plus underwear, accessories, fragrances and women's shoes.

Other location: *472 86th St between Fourth and Fifth Aves, Bay Ridge, Brooklyn (718-748-3266).*

Daffy's
111 Fifth Ave at 18th St (212-529-4477). Subway: L, N, R, 4, 5, 6 to 14th St–Union Sq. Mon–Sat 10am– 9pm; Sun noon–7pm. Disc, MC, V.
There are three floors packed with current mainstream fashions, from evening gowns and leather jackets to Calvin Klein and French lingerie, as well as men's suits and shirts. Prices are much lower than retail stores', and there are often substantial markdowns. The kids' clothes are fabulous. Check the phone book for other locations.

TJ Maxx
620 Sixth Ave between 18th and 19th Sts (212-229-0875). Subway: F to 14th St; L to Sixth Ave. Mon–Sat 9:30am–9pm; Sun 11am–7pm. AmEx, DC, MC, V.
This discount designer clothes store, with its brightly lit Woolworth's-like appearance, is less of an obvious treasure trove than Century 21 (*see above*), but if you're prepared to sift through the junk, you will undoubtedly find some fab-

Vintage and secondhand clothes

The pyramid rule of secondhand clothes means the less you browse, the more you have to pay. Although we've included them in our listings, the shops along lower Broadway tend to ask inflated prices for anything except the most mundane '70s disco shirts. The alternatives, too numerous and ever-changing to list here, are the many small shops in the East Village and on the Lower East Side. These nooks (along with the now-famous Domsey's in Brooklyn) are where real bargains can be found. Salvation Army and Goodwill stores are also worth checking out—as is anyplace with the word *thrift* in its name.

Alice Underground
481 Broadway at Broome St (212-431-9067). Subway: B, D, F, Q to Broadway–Lafayette St; 6 to Bleecker St. 11am–7:30pm. AmEx, MC, V.
A good selection of gear from the '40s through the '60s in all sorts of fabrics and in varied condition. Prices are high, but the bins at the front and back are always worth rummaging through. There's also a nice selection of bedding.

Allan & Suzi
416 Amsterdam Ave at 80th St (212-724-7445). Subway: 1, 9 to 79th St. Mon, Tue, Sat noon–7pm; Wed–Fri noon–8pm; Sun noon–6pm. AmEx, JCB, MC, V.
Models drop off their worn-once Comme des Garçons, Muglers and Gaultiers here. The platform-shoe collection is unmatched. A great store, but not cheap.

Anna
150 E 3rd St between Aves A and B (212-358-0195). Subway: F to Second Ave. Mon–Sat noon–7pm; Sun 1–7pm. AmEx, MC, V.
Anna is Kathy Kemp's middle name. Her shop, a haven for uptown fashion stylists and thrifters alike, usually stocks whatever is Kemp's current rage. Recently, she brought in reworked vintage clothing as well as some pieces by local designers.

Antique Boutique
712 Broadway between 4th St and Astor Pl (212-460-8830). Subway: N, R to 8th St–NYU; 6 to Astor Pl. Mon–Thu 11am–9pm; Fri, Sat 11am–10pm; Sun noon–8pm. AmEx, DC, Disc, JCB, MC, V.
This used to be one of the city's largest shops for vintage gear; now the collection at the recently revamped store has been banished to the basement. The good news is that much of it (generally in the '60s–'70s timeline) is sold by the pound. The main floor carries hip, up-and-coming designers as well as more vintage clothing.

Cheap Jack's
841 Broadway between 13th and 14th Sts (212-777-9564). Subway: L, N, R, 4, 5, 6 to 14th Street–Union Sq. Mon–Sat 11am–8pm; Sun noon–7pm. AmEx, MC, V.
A great vintage selection, but prices are exorbitant for anything nice. With army-surplus gear that runs into the high hundreds, cheap is the last thing Jack's is.

Domsey's Warehouse
431 Kent Ave at S 9th St, Williamsburg, Brooklyn (718-384-6000). Subway: J, M, Z to Marcy Ave. Mon–Fri 8am–5:30pm; Sat 8am–6:30pm; Sun 11am–5:30pm. No credit cards.

*Lab of luxury: Hunt for the trends at **DDC Lab**.*

The quality here has gone way down recently; maybe there's too much competition. Still, it's usually easy to turn up something worthwhile. Choose from a huge selection of used jeans, jackets, military and industrial wear, ball gowns, shoes and hats. Especially notable are the Hawaiian shirts, the sportsgear windbreakers and the unreal prices on cowboy boots.

Filthmart
531 E 13th St between Aves A and B (212-387-0650). Subway: L to First Ave. Mon, Tue 12:30–7pm; Wed–Sun 12:30–8pm. Disc, MC, V.
This newish East Village store specializes in white-trash and rock & roll memorabilia from the '60s through the early '80s. Expect lots of leather, denim and T-shirts. Also check out the excellent pinball-machine selection.

INA
101 Thompson St between Prince and Spring Sts (212-941-4757). Subway: C, E to Spring; N, R to Prince St. Noon–7pm. AmEx, MC, V.
In the market for an Alexander McQueen dress worn by Naomi Campbell? You'll find it at INA. For the past seven years, INA on Thompson has reigned over the downtown consignment scene. The cheery Soho location features drastically reduced couture pieces, while the Nolita site tends to carry clothing that's more trendy. And be sure to visit the new men's store on Mott Street.
Other locations: *21 Prince St between Mott and Elizabeth Sts (212-334-9048); INA Men, 262 Mott St between Prince and Houston Sts (212-334-2210).*

Rags-a-Go-Go
119 St. Marks Pl between First Ave and Ave A (212-254-4772). Subway: F to Second Ave; 6 to Astor Pl. Mon–Sat 1–9pm; Sun 1–8pm. AmEx, MC, V.
Do you like arranging your clothing by color? Then you'll love this place, where all the secondhand streetwear—sweatshirts, cords, tank tops, uniforms—are grouped according to hue. What's more, there's only one price for each type of clothing (e.g., all shirts are $12; all Ts are $6).
Other location: *75 E 7th St between First and Second Aves (212-254-4771).*

Resurrection
123 E 7th St between First Ave and Ave A (212-228-0063). Subway: F to Second Ave; L to First Ave; 6 to Astor Pl. Mon–Sat 1–9pm; Sun 1–8pm. AmEx, MC, V.
This vintage boutique is a Pucci wonderland; Kate Moss and Anna Sui are regulars. Owner Katy Rodriguez rents the space from the Theodore Wolinnin Funeral Home next door. Two dressing rooms take the place of the altar, and as you walk along the racks of leopard coats, 1940s dresses and beaded cardigans, you'll find yourself stepping on the metal outline of a coffin lifter. But don't worry: Rodriguez's shop looks more like a jewel box than a haunted house.
Other location: *217 Mott St between Prince and Spring Sts (212-625-1374).*

Screaming Mimi's
382 Lafayette St at 4th St (212-677-6464). Subway: N, R to 8th St–NYU; 6 to Astor Pl. Mon–Sat noon–8pm; Sun noon–6pm. AmEx, DC, Disc, MC, V.
This was where Cyndi Lauper shopped in the '80s. The prices are more reasonable for what you're getting, the selection is more carefully chosen than at the Broadway stores around the block, and the window displays are always worth a look.

Transfer International
594 Broadway between Prince and Houston Sts, suite 1002 (212-941-5472). Subway: B, D, F, Q to Broadway–Lafayette St; N, R to Prince St; 6 to Spring St. Tue–Sun 1–8pm. AmEx.
Well-connected Manhattanites Roberto Mitrotti and Linda Stein have collected celebrity castoffs from Ivana Trump,

Christie Brinkley, Trudie Styler and a host of others. This is a good bet for designer clothes, from Azzedine Alaïa to Zang Toi.

Fashion accessories

See **Jewelry,** *page 146;* **Lingerie,** *page 147;* **Shoes,** *page 150.*

Handbags

Amy Chan
247 Mulberry St between Prince and Spring Sts (212-966-3417). Subway: B, D, F, Q to Broadway–Lafayette St. Tue–Sat noon–7pm; Sun noon–5pm. AmEx, MC, V.
Although she had designed everything from shoes to waist and vest bags (years before Miu Miu and Helmut Lang), Amy Chan's career really took off a few years back when she launched a collection of handbags made from Chinese silks, sari fabric and feathers. Her bags are now the centerpiece of her 500-square-foot boutique.

Jamin Puech
252 Mott St between Houston and Prince Sts (212-334-9730). Subway: B, D, F, Q to Broadway–Lafayette St. Mon–Sat 11am–7pm; Sun noon–7pm. AmEx, MC, V.
Looking for a precious accessory or two? Make tracks to this tiny boutique, which sells exquisite creations by French partners Benoit Jamin and Isabel Puech. Look for flirty sequined bags, large leather totes and colorful boas.

Kate Spade
454 Broome St at Mercer St (212-274-1991). Subway: C, E, 6 to Spring St. Mon–Sat 11am–7pm; Sun noon–6pm. AmEx, MC, V.
Popular handbag designer Kate Spade sells her classic boxy tote as well as other chic numbers in this stylish store. Prices range from $80 to $400.

Kazuyo Nakano
223 Mott St between Prince and Spring Sts (212-941-7093). Subway: B, D, F, Q to Broadway–Lafayette St. 12:30–7pm. AmEx, MC, V.
Kazuyo Nakano started working in the assembly line at her father's kimono-bag factory in Kyoto straight out of high school. Now, nearly 20 years later, Nakano has her own handbag shop. The small store is filled with her fun and functional designs, many of them embroidered with flowers.

Hats

Amy Downs Hats
103 Stanton St at Ludlow St (212-598-4189). Subway: F to Second Ave. Wed–Sun 1–6pm. No credit cards.
Downs's soft wool and felt hats are neither fragile nor prissy. In fact, feel free to crumple them up and shove them into your bag (after purchasing them, of course)—they just won't die. Check out her trademark Twister, a cone-shaped hat with tassels.

Casa de Rodriguez
247 W 16th St between Seventh and Eighth Aves (212-989-0209). Subway: A, C, E, -to 14th St. By appointment only. MC, V.
Although they've closed their Soho shop, Jody and David Rodriguez haven't stopped selling their whimsical creations to stars like Missy Elliot. Jody has no millinery training; perhaps that's why she focuses more on the fabric of her hats than the design. With that in mind, prepare to have fun.

Put your best face forward

Here's where to look for perfumes, powders and other beauty potions

Manhattan is a makeup-lover's mecca. Department stores are a good source for the major names—as well as personal attention—but you will probably pay more than you would at some of the discount stores. Most drugstores stock a range of good, cheap makeup and general beauty products (*see* **Pharmacists**, *page 150*). Soho is the place where specialty lines such as 5S (Shiseido's kid sister), Make Up For Ever, M•A•C, Face Stockholm and Shu Uemura have set up boutiques in the past few years. And before we know it, Sephora will have popped up in every nabe, making dealing with pushy sales people—and searching high and low for unusual cosmetics lines—obsolete. Go on, give your makeup bag a makeover.

Alcone
235 W 19th St between Seventh and Eighth Aves (212-633-0551). Subway: 1, 9 to 18th St. Mon–Fri 11am–6pm; Sat noon–5pm. AmEx, MC, V.
Chelsea's little-known pro outlet Alcone offers brands and products you won't find elsewhere in the city, such as Visiora foundation and the German brand Kryolan. Alcone is full of products that seem as if they'd be at home only on a horror-movie set (fake-blood and bruise kits, for instance), but mere mortals like this shop for its premade palettes (trays of a dozen or more eye, lip and cheek colors). Not to miss: Alcone's own sponges.

Aveda
233 Spring St between Sixth Ave and Varick St (212-807-1492). Subway: C, E to Spring St; 1, 9 to Houston St. Mon, Tue, Thu, Fri 10am–7pm; Wed 9am–9pm; Sat 10am–6pm; Sun noon–6pm. AmEx, MC, V.
This is a spacious, tranquil boutique filled with an exclusive line of delicious-smelling hair- and skin-care products, makeup, massage oils, and cleansers, all made from flower and plant extracts. Check the phone book for other locations.

The Body Shop
773 Lexington Ave at 61st St (212-755-7851). Subway: N, R to Lexington Ave; 4, 5, 6 to 59th St. Mon–Sat 10am–8pm; Sun 11am–6pm. AmEx, Disc, MC, V.
The Body Shop, as most everyone knows, is the premier place for natural beauty products in no-nonsense, biodegradable plastic bottles. Grab a basket and start filling. Check the phone book for other locations.

Duane Reade
598 Broadway between Houston and Prince Sts (212-343-2567). Subway: B, D, F, Q to Broadway–Lafayette St. 24 hours. AmEx, Disc, MC, V.
Despite the number of high-end cosmetics shops that have put down roots in NYC, many New Yorkers head to Duane Reade for cheap staples: Revlon mascara, Wet 'n' Wild clear lip gloss and Cetaphil cleanser. Check the phone book for other locations.

Face Stockholm
110 Prince St at Greene St (212-966-9110). Subway: N, R to Prince St. Mon–Wed 11am–7pm; Thu–Sat 11am–8pm; Sun noon–7pm. AmEx, MC, V.
Along with a full line of shadows, lipsticks, tools and blushes (at very reasonable prices), Face offers two services: makeup applications ($40) and lessons ($75). Phone for an appointment or just stop by and check it out yourself. Check the phone book for other locations.

5S
98 Prince St between Mercer and Greene Sts (212-925-7880). Subway: N, R to Prince St. Mon–Sat 11am–7pm; Sun noon–6pm. AmEx, MC, V.
New makeup and skin-care line 5S, by Japanese cosmetics giant Shiseido, takes a novel approach to beauty. Customers can choose freely among the products, which are divided into five "senses of well-being" categories, ranging from energizing to nurturing.

Fresh
1061 Madison Ave between 80th and 81st Sts (212-396-0344). Subway: 6 to 77th St. Mon–Sat 10am–7pm; Sun noon–6pm. AmEx, MC, V.
Fresh, one of the soap industry's leaders, is a Boston company that bases its soaps, lotions and other products on natural ingredients such as honey, milk and sugar. Head to this bilevel store to stock up on cyclamen- and freesia-scented soap and to sample the company's new makeup and fragrance lines.

Kiehl's
109 Third Ave between 13th and 14th Sts (212-677-3171). Subway: L, N, R, 4, 5, 6 to 14th St–Union Sq. Mon–Wed, Fri 10am–6:30pm; Thu 10am–7:30pm; Sat 10am–6pm. AmEx, DC, MC, V.
Kiehl's is a New York institution; it has called its Third Avenue shop home since 1851. Stop by and sample the company's luxurious face moisturizer, lip balm or Creme with Silk Groom and you'll be hooked for life. The staff is knowledgeable and friendly, and extremely generous with free samples.

L'Occitane
1046 Madison Ave at 80th St (212-396-9097). Subway: 6 to 77th St. Mon–Sat 10am–7pm; Sun noon–6pm. AmEx, MC, V.
Fans of L'Occitane, a 25-year-old line of bath and beauty products made in Provence, flock to this shop to pick up their fix of brick-size soaps, massage balm and shea-butter hand cream. Check the phone book for other locations.

M•A•C
14 Christopher St between Sixth and Seventh Aves (212-243-4150). Subway: 1, 9 to Christopher St–Sheridan Sq. Mon–Sat 11am–7pm; Sun noon–6pm. AmEx, MC, V.
Makeup Art Cosmetics, a Canadian company, is committed to the development of cruelty-free products and is famous for its lipsticks and eyeshadows in otherwise unobtainable colors, particularly its durable, ultrasticky Lipglass. The Queen of New York, drag star Lady Bunny, used to give consultations here; current spokespersons are

RuPaul and k.d. lang. The enormous Soho branch is a bit like an art gallery and features nine makeover counters. **Other location:** *113 Spring St between Greene and Mercer Sts (212-334-4641).*

Make Up Forever

409 West Broadway between Prince and Spring Sts (212-941-9337). Subway: N, R to Prince St; C, E to Spring St. Mon–Sat 11am–7pm; Sun noon–6pm. AmEx, Disc, MC, V.
Make Up Forever, a French line introduced to the United States a few years ago, is popular with women and drag queens alike. Colors range from theatrical, bold purples and fuchsias to muted browns and soft pinks; the mascara is a must-have. Although the line is sold at Barneys and the Pierre Michel Salon, this is the brand's only New York boutique.

Ricky's

718 Broadway at Washington Pl (212-979-5232). Subway: N, R to 8th St–NYU. Mon–Thu 8am–11pm; Fri–Sun 8am–midnight. AmEx, DC, Disc, JCB, MC, V.
Stock up on tools and extras such as Tweezerman tweezers, cheap containers for traveling, empty palettes, odd-shaped cotton swabs (for instance, ones with a flat head) and makeup cases that look like souped-up tackle boxes. Still another draws here are the fake lashes, glitter, nail polish and other trendy items by Mattése, Ricky's in-house makeup line, which offers colors and packaging similar to M•A•C. Check the phone book for other locations.

Saks Fifth Avenue

See **Department stores**, *page 118 for listings.*
While most department stores in town devote their first floors to makeup, Saks Fifth Avenue's selection makes it one of the best. Saks stocks all the brands you'd expect (La Mer, Lancôme, Christian Dior, Yves Saint Laurent, Chanel) and plenty of hip surprises (Nars, Anna Sui, Stila, Bloom, Hard Candy). True, the store's lighting is the worst possible for testing makeup, but there are perks to shopping at Saks, such as free makeovers and incentive buys (spend $50, and you get free cosmetic goodies). Oh, and the occasional Jocelyne Wildenstein sighting.

Sephora

555 Broadway between Prince and Spring Sts (212-625-1309). Subway: N, R to Prince St. Mon–Wed, Sat 10am–8pm; Thu, Fri 10am–9pm; Sun noon–7pm. AmEx, Disc, JCB, MC, V.
Sephora, the French beauty chain that is slowly working its way across America (another one is set to open on Fifth Avenue in late 1999) has given downtown gals a reason to stay put: Sephora has everything. The 8,000-square-foot space looks like the first floor of a department store, but no one is standing behind the display cases (staffers hang back until you choose to seek them out). Fragrance is a big seller here, but the skin-care products and makeup have some calling Sephora "a makeup library."

Shu Uemura

121 Greene St between Prince and Spring Sts (212-979-5500). Subway: N, R to Prince St. Mon–Sat 11am–7pm; Sun noon–6pm. AmEx, MC, V.
The entire fantastic line of Shu Uemura Japanese cosmetics is on hand at this stark, well-lit Soho boutique. Most hit Shu Uemura for its selection of brushes, lipsticks, blushes and eye shadows, but for a real eye-opening experience, check out the best-selling eyelash-curler.

*Beauty call: Cultish **Kiehl's** offers some of the best products for skin, hair and face.*

Eugenia Kim

203 E 4th St between Aves A and B (212-673-9787).
Subway: F to Second Ave. Wed–Sun 2–8pm. AmEx,
DC, Disc, MC, V.
Spotted on the street in one of her own creations, Eugenia
Kim was besieged by shop owners who wanted to sell her
hats. Now, go directly to the source for her funky cowboy
hats, feather cloches and more.

The Hat Shop

120 Thompson St between Prince and Spring Sts (212-
219-1445). Subway: C, E to Spring St; N, R to Prince St.
Mon–Sat noon–7pm; Sun 1–6pm. AmEx, JCB, MC, V.
Linda Pagan isn't a hat designer herself, merely a hat junkie,
and her delightful boutique is a cross between a millinery
shop and a department store. Not only are customers able to
choose among 40 different designers, they receive scads of
personal attention, too.

Kelly Christy

235 Elizabeth St between Houston and Prince Sts
(212-965-0686). Subway: N, R to Prince St. Tue–Sat
noon–7pm; Sun noon–6pm. AmEx, MC, V.
The selection, for both men and women, is lovely, and the
atmosphere is relaxed. Try on anything you like; Christy is
more than happy to help and give the honest truth.

van der Linde Designs

Lombardy Hotel, 111 E 56th St between Park and
Lexington Aves, second floor (212-758-1686).
Subway: N, R to Lexington Ave; 4, 5, 6 to 59th St. By
appointment only. AmEx, MC, V.
Susan van der Linde is the protégée of designer Don Marshall (whose creations graced the heads of Joan Crawford
and Grace Kelly, among others). Her small boutique is akin
to an elegant '30s parlor. There are stunning cocktail hats,
rainwear and polar-fleece wrap hats—alternately very diva
and very ski bunny.

Worth & Worth

331 Madison Ave at 43rd St (212-867-6058).
Subway: S, 4, 5, 6, 7 to 42nd St–Grand Central. Mon–
Fri 9am–6pm; Sat 10am–5pm. AmEx, DC, MC, V.
This is the grandest men's hat shop in the city, where you'll
find the finest Panama hats under the sun and a vast assort-
ment of fedoras.

Flea markets

Although Mayor Giuliani has clamped down on
the number of illegal street vendors working in the
city, you might still get lucky: East Village vendors are persistent, if unreliable. Try along Second
Avenue and Avenue A at night or lower Broadway on weekend afternoons for used clothes,
records and magazines. And when the weather's
nice, there are sidewalk or stoop sales. Although
not as common in Manhattan, stoop sales are held
on Saturdays in parts of Brooklyn (Park Slope,
especially) and Queens. If you have a car, you'll
quickly spot the signs attached to trees and posts;
if not, local papers provide the hours, dates and
addresses. Sidewalk shopping is popular with the
natives, and they're serious, so head out early.
For bargain-hungry New Yorkers, rummaging
through flea markets qualifies as a religious experience. There's no better way to walk off that
two–Bloody Mary weekend brunch than by wan-

dering through aisles of vinyl records, 8-track
tapes, clothes, books and furniture.

Annex Antiques & Flea Market

Sixth Ave between 26th and 27th Sts (212-243-5343).
Subway: F to 23rd St. Sat, Sun 9am–5pm.
Designer Todd Oldham hunts regularly here, as do plenty
of models and the occasional dolled-down celebrity. This
market is divided into several sections: One charges $1, the
rest are free. But at all the sections you'll find heaps of secondhand clothing (some of it actually antique-quality), old-
fashioned bicycles, platform shoes, bird cages, funky tools
and those always-necessary accessories: hats, purses,
gloves and compacts. Don't forget to stop by the vintage
eyeglass-frame stand.

Antique Flea & Farmer's Market

P.S. 183, 67th St between First and York Aves
(212-721-0900). Subway: 6 to 68th St–Hunter College.
Sat 6am–6pm.
This is a small market, but one that's good for antique lace,
silverware and tapestries. Fresh eggs, fish and vegetables
are often also available.

The Garage

112 W 25th St between Sixth and Seventh Aves.
Subway: F to 23rd St; 1, 9 to 28th St.
This two-level indoor garage is a gold mine for the same
type of merchandise sold at the nearby outdoor flea market (*see* **Annex Antiques** *above*), along with the unusual: A pristine '60s map clock was unearthed here not too
long ago at a deep, deep discount. It's heaven, especially
on a cold day. And if you're desperate, there are bathrooms
on the lower level.

I.S. 44 Flea Market

Columbus Ave between 76th and 77th Sts
(212-721-0900). Subway: B, C to 72nd St; 1, 9 to 79th
St. Sun 10am–6pm.
Sadly, this flea isn't what it used to be. New merchandise,
like dried flowers, T-shirts and tube socks, has slowly
pushed out the secondhand wonders. But with more than
300 stalls, you're still likely to find *something*.

Park Slope Flea Market

Seventh Ave between 1st and 2nd Sts, Park Slope,
Brooklyn (718-330-9395). Subway: 2, 3, to Grand Army
Plaza. Sat 9am–6pm.
Keep in mind that the outer boroughs are where the best
deals are. If you don't mind the trip to this picturesque
neighborhood, this is quite a good market; some of the same
vendors who work out of the Soho Antique Fair (*see below*)
hawk their merchandise here—at substantially lower prices.

Soho Antique Fair & Collectibles Market

Grand St at Broadway (212-682-2000). Subway:
J, M, Z, N, R, 6 to Canal St. Sat, Sun 9am–5pm.
This flea market opened in 1992, and although it's smaller
than the sprawling Sixth Avenue market, you just might
walk away with more. Vintagewear, collectible radios, linens
and all manner of kitsch cover a parking lot. There isn't a
huge selection (when the weather's bad, the choice is hit-or-
miss), but prices are fair. Sunday is always best.

Florists

Although every corner deli sells flowers—especially carnations—they usually last just a few
days. For arrangements that stick around a while,
and don't contain baby's breath, check out some
of Manhattan's better florists.

Blue Ivy

206 Fifth Ave between 25th and 26th Sts, fifth floor
(212-448-0006). Subway: N, R to 28th St. Mon–Sat
9am–7pm. AmEx, CB, DC, Disc, MC, V.
Simon Naut, a former chief floral designer for the Ritz-Carlton Hotel, joined forces with graphic artist Michael Jackson to open this upscale floral shop. Arrangements start at $50.

City Floral

1661 York Ave between 87th and 88th Sts
(212-410-0303). Subway: 4, 5, 6 to 86th St. Mon–
Fri 8am–6:15pm; Sat 8am–5pm; Sun 9am–noon.
AmEx, CB, DC, Disc, JCB, MC, V.
City Floral, a full-service florist specializing in exotic flowers and gourmet fruit baskets, is a member of Interflora, a worldwide delivery network.

Elizabeth Ryan Floral Designs

411 E 9th St between Ave A and First Ave
(212-995-1111). Subway: L to First Ave; 6 to Astor Pl.
Mon–Fri 10am–7pm; Sat 10am–6pm. AmEx, MC, V.
Elizabeth Ryan has arranged her shop like one of her gorgeous bouquets, and the results are simply magical. Fork out $25 (or whatever you can afford) for an original bouquet and request whatever you're interested in.

Perriwater Ltd.

960 First Ave at 53rd St (212-759-9313). Subway:
E, F to Lexington Ave; 6 to 51st St. Mon–Fri 9am–6pm;
Sat 10am–6pm. AmEx, MC, V.
Patricia Grimley doesn't believe that white flowers should be reserved for weddings; she loves the pure effect of an all-white arrangement for any occasion.

Renny

505 Park Ave at 59th St (212-288-7000). Subway:
N, R to Lexington Ave; 4, 5, 6 to 59th St. Mon–Sat
9am–6pm. AmEx, MC, V.
"Exquisite flowers for the discriminating" is the slogan. Customers include David Letterman, Calvin Klein and myriad party-givers.

Spruce

75 Greenwich Ave between Seventh Ave South and
Eighth Ave (212-414-0588). Subway: 1, 9 to Christopher
St–Sheridan Sq. Mon–Fri 9am–8pm; Sat 11am–7pm.
AmEx, MC, V.
When those Korean-deli daisies don't cut it, stop by Spruce. An arrangement of roses encircled by a ring of wheatgrass can be whipped up on the premises.

VSF

204 W 10th St between Bleecker and W 4th Sts
(212-206-7236). Subway: A, C, E, B, D, F, Q to W 4th
St–Washington Sq. Mon–Fri 10am–5pm; Sat 11am–
4pm. AmEx, Disc, MC, V.
VSF stands for very special flowers, and very special they are. Dried-flower arrangements, exotic bonsai, miniature topiary and extravagant bouquets are the specialities.

Food and drink

A. Zito & Sons Bakery

259 Bleecker St at Seventh Ave (212-929-6139).
Subway: A, C, E, B, D, F, Q to W 4th St–
Washington Sq. Mon–Sat 6am–7pm; Sun 6am–
3pm. No credit cards.
Customers of this Bleecker Street bakery have included Frank Sinatra, who stopped by for a Sicilian loaf, and Bob Dylan, whose preference is for whole wheat. Tony Zito makes the best Italian bread in the Village, so if you're planning a picnic, this is the place to begin.

Balducci's

424 Sixth Ave at 9th St (212-673-2600). Subway:
A, C, E, B, D, F, Q to W 4th St–Washington Sq. 7am–
8:30pm. AmEx, MC, V.
The Balducci family's grocery store has grown over three generations into a gourmet emporium that offers every luxurious foodstuff imaginable, from exotic fruit and freshly picked funghi to edible flowers and properly hung game. It also sells its own brand of pasta and sauces, preserves and salamis.

Dean & DeLuca

560 Broadway at Prince St (212-431-1691).
Subway: N, R to Prince St. Mon–Sat 10am–8pm; Sun
10am–7pm. AmEx, MC, V.
Dean & DeLuca is consolidating its position as the designer deli. The cheese counter is almost legendary. The uninitiated will be amazed by the range and quality of the stock, but this is the place to come for every kind of gourmet delicacy from raspberry vinegar to pâté de foie gras. This location is the only Dean & DeLuca grocery in the city; check the phone book for Dean & DeLuca café locations.

Foodworks

10 W 19th St between Fifth and Sixth Aves
(212-352-9333). Subway: F to 23rd St. Mon–Fri 8am–
8:30pm; Sat, Sun 11am–6:30pm. AmEx, MC, V.
This is a Flatiron standby for gourmet sandwiches, soups and sushi to go. There's also a nice selection of flowers and Japanese candy.

Gourmet Garage

453 Broome St at Mercer St (212-941-5850).
Subway: N, R to Prince St. Mon–Sun 7am–9pm. AmEx,
Disc, MC, V.
A converted garage full of gourmet goodies, this was the first store in Manhattan to sell fresh food at wholesale prices but in retail quantities. The Starving Artist sandwiches are delish, as is the vast assortment of olives. Check the phone book for other locations.

Grace's Marketplace

1237 Third Ave at 71st St (212-737-0600).
Subway: 6 to 68th St–Hunter College. Mon–Sat
7am–8:30pm; Sun 8am–7pm. AmEx, DC, MC, V.
A schism in the Balducci family (owners of the famous grocery of the same name, see above) caused Grace to move to the Upper East Side, where she has established an admirable food store with a selection of all sorts of fabulous foods comparable to that in the Village store. Her Marketplace is the best bet for one-stop gourmet shopping in the neighborhood, but it is expensive.

Greenmarket

Information 212-477-3220. Mon–Fri 9am–6pm.
There are more than 20 open-air markets, sponsored by city authorities, in various locations and on different days. The most famous is the one at Union Square, on East 14th Street (Mon, Wed, Fri, Sat 8am–6pm), where small producers of organic cheeses, honey, vegetables, herbs and flowers sell their wares from the backs of their flat-bed trucks. Arrive early, before the good stuff sells out.

Guss' Pickles

35 Essex St between Grand and Hester Sts
(212-254-4477). Subway: F to East Broadway. Mon–
Thu, Sun 9am–6pm; Fri 9am–3:30pm. MC, V.
Once upon a time there was a notorious rivalry between two pickle merchants, Guss and Hollander, but eventually it was settled. Guss put his name over the door of the old Hollander store and became the undisputed Pickle King, selling them sour or half-sour and in several sizes. Also excellent are the sauerkraut, pickled peppers and watermelon rinds.

Kam Man Food Products

200 Canal St at Mott St (212-571-0330). Subway: J, M, Z, N, R, 6 to Canal St. 9am–9pm. MC, V.
A selection of fresh and preserved Chinese, Thai and other Asian foods, as well as utensils and kitchenware.

Kitchen Market

218 Eighth Ave between 21st and 22nd Sts (212-243-4433). Subway: C, E, 1, 9 to 23rd St. Mon–Sat 9am–10:30pm; Sun 11am–10:30pm. No credit cards.
This colorful *mercado* sells a small but far-reaching selection of moles, salsas and tortillas, as well as all sorts of Mexican tchotchkes. Other must-have items for a south-of-the-border kitchen include cactus leaves, tomatillos, jicama and a range of fresh and dried chilies.

Li-Lac

120 Christopher St between Bleecker and Hudson Sts (212-242-7374). Subway: 1, 9 to Christopher St–Sheridan Sq. Mon–Fri 10am–8pm; Sat noon–8pm; Sun noon–5pm. AmEx, Disc, MC, V.
Handmade chocolates par excellence are the specialty here.

McNulty's Tea and Coffee

109 Christopher St between Bleecker and Hudson Sts (212-242-5351). Subway: 1, 9 to Christopher St–Sheridan Sq. Mon–Sat 10am–9pm; Sun 1–7pm. AmEx, Disc, MC, V.
The original McNulty began selling tea here in 1895; in 1980, the shop was taken over by the Wong family. Of course, coffee is included in the bevy of stimulants, but the real draw is the tea. From the rarest, the White Flower Pekoe (it's harvested once a year in China and costs $25 per pound), to a simple Darjeeling or a box from Fortnum & Mason, this is a tea haven.

Myers of Keswick

634 Hudson St between Horatio and Jane Sts (212-691-4194). Subway: A, C, E to 14th St; L to Eighth Ave. Mon–Fri 10am–7pm; Sat 10am–6pm; Sun noon–5pm. AmEx, V.
Can't live without Heinz beans, treacle sponge or rice pudding? Hungry for Bovril, Bird's custard or Ribena? Sate yourself at Myers of Keswick, popularly known as the English Shop, a little corner of Coronation Street in the Big Apple.

Raffeto's Corporation

144 Houston St at MacDougal St (212-777-1261). Subway: A, C, E, B, D, F, Q to W 4th St–Washington Sq. Tue–Fri 9am–6:30pm; Sat 9am–6pm. No credit cards.
In business since 1906, Raffeto's is the source of much of the designer pasta that is sold in gourmet shops all over town. The staff sells special ravioli, tortellini, fettuccine, gnocchi and manicotti in any quantity to anyone who calls in, with no minimum order.

Russ & Daughters

179 Houston St between Allen and Orchard Sts (212-475-4880). Subway: F to Second Ave. Mon–Sat 9am–7pm; Sun 8am–5:30pm. MC, V.
This New York institution, founded in 1914, still boasts Sunday-morning lines of loyal customers waiting patiently for the most delicious smoked fish, gefilte fish, herring and whitefish salad in the city. A treasure.

Zabar's

2245 Broadway at 80th St (212-787-2000). Subway: 1, 9 to 79th St. Mon–Fri 8am–7:30pm; Sat 8am–8pm; Sun 9am–6pm. AmEx, MC, V.
By common consensus, this is the best food store in the city and, naturally therefore, the world. Zabar's is not only an excellent delicatessen but a great grocer and a first-class fish shop. The variety and quality of the coffee and the cookies, cheeses and croissants is breathtaking: Sniff the air and you'll understand why Zabar's is heaven.

Liquor stores

Most supermarkets and corner delis sell beer and aren't too fussy about ID, though you do need to show proof that you are over 21 if asked (and don't carry opened alcohol containers in the streets—that's a sure bust these days). To buy wine or spirits, you need to go to a liquor store. Most liquor stores don't sell beer, nor are they open on Sundays.

Astor Wines & Spirits

12 Astor Pl at Lafayette St (212-674-7500). Subway: N, R to 8th St–NYU; 6 to Astor Pl. Mon–Sat 9am–9pm. AmEx, JCB, MC, V.
This is a modern wine supermarket that would serve as the perfect blueprint for a chain, were it not for a law preventing liquor stores from branching out. There's a wide range of wines and spirits.

Best Cellars

1291 Lexington Ave between 86th and 87th Sts (212-426-4200). Subway: 4, 5, 6 to 86th St. Mon–Thu 10am–9pm; Fri, Sat 10am–10pm. AmEx, MC, V.
This wine shop stocks only 100 selections, but each one is delicious and has been tasted by the owners (who tested more than 1,500 bottles). The best part is that they're all under $10.

Sherry-Lehmann

679 Madison Ave at 61st St (212-838-7500). Subway: N, R to Lexington Ave; 4, 5, 6 to 59th St. Mon–Sat 9am–7pm. AmEx, MC, V.
Perhaps the most famous of New York's numerous liquor stores, Sherry-Lehmann has a vast selection of Scotches, brandies and ports, as well as a superb range of French, American and Italian wines.

Warehouse Wines & Spirits

735 Broadway between 8th St and Waverly Pl (212-982-7770). Subway: N, R to 8th St–NYU; 6 to Astor Pl. Mon–Thu 9am–8:45pm; Fri, Sat 9am–9:45pm. AmEx, MC, V.
For the best prices in town for wine and liquor, look no further. Grab a cart, because you'll need it.

Gifts

See **Specialty shops and services,** *page 151.*

Alphabets

47 Greenwich Ave between Charles and Perry Sts (212-229-2966). Subway: 1, 9 to Christopher St–Sheridan Sq. Sun–Thu noon–8pm; Fri, Sat noon–10pm. AmEx, MC, V.
Hilarious postcards, wrapping paper and tiny treasures fill the packed shelves here, together with a range of Josie and the Pussycats T-shirts and offbeat souvenirs of New York. **Other locations:** *115 Ave A between 7th St and St Marks Pl (212-475-7250); 2284 Broadway at 82nd St (212-579-5702).*

Breuklen

355 Atlantic Ave between Hoyt and Bond Sts, Brooklyn (718-246-0024). Subway: A, C, G to Hoyt–Schermerhorn. Tue–Sun noon–7pm. AmEx, DC, Disc, MC, V.
This contemporary design store crops up unexpectedly in the middle of Atlantic Avenue's popular three-block stretch of antiques stores. While the collection isn't limited to any single style, everything—pet dishes, table lamps, tumblers—follows a simple, clean, pared-down aesthetic.

Cobblestones
314 E 9th St between First and Second Aves (212-673-5372). Subway: 6 to Astor Pl; L to First Ave. Tue–Sat 1–7pm; Sun 1–6pm. AmEx, MC, V.
A thrift store of sorts, this wonderful place stocks everything from elegant cigarette holders to antique lingerie and shoes. Gazing into the glass cases filled with bejeweled chokers can take the better part of a day.

Daily 235
235 Elizabeth St between Prince and Houston Sts (212-334-9728). Subway: B, D, F, Q to Broadway–Lafayette St. Mon–Sat 1–8pm; Sun 1–6pm. AmEx, Disc, MC, V.
This store is stocked with stuff you can't possibly need but buy anyway. There's soap, matchbook-size games, condoms, books on photography, voodoo dolls—and that's just a sampling of the goods.

Ether
28 Prince St between Mott and Elizabeth Sts (212-625-3847). Subway: 6 to Spring St. Sun–Fri 1–8pm; Sat noon–8pm. AmEx, MC, V.
Shop under the spell of trippy lighting for glow-in-the-dark pajamas, space-age jewelry, funky calculators and various futuristic gadgets.

Hammacher Schlemmer
147 E 57th St between Third and Lexington Aves (212-421-9000). Subway: E, F to Lexington Ave; 4, 5, 6 to 59th St. Mon–Sat 10am–6pm. AmEx, JCB, DC, Disc, MC, V.
Here are six floors of bizarre toys for home, car, sports and leisure, each one supposedly the best of its kind. It's the perfect place to buy a gift that will permanently attach a smile to anyone's face—especially the electric nose-hair remover.

Love Saves the Day
119 Second Ave at 7th St (212-228-3802). Subway: 6 to Astor Pl. Mon–Sat 1–9pm; Sun 1–7pm. AmEx, MC, V.
This shop has more kitsch toys and tacky novelties than you can shake an Elvis doll at. There are Elvis lamps with pink shades, Elvis statuettes, ant farms, lurid machine-made tapestries of Madonna, glow-in-the-dark crucifixes and Mexican Day of the Dead statues.

MoMA Design Store
44 W 53rd St between Fifth and Sixth Aves (212-767-1050). Subway: E, F to Fifth Ave. 10am–6:30pm. AmEx, JCB, MC, V.
At the Museum of Modern Art's design store, you'll find calendars, glasses, CD racks—you name it—in the most whimsical shapes and colors.

Moss
146 Greene St between Houston and Prince Sts (212-226-2190). Subway: N, R to Prince St. Tue–Fri 11am–7pm; Sat, Sun noon–6pm. AmEx, MC, V.
Insist on the best design for even the most prosaic objects? Murray Moss's emporium features the best of what the contemporary design world has to offer, including stark clocks, curvy chairs and the most witty salt and pepper shakers.

Mxyplyzyk
123–125 Greenwich Ave at 13th St (212-989-4300). Subway: 1, 9 to Christopher St–Sheridan Sq. Mon–Sat 11am–7pm; Sun noon–5pm. AmEx, MC, V.
This West Village store (its name doesn't mean anything, although it's similar to the name of a character from Superman comics) offers a hodgepodge of lighting, furniture, toys, stationery, housewares and gardening items.

*Strung out: Near the legendary Chelsea Hotel, **Dan's Chelsea Guitars** has got the goods.*

Pop Shop

292 Lafayette St between Houston and Prince Sts (212-219-2784). Subway: B, D, F, Q to Broadway–Lafayette St. Tue–Sat noon–7pm; Sun noon–6pm. AmEx, MC, V.

The famed late pop iconographer Keith Haring's art lives on here. The Pop Shop sells T-shirts, bags, pillows and jigsaw puzzles—all emblazoned with Haring's famous cartoony babies.

Shi

233 Elizabeth St between Prince and Houston Sts (212-334-4330). Subway: B, D, F, Q to Broadway–Lafayette St. Tue–Sat noon–7pm; Sun noon–6pm. AmEx, MC, V.

At Shi, which means "is" in Chinese, everything has been selected for its unique design value, from the bullet-shaped hanging glass vases to the Cinzano ashtray.

SonyStyle

550 Madison Ave at 55th St (212-833-8800). Subway: E, F to Fifth Ave. Mon–Sat 10am–7pm; Sun noon–6pm.

For the latest from Sony, including futuristic boom boxes, paper-thin TV screens, innovative earphones and Sony's own VAIO personal computer line (created to interact with other company products), stop by this two-story midtown shop at the corporate headquaters.

Children's toys

Enchanted Forest

85 Mercer St between Spring and Broome Sts (212-925-6677). Subway: 6 to Prince St. Mon–Sat 11am–7pm; Sun noon–6pm. AmEx, DC, Disc, JCB, MC, V.

Browse through this gallery of beasts, books and handmade toys in a magical forest setting.

FAO Schwarz

767 Fifth Ave at 58th St (212-644-9400). Subway: E, F, N, R to Fifth Ave; 4, 5, 6 to 59th St. Mon–Sat 10am–7pm; Sun 11am–6pm. AmEx, DC, Disc, JCB, MC, V.

This famous toy store, which has been supplying New York kids with toys and games since 1862, stocks more stuffed animals than you could imagine in your worst nightmare. There are also kites, dolls, games, miniature cars, toy soldiers, bath toys and so on.

Tiny Doll House

1146 Lexington Ave between 79th and 80th Sts (212-744-3719). Subway: 6 to 77th St. Mon–Fri 11am–5:30pm; Sat 11am–5pm. AmEx, MC, V.

Everything in this shop is tiny: miniature furniture and furnishings for dollhouses, including chests, beds, kitchen fittings and cutlery. Even adults will love it.

Gift deliveries

Baskets by Wire

Call 212-724-6900 or 718-746-1200. Mon–Sat 8am–7pm; Sun 8am–2pm. AmEx, DC, Disc, MC, V.

Fruit, gourmet food, flowers and Mylar balloon bouquets are delivered nationwide.

Select-a-Gram

Call 800-292-1562 or 212-874-4464. Mon–Sat 9am–6pm. AmEx, DC, MC, V.

Create your own gift basket with anything from champagne and caviar to jelly beans, T-shirts and stuffed animals. Nationwide delivery.

Studio stores

Disney Store

711 Fifth Ave at 55th St (212-702-0702). Subway: E, F to Fifth Ave. Mon–Sat 10am–8pm; Sun 11am–7pm. AmEx, Disc, Disney, MC, V.

This is where all your favorite Disney characters come to life (in great quantity)—Mickey, Minnie, Goofy, etc. At the Fifth Avenue store, the largest of them all, you can buy merchandise previously available only by catalog. Check the phone book for other locations.

Warner Bros. Studio Store

1 E 57th St at Fifth Ave (212-754-0300). Subway: E, F, N, R to Fifth Ave; 4, 5, 6 to 59th St. Mon–Sat 10am–8pm; Sun noon–8pm. AmEx, DC, JCB, MC, V.

The outlet for anything and everything that has a Warner Bros. character slapped on it features baseball hats, T-shirts and a few surprises. Check the phone book for other locations.

Hair

Model discounts

Swanky salons free up their $200 chairs one night a week for those willing to become cut or color guinea pigs for trainees. Not to worry—there's much supervision, and the results are usually wonderful. Best of all, it costs a fraction of the usual price. All of the following have model nights, with prices ranging between $10 and $45 (often payable in cash only). Phone for details about their next model night; you may well have to get yourself on a waiting list.

Bumble & Bumble (212-521-6500)
Peter Coppola Salon (212-988-9404)
Frédéric Fekkai Beauté de Provence (212-753-9500)
Louis Licari (212-327-0639)
Oscar Blandi Salon (212-593-7930)
Vidal Sassoon (212-929-9668/212-223-9177)

Salons

In addition to the salons listed above, which all offer superb cuts and color, these salons below are a few NYC standouts.

Glow

36 E 23rd St between Park and Madison Aves, tenth floor (212-228-1822). Subway: N, R, 6 to 23rd St. Tue–Sat 11am–7pm. MC, V.

It's not often that your hair color looks the same inside the salon as it does outside. But it will after a visit to Glow, a salon suffused with natural light. Cuts start at $85, highlights at $125.

Prive

310 West Broadway between Grand and Canal Sts (212-274-8888). Subway: A, C, E to Canal St. Tue–Fri 10am–8pm; Sat 10am–7pm; Sun 11am–6pm. AmEx, CB, Disc, MC, V.

No need to head uptown for luxe locks. Laurent D., famous for tending to the tresses of celebs like Gwyneth Paltrow, scored prime retail space in the Soho Grand Hotel for his first New York salon. Haircuts with Laurent cost $185, with others $90 to $125. Highlights start at $125.

Studio 303

Chelsea Hotel, 222 W 23rd St between Seventh and Eighth Aves (212-633-1011). Subway: C, E, 1, 9 to 23rd St. Tue–Fri noon–8pm; Sat 11am–6pm. No credit cards.
Owned by three ex-Racine stylists, Studio 303 is located in the wonderfully spooky Chelsea Hotel. Haircuts start at $60. Highlights start at $110.

Wardwell Salon

200 W 80th St between Amsterdam Ave and Broadway (212-362-7617). Subway: 1, 9 to 79th St. Tue–Sat 11am–8pm.
Deborah Wardwell gave up a career in magazines to open her own salon. She reserves an hour for each haircut and does color as well; the results are breathtaking. Haircuts start at $70; highlights cost $125 and up.

Ultra

233 E 4th St between Aves A and B (212-677-4380). Subway: F to Second Ave. Tue, Wed, Fri 11am–7pm; Thu noon–8pm; Sat 10am–4pm. Disc, MC, V.
It's no wonder the music industry flocks to Ultra. This tiny salon's anonymous, mint-green storefront has the feel of a low-profile club. Cuts start at $65, color at $50, highlights $125 and up.

Cheap cuts

Astor Place Hair Designers

2 Astor Pl at Broadway (212-475-9854). Subway: N, R to 8th St–NYU; 6 to Astor Pl. Mon–Sat 8am–8pm; Sun 9am–6pm. No credit cards.
The classic New York hair experience. An army of barbers does everything from neat trims to shaved designs, all to pounding music—usually hip-hop. You can't make an appointment; just take a number and wait with the crowd outside. Sunday mornings are quiet. Cuts cost from $11.

Ginger Rose on Bleecker

154 Bleecker St between Thompson St and La Guardia Pl (212-677-6511). Subway: A, C, E, B, D, F, Q to W 4th St–Washington Sq. 10am–8pm.
Similar to Astor; haircuts here start at $10.

Jean Louis David

1180 Sixth Ave at 46th St (212-944-7389). Subway: B, D, F, Q to 47–50th Sts–Rockefeller Ctr. Mon–Fri 10am–7pm.
Things move fast at this chain. Models flicker in and out of view on a television screen. Stylists scurry about in white lab coats. Best of all, a shampoo, trendy cut and blowout can be yours, without scheduling an appointment, for under $30.

Home furnishings

ABC Carpet & Home

888 Broadway at 19th St (212-473-3000). Subway: N, R to 23rd St. Mon–Fri 10am–8pm; Sat 10am–7pm; Sun 11am–6:30pm. AmEx, MC, V.
The selection is unbelievable, and often so are the prices. But this New York shopping landmark really does have it all: accessories, carpeting, linens, antique and reproduction furniture, and more. If you are determined to get cheaper prices, you can trek to ABC's new warehouse outlet in the Bronx (call 718-842-8770 for hours and directions).

Area I.D. Moderne

262 Elizabeth St between Houston and Prince Sts (212-219-9903). Subway: B, D, F, Q to Broadway–Lafayette St. Tue–Sun noon–7pm. AmEx, MC, V.

Area I.D. sells ready-made furniture (think '50s modern) and home accessories but also offers interior-decoration and design services. What sets this store apart from the crowd is that all of its furniture has been reupholstered in luxurious fabrics (Ultrasuede and mohair, for example).

Bennison Fabrics

76 Greene St between Spring and Broome Sts (212-941-1212). Subway: C, E to Spring St. Mon–Fri 9am–5pm. MC, V.
An unusual downtown shop with a classic but innovative range of fabrics silk-screened in England. Prices are steep, but the fabrics—usually 70 percent linen, 30 percent cotton—end up in some of the best-dressed homes in town.

Fishs Eddy

889 Broadway at 19th St (212-420-9020). Subway: N, R to 23rd St. Mon–Sat 10am–9pm; Sun 11am–8pm.
Fishs Eddy sells virtually indestructible, well-priced china that you may also find in your favorite hotel or diner.
Other location: *2176 Broadway at 77th St (212-873-8819).*

Gracious Home

1217 and 1220 Third Ave between 70th and 71st Sts (212-988-8990). Subway: 6 to 68th St–Hunter College. Mon–Fri 8am–7pm; Sat 9am–7pm; Sun 10am–6pm. AmEx, DC, MC, V.
If you need a new curtain rod, place mat or drawer pull—or any other household accessory—this is the place to find it. (They'll even deliver to your hotel at no charge.)
Other location: *1992 Broadway at 67th St (212-231-7800).*

Knoll

105 Wooster St at Prince St (212-343-4000). Subway: N, R to Prince St. Mon–Fri 10am–6pm. AmEx.
Knoll sells classic and contemporary furniture that you'll find in almost every Soho loft.

Portico Home

72 Spring St between Broadway and Lafayette St (212-941-7800). Subway: 6 to Spring St. Mon–Sat 10am–7pm; Sun noon–6pm. AmEx, Disc, MC, V.
Portico features clean, country-chic furniture and bed and bath accessories. Check the phone book for other locations.

Rhubarb Home

26 Bond St between Lafayette St and Bowery (212-533-1817). Subway: B, D, F, Q to Broadway–Lafayette St; 6 to Bleecker St. Mon–Sat noon–7pm; Sun 2–6pm. AmEx, DC, MC, V.
Stacy Sindlinger scouts flea markets and yard sales in Ohio for impeccably battered furniture. Chipped work tables, French Deco mirrors, even a baker's table have all been in her shop at one time or another.

Totem Design

71 Franklin St between Broadway and Church St (212-925-5506). Subway: 1, 9 to Franklin St. Mon–Sat 11am–7pm; Sun noon–5pm. AmEx, MC, V.
Totem offers sleek, one-of-a-kind furniture, lighting and accessories that will blend seamlessly with whatever flea market finds move your apartment. It has several quirky and not-too-pricey accessories to choose from.

Urban Archeology

143 Franklin St between Varick and Hudson Sts (212-431-4646). Subway: 1, 9 to Franklin St; A, C, E to Canal St. Mon–Fri 8am–6pm; Sat 10am–4pm. AmEx, MC, V.
Old buildings saved! Or rather, picked into pieces and sold for parts. From Corinthian columns and lobby-size chandeliers to bathtubs and doorknobs, this store carries refur-

bished architectural artifacts as well as reproductions of popular favorites.

Other locations: *239 E 58th St between Second and Third Aves (212-371-4646); 285 Lafayette between Prince and Houston Sts (212-431-6969).*

White Trash

304 E 5th St between First and Second Aves (212-598-5956). Subway: F to Second Ave; 6 to Astor Pl. Tue–Sat 2–9pm; Sun 1–8pm. MC, V.
After holding a monthly yard-sale event at First Avenue and 4th Street for a while, "white trash" connoisseurs Kim Wurster and Stuart Zamksy opened this popular store, to the delight of those in dire need of Jesus night-lights, Noguchi lamps and 1950s kitchen tables. Great prices.

Wyeth

151 Franklin St between Varick and Hudson Sts (212-925-5278). Subway: 1, 9 to Franklin St; A, C, E to Canal St. Mon–Sat 11–6. AmEx, DC, MC, V.
This Tribeca shop is known for its collection of metal lamps, chairs and tables stripped of old paint, sanded, and burnished to a soft finish, with the hardware nickel-plated.

Personal home-design shopper

Design Find

516-365-4321. By appointment only.
Interior designer Lauren Rosenberg-Moffit claims to know Manhattan like the back of her hand and will escort you on a memorable shopping tour of the city's showrooms, antiques markets and back-alley stores, bringing you discounts of up to 20 percent. Her fee varies according to your needs.

Jewelry

Bulgari

730 Fifth Ave at 57th St (212-315-9000). Subway: N, R to Fifth Ave. Mon–Sat 10am–6pm. AmEx, DC, JCB, MC, V.
Bulgari offers some of the world's most beautiful adornments; you'll find everything from watches and chunky gold necklaces to leather goods and stationery at the recently opened flagship store.

Other location: *783 Madison Ave between 66th and 67th Sts (212-717-2300).*

Cartier

653 Fifth Ave at 52nd St (212-446-3459). Subway: E, F to Fifth Ave. Mon–Sat 10am–5:30pm. AmEx, DC, JCB, MC, V.
Cartier bought its Italianate building, one of the few survivors of this neighborhood's previous life as a classy residential area, for two strands of Oriental pearls. All the usual Cartier items—jewelry, silver, porcelain—are sold within.

Other location: *Trump Tower, 725 Fifth Ave at 56th St, main floor (212-308-0843).*

Clear Metals

72 Thompson St between Spring and Broome Sts (212-941-1800). Subway: 6 to Spring St. Tue–Fri 12:30–6:30pm; Sat 12:30–7pm; Sun, Mon 12:30–6pm. AmEx, Disc, MC, V.
Metalsmith Barbara Klar creates modernist silver forms that are engraved with signs and symbols. Her wedding rings are contemporary and lovely.

Fragments

107 Greene St between Prince and Spring Sts (212-334-9588). Subway: N, R to Prince St. Mon–Fri 11am–7pm; Sat noon–7pm; Sun noon–6pm. AmEx, MC, V.

In a word, Fragments rocks. And we're not just talking diamonds. Over the years, buyers Janet Goldman and Jimmy Moore have assembled an exclusive stable of 35 artists. The jewelers first show their designs (which are never *too* trendy) at the Soho store, before Goldman and Moore sell them to department stores like Barneys.

Kara Varian Baker

215 Mulberry St between Prince and Spring Sts (212-431-5727). Subway: 6 to Spring St. Wed, Thu noon–7pm; Fri noon–5:45pm; Sat noon–7pm; Sun noon–5pm. AmEx, Disc, MC, V.
Kara Varian Baker's store feels more like a New Age living room than like a trendy boutique. Famous for her chunky sterling-silver lockets (about $600), Baker designs classics, such as pearl necklaces, and avant-garde pieces with colorful stones.

Ilias Lalaounis

733 Madison Ave at 64th St (212-439-9400). Subway: N, R to Lexington Ave; 4, 5, 6 to 59th St. Mon–Sat 10am–5:30pm. AmEx, MC, V.
This Greek jewelry designer's work is inspired by his native country's ancient symbols as well as American Indian and Arab designs. Expensive.

L'Atelier

89 E 2nd St between First Ave and Ave A (212-677-4983). Subway: F to Second Ave. Mon–Fri 10am–7pm; Sat noon–6:30pm. AmEx, MC, V.
Everything at this small East Village jewel box is made onsite of precious metals.

Manny Winick & Son

19 W 47th St at Fifth Ave (212-302-9555). Subway: B, D, F, Q to 47–50th Sts–Rockefeller Ctr. Mon–Fri 10am–5:30pm; Sat 10am–4:30pm. AmEx, Disc, MC, V.
Fine jewelry made from precious metals is sold alongside more sculptural contemporary pieces.

Piaget

730 Fifth Ave at 57th St (212-246-5555). Subway: E, F, N, R to Fifth Ave; 4, 5, 6 to 59th St. Mon–Sat 10am–6pm. AmEx, MC, V.
This giant boutique full of glittering jewels would surely make Holly Golightly swoon. Piaget has a diamond (or an emerald) for every girl.

Push

240 Mulberry St between Prince and Spring Sts (212-965-9699). Subway: 6 to Spring St. Tue–Sat noon–7pm; Sun 1–6pm. AmEx, JCB, MC, V.
Karen Karch's charming rings, most of which have diamonds set in simple, narrow settings (and sell for $500–$1,100), make spending two months' salary on an engagement band obsolete. If you're not getting hitched, the store still has plenty to offer.

Reinstein/Ross

122 Prince St between Greene and Wooster Sts (212-226-4513). Subway: N, R to Prince St. Mon–Sat 11:30am–6:30pm; Sun noon–6pm. AmEx, MC, V.
Most of the sleek, handmade engagement and wedding bands at Reinstein/Ross are made with the store's custom alloys, such as 22-karat "apricot" gold. This touch and others make this the jeweler of choice for simple, detail-oriented jewelry fans.

Other location: *29 E 73rd St between Fifth and Madison Aves (212-772-1901).*

Robert Lee Morris

400 West Broadway between Spring and Broome Sts (212-431-9405). Subway: C, E to Spring St; N, R to

Prince St. Mon–Fri 11am–6pm; Sat 11am–7pm; Sun noon–6pm. AmEx, MC, V.
Robert Lee Morris is one of the foremost contemporary designers; his bright Soho gallery is filled with strong, striking pieces.

Ted Muehling

47 Greene St between Broome and Grand Sts (212-431-3825). Subway: N, R to Prince St. Tue–Fri, Sat noon–6pm. AmEx, MC, V.
Ted Muehling creates beautiful organic shapes in the studio behind the store, which sells the work of other artists, too.

Tiffany & Co.

757 Fifth Ave at 57th St (212-755-8000). Subway: N, R to Fifth Ave. Mon–Wed, Fri, Sat 10am–6pm; Thu 10am–7pm. AmEx, DC, JCB, MC, V.
Tiffany's heyday was around the turn of the century, when Louis Comfort Tiffany was designing his famous lamps and sensational Art Nouveau jewelry. Today, the big stars are Paloma Picasso and Elsa Peretti. Three stories are stacked with precious jewels, silver accessories, chic watches, stationary and porcelain. Don't forget your credit cards.

Laundry

Most neighborhoods have coin-operated laundromats, but in New York it costs about the same amount to drop off your wash and let someone else do the work. We recommend **Ecomat** (800-299-2309): It's one of the city's only laundries to use ecologically sound detergents. Check the phone book for the Upper West Side, East Village, Tribeca and other locations and establishments.

Leather goods and luggage

Need more luggage because you bought too much stuff? Before you head for the nearest Samsonite dealer, check out the plethora of shops on Orchard and Canal Streets that sell cheapo luggage. None stand out, but they are good, quick fixes. Other, more expensive options are listed below.

Bag House

797 Broadway at 11th St (212-260-0940). Subway: L, N, R, 4, 5, 6 to 14th St–Union Sq. Mon–Sat 11am–7pm; Sun 1–6pm. AmEx, MC, V.
All manner of bags, from the tiniest tote to something you could stow a small family in, are available here.

Coach

342 E 57th St at Madison Ave (212-754-0041). Subway N, R to Lexington Ave; 4, 5, 6 to 59th St. Mon, Tue, Sat 10am–7pm; Wed–Fri 10am–8pm; Sun 11am–6pm. AmEx, MC, V.
The colorful, butter-soft leather briefcases, wallets and handbags found here are exceptional. This and the 63rd Street (off Madison Avenue) locations are the only Coach stores in Manhattan to stock the company's outerwear collection. Check the phone book for other Coach locations.

Il Bisonte

72 Thompson St between Spring and Broome Sts (212-966-8773). Subway: C, E to Spring St. Tue–Sat noon–6:30pm; Mon, Sun noon–6pm. AmEx, MC, V.
Stylish, tough bags, belts and saddlebags from the famous Florentine company are sold here.

Innovation Luggage

10 E 34th St between Madison and Fifth Aves (212-684-8288). Subway: B, D, F, Q, N, R to 34th St–Herald Sq. Mon–Fri 9am–8pm; Sat 10am–7pm; Sun 11am–6pm. AmEx, DC, Disc, MC, V.
Need a new suitcase? For the newest (but not necessarily chicest) models, stop by Innovation Luggage. This chain carries an enormous selection of top-brand luggage, including Tumi, Samsonite, Andiamo and Dakota. Check the phone book for other locations.

Jutta Neumann

317 E 9th St between First and Second Aves (212-982-7048). Subway: L to First Ave; 6 to Astor Pl. Tue–Sat noon–8pm. AmEx, MC, V.
Neumann designs leather sandals ($140–$325) and bags ($100–$500) as well as belts and jewelry. Haven't you always wanted a leather choker?

Lingerie

Between the Sheets

241 E 10th St between First and Second Aves (212-677-7586). Subway: L to First Ave, 6 to Astor Pl. Tue–Sun 1–8pm. MC, V.
Sylvia Shum stocks American and European brands of bras and panties, along with silk slips, lacy cotton camisoles and teddies. Everything's extra pretty—she knows that many of her clients wear their underthings on the outside.

Enelra

485 E 7th St between First and Second Aves (212-473-2454). Subway: F to Second Ave; 6 to Astor Pl. Sun–Wed noon–8:30pm; Thu, Fri noon–9:30pm; Sat noon–9pm. AmEx, MC, V.
During the 1980s, Madonna was a regular. Plenty of corsets, bras and slinky slips, as well as fluffy marabou mules.

La Petite Coquette

51 University Pl between 9th and 10th Sts (212-473-2478). Subway: N, R to 8th St–NYU; 6 to Astor Pl. Mon–Wed, Fri, Sat 11am–7pm; Thu 11am–8pm; Sun noon–6pm. AmEx, MC, V.
There are too many goodies for the eye to take in at Rebecca Apsan's tiny lingerie boudoir. Customers can flip through panels of pinned-up bras and underpants before making a selection. Once you know what you like, she'll order it for you.

Le Corset by Selima

80 Thompson St between Spring and Broome Sts (212-334-4936). Subway: C, E to Spring St. Mon–Wed, Fri, Sat 11am–7pm; Thu 11am–8pm; Sat noon–7pm; Sun noon–6pm. AmEx, DC, MC, V.
This spacious one-room boutique stocks antique camisoles, Renaissance-inspired girdles and of-the-moment lingerie designers such as Collette Dinnigan.

Lingerie & Co

1217 Third Ave between 70th and 71st Sts (212-737-7700). Subway: 6 to 68th St–Hunter College. Mon–Sat 9:30am–7pm; Sun noon–5pm. AmEx, Disc, MC, V.
Sibling team Mark Peress and Tamara Watkins take a look at your body (and ask a few questions) before they announce their lingerie recommendations.

Religious Sex

7 St. Marks Pl between Second and Third Aves (212-477-9037). Subway: 6 to Astor Pl. Mon–Wed noon–8pm; Thu–Sat noon–9pm; Sun 1–8pm.
Religious Sex is a playpen for the fetishist in all of us. The store carries a nightie with FUCK printed all over it, panties

that are smaller than eye patches and rubber corsets that will all but ensure a dangerous liaison.

Victoria's Secret
565 Broadway at Prince St (212-274-9519). Subway: N, R to Prince St. Mon–Sat 10am–8pm; Sun noon–7pm. AmEx, Disc, MC, V.
There's lots of colored satin and plenty of sales at this lingerie chain. There's always a risk, however, that your boyfriend might have seen your floral-print ensemble before—on another woman. Still, good for a quick fix. Check the phone book for other locations.

Music

Superstores

HMV
57 W 34th St at Sixth Ave (212-629-0900). Subway: B, D, F, Q, N, R, to 34th St–Herald Sq; 1, 2, 3, 9 to 34th St–Penn Station. Mon–Sat 9am–10pm; Sun 11am–9pm. AmEx, Disc, MC, V.
One of the biggest record stores in North America, HMV has a jaw-dropping selection of vinyl, cassettes, CDs and videos. Check the phone book for other locations.

Tower Records
692 Broadway at 4th St (212-505-1500). Subway: N, R to 8th St–NYU. 9am–midnight. AmEx, Disc, MC, V.
All the current sounds on CD and tape. Visit the clearance store down the block on Lafayette Street for marked-down stuff in all formats, including vinyl (especially classical). **Other locations:** *1961 Broadway at 66th St (212-799-2500); Trump Tower, Fifth Ave between 56th and 57th Sts, garden level (212-838-8110).*

Virgin Megastore
52 E 14th St at Broadway (212-598-4666). Subway: L, N, R, 4, 5, 6 to 14th St–Union Sq. Mon–Sat 9am–1am; Sun 10am–11pm. AmEx, Disc, JCB, MC, V.
As enormous record stores go, this one is pretty good. Check out the Virgin soda machine and keep an eye out for dates of in-store performances. Books and videos are available. **Other location:** *1540 Broadway between 45th and 46th Sts (212-921-1020).*

Multigenres

Bleecker Bob's
118 W 3rd St between MacDougal St and Sixth Ave (212-475-9677). Subway: A, C, E, B, D, F, Q to W 4th St–Washington Sq. Sun–Thu noon–1am; Fri, Sat noon–3am. AmEx, MC, V.
Bleecker Bob's is an institution, but unfortunately it has coasted on its reputation for at least a decade. Still, it's the place to go when you really can't find what you want anywhere else.

Etherea
66 Ave A between 4th and 5th Sts (212-358-1126). Subway: F to Second Ave. Mon–Thu noon–10:30pm; Fri, Sat noon–11:30pm; Sun noon–10pm. AmEx, DC, MC, V.
Etherea has taken over the space that used to be Adult Crash. The store is dominated by indie, experimental, electronic and rock records.

J&R Music World
23 Park Row between Beekman and Ann Sts (212-238-9000). Subway: J, M, Z to Chambers St; 4, 5, 6 to Brooklyn Bridge–City Hall; 2, 3 to Park Pl. Mon–Wed, Fri, Sat 9am–7pm; Sun 10:30am–6:30pm. AmEx, Disc, MC, V.
Part of the massive, block-long home-electronics emporium, J&R's record department features box sets, jazz, Latin and popular titles by all the big names.

Mondo Kim's
6 St. Marks Pl between Second and Third Aves (212-598-9985). Subway: 6 to Astor Pl. 9am–midnight. AmEx, MC, V.
This minichain of movie-and-music stores offers a great selection for collector geeks: indie, electronic, prog, kraut, soundtracks and used CDs.
Other locations: *144 Bleecker St between La Guardia Pl and Thompson St (212-387-8250); 350 Bleecker St at 10th St (212-675-8996).*

Other Music
15 E 4th St between Broadway and Lafayette St (212-477-8150). Subway: N, R to 8th St; 6 to Astor Pl. Mon–Thu, Sat noon–9pm; Fri 1–10pm; Sun noon–7pm. AmEx, MC, V.
Excluding the big chains, perhaps the most famous record store in NYC is Other. No other venue has risen to the challenge of late-'90s genremania quite like this joint. Owned by three former Kim's slaves (*see* **Mondo Kim's** *above*), it stocks a full selection of indie, ambient, psychedelia, noise and French pop.

Rocks in Your Head
157 Prince St between Thompson St and West Broadway (212-475-6729). Subway: A, C, E, B, D, F, Q to W 4th St–Washington Sq; C, E to Spring St. Noon–9pm. MC, V.
Along with lots of new and used CDs and vinyl, this basement store has books, snappy Built by Wendy guitar straps and indie Ts.

Shrine
441 E 9th St between First Ave and Ave A (212-529-6646). Subway, 6 to Astor Pl. Sun–Thu noon–10pm; Fri, Sat noon–11pm. AmEx, MC, V.
Located in the former Etherea space, Shrine has purged itself of all traces of indie-electronica sleekness. Although you'll find most of the CD offerings elsewhere, Shrine boasts a terrific folk section.

St. Marks Sounds
16 St. Marks Pl (212-677-2727) and 20 St. Marks Pl (212-677-3444) between Second and Third Aves. Subway: N, R to 8th St–NYU; 6 to Astor Pl. Mon–Fri noon–10:00pm; Sat noon–11pm; Sun noon–9pm. No credit cards.
Sounds, consisting of two neighboring stores, is the best bargain on the block. The eastern branch stocks the catalog; new releases take up the west.

Subterranean Records
5 Cornelia St between W 4th and Bleecker Sts (212-463-8900). Subway: A, C, E, B, D, F, Q to W 4th St–Washington Sq. Sun–Tue noon–7pm; Wed–Sat 11am–8pm. AmEx, MC, V.
"Bleecker Street" is synonymous with "bootlegs," even at this just-off-Bleecker shop, where you'll find semilegitimate recordings.

Venus Records
13 St. Marks Pl between Second and Third Aves (212-598-4459). Subway: N, R to 8th St–NYU; 6 to Astor Pl. Sun–Thu noon–7pm; Fri, Sat noon–11pm. AmEx, Disc, MC, V.
The basement is filled with excellent vinyl—hardcore, country, rock, jazz—and the main floor stocks secondhand CDs. Prices are usually good. It gets crowded on weekends.

*Waxy buildup: Find the latest in hip-hop, acid jazz and reggae at **Fat Beats**.*

Classical

Gryphon Record Shop

*233 W 72nd St between Broadway and West End Ave
(212-874-1588). Subway: 1, 2, 3, 9 to 72nd St. Mon–
Sat 11am–7pm; Sun 12:30–6:30pm. MC, V.*
This solidly classical store, with a sprinkling of jazz and
show music, sells vinyl only.

Dance

Dance Tracks

*91 E 3rd St at First Ave (212-260-8729). Subway: F to
Second Ave. Mon–Thu noon–9pm; Fri noon–10pm; Sat
noon–8pm; Sun 1–6:30pm. AmEx, Disc, MC, V.*
Stocked with Euro imports hot off the plane (nearly as cheap
to buy here) and with fast-flowing racks of domestic house,
dangerously enticing bins of Loft/Paradise Garage classics
and private decks to listen on, Dance Tracks is a must.

OSSOM

*241 Lafayette St between Prince and Spring Sts
(212-343-0532). Subway: 6 to Spring St. Mon–Sat
1–8pm; Sun 2–7pm. AmEx, DC, Disc, MC, V.*
Liquid Sky has expanded its wares (and its space) with
OSSOM (One Sound System One Music). OSSOM is a
shrine to dance music: It features techno, house, drum 'n'
bass and brakes.

Satellite Records

*342 Bowery between Great Jones and Bond Sts
(212-780-9305). Subway: F to Second Ave. Mon–Sat
1–9pm; Sun 2–8pm. AmEx, Disc, MC, V.*
The racks here are a mess, but sort through them and you'll
eventually find every 12-inch you've ever wanted.

Hip-Hop and R&B

Beat Street

*494 Fulton St between Bond St and Elm Pl, Brooklyn
(718-624-6400). Subway: A, C, G toHoyt–Schermerhorn;
2, 3 to Hoyt St. Mon–Sat 9:30am–7pm; Sun
9:30am–6pm. AmEx, MC, V.*
Grooves are the specialty in the block-long basement at Beat
Street; this is the first stop for DJs in search of killer break-
beats and samples.

Fat Beats

*406 Sixth Ave between 8th and 9th Sts, second floor
(212-673-3883). Subway: A, C, E, B, D, F, Q to W 4th
St–Washington Sq. Mon–Thu noon–9pm; Fri, Sat
noon–10pm; Sun noon–8pm. MC, V.*
Hip-hop central: This small store carries a large selection of
the latest in hip-hop, acid jazz and reggae.

Jazz

Jazz Record Center

*236 W 26th St between Seventh and Eighth Aves,
room 804 (212-675-4480). Subway: C, E to 23rd St; 1,
9 to 28th St. Tue–Sat 10am–6pm. AmEx, MC, V.*
Quite simply, it's the best jazz store in the city, selling current and out-of-print records. You can have your purchases
shipped worldwide.

Latin and world

Record Mart/Times Square

*Times Square subway station, near the N and R
platform (212-840-0580). Subway: N, R, S, 1, 2, 3, 9 to
42nd St–Times Sq. Call for hours. MC, V.*

It costs the price of a subway token to get in, but Record Mart stocks the largest selection of Latino and Caribbean music in the city, much of it on vinyl.

Vintage and miscellaneous

Footlight Records
113 E 12th St between Third and Fourth Aves (212-533-1572). Subway: L, N, R, 4, 5, 6 to 14th St–Union Sq. Mon–Fri 11am–7pm; Sat 10am–6pm; Sun noon–5pm. AmEx, DC, MC, V.
This spectacular store specializes in vocalists, Broadway cast recordings, film soundtracks, bossa nova and French pop.

Pharmacists

Boyd's Chemists
655 Madison Ave between 60th and 61st Sts (212-838-6558). Subway: N, R to Lexington Ave; 4, 5, 6 to 59th St. Mon–Fri 8:30am–7:30pm; Sat 9:30am–7pm; Sun noon–6pm. AmEx, DC, Disc, JCB, MC, V.
This 50-year-old pharmacy, boutique and salon stocks the largest selection of hair accessories and eye shadow ever assembled under one roof. It also offers facials, makeovers, manicures and so on. Boyd's has its own cosmetics line, Renoir, which includes all the hot matte shades from the 1960s that are so hard to find.

C.O. Bigelow Apothecaries
414 Sixth Ave between 8th and 9th Sts (212-533-2700). Subway: A, C, E, B, D, F, Q to W 4th St–Washington Sq. Mon–Fri 7:30am–9pm; Sat 8:30–7pm; Sun 8:30am–5:30pm.
One of the grand old New York pharmacies, this is the place to find soaps, creams, hygiene products, over-the-counter remedies, hair accessories, makeup—you name it—from almost any brand under the sun. There's an especially good selection of items by old-time soap and perfume houses.

Duane Reade
224 W 57th St at Broadway (212-541-9708). Subway: B, D, E to Seventh Ave. 24hrs. AmEx, Disc, MC, V.
This branch of Duane Reade—one of New York's biggest drugstore chains—offers an all-night full-service pharmacy. Check the phone book for other locations.

Repairs

Cameras and camcorders

Panorama Camera Center
124 W 30th St between Sixth and Seventh Aves (212-563-1651). Subway: 1, 9 to 28th St. Mon–Fri 9am–6pm; Sat 11am–3pm. AmEx, MC, V.
All kinds of camera and camcorder problems can be solved here, with an eye to speed if necessary.

Computers

Emergency Computer Repairs
250 W 57th St between Eighth and Ninth Aves (212-586-9319, 800-586-9319). Subway: A, C, B, D, 1, 2, 3, 9 to 59th St–Columbus Circle; N, R to 57th St. Mon–Sun noon–midnight. AmEx, Disc, MC, V.
Specialists in Apples, IBMs and all related peripherals, ECR's staffers can recover your lost data and soothe you through all manner of computer disasters. They perform on-site repairs.

Leather

R&S Cleaners
176 Second Ave at 11th St (212-674-6651). Subway: L, N, R, 4, 5, 6 to 14th St–Union Sq. Mon–Fri 8am–5:30pm; Sat 9:30am–3pm. No credit cards.
R&S specializes in cleaning, repairing and tailoring leather jackets. Prices start at $35, and cleaning generally takes about a week.

Clothes

Raymond's Tailor Shop
306 Mott St between Houston and Bleecker Sts (212-226-0747). Subway: B, D, F, Q to Broadway–Lafayette St; 6 to Bleecker St. Mon–Fri 7:30am–7:30pm; Sat 9am–6:30pm. No credit cards.
Raymond's can alter or repair "anything that can be worn on the body." There's also an emergency service; delivery and collection are free in much of Manhattan.

Shoes

Andrade Shoe Repair
103 University Pl between 12th and 13th Sts (212-529-3541). Subway: L, N, R, 4, 5, 6 to 14th St–Union Sq. Mon–Fri 7:30am–7pm; Sat 9am–6pm. No credit cards.
Andrade is your basic—and trustworthy—shoe-repair chain. See phone book for other locations.

Shoe Service Plus
15 W 55th St between Fifth and Sixth Aves (212-262-4823). Subway: E, F to Fifth Ave. Mon–Fri 7:30am–7pm; Sat 10am–5pm. AmEx, MC, V.
This shop is bustling with customers. And no wonder: The staff here will give just as much attention to your battle-weary boots as to your pricey Manolos.

Watches

Falt Watch Company
Grand Central Terminal, 42nd St at Park Ave, third floor (212-697-6380). Subway: S, 4, 5, 6, 7 to 42nd St–Grand Central. Tue–Fri 10am–5pm. No credit cards.
The staff will repair just about any watch.

Shoes

West 8th Street has shoe stores lining both sides of the block between Broadway and Sixth Avenue where you'll find sneakers, boots and designer knockoffs. All the shops sell pretty much the same stuff, so if one doesn't have your size, just stop in the store next door. For shoe repairs, *see* **Repairs,** *above.*

Billy Martin's
810 Madison Ave at 68th St (212-861-3100). Subway: 6 to 68th St–Hunter College. Mon–Fri 10am–7pm; Sat 10am–6pm. AmEx, DC, MC, V.
Founded in 1978 by many-time Yankee manager Billy Martin and ex–Yankee slugger Mickey Mantle, this Western super-store features heaps of cowboy boots in all colors and sizes.

David Aaron
529 Broadway between Prince and Spring Sts (212-431-6022). Subway: N, R to Prince St. Mon–Thu 11am–8pm; Fri, Sat 11am–8:30pm; Sun 11am–7:30pm. AmEx, MC, V.

Want the latest footwear fashions for a bargain? Stop by this shop, which blatantly copies the hottest styles mere weeks after the originals appear in stores.

Jimmy Choo

5 E 51st St at Fifth Ave (212-593-0800). Subway: E, F to Fifth Ave. Mon–Sat 10am–6pm. AmEx, MC, V.
Jimmy Choo, a shoe whiz who opened his first store in London less than four years ago, is conquering America with his year-old shoe emporium. The plush space features Choo's chic boots, sexy pumps and kittenish flats—none of which sell for less than $300.

J.M. Weston

812 Madison Ave at 68th St (212-535-2100). Subway: 6 to 68th St–Hunter College. Mon–Wed, Fri, Sat 10am–6pm; Thu 10am–7pm. AmEx, MC, V.
Weston shoes appeal to such diverse men as Woody Allen, Yves Saint Laurent and the king of Morocco. The beautiful handmade shoes are available in 34 styles. "Westons don't fit you; you fit them," notes Robert Deslauriers, the man who established the Manhattan store. The shop also stocks women's shoes—and they're also expensive.

John Fluevog

104 Prince St between Mercer and Greene Sts (212-431-4484). Subway: N, R to Prince St. Mon–Sat 11am–7pm; Sun noon–6pm. AmEx, JCB, MC, V.
Fluevog is unique, stylish, often outrageous and definitely unmissable.

Manolo Blahnik

31 W 54th St between Fifth and Sixth Aves (212-582-3007). Subway: E, F to Fifth Ave. Mon–Fri 10:30am–6pm; Sat 10:30am–5pm. AmEx, MC, V.
From the high priest of style, timeless shoes in innovative designs and maximum taste will put style in your step.

McCreedy & Schreiber

37 W 46th St between Fifth and Sixth Aves (212-719-1552). Subway: B, D, F, Q to 47–50th Sts–Rockefeller Ctr; 7 to Fifth Ave. Mon–Sat 9am–7pm; Sun 11am–5pm. AmEx, DC, Disc, MC, V.
This well-known quality men's shoe store is good for all traditional American styles: Bass Weejuns, Sperry Topsiders, Frye boots and the famous Lucchese boots, in everything from goatskin to crocodile.
Other location: *213 E 59th St between Second and Third Aves (212-759-9241).*

Robert Clergerie

681 Madison Ave between 61st and 62nd Sts (212-207-8600). Subway: N, R to Lexington Ave; 4, 5, 6 to 59th St. Mon–Sat 10am–6pm. AmEx, MC, V.
The most sophisticated feet in Manhattan make tracks to this little boutique, which carries the full line of this minimalist-minded French shoe and sandal maker.

Sigerson Morrison

242 Mott St between Houston and Prince Sts (212-219-3893). Subway: B, D, F, Q to Broadway–Lafayette St. Mon–Sat 11am–7pm; Sun noon–6pm. AmEx, MC, V.
Stop by this cultish shoe store for delicate but fashion-forward women's styles in the prettiest colors, among them ruby red, shiny pearl, crocodile olive and burnt orange.

Stephane Kélian

158 Mercer St between Prince and Houston Sts (212-925-3077). Subway: N, R to Prince St. Mon–Sat 11am–7pm; Sun noon–6pm. AmEx, DC, MC, V.
Check out this funky French shoe master's latest looks for men and women at his recently relocated Soho boutique.
Other location: *717 Madison Ave at 67th St (212-980-1919).*

Timberland

709 Madison Ave at 63rd St (212-754-0434). Subway: N, R to Fifth Ave; 4, 5, 6 to 59th St. Mon–Sat 9:30am–7pm; Sun noon–6pm. AmEx, MC, V.
The complete American line of Timberland shoes and boots for men and women is sold here. The company's ruggedly elegant apparel is also available.

Tootsi Plohound

413 West Broadway between Prince and Spring Sts (212-925-8931). Subway: N, R to Prince St; C, E to Spring St. Mon–Fri 11:30am–7:30pm; Sat 11am–8pm; Sun noon–7pm. AmEx, MC, V.
One of the best places for the latest in shoe styles, Tootsi carries a wide range of trendy imports for both women and men. Prices for some pairs are tolerable, but beware of the impulse to splurge.
Other locations: *137 Fifth Ave between 20th and 21st Sts (212-460-8650); 38 E 57th St between Park and Madison Aves (212-231-3199).*

V.I.M.

686 Broadway between 3rd and 4th Sts (212-677-8364). Subway: N, R to 8th St–NYU; B, D, F, Q to Broadway–Lafayette St; 6 to Bleecker St. Mon–Sat 10am–8pm; Sun 11am–7pm. AmEx, MC, V.
Sneakers are treated like hit singles here, with a "latest release" display. One of the largest selections of athletic footwear in the city, complete with overhead monorail delivery system. Check the phone book for other locations.

Spas

Feeling frazzled? Pamper your weary body with a visit to a spa. After long days of battling vicious city crowds and being always on the go, you may soon find yourself feeling like a hardened New Yorker. So indulge yourself as they do. Most treatments start at $60, but no matter how ridiculously relaxed you feel afterwards, don't forget to leave a tip (15 to 20 percent).

Anushka Day Spa

241 E 60th St between Second and Third Aves (212-355-6404). Subway: N, R to Lexington Ave; 4, 5, 6 to 59th St. Mon, Sat 9am–6pm; Tue, Thu 10am–8pm; Wed, Fri 9am–7pm. AmEx, MC, V.
To get rid of vacation cellulite, it's best to see a specialist: The body contouring experts at the Anushka Day Spa will reveal more than you ever wanted to know about the horror of cottage-cheese thighs.

The Aveda Institute

233 Spring St between Sixth Ave and Varick St (212-807-1492). Subway: C, E to Spring St; 1, 9 to Houston St. Mon–Fri 10am–7pm; Sat 9am–6pm; Sun noon–6pm. AmEx, MC, V.
The treatments at Aveda are done with the company's popular botanical products. Simple, airy rooms house the treatment facilities, a hair salon and a store.

Avon Centre Spa and Salon

Trump Tower, 725 Fifth Ave between 56th and 57th Sts, sixth floor (212-755-2866). Subway: E, F to Fifth Ave. Mon–Wed, Fri, Sat 9am–6pm; Thu 9am–8pm. AmEx, MC, V.
Your fears of finding an army of door-to-door Avon ladies will dissolve as soon as you enter. This spa offers numerous treatments, but the real draw is the changing area, which houses the most perfect bathroom: thick carpeting, jars of products and glass-door showers.

Away Spa

W Hotel, 541 Lexington Ave at 50th St, fourth floor (212-407-2970). Subway: E, F to Lexington Ave; 6 to 51st St. Mon–Fri 6am–10pm; Sat, Sun 8:30am–7pm.

This stylish spa, which opened in January 1999, offers a range of alternative services (such as the Star of India full-body treatment). But it doesn't skimp on the basics.

Bliss Spa

568 Broadway at Prince St, second floor (212-219-8970). Subway: N, R to Prince St. Mon–Fri 9:30am–8:30pm. Sat 9:30am–6:30pm. AmEx, MC, V.

The trendy, luxurious Bliss Spa is popular for more than just its mighty massages and beautifying facials; the Bliss lounge boasts a famous buffet loaded with fresh cucumbers, chilled water with lemon slices, chocolates and cheese and crackers. It takes weeks to get an appointment, but smart customers know that regular Blissers often cancel, so you may luck out with a day-you-call appointment.

Carapan

5 W 16th St between Fifth and Sixth Aves (212-633-6220). Subway: F to 14th St; L to Sixth Ave. 10am–9:45pm. AmEx, MC, V.

Carapan, which means "a beautiful place of tranquillity where one comes to restore one's spirit" in the language of the Pueblo Indians, offers reiki, craniosacral therapy and manual lymphatic drainage.

Frédéric Fekkai
Beauté de Provence

15 E 57th St between Fifth and Madison Aves (212-753-9500). Subway: N, R to Fifth Ave; 4, 5, 6 to 59th St. Mon, Tue, Sat 9am–6pm; Wed, Fri, 9am–7pm; Thu 9am–8pm. AmEx, MC, V.

It isn't exactly like a trip to France, but the salon is modeled after Fekkai's hometown of Aix-en-Provence. Fekkai is known for its hair services, but the treatments at this upscale oasis are equally delectable.

Georgette Klinger

501 Madison Ave at 53rd St (212-838-3200). Subway: E, F to Fifth Ave. Mon, Wed 9:30am–8pm; Tue, Thu, Fri 9:30am–6pm; Sat 9am–5pm; Sun 10am–5pm. AmEx, MC, V.

One of the best facials in town can be had at this 50-year-old institution.
Other location: *978 Madison Ave between 76th and 77th Sts (212-744-900).*

Soho Sanctuary

119 Mercer St between Prince and Spring Sts (212-334-5550). Subway: N, R to Prince St; C, E to Spring St. Tue–Fri 9am–9pm; Sat 10am–6pm; Sun noon–6pm. AmEx, MC, V.

This women-only spa–yoga studio has a crunchy, feel-good vibe. And *feel-good* is the only way to describe the heavenly treatments given here.

The Spa at Equinox

140 E 63rd St at Lexington Ave, lower level (212-750-4671). Subway: N, R to Lexington Ave; 4, 5, 6 to 59th St. Mon–Thu 9am–10pm; Fri 9am–9pm; Sat, Sun 9am–8pm. AmEx, Disc, MC, V.

Once you make your way through the first-floor gym facilities, head downstairs, where you'll find a candlelit spa. The new vitamin C facial is excellent for keeping skin tight and smooth.

Woodstock Spa and Wellness Center

The Benjamin Hotel, 125 E 50th St at Lexington Ave (212-813-0100). Subway: E, F to Lexington Ave; 6 to 51st St. Mon–Fri 8am–9pm; Sat, Sun 9am–6pm. AmEx, MC, V.

Although the spa is new to Manhattan, it is a branch of an established Long Island retreat. The emphasis is on health, and personal training and yoga are offered in the hotel's fitness center, in addition to spa treatments.

Specialty shops and services

See **Gifts,** *page 142.*

Arthur Brown & Brothers

2 W 46th St between Fifth and Sixth Aves (212-575-5555). Subway: B, D, F, Q to 47–50th Sts–Rockefeller Ctr; 7 to Fifth Ave. Mon–Fri 9am–6:30pm; Sat 10am–6pm. AmEx, DC, Disc, MC, V.

Pens of the world are all on the same page at Arthur Brown, which has one of the largest selections anywhere, including Mont Blanc, Cartier, Dupont, Porsche and Schaeffer.

Big City Kite Company

1210 Lexington Ave at 82nd St (212-472-2623). Subway: 4, 5, 6 to 86th St. Mon–Fri 11am–6:30pm; Thu 11am–7:30pm; Sat 10am–6pm. AmEx, Disc, JCB, MC, V.

Act like a kid again and fly a kite. There are more than 150 to choose from.

Condomania

351 Bleecker St at 10th St (212-691-9442). Subway: 1, 9 to Christopher St–Sheridan Sq. Sun–Thu 11am–11pm; Fri, Sat 11am–midnight. AmEx, MC, V.

Condoms in all shapes, sizes, flavors and colors are sold in this West Village store.

Dan's Chelsea Guitars

220 W 23rd St between Seventh and Eighth Aves (212-675-4993). Subway: A, C, E, 1, 9 to 23rd St. Mon–Sat 11am–7pm. AmEx, MC, V.

Next to the rockin' Chelsea Hotel, this tiny shop has for sale as many great vintage guitars and amps as they can cram in.

Evolution

120 Spring St between Greene and Mercer Sts (212-343-1114). Subway: C, E to Spring St. 11am–7pm. AmEx, Disc, JCB, MC, V.

If natural history is an obsession, look no further. Insects in Plexiglas, giraffe skulls, seashells and wild-boar tusks are among the items for sale in this relatively politically correct store—the animals died of natural causes or were culled.

Frenchware

110 Greene St between Prince and Spring Sts (212-625-3131). Subway: N, R to Prince St. Tue–Sun 11am–7pm. AmEx, JCB, MC, V.

If names like Tintin, Astérix and Le Petit Prince give you a happy jolt, here's a flash: Frenchware, a dazzling den for Francophiles, carries all that loot and a lot more.

Game Show

1240 Lexington Ave at 83rd St (212-472-8011). Subway: 4, 5, 6 to 86th St. Mon–Wed, Fri, Sat 11am–6pm; Thu 11am–7pm; Sun noon–5pm. AmEx, MC, V.

Every board game imaginable is for sale here, guaranteed to leave you alternately intrigued and offended (some are quite naughty).
Other location: *474 Sixth Ave between 11th and 12th Sts (212-633-6328).*

Goldberg's Marine Distributors

12 W 37th St between Fifth and Sixth Aves (212-594-6065). Subway: B, D, F, Q to 34th St. Mon–Fri 9am–6pm; Sat, Sun 10am–4pm. AmEx, Disc, MC, V.

"Where thousands of boaters save millions of dollars" is Goldberg's slogan. Get your marine supplies, fishing gear, nautical fashion and deck shoes here.

Jerry Ohlinger's Movie Material Store
242 W 14th St between Seventh and Eighth Aves (212-989-0869). Subway: A, C, E, 1, 2, 3, 9 to 14th St; L to Eighth Ave. 1–7:45pm. AmEx, Disc, MC, V.
Ohlinger has an extensive stock of "paper material" from movies past and present, including photos, programs, posters and fascinating lists of information on the stars.

Karen's for People & Pets
1195 Lexington Ave between 81st and 82nd Sts (212-628-2312). Subway: 4, 5, 6 to 86th St. Mon–Fri 8am–6pm; Sat 9am–6pm. AmEx, MC, V.
Karen designs and manufactures witty clothing, accessories and even fitted sheets for the dog, cat or canary in your life.

Kartell
45 Greene St between Broome and Grand Sts (212-966-6665). Subway: A, C, E to Canal St. Tue–Sat 11am–7pm; Sun noon–6pm. AmEx, MC, V.
If you think "good plastic" is an oxymoron, a visit to Kartell, which offers furniture crafted from the most durable of substances, will set you straight.

Kate's Paperie
561 Broadway at Prince St (212-941-9816). Subway: N, R to Prince St. Mon–Thu 10:30am–7pm; Fri, Sat 10:30am–8pm; Sun 11am–7pm. AmEx, MC, V.
Kate's is the ultimate paper mill—there are more than 5,000 papers to choose from. It also serves as the best outpost for stationery, journals, photo albums, stamps and more. Check the phone book for other locations.

Lucky Wang
100 Stanton St between Orchard and Ludlow Sts (212-353-2850). Subway: F to Second Ave. Wed–Fri noon–7pm; Sat 1–7pm; Sun noon–6pm. AmEx, MC, V.
Emily Wang and Kit Lee, the duo behind the recent rage for Astroturf-like bags, opened their first showroom and retail space in February '98 (their zany accessories have been sold for years at FAB208, Patricia Field and TG-170). Along with the fuzzy purses and pouches, the stock includes plush vests, pillows, hats and lamps.

Metropolitan Opera Shop
136 W 65th St at Broadway (212-580-4090). Subway: 1, 9 to 66th St–Lincoln Ctr. Mon–Sat 10am–9:30pm; Sun noon–6pm. AmEx, Disc, MC, V.
Located in the Metropolitan Opera, this shop sells CDs, cassettes and laser discs of every opera imaginable. There's also a wealth of opera memorabilia.

Nat Sherman
500 Fifth Ave at 42nd St (212-764-5000). Subway: S, 4, 5, 6, to 42nd St–Grand Central. Mon–Fri 9am–7pm; Sat 10am–6:30pm; Sun 11am–5pm. AmEx, DC, MC, V.
Just across the street from the glorious New York Public Library, Nat Sherman specializes in slow-burning cigarettes, cigars and smoking accoutrements from cigar humidors to smoking chairs. Upstairs is the famous smoking room, where you can test your tobacco.

Paramount Vending
1158 Second Ave at 61st St (212-935-9577). Subway: N, R to Lexington Ave; 4, 5, 6 to 59th St. Mon–Fri 10am–6pm. AmEx, Disc, MC, V.
Looking for a secondhand jukebox or pinball machine? Here's the place.

*Star material: **Jerry Ohlinger's** has memorabilia from all your favorite flicks.*

Pearl Paint
308 Canal St between Church St and Broadway (212-431-7932). Subway: J, M, Z, N, R, 6 to Canal St. Mon–Fri 9am–7pm; Sat 9am–6:30pm; Sun 9:30am–6pm. AmEx, Disc, MC, V.
This artist's mainstay is as big as a supermarket and features everything you could possibly need to create your masterpiece—even if it's just in your hotel room.

Pearl River Mart
277 Canal St at Broadway (212-431-4770). Subway: J, M, Z, N, R, 6 to Canal St. 10am–7:15pm. AmEx, MC, V.
In this downtown emporium you can find all things Chinese, from clothing to pots, woks, teapots, groceries, bonsai, medicinal herbs, bedroom slippers and traditional stationery.

Poster America Gallery
138 W 18th St between Sixth and Seventh Aves (212-206-0499). Subway: 1, 9 to 18th St. Tue–Sat 11am–6pm; Sun 11am–5pm. AmEx, MC, V.
This gallery stocks original advertising posters from both sides of the Atlantic, dating as far back as 1880.

Quark Spy Center
537 Third Ave at 35th St (212-889-1808). Subway: 6 to 33rd St. Mon–Fri 9am–6pm; Sat by appointment only. AmEx, MC, V.
Quark is a little creepy but worth a visit if you're curious or interested in donning some body armor or bugging your ex-spouse's house. For those with elaborate James Bond fantasies.

Rand McNally Map & Travel Center
150 E 52nd St between Lexington and Third Aves (212-758-7488). Subway: E, F to Lexington Ave; 6 to 51st St. Mon–Fri 9am–7pm; Sat 10am–6pm; Sun noon–5pm. AmEx, Disc, MC, V.
Rand McNally stocks maps, atlases and globes, even those from rival publishers.

Other location: *555 Seventh Ave at 40th St (212-944-4477).*

Stack's Coin Company
123 W 57th St between Sixth and Seventh Aves (212-582-2580). Subway: B, Q, N, R, S to 57th St. Mon–Fri 10am–5pm. No credit cards.
The largest and oldest coin dealer in the United States, Stack's deals in rare and ancient coins from around the world.

Waterworks Collection
475 Broome St between Greene and Wooster Sts (212-274-8800). Subway: C, E to Spring St. Mon–Sat 10am–6pm; Sun noon–6pm. AmEx, MC, V.
Given their awkward shapes and sizes, bathrooms can be the hardest rooms to organize. With that in mind, the folks at Waterworks stock an array of items, from secretaries to silver-plated shaving brushes, that make bathrooms livable.

Sports

Blades Downtown
659 Broadway between Bleecker and Bond Sts (212-477-7350). Subway: B, D, F, Q to Broadway–Lafayette St; 6 to Bleecker St. Mon–Sat 11am–9pm; Sun noon–7pm. AmEx, JCB, MC, V.
This is where to come for those pesky in-line skates, as well as a wide range of skateboard and snowboard equipment and clothing. Check the phone book for other locations.

Gerry Cosby
3 Pennsylvania Plaza, inside Madison Square Garden (212-563-6464). Subway: A, C, E, 1, 2, 3, 9 to 34th St–Penn Station. Mon–Fri 9:30am–7:30pm; Sat 9:30am–6pm; Sun noon–5pm. AmEx, Disc, MC, V.
Cosby features a huge selection of official team wear and other sporting necessities.

Modell's
1535 Third Ave at 86th St (212-996-3800). Subway: 4, 5, 6 to 86th St. Mon–Sat 9:30am–9pm; Sun 11am–6:30pm. AmEx, Disc, MC, V.
Modell's sells a comprehensive range of sporting equipment and clothing at competitive prices. Check the phone book for other locations.

Niketown
6 E 57th St between Fifth and Madison Aves (212-891-6453). Subway: N, R to Fifth Ave. Mon–Fri 10am–8pm; Sat 10am–7pm; Sun 11am–6pm. AmEx, Disc, JCB, MC, V.
Every 20 minutes, a huge screen drops down and plays a Nike ad. There are interactive CD-ROMs to help you make an informed shoe choice. Don't scoff: There are 1,200 kinds of footwear to choose from.

Paragon Sporting Goods
867 Broadway at 18th St (212-255-8036). Subway: L, R, 4, 5, 6 to 14th St–Union Sq. Mon–Sat 10am–8pm; Sun 11am–6:30pm. AmEx, Disc, MC, V.
A full line of sports equipment and sportswear is available at this three-floor store. There's a good range of swimwear, surfwear, tennis rackets, climbing gear and shoes.

Tattoos and piercing

Tattooing was made legal in New York only in April 1998; piercing is completely unregulated, so be discriminating, especially if your venue is located on St. Marks Place.

Fun City
124 MacDougal St between Bleecker and 3rd Sts (212-674-0754). Mon–Fri noon–midnight; Sat, Sun noon–2am. Subway: A, C, E, B, D, Q, F to W 4th St–Washington Sq. AmEx, MC, V.
The setting isn't that of a doctor's office, but the folks at Fun City can be trusted. While both locations offer tattoos, piercing is offered only at the MacDougal Street location only.
Other location: *94 St. Marks Pl between First and Second Aves (212-353-8282).*

Gauntlet
144 Fifth Ave at 19th St (212-229-0180). Subway: N, R to 23rd St. Mon–Sat 12:30–7:30pm; Sun 12:30–7pm. MC, V.
A place with unrivaled experience, Gauntlet is where to go if you aren't satisfied with the holes you were born with. A Prince Albert costs $35, though navels, nipples and noses remain the more popular perforations.

NY Adorned
47 Second Ave at 3rd St (212-473-0007). Subway: F to Second Ave. Sun–Thu noon–8pm; Fri, Sat noon–10pm. AmEx, MC, V.
The waiting area of this beautiful store seems more like the lobby of a clean hipster hotel. Along with piercing, Adorned offers tattooing and henna designs.

Venus Body Art
199 E 4th St between Aves A and B (212-473-1954). Subway: F to Second Ave. 1–9pm. AmEx, MC, V.
Venus has been tattooing and piercing New Yorkers since 1993, long before body art became de rigueur. It offers an enormous selection of jewelry to choose from—diamonds in your navel and platinum in your tongue, anyone? Piercings range from $15 to $35, plus jewelry.

Video

Current ID (such as a passport) plus a credit card, and sometimes proof of address, are needed if you want to rent a video from any of the following outlets. American videos are NTSC format and don't work in British or Australian VCRs, which are PAL.

Columbus TV & Video Center
552 Columbus Ave at 86th St (212-496-2626). Subway: B, C, 1, 9 to 86th St. Mon–Fri 9am–7pm; Sat 9am–6pm. AmEx, Disc, MC, V.
All types of VCRs and TVs are available for rent.

Evergreen Video
37 Carmine St between Bleecker and Bedford Sts (212-691-7362). Subway: A, C, E, B, D, F, Q to W 4th St–Washington Sq. Mon–Thu 10am–10pm; Fri, Sat 10am–11pm; Sun noon–10pm. AmEx, MC, V.
Steve Feltes launched Evergreen as a mail-order company, renting and selling videos of independent and foreign films. It grew into a rental business, due to the popularity of its owner and local demand for offbeat titles. Evergreen remains the best place to purchase hard-to-find DVDs and videos, and the staff can order whatever you can't find.

Mondo Kim's
6 St. Marks Pl between Second and Third Aves (212-505-0311). Subway: 6 to Astor Pl. 9am–midnight. AmEx, MC, V ($20 minimum).
If Kim's doesn't have it, no one else will. Kim's stocks more than 7,000 titles and specializes in cult, classic and foreign films. Check the phone book for other locations (FYI, the additional stores are just called Kim's Video).

Tower Video

383 Lafayette St at 4th St (212-505-1166).
Subway: 6 to Bleecker St. 9am–midnight. AmEx, MC, V.
This branch of Tower has the same sort of sensiblity as the
record stores. Tower Video sells and rents pretty much every
type out there: cultural, exercise, theatrical, special interest,
music, the lot.
Other locations: *1961 Broadway at 66th St (212-496-
2500); Trump Tower, 1721 Fifth Ave between 56th and
57th Sts (212-838-8110).*

Weddings and formalwear

So you're planning on getting hitched? In Manhattan? Whether it's a complicated affair or just a
laid-back trip to City Hall, look no further. If you
don't want to buy your outfit for the big day, *see*
Clothing rental, *page 135.* But if Manhattan
isn't where you'll be tying the knot, it's still a great
place to look for what you'll wear on the big day.
For rings, *see* **Jewelry,** *page 146,* for flowers, *see*
Florists, *page 140.* Most bridal shops stock veils,
but if you're in the mood for something different,
see **Hats,** *page 137.*

Bridal wear

Blue

*125 St. Marks Pl between First Ave and Ave A
(212-228-7744). Subway: F to Second Ave, L to First
Ave, 6 to Astor Pl. Mon–Sat noon–8pm; Sun noon–
6pm. AmEx, MC, V.*
This is a must if you're in the market for a wedding or cocktail dress, a fancy suit or just a pick-me-up. And if your size
isn't available, owner Christina Karas will custom-make
whatever style you fancy.

Ghost Tailor

*853 Broadway between 13th and 14th Sts, fourth floor
(212-645-1930). Subway: L, N, R, 4, 5, 6 to 14th
St–Union Sq. By appointment only. Cash only.*
Ghost sells gorgeous, custom-made dresses for brides who
are anything but conventional.

Kleinfeld

*82nd St and Fifth Ave, Bay Ridge, Brooklyn
(718-833-1100). Subway: R to 86th St. By appointment
only. AmEx, Disc, MC, V.*
Kleinfeld, which opened in 1940 as a fur store, is one of the
biggest names in the wedding business, carrying everything
from veils and pumps to gowns.

Legacy

*109 Thompson St between Spring and Prince Sts
(212-966-4827). Subway: N, R to Prince St; C, E to
Spring St. Noon–7pm. AmEx, MC, V.*
Rita Brookoff carries a number of dresses by little-known
designers, including Parisian Stella Cadente.

Pierre Garroudi

*530 W 25th St between Tenth and Eleventh Aves
(212-475-2333). Subway: C, E to 23rd St. 10am–8pm.
AmEx, MC, V.*
This remote area of Chelsea has become a choice neighborhood for designers who want to leave Soho. Garroudi spent
five years there before signing the lease for a new space—
15 times larger than his previous boutique. For the Iranian-
born designer, the space means scads more room for his
signature slinky, low-cut gowns ($1,200 and up) and men's
suits ($1,500 and up).

Other location: *139 Thompson St between Houston
and Prince Sts (212-475-2333).*

Tati

*475 Fifth Ave at 41st St (212-481-TATI). Subway:
S, 4, 5, 6, 7 to 42nd St–Grand Central. Mon–Wed, Fri
10am–7pm; Thu 10am–8pm; Sat 10am–6pm; Sun
11am–6pm. AmEx, MC, V.*
To the French, the name Tati has the same significance
Kmart has in the U.S. But when the discount retailer made
its stateside debut, it took the high road; it's more the caliber
of Kleinfeld. Tati is your one-stop bridal shop; it has everything from ring pillows to gowns.

Vera Wang Bridal House

*991 Madison Ave at 77th St (212-628-3400). Subway: 6
to 77th St. By appointment only. AmEx, MC, V.*
Wang's dresses are lusted-after by America but sold only to
the few who can afford them at her famous boutique.

Wearkstatt

*33 Greene St at Grand St (212-334-9494). Subway:
N, R, 6 to Canal St. Tue, Wed, Fri 11am–7pm; Thu
11am–8pm; Sat 10am–6pm. AmEx, MC, V.*
Hubby-and-wife duo Jonas and Ursula Hegewisch offer off-
the-rack and custom styles with an edge.

Groom wear

Brooks Brothers

*346 Madison Ave at 44th St (212-682-8800).
Subway: 4, 5, 6, 7 to 42nd St–Grand Central. Mon–Wed,
Fri, Sat 9am–7pm; Thu 9am–8pm; Sun noon–6pm.
AmEx, Disc, MC, V.*
This famous men's store is still where prepsters head for
high quality button-down shirts and chinos, but it's also the
place for anyone to buy a classic men's tuxedo. The staff will
almost guarantee it'll last you for decades.
Other locations: *1 Liberty Plaza between Church and
Liberty Sts (212-267-2400); 666 Fifth Ave at 53rd St
(212-261-9453).*

D/L Cerney

*13 E 7th St between Second and Third Aves (212-673-
7033). Subway: 6 to Astor Pl. Noon–8pm. AmEx, MC, V.*
This vintage shop specializes in menswear from the 1940s
to the 1960s, plus new, timeless original designs—for the
swanky groom.
Other location: *222 West Broadway between Franklin
and White Sts (212-941-0530).*

Ceremonies

Civil Marriage Ceremony

City Hall (212-669-2400).
To get married in NYC, find your nearest municipal wedding chapel by calling the number above. (In Manhattan, it's
the Municipal Building at 1 Centre Street.) You'll need a $30
money order to cover the marriage license. You can get married after 24 hours. The ceremony costs $25, and you don't
need a blood test.

Judges

You can reach the Honorable Howard Goldfluss, who once
appeared on Geraldo Rivera's show, at 718-884-4239. If the
waiting list too long, phone 212-417-4434 for a list of former judges willing to perform wedding ceremonies.

Marcy Blum & Associates

212-688-3057
This international wedding consultant will arrange every
last detail for people who want a romantic experience without the traditional complications.

Restaurants

Chow, Manhattan: When you savor New York, you taste the whole world

Listen to New Yorkers talk about the restaurants they love, and you'll hear something more than just individual taste and habit, or civic pride. Like everything else in this city, dining out is part spectacle and sport, part protected solace. More than in most cities, restaurants are central to everyday life here. New Yorkers wear a good deal on their sleeves—mainly because they don't have room in their closets at home—and where you eat has a lot to do with how you like, or can afford, to live. Everyone eats out occasionally; some people do it all the time. To satisfy this voracity there is, famously, all manner of eating to be done in New York; the renowned hot dog competes for attention with the rarefied talents of the best chefs on the planet. Papaya King for lunch; Daniel for dinner.

Newcomers immediately adopt restaurants as their own, while born-and-bred New Yorkers are forever updating their lists as tastes and neighborhoods change. The one rule to enjoyment is to embrace the vastness: the authentic Greek grill in Astoria, the intensely hip downtown spot, whose star will burn out before you have time to tell friends about it; and the midtown joint that somehow escaped the wrecking ball and is still serving steaks to old men who ate there when they were young. New York is a city of unparalleled contrasts, and the best way to experience it is to eat out.

It's as hard as ever to get a table in a restaurant that's hot, but it's also a good idea to call ahead and check if the place that was sizzling last week is still in business. To snare a table at one of the city's premier eateries, you'll often need to reserve weeks in advance (and then get a table at 5:30 or 10pm). Many smaller restaurants and bistros prefer to operate on a first-come, first-served basis, and you may have to wait at the bar. Book ahead, when possible, at all the restaurants listed in the **Celebrated chefs**, **Landmark restaurants** and **Chic** sections below (though it's smart to call any restaurant and inquire about reservations before you make a trip).

While you're in the city, peruse the food columns of *The New York Times* and *New York* magazine. The listings in the Eat Out section of *Time Out New York* are more up-to-date than any annual guide to such a frenetic and constantly changing scene could hope to be. There's also the new *Time Out New York Eating & Drinking Guide 2000,* which lists 2,000 reviews of restaurants

and bars; it's for sale at newsstands for $9.95. And of course, there's the handy pocket *Zagat Survey* ($11.95) for a yearly overview of what restaurant-goers have to say.

During early July, the city proclaims Restaurant Week. Some of its finest establishments offer a prix-fixe lunch, which in 1999 cost $19.99 (many restaurants run the special throughout the summer). It's a great way to sample the talents of chefs who are otherwise unaffordable. Needless to say, you should make reservations well in advance.

Few New York restaurants add a service charge to your bill, but it is customary to double the 8.25-percent local sales tax as a tip. Many small places accept cash only, and some cards—American Express, Visa and Mastercard—are more welcome than others. Ask before you sit down.

As in every other financial transaction in the Big Apple, restaurant customers complain vociferously if they feel that they're not getting a fair deal. Don't be afraid of offending your waiter by moaning, but never withhold a tip.

Prices below indicate the average cost of a main course at dinner, unless otherwise specified.

Celebrated chefs

An American Place

125 E 50th St at Lexington Ave (212-888-5650). Subway: 6 to 51st St; E, F to Lexington Ave. Lunch: Mon–Fri 11:45am–3pm. Dinner: Sun–Thu 5:30–10:30pm; Fri, Sat 5:30–11pm. Average main course: $30. AmEx, CB, DC, Disc, MC, V.
Larry Forgione has expanded his business into a line of jams and a fellow midtown restaurant, the **Coach House** (212-696-1800), but the Place is still the spot to taste the talents of the godfather of new American cuisine. The patriotic premise at this New York institution, which recently relocated to the Benjamin Hotel, is that produce, wine and inspiration need not come from anywhere but home.

Aureole

34 E 61st St between Madison and Park Aves (212-319-1660). Subway: 4, 5, 6 to 59th St; N, R to Lexington Ave. Lunch: Mon–Fri noon–2:30pm. Dinner: Mon–Sat 5:30–11pm. Four-course prix fixe: $65. AmEx, Disc, MC, V.
Few chefs reflect the character of New York better than Charlie Palmer: His French-inspired American cuisine is big and bold, yet utterly sophisticated. Do your best to snare a seat in his duplex townhouse restaurant and savor meaty, pan-seared sea scallops entangled in potato wisps, top-notch wild game and some of the most visually stunning desserts in the city.

*Super Mario: Celeb chef Mario Batali serves superb pasta and other Italian specialties at **Babbo**.*

Babbo

110 Waverly Pl between Sixth Ave and MacDougal St (212-777-0303). Subway: A, C, E, B, D, F, Q to W 4th St–Washington Sq. Mon–Sat 5:30–11:30pm; Sun 5–11pm. Average main course: $20. AmEx, MC, V.
Babbo's soft yellow walls, beautiful flower displays and sun-gulping skylight make it one of the Village's most inviting restaurants. But it's the creative, aggressive Italian cuisine and the top-notch service that really set it apart. Chef Mario Batali (**Pó**, *see page 176*) mans the range while restaurateur Joe Bastianich (**Becco, Frico Bar**, *see* **Felidia** *below*) minds the crowds, keeping the split-level space as smooth as Batali's silky pasta.

Bouley Bakery

120 West Broadway at Duane St (212-964-2525). · Subway: 1, 9 to Franklin St. Lunch: 11am–3pm. Dinner: Mon–Sat 5:30–11pm; Sun 5–11pm. Average main course: $32. AmEx, Disc, MC, V.
One of *People* magazine's "50 Sexiest People," überchef David Bouley is biding his time with this charming bakery-restaurant while preparing to unveil a cooking school, an Austrian eatery and his flagship French restaurant. As for the bakery, don't let the name fool you: Both the French-American food and the prices are very upscale.

Chanterelle

2 Harrison St at Hudson St (212-966-6960). Subway: 1, 9 to Franklin St. Lunch: Tue–Sat noon–2:30pm. Dinner: Mon–Sat 5:30–11pm. Prix-fixe lunch: $35. Prix-fixe dinners: $75, $89. AmEx, Disc, MC, V.
Karen and David Waltuck's elegant but spare space in Tribeca's landmark Mercantile Exchange Building mirrors the restaurant's refined cuisine. If you want architectural fusion creations, go elsewhere, but if you want immaculately prepared modern takes on classic French dishes, such as grilled sea bass or tender rack of lamb, come to Chanterelle.

Daniel

60 E 65th St between Madison and Park Aves (212-288-0033). Subway: 6 to 68th St. Mon–Sat noon–11pm. Three-course prix fixe: $75. AmEx, DC, MC, V.
A native of Lyon, chef Daniel Boulud has won critical acclaim for his ability to elevate classic peasant dishes to haute cuisine. Because of his skill, Daniel is revered as one of the country's finest French restaurants. Last year, the eatery moved to a larger, more opulent space in the renovated former site of Le Cirque, where Boulud used to work. But despite the bigger, renaissance-inspired digs, reservations are still hard to come by. For a slightly more casual take on Boulud's cuisine, try **Café Boulud** (*see* **French**).

Felidia

243 E 58th St between Second and Third Aves (212-758-1479). Subway: N, R to Lexington Ave; 4, 5, 6 to 59th St. Lunch: Mon–Fri noon–3pm. Dinner: Mon–Thu 5–11pm; Fri, Sat 5–11:30pm. Average main course: $28. AmEx, Disc, MC, V.
Lidia Bastianich is considered the mother of authentic Italian restaurant cuisine in New York. At her flagship restaurant—and her more affordable projects, **Becco** (212-397-7597) and **Frico Bar** (212-564-7272)—the menu of hearty dishes is predominantly northern Italian; the recipes were handed down by her Istrian grandmother.

Gotham Bar and Grill

12 E 12th St between University Pl and Fifth Ave (212-620-4020). Subway: L, N, R, 4, 5, 6 to 14th St–Union Sq. Lunch: Mon–Fri noon–2:30pm. Dinner: Sun–Thu 5:30–10pm; Fri, Sat 5:30–11pm. Average main course: $29. AmEx, Disc, MC, V.
Crispy sweetbreads, towering seafood salads, deadly chocolate bread pudding—Gotham's acclaimed take on American cooking is neither meek nor limited to steak and potatoes.

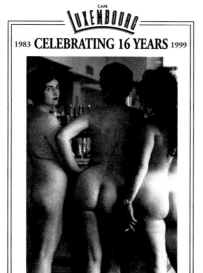

Alfred Portale's tall, architectural concoctions have been imitated all over town, but nothing tastes as good as the real thing.

Jean Georges

Trump International Hotel, 1 Central Park West between 59th and 60th Sts (212-299-3900). Subway: A, C, B, D, 1, 2, 3, 9 to 59th St–Columbus Circle. Breakfast: Mon–Fri 6:30–10am; Sat 6:30am–noon; Sun 8am–3pm. Lunch: Mon–Fri noon–2:30pm. Dinner: Mon–Sat 5:30–11pm; Sun 5:30–9:30pm. Average main course: $35. AmEx, MC, V.

Alsace-born Jean-Georges Vongerichten pulls out all the stops in his immaculate flagship restaurant. The setting is sleek and spare but the service elegant: Waiters present eminently creative food in traditional French fashion, complete with tableside trollies and silver dish hoods. To appreciate the breadth of Vongerichten's skills, also try his Asian fusion fare at **Vong** (212-486-9592), his sophisticated bistro cuisine at **Jo Jo** (212-223-5656) and his Mediterranean tastes at **Mercer Kitchen** (*see page 161*).

Mesa Grill

102 Fifth Ave between 15th and 16th Sts (212-807-7400). Subway: F to 14th St. Lunch: Mon–Fri noon–2:30pm. Brunch: Sat, Sun 11:30am–3pm. Dinner: 5:30–10:30pm. Average main course: $25. AmEx, Disc, MC, V.

Thanks to his imaginative use of traditional Southwestern ingredients (such as blue corn and jalapeños), chef Bobby Flay continues to keep Mesa Grill—and the newer **Mesa City** (212-207-1919) on the short list of perennially popular Manhattan restaurants. Large parties and couples alike will find this high-ceilinged, colorful restaurant inviting and memorable.

Nobu

105 Hudson St at Franklin St (212-219-0500). Subway: 1, 9 to Franklin St. Lunch: Mon–Fri 11:45am–2:15pm. Dinner: 5:45–10:15pm. Average main course: $18. AmEx, DC, MC, V.

The original Nobu is still packed nightly with high-powered New Yorkers and Hollywood honchos (and probably friends of partner Robert De Niro). Welcome the chance to pay through the nose for one of Nobu Matsuhisa's masterful tasting menus, and forget about being satisfied by any lesser sushi ever again. (*See* **Next Door Nobu**, *page 177*.)

Patria

250 Park Ave South at 20th St (212-777-6211). Subway: 6 to 23rd St. Lunch: Mon–Fri noon–2:45pm. Dinner: Mon–Thu 6–11pm; Fri, Sat 5:30pm–midnight; Sun 5:30–10:30pm. Three-course prixe fixe: $54. AmEx, DC, MC, V.

Park Avenue South's restaurant canyon keeps expanding, but the crowds haven't diminished at Patria. They come for the wild nuevo-Latino inventions of chef Douglas Rodriguez: fish and fruit fusion, assorted seafood ceviches, chocolate "cigars"—all in swinging, split-level surroundings.

Landmark restaurants

'21'

21 W 52nd St between Fifth and Sixth Aves (212-582-7200). Subway: B, D, F, Q to 47–50th Sts–Rockefeller Ctr. Lunch: Mon–Fri noon–2:30pm. Dinner: Mon–Thu 5:30–10pm; Fri, Sat 5:30–11:15pm. Average main course: $35. AmEx, MC, V.

The unofficial mess hall of capitalism and a hallowed haunt of old-boydom has a new chef and a few nouveau infiltrators, like Hawaiian snapper tartare with papaya and mango. But toys still hang from the low ceiling, and you can still order chicken hash and the famous burger, which is the size and weight of a newborn. The other traditions of this former speakeasy—the money chatter, swank and cheer—remain as present as the smell of well-prepared sirloin.

Café des Artistes

1 W 67th St between Columbus Ave and Central Park West (212-877-3500). Subway: 1, 9 to 66th St–Lincoln Ctr. Brunch: Sat 11am–2:45pm; Sun 10am–2:45pm. Lunch: Mon–Fri noon–3pm. Dinner: Mon–Sat 5:30–11:45pm; Sun 5:30–10:45pm. Average main course: $28. Prix-fixe lunch: $19.50. Prix-fixe dinner: $37.50. AmEx, DC, MC, V.

Eat at this Upper West Side holdout for the murals of frolicking, naked nymphs and a sense of history, because you'll be served upscale cafeteria food: A couple of roast potatoes, a broccoli stalk and a quarter of fennel thoughtlessly accompanies the dover sole meunière, the calf's liver and pretty much everything else on the menu, but you'll find plenty of pleasant entrées, including roast duckling and sturgeon schnitzel.

Four Seasons

99 E 52nd St between Park and Lexington Aves (212-754-9494). Subway: E, F to Lexington Ave; 6 to 51st St. Lunch: Mon–Fri noon–2:30pm. Dinner: Mon–Fri 5–9:30pm; Sat 5–11pm. Average main course: $39. AmEx, DC, Disc, JCB, MC, V.

The only restaurant in Manhattan to have been granted official landmark status, the 39-year-old, Philip Johnson-designed Four Seasons plays host to power-lunching publishing execs by day and free-spending tourists at night. The tycoons gather in the manly Grill Room amid plenty of leather and steel, while civilians repair to the Pool Room, home to an impressive modern art collection and a large illuminated pool.

Oyster Bar

Grand Central Terminal lower level, 42nd St and Park Ave (212-490-6650). Subway: S, 4, 5, 6, 7 to 42nd St–Grand Central. Mon–Fri 11:30am–9:30pm. Average main course: $25. AmEx, Disc, DC, MC, V.

Back to its original splendor after suffering a fire in 1997, this Grand Central institution serves fine, straightforward seafood under vaulted ceilings. The Oyster Bar can be noisy and pricey (oysters Rockefeller, $14.95), but no experience is more placid and dignified than stopping here after the early dinner rush to be alone with a plate of perfect half shells on ice.

Tavern on the Green

Central Park West at 67th St (212-873-3200). Subway: 1, 9 to 66th St–Lincoln Ctr. Brunch: Sat, Sun 10:30am–3:30pm. Lunch: Mon–Fri 11:30am–3:30pm. Dinner: 5:30–10:45pm. Average main course: $28. AmEx, Disc, MC, V.

Tavern on the Green is one of the prettiest places in the city—think Christmas lights year-round and chandeliers dripping with crystal. The food is notoriously average, no doubt due to the restaurant's enormous size (1,500 meals are served here per night), but the fairy-tale setting is enchanting and romantic. To complete the effect, take a horse-drawn carriage home through the park—but negotiate the price beforehand.

Windows on the World

1 World Trade Center, West St between Liberty and Vesey Sts, 107th floor (212-938-1111). Subway: C, E to World Trade Ctr; 1, 9, N, R to Cortlandt St. Brunch: Sun 11am–3pm. Lunch at bar only: Mon–Fri noon–2pm. Dinner: Mon–Thu 5–9pm; Fri, Sat 5–10:30pm. Average main course: $30. AmEx, DC, MC, V.

Thanks to former '21' chef Michael Lomonaco, Windows finally has food to match its spectacular view. Not that most New Yorkers would know. Perched atop the World Trade Center, the restaurant caters mostly to European tourists who don't mind vertigo from the bill or the hotel-dining-room decor. Still, there's no knocking the heavenly panorama.

Chic

Asia de Cuba

Morgans Hotel, 237 Madison Ave between 37th and 38th Sts (212-726-7755). Subway: 6 to 33rd St. 5:30pm–midnight. Average main course: $20. AmEx, MC, V.

Never mind that Asia de Cuba's Chino-Latino cuisine sometimes misses more than it hits. What matters is that this restaurant is flat-out fun. The kinetic bar scene; the long, lit-from-beneath family-style table; and the hologram waterfall make the bilevel, Philippe Starck–designed space as electric as the sparklers poking out of the Guava Dynamite dessert.

Balthazar

80 Spring St between Crosby St and Broadway (212-965-1414). Subway: C, E, 6 to Spring St. Mon–Thu noon–2am; Fri noon–3am; Sat, Sun 11:30am–2am. Average main course: $20. AmEx, MC, V.

Forget seating hierarchies and canoodling celebrities: This replica of a Parisian brasserie has risen above the hype and settled into its true calling—as a nonstop pleasure ride of early-morning pastries, evening oysters and cocktails, and late-night indulgences. Ironically, as Balthazar mellows, it's becoming more exciting to those who arrive with hungry mouths and stomachs rather than just eyes and egos.

Bond Street

6 Bond St between Broadway and Lafayette St (212-777-2500). Subway: 6 to Bleecker St. Mon–Sat 6–11:30pm; Sun 6–10:30pm. Average main course: $20. AmEx, MC, V.

Perhaps the only thing more attractive than Bond Street's stylish staff is the space itself: three floors of Japanese-inspired design, complete with a candlelit basement-level lounge. In addition to a full bar and a wide array of sake, the cocktail den also offers sublime sushi. In the dining room, expect top-notch Nobu-esque Japanese cuisine.

Bottino

246 Tenth Ave between 24th and 25th Sts (212-206-6766). Subway: C, E to 23rd St. Mon–Sun 6–11:30pm. Average main course: $18. AmEx, DC, MC, V.

Stop searching for New York's most pleasant garden—you'll find it at Bottino. Housed in a former hardware store, this art-world playpen fuses worn-down rusticity, simple Tuscan elegance and a backyard that any villa owner would be proud to call his own.

Clementine

1 Fifth Ave at 8th St (212-253-0003). Subway: N, R to 8th St. Mon–Fri noon–4am; Sat, Sun 5pm–4am. Average main course: $21. AmEx, DC, Disc, MC, V.

If you can stand the mad crush at the bar and the beeping cell phones, Clementine will reward you with some of the more interesting cooking in the city. Ask to sit in the Deco dining room (the front lounge is crowded and smoky) and enjoy John Shenk's boldly flavored creations, such as spicy tuna sashimi and barbecued sparerib salad. Or, come after a night of bar-hopping, and sample Clementine's more affordable late-night menu.

Elaine's

1703 Second Ave between 88th and 89th Sts (212-534-8103). Subway: 4, 5, 6 to 86th St. 6pm–2am. Average main course: $22. AmEx, Disc, MC, V.

Elaine's is the dinosaur of high-society restaurants, and even after all these years, it still pulls in an A-list crowd. The food, though respectable, isn't what counts. What does is the outspoken proprietress, Elaine Kaufman, and a stellar cast of characters that on any given night might include Woody Allen, Barbra Streisand or George Plimpton.

Restaurant Florent

69 Gansevoort St between Greenwich and Washington Sts (212-989-5779). Subway: A, C, E to 14th St; L to Eighth Ave. 24 hours. Average main course: $10. No credit cards.

After a night of club-hopping in west Chelsea or drinking in the lounges that line the cobblestoned streets of the hip Meatpacking District, stop by Florent—it opened long before the recent rash of trendy nightspots. It's open 24 hours, and the omelettes and frites on its French-bistro menu will help absorb all that beer sloshing around in your gut.

Markt

401 W 14th St at Ninth Ave (212-727-3314). Subway: L to Eighth Ave; A, C, E to 14th St. Mon–Fri 5pm–1am; Sat, Sun 10am–1am. Average main course: $16. AmEx, Disc, DC, MC, V.

If you can squeeze by the packed bar scene at this 4,500-square-foot Belgian brasserie in the heart of the Meatpacking District, enjoy a meal in the rollicking wood-paneled dining room. Sample a hit parade of Belgian staples, including decent pommes frites, fancified waterzooi (a creamy seafood stew), steamed mussels and plenty of Belgian beer.

Mercer Kitchen

The Mercer, 99 Prince St at Mercer St (212-966-5454). Subway: N, R to Prince St. Mon–Sat 8am–midnight; Sun 6–11pm. Average main course: $20. AmEx, DC, MC, V.

Just as hard to get into as Jean Georges, chef Vongerichten's new subterranean canteen in the Mercer hotel is, thankfully, substantially softer on the wallet. The menu options run the gamut from an irresistible Alsatian pizza (onion, bacon and fromage blanc) to Maine cod roasted in a fig leaf. The staff, straight from an Obsession ad, rarely smiles. But the dressed-in-black crowd, giddy just to be waiting at the bar, doesn't seem to mind.

Odeon

145 West Broadway between Thomas and Duane Sts (212-233-0507). Subway: 1, 2, 3, 9 to Chambers St. Mon–Thu noon–2am; Fri noon–3am; Sat 11:30am–3am; Sun 11:30am–2am. Average main course: $15. AmEx, DC, MC, V.

More than a decade after appearing on the cover of *Bright Lights, Big City,* Odeon remains one of Tribeca's biggest draws. The large, Deco dining room is always energizing, and the bistro food is always reliable. Jay McInerney might be a relic of the '80s, but Odeon, thankfully, is not.

Pop

127 Fourth Ave between 12th and 13th Sts (212-767-1800). Subway: L, N, R, 4, 5, 6 to 14th St–Union Sq. Mon–Sat 6pm–midnight. Average main course: $25. AmEx, DC, MC, V.

This sceney, industrial-mod restaurant (brought to you by the owner of the Lemon) offers a vaguely Mediterranean menu that sometimes promises more than it delivers. But some dishes—the appetizer of giant shaved clam with seaweed salad and ginger juice, for instance—live up to their billing.

Raoul's

180 Prince St between Sullivan and Thompson Sts (212-966-3518). Subway: C, E to Spring St. 6pm–2am. Average main course: $22. AmEx, DC, MC, V.

The Elaine's of downtown, Raoul's is a time-tested favorite that is constantly packed for dinner. Quirky as only an established joint can be, it has a good bar scene for after-work gallery types and late-night club crawlers. Then there's the dark, romantic dining room, which serves excellent French bistro food—and there's a tarot-card reader upstairs.

Vandam

150 Varick St at Vandam St (212-352-9090).
Subway: 1, 9 to Houston St. Mon–Sat 6pm–2am.
Average main course: $22. AmEx, MC, V.
Manhattan's newest arrival from Planet Balthazar combines
all the familiar ingredients: mirrored banquettes, a buzzing
Wall Street crowd and rich food. Vandam doesn't always hit
the mark, but its menu offers a pleasant Latin-American
twist on French standards. Foie gras is dusted with yucca,
and seared duck breast is coated in tamarind sauce and
served with quinoa.

Waterloo

145 Charles St at Washington St (212-352-1119).
Subway: 1, 9 to Christopher St–Sheridan Sq. Dinner:
Tue–Sun 6pm–2am. Average main course: $15.
AmEx, MC, V.
Located on a serene corner in the far West Village, this minimalist Belgian brasserie is at once soothing and madden-
ing. Because reservations are accepted only for parties of
six or more, expect a long wait at the bar. But when you've
got a big pot of mussels (the best item on the menu) and a
cannister of frites on the table, and the retractable facade
is rolled up to let in a warm breeze, you won't want to be
anywhere else.

Cheap eats

Amarin Cafe

617 Manhattan Ave between Driggs and Nassau
Sts, Williamsburg, Brooklyn (718-349-2788). Subway:
G to Metropolitan Ave, L to Lorimer St. 11am–11pm.
Average main course: $6.50. Cash only.
Amarin's bland decor—beige and Formica everything—is
probably an asset: If the atmosphere were half as enticing
as the food, you'd never get a table. Munch on piquant green-
papaya salad, light and fresh vegetarian pad thai and perfectly seasoned fish cakes—all of which seem to have been
airlifted in from the Gulf of Thailand.

B. Frites

1657 Broadway between 51st and 52nd Sts
(212-767-0858). Subway: 1, 9 to 50th St. Mon–Thu
11am–midnight; Fri, Sat 11am–1am; Sun 11am–
11pm. Frites: $2.50–$4.50. Cash only.
On the surface, B. Frites has all the charm of a McDonald's—
industrial cleanliness, a kitschy logo and a bank of high-
power stainless-steel deep-fryers. But the Belgian-style frites
here, all of which are fried to order, are as crisp, golden and
delicious as any in the city. Best of all are the frite containers themselves: straight-edged cones equipped with built-in
wells for B. Frites' ten mayonnaise-based sauces.

Ecco-La

1660 Third Ave at 93rd St (212-860-5609).
Subway: 6 to 96th St. Lunch: 11:30am–3:45pm.
Dinner: Sun–Thu 4–11:30pm; Fri, Sat 4pm–midnight.
Average main course: $11. AmEx.
The front room at Ecco-La is cheerful, noisy and boldly colorful; the back one is quiet, with gilt-framed pictures and
upholstered chairs. Choose your room according to your
mood and enjoy the simple menu, which offers endless variations of pastas and sauces, most for under $10.

Eisenberg's Sandwich Shop

174 Fifth Ave between 22nd and 23rd Sts (212-675-
5096). Subway: N, R to 23rd St. Mon–Fri 6am–5pm; Sat
7am–4pm. Average main course: $5. No credit cards.
You've got two reasons to stop by this time warp of a
restaurant: its chicken and tuna salads. You won't find a
better version of either anywhere in the city. The narrow,
cramped space looks as though it hasn't changed in 50
years, and so does the staff.

Elvie's Turo-Turo

214 First Ave between 12th and 13th Sts
(212-473-7785). Subway: L to First Ave. Mon–Sat
11am–9pm; Sun 11am–8pm. Average main course:
$5. No credit cards.
This Filipino buffet-style diner caters to hungry New Yorkers from all walks of life. They come for Elvira Samora
Cinco's stews, grills, barbecued pork and seafood—a choice
of two served on a mountain of rice costs just $5.

La Taza de Oro

96 Eighth Ave between 14th and 15th Sts
(212-243-9946). Subway: C, E to 14th St; L to Eighth
Ave. Mon–Sat 6am–11:30pm. Average main course:
$8. No credit cards.
You don't need to be able to speak Spanish to get by at this
Puerto Rican lunch counter. Just remember three words in
English: rice and beans. They simply don't get any better
than this. Don't miss the vinegary avocado salad, either.

Mama's Food Shop

200 E 3rd St between Aves A and B (212-777-
4425). Subway: F to Second Ave. Mon–Sat 11am–11pm.
Average main course: $6. No credit cards.
An instant institution in the East Village, this pint-size
eatery offers a taste of the South, cafeteria-style. Maybe it's
the mother-size portions of mashed potatoes, macaroni,
fried chicken and meatloaf, or the portraits of various
moms on the walls, but the regulars keep coming back for
a dose of comfort.

Mamoun's Falafel

119 MacDougal between W 3rd and Minetta Lane
(212-674-8685). Subway: A, C, E, B, D, F, Q to W 4th
St.–Washington Sq. 11am–1am. Average falafel: $2.50.
No credit cards.
In the heart of New York University territory, this hole-in-
the-wall joint quickly serves up some of the best falafel in
the city. Mamoun's is also one of the few places that has real
shwarma (spit-roasted layers of marinated lamb), instead of
the oversize-hot-dog-on-a-spike known as a *gyro.*

Margon

136 W 46th St between Sixth and Seventh Aves
(212-354-5013). Subway: N, R to 49th St. Mon–Fri
6am–4:45pm; Sat 7am–2:30pm. Average main course:
$7. No credit cards.
Margon is a packed Cuban joint that offers blessed deliver-
ance from the usual midtown lunch hustle. Line up for Cuban
sandwiches, octopus salad, tripe and pig's feet, or soft beef
pot roast—all of it served with great amounts of beans
(black or red) and rice. Sharing tables with strangers is
encouraged, so don't hog the hot sauce.

Panna II

93 First Ave between 5th and 6th Sts (212-598-
4610). Subway: F to Second Ave. Noon–midnight.
Average main course: $5. No credit cards.
At Panna II you'll find an Indian restaurant American-style,
with riotous paper decorations, loud, piped-in sitars and a
typically East Village mix of customers. And the waiters
serve North Indian specialities at a rapid clip.

Pepe Rosso

149 Sullivan St between Houston and Prince Sts (212-
677-4555). Subway: E to Spring St; 1, 9 to Houston St.
11am–11pm. Average main course: $7. Cash only.
This budding chainlet turns out the best kind of Italian cooking: pure, unpretentious and deeply flavorful. Squeeze in
with the scruffy young Italians who come to the Soho branch
with religious regularity, and order an absurdly large plate
of pillowy handmade gnocchi or pungent pesto pasta.
Other locations: *110 St. Marks Pl between Ave A and*
First Ave (212-677-6563); 559 Hudson St between Perry

and W 11th Sts (212-255-2221); 253 Tenth Ave between 24th and 25th Sts (212-242-6055).

Pommes Frites

123 Second Ave between 7th and 8th Sts (212-674-1234). Subway: 6 to Astor Pl. Sun–Thu 11:30am–midnight; Fri, Sat 11:30am–1am. Regular fries: $2.50. Cash only.

It's midnight, you're drunk, and you need fried food: Welcome to Nirvana. Pommes Frites' Belgian-style fries are so good—hot, crispy and salty—that this storefront doesn't sell anything else, except a selection of 28 mostly mayo-based toppings.

Contemporary American

11 Madison Park

11 Madison Ave at 24th St (212-889-0905). Subway: N, R, 6 to 23rd St. Mon–Thu 11:30am–11pm; Sat 5:30–11pm; Sun 5:30–10pm. Average main course: $26. AmEx, Disc, DC, MC, V.

Big enough to house a T. rex, 11 Madison feels a little like a bank: plenty of marble, soaring ceilings and lots of suits. But it's hard to argue with this latest effort from Danny Meyer (Union Square Café, **Gramercy Tavern**, *see below*). Its French-inspired menu, friendly service and superior wine-by-the-glass selection made it an instant player on NYC's restaurant scene. The Indian-inspired **Tabla** is at the same location (*see page 175*).

Avenue

520 Columbus Ave at 85th St (212-579-3194). Subway: B, C to 86th St. 5pm–midnight. Average main course: $14. AmEx, MC, V.

Catering to the neighborhood's stroller-pushing, chino-sporting residents, Avenue hawks food for every mood, hour and price range, from homemade sugared doughnuts to grilled foie gras. Bring your morning paper, Broadway program or toddler and settle in.

Blue Ribbon Bakery

33 Downing St at Bedford St (212-337-0404). Subway: 1, 9 to Houston St. Tue–Sun noon–2am. Average main course: $19. AmEx, DC, MC, V.

Far more than just a bakery, the Bromberg brothers' split-level restaurant rewards you with a wealth of choices—everything from straight-ahead entrées (rack of lamb, striped bass) to a medley of charcuterie-style tasting plates, including sumptuous house-cured sausages, smoked seafood and Mediterranean vegetables. But remember, whether you sit in the upstairs café or in the inviting, brick-lined cellar, prices add up quickly.

Boughalem

14 Bedford St between Sixth Ave and Downing St (212-414-4764). Subway: 1, 9 to Houston St. Tue–Sun 6pm–midnight. Average main course: $16. Cash only.

If Martha Stewart were to open a bistro, it might look something like Boughalem: glossy white walls, candlelit tables, bouquets of narcissuses and a location on one of the West Village's most precious streets. The menu won't throw you many curves (filet mignon, seared sea scallops, etc.), but Boughalem's charm is undeniable.

Cena

12 E 22nd St between Broadway and Park Ave South (212-505-1222). Subway: 6 to 23rd St. Mon–Thu noon–10:30pm; Fri noon–11pm; Sat 5:30–11pm; Sun 5:30–10:30pm. Average café main course: $14; Average main course: $26. AmEx, DC, MC, V.

Even though he recently arrived from Montreal, acclaimed Canadian chef Normand Laprise might already be the most daring toque in town. Savor his jalapeño compote, cara-melized kumquats or licorice-infused duck jus in Cena's airy dining room or relaxed café, and you will wonder why he didn't cross the border sooner.

City Hall

131 Duane St between Church St and West Broadway (212-227-7777). Subway: 1, 2, 3, 9 to Chambers St. Mon–Thu noon–11pm; Fri noon–midnight; Sat 5:30pm–midnight. Average main course: $25. AmEx, MC, V.

A spacious, spit-polish-clean interior decorated with illuminated photographs from the '20s makes this Old New York–style restaurant feel more 57th Street than turn-of-the-century. Nonetheless, its throwback menu is hard to resist: heaps of oysters, made-to-order chowders and a large selection of steaks and chops.

First

87 First Ave between 5th and 6th Sts (212-674-3823). Subway: 6 to Astor Pl. Dinner: Mon–Thu 6pm–2am; Fri, Sat 6pm–3am; Sun 4pm–1am. Average main course: $15. AmEx, MC, V.

You can be fairly certain of two things after dining at First: You will be both drunk and full. Order a round of teeny-weeny martinis (served on a mound of ice in glass beakers), and then indulge in Sammy DeMarco's creative, stick-to-your-ribs food. Hang around the mod-Gothic dining room long enough, and you'll spot many of the city's best chefs stopping by for a late-night snack.

Gramercy Tavern

42 E 20th St between Broadway and Park Ave South (212-477-0777). Subway: 6 to 23rd St. Restaurant lunch: noon–2pm. Dinner: Sun–Thu 5–10pm; Fri, Sat 5:30–11pm. Three-course prix-fixe dinner: $62. Tavern: Sun–Thu noon–11pm; Fri, Sat noon–midnight. Average main course: $16. AmEx, DC, MC, V.

Sitting down to an elegant meal in Manhattan doesn't have to mean dealing with stiff waiters and frosty hostesses. At Gramercy Tavern, the city's most welcoming upscale restaurant, you'll be set at ease by a bright, jovial dining room, a casual bar and relaxed but professional service. And the market-inspired haute cuisine (also available in the restaurant's no-reservations-necessary tavern) will send you into culinary heaven.

Indigo

142 W 10th St between Greenwich Ave and Waverly Pl (212-691-7757). Subway: 1, 2, 3, 9 to 14th St. Dinner: Mon–Thu 6–11pm; Fri, Sat 6–11:30pm; Sun 6–10:30pm. Average main course: $14. AmEx.

Indigo serves delicious French-American cuisine by Scott Bryan, the chef at **Veritas** (*see below*). West Villagers love the bold dishes—like wild mushroom strudel and roast pork loin—and the affordable prices.

Max & Moritz

426A Seventh Ave between 14th and 15th Sts, Park Slope, Brooklyn (718-499-5557). Subway: F to Seventh Ave–Park Slope. Mon–Fri 5:30–11pm; Sat, Sun 11am–11pm. Average main course: $13. AmEx, MC, V.

The pride of Park Slope, this stylish yet relaxed bistro has won a devoted clientele with its exceptional comfort fare, from warm goat-cheese cake to roasted monkfish with spinach puree. In Manhattan, such choices would run $30 an entrée—and you wouldn't be able to get in anyway.

Park View at the Boathouse

Central Park Lake, Park Drive North and E 72nd St (212-517-2233). Subway: 6 to 68th St–Hunter College. Mon–Fri noon–10pm; Sat, Sun 11am–10pm. Average main course: $21. AmEx, MC, V.

Under the stewardship of former JUdson Grill chef John Villa, the Boathouse finally has food to match its idyllic Central Park setting. Escape for a midweek lunch, order the Gulf shrimp rice-paper rolls and watch the ducks float by.

Radio Perfecto

190 Ave B between 11th and 12th Sts (212-477-3366). Subway: L to First Ave. 6pm–midnight. Average main course: $9. Cash only.
Excellent roast chicken, fair prices and an inventive decor make this midsize bistro a welcome addition to Alphabet City's burgeoning restaurant scene. For dessert, try the peanut-butter surprise, a warm, gooey brownie bursting with coconut, chocolate chips and peanut butter.

Rialto

265 Elizabeth St between Houston and Prince Sts (212-334-7900). Subway: B, D, F, Q to Broadway–Lafayette St. 11am–1am. Average main course: $14. AmEx, DC, MC, V.
With curvy red banquettes that look as if they spun off a Tilt-a-Whirl, a magnificent back garden and a sardonic staff, Rialto is a bistro with some bite. Expect a beautiful (and noisy) clientele, but don't expect food for waifs: Rialto's chicken-fried pork chops and creamy garlic soup will help you fill out your leather pants.

River Café

1 Water St at Cadman Plaza West, Brooklyn (718-522-5200). Subway: A, C to High St. Brunch: Sat noon–2:30pm; Sun 11:30am–2:30pm. Lunch: Mon–Fri noon–2:30pm. Dinner: Mon–Sun 6–11pm. Three-course prix-fixe dinner: $68. AmEx, DC, MC, V.
The irony of Manhattan's awe-inspiring skyline is that you have to leave it in order to enjoy it. Hop across the Brooklyn Bridge to this romantic restaurant abutting the East River. In winter, ask for a window table; in summer, enjoy American cuisine in the open air, with the lights of the Brooklyn Bridge and of the looming metropolis shining on your table.

Verbena

54 Irving Pl between 17th and 18th Sts (212-260-5454). Subway: L, N, R, 4, 5, 6 to 14th St–Union Sq. Lunch: Sat, Sun noon–2:45pm. Dinner: Mon 5:30–10pm; Tue–Thu 5:30–10:30pm; Fri, Sat 5:30–11pm; Sun 5:30–9:30pm. Average main course: $25. AmEx, DC, MC, V.
The theme here is flora, from the flowers pressed in glass on the walls to the back courtyard herb garden. Chef Diane Forley's menu relies on the creative use of her homegrown herbs for such dishes as a rolled herb soufflé and butternut squash ravioli flavored with sage.

Veritas

43 E 20th St between Broadway and Park Ave South (212-353-3700). Subway: 6 to 23rd St. Mon–Fri noon–10:30pm; Sat 6–10:30pm; Sun 5–10pm. Three-course prix-fixe dinner: $62. AmEx, MC, V.
The modern decor at this intimate restaurant is on the spartan side, but chef Scott Bryan's food certainly is not. Take your pick from a 1,300-bottle wine list, and savor such hearty but elegant dishes as warm truffled oysters in a creamy Riesling broth and braised veal with baby vegetables and amazingly creamy pureed celery root.

Wild Blue

1 World Trade Center, 107th floor (212-524-7107). Subway: C, E to World Trade Center; N, R, 1, 9 to Cortlandt St. Mon–Sat 5:30–10:30pm. Average main course: $23. AmEx, DC, Disc, JCB, MC, V.
Ignore the badly dressed stargazers who crowd the 107th floor of 1 World Trade Center, and hide at this relaxed American bistro. Like its down-the-hall sibling, Windows on the World, Wild Blue trades on chef Michael Lomonaco's spirited American cuisine and, of course, glittery views of the city. Don't miss the revolving menu specials, like the

wild mushroom–and–oxtail ravioli appetizer, the charred rib steak or the knockout side of mustard-and-honey-roasted young beets.

Delis

Carnegie Deli

854 Seventh Ave between 54th and 55th Sts (212-757-2245). Subway: N, R to 57th St. 6:30am–4am. Average main course: $10. No credit cards.
The decor is unprepossessing and the waiters are infamously rude at this Theater District deli, but the supersize sandwiches, piled high with corned beef and other typical New York deli meats, are worth any visual or emotional distress you may suffer.

Ess-a-Bagel

359 First Ave at 21st St (212-260-2252). Subway: 6 to 23rd St. Mon–Sat 6:30am–10pm; Sun 6:30am–5pm. Plain bagel: 50¢.
Let's talk about what a bagel should be: huge, with a crust that's a little chewy but breaks. There should be no—or almost no—space in the hole. And a thick layer of *plain* cream cheese. At Ess-a-Bagel's original downtown location, the ideal bagel is served by fat-fingered guy who makes dumb jokes. Perfection at 60¢ a pop.
Other location: *831 Third Ave between 50th and 51st Sts (212-980-1010).*

Katz's Deli

205 E Houston St at Ludlow St (212-254-2246). Subway: F to Second Ave. Sun–Tue 8am–10pm; Wed, Thu 8am–11pm; Fri, Sat 8am–3am. Average main course: $8. AmEx, MC, V.
This venerable New York deli, famous for its old-style cafeteria decor and superb salamis and hot dogs, stands at the invisible portals of the Lower East Side. Order a sandwich piled high with thick slabs of pastrami or corned beef; a platter of salami and eggs; or an egg cream, an old-fashioned drink with a misleading name.

Second Avenue Deli

156 Second Ave at 10th St (212-677-0606). Subway: 6 to Astor Pl. Sun–Thu 7am–midnight; Fri, Sat 7am–2am. Average main course: $14. AmEx, Disc, MC, V.
The dwindling number of authentic Jewish delicatessens in town makes this one a mandatory East Village stop; it's been serving since 1954 (but was recently renovated, so it looks brand-new). Soothe your soul with a matzo ball soup, and then embark on a trip down heartburn lane with a hot corned beef sandwich, some knishes and a serving of chopped liver. Prices are a bit steep, but most customers will find the large portions easy to share.

Stage Deli

834 Seventh Ave between 53rd and 54th Sts (212-245-7850). Subway: N, R to 57th St. 6am–2am. Average main course: $15. AmEx, Disc, MC, V.
Famous for its monolithic sandwiches and top-quality deli food, Stage Deli serves much the same menu as nearby rival Carnegie at the same high prices. Visit both and decide which is better. Expect to see many tourists.

Diners

Cheyenne Diner

411 Ninth Ave at 33rd St (212-465-8750). Subway: A, C, E to 34th St–Penn Station. 24 hours. Average main course: $7. AmEx, DC, MC, V.
Cheyenne is the kind of place that cigarette-ad location scouts would give a lung for; it's also a rare piece of the

*Gallic symbol: The irresistibly French **Balthazar** looks like it was Fed Exed straight from Paris.*

heartland in NYC—a silver-sided, pink-neon breadbox of a diner. Brunch specials ($6.95) include juice, fruit salad, coffee and megacaloric helpings of eggs and meat. Indulge, and enjoy the delightfully crappy mise-en-scène of Ninth Avenue.

Comfort Diner

214 E 45th St between Second and Third Aves (212-867-4555). Subway: S, 4, 5, 6, 7 to 42nd St–Grand Central. Mon–Fri 7:30am–11pm; Sat, Sun 9am–11pm. Average main course: $15. AmEx, Disc, MC, V.

This retro diner is inspired by, rather than torn from, the pages of history. The red lights along the wall look as if they were swiped from a Cadillac's tailfin, and the terrazzo tabletops resemble old diner floors. All you really need to know is that this is one of the friendliest spots in east midtown. It's perfect for a cup of joe–and–waffle breakfast, or a memory-jogging bite of grilled s'mores.

Other location: *142 E 86th St at Lexington Ave (212-369-8628).*

Diner

85 Broadway at Berry St, Williamsburg, Brooklyn (718-486-3077). Subway: L to Bedford Ave. Mon–Sat 11am–midnight; Sun 11am–10:30pm. Average main course: $10. Cash only.

As if Williamsburg weren't hip enough, this 72-year-old dining car gives you one more reason to bail on Manhattan. Run by a couple of former bartenders from Balthazar and Odeon, Diner doles out moules frites, martinis and—true to its name—late-night burgers.

Empire Diner

210 Tenth Ave at 22nd St (212-243-2736). Subway: C, E to 23rd St. 24 hours; closed Mon 4am–Tue 8am. Average main course: $10. AmEx, Disc, MC, V.

This west Chelsea all-nighter is the essence of preserved Americana. Come at night, when the place glows, and sample some above-average diner fare. At 3am, everything tastes fine and a little illicit. It's a shame the rest of the city isn't like this—shiny and as edgily smooth as early Tom Waits.

Jones Diner

371 Lafayette St at Great Jones St (212-673-3577). Subway: 6 to Astor Pl. Mon–Sat 6am–6pm. Average main course: $6. No credit cards.

This brick-and-aluminium shanty has been on this corner for 80 years and, fortunately, shows every bit of it. Though the dingy facade keeps newcomers away, the craggy regulars are devoted to the basic and ultracheap sandwiches, breakfast specials and burgers.

M&G Soul Food Diner

383 W 125th St at Morningside Ave (212-864-7326). Subway: B, C to 116th St. 24 hours. Average main course: $9. No credit cards.

Who doesn't order fried chicken just for the crispy coating? At this Harlem diner, the chicken pieces are almost more deeply seasoned crust than meat—which is a good thing. Sit at the Formica-topped counter, and soon you'll be swaying to the jukebox tunes of Marvin Gaye and Curtis Mayfield.

Moondance

80 Sixth Ave between Grand and Canal Sts (212-226-1191). Subway: A, C, E to Canal St. Mon–Fri

8:30am–11pm; Sat, Sun 24 hours. Average main course: $9. AmEx, Disc, MC, V.
Here, the good, cheap diner specials come with a retro New Wave vibe. The best deal in the house is the appetizer for two: a cholesterol jackpot of fried onion rings, chicken fingers, mozzarella sticks and potato pancakes ($6.75). Look for the young things on rock & roll budgets who gather here, droopy-eyed, on Saturday mornings.

Tom's Restaurant
2880 Broadway at 112th St (212-864-6137). Subway: 1, 9 to 110th St–Cathedral Pkwy. Mon–Wed, Sun 6am–1:30am; Thu–Sat 24 hours. Average main course: $7. No credit cards.
Columbia University students come to this diner on a weekly, if not daily, basis for the grilled cheese sandwiches, hamburgers, fries and milk shakes. Suzanne Vega sang about it, and the characters on *Seinfeld* used it as the seat for all their neurotic get-togethers (an exterior shot of Tom's preceded all diner scenes).

Southern

Charles' Southern Style Kitchen
2841 Frederick Douglass Blvd between 151st and 152nd Sts (212-926-4313). Subway: A, C, B, D to 155th St. Mon 6pm–midnight; Tue–Sat 4pm–4am; Sun 1–8pm. Average main course: $7. AmEx, MC, V.
Buttressed by an all-you-can-eat-buffet dining room, this fluorescent-lit take-out sells the best fried chicken in New York, hands down. Marinated for eight hours and then dunked in an oil-filled cast-iron skillet, the intensely crunchy and well-seasoned poultry proves that the South ain't got nothing on Harlem.

Great Jones Café
54 Great Jones St between Bowery and Lafayette St (212-674-9304). Subway: 6 to Bleecker St. Brunch: Sat, Sun 11:30am–4pm. Dinner: Mon–Thu 5pm–midnight; Fri, Sat 5pm–1am. Average main course: $8. No credit cards.
Tiny but easy to spot by its bright-orange exterior and bust of Elvis in the front window, Great Jones is one of the best Cajun restaurants in the city. The basic menu is small and painted on the wall; the changing specials almost always include some kind of catfish and a po'boy (French-bread sandwich) or two.

The Hog Pit
22 Ninth Ave at 13th St (212-604-0092). Subway: A, C, E to 14th St. Tue–Sun 5–11pm. Average main course: $12. AmEx, MC, V.
This honky-tonk eatery in the Meatpacking District feels like a sleepy roadside bar in the middle of the South: Cow skulls adorn the walls, Hank Williams Jr. plays on the juke, and an American flag hangs over a window. The belt-loosening soul food—including golden-brown hush puppies and excellent chicken-fried steak—is just as down-home.

Justin's
31 W 21st St between Fifth and Sixth Aves (212-352-0599). Subway: F to 23rd St. Mon–Sat 5:30pm–midnight; Sun 5:30–11pm. Average main course: $23. AmEx, Disc, MC, V.
These days, it seems that anything Sean "Puffy" Combs touches turns to gold. The rap impresario helped open this slick, new Southern-style hot spot (he's a managing partner), and so far, so good. The food—such as smothered chicken livers and fried chicken with waffles—is surprisingly yummy, but the real reason to come is to rub shoulders with Puff Daddy and other rap-world players.

Mekka
14 Ave A between Houston and 2nd Sts (212-475-8500). Subway: F to Second Ave. Brunch: Sun noon–3:30pm. Dinner: Sun–Thu 5:30–11pm; Fri, Sat 5:30pm–2am. Average main course: $13. AmEx, DC, MC, V.
Mekka has got a chic clientele, a nightclub vibe and a DJ who starts at 10pm on weekends. The hip-hop and Caribbean music go perfectly with the food—a combo of traditional soul food and island references. Sit in the back garden and wash down your barbecued pork and po'boys with a Mambo beer.

Pink Tea Cup
42 Grove St between Bedford and Bleecker Sts (212-807-6755). Subway: 1, 9 to Christopher St–Sheridan Sq. Sun–Thu 8am–midnight; Fri, Sat 8am–1am. Average main course: $12. No credit cards.
Within these pink West Village walls is a charmingly intimate restaurant that's a hot spot for brunch. There will most certainly be a line on weekends; use the wait as an opportunity to decide whether you want grilled pork chops or fried chicken with your pancakes.

Sylvia's
328 Lenox Ave between 126th and 127th Sts (212-996-0660). Subway: 2, 3 to 125th St. Mon–Sat 7:30am–10:30pm; Sun 12:30–7pm. Average main course: $11. AmEx, Disc, MC, V.
Harlem's most famous dining spot has become a bit touristy (tour buses wait patiently outside the place). But no matter; the ribs are still tender, sweet and way ahead of any downtown contenders, and the collard greens would sate any Southerner.

Virgil's Real BBQ
152 W 45th St between Broadway and Sixth Ave (212-921-9494). Subway: N, R, S, 1, 2, 3, 9, 7 to 42nd St–Times Sq. Sun 11:30am–10pm; Mon 11:30am–11pm; Tue–Sat 11:30am–midnight. Average main course: $15. AmEx, MC, V.
A two-story barbecue emporium, this always-mobbed Times Square restaurant serves the best smoked spareribs, brisket and pulled pork in Manhattan. Bring a monstrous appetite, and Virgil's will take care of the rest. For all those staying in midtown hotels: Virgil's has take-out.

Seafood

Aquagrill
210 Spring St at Sixth Ave (212-274-0505). Subway: C, E to Spring St. Brunch: Sat, Sun noon–4pm. Lunch: Mon–Fri noon–3pm. Dinner: Mon–Thu 6–10:30pm; Fri, Sat 6–11:45pm; Sun 6–10:30pm. Average main course: $22. AmEx, MC, V.
A primary fixture in Soho's world of the raw and the booked, Aquagrill is distinguished by location and extremely fresh aquatic fare. A briny-to-creamy range of oysters is shipped in every day, from locations as far away as Chile and Japan.

Blue Water Grill
31 Union Sq West at 16th St (212-675-9500). Subway: L, N, R, 4, 5, 6 to 14th St–Union Sq. Mon–Thu 11am–12:30am; Fri, Sat 11am–1am; Sun 11am–11pm. Average main course: $20. AmEx, MC, V.
Like Banana Republic, this cavernous, marbled restaurant (housed in a former bank) appeals to a young, attractive clientele in search of something stylish but not too daring. Sample the wide selection of fresh oysters and nicely prepared fish entrées, and soak up the dining room's incessant buzz.

Estiatorio Milos

*125 W 55th St between Sixth and Seventh Aves
(212-245-7400). Subway: B, D, E to Seventh Ave. Lunch:
Mon–Fri noon–3:15pm. Dinner: Mon–Sat 5:30pm–
midnight; Sun 5–10:45pm. Average main course: $45.
AmEx, MC, V.*

At this chic Greek seafood restaurant in musty midtown, fish is not ordered; it is chosen, market-style, from the mountains of ice in the back of this soaring space and then paid for by the pound. The easygoing, attentive staff and big round tables of happy Greek-Americans make for a boisterous evening. Go with a group and share a red snapper, some delicate pompano and exotic Mediterranean sea bass.

Johnny's Reef

*2 City Island Ave at Belden's Point, City Island, Bronx
(718-885-2086). Travel: 6 to Pelham Bay Park,
then Bx29 bus to City Island. Sun–Thu 11am–
midnight; Fri, Sat 11am–1am. Average main course:
$10. No credit cards.*

This cheapo fry-fest is one of the best ways to take part in a central ritual of New York life—constantly planning to escape, but never going very far. City Island feels like a sleepy shoreside vacation spot, but it's accessible by mass transit. The main drag is lined with clam shacks, but go to the end, to Johnny's, for all manner of fried sea life, which you eat outside among the throng of locals and low-circling seagulls.

Le Bernardin

*155 W 51st St between Sixth and Seventh Aves
(212-489-1515). Subway: B, D, F, Q to 47–50th Sts–
Rockefeller Ctr. Lunch: Mon–Fri noon–2:30pm. Dinner:
Mon 6–10:30pm; Tue–Thu 5:30–10:30pm; Sat, Sun
5:30–11pm. Average main course: $42 lunch, $70
dinner. AmEx, Disc, MC, V.*

The unimpressive corporate decor matters little at this midtowner—especially once you've sat down and had some of the best fish you've ever tasted. Chef Eric Ripert dazzles with appetizers such as escabèche of chilled baby oysters and entrées like the whole red snapper baked in a rosemary-and-thyme salt crust (which you must order 24 hours in advance, s'il vous plaît).

Lundy Bros.

*1901 Emmons Ave at Ocean Ave, Sheepshead Bay,
Brooklyn (718-743-0022). Subway: D, Q to Sheepshead
Bay. Brunch: Sun 11am–2pm. Lunch: Mon–Sat
noon–3:15pm. Dinner: Mon–Thu 5–10pm; Fri, Sat
5pm–midnight; Sun 3–9pm. Average main course: $16.
AmEx, MC, V.*

After a 17-year absence, more than just the Lundy name has been revived. This Sheepshead Bay waterfront institution is throbbing with customers—families at big tables, couples at the raw bar—and a good time is being had by all. The combination dinners of chowder, lobster and chicken satisfy, as does the reconstructed spirit of a time when Brooklyn was the world.

Pearl Oyster Bar

*18 Cornelia St between W 4th and Bleecker Sts
(212-691-8211). Subway: A, C, E, B, D, F, Q to West
4th St–Washington Sq. Lunch: Mon–Fri noon–2:30pm.
Dinner: Mon–Sat 6–11pm. Average main course:
$17. MC, V.*

Pearl is just what the name suggests: miniature (a long bar with stools and one solitary table), gleaming (simple shades of white and silver, the dewy sheen of oysters) and a rare find (straightforward, not too pricey). The sea bass is perfectly charred on the outside, moist and laced with herbs on the inside. And how's this for simple pleasures: a plate of littlenecks on ice, a bowl of scallop chowder and a cold German pilsner.

Trata

*1331 Second Ave between 70th and 71st Sts
(212-535-3800). Subway: 6 to 68th St–Hunter College.
Noon–midnight. Average main course: $17.
AmEx, MC, V.*

This mid-priced Greek restaurant, staffed by veterans of Estiatorio Milos, will leave you wondering why anybody has ever felt the need for a cooking appliance other than a charcoal grill. Octopus, fresh sardines, peppers and a wide selection of fresh fish all come off that happy, warm place to be drizzled with olive oil, lemon and herbs. Only the impersonal dining room detracts from Trata's blessed simplicity.

Steak houses

Ben Benson's Steak House

*123 W 52nd St between Sixth and Seventh Aves
(212-581-8888). Subway: N, R to 49th St. Mon–Thu
11:45am–11pm; Fri 11:45am–midnight; Sat
5pm–midnight; Sun 5–10pm. Average main course:
$30. AmEx, MC, V.*

Teeming with men in pinstripes, this traditional steak house features a menu of luscious classics, including shimmery oysters on the half shell and hearts of romaine served in a tangy Caesar dressing. When it's time for steak, get the juicy porterhouse for two, and don't forget mashed potatoes with horseradish and the superb creamed spinach. The career waiters in tan smocks will be sure to keep things moving.

Old Homestead

*56 Ninth Ave between 14th and 15th Sts (212-242-9040). Subway: A, C, E to 14th St; L to Eighth Ave.
Lunch: Mon–Fri noon–4pm. Dinner: Mon–Fri
5–10:45pm; Sat 1–11:45pm; Sun 1–9:45pm. Average
main course: $30. AmEx, CB, DC, MC, V.*

There are plenty of pleasures at the oldest steak house in the city (founded 1868), but many come for the Kobe—that coddled, beer-fed bovine of mythological softness. A Kobe steak is $110, but it's so finely marbled and tender, it's the Grail for carnivores. Still, you'll be forgiven if you opt instead for a more classic porterhouse for two ($58) and soak in the meaty history of the room.

Palm

*837 Second Ave between 44th and 45th Sts (212-687-2953). Subway: S, 4, 5, 6, 7 to 42nd St–Grand
Central. Mon–Fri noon–11:30pm; Sat 5–11:30pm.
Average main course: $29. AmEx, MC, V.*

A total of 15 other Palms have appeared around the U.S., but this 70-year-old speakeasy is the original. **Palm Too** (212-697-5198) opened across the street in 1973, and the two are basically identical: no frills, with stern Italian waiters in flesh-colored jackets and yellowed walls bearing cartoons and caricatures of such past regulars as Jackie Gleason and J. Edgar Hoover. Palm Too, however, is open on Sundays (2–10pm). Go supple (filet mignon, $29) or savory (New York strip, $29), but either way, have the cheesecake.

Peter Luger

*178 Broadway, between Driggs and Bedford Aves,
Williamsburg, Brooklyn (718-387-7400). Subway: J to
Marcy Ave. Mon–Thu 11:45am–9:45pm; Fri, Sat
11:45am–10:45pm; Sun 1–9:45pm. Average main
course: $29. No credit cards.*

Is the hike to this Williamsburg institution worth it? Without question. Pulled from a bank of infernal broilers, the massive porterhouses emerge a crunchy dark brown, still tender pink on the inside. Dripping with fat and melted butter, this huge steak (the only cut the 110-year-old restaurant serves) awakens bone-gnawing urges you thought mankind had abandoned in the Paleolithic era.

Smith & Wollensky
797 Third Ave at 49th St (212-753-1530). Subway:
E, F to Lexington Ave; 6 to 51st St. Mon–Fri
11:30am–11pm; Sat, Sun 5–11pm. Average main
course: $55. AmEx, Disc, MC, V.
Smith & Wollensky, one of the most enduringly popular midtown steak houses, refuses to catch up with the times. The
ratio of men to women is still grossly uneven, and the decor
is still defiantly conservative. Thankfully, though, the steaks
are still unmanageably large and available in a great choice
of cuts, from sirloin to filet mignon.

Sparks
210 E 46th St between Second and Third Aves
(212-687-4855). Subway: S, 4, 5, 6, 7 to 42nd St–
Grand Central. Lunch: Mon–Fri noon–3pm. Dinner:
Mon–Thu 5–11pm; Fri, Sat 5–11:30pm. Average main
course: $25. AmEx, CB, DC, MC, V.
So maybe Big Paul Castellano did ingest his last saturated
fats here before being unceremoniously gunned down. But
there's really no dark mystery at Sparks, home of bulging
jeroboams, gargantuan family dinners and long lines. What's
here is a 30-year history of good steaks in a setting of comfortably familiar swank. Waiters are happy to improvise lavish, off-the-menu chopped salads—and what better warm-up
for a black-and-blue (charred outside, rare inside) sirloin than
a salad thick with bacon and blue cheese?

Chinese

20 Mott Street
20 Mott St between Pell St and Bowery (212-964-0380).
Subway: J, M, Z, N, R, 6 to Canal St. 9am–11pm.
Average main course: $9. AmEx, Disc, MC, V.
Come early to this three-story dim sum emporium—one of
the most popular in Chinatown. The mouthwatering,
appetizerlike dumplings, rolls and buns are served from carts
that periodically stop at each table. The menus are in Chinese and the waiters can be unhelpful, but the dim sum selection, including duck feet and jellyfish, is extensive,
guaranteeing a full stomach and a good time.

Broadway Cottage
2690 Broadway at 103rd St (212-316-2600, 2601).
Subway: 1, 9 to 103rd St. Mon–Thu 11:30am–11:30pm;
Fri, Sat 11:30am–midnight; Sun noon–11:30pm.
Average main course: $7. AmEx, MC, V.
Innumerable "cottage" Chinese restaurants dot the city, but
they aren't all created equal. While many people go to these
restaurants for the free, cheap-tasting, all-you-can-drink white
wine, Broadway Cottage is worth a visit for the attentive and
polite service and for such satisfying dishes as pan-fried scallion pancakes and crispy sweet-and-sour prawns with walnuts.

Home's Kitchen
222 E 21st St between Broadway and Park Ave
South (212-475-5049). Subway: 6 to 23rd St. 11am–
11pm. Average main course: $7. AmEx, MC, V.
It's hard to find good Peking duck—the kind that's crispy on
the outside, meaty and juicy on the inside. But Home's
Kitchen serves the real thing. Start with dumplings (steamed
or fried), and get the Peking duck to share. The dumplings
are filled to the dough with well-seasoned meat (a rarity), and
the crispy, rich duck comes with all the fixings.

Joe's Shanghai
9 Pell St between Mott St and Bowery (212-233-8888).
Subway: J, M, Z, N, R, 6 to Canal St. 11am–11:15pm.
Average main course: $12. No credit cards.
Although you'll find such dishes as fried pork dumplings
and cold chicken in wine, the main attractions at Joe's are the
steamed buns, which hold inside them a mouthful of hot
soup and morsels of pork or crabmeat. Don't shove the whole

dumpling into your mouth or you'll burn yourself; hold it on
the spoon, take a tiny bite and then drink the liquid that collects in the utensil's well.
Other locations: *24 W 56th St between Fifth and*
Sixth Aves (333-3868); 82–74 Broadway between 45th and
Whitney Aves, Queens (718-639-6888); 136–21 37th Ave
between Main and Union Sts, Queens (718-539-3838).

New Chao Chow Restaurant
111 Mott St between Canal and Hester Sts (212-226-
2590/8222). Subway: J, M, Z, N, R, 6 to Canal St.
8:30am–10pm. Average main course: $5. No credit cards.
Ignore the unimpressive decor at this cheap noodle shop,
where no dish tops $9, and focus instead on the soups, which
are the true draw. Try the Chao Chow fishball, noodles in
chicken broth topped with more than enough fishballs to
satiate any seafood lover's craving.

Red Hot Szechuan
347 Seventh Ave at 10th St, Park Slope, Brooklyn
(718-369-0700). Subway: F to Seventh Ave. Mon–Thu
11:30am–10:30pm; Fri, Sat 11:30am–11pm; Sun
2–10:30pm. Average main course: $8. AmEx, MC, V.
This Park Slope restaurant does Chinese right—and it's a good
value, too. Red Hot offers a full selection of vegetarian dishes
(including some Buddhist cuisine) and a brunch that can't be
beat: You get your choice of various main dishes, plus egg drop
or wonton soup, and vegetable, plain or brown rice for $4.15!
Be sure to try the steamed celery–with–sesame sauce appetizer; in summer, there's lobster, served however you like it.

Shun Lee Palace
155 E 55th St between Lexington and Third Aves
(212-371-8844). Subway: 4, 5, 6 to 59th St; N, R to
Lexington Ave. Noon–11:30pm. Average main course:
$20. AmEx, DC, MC, V.
In this city of a thousand cheap, accessible Chinese food
joints, it might seem silly to venture to this place on the posh
East Side, where main courses can cost as much as $30. But
you'll see why when you try the food, such as the crab seasoned with ginger and scallion or the roast squab. And if
Shun Lee's elegance doesn't surprise you, maybe the cour-
teous and friendly service will.

Eastern European

Firebird
365 W 46th St between Eighth and Ninth Aves
(212-586-0244). Subway: A, C, E to 42nd St–Port
Authority. Lunch: Tue–Sat 11:45am–2:15pm. Dinner:
Sun–Thu 5–10:15pm; Fri, Sat 5–11:15pm. Average
main course: $24. AmEx, Disc, MC, V.
Located on Restaurant Row in the Theater District, Firebird
dedicates itself to old-style Russian extravagance. If you're
not up to trying some of the grander main courses (such as
marinated lamb), order from the zakuska menu (a sort of
Russian tapas), which changes daily.

Rasputin
2670 Coney Island Ave at Ave X, Brighton Beach,
Brooklyn (718-332-8333). Subway: F to Ave X; D to Neck
Rd. Mon–Thu 11am–midnight; Fri–Sun 11am–3am.
Average main course $45. AmEx, MC, V.
Come to this restaurant in Brooklyn's Little Odessa for an
authentic Russian evening—some dining and dancing and
much smoking and drinking. Order typical Russian dishes
such as boiled tongue, radish salad and caviar before heading to the crowded dance floor. Arrive early if you want to
catch the Vegas-style floor show.

Russian Samovar
256 W 52nd St between Broadway and Eighth Ave
(212-757-0168). Subway: C, E to 50th St. Lunch:

Tue–Sat noon–3pm. Dinner: Mon 5–11:30pm; Tue–Thu, Sun 5pm–midnight; Fri, Sat 5pm–12:30am. Average main course: $18. AmEx, MC, V.
You may not recognize them, but this mid-priced Theater District restaurant is where Russia's beautiful people go when they are in town. Mikhail Baryshnikov is an investor.

Ukrainian East Village Restaurant
140 Second Ave between 8th and 9th Sts (212-529-5024). Subway: 6 to Astor Pl. Noon–11pm. Average main course: $7. No credit cards.
Experience true Ukrainian dining and service at this plain-looking restaurant tucked away behind the Ukrainian National Home. Order the combo platter and fill up on stuffed cabbage, kielbasa, four types of pierogi and a choice of potatoes or kasha (buckwheat). And if you're full, don't let the grand-motherlike waitresses convince you otherwise.

Veselka
144 Second Ave at 9th St (212-228-9682).
Subway: 6 to Astor Pl. 24 hours. Average main course: $10. AmEx, MC, V.
This bohemian Ukrainian coffee shop, open around the clock, was recently renovated, so it might not seem like the old East Village hangout it actually is. After a tour of the small shops in the vicinity, stop here for a cheap bowl of chicken soup and a slab of challah bread.

Ethiopian

Ghenet
284 Mulberry St between Houston and Prince Sts (212-343-1888). Subway: B, D, F, Q to Broadway–Lafayette St; N, R to Prince St. Tue–Sun noon–10:30pm. Average main course: $9. AmEx, MC, V.
Get off the bistro bus and head to this stylish and authentic Ethiopian restaurant. Ghenet serves up dark, spicy stews that you eat sans utensils with spongy injera bread. Weekly menu additions (such as a traditional bean spread), which

you won't find on any other Ethiopian menu in the city, necessitate repeat visits.

French

Alison on Dominick
38 Dominick St between Varick and Hudson Sts (212-727-1188). Subway: 1, 9 to Canal St. Dinner: Mon–Thu 5:30–9:30pm; Fri, Sat 5:15–10:30pm; Sun 5:15–9:30pm. Average main course: $27. AmEx, DC, MC, V.
This French country restaurant is one of the most romantic hideaways in the city, with light—almost healthy—versions of southwestern French cuisine and a quiet, jazz-tinged atmosphere.

Café Boulud
20 E 76th St between Fifth and Madison Aves (212-772-2600). Subway: 6 to 77th St. Tue–Sat noon–11pm; Sun, Mon 5:45–11pm. Average main course: $28. AmEx, DC, MC, V.
A café in name only, Daniel Boulud's remodeled take on his haute-cuisine temple still attracts a sea of expensive suits and diamond rings, while charging lower (if not low) prices. The decor is now more modern and spare, but Boulud's superior French cooking—including signature dishes as well as a range of vegetarian options—remains some of the finest in New York.

Casimir
103–105 Ave B between 6th and 7th Sts (212-358-9683). Subway: F to Second Ave. Sun–Thu 5:30pm–midnight; Fri, Sat 5:30pm–1am. Average main course: $13. AmEx.
Tin ceilings, waning yellow light and plenty of young French guys sporting that just-rolled-out-of-bed look instill Casimir with the homey familiarity you'd expect from a bistro. The impressive food—cassoulet, roasted cod, etc.—is just as welcoming, as is the Moroccan lounge next door and the garden out back.

*Hot chicks! Ground chick peas make for first-rate falafel at **Mamoun's** in the Village.*

Flea Market

131 Ave A between 8th and 9th Sts (212-358-9280). Subway: 6 to Astor Pl. Brunch: Sat, Sun 10am–4pm. Lunch: Mon–Fri 9am–4:30pm. Dinner: Mon–Fri 5:30pm–midnight; Sat, Sun 5pm–midnight. Average main course: $13. AmEx.

Named for the vintage bric-a-brac scattered about, Flea Market whips up traditional French bistro fare with authenticity and plenty of rich sauces. No matter what you choose—the steak au poivre and sautéed skate with roasted-garlic mashed potatoes are delicious—your fork will inevitably trespass onto your companion's plate. In summer, choose a table near the doors and watch motley East Villagers traipse by.

Jean Claude

137 Sullivan St between Houston and Prince Sts (212-475-9232). Subway: C, E to Prince St; 1, 9 to Houston St. Mon–Thu 6:30–11pm; Fri, Sat 6:30–11:30pm; Sun 6–10:30pm. Average main course: $18. No credit cards.

Perpetually mobbed, Jean-Claude Iacovelli's trendy bistro is a Soho favorite, thanks to the mix of beautiful customers, relaxed waiters and an affordable menu of imaginative continental and nouvelle cuisine.

Jules

65 St. Marks Pl between First and Second Aves (212-477-5560). Subway: 6 to Astor Pl. 11am–2am. Average main course: $16. AmEx.

Jules may be at its best at Sunday brunch-time, when the sun shines through the lace curtains and an accordionist wanders around the room. Regulars favor the goat-cheese omelette, steak frites and the salad frisée aux lardons.

La Forêt

1713 First Ave between 88th and 89th Sts (212-987-9839). Subway: 4, 5, 6 to 86th St. Tue–Sun 6–11pm. Average main course: $14. Cash only.

Good, affordable bistros might not make waves south of 14th Street, but on this restaurant-starved strip of First Avenue, La Forêt is a godsend. Bouley-trained chef Vladimir Ribartchouk prepares creative French-inspired cuisine at eminently fair prices. It's reason enough to say so long to Soho.

Le Cirque 2000

New York Palace Hotel, 455 Madison Ave between 50th and 51st Sts (212-303-7788). Subway: 6 to 51st St. Lunch: Mon–Sat 11:45am–2:45pm; Sun 11:30am–2:30pm. Dinner: Mon–Sat 5:45–11pm; Sun 5:30–10:30pm. Average main course: $35. AmEx, MC, V.

Step into Sirio Maccioni's revamped Le Cirque, and you'll be surprised by the loony, futuristic redesign of Stanford White's decor. But then chef Sottha Khunn's menu will grab your attention, from the exquisite sautéed foie gras and lobster salad to the "juggler's ball" of pink meringue filled with lemon curd and vanilla ice cream.

Better late than ever

Satisfy your midnight cravings at these great after-hours restaurants

Never mind what your mom told you—it's never too late to sit down to a good meal. Especially in New York City. You can stumble out of a bar at 2am, or leave a dance club at 6am, or wake up in a jet-lag fit sometime in between—and still you can find some of the best food in the world.

For a quick bite, just breeze into one of the city's myriad pizza joints and pick up a satisfying slice smothered in mozzarella and tangy tomato sauce. If you want to sit down and spend a few more bucks, you've got plenty of options. Many of the city's best chefs like to wind down in Soho at **Blue Ribbon** (97 Sullivan Street between Prince and Spring Streets, 212-274-0404), a tiny, up-all-night bistro where you can dig into rack of lamb, fried chicken, matzo ball soup or even a raw-bar platter of oysters on the half shell. Once the Wall Street hordes have trucked off to bed, the usually impenetrable **Balthazar** (80 Spring Street between Crosby Street and Broadway, 212-965-1414) settles into a quiet groove. Grab a booth in the stunning brasserie and graze on perfectly poached eggs with rich boudin noir, puffy batter-dipped onion rings or an irresistible Monte Cristo sandwich.

If you're craving Asian food, you can get your fix at a number of Chinatown restaurants. One of the best is **New York Noodle Town** (28 1/2 Bowery at Bayard Street, 212-349-0923), where fans savor the famous barbecued pork (encased in a crackling, salty skin) and perhaps the best softshell crabs in the city. Farther uptown, on 32nd Street, several Korean restaurants operate 24 hours. At **Kang Suh** (1250 Broadway at 32nd Street, 212-564-6845) you can chow down on kimchee while barbecuing a bevy of marinated meats on a built-in grill at your own table.

Finally, you can hit one of New York's numerous diners. In the East Village, most locals and barhoppers end their nights at **Veselka** (144 Second Avenue at 9th Street, 212-228-9682), an affordable Polish mecca serving blintzes, pierogi, kielbasa and American standards like cheeseburgers and chicken soup. Across the island, in the middle of the Meatpacking District, clubhoppers, models, actors and industry insiders inevitably wrap up their evenings at **Restaurant Florent** (69 Gansevoort Street between Greenwich and Washington Streets, 212-989-5779), a funky, chrome-paneled French diner that's as much a party as a restaurant. Take your pick among mussels, fries, omelets, burgers, etc.—like Manhattan itself, Florent will give you pretty much anything you want.

Star of David: Sample sublime loaves and four-star cuisine at David Bouley's **Bouley Bakery**.

Les Deux Gamins

170 Waverly Pl at Grove St (212-807-7047).
Subway: 1, 9 to Christopher St–Sheridan Sq. 8am–
midnight. Average main course: $14. AmEx.
Watch the Village go by as you soak up atmosphere that's très Parisian and bistro food that's almost as authentic.

Lucien

14 First Ave between 1st and 2nd Sts (212-260-6481).
Subway: F to Second Ave. Mon–Fri noon–2am; Sat, Sun
11am–2am. Average main course: $14. AmEx.
Lucien's menu doesn't stray too far from the bistro formula: steak frites, moules marinières, tarte tatin. But as at most memorable bistros, the menu isn't really the point. Comfort, familiarity and flair are, and Lucien scores high in these departments. The food's reliable, too. On a typical night, after normal dinner hours, the banquettes are still filled with East Village locals, clearly relishing their newest home.

Palacinka

28 Grand St between Sixth Ave and Thompson St
(212-625-0362). Subway: C, E to Spring St. 10am–
10pm. Average crepe: $6.50. Cash only.
More European than Euro, this chic-but-bohemian café on the edge of Soho seduces stray shoppers with an array of wonderful buckwheat crepes. Uncap a bottle of Pellegrino, and enjoy tender pancakes filled with everything from spinach, garlic, lemon and feta to brandied pear with almond cream.

Patois

255 Smith St between Douglass and DeGraw Sts,
Carroll Gardens, Brooklyn (718-855-1535). Subway: F to
Carroll St. Brunch: 11am–3pm. Dinner: Tue–Thu 6–
10:30pm; Fri, Sat 6–11:30pm. Average main course:
$23. AmEx, MC, V.
With its fashionably worn vintage furniture and fair prices, Patois, a new Carroll Gardens bistro, feels as if it's been a part of the neighborhood for years. The tables are filled by 8pm for the superb French fare, which includes a crustless tart with layers of thinly sliced leek and potato blended with melted Roquefort, and duck ravioli with diced pumpkin.

Payard Patisserie & Bistro

1032 Lexington Ave between 73rd and 74th Sts (212-
717-5252). Subway: 6 to 77th St. Mon–Sat 7am–11pm.
Average main course: $40. AmEx, DC, MC, V.
Opened in 1997 by François Payard, the former pastry chef at Daniel, this hybrid restaurant is a sugar wonderland that would make Willy Wonka jealous. The stunning confections in the polished glass display cases include myriad handmade chocolates, moonpie-size macaroons and lush homemade sorbets and ice creams. The bustling bistro also serves top-notch provincial French cooking, but the huge assortment of traditional pastries and crisp fruit tarts reminds you that you were right as a kid: Dessert should come first.

Provence

38 MacDougal St between Houston and Prince Sts
(212-475-7500). Subway: C, E to Spring St. Lunch:
Noon–3pm. Dinner: Mon–Sat 5:30–
10:30pm. Average main course: $20. AmEx.
Provence has been a Soho institution since 1986, thanks to its informal, flirtatious staff and superb Provençal food. During the warm months, try to sit in the garden out back.

Rive Gauche

560 Third Ave at 37th St (212-949-5400). Subway:
6 to 33rd St. Mon–Fri noon–11pm; Sat 11:30am–
midnight; Sun 11:30am–11pm. Average main course:
$18. AmEx, DC, Disc, MC, V.
So what if Rive Gauche's tie-clipped waiters, angled mirrors and whirring ceiling fans make it feel suspiciously like

*Rocking good time: Enjoy potent margaritas and creative Mexican food at **Rocking Horse Cafe**.*

any number of Soho bistros? In a neighborhood as restaurant-deprived as Murray Hill, it's impossible to resist this eatery's pleasantly noisy atmosphere and menu of modern French standards.

Greek

Agrotikon
322 E 14th St between First and Second Aves (212-473-2602). Subway: L to First Ave. Tue–Sun 5pm–midnight. Average main course: $16. AmEx, MC, V.
Cheaper and more adventurous than an haute Greek place like Periyali (*see below*), Agrotikon is a happy and relatively recent addition to 14th Street. Dolmades are wonderful here, as is the sheep's milk cheese saganaki. For fish, choose grilled over baked. Or try the fisherman's pie—a stew with chunks of fish and squid baked under garlic-cod mashed potatoes. The chocolate baklava is a true original.

Elias Corner for Fish
24-02 31st St at 24th Ave Astoria, Queens (718-932-1510). Subway: N to Astoria Blvd. 4pm–midnight. Average main course: $15. No credit cards.
This newly expanded but still simple Greek seafood restaurant doesn't take reservations, so there may be a wait; use the time in the lobby to select the right fish from the glass case. There's no menu, but no matter: Everything comes in extremely fresh and leaves the grill perfectly charred and full of flavor. The crowds come for swordfish kebabs and whole red mullet, snapper and striped bass. Treat the waitresses nicely, and perhaps they'll bring a platter of fried dough with honey, a free dessert that's as sweet as the mood here.

Meltemi
905 First Ave at 51st St (212-355-4040). Subway: 6 to 51st St; E, F to Lexington Ave. Noon–11pm. Average main course: $20. AmEx, MC, V.
Meltemi's airy look befits its Sutton Place location, but the atmosphere here comes from its Greek customers and

authentic food. The exacting chef really knows his way around a grill, and the squid are perfect: Cooked over charcoal until just moist, they're sweet and tender to the point of indecency.

Molyvos
871 Seventh Ave between 55th and 56th Sts (212-582-7500). Subway: N, R, S to 57th St; B, D, E to Seventh Ave. Lunch: Mon–Fri noon–3pm. Dinner: 5:30–11:30pm. Average main course: $20. AmEx, DC, Disc, MC, V.
This midtown taverna offers superior Greek home cooking refined for Manhattan taste buds. Instead of bread and butter, expect a basket of warm, chewy pita and a ramekin of pungent feta–and–roasted red pepper spread. Homey entrées include baby chicken bathed in a tangy lemon-dill cream sauce; desserts are irresistibly sweet. Like everything at Molyvos, they're not fancy—just plain delicious.

Periyali
35 W 20th St between Fifth and Sixth Aves (212-463-7890). Subway: N, R to 23rd St. Lunch: Mon–Fri noon–3pm. Dinner: Mon–Fri 5:30–11pm; Sat 5:30pm–midnight. Average main course: $20. AmEx, DC, MC, V.
Periyali was one of the first restaurants in Manhattan to elevate Greek cuisine above the level of coffee-shop spanikopita. And though the best Greek cooking is now available more cheaply in Astoria, this traditional coal-grill place is still a good upscale spot for moussaka, taramasalata, grilled meat and vegetable appetizers.

Indian

Café Spice
72 University Pl at 11th St (212-253-6999). Subway: L, N, R, 4, 5, 6 to 14th St–Union Sq. Mon–Thu 11:30am–10:30pm; Fri 11:30am–11:30pm; Sat noon–11:30pm; Sun 1–10:30pm. Average main course: $15. AmEx, MC, V.

In a design-conscious setting that's more Pottery Barn than 6th Street, the folks from uptown's Dawat offer affordable (and high-quality) renditions of prawn curry, tandoori chicken, poori and even wraps. All entrées include a square-meal accompaniment of naan, lentils, veggies and basmati rice.

Dawat
210 E 58th St between Second and Third Aves (212-355-7555). Subway: 4, 5, 6 to 59th St; N, R to Lexington Ave. Lunch: 11:30am–2.45pm. Dinner: Sun–Thu 5:30–10.45pm; Fri, Sat 5:30–11:15pm. Average lunch: $12.95; dinner: $35. AmEx, DC, MC, V.
Once considered one of the city's best Indian restaurants, Dawat has slipped in recent years. Still, it offers a long and diverse menu within its pretty peach walls. Dinner is pricey here, but the prix-fixe lunches ($12.95–$13.95) are one of east midtown's few midday bargains.

Haveli
100 Second Ave between 5th and 6th Sts (212-982-0533). Subway: 6 to Astor Pl. Noon–midnight. Average main course: $9. AmEx, MC, V.
The best thing about 6th Street's Little Delhi isn't even on 6th; it's just around the corner. In fact, Haveli is better than the neighborhood deserves. Behind the shattered-on-purpose wall of glass, all the standards are a notch above average with only a moderate price hike.

Jackson Diner
37-47 74th St between Roosevelt and 37th Aves, Jackson Heights, Queens (718-672-1232). Subway: E, F, G, R to Roosevelt Ave–Jackson Hts; 7 to 74th St–Broadway. Sun–Thu 11:30am–10pm; Fri, Sat 11:30am–10:30pm. Average main course: $9. Cash only.
After 14 years in business, Jackson Heights's esteemed house of dosas and dal has relocated to spacious digs down the block. The stylish lighting and chichi banquettes look thoroughly Manhattan, but thankfully, the low-priced Indian cuisine remains unmistakably Queens.

Nirvana
30 W 59th St between Fifth and Sixth Aves (212-486-5700). Subway: N, R to Fifth Ave. Noon–1am. Average main course: $18. AmEx, DC, Disc, MC, V.
The high-rent panorama of Central Park is the real attraction here; the menu is virtually identical to every place on 6th Street—despite the elephantine prices. If you're determined to have your curry with a view, go for the "theater dinner," which is served all day. For $5 more than a main course, you'll also receive an appetizer sampler, dessert and coffee.

Tabla
11 Madison Ave at 25th St (212-889-0667). Subway: N, R, 6 to 23rd St. Mon–Fri noon–11pm; Sat 5:30–11pm. Three-course prix fixe: $52. AmEx, Disc, DC, MC, V.
Danny Meyer's beautiful new Indian fusion restaurant offers something for everybody. Munch on freshly baked olive oil–and–rosemary naan with lemon-chive raita at the downstairs bread bar, or venture upstairs to the dining room for some of the most stimulating food in the city, like a Goan-spiced Maine crab cake with avocado salad and a tamarind glaze. Whatever you decide on, prepare to leave happy and full.

Thali
28 Greenwich Ave between 10th and Charles Sts (212-367-7411). Subway: A, C, E, B, D, F, Q to W 4th St–Washington Sq. Lunch: Mon–Sat noon–3pm; Dinner: Mon–Sat 6–9:30pm; Sun 5–10pm. Average main course: $10. No credit cards.
There is no menu at this sparsely decorated, closet-size vegetarian restaurant. Just sit down and order tea, and within minutes a server brings a thali, a traditional Indian meal consisting of vegetable curries, a lentil dish, chutney, pickles, bread, a pile of rice and dessert, served on a large silver tray.

You can be sure the food is fresh—the place has no storage area, so it is all bought and prepared on the same day.

Italian

al di lá
248 Fifth Ave at Carroll St, Park Slope, Brooklyn (718-783-4565). Subway: M, N, R to Union St. Mon, Wed, Thu 6–10:30pm; Fri, Sat 6–11pm; Sun 6–10pm. Average main course: $12. MC, V.
All the pieces come together at this Park Slope trattoria. The rustic decor lures you in, while the food—quality ingredients crafted by expert hands—keeps you there for hours. Hanger steak tagliata is delicious, but so is everything else.

Andy's Colonial
2257 First Ave at 116th St (212-410-9175). Subway: 6 to 116th St. Mon–Fri 11am–9pm; Sat 5–10pm. Average main course: $15. No credit cards.
At this eight-table wood-paneled bar-restaurant, there are no printed menus: Co-owner Joe Medici (your bartender and waiter) will hand you a short list of Italian specials. If those don't interest you, Joe will offer you any kind of chicken or veal—cooked by his 81-year-old father.

Bamonte's
32 Withers St between Union Ave and Lorimer St, Williamsburg (718-384-8831). Subway: L to Lorimer St. noon–11pm. Average main course: $14. MC, V.
You may never achieve the perfect Frankie Valli hair or pinkie-ring panache of many of the customers at Bamonte's, but that shouldn't keep you from this colorful 98-year-old eatery on a rowhouse lined block of Williamsburg. Come on a weeknight, and join the long tables of done-up ladies and clamoring fellas passing platters of light, crispy zucchini fritters, garlic-laden roasted peppers and spaghetti with meat sauce.

Barolo
398 West Broadway between Spring and Broome Sts (212-226-1102). Subway: C, E to Spring St. Mon–Fri 10am–midnight; Sat, Sun 10am–1am. Average main course: $20. AmEx, Disc, MC, V.
This Soho attraction draws a swanky crowd that's heavily into money and looks. You can comfortably chat on your cell phone while digging into penne with lamb and artichokes. It's a perfect summer choice, due to the enormous garden in the back, complete with lush trees lit with tiny lights.

Bona Fides
60 Second Ave between 3rd and 4th Sts (212-777-2840). Subway: 6 to Astor Pl. Dinner: Sun–Thu 5–11pm; Fri, Sat 5pm–midnight. Average main course: $9. AmEx, DC, MC, V.
A mellow and unremarkably pretty place with a long dining room and a partially tented garden, this East Village Italian restaurant serves meals that never exceed the $10 mark and include free bruschetta. Even regular diners still regard Bona Fides as a place they have just stumbled upon, wondering at their luck.

Carmine's
2450 Broadway between 90th and 91st Sts (212-362-2200). Subway: 1, 2, 3, 9 to 96th St. Mon–Thu 5–11pm; Fri 5pm–midnight; Sat 5pm–1am; Sun 2–10pm. Average main course: $20. AmEx, MC, V.
Plenty of pasta and garlic are the hallmarks of Manhattan's two Carmine's, both southern Italian eateries that serve gargantuan portions of noodles in a warm, raucous setting. The reservation policy can be tricky; call ahead, and if you can't get a table, be ready to wait.
Other location: *200 W 44th St between Broadway and Eighth Ave (212-221-3800).*

Frank

88 Second Ave between 5th and 6th Sts
(212-420-0202). Subway: 6 to Astor Pl. 10:30–1am.
Average main course: $9. Cash only.
Inspired by his Neapolitan grandmother's cooking, chef-owner
Frank Prisinzano serves superb, straightforward food at no-
nonsense prices. Just as homespun is the storefront space—it's
chock-full of antique knickknacks and family photographs.
It's also chock-full of customers, so be prepared to wait.

Il Bagatto

192 E 2nd St between Aves A and B (212-228-0977).
Subway: F to Second Ave. Tue–Thu 7pm–midnight;
Fri, Sat 7pm–1am; Sun 6–11pm. Average main course:
$12. No credit cards.
There are few convincing reasons to send anyone with lin-
gering fears about Alphabet City into its bowels. Count the
spinach gnocchi at the dark and cozy Il Bagatto as one of
them. These plump morsels are made fresh at least four
times a week and are served in a ripe, creamy Gorgonzola
sauce. Other dishes worth the trek: the antipasto Il Bagatto,
a sampler of the house antipasti; and the stracceti ai ros-
marino, a round of beef sliced paper-thin.

La Focacceria

128 First Ave between St. Marks Pl and 7th St
(212-254-4946). Subway: 6 to Astor Pl. Mon–Thu
10am–10pm; Fri, Sat 10am–11pm. Average main
course: $7. No credit cards.
First, order a half carafe of the delicious house chianti, then
fill your tumbler and drink to the abolition of long-stemmed
glasses and overpriced wine lists. Now, scan the food choices
on the wall. (This brightly lit pasta factory has been here
since 1914 and still hasn't gotten around to printing a menu.)
Everything's so cheap, you can probably afford to order
appetizers, pasta and a main course, but portions are big
enough that you don't have to.

La Mela

137 Mulberry St between Grand and Broome Sts
(212-431- 9493). Subway: B, D, Q to Grand St. Noon–
11pm. Average main course: $13. AmEx, DC, MC, V.
Located on the main strip in Little Italy, La Mela looks a bit
touristy, but you'll still find many old-timers ordering wine
by the color to go with mounds of traditional Italian
antipasti, heaps of pasta (lasagna, tortellini, ravioli and
spaghetti) and large plates of desserts.

Le Madri

168 W 18th St between Sixth and Seventh Aves
(212-727-8022). Subway: 1, 9 to 18th St. Lunch: Noon–
3pm. Dinner: 5:30–11pm. Average main course: $25.
AmEx, DC, MC, V.
You'll be hungry after an arduous day of shopping at
Loehmann's. Just a few steps away is this spotless, classy
Tuscan restaurant serving exciting pastas, pizzas, bread salads and grilled vegetables. The garden patio opens with the
arrival of warm weather.

Orologio

162 Ave A between 10th and 11th Sts (212-228-6900).
Subway: 6 to Astor Pl; L to First Ave. Dinner: Sun–Thu,
5:30pm–midnight; Fri, Sat 5:30pm–1am. Average
main course: $10. No credit cards.
Orologio is one of the many restaurants that have sprouted
in the past five years on the formerly desolate and now gentrified Avenue A. There's little elbow room at this trattoria,
which offers a modestly priced wine list and cheap pasta
that's always properly al dente and never swimming in sauce.

Osteria al Doge

142 W 44th St between Broadway and Sixth Ave
(212-944-3643). Subway: N, R, S, 1, 2, 3, 9, 7 to 42nd
St–Times Sq. Mon–Sat noon–11:30pm, Sun 5–11pm.
Average main course: $16. AmEx, Disc, MC, Visa.
The walls at Osteria al Doge are lined with pictures of
Venice, and whether you sit at one of the long wooden tables
up-front or at a comfy leather banquette toward the back,
you'll feel you're enjoying a solid meal in the canal-lined city
(just ignore those *New Yorker* editors scattered about). The
house antipasto is always reliable, as are the pastas.

Piadina

57 W 10th St between Sixth and Seventh Aves (212-
460-1017). Subway: A, C, E to 14th St. 5:30–11:30pm.
Average main course: $12. No credit cards.
At times, Piadina feels less like a restaurant than a commis-
sary for the fashion industry. Even if you're wearing chinos
instead of Helmut Lang, you'll love this eatery's worn-in
Euro-bohemian vibe, candlelit glow and impressive Tuscan
food. Start off with warm polenta bathed in Gorgonzola
cream sauce, move on to spinach gnocchi, and try not to stare
too much at that model sitting at the next table.

Pó

31 Cornelia St between Bleecker and W 4th Sts
(212-645-2189). Subway: A, C, E, B, D, F, Q to W 4th
St–Washington Sq. Lunch: 11:30am–2pm Wed–Sun.
Dinner: Tue–Thu 5:30–11pm; Fri, Sat 5:30–11:30pm;
Sun 5–10pm. Average main course: $23. AmEx.
Chef Mario Battali, who has his own show on cable's Food
Network, makes this tiny West Village restaurant an unfor-
gettable treat. The complimentary rosemary-laced white
bean bruschetta that's brought to the table as you're seated
is a harbinger of the simple masterpieces to come.

Trattoria Dell'Arte

900 Seventh Ave between 56th and 57th Sts (212-245-
9800). Subway: N, R, S to 57th St. Brunch: Sat, Sun
11:45am–3:30pm. Lunch: Mon–Fri 11:30am–2:30pm.
Dinner: Mon–Sat 5–11:30pm. Average main course: $25.
AmEx, Disc, MC, V.
Decorated with artwork of body parts, including a huge nose
near the bar, this trilevel pretheater spot is popular with celebrities. Hope to get seated downstairs, though the contemporary
Italian food will taste great no matter where you are.

Pizza

John's Pizzeria

278 Bleecker St between Sixth and Seventh Aves
(212-243-1680). Subway: A, C, E, B, D, Q to West 4th
St–Washington Sq; 1, 9 to Christopher St–Sheridan Sq.
Mon–Sat 11:30am–midnight; Sun noon–midnight.
Medium pizza: $10. No credit cards.
The brick-oven pizza at John's has long been a contender for
annual best-pizza awards. Although there are two newer
uptown branches, head to the original in the Village, which
has been expanded. Find the oldest part of the restaurant and
sit in a scratched wooden booth. Someone will inevitably play
Sinatra on the jukebox, and your thin-crust pizza, which can
easily be shared by two, will arrive within minutes.
Other locations: *408 E 64th St between First and York*
Aves (212-935-2895); 48 W 65th St between Central
Park West and Columbus Ave (212-721-7001).

Lombardi's

32 Spring St between Mott and Mulberry Sts
(212-941-7994). Subway: 6 to Spring St. Mon–Thu
11:30am–11pm; Fri, Sat 11am–midnight; Sun
11:30am–10pm. Large pizza: $12.50. No credit cards.
This narrow pizzeria in Little Italy opened at the turn of
the century as a pasta restaurant. Closed in the late 1980s,
Lombardi's reopened four years ago to sell only pizza and
quickly became a hit with the locals. The pizza, made with
fresh ingredients, is baked in a coal oven and has a thin but
chewy crust.

Patsy Grimaldi's

19 Old Fulton St between Front and Water Sts,
Brooklyn Heights, Brooklyn (718-858-4300). Subway:
A, C to High St. Mon–Thu 11:30am–11pm; Fri
11:30am–midnight; Sat 2pm–midnight; Sun 2–
11pm. Large pizza: $12. No credit cards.
Make a detour to this bustling sit-down pizzeria near the
tranquil waterfront facing downtown Manhattan. The thin
brick-oven pizza, piled with fresh mozzarella and tomatoes,
has a delicious, slightly oily crust that could be eaten on
its own.

Patsy's Pizzeria

2287 First Ave between 117th and 118th Sts
(212-534-9783). Subway: 6 to 116th St. 11am–
midnight. Large pizza: $10. No credit cards.
No matter how hard you try, you'll never find coal-oven
pizza in Manhattan that can measure up to a pie at Patsy's.
Not only are all the ingredients perfect on their own; they're
even better blended together on a blackened, blistered
crust (which somehow is still moist and chewy). But the
purity of the design evident in the pizza is less apparent
in the decor. Expect a crude wood counter, a hulking oven,
random oil paintings and a few pictures of the late, great
Frank Sinatra.

Totonno's

1524 Neptune Ave between 15th and 16th Sts, Coney
Island, Brooklyn (718-372-8606). Subway: B, D, F, N to
Stillwell Ave–Coney Island. Thu–Sun noon–8:30pm.
Large pizza: $14.50 AmEx, DC, MC, V.
Pizza lovers in search of the best New York pie no longer
need to make the pilgrimage to Coney Island. After almost
75 years at the beach, the Pero family brought its delicious
pies to Manhattan in 1997. The tomatoes are just as fresh
and the mozzarella just as creamy, but the dining experience
is more memorable in funky Luna Park.
Other location: *1544 Second Ave between 80th*
and 81st Sts (212-327-2800).

Japanese

Honmura An

170 Mercer St between Prince and Houston Sts
(212-334-5253). Subway: N, R to Prince St. Lunch:
Wed–Sat noon–2:30pm. Dinner: Tue–Thu 6:30–10pm;
Fri, Sat 6–10:30pm; Sun 6–9:30pm. Average main
course: $20. AmEx, DC, MC, V.
There's quiet, Zenlike harmony just off Houston—for a price.
Start with edamame pea pods, then get into buckwheat noodles like you've never tasted, including hearty nabeyaki udon
with chicken and shrimp.

Next Door Nobu

105 Hudson St at Franklin St (212-334-4445). Subway:
1, 9 to Franklin St. Mon–Thu 5:45pm–midnight; Fri, Sat
5:45pm–1am; Sun 5:45–11pm. Average main course:
$18. AmEx, DC, MC, V.
Drew Nieporent could have pitched a tent outside Nobu and
packed it nightly. But his annexed eatery is every bit as
attractive as its Japanese parent and twice as accessible: The
70-seat restaurant is open till 1am on weekends (midnight
during the week), and reservations are not accepted. Sit at
the pounded-wok raw bar for sushi and shellfish, or snare a
table and try affordable udon and soba noodle creations;
steamed, grilled or fried whole fish; and such familiar Nobu
specialties as broiled black cod with miso.

Oikawa

805 Third Ave at 50th St (212-980-1400). Subway:
6 to 51st St; E, F to Lexington Ave. Lunch: Mon–Fri
11:30am–2:30pm. Dinner: Mon–Sat 5:30pm–12:30am;
Sun 5:30–11pm. Average main course: $18.50. AmEx,
DC, MC, V.
Located in a glassy, mall-like midtown building, Oikawa may
look sterile, but the food is thrilling. Sample the shredded jellyfish, chopped shark fin with plum sauce, or squid with
spicy cod roe. Even the sushi is pretty creative; try the
salmon-and-eel roll, gently fried, tempura-style.

Omen

113 Thompson St between Prince and Spring Sts
(212-925-8923). Subway: C, E to Spring St.
5:30–10:30pm. Average main course: $18. AmEx.
Not even the salads are bad omens at this calm Soho eatery.
The house salad is enlivened with seaweed and baby scallops, a perfect accompaniment to an assortment of sashimi.
Order the herby chiso rice on the side.

Sandobe Sushi

330 E 11th St between First and Second Aves
(212-780-0328). Subway: L to First Ave, 6 to Astor Pl.
5:30pm–1am. Average main course: $11. No credit cards.
When you leave this three-room restaurant, you will feel fool-
ish for ever having eaten mediocre sushi. Chef Kirjin Kim's
menu is incredibly delicious, especially considering his fish
is some of the cheapest in the city. There are lush, generous
slabs of tuna and salmon, but the real stars here are the rolls,
in all the colors of the sushi rainbow.

Takahachi

85 Ave A between 5th and 6th Sts (212-505-6524).
Subway: 6 to Bleecker St. 5:30pm–12:45am. Average
main course: $14. AmEx, MC, V.
Fresh slivers of fish and waiters in matching T-shirts are
about the only consistent elements here; everything else is
Avenue-A eclectic. Early-bird specials ($13 until 7pm) are a
good value and a smart way to beat the dinner rush.

Tomoe Sushi

172 Thompson St between Houston and Bleecker
Sts (212-777-9346). Subway: A, C, E, B, D, F, Q to W
4th St–Washington Sq; 1, 9 to Houston St. Lunch:
Wed–Sat 1–3pm. Dinner: Mon, Wed–Sat 5–11pm.
Average main course: $18. AmEx.
The fussy folks here take only AmEx and expect you to wait
outside in the cold for a table. Everyone puts up with it, though,
because the bargain sushi is always as big as your fist, and,
sometimes, it's among the silkiest and tastiest in the city.

Yama

122 E 17th St at Irving Pl (212-475-0969). Subway:
L, N, R, 4, 5, 6 to 14th St–Union Sq. Lunch: Mon–Fri
noon–2:20pm. Dinner: Mon–Thu 5:30–10:20pm;
Fri, Sat 5:30–11:20pm. Average main course: $16.
AmEx, MC, V.
Good, fresh sushi and big bento-box dinner deals keep this
place packed. The Irving Place location, where writer Washington Irving once lived, doesn't take reservations, so expect
a wait (but if you have to line up outside, you couldn't pick
a prettier block). The newer, larger Carmine Street location
does accept reservations.
Other location: *38–40 Carmine St between Bleecker and*
Bedford Sts (212-989-9330).

Kosher

Le Marais

150 W 46th St between Sixth and Seventh Aves
(212-869-0900). Subway: N, R, S, 1, 2, 3, 9, 7 to 42nd
St–Times Sq. Sun–Thu noon–midnight; Fri noon–3pm.
Average main course: $22. AmEx, DC, MC, V.
A kosher French bistro might seem like an oxymoron (mar-
garine on a baguette, anyone?), but the pretheater crowds are
a testament to Le Marais's strengths. Bistro staples such as

steak, lamb and chicken are as good as those at the nonkosher bistro **Les Halles** (212-679-4111), owned by the same people.

Ratner's

138 Delancey St between Norfolk and Suffolk Sts (212-677-5588). Subway: F to Delancey St; J, M, Z to Essex St. Sun–Thu 6am–11pm; Fri 6am–3pm; Sat 7pm–1am; Average main course: $12. AmEx, Disc, MC, V.
This restaurant is one of the few reminders that the Lower East Side once housed one of the world's largest Jewish communities. Come to Ratner's for the plain or fruit-filled cheese blintzes, or the pierogi. Don't expect any meat specialities, however, since dairy products and fish are used here.

Sammy's Roumanian

157 Chrystie St at Delancey St (212-673-0330). Subway: F to Delancey St; J, M, Z to Essex St. Sun–Thu 3–11pm; Fri, Sat 3pm–midnight. Average main course: $22. AmEx, MC, V.
Your arteries will immediately begin to thicken after a meal at Sammy's, which includes obscenely long steaks, chopped liver that's mixed at the table with schmaltz (yellow rendered chicken fat) and a bottle of vodka served in an ice block. The sour pickles and peppers will help cut the massive quantities of fat you're ingesting, and the loud band playing Yiddish standards will keep you from thinking about that impending heart attack.

Mexican

Rosa Mexicano

1063 First Ave at 58th St (212-753-7407). Subway: 4, 5, 6 to 59th St; N, R to Lexington Ave. Dinner: 5pm–midnight. Average main course: $20. AmEx, DC, MC, V.
When Josefina Howard cooks Mexican food, the result isn't leaden dishes smothered in melted cheese, but a mix of vibrant flavors that jump off the plate. Savor her renowned guacamole, prepared tableside, and you'll forget just how far north of the border you really are.

Zarela

953 Second Ave between 50th and 51st Sts (212-644-6740). Subway: E, F to Lexington Ave; 6 to 51st St. Lunch: Mon–Fri noon–3pm. Dinner: Mon–Thu 5–11pm; Fri, Sat 5–11:30pm; Sun 5–10pm. Average main course: $14. AmEx, DC.
Distinguished by its authentic menu, this upscale but festive Mexican restaurant has two floors, the upper being quieter. Owner Zarela Martinez is serious about the food she offers and has even penned a cookbook, *Food from My Heart.*

Zócalo

174 E 82nd St between Lexington and Third Aves (212-717-7772). Subway: 4, 5, 6 to 86th St. 6pm–midnight. Average main course: $20. AmEx, MC, V.
At this candlelit spot (with orange walls and a green ceiling), you can expect the kind of food that Mexicans eat in their homes. Empanadas are filled with such ingredients as oysters or zucchini, and the pozole (pork and hominy stew) is a great choice after too many margaritas.

Pan-Asian

Bop

325 Bowery at 2nd St (212-254-7887). Subway: 6 to Bleecker St. 6pm–midnight. Average main course: $16. AmEx, MC, V.
Do-it-yourself Korean barbecue and a stylish cocktail lounge are the new draws at Bop, which has relocated to an airy, bilevel space on the Bowery. But if soy-marinated beef and soju (a potato-based Korean liquor) aren't your thing, don't worry: You can still get bibimbop, kimchi and several other Korean staples.

Dok Suni's

119 First Ave between 7th St and St. Marks Pl (212-477-9506). Subway: 6 to Astor Pl. 4:30–11:30pm. Average main course: $12. No credit cards.
Korean "home cooking" might not resemble anything you've ever cooked at home, but this woody East Villager is down-

*Home sweet chrome: Stop by the 24-hour **Empire Diner** for classic American eats.*

town-homey, featuring an ample menu of stir-fried kimchi with rice, braised short ribs, grilled squid and other straight-forward alternatives to Chinese take-out.

The Elephant

58 E 1st St between First and Second Aves
(212-505-7739). Subway: F to Second Ave. Mon–Thu
11:30am–1am. Fri, Sat 11:30am–2:30am. Sun
3pm–1am. Average main course: $12. AmEx.
This French-Thai bistro looks tiny, but it thinks huge. Both the cuisine—ambitious, often sculptural fusion dishes such as charcoal-grilled chicken marinated in lemongrass, and steamed mussels in coconut-milk broth—and the zebra-striped furniture scream for attention. And they get it: The place packs in a hip local crowd every night.

Kelley & Ping

127 Greene St between Houston and Prince Sts
(212-228-1212). Subway: N, R to Prince St. Lunch:
1:30am–5pm. Dinner: 6–11:30pm. Average main
course: $13. AmEx, MC, V.
This cool spot is part Saigon corner deli, part pan-Asian noodle bar. Nothing beats the cold weather like an oversize bowl of steaming soup with chow fun noodles and shredded pork. It's no mystery why K&P gets packed at lunchtime: The cheap (for Soho) prices and efficient service make it one of the area's most reliable places for a quick, filling and flavorful meal.

Penang

109 Spring St between Greene and Mercer Sts
(212-274-8883). Subway: N, R to Prince St. Mon–Thu
11:30am–midnight; Fri, Sat 11:30am–1am; Sun
1pm–midnight. Average main course: $13. AmEx, MC, V.
The Penangs are separately owned but share a transporting, slightly silly decor and a menu of serious Malaysian intrigue. Ask for traditional fish-head soup, or stick to more approachable fare, such as spring rolls with jicama or a whole striped bass in banana leaves.
Other locations: *240 Columbus Ave at 71st St*
(212-769-3988); 1596 Second Ave between 82nd and
83rd Sts (212-585-3838); 38-04 Prince St at Main St,
Flushing, Queens (718-321-2078).

Pho Bang

117 Mott St at Hester St (212-966-3797). Subway:
J, M, Z, N, R, 6 to Canal St. 10am–10pm. Average main
course: $8. No credit cards.
The Bang family has six Vietnamese restaurants in the metropolitan area, but this is where to get the greatest Bang for your buck: For $5.95, you get logs of beef stuffed with onions, which you roll with squares of vermicelli rice noodles and crisp greens, and then dunk in a sweet fish sauce. But think twice before ordering the salty lemonade.

Ruby Foo's

2182 Broadway at 77th St (212-724-6700). Subway:
1, 9 to 79th St. Mon–Thu 11:30am–12:30am; Fri, Sat
11:30am–1am; Sun 11:30am–midnight. Average main
course: $15. AmEx, MC, V.
Ruby Foo's sweeping pan-Asian decor evokes both classic chop-suey houses and the decadence of sister rooms Blue Water Grill and Park Avalon. Chef Junnajet Hurapan adds to the convivial spirit, mixing clever dim sum and meaty sushi on an East-meets-East fusion menu designed for sharing.

South American/Caribbean

Cafe Habana

17 Prince St at Elizabeth St (212-625-2002).
Subway: 6 to Spring St. 9am–midnight. Average main
course: $7. AmEx, MC, V.
Leave it to the owners of Rialto to make rice and beans cool. Inspired by a 1960s Miami Beach aesthetic, the Nolita restau-rateurs have stocked this tiny lunch counter with an appetizing mix of hip customers, turquoise tiles, char-grilled burgers, crisp Cubano sandwiches and Day-Glo Mexican sodas. You'll never look so good slumming it anywhere else.

Campo

89 Greenwich Ave between 12th and Bank Sts
(212-691-8080). Subway: A, C, E to 14th St; L to Eighth
Ave. Mon–Fri 11:30am–11pm; Sat 10am–11:30pm; Sun
10am–11pm. Average main course: $16. AmEx, MC, V.
A modest restaurant with big intentions, Campo captures the flavors of heartland cooking from throughout the Americas. Its appetizer of crisp, light empanadas filled with a creamy corn puree is excellent, as is its smoked, shredded pork shoulder. The slightly cramped dining room doesn't quite make you feel as if you're in the American Southwest or out on the pampas, but the food is transporting enough.

Chimichurri Grill

606 Ninth Ave between 43rd and 44th Sts
(212-586-8655). Subway: A, C, E to 42nd St–Port
Authority. Mon–Sat noon–11:30pm; Sun noon–10:30pm.
Average main course: $18. AmEx, DC, MC, V.
The warm atmosphere in this compact, neatly appointed dining room is reason enough to squeeze into one of Chimichurri's 30 seats, but the simple, rich Argentinean cuisine clinches the deal. Main courses revolve around Argentinean beef, best accented with chimichurri, a pestolike mixture of garlic, olive oil, oregano, parsley and roasted red peppers.

Coco Roco

392 Fifth Ave between 6th and 7th Sts, Park Slope,
Brooklyn (718-965-3376). Subway: F to Seventh Ave.
Sun–Thu noon–10pm; Fri, Sat noon–11pm. Average
main course: $7. AmEx, Disc, MC, V.
Slowly rotating skewers of dripping, charred chicken will mesmerize you at this Peruvian outpost. But it's the other dishes on the menu that make Coco Roco the best South American joint this side of Patria: fluffy papa rellenas stuffed with pork, roast corn and piquant salsa; pulpo al olivo, tender octopus in a creamy, mild olive sauce; arroz chaufa de mariscos, a massive paella; and tacu-tacu de pescado, sweet potato–crusted red snapper—to name but a few.

El Castillo de Jagua

113 Rivington St between Essex and Ludlow Sts
(212-982-6412). Subway: J, M, Z, N, R, 6 to Canal St.
10am–11pm. Average main course: $8. No credit cards.
Travelers, take note: A fail-safe means of finding a cheap, delicious meal is to eat where the cops eat. At this blue-collar restaurant, policemen sit shoulder to shoulder with local Dominicans. Order a sumptuous meal of chuletas (fried pork chops) or two eggs sunny-side-up over a heaping portion of rice and beans, and sway to the Latin rhythms on the jukebox.

El Pollo

1746 First Ave between 90th and 91st Sts (212-
966-7810). Subway: 4, 5, 6 to 86th St. 11:30am–11pm.
Average main course: $9. AmEx, MC, V.
A good, cheap meal is a rarity on the Upper East Side, which explains why El Pollo has such a cultish following. Its marinated chicken is carefully roasted to dripping perfection, and the birds are so cheap, you'll want to order more—say, the menudencias fritas, a melange of chicken hearts, liver, gizzards and necks, gently sautéed. Portions are large, so choose carefully or be prepared to cart around your leftovers.

Ipanema

13 W 46th St between Fifth and Sixth Aves (212-730-
5848). Subway: B, D, F, Q to 42nd St. Average main
course: $14. AmEx, DC, Disc, MC, V.
Ipanema is one of the best places on 46th Street's Little Brazil and an ideal pretheater or mid-shopping pit stop. Try shrimp in its many incarnations (garlicky and grilled as an appe-

Want a quickie?

When New Yorkers are in a hurry, they grab a sandwich

In New York, where people barely have time to breathe during the workweek, much less eat, it's the sandwich that's the midday meal of choice: It's quick, filling and cheap. Most New Yorkers in a hurry stop by any of the countless corner delis throughout the city to pick up a decent turkey-on-rye or a ham-and-cheese-on-sourdough for an affordable price (usually around $5). But if you're willing to look a bit harder, you'll find sandwich shops whose products stand up to any of the city's ballyhooed culinary creations. You'll discover teetering Italian heroes stacked with soppressata, provolone and prosciutto, or choice gourmet creations filled with marinated portobellos, caramelized onions and arugula.

For some of the city's more authentic and flavorful sandwiches, head to the outer boroughs. At **Joe's Busy Corner** (552 Driggs Avenue between 7th and 8th Streets, Williamsburg, Brooklyn, 718-388-6372), freshly made mozzarella is smoked out front on the sidewalk, while the chatty Italian countermen inside assemble hulking heroes layered with shaved prosciutto, pepperoni, roasted peppers and just enough balsamic vinegar and olives to add some kick. Italophiles will find an equally satisfying taste of the old country in the Bronx at **Mike's Deli** (inside the **Arthur Avenue Market**, 2344 Arthur Avenue between 186th Street and Crescent Avenue, Bronx, 718-295-5033). Cured sausages and prosciutto hang like vines from the ceiling, yet the shop's best creation might be its vegetarian schiaccata ($5), a square of homemade foccacia studded with sun-dried tomatoes, sliced open and stacked high with grilled zucchini and eggplant, roasted red peppers, marinated red onion, tomato and fresh mesclun. Craving something American? Go straight to **Brennan & Carr** (3432 Nostrand Avenue at Avenue U, Marine Park, Brooklyn, 718-769-1254), a 62-year-old ranch-style restaurant where thinly sliced medium-rare roast beef is piled onto kaiser rolls and dipped into its own juices.

In Manhattan, locals can't get enough of **Così** (165 East 52nd Street between Lexington and Third Avenues, 212-758-7800; 11 West 42nd Street between Fifth and Sixth Avenues, 212-398-6660; 38 East 45th Street between Madison and Vanderbilt Avenues, 212-949-7400; 257 Park Avenue South between 21st and 22nd Streets, 212-598-9300; 3 East 17th Street between Fifth Avenue and Union Square West, 212-414-8476). At these sporty French sandwich shops, incredibly tasty warm flatbread (baked fresh in a stone ovens) is sliced open and stuffed with any number of fillings, including pesto chicken salad, smoked ham and marinated mushrooms. Far less stylish, but just as delicious, is **Cuchifrito** (351 East 13th Street between First and Second Avenues, 212-475-4508), a tiny Cuban take-out in the East Village. Admire the roasted plantains and savory stews, and then order the cubano, a foot-long section of French bread bulging with crispy, succulent chunks of roasted pork, thin slices of ham, tart pickles, mayo and melted Swiss cheese.

Soho shoppers can head a few blocks east to Little Italy and stop by the **Italian Food Center** (186 Grand Street at Mulberry Street, 212-925-2954) for delicious Italian heroes big and heavy enough to double as barbells. Or they can go to **Bread & Butter** (229 Elizabeth Street between Houston and Prince Streets, 212-925-7600). A lazy, country-style shop frequented by neighborhood artists and celebs like Vincent Gallo, B&B makes superb sandwiches on grilled baguettes that are layered with marinated artichokes, fresh arugula, smoky bacon, shaved turkey and other top-quality ingredients. If that's not enough to win you over, try their massive bags of homemade thick-cut fries. You and your personal trainer will wish you'd never discovered how good they are.

*Be like Mike: Order a supreme foccacia sandwich at **Mike's Deli** in the Bronx.*

tizer, or served in a coconut with olives and mashed potatoes). It's odd to find Brazilian flair in midtown, but Ipanema lives up to its name.

Jimmy's Bronx Cafe
281 W Fordham Rd between Cedar Ave and Major Deegan Expwy, Bronx (718-329-2000). Subway: 1, 9 to 207th St. Cafe: Mon–Wed 10am–2am; Thu–Sun 10am–4am. Patio: Thu–Sat 9pm–4am; Sun 5pm–4am. Average main course: $7. AmEx, DC, MC, V.
Enough with the Yankees and the zoo. The best reason to visit the Bronx is Jimmy's. Taking up an entire block, this Puerto Rican entertainment mecca is part sports bar, part criollo dining room and part nightclub. It's as popular with Latino families; recording artists, such as Tito Puente; and members of the Yanks—their signed jerseys line the sports-bar section of the complex.

Victor's Café
236 W 52nd St between Broadway and Eighth Ave (212-586-7714). Subway: C, E to 50th St. Sun–Thu noon–midnight; Fri, Sat noon–1am. Average main course: $20. AmEx, DC, MC, V.
Nearly 30 years old, this estimable Theater District restaurant is the father of all Manhattan Cubans. Get into the mood with a mojito, Hemingway's favorite pre-Castro cocktail, and then let yourself go with a helping of regional flavors, from porky and spicy to sweet and, well, porky.

Spanish

El Faro
823 Greenwich St at Horatio St (212-929-8210). Subway: A, C, E to 14th St; L to Eighth Ave. Mon–Thu 11:30am–midnight; Fri, Sat 11:30am–1am. Average main course: $19. AmEx, Disc, MC, V.
Ancient and constant, this West Villager is widely regarded as having some of the best Spanish food in the borough of Manhattan.

El Quixote
226 W 23rd St between Seventh and Eighth Aves (212-929-1855). Subway: 1, 9 to 23rd St. Sun–Thu noon–midnight; Fri, Sat noon–1am. Average main course: $16. AmEx, DC, Disc, MC, V.
It's in the eternally quirky Chelsea Hotel, but El Quixote is straight-faced, old-school Spanish. With its endearingly serious uniformed waiters, murals starring the ubiquitous Mr. La Mancha, and its huge platters of paella and cut-rate lobster specials, El Quixote proves it's hip to be square.

Ñ
33 Crosby St between Broome and Grand Sts (212-219-8856). Subway: 6 to Spring St. 5pm–midnight. Average main course: $15. No credit cards.
Straight out of an Almodóvar movie, Ñ (pronounced en-yay) has yellow and red polka-dotted walls and copper-penny sculptures. It's a narrow, cool, dark spot, great for beating the heat of a Soho summer with a pitcher of sangria, or for cozying up in cooler seasons with copious tapas. Tuck yourself into a table and try the pan con tomate and the marinated anchovies called boquerones.

Rio Mar
7 Ninth Ave at Little W 12th St (212-243-9015). Subway: A, C, E to 14th St. Noon–3am. Average main course: $14. AmEx.
On a desolate, ragged stretch of the Meatpacking District sits Rio Mar, partying all by itself. It's an unexpected home of sangria by the pitcher, fantastically oily and garlicky tapas, a nearly all-Spanish jukebox and a hell of a lot of up-late fun.

Tapas Lounge
1078 First Ave between 58th and 59th Sts (212-421-8282). Subway: N, R to Lexington Ave; 4, 5, 6 to 59th St. Sun–Tue 5:30pm–midnight; Wed–Sat 5:30pm–3am. Average main course: $12. AmEx.
Little Spanish snacks are the familiar premise around which the guys at Tapas Lounge have built an ongoing party. Music, chatter, low lighting, low seating and a higher than expected pretty-people quotient for this residential Siberia all add to the good time. The look is midway between a fetishist's dark chamber and a theme-park lounge, but the paella is moist and huge. Where else in the neighborhood can you stay up till 3am smoking Turkish tobacco in a hookah?

Vegetarian

Angelica Kitchen
300 E 12th St between First and Second Aves (212-228-2909). Subway: L to First Ave; N, R, 4, 5, 6 to 14th St–Union Sq. 11:30am–10:30pm. Average main course: $10. No credit cards.
The best vegan restaurant in the city, this soothing oblong fishbowl serves up tasty dishes such as the velvety sesame-noodle dish Soba Sensation, the (huge) Wee Dragon bowl and an array of cheesy cheeseless specials. If you are a vegan, vegetarian or health-food enthusiast, you must pay Angelica a visit.

B&H Dairy
127 Second Ave between 7th St and St. Marks Pl (212-505-8065). Subway: 6 to Astor Pl. Mon–Sat 6:30am–10pm; Sun 7am–10pm. Average main course: $8. No credit cards.
B&H looks just like a standard ham 'n' eggs American diner but serves an astonishing range of hearty vegetarian soups, juices, great homemade challah bread and veggie burgers. It's the antidote to prissy, self-righteous vegetarian dining.

Kate's Joint
58 Ave B between 4th and 5th Sts (212-777-7059). Subway: F to Second Ave. Mon–Wed 8:30am–11pm; Thu–Sun 8:30am–midnight. Average main course: $9. AmEx, DC, MC, V.
Kate's is a lazy, laid-back Alphabet City family business, with a comfy living-room area at the front. Kate, the chef, is a master at faux meat. Try her mock popcorn shrimp with Abijah's Secret Sauce and her faux Jamaican patties. Watch out for her kids.

Strictly Roots
2058 Adam Clayton Powell Blvd between 122nd and 123rd Sts (212-864-8699). Subway: 2, 3 to 125th St. Mon–Sat 11am–11pm; Sun noon–7pm. Average main course: $8. No credit cards.
This Harlem diner serves "nothing that crawls, swims, walks or flies." Delicious food such as the mock-beef stew make it worth a visit, but don't miss the frothy shakes with names like Bad Man, served by friendly Rasta dudes.

Zen Palate
34 Union Sq East at 16th St (212-614-9291). Subway: L, N, R, 4, 5, 6 to 14th St–Union Sq. Lunch: Mon–Sat 11:30am–3pm. Dinner: Mon–Sat 5:30–11pm; Sun 5–10:30pm. Average main course: $13. AmEx, DC, MC, V.
Decorated like delicate Japanese bistros, these restaurants have quickly become favorites among many New Yorkers, vegetarian or not. Despite selections with names such as Shredded Melody, the food is good, and each branch is perennially packed.
Other locations: *663 Ninth Ave at 46th St (212-582-1669); 2170 Broadway between 76th and 77th Sts (212-501-7768).*

Cafés & Bars

Of all the gin joints in the world, you have to walk into these

Cafés

For a while there, it seemed as if New Yorkers were trying to classify coffee bars as more of a trend than a habit. But with Starbucks and other chains still gobbling up retail space, the citywide addiction is out in the open, and it's safe to say that New Yorkers are permanently hooked on joe. The question is how you want to get your fix: The trendy crowd likes its lattes in laid-back lounges that offer a profusion of sofas and magazines. Foodies want a bite to eat while they're sipping their brew, and many cafés offer delectable home-made desserts and sandwiches. Those on the run can stop into a coffee bar and get a double espresso to go. And traditionalists can still find a string of old-fashioned cafés on Bleecker Street in the West Village, where you can sit with your espresso and watch the crowds go by.

Big Cup
228 Eighth Ave between 21st and 22nd Sts (212-206-0059). Subway: C, E to 23rd St. Mon–Thu 7am–1am; Fri 7am–2am; Sat, Sun 8am–2am. No credit cards.

This Chelsea coffee shop is a popular morning hangout for the local gay population. The café has a comfortable mix of living-room furniture that makes it an ideal place to skim the newspaper while inhaling a muffin and some coffee.

Cafe Gitane
242 Mott St between Houston and Prince Sts (212-334-9552). Subway: N, R to Prince St; B, D, F, Q to Broadway–Lafayette St. 9am–midnight. No credit cards.

Walk by this Frenchy café on a sunny day, and you'll feel as if you've discovered the source of downtown cool. Hipsters lounge outside on small benches; inside, they sip café au lait, smoke and skim the many fashion glossies the café offers as reading material. Don't be afraid to join the scene—these pretty young things don't bite (and you might get some swell fashion ideas too).

Café Lalo
201 W 83rd St between Amsterdam Ave and Broadway (212-496-6031). Subway: 1, 9 to 86th St. Mon–Thu, Sun 9am–2am; Fri, Sat 9am–4am. No credit cards.

This perennially popular Upper West Side café has one of the city's largest dessert selections—all sorts of chocolate and fruit cakes, plus all-American pies, such as pecan and apple. In summer, the long windows open onto the tree-lined street, European-style. Classical melodies are the music of choice here.

*Feeling Hungary? Fuel up on pastries with Columbia students at **Hungarian Pastry Shop**.*

Caffe Reggio

*119 MacDougal St between W 3rd and Bleecker Sts
(212-475-9557). Subway: A, C, E, B, D, F, Q to West
4th St–Washington Sq. Mon–Thu, Sun 10am–2am;
Fri, Sat 10am–4am. No credit cards.*
A favorite spot with tourists and New Yorkers who don't
live downtown (if they did, they'd know of more chic and
less crowded places to go), Caffe Reggio is a great spot for
people-watching and coffee-drinking.

Ceci-Cela

*55 Spring St between Lafayette and Mulberry Sts
(212-274-9179). Subway: 6 to Spring St. Mon–Sat
7am–7pm; Sun 8am–7pm. MC, V.*
Tucked in a narrow space away from the weekend throngs
of Soho, Ceci-Cela offers its own French pastries and crispy
croissants in a cozy and relaxed setting. Get some dessert to
go, or walk to the back room, where there are a few rattan
tables and waitress service.

City Bakery

*22 E 17th St between Fifth Ave and Broadway
(212-366-1414). Subway: L, N, R, 4, 5, 6 to 14th
St–Union Sq. Mon–Sat 7:30am–6pm. AmEx, MC, V.*
Don't be intimidated by the drafty, industrial decor of this Flatiron
bakery. The rich tarts found here are some of the best in the
city, scoring high marks for taste, originality and design.
Make a detour on Saturday morning before heading to Union
Square's outdoor farmer's market and order a coffee and a
tart. Before you know it, you'll be craving chef/owner Maury
Rubin's pastry cookbook, available in the store.

Cupcake Café

*522 Ninth Ave at 39th St (212-465-1530). Subway:
A, C, E to 42nd St. Mon–Fri 7am–7pm; Sat 8am–7pm;
Sun 9am– 5pm. No credit cards.*
There's little room for loungers at this off-the-beaten-track
bakery in Hell's Kitchen; it only has a few shabby tables.
Cupcakes and cakes are exquisitely decorated with rich, but-
tery frosting swirled into colorful flowers. If you can't stom-
ach so much fat, try a freshly made doughnut or muffin.

DeRoberti's

*176 First Ave at 11th St (212-674-7137). Subway:
L to First Ave. Tue–Thu, Sun 9am–11pm; Fri, Sat
9am–midnight. MC, V.*
Located in a pocket of the East Village that closely resembles Little Italy, DeRoberti's is a decades-old patisserie where
espresso, cappuccino and Italian desserts, such as cannoli
and hazelnut meringue, are served in a beautiful old-
fashioned setting.

Drip

*489 Amsterdam Ave between 83rd and 84th Sts
(212-875-1032). Subway: 1, 9 to 86th St. Mon–Thu
7am–1am; Fri, Sat 7am–3am; Sun 7am–midnight.
MC, V.*
Brightly colored pleather couches fill this coffee lounge and
bar. Its walls display junk food props, such as Cap'n Crunch
cereal boxes and Orangina soda bottles. The list of coffees—
espresso, cappuccino, au lait, mochaccino—is short, but suf-
ficient. At the back is a "love life" notice board, where you
can fill out a questionnaire about the mate of your dreams.

DT/UT

*1626 Second Ave at 84th St (212-327-1327). Subway:
4, 5, 6 to 86th St. Mon–Thu, Sun 7:30am–midnight; Fri,
Sat 8:30am–2am. No credit cards.*
The name of this brick-walled space, decorated with Gothic
candles and primitive art, is an abbreviation for down-
town/uptown. Plop into a couch or easy chair and choose
from a tantalizing array of baked goods—perfect accom-
paniments for the many different types of coffee listed on
the blackboard.

Kreme of the crop: Hot and cheap, **Krispy Kreme** doughnuts melt in your mouth.

Felissimo

*10 W 56th St between Fifth and Sixth Aves
(212-956-0082). Subway: N, R to Fifth Ave. Mon–Sat
10:30am–6pm. AmEx, DC, Disc, MC, V.*
The newly renovated Felissimo is a chic bazaar occupying a
narrow townhouse off the deluxe shopping extravaganza
that is Fifth Avenue. The simple Japanese-inspired decor is
wonderfully soothing; this is a great place to rest your tired
feet. On the top floor, you'll find a tranquil café serving sandwiches, cakes and tea. Sometimes a tarot-card reader takes
up residence in one corner, selling a glimpse of the future to
the forever hopeful.

Hungarian Pastry Shop

*1030 Amsterdam Ave at 111th St (212-866-4230).
Subway: 1, 9 to 110th St. Mon–Fri 8am–
11:30pm; Sat 8:30am–11:30pm; Sun 8:30am–10pm.
No credit cards.*
A Morningside Heights original, this plain-looking coffee
shop offers coffee, tea and many pastries (made in-house) to
Columbia University students and teachers. Ignore the pre-
tentious students around you reading Kant and pull out that
Jackie Collins novel you've been meaning to peruse.

'Ino

*21 Bedford St between Houston and Downing Sts
(212-989-5769). Subway: 1, 9 to Houston St. Mon–Thu
8am–2am; Fri, Sat 11am–2am. No credit cards.*
Around the corner from Film Forum, this tiny wine bar offers
inspired Italian snacks for the price of a medium popcorn.
In addition to a selection of excellent—but small—bruschetta that changes daily, 'Ino serves crisp panini and 20 wines
(all available by the half carafe, and most by the glass).

Krispy Kreme

*265 W 23rd St between Seventh and Eighth Aves
(212-620-0111). Subway: A, C, E, 1, 9 to 23rd St.
Sun–Thu 6am–midnight; Fri–Sat 6am–2am.
No credit cards.*
Sink your teeth into a fresh, hot Krispy Kreme and you'll for-
get about bagels altogether. Purists stick to the feathery light

glazed doughnuts at this ever-expanding chain, but a warm jelly-filled or moist cake version will do you just as well.
Other locations: *38 E 8th St (212-620-0111); 141 W 72nd St (212-724-1100); 1497 Third Ave (212-879-9111); 280 W 125th St (212-531-0111).*

Limbo
47 Ave A between 3rd and 4th Sts (212-477-5271). Subway: F to Second Ave. Mon–Fri 7am–midnight; Sat, Sun 8am–midnight. No credit cards.
To get a real sense of the East Village, come to this stylish coffee hangout. Freelance writers, actors and artists sit for hours, drinking large cups of tea or coffee, reading scripts and typing manuscripts on their portable computers. A packed schedule of book, poetry and tarot-card readings attracts crowds in the evenings.

Once Upon a Tart
135 Sullivan St between Houston and Prince Sts (212-387-8869). Subway: N, R to Prince St; C, E to Spring St. Mon–Fri 8am–8pm; Sat 9am–8pm; Sun 9am–6pm. AmEx, MC, V.
Waiting for the shops in Soho to open, which many do notoriously late? Stop by this small, tin-ceilinged café first for a steaming cup of café au lait or cappuccino. At breakfast, try one of the café's excellent muffins or scones. Later in the day, order a sandwich, packed with fresh ingredients, or sample one of many excellent vegetable or grain salads.

Tea & Sympathy
108 Greenwich Ave at 13th St (212-807-8329). Subway: A, C, E, 1, 2, 3, 9 to 14th St. Mon–Sat 11:30am–10:30pm; Sun 11:30am–10pm. No credit cards.
Visit this cramped, homestyle English nook during the week—on weekends the wait is annoyingly long—and order delights from Blighty, including beans on toast and cucumber sandwiches. Afternoon tea consists of an assortment of finger sandwiches, two cakes, two scones, clotted cream, jam and a pot of tea. Here, Britannia rules.

Wild Lily Tea Room
511 W 22nd St between Tenth and Eleventh Aves (212-691-2258). Subway: C, E to 23rd St. 11am–11pm. MC, V.
Suffering sensory overload after gallery-hopping in Chelsea? Recalibrate your yin and yang at this serene, multilevel space where the sound of the gurgling water in a small indoor fish pond blends with the clink of handcrafted china. Choose between dainty tea sandwiches, scones and more than 40 different types of tea, including Chinese, Japanese, Indian and herbal varieties.

Bars

Whether your taste runs to dingy gin mill, fabulous lounge or alehouse, New York is a damn fine drinking town (*see chapter* **Ale, ale the gang's all here**, *page 186, and* **This ain't no disco**, *pages 210–211*). In the past year, a number of bars have set up shop in the once run-down, but now trendy Lower East Side. Upscale restaurants continue to open with drinking dens attached, but the brewhouse and cigar-bar fads are fading, and the cosmopolitan—the early-'90s libation of choice—is now officially tired. The rest of the bars here should quench the thirst of any type of drinker, from the polite sipper to the perennially pickled hooch hound.

288
288 Elizabeth St between Houston and Bleecker Sts (212-260-5045). Subway: B, D, F, Q to

*Drink to your health: Weekend DJs and Rx paraphernalia add to the atmosphere at **Barmacy**.*

Broadway–Lafayette St; 6 to Bleecker St. Noon–4am.
No credit cards.
Also called Tom & Jerry's, this is a cavernous drinking hall
that gets smoky and loud. It also serves a great Guinness to
an arty, slightly slackerish crowd.

Baby Jupiter
170 Orchard St at Stanton St (212-982-2229). Subway:
F to Second Ave. 11am–4am. MC, V.
Impressive (and affordable) Asian-Cajun cuisine and a raucous back room featuring local unsigned bands have made
Baby Jupiter an excellent addition to the batch of no-cover
music venues on the Lower East Side.

Barmacy
538 E 14th St between Aves A and B (212-228-2240).
Subway: L to First Ave. Mon–Fri 5:30pm–4am; Sat,
Sun 7:30pm– 4am. No credit cards.
Formerly (you guessed it) a pharmacy, Barmacy is American-
kitsch queen Deb Parker's latest project (she also owns
Beauty Bar a few blocks west). Packed to the hilt with 1950s
Rx paraphernalia, it remains a fun and trendy spot (when
taken in the right dosage). The decor includes ads for pros-
thetics and adult diapers. They use beakers instead of glasses and, thankfully, good DJs play on the weekends.

Botanica
47 E Houston St between Mott and Mulberry Sts
(212-343-7251). Subway: B, D, F, Q to
Broadway–Lafayette St. 5pm–4am. No credit cards.
It's easy to choke on the bohemian atmosphere here, but
besides a few modern beatniks and a lot of Gitanes smoke,
Botanica is a fine neighborhood gin mill with plenty of
couches and good DJs most nights.

Bubble Lounge
228 West Broadway between Franklin and White Sts
(212-431-3433). Subway: 1, 9 to Franklin; A, C, E to
Canal St. Mon–Thu 5:30pm–4am; Fri, Sat 4:30pm–
4am; Sun 4:30pm–1am. AmEx, DC, MC, V.
Tribeca's very own cigar-and-champagne bar has the requisite sofas, wing-back chairs, Persian rugs and chandeliers,
and it's made more bearable by the live jazz and good, caviar-
heavy bar menu.

Chumley's
86 Bedford St between Barrow and Grove Sts (212-
675-4449). 1, 9 to Christopher St–Sheridan Sq. Mon–Fri
5pm–midnight; Sat, Sun 5pm–2am. No credit cards.
Someone needs to tell Chumley's that the days of prohibition are over. This ex-speakeasy still doesn't have a sign over
the door, so it's easy to walk straight past it. Inside is a pub-
restaurant with book-lined walls and a cozy atmosphere. The
food is passable and well priced.

Double Happiness
174 Mott St between Broome and Grand Sts
(212-941-1282). Subway: B, D, Q to Grand St. Sun–
Thu 5pm–2am; Fri, Sat 5pm–4am. MC, V.
With its low ceilings, seductively dank vibe and multitude
of hidden nooks, this former mob hangout in the middle of
Chinatown offers the perfect atmosphere for intimate conversation or loud chatter. And expect some good people-
watching while you're there: It attracts a crowd as hip as that
at its Lower East Side sibling, **Orchard Bar** (212-673-5350).

Fanelli's
94 Prince St at Mercer St (212-226-9412). Subway:
B, D, F, Q to Broadway–Lafayette St; N, R to Prince St.
Mon–Thu 10am–2am; Sat 11am–3am. AmEx, DC,
Disc, MC, V.
Fanelli's is the oldest and one of the best bars in Soho. It has
a great wooden bar, local beers, wonderful barmen, a tiled floor
and framed pictures of boxers on the walls. It's decidedly

I like to watch

Catch all the action (and down a few) at a mega sports bar

New York may or may not be the sports capital of the world, but it's almost certainly the
sports-bar capital. Hundreds of New York
bars provide TV sports as a drinking companion, but some go to extremes to take you
to big-screen sports heaven—and to provide
an audience for your illuminating (if not
always sober) insights into the big game.

The **All-Star Cafe**, 1540 Broadway at 45th
Street (212-840-TEAM), is the prototype for
these spaceship-like spaces, overflowing with
TV sets, electronic score tickers and overpriced
fried food. This theme restaurant also features
plenty of cool memorabilia from sports celebrities hanging on the walls, à la the Hard Rock
Cafe. **Mickey Mantle's**, 42 Central Park
South near Sixth Avenue (212-688-7777), has
ten huge screens. **The Sporting Club**, 99
Hudson Street at Franklin Street (212-219-
0900), has "only" nine televisions, but throws
in trivia betting machines at the bar.

If you're feeling the urge to actually participate in a sport, check out **Hackers Hitters
& Hoops**, 123 West 18th Street between Sixth
and Seventh Avenues (212-929-7482), a bar
with a sporting club attached. It boasts one
basketball court, two baseball batting cages, a
golf simulator, a mini-golf game and two giant
screens, for the lazy members in your group. If
you get tired of the televisual glitz of American sports, there's always **McCormack's**, 365
Third Avenue at 27th Street (212-683-0911), or
British Open, 320 East 59th Street between
First and Second Avenues (212-355-8467), these
are the best places to watch British football in
the company of some expatriate hooligans.

unpretentious and a favorite with art-gallery owners. The food
is good, but many use it as ballast for shots of Jack.

Fez
Inside Time Café, 380 Lafayette St at Great Jones St
(212-533-7000). Subway: 6 to Astor Pl. Mon–Thu, Sun
6pm–2am; Fri, Sat 6pm–4am. AmEx, MC, V.
Downstairs you'll find music and readings, but the bar is
perfect for a good old lounge. Deep sofas, low tables, good
low lighting and a slight Moroccan theme (copper tables and
paintings of Maghreb mamas) all conspire to keep you
reclining long into the night.

Global 33
93 Second Avenue between 5th and 6th Sts
(212-477-8427). Subway: 6 to Astor Pl. Mon–Thu
6pm–1am; Fri, Sat 6pm–2am. AmEx.

The big modernist clocks in Global 33's back room tell you the time in Monte Carlo, Shanghai, Tangier, Istanbul and Havana—helpful if you're on an international espionage mission. But even if you're not, the sleek 1960s design practically forces you to drink a sophisticated cocktail.

Great Lakes
284 Fifth Ave at 1st St, Park Slope, Brooklyn (718-499-3710). Subway: F to Seventh Ave. Mon–Fri 6pm–4am; Sat, Sun 1pm–4am. No credit cards.
Spend enough nights dealing with bitchy hostesses, cocky bartenders and glamorama crowds, and you begin to crave a bar like Great Lakes. This sparsely decorated outpost evokes the simple feel of the Midwest, while attracting a loyal clientele that comes for the booze, conversation and live music.

The Greatest Bar on Earth
Windows on the World, 1 World Trade Center, West St between Liberty and Vesey Sts, 107th floor

(212-524-7011). Subway: C, E to World Trade Ctr; N, R, 1, 9 to Cortlandt St. Mon–Thu 4pm–midnight; Fri 4pm–2am; Sat noon–2am; Sun 11am–11pm. AmEx, DC, Disc, MC, V.
No, this postmodern saloon in the sky certainly doesn't live up to the hyperbolic name, but it's nicely unearthly. And its Monday "Little Debbie" funk nights brings an unlikely hip crowd to the Wall Street area. Go ahead, get high among the odd spiky sculptures in the sky, and the whole city below appears festive.

Joe's
520 E 6th St between Aves A and B (212-473-9093). Subway: F to Second Ave. Noon– 4am. No credit cards.
Joe's bar (as opposed to **Joe's Pub**, *see next page*) is an East Village refuge for barflies young and old, with Hank Williams and Dolly Parton on the jukebox a pool table in the back.

Ale, ale the gang's all here
Hey, Bud, join your pint-swilling pals at one of NYC's best beer halls

Over the past few years, New York has gone gaga over martinis, studied up on single-malt scotches and even taken a shine to small-batch bourbons. Still, a hefty portion of the city has remained interested not in "having a cocktail," but in just plain old drinking—beer, that is. And for them, there's countless bars all over town where one can tip back a pint, pour a pitcher or chug from a mug. Below are some of the best.

Burp Castle
41 E 7th St between First and Second Aves (212-982-4576). Subway: 6 to Astor Pl. Hours vary. AmEx, Disc, MC, V.
The bartenders dressed in cassocks and the Brueghelesque murals of drunk monks hanging on the walls help make Burp Castle one of the city's weirder theme bars, but they also illustrate the proud, 900-year tradition of beer-brewing Belgian Trappist monks. Famed for its massive beer selection (more than 135 varieties) and knowledgeable staff, the Burp Castle is a beer nut's haven.

The Ginger Man
11 E 36th St between Fifth and Madison Aves (212-532-3740). Subway: 6 to 33rd St. Mon–Wed 11am–2am; Thu, Fri 11:30am–4am; Sat 12:30pm– 4am; Sun 3pm–midnight. AmEx, DC, MC, V.
One of the best places to grab a cold pint on the East Side, the Ginger Man combines the feel of a down-to-earth pub with the elegance of one of the city's finer restaurants. Even when the after-work crowd pours into this cavernous place, you should be able to find a spot in a snug booth or on a capacious leather couch. New brews are added regularly to the list of more than 150 beers, and the Irish-slanted pub menu includes a hearty Guinness stew.

Lakeside Lounge
162 Ave B between 10th and 11th Sts (212-529-8463). Subway: L to First Ave. 4pm– 4am. No credit cards.
Who says New York is a pricey town? At this Alphabet City favorite you can relive your high school and college days with ice cold cans of Milwaukee's Best for $1.50 each. Better yet, you can drain that beer while watching some of New York's finest underground rock & roll bands, which often play for free in the back room.

Phebe's
361 Bowery at 4th St (212-473-9008). Subway: 6 to Astor Pl. Mon–Fri 4pm–4am; Sat, Sun 5pm–4am. AmEx, MC, Visa.
When you're intent on getting hammered (but not on cleaning out your checking account), swallow your hipster pride and head to Phebe's. The waitresses at this sprawling, raucous bar will set down a stack of plastic cups and keep on dropping off $5 pitchers of Bud until you're as loud, drunk and idiotic as all the other happy customers.

Sparky's Ale House
481 Court St at Nelson St, Carroll Gardens, Brooklyn (718-624-5516). Subway: F to Smith–9th Sts. Mon–Fri 4pm–4am; Sat 3pm–4am; Sun 2pm–4am. No credit cards.
Tucked away in Carroll Gardens, Sparky's is a genuine neighborhood bar with Foosball, darts, pool, 30 beers on tap and 100 different bottles. The friendly bartenders don't flinch when the laid-back customers arrive with dogs in tow, and regulars can join Sparky's Mug Club—members are allowed to keep their own glasses behind the bar.

Subway Inn
143 E 60th St between Lexington and Third Aves (212-223-8929). Subway: 6 to 59th St; N, R to Lexington Ave. Mon–Sat 8am–4am; Sun noon– 4am. No credit cards.
Hidden in plain sight on one of NYC's busiest corners lies this dark sanctuary, completely removed from the surrounding Upper East Side melee. The bar's utility-grade name (displayed beaconlike with a vintage pink neon sign) attracts exactly the crowd you'd expect: construction workers, Vietnam vets, businessmen grabbing a quick one and other thirsty souls who aren't exactly looking to see and be seen. Join them all and down a hefty mug of Bud or Schaefer for only a buck.

*Make it a double: Subterranean **Double Happiness** attracts a cool crowd to Chinatown.*

Joe's Pub

425 Lafayette St between 4th St and Astor Pl (212-539-8770). Subway: 6 to Astor Pl. 5pm–4am. AmEx, MC, V.
Located in the majestic Joseph Papp Public Theater, this bar/performance space attracts A-list entertainers and patrons—therefore, the doormen sometimes make it difficult to gain entry. Once you're inside, you'll love the bar's warm, low lighting and stylishly loungey decor.

Junno's

64 Downing St between Bedford St and Seventh Ave South (212-627-7995). Subway: 1, 9 to Houston St. Mon–Thu 5:30pm–2am; Fri, Sat 5:30pm–4am. AmEx, MC, V.
Junno Lee's restaurant/lounge is glossier—and more legal—than the speakeasy he once operated out of a Sixth Avenue apartment. The airy space houses a bright blue bar and a restaurant serving French- and Korean-inflected Japanese cuisine, with an emphasis on seafood. But Lee clearly still has a serendipitous streak: He'll drag out a karaoke machine late at night when the drinking crowd takes over the joint.

Landmark Tavern

626 Eleventh Ave at 40th St (212-757-8595). Subway: A, C, E to 42nd St–Port Authority. Mon–Thu, Sun noon–11pm; Fri, Sat noon–midnight. No credit cards.
One of the most beautiful and tranquil of the town's old saloons, the 131-year-old Landmark has tin ceilings, wood-burning potbelly stoves and about five dozen single-malt Scotches on hand.

Lansky Lounge

104 Norfolk St between Delancey and Rivington Sts (212-677-9489). Subway: F to Delancey St; J, M, Z to Essex St. Sun–Thu 8pm–4am; Sat 10pm–4am. No credit cards.
Named after Meyer Lansky, the legendary Jewish gangster who used to eat at the adjoining Ratner's restaurant, Lansky has a hidden entrance and a 1930s backroom feel. It also has steep drink prices and an intermittent cover charge, sug-

gesting that the owners think this place is cooler than it actually is. And remember—don't go on Friday nights: The club is kosher and closed for the Jewish Sabbath.

Lot 61

550 W 21st St at Eleventh Ave (212-243-6555). Subway: C, E to 23rd St. Sun–Thu 6pm–3am; Fri–Sat 6pm–3:30am. AmEx, MC, V.
Feeding off West Chelsea's thriving art scene, this former truck garage attracts an art gallery–type clientele—and it *looks* like a gallery, right down to its collection of commissioned works by big-name artists. Sliding scrims and funky furniture give depth to the warehouse-size space, while a menu of eclectic appetizers gives you something to talk about besides last night's opening. But be warned: Tons of "private parties" can make it difficult to get in.

Max Fish

178 Ludlow St between Houston and Stanton Sts (212-529-3959). Subway: F to Second Ave. 5:30pm–4am. No credit cards.
Before stumbling on to the Lower East Side's newest bars on Ludlow and Orchard Streets, enjoy a cheap beer at this seven-year-old institution, which caters to a cool bunch of musicians and artists who have remained loyal regulars.

McSorley's Old Ale House

15 E 7th St between Second and Third Aves (212-473-9148). Subway: 6 to Astor Place; N, R to 8th St. Mon–Sat 11–1am; Sun 1pm–1am. No credit cards.
The oldest pub in Manhattan now admits women—and to judge by the usual crowd, these are mainly women who like their men in baseball caps and sloppy stages of inebriation. Still, it's a classic place for a mug of warm ale and a whiff of times gone by.

Milano's

51 E Houston St between Mott and Mulberry Sts (212-226-8632). Subway: N, R to Prince St; B, D, F, Q to Broadway–Lafayette St; 6 to Bleecker St. Mon–Sat 8–4am; Sun noon–4am. No credit cards.

Have yourself a New York moment and a great pint of Guinness at this Irish/Italian dive bar on the cusp of Little Italy. Frank Sinatra's on the walls and on the jukebox, and the die-hard barflies are always ready for boozy conversation, should you be in the mood.

North Star Pub

93 South St at Fulton St (212-509-6757). Subway: A, C to Broadway–Nassau St; 2, 3, 4, 5, J, M, Z to Fulton St. 11:30am–midnight. AmEx, DC, MC, V.
Popular with homesick Brits and local Anglophiles, this waterfront pub is the genuine article (you can order imported Brit beer and HP sauce to drench your pub grub with).

Oak Room

Algonquin Hotel, 59 W 44th St between Fifth and Sixth Aves (212-840-6800). Subway: B, D, F, Q to 42nd St; 7 to Fifth Ave. 11:30am–1am. AmEx, DC, Disc, MC, V.
Once home to Dorothy Parker's legendary literary Round Table, the Oak Room recently underwent a major renovation. The patina of cigar smoke and spilled highballs has been removed, but the clubby atmosphere of one of New York's finest hotel bars remains.

Old Town Bar

45 E 18th St between Broadway and Park Ave South (212-529-6732). Subway: L, N, R, 4, 5, 6 to 14th St–Union Square. Mon–Sat 11:30am–midnight; Sun 1–10pm. AmEx, MC, V.
Having aged like a fine whiskey, this wood-paneled bar is still going strong after more than a century. The two floors fill up with regulars and after-work mobs, but make your way to the long bar, order some stiff drinks and a top-notch burger, and you'll feel welcome.

P.J. Clarke's

915 Third Ave at 55th St (212-355-8857). Subway: 6 to 51st St; E, F to Lexington Ave. 10am–4am. AmEx, DC, MC, V.
This classic mahogany and cut-glass saloon dates from the days when Third Avenue was darkened by an elevated train and every corner had a watering hole. It survived prohibition; it also served as the location for the film *The Lost Weekend.* The whiskey's still good, and even the urinals should be a landmark.

Rudy's

627 Ninth Ave between 44th and 45th Sts (212-974-9169). Subway: A, C, E to 42nd St. 10am–4am. No credit cards.
Ninth Avenue may finally be getting its share of hip lounges, but the best place to be is parked at the bar at this unchanging institution. The red banquettes are full of customers, because the beer is cheap, the hot dogs are free and the jukebox is full of great jazz. Then there's the human jazz of Rudy's dedicated regulars, young and old.

Sophie's

507 E 5th St between Aves A and B (no phone). Subway: F to Second Ave. 11am–4am. No credit cards.
Expect to find a young crowd here on weekends, when this seasoned East Village dive bar is packed with coeds looking for cheap draft beer and a turn at the pool table.

Spy

101 Greene St between Prince and Spring Sts (212-343-9000). Subway: N, R to Prince St; 6 to Spring St. 8pm–4am. AmEx, DC, MC, V.
Spy is appropriately decadent, with grandiose chandeliers and overstuffed seating. Even with the proliferation of sofas, this is really no place to relax—you've got far too much posing to do. Drop by any evening, and you're sure to spy a model or two.

Swim

146 Orchard St between Stanton and Rivington Sts (212-673-0799). Subway: F to Second Ave. Noon–4am. AmEx, DC, MC, V.
Swim isn't the first Lower East Side bar to have a do-it-yourself design scheme, a DJ-driven soundtrack and reedy patrons. But it does distinguish itself in one way: It serves sushi. Climb to the second floor of the slim duplex to nosh on a spicy tuna roll at one of several blond-wood tables. You'll find better sushi north of Houston, but who wants to walk that far at 2am?

Temple Bar

332 Lafayette St between Bleecker and Houston Sts (212-925-4242). Subway: 6 to Bleecker St. Mon–Thu 5pm–1am; Fri, Sat 5pm–2am; Sun 7pm–1am. AmEx, DC, MC, V.
Temple's bartenders are dedicated masters of their trade, and the decor is sophisticated and opulent, lending an otherworldly air to what could become a long, dark night of expensive drinking.

Tonic

107 Norfolk St between Delancey and Rivington Sts (212-358-7504). Subway: F to Delancey St. 11am–3am. No credit cards.
Housed in a former Lower East Side kosher winery, Tonic is equal parts hair salon, café, performance space and bar. Most intriguing is the downstairs cocktail lounge, which utilizes remnants of the Kedem winery, including circular booths built within 2,500-gallon hardwood wine casks.

Vasac

108 Ave B at 7th St (212-473-8840). Subway: L to First Ave. Noon–4am. AmEx, DC, Disc, MC, V.
Also called 7B and the Horseshoe Bar, Vasac, with its spit-and-sawdust atmosphere, has been featured in countless films. The formerly edgy crowd has been replaced by a younger, bridge-and-tunnel set that likes to rock out to Dinosaur Jr and Superchunk on the alterna-heavy jukebox.

Welcome to the Johnsons

123 Rivington St between Norfolk and Essex Sts (212-420-9911). Subway: F to Delancey St. 6pm–4am. No credit cards.
Anyone who's ever rolled around on a plastic-wrapped couch while making out in a basement rec room will feel a twinge of nostalgia at Welcome to the Johnsons. Named for a hypothetical suburban American family, the laid-back bar conjures up memories of a Van Halen–saturated youth with simulated wood-paneled walls, basketball trophies, a Ms. Pac-Man machine, an avocado-green fridge and, of course, plenty of Budweiser.

The Whiskey Bar

Paramount Hotel, 235 W 46th St between Broadway and Eighth Ave (212-819-0404). Subway: C, E to 50th St. 4pm–3am. AmEx, MC, V.
Join all the rock stars and other sporty young guests of the Paramount at this dark, loungey bar run by hotshot Rande Gerber (also known as Cindy Crawford's husband). The rock & roll photos on the wall are attractive but don't draw nearly as much attention as the catsuit-wearing waitresses.

White Horse

567 Hudson St at 11th St (212-243-9260). Subway: A, C, E to 14th St; L to Eighth Ave. Mon–Wed 11am–2am; Thu–Sat 11am–4am; Sun noon–2am. No credit cards.
The White Horse is best visited on weekdays—in the evenings and on weekends the crowd becomes cheesy and noisy. It is one of New York's oldest pubs and is famous for being the site where Dylan Thomas had his final whiskey before he died in 1953. Don't expect anything special from the food.

*Tails of the city: Radio City's legendary **Rockettes** take their act outdoors.*

Arts & Entertainment

Art Galleries

From the plush halls of uptown galleries to poky artist-run spaces in Brooklyn, art shows everywhere in New York

Blessed with an abundance of galleries that exhibit everything from old and modern masters to contemporary experiments in new media, New York is an art lover's dream. You'll find galleries not just amid the refined residences of upper Madison Avenue and the glossy boutiques of 57th Street but also in areas you might not expect: in postindustrial West Chelsea, on the scruffy Lower East Side, in the meatpacking hinterland of Greenwich Village, even under the ramps that lead up to the Brooklyn Bridge. Real-estate values have forced relocations and forged a few new partnerships. While uptown galleries remain stable and sedate, occasionally taking on new artists, gallery owners in the cast-iron district of Soho—until recently the world capital of the contemporary art market—have had to compete with an increasing number of retail shops, restaurants and hotels invading their Dickensian streets. Consequently, dozens of Soho galleries have defected to more spacious (and quieter) quarters in West Chelsea, the former warehouse district now almost entirely dedicated to the exhibition and sale of contemporary art. There are still notable holdouts in Soho, though, and on weekends the neighborhood fills with a colorful mix of shoppers, tourists and art enthusiasts—often the same people.

Tribeca has its own odd assortment of small galleries and fine, art-friendly restaurants, and with more artists priced out of Manhattan studios, the areas of Brooklyn known as Williamsburg and Dumbo (Down Under the Manhattan and Brooklyn Bridge Overpass) have begun to offer freewheeling, often festive delights in quirky new artist-run spaces. In fact, the art world's current structure resembles that of the film industry: uptown corporate studios bearing the names Gagosian, PaceWildenstein and Marlborough; major independent productions in Chelsea and Soho; and smaller art-house upstarts and satellite productions on the fringes.

There has also been a curatorial shift. Many galleries have reduced their emphasis on American (particularly New York) artists and taken on a more global perspective. Photography is enjoying a renaissance, along with so-called "outsider art." And traditional, object-oriented exhibitions share the bill with multidisciplinary, often site-specific artworks that incorporate several media at once

(especially video), adding quite a theatrical flavor to viewing and collecting.

Gallerygoers should check the weekly reviews and listings in *Time Out New York*, the reviews in the Weekend section of Friday's *New York Times*, the monthly notices in such glossies as *Artforum* ($7), *Flash Art* ($7) and *Art in America* ($5), and the magazine section of the website www.artnet.com. The *Art Now Gallery Guide*, free for the asking at most galleries (or $1.50 at museum bookstores), dependably lists current exhibitions and gallery hours each month and includes helpful neighborhood maps. For an overview of the art market, look to the monthlies *Art and Antiques* ($3.95), *Art & Auction* ($6) and *Art News* ($6).

Opening times listed are from September to May or June. Summer visitors should keep in mind that most galleries are open Monday to Friday from late June to early September; some close at the end of August. Call before visiting.

Upper East Side

Most galleries on the Upper East Side are well established and sell masterworks priced for millionaires. Still, anyone can look for free, and many works are treasures that could swiftly vanish into someone's private collection. Check the auctionhouse ads for viewing schedules of important collections before they go on the block.

Gagosian
980 Madison Ave at 76th St (212-744-2313).
Subway: 6 to 77th St. Sept–Jun Tue–Sat 10am–6pm.
The prince of the 1980s, Larry Gagosian is still one of New York's major players in contemporary art, showing new work by such artists as Francesco Clemente and David Salle; he has also been hugely successful in the resale market.

Leo Castelli
59 E 79th St, between Madison and Park Aves (212-249-4470). Subway: 6 to 77th St. Sept–Jun Tue–Sat 10am–6pm.
After 30 odd years in Soho, the revered Castelli has moved back to his original uptown space. This world-famous gallery—known for representing such seminal Pop figures as Jasper Johns and Roy Lichtenstein, as well as conceptual artists Lawrence Weiner and Joseph Kosuth—seems more like a museum than a contemporary gallery.

*The rag and bone shop of art: Cameroonian artist Pascale Marthine Tayou unpacks at Soho's **Lombard Freid Fine Arts**.*

M. Knoedler & Co. Inc.

*19 E 70th St between Fifth and Madison Aves
(212-794-0550). Subway: 6 to 68th St. Sept–May
Tue–Fri 9:30am–5:30pm; Sat 10am–5:30pm.*
Knoedler shows name abstractionists and Pop artists and a selection of new contemporaries, including Frank Stella, Nancy Graves, Robert Rauschenberg, Richard Diebenkorn, Howard Hodgkin and Caio Fonseca.

Michael Werner

*21 E 67th St between Fifth and Madison Aves
(212-988-1623). Subway: 6 to 68th St. Sept–May
Mon–Sat 10am–6pm.*
The genteel Werner's Manhattan addition to his successful operation in Germany is a small but elegant space with finely curated exhibitions of work by such protean European art stars as Marcel Broodthaers, Sigmar Polke and Per Kirkeby.

Salander-O'Reilly Galleries

*20 E 79th St at Madison Ave (212-581-2268). Subway:
6 to 77th St. Winter Tue–Sat 10am–5:30pm.*
An extensive artist base, including important European and American realists, makes these galleries a must.

57th Street

The home of Carnegie Hall, exclusive boutiques and numerous art galleries, 57th Street is a beehive of cultural and commercial activity—ostentatious and expensive but fun.

André Emmerich

*41 E 57th St between Fifth and Madison Aves
(212-752-0124). Subway: 4, 5, 6 to 59th St; N, R to Fifth
Ave. Sept–May Tue–Sat 10am–5:30pm.*
Now a division of Sotheby's, this blue-chip gallery divides its interest between important modern painting, particular-

ly from the Surrealist school, and contemporary sculpture. Various works by Man Ray and David Hockney are on display, as well as pieces by Anthony Caro, Dorothea Rockburne and Judy Pfaff, among others.

DC Moore Gallery

*724 Fifth Ave between 55th and 56th Sts
(212-247-2111). Subway: E, F, N, R to Fifth Ave.
Tue–Sat 10am–5:30pm.*
This airy gallery overlooking Fifth Avenue shows prominent 20th-century and contemporary artists such as Milton Avery, Paul Cadmus, Robert Kushner, Jacob Lawrence and George Platt Lynes.

Lawrence Rubin Greenberg Van Doren

*730 Fifth Ave at 57th St (212-445-0444). Subway: N, R
to Fifth Ave. Tue–Sat 10:30am–5:30pm.*
This new 57th Street gallery looks as though it's going to be a mainstay, showing such diverse artists as Vibeke Tandberg and Roy Lichtenstein.

Marian Goodman

*24 W 57th St between Fifth and Sixth Aves
(212-977-7160). Subway: B, Q, N, R to 57th St.
Mon–Sat 10am–6pm.*
Work by acclaimed European contemporary painters, sculptors and conceptualists predominates here, usually in striking installations. The impressive roster of gallery artists includes Anselm Kiefer, Christian Boltanski and Rebecca Horn, as well as Jeff Wall, Juan Muñoz and Gabriel Orozco. This is a 57th Street must.

Mary Boone

*745 Fifth Ave between 57th and 58th Sts, fourth
floor (212-752-2929). Subway: E, F, N, R to Fifth Ave.
Tue–Fri 10am–6pm; Sat 10am–5pm.*
This former Soho celeb continues to attract major attention. Boone's list of contemporaries currently includes Eric Fischl, Ross Bleckner, Barbara Kruger and hipster

*Downtown **Gavin Brown**: This British gallerist shows the hip and the infamous.*

Damian Loeb; she has also begun supporting the ideas of independent curators by organizing stellar group shows that include new photography, sculpture and painting.

Marlborough
40 W 57th St between Fifth and Sixth Aves, second floor (212-541-4900). Subway: B, Q, N, R to 57th St. Sept–May Mon–Sat 10am–5:30pm.
This monolithic international gallery shows work by modernist bigwigs Larry Rivers, Red Grooms, Marisol, Alex Katz, Francis Bacon, R.B. Kitaj, Kurt Schwitters, Magdalena Abakanowicz and more—much more. **Marlborough Graphics**, at the same address, is just as splendiferous.

PaceWildenstein
32 E 57th St between Madison and Park Aves (212-421-3292) www.pacewildenstein.com. Subway: 4, 5, 6 to 59th St; N, R to Fifth Ave. Sept–May Tue–Fri 9:30am–6pm; Sat 10am–6pm.
The heavyweight of dealerships, this corporate giant offers work by some of the most significant artists of the century: Picasso, Mark Rothko, Alexander Calder, Ad Reinhardt, Lucas Samaras, Agnes Martin and Chuck Close, along with Julian Schnabel, Kiki Smith and Elizabeth Murray. **Pace Prints and Primitives**, at the same address, publishes prints from Old Masters to big-name contemporaries, and has a fine collection of African art.

Yoshii
20 W 57th St between Sixth and Seventh Aves (212-265-8876). Subway: B, Q, N, R to 57th St. Tue–Sat 10am–6pm.
This smallish gallery presents lively shows by contemporaries in painting, photography, sculpture and installation, as well as terrific historical surveys featuring work by such important modernists as Picasso and Giacometti.

Chelsea

The growth of the West Chelsea art district has been nothing short of phenomenal. Until 1993, the nonprofit Dia Art Center was the area's only major claim to art. Now new galleries seem to open every month. All this activity has inevitably attracted trendy restaurants and shops such as Comme des Garçons; despite the gentrification, the area retains its frontier feeling. Some galleries have such distinctive architecture that it's worth a trip just to see them—and to catch the light from the nearby Hudson River. Take the C or E trains on the Eighth Avenue line, although a taxi or the 23rd Street crosstown bus will bring you closer—the blocks between avenues will bring you long.

303 Gallery
525 W 22nd St between Tenth and Eleventh Aves (212-255-1121). Subway: C, E to 23rd St. Tue–Sat 10am–6pm.
This cutting-edge gallery features international artists working in several media; all have garnered critical acclaim. They include photographers Thomas Ruff, Maureen Gallace, Thomas Demand and Collier Schorr; sculptor Daniel Oates; painters Sue Williams and Karen Kilimnik; and video artist Doug Aitken.

AC Project Room
453 W 17th St between Ninth and Tenth Aves, second floor (212-645-4970). Subway: A, C, E to 14th St; L to Eighth Ave. Tue–Sat 10am–6pm.

This innovative artist-run space, a recent addition to Chelsea, hooks up with a cross-generational mix of New York City artists working in diverse forms.

Alexander and Bonin
132 Tenth Ave between 18th and 19th Sts (212-367-7474) www.alexanderandbonin.com. Subway: A, C, E to 14th St; L to Eighth Ave. Tue–Sat 10am–6pm.
This is a long, cool drink of an exhibition space featuring contemporary painting, sculpture, photography and works on paper by an interesting group of international artists, including Doris Salcedo, Willie Doherty, Paul Thek, Mona Hatoum, Rita McBride, Silvia Plimack Mangold and Jennifer Bolande.

Andrea Rosen Gallery
525 W 24th St between Tenth and Eleventh Aves (212-627-6000). Subway: C, E to 23rd St. Sept–June Tue–Sat 10am–6pm; summer hours Mon–Fri 10am–6pm.
Count on this place to show you the young heroes of the decade; this is where Rita Ackermann's endearing but unsettling waifs, John Currin's equally unsettling young babes, Andrea Zittel's compact model homes and Wolfgang Tillmans's disturbing fashion photos all found their way into the limelight.

Barbara Gladstone
515 W 24th St between Tenth and Eleventh Aves (212-206-9300). Subway: C, E to 23rd St. Tue–Sat 10am–6pm.
Gladstone is strictly blue-chip and presents often spectacular shows of high-quality painting, sculpture, photography and video by established artists, including Richard Prince, Matthew Barney, Rosemarie Trockel, Anish Kapoor, Ilya Kabokov and Vito Acconci.

Bill Maynes
529 W 20th St between Tenth and Eleventh Aves, eighth floor (212-741-3318). Subway: C, E to 23rd St. Tue–Sat 11am–6pm.
Maynes is a bright, energetic fellow whose lovely gallery offers a great downtown view toward New York Harbor. He shows youngish American painters and sculptors who take traditional media to quirky, emotionally affecting new heights.

Bonakdar Jancou Gallery
521 W 21st St between Tenth and Eleventh Aves (212-414-4144). Subway: C, E to 23rd St. Tue–Sat 10am–6pm.
In her dreamy new skylighted Chelsea gallery, British-born Bonakdar presents odd, often rather disturbing—and just as often quite distinguished—installations by such vanguard artists as Damien Hirst, Charles Long, Uta Barth and Matt Collishaw.

Brent Sikkema
530 W 22nd St between Tenth and Eleventh Aves (212-929-2262). Subway: C, E to 23rd St. Tue–Sat 10am–6pm.
Former owner of the late Soho gallery Wooster Gardens, Brent Sikkema recently followed the mass exodus to Chelsea, mounting evocative and politically charged shows of work by American, British and European artists, including Kara Walker and Yinka Shonibare.

Cheim & Read
521 W 23rd St between Tenth and Eleventh Aves (212-242-7727). Subway: C, E to 23rd St. Tue–Sat 10am–6pm.
Louise Bourgeois and Jenny Holzer are examples of the high-profile artists these expatriates from 57th Street's Robert Miller Gallery have put on view in their cool and sensibly

*Rock and **Roebling Hall**: This subterranean art space is a Williamsburg must.*

human-scale room. Look for a high concentration of photographers such as Jack Pierson, Adam Fuss and August Sander, along with such contemporary sculptors and painters as Lynda Benglis and Louise Fishman.

Cristinerose Gallery
529 W 20th St between Tenth and Eleventh Aves, second floor (212-206-0297). Subway: C, E to 23rd St. Tue–Fri 10am–6pm; Sat 11am–6pm.
This quirky gallery consistently mounts engaging shows, spotlighting high-IQ artists whose focus is on materials or the media—thankfully not both at once.

Gavin Brown's enterprise
436 W 15th St between Ninth and Tenth Aves (212-627-5258). Subway: A, C, E to 14th St; L to Eighth Ave. Tue–Sat 10am–6pm.
Londoner Gavin Brown champions young hopefuls in an admirably antiestablishment gallery that has managed both to establish such artists as Rirkrit Tiravanija and Elizabeth Peyton, and to showcase more established talents such as Stephen Pippin and Peter Doig. Stop by to look at the art and have a drink at the gallery's chic bar.

Greene Naftali
526 W 26th St between Tenth and Eleventh Aves, eighth floor (212-463-7770). Subway: C, E to 23rd St. Tue–Sat 10am–6pm.
Carol Greene's airy aerie has wonderful light, a spectacular view and a history of rock-'em-sock-'em group shows of a somewhat conceptualist nature, as well as fine solo work by American painters and installation specialists.

Henry Urbach Architecture
526 W 26th St between Tenth and Eleventh Aves (212-627-0974). Subway: C, E to 23rd St. Wed–Sat noon–6pm.
Urbach mounts quirky, conceptual shows that almost always have a photographic or architectural bent.

Jessica Fredericks
504 W 22nd St between Tenth and Eleventh Aves (212-633-6555). Subway: C, E to 23rd St. Tue–Sat 11am–6pm.
Fredericks and partner/spouse Andrew Freiser live and work out of this small gallery on the ground floor of an art-dedicated townhouse. They have been effective in developing a new generation of collectors for work by both midcareer and emerging artists from New York and Los Angeles, with a roster that includes Michael Bevilacqua, Marnie Weber, Robert Overby and John Wesley.

John Weber
529 W 20th St between Tenth and Eleventh Aves, second floor (212-691-5711). Subway: C, E to 23rd St. Sept–May Tue–Sat 10am–6pm.
Weber shows strong conceptual and minimalist work, with an emphasis on sculpture. Artists include Hans Haacke, Daniel Buren and Alice Aycock.

Klemens Gasser & Tanja Grunert, Inc.
524 W 19th St between Tenth and Eleventh Aves (212-807-9494). Subway: C, E to 23rd St. Tue–Sat 10am–6pm.

Grunert ran a gallery in Cologne for 12 years and was joined by her husband, Gasser, several years ago. Having recently moved to New York, this international couple have now opened shop in Chelsea, where they continue to present consistently good shows that focus on European artists.

Linda Kirkland

504 W 22nd St between Tenth and Eleventh Aves (212-627-3930). Subway: C, E to 23rd Street. Tue–Sat 11am–6pm.
The brains behind the conversion of this 1860 townhouse, Kirkland runs a nifty operation on the third floor, which she gives over to the work of the fastest emerging artists on the street as well as to group shows in all media.

Luhring Augustine

531 W 24th St between Tenth and Eleventh Aves (212-206-9100). Subway: C, E to 23rd St. Sept–May Tue–Sat 10am–6pm; summer hours Mon–Fri 10am–6pm.
Luhring Augustine's gracious, skylighted Chelsea gallery (designed by the area's architect of choice, Richard Gluckman) features work from an impressive stable of artists that includes the Germans Albert Oehlen, Gerhard Richter and Günther Förg; Britons Rachel Whiteread, Fiona Rae and Richard Billingham; and Americans Janine Antoni, Christopher Wool, Larry Clark and Paul McCarthy.

Marlborough Chelsea

211 W 19th St between Seventh and Eighth Aves (212-463-8634). Subway: 1, 9 to 18th St. Tue–Sat 10am–5:30pm.
This satellite branch of the 57th Street gallery (*see* **57th Street,** *page 193*) displays new sculpture and painting.

Matthew Marks

523 W 24th St between Tenth and Eleventh Aves (212-243-0200). Subway: C, E to 23rd St. Tue–Sat 10am–6pm; summer hours Mon–Fri 10am–6pm.
The driving force behind Chelsea's rebirth as an art center, the ambitious Marks has two galleries. The first is a beautifully lit, glass-fronted converted garage devoted to large-scale works by such blue-chip modernist heroes as Willem de Kooning, Ellsworth Kelly, Brice Marden, Terry Winters and Richard Serra. The second is a 9,000-square-foot, two-story space featuring new work by contemporary painters, photographers and sculptors, including Lucian Freud, Nan Goldin, Roni Horn, Gary Hume, Andreas Gursky, Katharina Fritsch and Tracey Moffat.
Other location*: 522 W 22nd St between Tenth and Eleventh Aves (212-243-1650). Tue–Sat 11am–6pm.*

Max Protetch Gallery

511 W 22nd St between Tenth and Eleventh Aves (212-633-6999). Subway: C, E to 23rd St. Tue–Sat 10am–6pm.
Protetch, relocated from Soho, has been hosting excellent group shows of contemporary work imported from China and elsewhere; he also exhibits important new painting, sculpture and ceramics. This is also one of the few galleries that also leaves room for architectural drawings and installations.

Metro Pictures

519 W 24th St between Tenth and Eleventh Aves (212-206-7100). Subway: C, E to 23rd St. Sept–May Tue–Sat 10am–6pm. Summer hours Tue–Fri 10am–6pm; closed August.
This great playground for artists features the hip, keenly critical, cutting-edge work of Cindy Sherman, Fred Wilson and Laurie Simmons, along with Carroll Dunham's wildly polymorphous painting, Mike Kelley's sublime conflation of pathos and perversity, Jim Shaw's California kitsch, and Tony Oursler's eerie and eye-popping video projections.

Murray Guy

453 W 17th St between Ninth and Tenth Aves (212-463-7372). Subway: A, C, E to 14th St; L to Eighth Ave. Tue–Sat 10am–6pm.
This dynamic duo mounts elegant shows with such artists as Francis Cape, Mette Tronvoll and Beat Streuli.

Pat Hearn Gallery

530 W 22nd St between Tenth and Eleventh Aves (212-727-7366). Subway: C, E to 23rd St. Tue–Sat 11am–6pm.
This vanguard gallery owner helped establish the East Village and Soho art scenes before moving up to Chelsea to continue presenting her roster of rigorous abstractionists and conceptualists. Hearn represents Mary Heilmann, Jutta Koettker, Joan Jonas, Renee Green and Lincoln Tobier.

Patrick Callery

433 W 14th St at Washington St (212-741-6364). Subway: A, C, E to 14th St; L to Eighth Ave. Tue–Sat 11am–6pm.
Formerly of Boesky and Callery, Patrick Callery mounts work by artists across generations, both established and emerging, who work in a wide variety of media. Be sure to check out this newcomer to the Meatpacking District.

Paul Morris Gallery

465 W 23rd St between Ninth and Tenth Aves (212-727-2752). Subway: C , E to 23rd St. Tue–Sat 11am–6pm.
Morris's new gallery in Chelsea's London Terrace complex is a shoebox compared to his former digs on West 20th Street, but his roster of emerging talents makes the traditional art exhibited in larger surrounding galleries look terribly stuffy and old-hat.

Paula Cooper Gallery

534 W 21st St between Tenth and Eleventh Aves (212-255-1105). Subway: C, E to 23rd St. Tue–Sat 10am–6pm; call gallery for summer hours.
Cooper opened the first art gallery in Soho and, as an early settler in West Chelsea, built one of the grander temples for the predominantly minimalist, largely conceptual work of artists whose careers have flourished under her administration. They include Donald Judd, Carl Andre, Tony Smith, Jonathan Borofsky, Dan Walsh and Robert Gober, as well as photographers Andres Serrano and Zoe Leonard.

Postmasters Gallery

459 W 19th St between Ninth and Tenth Aves (212-727-3323). Subway: C, E to 23rd St. Tue–Sat 11am–6pm.
Another Soho-gone-Chelsea addition, this intriguing international gallery, run by Magdalena Sawon, presents cutting-edge, techno-savvy art, most of which has insistent conceptual leanings. Artists include Spencer Finch, Sylvie Fleury, Alix Pearstein and Claude Wampler.

Robert Miller

526 W 26th St between Tenth and Eleventh Aves (212-980-5454). Subway: C, E to 23rd St. Sept–May Tue–Sat 10am–6pm.
This gallery used to be a 57th Street stalwart but recently contracted the Chelsea bug. Check out Miller's new space, where you'll see work by artists as familiar to museums as to private collections: Lee Krasner, Al Held, Alice Neel, Joan Mitchell and Philip Pearlstein, as well as popular contemporaries such as Diane Arbus, Robert Mapplethorpe and Bruce Weber.

Rupert Goldsworthy Gallery

453 W 17th St between Ninth and Tenth Aves, second floor (212-414-4560). Subway: A,C, E to 14th St; L to Eighth Ave. Tue–Sat 11am–6pm.

This British gallerist has been in the business for years and has the eye to show for it. You won't be disappointed with his cool, often theme-based shows.

Venetia Kapernekas Fine Arts, Inc.
526 W 26th St between Tenth and Eleventh Aves, suite 814 (212-462-4150). Subway: C, E to 23rd St. Tue–Sat 11am–6pm.
This newcomer to the building (which also has the Robert Miller and Greene Naftali galleries) adds some flare, hanging cross-generational shows with work by twentysomething artists like Jeremy Blake and those more established, such as video artist Michel Auder.

Soho

Despite its "mallification," you can find something of interest and import on every street in Soho, along with such solid institutions as the downtown branch of the Guggenheim, the Museum of African Art and the New Museum for Contemporary Art. What follows is a selection of the most consistently rewarding galleries in the community.

American Fine Arts, Colin deLand
22 Wooster St at Grand St (212-941-0401). Subway: A, C, E to Canal St. Tue–Sat noon–6pm.
Dealer Colin deLand mounts what are arguably the most unusual exhibitions in Soho. His shows retain a refreshingly ad-hoc feel that belies the consistently strong quality of the work. Artists include filmmaker John Waters and the subversive collective Art Club 2000.

Anton Kern
558 Broadway between Prince and Spring Sts (212-965-1706). Subway: 6 to Spring St; B, D, F, Q to Broadway–Lafayette St; N, R to Prince St. Tue–Sat 10am–6pm.
The son of artist Georg Baselitz and a Gladstone Gallery protégé, Kern presents installations by young American and European artists whose futuristic, site-specific installations have provided the New York art world with some of its most visionary shows.

Basilico Fine Arts
26 Wooster St at Grand St (212-966-1831). Subway: A, C, E to Canal St. Tue–Sat 10am–6pm; August by appointment only.
Stefano Basilico's high-concept gallery has a group of strong contenders for future art-stardom, most of them artists working in various media who turn 1960s conceptualism into visual pleasure for the millennium. Expect the unexpected—maybe the unheard-of.

Bronwyn Keenan
3 Crosby St at Howard St (212-431-5083). Subway: J, M, Z, N, R, 6 to Canal St. Tue–Sat 11am–6pm.
Among the younger dealers in New York, Keenan may have the sharpest eye for new talent. While work can be inconsistent, shows tend to be bigger than the sum of their parts, making this gallery a worthwhile stop more often than not.

Casey M. Kaplan
48 Greene St between Broome and Grand Sts, fourth floor (212-226-6131). Subway: C, E, 6 to Spring St; J, M, Z, N, R, 6 to Canal St. Sept–Jun Tue–Sat 10am–6pm.
In only four years, twentysomething Kaplan has made his gallery one of the brightest spots on the Soho art map, introducing work by artists based primarily in New York and Los Angeles. Among the most notable: Amy Sillman, Amy Adler and Anna Gaskell.

Charles Cowles
420 West Broadway between Prince and Spring Sts, fifth floor (212-925-3500). Subway: C, E, 6 to Spring St; N, R to Prince St. Sept–Jun Tue–Sat 10am–6pm; summer hours Mon–Fri 10am–5pm.
This gallery shows modern and contemporary paintings, sculptures and installations, including pieces by David Bates, Patrick Ireland, Beverly Pepper, Darren Watterston, Vernon Fisher, Charles Arnoldi, Howard Ben Tré. You might also catch the fabulous blown-glass works by Dale Chihuly.

CRG Art
93 Grand St between Mercer and Greene Sts (212-966-4360). Subway: J, M, Z, N, R, 6 to Canal St. Sept–May Tue–Sat 11am–6pm.
Carla Chammas, Richard Desroche and Glenn McMillan's premises represent such eminent risk-takers as Cathleen Lewis, Mona Hatoum and Sam Reveles.

Curt Marcus Gallery
578 Broadway between Houston and Prince Sts (212-226-3200). Subway: 6 to Bleecker St; B, D, F, Q to Broadway–Lafayette St; N, R to Prince St. Sept–May Tue–Sat 10am–6pm.
This is a place for the peculiar but appealing, from Richard Pettibone's Shakerish objects to the mysterious pinhole photography of Barbara Ess and the intricate inkblots of film-maker/conceptualist Bruce Connor.

David Zwirner
43 Greene St between Broome and Grand Sts (212-966-9074). Subway: A, C, E, J, M, Z, N, R, 6 to Canal St. Sept–May Tue–Sat 10am–6pm; summer hours Mon–Fri 10am–6pm.
This maverick German expatriate's shop has been the hot spot on Greene Street since it opened six years ago, offering shows that serve as a barometer of what's important in art, not just in New York but internationally. The stable of cutting-edge talent includes Raymond Pettibon, Jason Rhoades, Toba Khedoori and Stan Douglas.

Deitch Projects
76 Grand St between Wooster and Greene Sts (212-343-7300). Subway: A, C, E, J, M, Z, N, R, 6 to Canal St. Tue–Sat noon–6pm.
Jeffrey Deitch is known for spotting new talent and setting trends; his project space attracts stellar crowds to its openings and continues to focus on emerging artists who create elaborate, often outrageously provocative multimedia installations. Of late, Deitch's roster of the young and hip has included street artist Barry McGee and sex-obsessed painter Cecily Brown.

Friedrich Petzel
26 Wooster St between Grand and Canal Sts (212-334-9466). Subway: A, C, E to Canal St. Sept–Jun Tue–Sat 10am–6pm; call for summer hours.
Locals have nicknamed this "the morphing gallery" for its emphasis on the conceptually based art of mutating forms seen in work by Victor Estrada and Jorge Pardo. But Petzel has now taken on painter Richard Phillips and up-and-coming photographers Sharon Lockhart and Dana Hoey, putting him on the leading edge of his generation of dealers.

Gagosian
136 Wooster St between Houston and Prince Sts (212-228-2828). Subway: C, E to Spring St; N, R to Prince St. Sept–Jun Tue–Sat 10am–6pm; summer hours Mon–Fri 10am–6pm.
A branch of Larry Gagosian's uptown gallery, this dazzling ground-floor space provides a perfect setting for the imposing (at times, mammoth) pieces it houses—by such names as Damien Hirst, Richard Serra and Andy Warhol as well as newcomers Ellen Gallagher and Britain's fraternal team Jake and Dinos Chapman.

Holly Solomon Gallery

172 Mercer St at Houston St (212-941-5777).
Subway: 6 to Bleecker St; B, D, F, Q to Broadway–
Lafayette St; N, R to Prince St. Sept–May Tue–Sat
10am–6pm; call for summer hours.
Solomon's dramatic space shouldn't be missed. The reign-
ing doyenne of the Soho scene shows distinctive work in all
media by a quirky selection of artists including Nam June
Paik, Izhar Patkin and Nick Waplington.

Lehmann Maupin

39 Greene St between Broome and Grand Sts
(212-965-0753). Subway: A, C, E, N, R, J, M, Z to Canal
St; 6 to Spring St. Tue–Sat 10am–6pm.
This flexible project space, designed by famed architect Rem
Koolhaas, features epic group shows of hip Americans and
Europeans. It may be the most eclectic of the high-end gal-
leries in Soho.

Nolan/Eckman

560 Broadway at Prince St, sixth floor (212-925-
6190). Subway: 6 to Spring St; B, D, F, Q to
Broadway–Lafayette St; N, R to Prince St. Sept–May
Tue–Fri 10am–6pm; Sat 11am–6pm.
This small but high-level gallery shows primarily work on
paper by established contemporary artists from the U.S.
and Europe.

PaceWildenstein

142 Greene St between Prince and Houston Sts
(212-431-9224). Subway: 6 to Bleecker St; B, D, F, Q to
Broadway–Lafayette St; N, R to Prince St. Sept–June
Tue–Sat 10am–6pm; summer hours Mon–Fri
10am–5pm.
This luxurious downtown branch of the famous 57th Street
gallery is where you'll find grand-scale installations by such
big-time contemporaries as Robert Irwin, Sol Lewitt, Joel
Shapiro, Julian Schnabel, George Condo, John Chamberlain
and Robert Whitman.

Paul Kasmin

74 Grand St between Wooster and Greene Sts
(212-219-3219). Subway: A, C, E, J, M, Z, N, R, 6 to
Canal St. Sept–May Tue–Fri 10am–6pm; Sat
11am–6pm.
Here you'll get well-chosen group shows of gallery artists
with established names like Donald Sultan and Donald
Baechler. Also look for solo exhibitions by Alessandro
Twombly, Suzanne McClelland, Nancy Rubins, Elliott Puck-
ette and Aaron Ross, whose reputations—and prices—
increase with every new appearance. Catch them now.

Ronald Feldman Fine Arts

31 Mercer St between Grand and Canal Sts
(212-226-3232). Subway: J, M, Z, N, R, 6 to Canal St.
Sept–Jun Tue–Sat 10am–6pm; call for summer hours.
Feldman's history in Soho is marked by landmark shows of
such artists as Komar & Melamid, Ida Applebroog, Leon
Golub and Hannah Wilke, but also includes more avant-
garde installations by Eleanor Antin, Roxy Paine, Nancy
Chunn and Carl Fudge.

Sean Kelly

43 Mercer St between Broome and Grand Sts
(212-343-2405). Subway: J, M, Z, N, R, 6 to Canal St.
Sept–Jun Tue–Sat 11am–6pm; summer hours Mon–Fri
10am–5pm.
This Brit expat's project-oriented gallery offers exhibitions
by established conceptualists, including Ann Hamilton,
Lorna Simpson and Marina Abramovic. It also showcases
emerging talents such as Cathy de Monchaux and James
Casebere.

Sonnabend Gallery

420 West Broadway between Prince and Spring Sts,
third floor (212-966-6160). Subway: C, E, 6 to Spring St;
N, R to Prince St. Sept–Jun Tue–Sat 10am–6pm;
summer hours Tue–Fri 11am–5pm.
Visit this elegant old standby for strong new work from
artists such as Haim Steinbach, Ashley Bickerton, Gilbert &
George, John Baldessari and Matthew Weinstein.

Sperone Westwater

142 Greene St between Houston and Prince Sts
(212-431-3685). Subway: 6 to Bleecker St; B, D, F, Q to
Broadway–Lafayette St; N, R to Prince St. Sept–mid-Jun
Tue–Sat 10am–6pm; summer hours Mon–Fri
10am–6pm.
This is a stronghold of painting and one of the best places
to see work by the Italian neo-Expressionists Francesco
Clemente, Sandro Chia, Luigi Ontani and Mimmo Paladino.
Among the gallery's other illustrious contemporaries are
Frank Moore, Jonathan Lasker, Susan Rothenberg and
Richard Tuttle.

Tribeca

Apex Art

291 Church St at Walker St (212-431-5270). Subway:
1, 9 to Franklin St. Sept–Jun Tue–Sat 11am–6pm;
summer hours Wed 6–8pm, Thu–Sat 11am–6pm.
This is an interesting gallery, where the impulse comes from
independent critics who experiment with cleverly themed
shows in all media.

Get down: You'll see new heights in
*curatorial experimentation at **Apex Art**.*

Brooklyn

Artists living and/or working in the postindustrial blue-collar neighborhoods of Brooklyn have opened up quite a few galleries. Some summer weekends, area artists sponsored by the Dumbo Arts Center hold group exhibitions in their studios or big, carnival-style art fairs. *See* **A view from the bridge,** *pages 80–81,* for more on the Williamsburg galleries (and neighborhood art-friendly bars and restaurants).

Flipside
84 Withers St between Leonard and Lorimer Sts,
Williamsburg, third floor (718-389-7108). Subway: L to
Lorimer St. Sun 1–6pm; closed July and August.
This intimate artist-run gallery features work in all media by accomplished homegrown talent.

GAle GAtes et al.
37 Main St between Front and Water Sts,
Dumbo (718-522-4596). Subway: F to York St. Wed–Sun
noon–6pm.
The first and most energetic gallery to open in Dumbo, this huge nonprofit complex on the Brooklyn waterfront hosts group exhibitions and performances of all sorts by a wide variety of local artists.

Momenta
72 Berry St between N 9th and N 10th Sts,
Williamsburg (718-218-8058). Subway: L to Bedford
Ave. Mon, Fri–Sun noon–6pm.
The most imaginative and professional organization in Williamsburg, Momenta presents strong solo and group exhibitions by an exhilarating mix of up-and-coming artists. Catch their work here before it's snapped up by Manhattan dealers.

Pierogi 2000
167 N 9th St between Bedford and Driggs Aves,
Williamsburg (718-599-2144). Subway: L to Bedford Ave.
Sept–Jun Mon, Sat, Sun noon–6pm and by appointment.
Monthly openings at this artist-run gallery tend to attract the whole neighborhood.

Roebling Hall
390 Wythe Ave at S 4th St, Williamsburg
(718-599-5352). Subway: L to Bedford Ave. Sat–
Mon noon–6pm.
Directors Joel Beck and Christian Viveros-Fauné cook up cutting-edge, alternative shows at this Williamsburg hot spot—a must-see on the Brooklyn gallery circuit.

The Rotunda Gallery
33 Clinton St between Pierrepont St and Cadman
Plaza West, Brooklyn Heights (718-875-4047)
www.brooklynx.org/rotunda. Subway: 2, 3, 4, 5 to
Borough Hall. Tue–Fri noon–5pm; Sat 11am–4pm.
This beautiful Brooklyn Heights gallery is the borough's oldest and foremost nonprofit exhibition space. Monthly shows feature innovative sculpture, painting, site-specific installation, photography and video by Brooklyn-based artists, always in top-quality presentations.

Nonprofit spaces

New York may have more commercial galleries than you can count, but they haven't overwhelmed either the significance or the mission of the city's best nonprofit spaces. Museumlike alternatives that are supported by a combination of public and private funds, these highly valued organizations showcase avant-garde work of both past and present in expertly curated, sometimes eventful contexts.

Alternative Museum
594 Broadway near Prince St, suite 402
(212-966-4444). Subway: 6 to Spring St; N, R to Prince
St. Tue–Sat 11am–6pm; call for summer hours from
Jun–Jul; closed August.
The Alternative Museum has a reputation for exhibitions with humanitarian and sociopolitical concerns, especially by artists who are well beyond the mainstream.

Art in General
79 Walker St between Broadway and Lafayette St
(212-219-0473) www.artingeneral.org. Subway: J, M, Z,
N, R, 6 to Canal St. Sept–May Tue–Sat noon–6pm;
closed Jun–Aug.
On its fourth and sixth floors, this venerable Tribeca institution holds exhibitions of contemporary work-in-development by emerging and underrecognized artists, with an emphasis on cultural diversity. It also sponsors eye-catching window installations at street level year-round.

Artists Space
38 Greene St between Grand and Broome Sts
(212-226-3970) www.artistsspace.org. Subway: A, C,
E, N, R to Canal St. Sept–Jul Tue–Sat 10am–6pm;
closed August.
Laurie Anderson, Jonathan Borofsky, Cindy Sherman, Robert Longo and David Salle all had exhibitions here early in their careers. The emphasis is on innovative work in all forms, so expect performance art, installations and video art, and some terrific curatorial adventures.

Dia Center for the Arts
548 W 22nd St between Tenth and Eleventh Aves
(212-989-5566) www.diacenter.org. Subway: C, E to
23rd St. Mid-Sept–mid-Jun Wed–Sun noon–6pm. $6,
$3 concessions.
Dia presents commissioned work by major contemporaries. Shows remain on view throughout a season; there's a program that includes poetry readings, panels and long-term temporary installations in a new annex across the street. The 1999–2000 schedule includes the final part of German artist Thomas Schütte's three-part installation and the second part of a two-part installation by that wizard of perception Robert Irwin. And don't miss the wondrous glass house by Dan Graham, permanently installed on the roof.

The Drawing Center
35 Wooster St between Broome and Grand Sts
(212-219-2166). Subway: C, E, 6 to Spring St; A, C, E,
N, R to Canal St. Tue–Fri 10am–6pm; Sat 11am–
6pm; closed August.
Exhibitions here are devoted to work on paper by emerging international talent, which the Center promotes in its group shows. It also holds important historical exhibitions. **The Drawing Room,** a project space at 40 Wooster Street, features site-specific solo shows by both emerging and established artists of all stripes.

Exit Art: The First World
548 Broadway between Prince and Spring Sts,
second floor (212-966-7745). Subway: 6 to Bleecker St;
B, D, F, Q to Broadway–Lafayette St. Tue–Thu
10am–6pm; Fri 10am–8pm; Sat 11am–6pm;
call for summer hours.
Expect the best in multimedia cross-pollinations and culture clashes at this sprawling alternative space. Shows have big themes (and sometimes living organisms) and include dozens of artists. Exit Art is noisy and colorful and fun—and it can

easily overwhelm. There's also a charming tapas bar and a shop that sells artists' work.

Grey Art Gallery and Study Center at New York University

100 Washington Sq East between Waverly and Washington Pls (212-998-6780) www.nyu.edu/greyart. Subway: A, C, E, B, D, F, Q to W 4th St–Washington Sq; N, R to 8th St. Tue, Thu, Fri 11am–6pm; Wed 11am–8pm; Sat 11am–5pm. Closed mid-Jul–Aug. Suggested donation $2.50.

NYU's recently renovated museum-laboratory has a collection comprising nearly 6,000 works that cover all the visual arts. During the 1999–2000 season, look for two promising shows, "Inverted Odysseys: Claude Cahun, Maya Deren, Cindy Sherman" and "Sheer Realities: Power and Clothing in the Nineteenth Century Philippines."

International Center of Photography

1130 Fifth Ave at 94th St (212-860-1777). Subway: 6 to 96th St. Tue–Thu 10am–5pm; Fri 10am–8pm; Sat, Sun 10am–6pm. $6, students and seniors $4; voluntary contribution Fri 5–8pm.

The center began in the 1960s as the International Fund for Concerned Photography. Its collection contains work by photojournalists Robert Capa, Werner Bischof, David Seymour and Dan Weiner, who were all killed on assignment. Their work was preserved and exhibited by Cornell Capa, brother of Robert, who went on to found the ICP in 1974. Given this history, it's no surprise that exhibitions are particularly strong on news and documentary photography. The library houses thousands of biographical and photographic files, as well as back issues of photography magazines. There's also a bookshop, space for video installations and a small screening room. ICP's branch gallery in midtown has two floors of exhibition space for retrospectives devoted to single artists, such as the ever-popular Weegee, as well as a screening room and its own bookshop. Exhibitions change throughout the year.
Other location: ICP Midtown, *1133 Sixth Ave at 43rd St (212-768-4682). Subway: B, D, F, Q to 42nd St; 7 to Fifth Ave. Tue–Thu 10am–5pm; Fri 10am–8pm; Sat, Sun 10am–6pm. $6, students and seniors $4; voluntary contribution Fri 5–8pm.*

Sculpture Center

167 E 69th St between Lexington and Third Aves (212-879-3500). Subway: 6 to 68th St. Tue–Sat 11am–5pm.

This is one of the best places to see contemporary work by emerging and midcareer sculptors. The Sculpture Center also runs an ongoing project on Roosevelt Island.

Thread Waxing Space

476 Broadway between Grand and Broome Sts, second floor (212-966-9520). Subway: 6 to Spring St; J, M, Z, N, R to Canal St. Tue–Sat 10am–6pm.

This truly dynamic block-long multimedia space for contemporary art also hosts video, performance, poetry and lecture series, as well as the occasional musical evening.

White Columns

320 W 13th St between Eighth Ave and Hudson St (212-924-4212). Subway: A, C, E to 14th St; L to Eighth Ave. Sept–Jun Wed–Sun noon–6pm.

Group shows organized by up-and-coming curators and presented by this venerable alternative organization, which recently acquired this location, have helped launch the careers of a number of important artists. Always a lively scene.

Photography

In the past decade, there has been a renewal of interest in art photography in New York, along with notable strides forward in the medium. For an overview, look for the bimonthly directory *Photography in New York International* ($2.95). See chapter **Museums** *for public collections.*

Janet Borden

560 Broadway at Prince St (212-431-0166). Subway: 6 to Bleecker St; N, R to Prince St; B, D, F, Q to Broadway–Lafayette St. Sept–Jun Tue–Sat 11am–5pm; summer hours Tue–Fri 11am–5pm; closed August.

No tour of contemporary photography can be complete without a visit to this Soho stalwart, where the latest work by Oliver Wassow, Jan Groover, Tina Barney, Sandy Skoglund and David Levinthal, among others, is regularly on view.

James Danziger

851 Madison Ave between 70th and 71st Sts (212-734-5300). Subway: 6 to 68th St. Tue–Sat 10am–6pm; Sun noon–5pm.

With a vast collection that ranges from the classic to the trendy, this uptown gallery shows such photographers as Ansel Adams, Andre Kertesz, Walker Evans, Richard Avedon and Annie Liebovitz.

Edwynn Houk Gallery

745 Fifth Ave between 57th and 58th Sts, fourth floor (212-750-7070). Subway: N, R to Fifth Ave. Sept–Jul Tue–Sat 11am–6pm; closed last three weeks of August.

This highly respected specialist in 20th-century vintage and contemporary photography has two professional-looking new rooms in which to show such artists as Sally Mann, Dorothea Lange, Man Ray, Alfred Stieglitz, Brassai, Cartier-Bresson, Danny Lyon and Elliott Erwitt, all of whom command over-the-top dollar.

Howard Greenberg & 292 Gallery

120 Wooster St between Prince and Spring Sts, second floor (212-334-0010). Subway: N, R to Prince St; C, E to Spring St. Tue–Sat 10am–6pm.

These connecting galleries exhibit one enticing show after another of name 20th-century photographers, including Berenice Abbot, William Klein, Robert Frank, Ralph Eugene Meatyard and Imogen Cunningham.

Julie Saul Gallery

560 Broadway at Prince St (212-431-0747). Subway: 6 to Bleecker St; B, D, F, Q to Broadway–Lafayette St; N, R to Prince St. Tue–Sat 11am–6pm.

Come here for well-conceived contemporary photography shows, featuring clean and smart installations.

PaceWildensteinMacGill

32 E 57th St between Madison and Park Aves (212-759-7999). Subway: 4, 5, 6 to 59th St; N, R to Lexington Ave. Sept–late Jun Tue–Fri 9:30am–5:30pm; Sat 10am–6pm; summer hours Mon–Thu 9:30am–5:30pm; and Fri 9am–4pm.

This gallery never misses. Look for such well-known names as Weegee, William Wegman, Lisette Model, Joel-Peter Witkin and Walker Evans, in addition to important contemporaries like Harry Callahan, Philip-Lorca DiCorcia and William Christenberry.

Yancey Richardson Gallery

560 Broadway at Prince St (212-343-1255). Subway: 6 to Bleecker St; N, R to Prince St; B, D, F, Q to Broadway–Lafayette St. Tue–Sat 11am–6pm.

An intimate gallery showing contemporary, often experimental American, European and Japanese photographers, each with a solid following.

Books & Poetry

From world-class authors to hip-hop poetry slammers, literary New York covers every page in the book

"I have taken a liking to this abominable place," confessed Mark Twain about the city in which he married, made his fortune and died. His conversion was probably helped by the fact that New Yorkers took such a liking to him. Known as "the belle of New York," Twain was wined and dined and frequently quoted in the press. Far from the old Mississippi, the author was a bona fide celebrity.

New York has always been a literary town, a place where the published few are sought-after guests at dinner parties, and where both best-selling authors and up-and-comers gather at writers' haunts like Elaine's to exchange gossip and be seen. Why, Norman Mailer once even ran for mayor. As the publishing capital of the United States, New York creates literary stars the way Los Angeles creates movie stars. Million-dollar advances and Hollywood options bring fame and gossip-column coverage to authors (and, in some cases, to their editors). The literary crème de la crème mingles in the fashion world; even the lavish literary breakfasts hosted from 1994 to '97 by Harry Evans, then Random House president and publisher, were held not within the book-lined walls of some dusty scholarly establishment but at the ultrachic department store Barneys.

Still, you don't have to be part of the literati to get literary satisfaction in New York. Whether you want to hear Walter Mosley or Dorothy Allison reading from their latest novels, poets trying out their new work or speakers dazzling audiences with intellectual pyrotechnics, there's always a place to do so, often for free. It's one of the best entertainment deals in the city.

Spoken word, formerly known as performance poetry, has become a popular New York pastime. Not since the Beats reinvented the American oral tradition have poets attracted so much media attention or been as fashionable. Walk into the Nuyorican Poets Cafe on any Friday night and it's standing-room only; poetry has even invaded clubland.

Spoken word's mainstays are the often-raucous slams (in which selected audience members award points to competing poets) and open-mike nights (when unknowns get five minutes to do their thing before the crowd). Reg E. Gaines, who made a big name for himself and for the downtown spoken-word world with his rap-inspired poetry for the smash-hit musical *Bring in 'da Noise, Bring in 'da Funk*, is a graduate of this scene. You'll find the most innovative performance poetry in the ongoing reading series and festivals; in these, poets cross-pollinate their verses with performance art, theater, dance and music, particularly rap and jazz.

Dead poets (and novelists) are getting an airing, too, in the form of marathon readings, a truly New York tradition. Some annual readings star a stream of big-name personalities. Past readers at Symphony Space's Joycean Bloomsday event have included Jason Robards and Claire Bloom. You can also celebrate Good Friday with Dante's *Inferno* at the Cathedral of St. John the Divine, complete with devil's food cake, or ring in the New Year with *Finnegans Wake* or some other hefty modernist tome at the Paula Cooper Gallery. Also, watch for one-time-only marathons, usually in celebration of a literary anniversary.

New York's bookstores—especially the superstores—have become meccas for anyone seeking a good read, a cappuccino and a comfortable lounge chair, or a café table around which to spend a literate evening with like-minded friends. Some of these stores have become known among bookishly inclined lonely hearts as hot pickup spots (some Barnes & Noble stores stay open until midnight). Many feature literary events, including author readings, talks and signings, and discussions of arcane matters, such as setting and location in fiction.

April is National Poetry Month; poets can be found reading throughout the city. The last Sunday in September, the New York Is Book Country publishers' festival takes over Fifth Avenue. All the major houses exhibit their latest wares and authors as they prove that literacy can be lots of fun.

For the most comprehensive listings of book and poetry events, get the monthly *Poetry Calendar*, free at poetry venues and in many bookstores, or find it online at the Academy of American Poets site (www.poets.org). For more selective listings, check the Books and Around Town sections of *Time Out New York* and the Spoken Word section in *The New York Times*. Some reading series take long summer breaks, so call to check events before setting out. Also, the New York Public Library hosts poetry and author readings, listed in *Events for Adults,* available free at all branches.

Author readings

In today's cutthroat publishing climate, where books either make the best-seller lists or die early deaths, authors are clamoring for the chance to promote their latest titles at bookstores, some of which schedule almost daily events. These are always free, usually in the early evening and well-attended; arrive early if you want a seat. At the superstores, events range from lowbrow to highbrow: You're as likely to catch a supermodel promoting her new exercise book as you are one of your favorite novelists. The following offer frequent author readings, talks and signings.

Barnes & Noble superstores

33 E 17th St at Union Sq (212-253-0810). Subway: L, N, R, 4, 5, 6 to Union Sq. 10am–10pm.
Calendars of events for each branch are available in-store.
Other location: *2289 Broadway at 82nd St (212-362-8835). Check phone book for more locations.*

Borders Books and Music

5 World Trade Center at Church and Vesey Sts (212-839-8049). Subway: C, E, to World Trade Center; N, R, 1, 9, to Cortland St. Mon–Fri 7am–8:30pm; Sat 10am–8:30pm; Sun 11am–8:30pm.
Calendars of events for each branch are available in-store.
Other locations: *461 Park Ave at 57th St (212-980-6785); 576 Second Ave at 32nd St (212-685-3938).*

A Different Light

151 W 19th St between Sixth and Seventh Aves (212-989-4850). Subway: 1, 9 to 18th St. 10am–midnight.
This gay and lesbian bookstore hosts frequent readings.

Posman Books

1 University Pl between Waverly Pl and 8th St (212-533-2665). Subway: N, R to 8th St. Mon–Fri 9am–9pm; Sat 11am–7pm; Sun noon–7pm.
A haunt of New York University students, Posman presents lesser-known novelists and poets.

Rizzoli Bookstore

454 West Broadway between Prince and Houston Sts (212-674-1616). Subway: N, R to Prince St; B, D, F, Q to Broadway–Lafayette St. Mon–Sat 10:30am–8pm, Sun noon–7pm.
Soho's arty bookstore and its midtown sister are on the author-tour map of high-profile novelists, photographers and artists.
Other locations: *31 W 57th St between Fifth and Sixth Aves (212-759-2424); 200 Vesey St at the World Financial Center (212-385-1400).*

Three Lives & Co.

154 W 10 St at Waverly Pl (212-741-2069). Subway: 1, 9 to Christopher St–Sheridan Sq; A, C, E, B, D, F, Q to W 4th St–Washington Sq. Mon, Tue 1–8pm; Wed–Sat 11am–8:30pm; Sun 1–7pm.
Hear established novelists read in this cozy West Village bookstore.

Reading series

The following host fiction and poetry readings; some also offer lectures. For spoken-word poetry, *see* **Spoken word**.

The Algonquin

59 W 44th St between Fifth and Sixth Aves (212-840-6800, 800-555-8000). Subway: B, D, F, Q to 42nd St. Mon 7pm. $20.

*Spiel this book: Authors stump at **Barnes & Noble** to promote their latest offerings.*

This literary landmark hosts the Spoken Word on Monday nights, and many big names pass through. Past evenings have included Israel Horovitz's birthday party and a night of Irish poetry hosted by Frank McCourt.

New School for Social Research
66 W 12th St between Fifth and Sixth Aves (212-229-5488). Subway: F to 14th St; L to Sixth Ave. Admission varies.
This occasional spoken-word series is sometimes organized by one of New York's slickest and most venerable spoken-word-and-music artists, Sekou Sundiata, a New School faculty member. The school also holds lecture series. The Academy of American Poets schedules occasional readings here (at the Tishman Auditorium) by some of the country's best-known poets.

92nd Street Y Unterberg Poetry Center
1395 Lexington Ave at 92nd St (212-996-1100). Subway: 6 to 96th St. Admission varies.
The Academy of American Poets and the Y cosponsor regular readings, with such luminaries as Edward Albee, Athol Fugard, David Mamet and Alice Walker. Panel discussions and lectures by high-profile academics are also held.

Writer's Voice/West Side YMCA
5 W 63rd St between Central Park West and Columbus Ave (212-875-4128). Subway: A, C, B, D, 1, 9 to 59th St–Columbus Circle. $5.
Events include readings by poets, playwrights and novelists. The Y also offers highly regarded writers' workshops.

Spoken word

Dia Center for the Arts
548 W 22nd St between Tenth and Eleventh Aves (212-989-5566). Subway: C, E to 23rd St. Monthly on Fridays at 7pm. $5, students and seniors $2.50.
Dia's Readings in Contemporary Poetry series features established American poets. Past readers have included Adrienne Rich, Amiri Baraka and Jayne Cortez.

Dixon Place
258 Bowery between Houston and Prince Sts (212-219-3088). Subway: 6 to Spring St. Call for dates and times. Admission varies.
Ellie Covan hosts a performance salon in her loft, with open-mike night on the first Tuesday of each month. Poets mix with storytellers, fiction writers and performance artists, but

*Risen from the Ashes: Frank McCourt enjoys celebrity status at the **92nd Street Y**.*

not stand-up comics. Covan also hosts frequent readings at Locus Media, 594 Broadway between Houston and Prince Sts (212-219-3088).

A Gathering of Tribes
285 E 3rd St between Aves B and C (212-674-3778). Subway: F to Second Ave. Sun 5–7pm. Free.
Poetry readings and poetry parties are held on Sunday evenings. A Gathering of Tribes also publishes its own poetry magazine.

The Guitar and Pen
5804 Mosholu Ave at Broadway, Riverdale, Bronx (718-549-5192). Subway: 1, 9 to 242nd St. Thu 8:30pm. Free.
Exoterica organizes an eclectic mixture of free poetry readings here, ranging from Pulitzer Prize winners to Nuyorican slam champions. It also hosts a Tuesday-night reading at An Beal Bocht Café.
Other location: *An Beal Bocht Café, 445 W 238th St between Waldo and Greystone Aves, Bronx (718-549-5192). Subway: 1 to 238th St.*

KGB
85 E 4th St between Second and Third Aves (212-505-3360). Subway: 6 to Astor Pl; F to Second Ave. Mon 7:30pm. Free.
This weekly reading series in a funky East Village bar features luminaries of the downtown poetry scene.

Knitting Factory/AlterKnit Theater
74 Leonard St between Broadway and Church St (212-219-3006). Subway: A, C, E, N, R to Canal St; 1, 9 to Franklin St. Call for dates and times. Admission varies.
Weekly open-mike sessions (Fridays), plus occasional spoken-word specials, are held in one of downtown's most happening music venues. *See chapters Music and Dance.*

Mother
432 W 14th St at Washington St (212-366-5680). Subway: A, C, E to 14th St; L to Eighth Ave. Call for dates and times. Admission varies.
Verbal Abuse—one of the city's most interesting poetry series at one of New York's most interesting clubland spots—starts with an open mike sprinkled with invited readers and then settles into an hourlong lineup of top spoken-word poets. Performance is the key here; shock value is secondary. A words-and-music segment finishes up the night. Call club for dates and times. For the Verbal Abuse online magazine, log on to www.echonyc.com/interjackie.

Nuyorican Poets Cafe
236 E 3rd St between Aves B and C (212-505-8183). Subway: F to Second Ave. Call for dates and times. Admission varies.
The now-famous Nuyorican goes beyond open mikes and slams (open slam Wednesdays, "slam invitational" Fridays) with multimedia staged readings, hip-hop poetry nights and more. Elbow your way past the slumming media execs on the hunt for new talent.

Poetry Project
St. Mark's Church in-the-Bowery, 131 E 10th St at Second Ave (212-674-0910). Subway: 6 to Astor Pl, L to Third Ave. Call for dates and times. Admission varies.
The legendary Poetry Project, whose hallowed walls first heard the likes of Allen Ginsberg and Anne Waldman, is still a thriving center for hearing the new and worthy. Living legends like Jim Carroll and Patti Smith still read here.

Segue at Double Happiness
Double Happiness, 174 Mott St between Broome and Grand Sts (212-941-1282). Subway: B, D, Q to Grand St; 6 to Spring St. Oct–May Sat 4–6pm. $4.

*Tome sweet home: The **New York Public Library** features readings amid stacks of books.*

The Segue Foundation's long-standing poetry series now finds a home at funky, cavernous Double Happiness in Chinatown.

Strictly Roots

2058 Adam Clayton Powell Blvd at 123rd St (212-864-8699). Subway: A, C, B, D to 125th St. Second and last Thursdays of the month at 8pm. Contribution.

This Harlem bookstore's Word Thursdays feature spoken word, sometimes with music.

Talks and lectures

Although nowhere near as trendy as the city's poetry scene, the lecture world is still thriving, with people in-the-know talking about everything from poststructuralism to the Inner Smile. If you're into Self-Help/New Age, pick up a copy of the Open Center's catalog, available free in book and health-food stores. The following venues offer lectures of a more or less literary nature.

Brecht Forum

122 W 27th St between Sixth and Seventh Aves, tenth floor (212-242-4201) www.brechtforum.org. Subway: 1, 9 to 28th St.

This old-style leftist institution offers lectures, forums, discussions and bilingual poetry readings.

The Brooklyn Public Library

Grand Army Plaza, Eastern Pkwy and Flatbush Ave. Brooklyn (718-230-2100) www.brooklynpubliclibrary.org. Subway: 2, 3 to Grand Army Plaza.

Brooklyn's Public Library offers lectures and readings of impressive scope.

New School for Social Research

*See **Reading series** for listings.*

The New School hosts esoteric lectures by visiting savants.

92nd Street Y

*See **Reading series** for listings.*

Regular lectures by and dialogues between top-notch speakers on subjects ranging from the arts to feminism, politics and international scandals. People like Susan Sontag and Wole Soyinka have spoken.

New York Public Library, Celeste Bartos Forum

Fifth Ave between 40th and 42nd Sts (212-930-0855). Subway: B, D, F, Q to 42nd St; 7 to Fifth Ave. Admission varies.

Several annual lecture series feature renowned writers and thinkers, including quite a few Guggenheim fellows, speaking on issues of contemporary culture, science and the humanities.

Tours

Mark Twain Annual Birthday Tour

Meet at the southwest corner of Broadway and Spring St (212-873-1944). Subway: N, R to Prince St. Late November. $15.

The tour, led by Peter Salwen, a Twain aficionado, ends with a birthday toast at one of Twain's New York City homes.

Greenwich Village Past and Present

Meet at Washington Sq Arch, Washington Sq Park, Fifth Ave at Waverly Pl. Call Street Smarts at 212-969-8262 for more information. Subway: A, C, E, B, D, F, Q to W 4th St–Washington Sq. Sun 2pm.

This walk takes you past homes and hangout spots of Village writers past and present.

Cabaret
& Comedy

In New York's most intimate spots, you can sway and swoon to Gershwin or laugh till your belly aches

New York is the cabaret capital of the U.S., and quite possibly of the world. No other city supports a cabaret industry where you can pick from a dozen different shows on any given night. In the strict New York sense, the term *cabaret* covers both a venue and an art form. It's an intimate club where songs are sung, usually by one person, but sometimes by a small ensemble of performers. The songs are usually drawn from what's known as the Great American Songbook—the vast repertoire of the American musical theater—and are supplemented with the occasional new number by a contemporary composer. More than anything, cabaret is an act of intimacy: The best singers are able to draw the audience in until each member feels that he or she is being sung to directly in the most private of concerts.

The Golden Age of cabaret in New York was the 1950s and early 1960s. The advent of rock music and changing tastes eventually made cabaret an art form for the connoisseur, but today there are still plenty of fans and performers who keep it alive. Today's rooms basically fall into two groups: classic, elegant, expensive boîtes like the Oak Room and Cafe Carlyle, where you'll spend $30 to $50 just to get in and hear the likes of Bobby Short, Rosemary Clooney and Andrea Marcovicci; and less formal neighborhood clubs like Don't Tell Mama and Danny's Skylight Room, where up-and-coming singers—many of them enormously talented—perform for enthusiastic fans who pay much lower cover charges.

Classic cabaret

Cafe Carlyle
Carlyle Hotel, 35 E 76th St at Madison Ave (212-744-1600, 800-227-5737). Subway: 6 to 77th St. Tue–Sat 8:45, 10:45pm. Closed Jul–mid Sept. Cover $50, no drink minimum. AmEx, DC, MC, V.
The epitome of chic New York, especially when Barbara Cook, Bobby Short or Eartha Kitt do their thing (or Woody Allen, who's become a regular at the early show on Monday nights with his Dixieland band). Don't dress down; this is about plunking down some cash and remembering it's almost the new millennium. If you want to drink in some atmosphere more cheaply, Bemelmans Bar across the hall always has a fine pianist, such as Barbara Carroll or Peter Mintun, Tuesday to Saturday from 9:30pm to 1:30am with a $10 cover. *See chapter* **Accommodations**.

Delmonico Lounge
Hotel Delmonico, 502 Park Ave at 59th St (212-355-2500). Subway: N, R to Lexington Ave; 4, 5, 6 to 59th St. Show times vary. Cover $15–$25, no drink minimum. AmEx, DC, MC, V.
It doesn't get much more intimate than this tiny East Side hotel lounge, with its lush decor and cozy seating. Sit on one of the half-dozen bar stools, sip a martini and listen to one of the elegant chanteuses who sing here regularly.

The FireBird Cafe
363 W 46th St between Eighth and Ninth Aves (212-586-0244). Subway: A, C, E to 42nd St–Port Authority. Show times vary. Cover $30, $15 drink minimum. AmEx, DC, Disc, MC, V.
This classy joint, opened in early 1998, is next door to the regal-looking Russian restaurant of the same name. If the

Down-home singin': An NYC regular,
Amanda Green *blends cabaret and country.*

Knock on wood: Try to catch Andrea Marcovicci's luxurious voice at the **Oak Room**.

caviar and the mosaic reproduction of Klimt's *The Kiss* don't ignite your passions, rely on the first-rate performers, such as Phillip Officer, Steve Ross and the outrageous British trio Fascinating Aida.

Michael's Pub at Bill's Gay Nineties

57 E 54th St between Park and Madison Aves (212-758-2272). Subway: E, F, to Lexington Ave; 6 to 51st St. Tue–Sat 9, 11pm. Cover $20–$25, $15 drink minimum. AmEx, DC, Disc, MC, V.
Julie Wilson, the glamorous sylph with the gardenia in her hair, is widely considered one of cabaret's greatest interpreters, and she has made Michael's Pub her new home (though it's always a good idea to call first and make sure she's performing). After having spent decades a few blocks east, Michael's has moved into Bill's, a former speakeasy. Go see the inimitable Ms. Wilson for a glimpse of cabaret the way it's meant to be.

The Oak Room

Algonquin Hotel, 59 W 44th St between Fifth and Sixth Aves (212-840-6800). Subway: B, D, F, Q to 42nd St. Tue–Thu 9:30pm; Fri, Sat 9:30, 11:30pm, dinner compulsory at first Fri, Sat show. Cover $45, $15 drink minimum. AmEx, DC, Disc, MC, V.
This resonant banquette-lined room was recently renovated, and it is the place to savor the cream of cabaret performers, including Andrea Marcovicci, Maureen McGovern and Christine Andreas. *See chapter* **Accommodations**.

The Supper Club

240 W 47th St between Broadway and Eighth Ave (212-921-1940). Subway: C, E, 1, 9 to 50th St; N, R to 49th St. Show times vary. Cover $20, no drink minimum. AmEx, DC, MC, V.
This beautifully restored ballroom is the setting for dining and dancing to a 12-piece big band. The decor and better-than-average food attract a glamorous crowd of pre-theater dahlings. It also serves as a concert venue, hosting such performers as Ute Lemper and Marianne Faithfull, not to mention the occasional rock show. The strikingly azure Blue Room has recently reopened for more intimate sets by performers such as the talented pianist-singer Eric Comstock.

Emerging talents

Danny's Skylight Room

346 W 46th St between Eighth and Ninth Aves (212-265-8133). Subway: A, C, E to 42nd St–Port Authority. Show times vary. Cover $8–$15, no drink minimum. AmEx, DC, MC, V.
A pastel nook of the Grand Sea Palace restaurant, "where Bangkok meets Broadway" on touristy Restaurant Row, Danny's features pop-jazz, pop and cabaret, with the accent on the smooth. In addition to up-and-comers, this is a good place to catch a few mature cabaret standbys like Blossom Dearie and Barbara Lea.

Don't Tell Mama

*343 W 46th St between Eighth and Ninth Aves
(212-757-0788). Subway: A, C, E to 42nd St–Port
Authority. Show times vary. No cover for piano bar;
$6–$15 in cabaret room, two-drink minimum at tables
(no food served). AmEx, MC, V.*

Showbiz pros like to visit this Theater District venue. The
acts range from strictly amateurish to potential stars of
tomorrow. The nightly lineup can include pop, jazz or
Broadway singers, female impersonators, magicians, revues
or comedians.

55 Grove Street Upstairs at Rose's Turn

*55 Grove St between Seventh Ave and Bleecker
St (212-366-5438). Subway: 1, 9 to Christopher
St–Sheridan Sq. Show times vary. Cover $6–$15, two-
drink minimum. No credit cards.*

This is the oldest cabaret showroom in Greenwich Village
and where the Duplex started 40 years ago, before it moved
to newer quarters across Seventh Avenue (*see below*). It's a
dark room with zero atmosphere. The emphasis tends to be
on comedy, or pocket-size one-act musicals—like *Our Lives
& Times*, a hilarious spoof of current events—with only the
occasional musical.

Judy's Chelsea

*169 Eighth Ave between 18th and 19th Sts
(212-929-5410). Subway: C, E to 23rd St. Mon–Thu
9pm; Fri, Sat 9, 11pm. Cover $15, $10 food or drink
minimum. AmEx, MC, V.*

The venerable Theater-District haunt Judy's lost its lease in
1998, but it has since resurfaced downtown in a fabulous
space. Award-winning singer-songwriter Bonnie Lee
Sanders has played, while the geek-chic Lounge-O-Leers
keep piano-bar patrons laughing with grooved-out versions
of top 40 hits. Co-owner/singer Judy Kreston (just one of the
many Judys after whom the place is named) and pianist
David Lahm often perform on Saturday nights.

Triad

*158 W 72nd St between Broadway and Columbus
Ave (212-799-4599). Subway: B, C, 1, 2, 3, 9 to 72nd
St. Mon, Wed–Fri 8pm; Sat, Sun 3, 7:30pm. Cover
varies. AmEx, Disc, MC, V.*

This Upper West Side cabaret has been the launching pad
for many successful revues over the years, several of which
(*Forever Plaid, Forbidden Broadway*) have moved to larger
spaces Off Broadway. Dinner is available, and, in a smaller
spot downstairs, there's an occasional singer or benefit show.

Alternative venues

The Duplex

*61 Christopher St at Seventh Ave South
(212-255-5438). Subway: 1, 9 to Christopher St–
Sheridan Sq. Show times vary. Piano bar 9pm–4am daily.
Cover $6–$12, two-drink minimum. No credit cards.*

New York's oldest cabaret has been going for 40-plus years,
and it sets the pace for campy, good-natured fun. It attracts
a mix of regulars and tourists, who laugh and sing along
with classy drag performers, comedians and rising stars.

Joe's Pub

*425 Lafayette St between Astor Pl and E 4th St. (212-
260-2400). Subway: N, R to 8th St; 6 to Astor Pl. Cover
varies. AmEx, MC, V.*

This plush club in the Public Theater manages to be hip and
elegant at the same time. There's a great trend of recogniz-
ing new talent here: The incandescent Audra McDonald pre-
miered her CD; Jason Robert Brown, the young composer of
the Tony-nominated musical *Parade*, performed original
material. Theater legends Betty Comden and Adolph Green
(*On the Town, Singin' in the Rain*) have made an appear-

ance as well. The music schedule is as varied as the clientele; on noncabaret nights, you can rub elbows with celebs
like Puff Daddy and that guy from *Titanic*.

Torch

*137 Ludlow St between Rivington and Stanton Sts
(212-228-5151). Subway: F to Second Ave. No cover.
AmEx, DC, Disc, MC, V.*

Monday nights at this Lower East Side bar/restaurant are
where you'll find Nicole Renaud, an enchanting Parisian
songbird. Renaud's crystalline voice, clever playlist (music
from *The Umbrellas of Cherbourg*, anyone?) and bizarrely
beautiful costumes make for a decidedly different evening.
Best of all, there's no cover. Avoid the pricey food, but
splurge on a delicious Fleur-de-Lis cocktail and savor the
Gallic atmosphere.

Wilson's

*201 W 79th St between Broadway and Amsterdam Ave
(212-769-0100). Subway: 1, 9 to 79th St. Cover $5–$10,
no drink minimum. AmEx, DC, Disc, MC, V.*

Don't let the cruisy atmosphere at this Upper West Side bar
and bistro fool you. It's often home to Judy Barnett, whose
velvety powerhouse of a voice and inventive jazz arrangements will have you cheering.

Jazz

Almost all the established jazz clubs adhere to a
cabaret format. For information on some of the larger venues, including Birdland, Iridium and others,
see chapter **Music**.

Arthur's Tavern

*57 Grove St between Bleecker St and Seventh Ave
South (212-675-6879). Subway: 1, 9 to Christopher St–
Sheridan Sq. No cover, two-drink minimum at tables.
No credit cards.*

Arthur's is a funky, divey-looking joint in the Village, where
the schedule includes Dixieland bands and pianists Johnny
Parker and Al Bundy.

Five and Ten No Exaggeration

*77 Greene St between Spring and Broome Sts (212-925-
7414). Subway: N, R to Prince St. Tue–Sun 8pm. Cover
$5, $10 food or drink minimum. AmEx, DC, MC, V.*

At this warm, 1940s-style supper club, where the lamps wear
beaded fringes and the jiving swing survivors share their
pink-draped stage with an old Esso gas pump. Various artifacts in the club are for sale, including rhinestone earrings,
vintage radios and Coke signs.

Comedy venues

The business of comedy is booming in New York
City these days. Small, out-of-the-way clubs and
bars have been nurturing a new generation of performers with an avant-garde approach. Many of
the talented fringe performers who started out in
the alternative clubs of the Lower East Side are
gradually making their way into bigger clubs and
mainstream outlets. Marc Maron, who does edgy
stand-up, frequently appears on such talk shows
as *Late Show with David Letterman,* and the
Upright Citizens Brigade has a weekly half-hour
show on Comedy Central, as well as its own theater where the troupe performs and produces
shows for up-and-coming talent.

You can still catch off-beat talent at some smaller venues, along with established stars like Colin Quinn, Janeane Garofalo and David Cross. In the following clubs you can check out a wide range of comedy styles—from traditional stand-up to some very twisted entertainment.

Show times vary at the venues listed below; it's always best to call ahead.

Boston Comedy Club

82 W 3rd St between Thompson and Sullivan Sts (212-477-1000). Subway: A, C, E, B, D, F, Q to W 4th St–Washington Sq. $5 Sun–Thu; $10 Fri, Sat, two-drink minimum. AmEx, MC, V.
This rowdy basement-level room is a late-night option. The bill can include as many as ten different acts. The first show on Saturdays is a new-talent showcase.

Carolines on Broadway

1626 Broadway between 49th and 50th Sts (212-757-4100). Subway: C, E, 1, 9 to 50th St; N, R to 49th St. $20–$27, two-drink minimum. AmEx, DC, V.
A few blocks north of Times Square's Disneyfied madness, Caroline's colorful lounge is the place for up-and-coming TV faces such as MTV's Bill Bellamy or comics with broad appeal such as Wendy Liebman. Billy Crystal and Jay Leno honed their craft at the original Caroline's in Chelsea.

Chicago City Limits Theatre

1105 First Ave between 60th and 61st Sts (212-888-5233). Subway: N, R to Lexington Ave; 4, 5, 6 to 59th St. $20, no drink minimum. AmEx, MC, V.
Founded in the Windy City, this popular group moved to New York in 1979 and has been delighting audiences ever since with a combination of current events–driven sketch and audience-inspired improvisation.

Comedy Cellar

117 MacDougal St between W 3rd and Bleecker Sts (212-254-3480). Subway: A, C, E, B, D, F, Q to W 4th St–Washington Sq. $5 Sun–Thu; $10 Fri, Sat, two-drink minimum. AmEx, MC, V.
Amid the coffeehouses of MacDougal Street, this well-worn underground lair recalls the counterculture vibe of another era, before the neighborhood became besieged by out-of-towners every weekend. Still, the Comedy Cellar regularly provides an excellent roster of popular local talent.

Comic Strip Live

1568 Second Ave between 81st and 82nd Sts (212-861-9386). Subway: 4, 5, 6 to 86th St. $10 Sun–Thu; $14 Fri, Sat, $9 drink minimum. AmEx, DC, Disc, MC, V.
This saloonlike stand-up club is known for separating the wheat from the chaff, a blessing in a city with its share of comics high on ambition and short on talent. Monday is amateur night—comic hopefuls should sign up the Friday before.

Dangerfield's

1118 First Ave between 61st and 62nd Sts (212-593-1650). Subway: N, R to Lexington Ave; 4, 5, 6 to 59th St. $12.50 Sun–Thu; $15 Fri, Sat, no drink minimum. AmEx, DC, MC, V.
Opened by comedian Rodney Dangerfield more than 20 years ago, this glitzy lounge is now one of New York's oldest and most formidable clubs.

Gotham Comedy Club

34 W 22nd St between Fifth and Sixth Aves (212-367-9000). Subway: F, N, R, 1, 9 to 23rd St. $8–$12, two-drink minimum. AmEx, DC, MC, V.
The Gotham Comedy Club books a lineup of top comedians from all over the country, including stand-ups such as Todd Barry and Louis CK, who perform here regularly.

Laugh track: Janeane Garofolo cracks a joke at **Carolines on Broadway**.

New York Comedy Club

241 E 24th St between Second and Third Aves (212-696-5233). Subway: 6 to 23rd St. $5 Sun–Thu; $10 Fri, Sat, two-drink minimum. AmEx, MC, V.
A relative newcomer, the New York Comedy Club takes a democratic approach: a packed lineup and a bargain cover price.

Stand-Up NY

236 W 78th St at Broadway (212-595-0850). Subway: 1, 9 to 79th St. $7 Sun–Thu; $12 Fri, Sat, two-drink minimum. AmEx, MC, V.
A somewhat sterile but small and intimate place, Stand-Up NY always features a good mix of club-circuit regulars and new faces.

Surf Reality

172 Allen St between Stanton and Rivington Sts (212-330-8611). Subway: F to Second Ave. Call for ticket prices.
The center of the Lower East Side alternative universe, Surf Reality features a lot of comedy—but probably nothing like you've ever seen before. Bring an open mind and you'll surely be entertained.

Upright Citizens Brigade Theater

161 W 22nd St between Sixth and Seventh Aves (212-366-9176). Subway: 1, 9 to 23rd St. Call for ticket prices.
The home of Comedy Central's crazy and brilliant sketch group, the UCB Theater features inexpensive, high-quality sketch comedy seven nights a week. The original foursome still performs every Sunday for free; their disciples entertain the rest of the week.

Clubs

Despite the city's "quality of life" measures, New York's clublife still presents lots of wild nocturnal options

Under crackdown-loving Mayor Rudolph Giuliani (dubbed "Mayor Rapknuckles" in *The New York Times*), Manhattan, an island of anarchy since colonial days, has become more regimented, and the clubs have consequently lost some of their wildness. But there's still plenty out there—you just have to look a little harder. Many of the more risqué events shun publicity (and hence may not be listed here), so if you're interested in events of a semilegal nature, it's best to ask around. Also, because of the political climate, much of the scene revolves around lounges or DJ bars (*see* **This ain't no disco**, *pages 210–211*).

New Yorkers are a cynical bunch and hard to impress. But despite the perennial "been there, done that" attitude, New York's club scene is proud of its history and traditions. Most twentysomething natives grew up on disco and old-school rap, and DJs program a fair number of "classics" in their sets. While some clubs seem overly nostalgic for legendary, long-gone nightspots like Paradise Garage (a famed gay disco and the source of the British term for gospel-influenced vocal house music), classics give props to the past and connect the musical dots between then and now.

New York DJs are more eclectic than their counterparts elsewhere, spinning hip-hop, reggae, soul, house, disco, drum 'n' bass and Latin over the course of one night (though less so in the big clubs). The crowds, too, tend to be varied (though certain clubs are populated almost exclusively by white gay musclemen). A gay sensibility is common, and a "straight" night often means "mixed."

Although glamour-oriented clubs do have door policies, economic and fashion trends have persuaded most places to accept the money of the sartorially challenged. You still may want to dress up, though, as this situation can change like the weather. Particularly straight venues often refuse entry to groups of men in order to maintain a desirable gender balance and to prevent testosterone overload.

*Monster mash: Vampires and goths get down at Long Black Veil, Thursdays at **Mother**.*

This ain't no disco

To hear some diverse music, get your lounge act together

Clubland's clever response to the difficulty of obtaining a city license to allow dancing is the lounge: a bar that features many of the trappings of a club (DJs, doormen, velvet ropes, expensive drinks) but doesn't (well, can't) allow dancing. With the dearth of smaller dance clubs, lounges have also become places to hear more left-field music. Laid-back staff may look the other way if you start moving to the beat. Just don't plan to do any arabesques.

Beige
B Bar, 40 E 4th St at Bowery (212-475-2220). Subway: 6 to Bleecker St. Tue 11pm.
DJs serve up a groovy, just-this-side-of-camp soundtrack that can include anything from gay show-tune standards to 1980s electro-disco classics. Expect fashionistas, clubbies and off-duty drag queens. Hilarious and very visual.

bOb
235 Eldridge St between Houston and Stanton Sts (212-777-0588). Subway: F to Second Ave. 7pm–4am.
bOb features everything from the standard hip-hop/reggae/classics to exotica and film-noir soundtracks. The space doubles as an art gallery.

Double Happiness
173 Mott St between Broome and Grand Sts (212-941-1282). Subway: B, D, Q to Grand St; 6 to Spring St. 5pm–2am.

Owned by the same folks behind the similarly gorgeous Orchard Bar, Double Happiness is a classy, imaginative, tasteful and beautiful space. Low lighting and cozy booths add to the charm. It's a great place for an afternoon or early-evening tipple—just as well, since it closes disturbingly early. DJs spin eclectic, funky music, usually starting at about 9pm. Sundays, hosted by highly regarded Italian dance label Irma, are pretty popular right now.

Idlewild
145 E Houston St between Eldridge and Forsyth Sts (212-477-5005). Subway: F to Second Ave. Sun–Wed 8pm–3am, Thu–Sat 8pm–4am.
This space reopened in early 1998 as an impressively designed jet-themed bar. Idlewild (JFK International Airport's original name) looks just like a jet, with airplane seats, a curved, fuselage-shaped interior and a boarding-ramp entrance hall. All this wonderful decor makes the place in high demand for private parties, so you may have trouble getting in.

Kush
183 Orchard St between Houston and Stanton Sts (212-677-7328). Subway: F to Second Ave. 8pm–4am.
In a neighborhood overrun with pseudo-hip theme bars, Kush is hard to knock. Located on the main drag of the old Lower East Side bargain district, Kush is a beautifully designed bar that transports you to Morocco as soon as you enter. There are olives at the bar and cushions to sit on, and the music policy is commendably uncompromising. DJs spin mainly ethnic-influenced music—from rai and dub reggae to Arab-flavored dance music.

*Single Beige female: Poseurs, trendies, fashionistas and celebrities mingle at **Beige**.*

Lansky Lounge

104 Norfolk St at Delancey St (212-677-9489).
Subway: F to Delancey St; J, M, Z to Essex St.
Hours vary with event.
File under "Only in New York": Lansky Lounge is a
speakeasy (complete with live swing bands) in the back
of Ratner's, a legendary kosher restaurant. Though
Lansky caters to a hipster crowd (partly from the healthy
swing scene), it serves rabbi-supervised kosher drinks
and is closed on Jewish holidays—and never open Friday
nights. Its surreptitious entrance—through a basement
alley between buildings and up into the back of the
restaurant—adds novelty appeal.

Ludlow Bar

165 Ludlow St between Houston and Rivington Sts
(212-353-0536). Subway: F to Second Ave. 6pm–4am.
Ludlow is simply and tastefully appointed and features
some of the more progressive music you'll hear on the
Lower East Side—although, like most spots in the area,
it's often overrun by suburban wanna-bes. DJs spin
every night, playing jazz, trip-hop, hip-hop, loungecore,
drum 'n' bass, house, salsa, bossa nova and pretty much
anything that's groovy. The owners are presently in the
process of reopening the space once occupied by legendary after-hours joint Save the Robots. No firm details
on when that will happen, though; ask the staff here.

Niagara

112 Avenue A at 7th St (212-420-9517).
Subway: F to Second Ave. 4pm–4am.
Once King Tut's Wah-Wah Hut, a legendary hangout on
the '80s East Village art scene, this bar now caters to a
cross section of local (and slumming) punk rockers, swing
nationals, loungecore enthusiasts, preppies on parade and
the like. DJs spin everything from punk and garage rock
to Latin jazz, '60s soul and exotica.

Spy

101 Greene St between Prince and Spring
Sts (212-343-9000). Subway: N, R to Prince St.
Mon–Sun 5pm–4am.
Totally trendy a couple of years ago, Spy is still a good
bet for Soho people-watching. The former cabaret theater is laid out perfectly for it, with balconies and raised
banquettes. DJs spin mostly mainstream lounge music,
but then you'll also find major-league DJ/remixer Roger
Sanchez spinning on Fridays, too. Lots of celebrities
mixed in with the Eurotrash.

23 Watts

23 Watts St between West Broadway and
Thompson St (212-925-9294). Subway: C, E
to Spring St.
Formerly catering to models and their cigar-chomping
admirers as Chaos, 23 Watts opened in spring 1999 with
new decor; it now caters to…models and their cigar-
chomping admirers. Of course, where the models and
stockbrokers go, the hoi polloi follow. The music is generally on the mainstream side.

Void

16 Mercer St at Howard St (212-941-6492).
Subway: J, M, Z, N, R, 6 to Canal St. Wed, Thu
8pm–2am; Fri, Sat 8pm–3am.
Void, as you might expect from the name, is dark, stark
and minimalist. A giant video screen engulfs one wall,
and there are monitors embedded in the cocktail tables.
Musically, you get DJs spinning armchair techno or live
bands playing jazz.

In pre-Giuliani times, weapons were the only
items verboten in clubs, but the current climate has
forced some clubs to police their patrons' drug use
as well, so if getting high is your cup of E, be careful—and leave the guns and knives at home. Since
we're on the subject, it should be said that while
New York isn't nearly as dangerous as it used to
be, this is still a city where anything can happen.
If you're leaving a club in the middle of the night,
you might want to take a taxi or call a car service
as you leave (*see* **Getting around** *in chapter*
Directory). Here are two of the latter with easily
memorized numbers: Lower East Side Car Service
(212-477-7777) and Tel Aviv (212-777-7777).

Alcohol is sold until 4am, and some after-hours
clubs are open late enough to reopen their bars at
8am (noon on Sunday), the earliest allowed by law.
There are also a number of illegal drinking dens
(not surprisingly, we can't list these); ask around
at last call if you want another round. Wherever
you go, most people won't arrive before midnight
(some clubs don't fill up—or even open their
doors—until well past 4am). Still, one of the city's
most popular events, Body & Soul, is a reaction to
that; it runs Sundays from 3pm until 11pm, allow-
ing club dinosaurs and weekday clockpunchers to
be in bed early. (Some regulars, however, are most
certainly still celebrating Saturday night!)

Though Friday and Saturday are of course the
biggest nights to go out, many hipsters and locals
stick to midweek clubbing in order to avoid the
throngs of suburbanites (the "bridge-and-tunnel"
crowd) that overwhelm Manhattan every weekend, and many of the more interesting and unusual events happen during the week.

The club scene is mercurial: Parties move weekly, and clubs can differ wildly from night to night.
For example, a primarily gay establishment may
"go straight" once a week because a promoter can
fill the place on a slow night. Calling ahead is a
good idea, as is consulting *Time Out New York* or
the monthly style magazine *Paper*. The gay listings
magazine *HX (Homo Xtra)* is also good for club
reviews, albeit with a gym-queen-oriented slant (*see*
chapter **Gay & Lesbian**). Happy hunting.

Movable parties may change venues at a
moment's notice, and keeping up can be a challenge. Calling the various hot lines can help put
your finger on the pulse. These cover a wide range
of events. Rave clothing and record store **Liquid
Sky** has a popular phone line (212-226-0657), with
details of rave-oriented parties. **Mello**'s line (212-
631-1023) is also rave-oriented, but is geared more
toward clubs and is less artsy. Other rave lines
include **Satellite Productions** (212-465-3299),
Digital Domain (212-592-3676) and **Solar Luv**
(212-629-2078). **Urban Works** (212-629-1786) covers a variety of events from hip-hop and rave to gay
parties (such as Café Con Leche). **E-Man's** line
(212-330-8101) tracks a selection of underground

house clubs, mostly—but by no means exclusively—of the mixed-to-gay variety. **Giant Step**'s line (212-714-8001) focuses on acid jazz, drum 'n' bass, trip-hop and the like. **Mixed Bag Productions** (212-604-4224) has a role in many events: In addition to running Konkrete Jungle, Mixed Bag helps promote various jungle, acid jazz and trip-hop parties, including larger-scale ravelike events

Admission prices for the clubs listed below vary according to the night, but usually range from $5 to $25. When no closing time is listed, assume the club stays open until the party fizzles out. The term "club" is also used to describe discos and live music venues (*see chapter* **Music**).

Clubs

Cheetah
12 W 21st St between Fifth and Sixth Aves (212-206-7770). Subway: F, N, R to 23rd St. Hours vary with event.
While drink prices are outrageous and the crowd can tend toward model-worshippers and Eurotrash, the cheetah-print booths and indoor waterfall are fun. Purr, a hip-hop/R&B/classics party on Monday, is popular for its attractive, racially mixed crowd of trendy downtown heteros on the make. Plenty of models and celebs, too. Other nights, resident DJ Nelson "That Boy" Diaz is worth checking out for his masterful blending of salsa, merengue, house, disco, hip-hop and more.

Club New York
252 W 43rd St between Broadway and Eighth Ave (212-997-9510). Subway: A, C, E, N, R, 1, 2, 3, 9, 7 to 42nd St. Hours vary with event.
The very idea of Club New York triggers thoughts good and bad. In its prior incarnation, back when Times Square was an interesting sleaze zone and not a sanitized shopping mall, this was the legendary trannie hustler bar Sally's II, a major inspiration for the folks at Jackie 60 (*see* **Mother** *below*), among others. It was closed down as part of the city's war on non-tourist-friendly culture. Still, the fact that the place has reopened as a club has made more than a few cynics smile…a little. Granted, Club New York caters to a more mainstream, straight, well-behaved crowd than did Sally's. But much of the layout (including the fabulous circular bar) has been saved.

Coney Island High
15 St. Marks Pl between Second and Third Aves (212-674-7959). Subway: 6 to Astor Pl; N, R to 8th St. 11pm–4am alternate Saturdays.
Most of the week, Coney Island High is a vortex of punky rock posing, in the old Max's Kansas City/CBGB vein. You'll see lots of guys with eyeliner, bondage trousers and hair like Rod Stewart's; they're probably the owners. Coney Island High hosts a variety of (mainly rock-oriented) club nights, but ska, reggae, jungle, swing and even gay nights get plenty of time here. Live bands are as common as DJs.

Copacabana
617 W 57th St between Eleventh and Twelfth Aves (212-582-2672). Subway: A, C, B, D, 1, 9 to 59th St–Columbus Circle. Jun–Aug Tue 6pm–3am, Thu–Sat 6pm–4am; Sept–May Tue 6pm–3am, Fri 6pm–5am, Sat 10am–5pm.
The truly legendary Copa is an upscale disco catering to a 25-plus, mainly black and Hispanic clientele. Although this isn't the exact same space Barry Manilow sang in (the club moved across town to its present space a few years back), the look and feel have been preserved with remarkable faithfulness. Live bands play salsa and merengue every

night, and DJs fill the gaps with hip-hop, R&B, disco and Latin sounds. You saw it looking its best in Martin Scorsese's *GoodFellas*. The dress code requires customers to look "casual but nice": no jeans, sneakers or work boots, and gents must wear shirts with collars.

Don Hill's
511 Greenwich St at Spring St (212-334-1390). Subway: 1, 9 to Houston St. Tue–Sun 10pm–4am.
Don Hill's is half dance club, half live-music venue, and its best night, Squeezebox, combines both: It's a gay rock party, with live bands and a drag queen DJ spinning glammy, punky, scummy rock for a mixed (but queer in appearance and sensibility) crowd. Fashion and music celebrities regularly make appearances at this festive alternative to house music all night long.

Fahrenheit
349 Broadway at Leonard St (212-343-0957). Subway: A, C, E, 1, 2, 3, 9 to Chambers St. Hours vary with event.
Most of the time, Fahrenheit caters to mature, working- and middle-class Latino, African-American, Caribbean and African singles. The music generally ranges from hip-hop, R&B, house and classics to soca, reggae, African and Latin music.

Flamingo East
219 Second Ave between 13th and 14th Sts (212-533-2860). Subway: L to Third Ave; N, R, 4, 5, 6 to 14th St–Union Sq. Hours vary with event.
Long ago, this club and restaurant was some bon vivant's townhouse. Flamingo East still exudes that kind of swank atmosphere. The upstairs room features DJs spinning everything from loungecore and '80s pop to groovy disco and house (depending on the night), and you'll come across music-industry types as well as fashionistas. Wednesday night's Salon party offers some great drag shows, too. Once a month, the promoters clear the tables and chairs downstairs, set up a DJ booth and turn the restaurant area into a pumping deep-house dance floor.

The Greatest Bar on Earth
1 World Trade Center, West St between Liberty and Vesey Sts, 107th floor (212-524-7000). Subway: C, E to World Trade Center; N, R to Cortlandt St. Hours vary with event.
This restaurant and bar on top of the World Trade Center is the kind of place you'd take your cousins from Indiana, but in the last few years it has cleverly courted New York's trendies by adding loungecore, Latin and funk DJs to its lineup of middle-age crooners and cover bands. Wednesday night's Mondo 107 is the most popular night, with a mix of vintage exotica and newer stuff in that vein (Pizzicato Five, Dimitri from Paris, etc.). While it's probably peaked as a hot spot, it's still fun, especially for the view on a clear night.

Kit Kat Klub
124 W 43rd St between Sixth Ave and Broadway (212-819-0377). Subway: B, D, F, Q to 42nd St; N, R, S 1, 2, 3, 9, 7 to 42nd St–Times Sq. Fri–Sun 10pm–4am.
Originally the Henry Miller Theater, the building was home to Xenon during the disco era. Until recently, it hosted a revival of the musical *Cabaret,* throwing down the dance floor after the final curtain. The place still looks rough around the edges, but there's charm in the chaos and decrepitude. The crowd is pretty mainstream, but all sorts of special parties wind up here, so it's worth checking out.

Krystal's
89-25 Merrick Blvd between 89th and Jamaica Aves, Jamaica, Queens (718-523-3662). Subway: E, J, Z to Jamaica Center. Mon, Tue, Fri, Sat 10pm–4am.
If you don't mind trekking out to the boroughs, you can get a slightly grittier taste of the city's musical life. Krystal's, in the

Caribbean section of Queens, is where you'll hear a hot mix of hip-hop and reggae, played for a boisterous local audience.

La Nueva Escuelita
301 W 39th St at Eighth Ave (212-631-0588). Subway: A, C, E to 42nd St–Port Authority. Thu–Sun 10pm–5am.
Escuelita used to be a seedy Latin drag club. Now, it's a rather less seedy Latin drag club, but no less entertaining for that. Though it's oriented toward gay and lesbian Latinos, all are welcome. The music is generally high-energy, heavy on the merengue and banging Latin/tribal house. The drag shows are not to be missed. The Sunday tea dance is hosted by the incomparable Harmonica Sunbeam, a wacky drag queen comedienne with universal appeal.

Life
158 Bleecker St at Thompson St (212-420-1999). Subway: A, C, E, B, D, F, Q to W 4th St–Washington Sq. Mon–Wed 10pm–4am, Thu–Sun 10pm–6am.
Life opened in 1996 in Greenwich Village on the former site of the legendary jazz club the Village Gate. In a neighborhood already teeming with bars, the club initially attempted to keep the community happy by playing it safe musically and demographically. Interestingly, though there's plenty of Eurotrash and preppies, you'll often find some surprisingly bohemian and off-the-wall stuff going on here. Thursdays are hip, drawing a beautiful, jaded but decadent downtown crowd, heavy on gay and fashion types. The music is a blend of underground vocal and instrumental house, while the VIP lounge (and pretty much everyone is a VIP on this night) features classics of all kinds—disco one week, new wave the next. Boy's Life on Sundays caters to gay gym-bunnies. Wednesday night is also very hot at the moment, drawing a mixed-to-queer crowd into glam rock, punk and posing; meanwhile, young mod types dance to Britpop and '60s soul, while an underground house party in the club's Sullivan Street Room draws a mix of music-industry types and the hard-core dance crowd. Depending on the night, you may not get in unless you're dressed up or are looking particularly stylish.

The Lounge
Lenox Lounge, 288 Lenox Ave between 124th and 125th Sts (212-722-9566). Subway: 2, 3 to 125th St. Tue, Thu 11pm–4am.
Go to the heart of Harlem for this twice-a-week gay hip-hop club—a phenomenon that's not nearly as unique as you might think. House, reggae, R&B and disco classics are thrown into the musical mix, and there's a more party-minded atmosphere than at other spots in the area or, for that matter, at Chelsea gay clubs. It's a solidly black crowd, but new faces are welcome regardless of their complexion. DJs include NFX, Cat and veteran spinner Andre Collins.

Mother
432 W 14th St at Washington St (212-366-5680). Subway: A, C, E to 14th St; L to Eighth Ave. Hours vary with event.
Run by longtime club royalty Chi Chi Valenti and Johnny Dynell (a popular DJ), Mother is home to a variety of highly imaginative events, ranging from gay techno parties to modern-dance recitals and spoken-word evenings. Jackie 60, the club's nine-year-old Tuesday-night tradition will end just before New Year's Eve 1999, but the rest of the week here is often just as wild. Dynell pumps out hard but funky New York–style house, and all manner of performers do their thing on stage. Lots of artists, celebrities, freaks and club faces are regulars, though the club's longevity and many press clippings bring in the tourist crowd, too. Clit Club is a Friday-night lesbian institution, and Saturday's Click+Drag is a brilliant cross-breeding of technological and sexual fetishism (featuring Internet chat and dominatrices, among other hot-wired things). A vague dress code exists on Tuesdays and Saturdays—according to that week's theme—but is selectively enforced.

*Mixin' 'n' matchin': DJs work it nightly at the Lower East Side's **Ludlow Bar**.*

NV
289 Spring St at Hudson St (212-929-NVNV). Subway: 1, 9 to Houston St; C, E to Spring St. Wed–Fri 4:30pm–4am; Sat 8pm–4am.
NV, located just west of Soho, caters mainly to Eurotrash, yuppies, sports stars and model-worshippers, but worthwhile parties do take place on occasion. The Sunday-night Passion event draws an upscale, good-looking mixed-to-black crowd, there to groove to the music (hip-hop, R&B, classics) and each other.

Nell's
246 W 14th St between Seventh and Eighth Aves (212-675-1567). Subway: A, C, E to 14th St; L to Eighth Ave. 10pm–4am.
More than a decade old, Nell's is much the same as it's always been. Its formula: laid-back jazz and funky soul (often with live bands) upstairs, where there's a limited dining menu, and DJed hip-hop, R&B, reggae, house and classics below. The crowd is multiracial (leaning to black), dressed up, straight and ready to spend.

Night Strike
Bowlmor Lanes, 110 University Pl between 12th and 13th Sts (212-255-8158). Subway: L, N, R, 4, 5, 6 to 14th St–Union Sq. Mon 10pm.
Scenesters exchange their platforms for bowling shoes, while DJs spin house and techno. There's something humanizing

about a crowd of full-time nightcrawlers letting their hair down and hanging out the classic American white-trash way: drinking, bowling and shootin' the shit.

Ohm

16 W 22nd St between Fifth and Sixth Aves (212-229-2000). Subway: F, N, R to 23rd St.
Ohm is essentially an upscale space with no real built-in crowd; as such, everything from yuppie parties to underground house nights fill up the week. As of this writing, Thursday's Soul Circuit event looked to be the best bet, with two of New York's better deep-house DJs, Joe T. Turri and Rio, spinning the tunes.

Organic Grooves

Various locations and prices; call 212-439-1147 for details. Fri 10:30pm.
The Go Global folks throw their parties at any old space, from Lower East Side antique shops to Brooklyn's decrepit waterfront. DJ Sasha spins soupy, trippy dub funk and acid jazz, while live musicians noodle to the records. It's hippyish but funky nonetheless. The crowd tends toward the sexually straight and racially mixed (and it's not a bad-looking bunch, either).

Planet 28

215 W 28th St between Seventh and Eighth Aves (212-726-8820). Subway: A, C, E to 34th St–Penn Station; 1, 9 to 28th St. Hours vary with event.
Planet 28 features everything from gay, black voguing balls (the fierce Clubhouse event on Wednesday is as close to *Paris Is Burning* as you're likely to get) to rave and hip-hop nights. The events change often, so check ahead.

Roxy

515 W 18th St between Tenth and Eleventh Aves (212-645-5156). Subway: A, C, E to 14th St; L to Eighth Ave. Hours vary with event.
This warhorse of a club has had more lives than a cat. Originally a roller disco, it gained worldwide fame in the early '80s as the epicenter of the downtown hip-hop culture-clash, with Afrika Bambaataa on the wheels of steel. Later, it became a cheesy Latin freestyle club, then a hugely popular gay club. The queens have returned on Saturdays (perhaps getting the jump on an early-'90s revival), packing the place as they used to do. On Fridays, meanwhile, you'll find a straight suburban crowd getting down to commercial house, hip-hop, salsa, etc. The room is immense and impressive, and the sound system kicks ass. Worth a trip for first-timers.

Sapphire

249 Eldridge St between Houston and Stanton Sts (212-777-5153). Subway: F to Second Ave. 7pm–4am.
Sapphire was one of the first trendy Lower East Side DJ bars. As such, the crowd has evolved from downtown hipsters to uptown slummers to outer-borough weekend warriors. Over the past year or so, Sapphire went to considerable lengths (and expense) to obtain a cabaret license, so it's now a legitimate (though still very small) dance club. The music is fairly typical—hip-hop, reggae, acid jazz, R&B and disco classics—though Mondays and Tuesdays currently feature soulful underground house.

XVI

16 First Ave between 1st and 2nd Sts (212-260-1549). Subway: F to Second Ave. Hours vary with event.
The story goes that XVI's incredibly funky basement used to be some sort of Middle Eastern coke den that was accidentally discovered during renovation of the ground-floor storefront space. The place really is from a different time: all mirrored tiles, stone floors, exotic paintings and gaudy brick arches. DJs play on both levels, though the music tends to be considerably more pedestrian than the decor. The Vampyros Lesbos party is a Thursday-night homage to the

early-'70s soft-core porn/horror flicks of Spanish director Jess Franco; DJ Franc O spins a selection of loungecore, exotica, strip-hop and other kitschy, groovy stuff from Franco films and their ilk. The crowd, meanwhile, does its best to be decadent, while slides of soft-core nudes and album sleeves illuminate the walls.

Sound Factory

618 W 46th St between Eleventh and Twelfth Aves (212-643-0728). Subway: C, E to 50th St. Hours vary with event.
The long-awaited new incarnation of the legendary Sound Factory finally opened in January 1997. The space is different, but the sound system is allegedly the very same one. However, the club does not have DJ Junior Vasquez, and for many that means it will never be the Sound Factory. In any case, the new model is much more mainstream than its namesake. Unlike the original Factory's streetwise black and Latin gay audience, the new Factory crowd is mostly straight and suburban. DJ Jonathan Peters spins an attack-oriented and, frankly, cheesy brand of hard house, with snare rolls and breakdowns seemingly every other minute. Although closer to the politics of club promotion than its predecessor, the club is also keeping alive the long New York after-hours tradition of free munchies, offering a generous spread of fruit, cookies, potato chips, coffee and more, although it now has a full bar.

Speeed

20 W 39th St between Fifth and Sixth Aves (212-719-9867). Subway: B, D, F, Q to 42nd St; 7 to Fifth Ave. Hours vary with event.
Speeed opened early in 1998 with much fanfare, and then, well…While it never achieved "in" status, it has a full lineup, mostly mainstream parties with hip-hop on the ground floor and house in the basement. The club briefly changed its name to Creation and is referred to by either name. Events change often here, and worthwhile nights do pop up sometimes, so it's worth keeping in mind.

Studio 84

3534 Broadway at 145th St (212-234-8484). Subway: 1, 9 to 145th Street. Wed–Sun 9pm–4am.
Who needs techno when you've got merengue? That's the frenzied, 150-beats-per-minute dance music you hear blasting out of the speakers at this genuine Dominican dance hall. Though its light-speed tempo and insane arrangements can be daunting to first-timers, there's no denying its sex appeal. Salsa, Latin house, hip-hop and reggae are also played here, and Thursdays are gay.

Tatou

151 E 50th St between Third and Lexington Aves (212-753-1144). Subway: E, F to Lexington Ave; 6 to 51st St. Mon–Sat 5pm–4am.
A midtown supper club–cum–disco, Tatou is chiefly the domain of tourists, businessmen, Eurotrash and old-money types. The joint is pleasant enough in its own way: The upstairs lounge is comfy, and the DJs—who spin mostly well-known dance hits—are good at what they do. Downstairs, the dining room is turned over to dancing once the last table is cleared. If the neoswing thing is your bag, New York's top swing promoter runs Thursday nights. Dressing up, or casual but neat, is advised.

Thirteen

35 E 13th St at University Pl (212-979-6677). Subway: L, N, R, 4, 5, 6 to 14th St–Union Sq. Mon–Sun 10pm–4am.
This postage stamp–size joint is relatively new, but because the space has been a club for years (in the 1980s, it was Peggy Sue's, a preppy hangout populated by New York University students), Thirteen enjoys the status of having the city's smallest legal dance floor. A variety of nights offer everything from the usual hip-hop/R&B/classics formula to rock and house

music. Parties come and go, but one that has lasted is Sunday night's Shout!, which offers up Northern soul, freakbeat, 1960s psychedelic rock, garage punk and various other genres commonly (albeit often wrongly) associated with mods.

Tunnel

220 Twelfth Ave at 27th St (212-695-4682). Subway: C, E to 23rd St. Fri 10pm–6am, Sat 11pm–noon, Sun 10pm–4am.

A stunningly massive place with equally impressive decor—there's a unisex bathroom complete with a bar and banquettes, a coffeehouse and the mind-blowing, psychedelic Cosmic Cavern, designed by pop artist Kenny Scharf (floor-to-ceiling fake fur, Lava lamps, Internet terminals, black-light paintings and a fountain). The 1996 police raid dealt a blow to Tunnel's spirit (not to mention its trendy cachet) from which the club hasn't fully recovered. The place looks shabby these days; the main dance floor isn't very conducive to disco epiphanies, and the crowd is mostly quite mainstream. It's such an incredible space that it deserves at least one visit. Head for one of the many smaller rooms, which feature more interesting music, decor and people.

Twilo

530 W 27th St between Tenth and Eleventh Aves (212-268-1600). Subway: C, E to 23rd St. Hours vary with event.

With little else besides an immense sound system and dance floor, Twilo was designed to be a temple of music. Unfortunately, it wants to be both underground *and* trendy, a difficult feat. The result, sadly, is uneven music and crowds. Friday, the straight (i.e., mixed) night, draws lots of suburban ex-ravers who have graduated to disco shirts and club-babe outfits. The music can be excellent, but the hype-driven booking policy yields uneven results; the upstairs lounge, on the other hand, has hosted everything from drum 'n' bass to loungecore. On Saturdays, Twilo attempts to restore the magic of the old Sound Factory, with Junior Vasquez. But while the original Factory sound was hard, brutal and funky, Junior's music now is largely fluffy HiNRG, and his following has mutated from working-class, streetwise black and Latino gay kids to straight suburbanites and bourgeois white muscle clones more concerned with pecs and sex than dancing. Still, it's worth checking out who's playing on Fridays, and if you go on Saturday (suggested arrival time: 5am), you *will* feel as if you had a big night out.

205 Club

205 Chrystie St at Stanton St (212-473-5816). Subway: F to Second Ave. Hours vary with event.

The 205 Club, like Sapphire, is basically a nondescript bar that got hassled so much by the authorities for dancing patrons that it took the extraordinary step of obtaining a cabaret license. It's still a bit of a Bowery dive, but now you'll find everything from African music and reggae to hip-hop, drum 'n' bass and funk.

Vanity

28 E 23rd St between Madison Ave and Park Ave South (212-254-6117). Subway: N, R, 6 to 23rd St.

Vanity isn't much to look at, and the name is pretty tired, but as one of Manhattan's fairly few smallish dance clubs it fills a definite need. It actually has a pretty nice little dance floor and sound system, too. The most popular nights are Tuesdays, when Super Funk attracts a fun music-industry crowd (it's a good bet that you'll rub elbows at the bar with the likes of Todd Terry or Masters at Work) despite the name, you'll mostly hear deep but pumping house spun by guest DJs ranging from local up-and-comers to internationally known names like Benji Candelario. Friday night, the also-misnamed GBH (which stands for Great British House) features mostly American vocal house, spun by DJs who work at King Street and Northcott, two top New York labels (DJ Disciple is a monthly guest, and folks like Roger Sanchez

spin on occasion, too). Saturday, Sticky's program of electronica draws the sort of indie/alternative/student-oriented crowd that listens to the Chemical Brothers, DJ Icey, Fatboy Slim and the like.

Vinyl

6 Hubert St at Hudson St (212-343-1379). Subway: A, C, E to Canal St; 1, 9 to Franklin St. Hours vary with event.

This space has housed many clubs of note, including the legendary art-disco Area in the mid-'80s and the not-quite-as-legendary early-'90s underground dance club Shelter. Vinyl still features Timmy Regisford (the main man at Shelter and a sometime DJ at Area) on Saturdays, who spins Paradise Garage retreads and current R&B-flavored house (what the English call "garage") for a devoted crowd. Fridays alternate between Goa trance parties and biweekly stints by the brilliant Danny Tenaglia. Tenaglia is an extremely highly regarded spinner who grew up in the Garage and over the course of a ten-hour set spins everything from deep vocal house and Garage disco classics to hard but funky techno. Sunday afternoon's Body & Soul tea dance is probably the trendiest club in the world at the moment. Revered DJ/producer/remixer François K. (who actually filled in for Larry Levan at the Garage), along with Joe Claussell and veteran New York jock Danny Krivit, spin soulful house and Garage classics. It's similar to Shelter musically and conceptually, though the DJs' selections are more interesting. Ironically, Vinyl unintentionally became a bit like the alcohol-free Garage when the club's liquor license was revoked in 1997.

The Warehouse

141 E 140th St between Grand Concourse and Walton Ave, Bronx (718-992-5974). Subway: 4 to 138th St. Sat 10pm–6am.

Most New York itineraries fail to include a visit to a gay black hip-hop and house club in the South Bronx. But adventurous and streetwise visitors will find the Warehouse a uniquely New York experience. Plummeting crime rates notwithstanding, the South Bronx is still probably one of the city's—hell, the nation's—worst areas. Once inside the club, though, you'll find a peaceful, friendly, attitude-free crowd. It's overwhelmingly black and queer, but all are welcome. The ground floor vibrates to the sounds of top-shelf hip-hop and R&B—neither too commercial nor too obscure. Meanwhile, on the surprisingly large main floor, New York–style urban house, ranging from tribal and funky sample tracks to vocal anthems, rules.

Webster Hall

125 E 11th St between Third and Fourth Aves (212-353-1600). Subway: L, N, R, 4, 5, 6 to 14th St–Union Sq. Thu–Sat 10pm–4am.

Webster Hall is an out-and-out commercial nightclub worth visiting in a fun-night-out-with-your-friends sort of way. There are four or five different mainstream musical zones, and though the crowd is essentially a suburban influx, there are a few New York freaks, special attractions (like the trapeze artists) and rampant hetero hormones to amuse newcomers. As is often the case with mainstream spots, its not-on-the-map status among downtown hipsters makes it novel, and thus ripe for a comeback: DJ Young Richard, who made his name with his Makeup Room party when the club opened, has just started a new party here.

Wetlands

161 Hudson St at Laight St (212-966-4225). Subway: A, C, E, 1, 9 to Canal St.

Mainly a live rock venue, Wetlands was founded on admirably progressive ideals. It holds frequent fundraisers and implements environmentally correct policies (no plastic cups, a nonsmoking lounge, etc.). So yes, it's still kinda hippyish, but the place does host rap, reggae, jungle and trance nights, so it's worth checking out.

Dance

From uptown pirouettes to downtown postmodern moves, New York boasts the richest assortment of dance in the world

Dance in New York has never been bestowed with the same kind of generous government subsidies European companies receive. And it's true that the ranks of choreographers have diminished since the '80s. But no other city in the world boasts such a high caliber of established companies and emerging choreographers. Of the two major seasons—October to December and March to June—the spring stretch is decidedly richer. Not only does Paul Taylor regularly present his marvelous troupe each March, but local ballet companies—American Ballet Theatre and the New York City Ballet—are both onstage in full force. There are usually a few dance films and lectures presented each week, and if watching those beautiful bodies onstage makes you depressed, don't fret—enroll in a class! New York is jam-packed with wonderful dance schools and teachers. Choose from an aggressive rhythm tap class, a retro swing session or a modern dance class—from improvisation to the Martha Graham technique—or drop by a ballet studio for some serious barre work. Call ahead for schedules, but walk-ins are more than welcome at most schools (*see page 220*).

The Theater Development Fund's NYC/On Stage service (*see page 220*) offers information on all theater, dance and music events in town. For information on weekly performances, see *Time Out New York*, which covers everything from ballet to tap and modern dance, previews selected shows and lists dance classes. *The Village Voice* covers the downtown scene, and the Sunday *New York Times* includes a box of dance listings for the week. *Dance Magazine* ($3.95, monthly) is a good way to find out about a performance well ahead of time.

Venues

Brooklyn Academy of Music

Opera House: 30 Lafayette Ave between Flatbush Ave and Fulton St (718-636-4100) www.bam.org. $15–$60. Majestic Theater: 651 Fulton St between Ashland St and Rockwell Pl (718-636-4181). $10–40. Subway: D, Q, 2, 3, 4, 5, to Atlantic Ave; B, M, N, R to Pacific St. AmEx, MC, V.
Traveling to Brooklyn really isn't so difficult or scary, and BAM, as it's affectionately known, showcases many superb modern and out-of-town companies. BAM's Opera House, with its Federal-style columns and carved marble, is one of the most beautiful stages for dance in the city.

(Mark Morris, always loyal to his roots, still performs there when he's in town.) The Majestic Theater, just around the corner, originally opened in 1904 and has played host to modern choreographers Ralph Lemon and Susan Marshall, as well as a wealth of theater companies. The Next Wave Festival each autumn showcases both experimental and established dance and music groups, and during the spring, short festivals focus on ballet, tap, hip-hop and modern dance.

City Center Theater

131 W 55th St between Sixth and Seventh Aves (212-581-7907). Subway: B, D, E to Seventh Ave. $25–$50. AmEx, MC, V.
Before the creation of Lincoln Center changed the cultural geography of New York, this was the home of the New York City Ballet (originally known as the Ballet Society), the Joffrey Ballet and American Ballet Theatre. The lavish decor is all golden. So are the established companies that pass through—they tend to be on the mature side, including the Paul Taylor Dance Company and the Alvin Ailey American Dance Theater.

Joyce Theater

175 Eighth Ave at 19th St (212-242-0800) www.joyce.org. Subway: 1, 9 to 18th St; A, C, E to 23rd St. $17–$35. AmEx, DC, Disc, MC, V.
The Joyce, once a vacant movie house, is one of the finest theaters in town. It's intimate, but not too small; of the 472 seats, there's not a bad one in the house. Choreographers ranging from Doug Elkins and David Dorfman to the Bill T. Jones and the Martha Graham dance companies have performed recently. In residence is Eliot Feld's company, Ballet Tech. Feld, who began his performing career in George Balanchine's *The Nutcracker* and Jerome Robbins's *West Side Story*, presents his company in two monthlong seasons (one in March, the other in July). The Joyce also hosts a variety of out-of-town ensembles, along with a few staples, including the Pilobolus Dance Theatre in June and the Altogether Different Festival in January. During the summer, when many theaters are dark, the Joyce schedule often includes close to a dozen companies. The Joyce Soho offers rehearsal space for choreographers and also showcases work on residence.
Other location: *Joyce Soho, 155 Mercer St between Houston and Prince Sts (212-431-9233). Subway: B, D, F, Q to Broadway–Lafayette St; N, R to Prince St. $10–$15. No credit cards.*

Metropolitan Opera House

65th St at Columbus Ave (212-362-6000) www.metopera.org. Subway: 1, 9 to 66th St–Lincoln Ctr. $24–$145. AmEx, MC, V.
The Met hosts a range of top international companies, from the Paris Opéra Ballet to the Kirov Ballet. Each spring (May 8–July 1), the majestic theater hosts American Ballet Theatre, which presents full-length story classics. The acoustics are wonderful, but the theater is vast, so sit as close as you can afford.

*Arch deluxe: Pilobolus Dance Theatre performs each summer at the **Joyce Theater**.*

New York State Theater
65th St at Columbus Ave (212-870-5570). Subway: 1, 9 to 66th St–Lincoln Ctr. $10–$82. AmEx, MC, V (telephone sales only; $1 surcharge).
Both the neoclassical New York City Ballet and the New York City Opera headline at this opulent theater, which Philip Johnson designed to resemble a jewel box. NYCB hosts two seasons: Winter begins just before Thanksgiving, features more than a month of *Nutcracker* performances and runs until the beginning of March; the spring season usually begins in April or May and lasts eight weeks. Even from the inexpensive fourth-ring seats, the view is unobstructed, but the best seats in the house are in the first ring, where the music is best appreciated, and one can enjoy the dazzling patterns of the lovely corps de ballet. The stage, 89 by 58 feet, was made to George Balanchine's specifications.

Alternative venues

Aaron Davis Hall
City College, 135th St at Convent Ave (212-650-7148). Subway: 1, 9 to 137th St–City College. $15–$100. No credit cards.
It's a trek, but worth it. Troupes here often celebrate African-American life and culture. Among the companies that have appeared at Davis: the Bill T. Jones/Arnie Zane Dance Company and the Alvin Ailey Repertory Ensemble.

Merce Cunningham Studio
55 Bethune St between Washington and West Sts, 11th floor (212-691-9751). Subway: A, C, E to 14th St; 1, 9 to Christopher St–Sheridan Sq. $5–$30. No credit cards.
Located in the Westbeth complex on the edge of Greenwich Village (no matter which subway you take, be prepared for

More than a two-tutu town

New York's ballet companies tout the best dancers and choreographers

New York City's two major ballet companies—New York City Ballet (NYCB) and American Ballet Theatre (ABT)—dazzle in different ways. At ABT, it's all romance, with captivating productions of classic ballets such as *Romeo and Juliet, Swan Lake* and *Giselle*. Founded in 1939 by Mikhail Mordkin as Ballet Theatre, the com-

Pointe taken: **New York City Ballet***'s Darci Kistler sparkles in* Bugaku.

pany originally offered mainly classics and new works created by Mordkin in a traditional Russian style. The focus of ABT is still predominantly classical, although artistic director Kevin McKenzie occasionally slips in an evening of Twyla Tharp or individual works by Anthony Tudor. Here, it's the dancers who keep devoted fans in awe. Of the dashing men, look for performances featuring Angel Corella, Ethan Steifel, Vladimir Malakov and José Manuel Carreño. Of the women, Julie Kent, Susan Jaffe and Alessandra Ferri are astonishing. The youthful, dynamic Paloma Herrera dances here (often with Corella) and pay attention to the Russian beauty, Irina Dvorovenko.

At NYCB, it's the stunning choreography that matters. Here, the dancers themselves aren't publicized (although as the cast lists printed inside the door of the New York State Theater each week attest, they do matter). The company is famously spontaneous: You're likely to see a star or two, but perhaps more exciting is watching a corps dancer make a grand debut in a principal role. These are dancers to keep an eye on: Kyra Nichols, Maria Kowroski, Wendy Whelan, Miranda Weese, Monique Meunier, Peter Boal, Christopher Wheeldon and Benjamin Millepied. Each season features plenty of repertory works by NYCB founder George Balanchine, founding choreographer Jerome Robbins and current ballet master-in-chief Peter Martins, as well as "Diamond Project" premieres—past choreographers include Angelin Preljocaj, Kevin O'Day and David Parsons. Each December, catch performances of Balanchine's celebrated Christmas classic, *The Nutcracker*.

Other classical companies include Arthur Mitchell's famed Dance Theatre of Harlem and Eliot Feld's Ballet Tech, a young company made up of dancers plucked as children from auditions held in New York's public schools. There are also a handful of ballet performances held at the Clark Studio Theater, located in the David Rose Building, which is also home to the School of American Ballet (SAB), founded by Balanchine and Lincoln Kirstein. One of the most thrilling weekends for ballet addicts comes each June, when students from SAB present their annual workshop performances. As every dance fan knows, the next Darci Kistler might be waiting in the wings.

a good, wind-blown walk), the Cunningham Studio is rented by individual choreographers who don't feel like waiting to be asked to join Dance Theater Workshop's lineup. As can be imagined, the quality of performances ranges from wonderful to horrid. Since the stage and the seating area are in Cunningham's large studio, be prepared to take off your shoes. Arrive early, too, or you'll have to sit on the floor. For more details, contact the Cunningham Dance Foundation (212-255-8240).

Dance Theater Workshop

Bessie Schönberg Theater, 219 W 19th St between Seventh and Eighth Aves (212-691-6500/box office 212-924-0077). Subway: 1, 9 to 18th St; C, E to 23rd St. $12–$15. AmEx, MC, V.
Pointe shoes are generally looked down upon at this haven for experimental dance and theater. During popular shows, cushions are tossed on the floor for those without a seat (but reservations are taken). Drop by the intimate theater at any time for a schedule. It's one of the most user-friendly and best organized of the downtown venues, and a must-see if you're interested in exploring the full range of New York dance. You probably won't see performances by anyone now famous—but someday they might be. DTW has launched the careers of dozens of acclaimed artists, including Bill T. Jones, Mark Morris and, believe it or not, Whoopi Goldberg.

Danspace Project

St Mark's Church-in-the-Bowery, Second Ave at 10th St (212-674-8194). Subway: N, R, 4, 5, 6 to 14th St–Union Sq; L to Third Ave. $12. No credit cards.
This is a gorgeous, high-ceilinged sanctuary for downtown dance that is even more otherworldly when the music is live. Downtown choreographers are selected by the director, Laurie Uprichard, whose standards are, thankfully, high. Regular programs include Global Exchange/Danza Libre, which features international artists and collaborations between choreographers; City/Dans, which focuses on New York choreographers; and Lone Stars, which showcases local artists.

The Kitchen

512 W 19th St between Tenth and Eleventh Aves (212-255-5793). Subway: A, C, E to 14th St; L to Eighth Ave. $8–$25. AmEx, MC, V.
Best known as an avant-garde theater space, the Kitchen also features experimental choreographers from New York and elsewhere, occasionally including a multimedia element.

Martha @ Mother

432 W 14th St at Washington St (212-642-5005). Subway: A, C, E to 14th St; L to Eighth Ave. $15, $30. No credit cards.
Richard Move and Janet Stapleton present their hilarious award-winning series the first Wednesday of each month, portraying Martha Graham, the mother of modern dance. Move hosts the evening, joined by an ensemble of "Graham Crackers." Move introduces the evening's guest artists with short dance "herstory" lectures. Brilliant choreographers like Gus Solomons Jr., Keely Garfield and Jennifer Monson have presented their work in the past—and you'll probably catch a glimpse of Mikhail Baryshnikov in the audience—but no one can top Move. Innovative, fresh and highly recommended.

Movement Research at Judson Church

55 Washington Sq South at Thompson St (212-477-6854). Subway: A, C, E, B, D, F, Q to W 4th St–Washington Sq. Free.
Director Catherine Levine carries on the tradition of free Monday-night performances at the Judson Church, a custom started in the 1960s by avant-garde choreographers Yvonne Rainer, Steve Paxton and Trisha Brown. At least two chore-

Re-Joyce: The **Joyce Theater** delights fans.

ographers' works are shown each night. The series runs from September to June. MR also offers a vast selection of classes and workshops, which are held at Context Studio and Danspace Project. Lectures are also held from time to time.

New Jersey Performing Arts Center

1 Center St at the waterfront, Newark, NJ (973-642-8989). Travel: PATH train to Newark, then take the Loop shuttle bus two stops to the center. $15–$60. AmEx, D, MC, V.
The New Jersey Performing Arts Center serves as home base for the New Jersey Symphony Orchestra and has hosted Alvin Ailey American Dance Theater and Ballet Nacional de Cuba. Large, open theaters make NJPAC a choice venue for dance.

P.S. 122

150 First Ave at 9th St (212-477-5288). Subway: 6 to Astor Pl; F to Second Ave; L to First Ave. $9–$15. AmEx, MC, V.
Located in the heart of the East Village, P.S. 122 was once a public school (hence the P.S.) and is now a performance space. It's dedicated to presenting up-and-coming choreographers (as well as the occasional established talent) in new and unconventional works.

Playhouse 91

316 E 91st St between First and Second Aves (212-996-1100). Subway: 4, 5, 6 to 86th St. $15. AmEx, MC, V.
The annual monthlong 92nd Street Y Harkness Dance Project is presented uptown, at Playhouse 91. Last year's participants included the dance companies of the late Erick Hawkins, Ellen Cornfield and Maia Claire Garrison. The festival is held in early spring.

Symphony Space

2537 Broadway at 95th St (212-864-1414). Subway: 1, 2, 3, 9 to 96th St. $10–$20. AmEx, MC, V.
Located on a stretch of upper Broadway, this is a center for all the performing arts. The World Music Institute presents many international dance troupes here.

Summer performances

Central Park SummerStage

Central Park, Rumsey Playfield at 72nd St (212-360-2777). Subway: B, C to 72nd St. Free.
This outdoor dance series runs on Fridays in July and the first couple weeks in August. Temperatures can get steamy, but at least you're outside. The caliber of choreographers is improving: Last year's participants included Pascal Rioult, Ben Munisteri and the divine Molissa Fenley.

The mod squad

NY's modern dance scene thrives

It's difficult to say exactly where and when modern dance was born, but one thing's for sure: It was raised in New York, where it has flourished for nearly a century. Perhaps the most intriguing aspect of the contemporary dance scene in New York is that it's so varied; not only do the companies of late greats such as Martha Graham and José Limón perform annually at City Center or the Joyce Theater, but a variety of young choreographers can be seen nearly every night of the week. Well-known modern choreographers such as Paul Taylor, Merce Cunningham, Trisha Brown, Bill T. Jones and Mark Morris present their companies fairly regularly at the Brooklyn Academy of Music, City Center and the Joyce, while experimental downtown venues including P.S. 122, Movement Research at the Judson Church, Danspace Project at St Mark's Church and Dance Theater Workshop are excellent spaces to view the unexpected. These tickets are never more than $15—and though the choreographers are taken quite seriously, the crowds are, refreshingly, without airs.

Dances for Wave Hill
W 249th St at Independence Ave, Riverdale, Bronx (212-989-6830). Travel: 1, 9 to 231st St, then Bx7, Bx10 or Bx24 bus to 252nd St. $4. No credit cards.
This is a gorgeous setting for outdoor dance. The series, sponsored by Dancing in the Streets, runs in July.

Bargains

Theater Development Fund
1501 Broadway between 43rd and 44th Sts (212-221-0013). Subway: N, R, 1, 2, 3, 9, 7 to 42nd St–Times Sq. No credit cards.
TDF offers a book of four vouchers for $28, which can be purchased at the TDF offices by visitors who bring their passport or out-of-state driver's license. Each voucher is good for one admission at Off-Off Broadway music, theater and dance events, at venues such as the Joyce, the Kitchen, Dance Theater Workshop and P.S. 122. TDF also provides information by phone on all theater, dance and music events in town with its NYC/On Stage service (212-768-1818). See chapter **Theater.**

Dance shopping

Both the New York City Ballet and American Ballet Theatre have gift shops, open during intermission, selling everything from autographed pointe shoes to ballet-themed T-shirts, night-lights and jewelry.

Capezio Dance-Theater Shop
1650 Broadway at 51st St (212-245-2130). Subway: C, E, 1, 9 to 50th St; N, R to 49th St. Mon–Wed, Fri 9:30am–6:30pm; Thu 9:30am–7pm; Sat 9:30am–6pm; Sun 11am–5pm. AmEx, MC, V.
Capezio carries an excellent stock of professional-quality shoes and practice and performance gear, as well as dance duds that can actually be worn on the street. See the Yellow Pages for other locations.

KD Dance
339 Lafayette St at Bleecker St (212-533-1037). Subway: B, D, F, Q to Broadway–Lafayette St; 6 to Bleecker St. Mon–Sat noon–8pm. AmEx, MC, V.
This shop, owned by Tricia Kaye, former principal dancer and ballet mistress of the Oakland Ballet, and dancer David Lee, features the softest, prettiest dance knits available.

Dance schools

Most major companies have their own schools. Amateurs are welcome at the following (classes for beginners start at $10 per session):

Alvin Ailey American Dance Center
211 W 61st St between Amsterdam and West End Aves, third floor (212-767-0940). Subway: A, C, B, D, 1, 9 to 59th St–Columbus Circle.
Modern dance, tap, ballet.

American Ballet Theatre
890 Broadway at 19th St, third floor (212-477 3030). Subway: N, R to 23rd St; L to Sixth Ave.
Classical ballet.

Ballet Hispanico School of Dance
167 W 89th St between Columbus and Amsterdam Aves (212-362-6710). Subway: 1, 9 to 86th St.
All styles of Latin and Spanish dance, including Flamenco.

Merce Cunningham Studio
55 Bethune St at Washington St (212-691-9751). Subway: A, C, E, 1, 2, 3, 9 to 14th St; L to Eighth Ave.
Merce Cunningham technique.

Dance Space Inc.
622 Broadway between Bleecker and Houston Sts, sixth floor (212-777-8067). Subway: B, D, F, Q to Broadway–Lafayette St; 6 to Bleecker St.
Simonson jazz, yoga, modern dance, ballet and stretch.

DanceSport
1845 Broadway at 60th St (212-307-1111). Subway: A, C, B, D, 1, 9 to 59th St–Columbus Circle.
Ballroom and Latin.

Martha Graham School
316 E 63rd St between First and Second Aves (212-838-5886). Subway: 4, 5, 6 to 59th St; N, R to Lexington Ave.
Martha Graham technique.

Limón Institute
611 Broadway between Houston and Bleecker Sts, ninth floor (212-777-3353). Subway: B, D, F, Q to Broadway–Lafayette St; 6 to Bleecker St.
José Limón and Doris Humphrey technique.

Paul Taylor School
552 Broadway between Prince and Spring Sts, second floor (212-431-5562). Subway: B, D, F, Q to Broadway–Lafayette St; 6 to Bleecker St; N, R to Prince St.
Daily modern technique class.

Film & TV

If life is a movie, then New York City is the greatest set ever built

Visitors often feel as if they're in the middle of a movie or television show as soon as they set foot on the mean streets of New York. It's not just the heightened intensity and frenetic pace of Manhattan life, it's the fact that many of the city's street corners have been the site of quite a bit of cinematic drama, whether it's Lorraine Bracco taunting Ray Liotta in *GoodFellas* or Spike Lee tossing a trash can through a window in *Do the Right Thing*.

And the prospect of running into a film crew shooting here—whether for a Hollywood action flick, an angst-filled indie or a prime-time sitcom—is increasingly likely. The rise in film projects has been so meteoric in the past five years that New York could be renamed Cin City: Some 221 movies were made in 1998, more than in any previous year. With better relations between production companies and local labor unions, and a mayor determined to boost film and TV production, the film business is booming. Choice Hollywood projects—including mega-budget urban thrillers like Arnold Schwarzeneg-

ger's apocalyptic *End of Days* and vital, they-started-here biopics like *Man on the Moon*, the Milos Forman–Jim Carrey film about the late comedian Andy Kaufman—are back in force, while the indie community can often be found shooting on the Lower East Side and the East Village, making use of the areas' vibrant street culture. For information about being an audience member for NYC-based shows, *see* **Live, from New York...**, *page 224*.

For viewing the finished product, there are hundreds of screens throughout the metropolis, from the deluxe 12-plex movie mecca, Sony Lincoln Square, to one of the nation's premier homes for experimental film, the Anthology Film Archives. New Yorkers are famously knowledgeable about film; on opening nights of the current blockbuster (or Woody Allen picture), lines often wind around the corner and SOLD OUT signs are posted on ticket-sellers' windows. To guarantee seats for the latest *Titanic* on its first weekend, call the automated 777-FILM ticket system

*Masterpiece theater: The **Angelika** in Noho is New York City's premier art-film venue.*

Screen test

Settle into the best seats in these exceptional houses

We rate these New York cinemas tops for...

Blockbusters: The Ziegfeld; Sony Lincoln Square; Cineplex Odeon Chelsea

Foreign films: Paris; Angelika Film Center; BAM Rose Cinemas

Popcorn: Cineplex Odeon Waverly Twin

Romantic movies: The Ziegfeld

Cheap movies: Cineplex Odeon Encore Worldwide

Dinner dates: Screening Room

Midnight movies: Angelika Film Center

Classics: Film Forum

Campy revivals: A Different Light

well in advance. For information on TV stations, *see chapter* **Directory**.

New York is often used as a test market, so you can catch first-run films here long before they open in the rest of the country. Incidentally, the city also happens to be a great place to prepare for your own fabulous filmmaking career. Besides New York University's world-renowned graduate film program, several worthwhile shorter-term production courses and workshops, such as those offered by New York Film Academy and the Reel School, are worth investigating. Because the classes generally run from a week or two to several months, they are an excellent way to experience the filmmaking process without a long-term commitment.

Those who want to bring home some cinematic goodies should visit the mammoth Warner Bros. Studio Store (*see chapter* **Shopping & Services**) for everything from Bugs Bunny memorabilia to *Casablanca* swag. If you'd prefer to feel close to Mr. New York, Robert De Niro, you must make a trip to his elegant **Tribeca Grill** (375 Greenwich Avenue at Franklin Street; 212-941-3900). De Niro's production offices are upstairs, and his late father's brilliantly hued paintings decorate the bistro's walls.

For up-to-date listings, including the whereabouts of the nearest first-run cinema, check out the weekly *Time Out New York* or consult the film sections of *The Village Voice, New York* or *The New York Times*. For video-rental stores, *see chapter* **Shopping & Services**. And if you stumble across a film set, remember that when they yell "Action!" it's time to hush up and watch.

Popular cinemas

There are scores of first-run movie theaters throughout the city. New releases come and go relatively quickly; if a film does badly it might only show for a couple of weeks. Tickets usually cost $8–$9.75, with discounts for children and senior citizens (usually restricted to weekday afternoons). Friday is the opening night for most films, and the lines then can be staggeringly long. Be aware: There are "ticket buyers' lines" and "ticket holders' lines." The first showings on Saturday or Sunday (around noon) are less crowded, even for brand-new releases. Finally, since a handful of theaters in Manhattan are reserved-seating only, be sure to call ahead before you go.

Cineplex Odeon Encore Worldwide
340 W 50th St at Eighth Ave (212-50-LOEWS ext 610). Subway: C, E, 1, 9 to 50th St. $3.50; $6.50 concessions. AmEx, MC, V.
Although you won't see the latest openings, you can check out recent Hollywood releases—for only three-and-a-half bucks a shot—at this six-screen theater.

Sony Lincoln Square & Imax Theatre
1992 Broadway at 68th St (212-50-LOEWS ext 638). Subway: 1, 9 to 66th St–Lincoln Ctr. $9.50; $6 concessions. Imax tickets $9.50; $7.50 concessions. AmEx, MC, V.
Across Broadway from the high culture of Lincoln Center, Sony has constructed a cinematic entertainment center that's more a theme park than a dull old multiplex. There are fiberglass decorations that conjure up classic movie sets, enough popcorn vendors to bloat entire armies, a gift shop selling movie memorabilia and 12 fairly large screens (the one in the Loews Auditorium is the city's biggest for first-run features). The added attraction is the center's eight-story Imax screen, which, apart from being truly enormous, can also accommodate 3-D films (viewed through special headsets). Films screened here are the usual show-off-the-technology stuff (cities of the future and ultravivid underwater adventures) that last 35 to 45 minutes each. Services for the hearing-impaired are available.

United Artists Union Square 14
Broadway at 13th St (212-253-2225). Subway: L, N, R, 4, 5, 6 to 14th St–Union Sq. $9; $6.50 concessions. AmEx, MC, V.
This brand-new venue is distinctly lacking in character, but it does feature such amenities as comfortable stadium seating and digital sound in all 14 theaters.

The Ziegfeld
141 W 54th St between Sixth and Seventh Aves (212-777-FILM ext 602). Subway: B, D, E to Seventh Ave. $9.50; $6.50 concessions. AmEx, MC, V.
Rich in history and still the grandest picture palace in town (it is, after all, inspired by the Ziegfeld Follies), the Ziegfeld is often the venue for glitzy New York premieres. It is also a reserved-seating theater, so remember to order your tickets in advance.

Revival and art houses

In the past few years, New York City has seen a dramatic increase in the number of venues screening art films and old movies; the following are the most popular and reliable.

Angelika Film Center

18 W Houston St at Mercer St (212-777-FILM ext 531). Subway: 6 to Bleecker St; B, D, F, Q to Broadway–Lafayette St; N, R to Prince St. $8.50; $5 concessions. No credit cards.
Popular with local NYU students, the Angelika is a six-screen cinema with diverse programming, featuring primarily new American independent and foreign films. There's an espresso-and-pastry bar to hang out in before or after the show.

BAM Rose Cinemas

30 Lafayette Ave between Flatbush Ave and Fulton St, Fort Greene, Brooklyn (718-623-2770). Subway: B, M, N, R to Pacific St; D, Q, 2, 3, 4, 5 to Atlantic Ave; G to Fulton St. $8.50; $4 concessions. No credit cards.
First-run art flicks finally became available in Brooklyn when the beautiful, six-screen BAM Rose Cinemas was established in late 1998. The venue is affiliated with the venerable Brooklyn Academy of Music.

Cinema Classics

332 E 11th St between First and Second Aves (212-675-6692). Subway: L to First Ave. $5, includes double features; $4 concessions. No credit cards.
It may be shabby and cramped, but this tiny East Village venue is quickly making a name for itself with its roster of imaginative old-film programs. The $5 double bills can't be beat.

Cinema Village

22 E 12th St between Fifth Ave and University Pl (212-924-3363, box office 212-924-3364). Subway: L, N, R, 4, 5, 6 to 14th St–Union Square. $8; $4 concessions. No credit cards.
Cinema Village specializes in small, American independent and foreign films that don't find their way into the more mainstream Angelika and Lincoln Plaza cinemas. The theater also hosts mini-festivals (Hong Kong action films are a popular attraction) and runs midnight horror shows on weekends.

A Different Light

151 W 19th St between Sixth and Seventh Aves (212-989-4850). Subway: 1, 9 to 18th St. All films shown on video. Free.
A Different Light is a gay-themed bookstore that hosts delicious Sunday-night screenings of screamers like *A Star Is Born*, *All About Eve* or anything starring queer icons Bette Davis, Joan Crawford or Tallulah Bankhead. Get ready for some major audience participation.

Film Forum

209 W Houston St between Sixth Ave and Varick St (212-727-8110, box office 212-727-8112). Subway: 1, 9 to Houston St. $8.50; $4.50 concessions. No credit cards.
On Soho's edge, the three-screen Film Forum offers some of the best new films, documentaries and art movies around. Series or revivals, usually brilliantly curated, are also shown.

Lincoln Plaza Cinemas

30 Lincoln Plaza, entrance on Broadway between 62nd and 63rd Sts (212-757-2280, box office 212-757-0359). Subway: A, C, B, D, 1, 9 to 59th St–Columbus Circle. $9; $5 concessions. AmEx, MC, V for advance tickets; cash only at box office. All theaters are wheelchair accessible and equipped with assisted listening devices for the hearing impaired.

Commercially successful and worthy European art-house movies can be seen here alongside biggish American independent productions.

Quad Cinema

34 W 13th St between Fifth and Sixth Aves (212-255-8800, box office 212-255-2243). Subway: F to 14th St; L to Sixth Ave. $8; $4 concessions. No credit cards.
Four small screens show a broad selection of foreign films, American independents and documentaries—a preponderance dealing with sexual and political issues. Often, these are movies you can't see anywhere else. Children under five are not admitted.

Paris Theatre

4 W 58th St between Fifth and Sixth Aves (212-688-3800). Subway: N, R to Fifth Ave. $8.75; $5 concessions. No credit cards.
Situated beside Bergdorf Goodman and across from the Plaza Hotel, the Paris has a stylish program of European art-house movies, in addition to such eminently revivable films as Fellini's *8 1/2*.

Museums and societies

Special film series and experimental films often appear in museums and galleries other than those listed here. Check *Time Out New York* or *The Village Voice* for details. *See also chapter* **Museums**.

American Museum of the Moving Image

See chapter **Museums** *for listings.*
The first museum in the U.S. devoted to moving pictures is in Queens. More than 700 films and videos are shown each year, covering everything from Hollywood classics and series devoted to a single actor or director to industrial-safety films. The schedule is inspired and entertaining.

Anthology Film Archives

32 Second Ave at 2nd St (212-505-5110). Subway: F to Second Ave. $7.50; $3 concessions. No credit cards.
Anthology is one of New York's treasures, housing the world's largest collection of written material documenting the history of independent film and video. The Archives are sponsored by some of the biggest names in film and host a full program of screenings, festivals, talks and lectures.

Brooklyn Museum of Art

See chapter **Museums** *for listings.*
The Brooklyn Museum of Art's intelligent, eclectic roster concentrates primarily on the works of foreign filmmakers.

Film Society of Lincoln Center

Lincoln Center, 65th St between Broadway and Amsterdam Ave (212-875-5600). Subway: 1, 9 to 66th St–Lincoln Ctr. $8.50; $5 concessions. No credit cards.
The Society was founded in 1969 to promote film and support filmmakers. It operates the Walter Reade Theater (built in 1991), a state-of-the-art showcase for contemporary film and video—with the most comfortable theater seats in New York. The program is usually organized around a theme, often with a decidedly international perspective. Each autumn, the society hosts the New York Film Festival (*see page 225*).

The Solomon R. Guggenheim Museum

See chapter **Museums** *for listings.*
The Guggenheim is building a reputation for programming series that are both insightful and provocative, a notable example being 1998's well-received tribute to the motorcycle in cinema. It's worth a look.

Live, from New York…

Plan ahead and you can be the human laugh-track for several TV shows

Tickets are available for all sorts of TV shows recorded in New York studios. Should you need more information, contact the New York Convention & Visitors Bureau (*see chapter* **Directory**).

The Daily Show
356 W 58th St between Eighth and Ninth Aves (212-586-2477). Subway: A, C, B, D, 1, 9 to 59th St–Columbus Circle. Mon–Thu 5:30pm.

*I wanna be a star: An eager teen tries to be on **MTV**'s House of Style.*

If you're a fan of this Comedy Central series, reserve tickets three months ahead of time, or call on the Friday before you'd like to attend to see if there are any canceled tickets. You must be at least 18 with photo ID.

Late Night with Conan O'Brien
Mailing address: NBC, 30 Rockefeller Plaza, New York, NY 10112 (212-664-4000). Tue–Fri 5:30pm.
Send a postcard for tickets. A limited amount of same-day tickets are distributed at 9am. You must be at least 16.

Late Show with David Letterman
Mailing address: Ed Sullivan Theater, 1697 Broadway, New York, NY 10019. (212-975-1003). Mon–Thu 5:30pm, Fri 8pm.
Send a postcard with your name, address and telephone number six to eight months in advance; standby tickets are available at 9am. You can also apply for tickets on the CBS Web page (www.cbs.com). You must be at least 16 with photo ID.

MTV
1515 Broadway at 44th St (212-258-8000). Subway: N, R, S, 1, 2, 3, 9, 7 to 42nd St–Times Sq.
Watch the music channel for info about being in the audience or participating in a show.

The Ricki Lake Show
Mailing address: 226 W 26th St, 4th Floor, New York, NY 10001.
Send requests for tickets one month in advance by postcard. Standby tickets are available one hour before taping. You must be at least 18 with photo ID.

The Rosie O'Donnell Show
Mailing address: NBC, 30 Rockefeller Plaza, New York, NY 10112 (212-664-4000). Mon–Thu 10am.
A ticket lottery for the whole season is held in April and May; only postcards received during those months are accepted for the shows. You will be notified one to two weeks in advance of taping if you have seats. A few same-day standby seats are available at 8am (but get there at around 5am if you really want to go) from the 49th Street entrance. No children under five admitted.

Saturday Night Live
Mailing address: NBC, 30 Rockefeller Plaza, New York, NY 10112 (212-664-4000). Dress rehearsals at 7:30pm, live at 10pm.
A ticket lottery for the whole season is held in August, and only postcards received in the month of August are accepted for the shows. You will be notified one to two weeks in advance of taping if you have seats. A few same-day standby tickets, for either the dress rehearsal or the live show, are distributed at 9:15am (but get there at around 5am if you really want to go). You must be at least 16.

Spin City
The Silver Screen Studios at Chelsea Piers, Pier 62, 23rd St at West Side Hwy (212-336-6993). Subway: C, E to 23rd St. Fri 7pm.
Call for latest taping dates.

Imax Theater

American Museum of Natural History. See chapter
Museums *for listings. Museum admission plus $13
or more (varies). AmEx, DC, V.*
The Imax screen is four stories high and the daily programs
concentrate on the natural world. On weekends, it is usually crowded with children and their parents.

Metropolitan Museum of Art

See chapter **Museums** *for listings.*
The Met shows a full program of documentary films on
art (many of which relate to exhibitions on display) in the
Uris Center Auditorium (near the 81st Street entrance). In
addition, there are occasional themed series, with weekend
showings.

Millennium

*66 E 4th St between Second Ave and Bowery
(212-673-0090). Subway: F to Second Ave; 6 to Astor
Pl. Nonmembers $7, members $5. No credit cards.*
This media-arts center conducts filmmaking classes and
workshops, and screens avant-garde works, sometimes
introduced by the films' directors.

Museum of Modern Art

See chapter **Museums** *for listings.*
MoMA was one of the first museums to recognize film as an
art form. Its first director, Alfred H. Barr, believed that film
was "the only great art peculiar to the 20th century." The
museum has massive archives of films, to which film scholars and researchers have access (appointments must be
requested in writing). MoMA hosts about 25 screenings a
week, often in series on the work of a particular director or
other themes.

Museum of Television & Radio

See chapter **Museums** *for listings.*
Television and radio works, rather than film, are archived
here. The museum's collection includes more than 30,000 programs, which can be viewed at private consoles. In addition,
there are two small screening rooms and a 63-seat video theater where a number of programs are shown daily. Screenings are Tue–Sun at 2:30pm, Thu at 6pm and Fri at 7pm.

Whitney Museum of American Art

See chapter **Museums** *for listings.*
In keeping with its practice of showing the best in contemporary American art, the Whitney runs a varied schedule of
film and video works. Its exhibitions often have a strong
moving-image component, including the famous Biennial
showcase of contemporary artworks; entry is free with museum admission.

Foreign-language films

Most or all of the above institutions will screen
films in languages other than English, but the following show only foreign films.

Asia Society

See chapter **Museums** *for listings.*
The Society shows films from India, China and many other
Asian countries, as well as Asian-American films.

French Institute–Alliance Française

*55 E 59th St between Park and Madison Aves
(212-355-6160). Subway: N, R to Lexington Ave;
4, 5, 6 to 59th St. Tue–Fri 11am–7pm; Sat, Sun
11am–3pm. $7 nonmembers; free for members, $5.50
concessions. Membership $65 per year. AmEx, MC, V.*
The Institute—which is also known as the Alliance
Française—shows movies from back home. They're usually subtitled (and never dubbed).

Goethe-Institut/ German Cultural Center

See chapter **Museums** *for listings.*
A paragovernmental German cultural and educational organization, the Institut shows German films in various locations around the city, as well as in its own opulent auditorium.

Japan Society

*333 E 47th St between First and Second Aves
(212-752-0824). Subway: E, F to Lexington Ave; 6 to
51st St. $10; members, seniors and students $8.
AmEx, MC, V.*
The Japan Society Film Center organizes a busy schedule of
Japanese films, including two or three big series each year.

Libraries

Donnell Library Center

See chapter **Museums** *for listings.*
A branch of the New York Public Library, the Donnell shows
and circulates films.

Library for the Performing Arts

See chapter **Museums** *for listings.*
The library has an extensive collection of books, periodicals,
clippings and posters on film, as well as a vast catalog of
film memorabilia.

Film festivals

Every September and October for more than 25
years, the Lincoln Center Film Society has been
running the prestigious **New York Film Festival**. More than two dozen American and foreign
films are given New York, U.S. or world premieres,
and the festival usually features several rarely
seen classics. Tickets for films by known directors
are often hard to come by; tickets go on sale several weeks in advance. The Film Society, in collaboration with the Museum of Modern Art, also
sponsors the **New Directors, New Films** festival each spring, where you will catch works from
on-the-cusp filmmakers from around the world.

New York City also hosts several smaller but
just as highly anticipated festivals throughout the
year. March brings the annual **New York Jewish Film Festival** (212-875-5600). Held at Walter Reade Theater, it mostly screens works from
Jewish filmmakers living abroad. The **Gen Art
Film Festival** (212-791-2778), a weeklong late-
spring showcase of quality independent films, has
burst upon the scene in recent years. It's followed
by the more established **New Festival** (also
known as the New York Lesbian and Gay Film
Festival), which is held at the beginning of each
June (212-254-7228). **Bryant Park** (on Sixth
Avenue between 40th and 42nd Streets) has a
series of free summer Monday-night showings
(8:30pm) of classics like *Strangers on a Train* or
Casablanca on a giant screen. *See chapter* **New
York by Season** for details.

In addition, many of the art houses arrange their
own smaller festivals and series, often in conjunction with other institutions.

Gay & Lesbian

The vibrant world of queer New York runs rainbows around other cities

The much-chanted phrase "We're here, we're queer, get used to us" has become outdated. It's safe to say that New York is used to its boisterous rainbow contingent. From the offices of City Hall to the floor of the New York Stock Exchange, from the media and advertising conglomerates on Madison Avenue to the big design and fashion houses on Seventh Avenue, and from the bright lights of Broadway to the quiet white rooms of museums and art galleries, it is impossible to ignore the fact that openly gay men and women are a powerful part of what makes New York one of the world's financial and cultural centers. As the site of the 1969 Stonewall riots and the birthplace of the American gay-rights movement, New York City is a queer mecca and is home to more than 500 lesbian, gay, bisexual and transgender social and political organizations.

During the annual celebration of Gay Pride, which takes place the last weekend in June (although the festivities begin the week prior), the Empire State Building is lit up in glorious lavender (*see chapter* **New York by Season**). This amazing celebration draws hundreds of thousands of visitors into the city. The Pride march, which takes place on Sunday, draws between 250,000 and 500,000 spectators, and a number of Manhattan businesses now fly the lesbian- and gay-friendly rainbow flag in celebration. Pride is a great time to visit the Big Apple: You'll feel as though everyone here is queer. Arrive during the summer months and sample lesbian and gay resort culture on Fire Island, which is only a short trip from the center of town (*see page 228*); the stellar lineup of celluloid delights at the increasingly important New York Lesbian & Gay Film Festival (212-254-7228) in June; and the cross-dressing extravaganza Wig-

*Mother may I? At Jackie 60's home base, the sublime **Mother**, practically anything goes.*

stock (around Labor Day), presided over by the irrepressible Lady Bunny (*see chapter* **New York by Season**).

An essential stop for any lesbian or gay visitor to New York is the Lesbian & Gay Community Center (*see page 228*), a nexus of information and activity that serves as a meeting place for more than 300 groups and organizations. There, you can pick up copies of New York's free weekly gay and lesbian publications. And don't miss *Time Out New York's* lively Gay & Lesbian listings for the latest happenings around town.

Though the sizable gay and lesbian population of New York is quite diverse, the lesbian and gay club and bar scenes often don't reflect this, since they are frequently gender-segregated and, like their straight counterparts, tend to attract the single 35-and-under crowd. However, the social alternatives are plentiful—among them burgeoning queer coffee-bar, bookstore and restaurant scenes and dozens of gay and lesbian films and plays that are presented in mainstream venues (*see chapters* **Theater, Film & TV** *and* **Cabaret & Comedy**).

There's no doubt about it: New York is a non-stop city with a multitude of choices for queer entertainment. Enjoy!

Books and media

Publications

New York's gay weekly magazines are *HX* (*Homo Xtra*)—which includes extensive information on bars, dance clubs, sex clubs, restaurants, cultural events and group meetings, and loads of funny personals—and *HX for Her*, with lesbian listings. The newspaper *LGNY* (*Lesbian & Gay New York*) offers political coverage and serious articles. The *New York Blade News*, a sister publication of *The Washington Blade*, also focuses on queer politics and news. All four are free at gay and lesbian venues and shops.

National publications include the stylish *Out* ($4.95) and the newsy *The Advocate* ($3.95), both of which are published monthly. *Girlfriends* ($4.95) and *Curve* ($3.95) are colorful, fun monthly magazines for lesbians. Also look for the rather tacky (and irregularly published) *Bad Attitude* ($7) and the far better sex quarterly *On Our Backs* ($5.95).

Fodor's Gay Guide to New York City ($12) is an excellent source of opinionated information about queer NYC and the surrounding areas. Daniel Hurewitz's *Stepping Out,* which details nine walking tours of gay and lesbian NYC, is another invaluable source. Both books—as well as the above-mentioned magazines—are available at A Different Light and the Oscar Wilde Memorial Bookshop (*see below*).

Television

There's an abundance of gay-related broadcasting, though nearly all of it is poorly produced and appears on public-access cable channels. Programming varies by cable company, so you may not be able to watch all these shows on a hotel TV. Some of the funniest programs are to be found on Channel 35 (in most of Manhattan), which is where the infamous Robin Byrd hosts her *Men for Men* soft-core strip show. Manhattan Neighborhood Network (channels 16, 34, 56 and 57 on all Manhattan cable systems) has plenty of gay shows, ranging from drag queens milking their 15 minutes of fame to serious discussion programs. *HX* provides the most current TV listings.

Bookshops

Most New York bookshops have gay sections (*see chapter* **Shopping & Services**), but the following are exclusively lesbian and gay.

A Different Light Bookstore & Café
151 W 19th St between Sixth and Seventh Aves (212-989-4850). Subway: 1, 9 to 18th St. 10am–midnight. AmEx, Disc, MC, V.
This is the biggest and best gay and lesbian bookshop in New York. It's great for browsing and has plenty of free readings, film screenings and art openings. There are also useful bulletin boards with local information, a cute café and a gift shop filled with homo knickknacks.

Oscar Wilde Memorial Bookshop
15 Christopher St between Sixth and Seventh Aves (212-255-8097). Subway: 1, 9 to Christopher St–Sheridan Sq. Mon–Sat 11am–8pm; Sun noon–7pm. AmEx, Disc, MC, V.
New York's oldest gay and lesbian bookshop is chock-full of books and magazines, and offers many discounts.

Centers and phone lines

Audre Lorde Project Center
85 S Oxford St at Lafayette Ave, Brooklyn (718-596-0342). Subway: C to Lafayette Ave. Mon 10am–6pm; Tue–Thu 10am–9pm; Fri 10am–9pm; Sat 1:30–9pm.
Actually known by the unwieldy moniker the Audre Lorde Project Center for Lesbian, Gay, Bisexual, Two-Spirit & Transgender People of Color Community, this community center provides a plethora of resources for queer people of color. Call for information about events and group meetings.

Barnard Center for Research on Women
101 Barnard Hall, 3009 Broadway at 117th St (212-854-2067). Subway: 1, 9 to 116th St. Tue–Fri 9:30am–5pm, Mon 9:30am–9pm.
An academic center with a distinctly off-putting name, this is where to explore scholarly feminism—a calendar of classes, lectures and film screenings is available. The library has an extensive archive of feminist journals and government reports.

Gay Men's Health Crisis
129 W 24th St between Sixth and Seventh Aves (212-367-1000, AIDS advice hot line 212-807-6655). Subway: 1, 9 to 23rd St. Advice hot line Mon–Fri 9am–9pm, Sat noon–3pm. Recorded information in English and Spanish at other times. Office Mon–Fri 10am–6pm.

This was the first organization in the world to take up the challenge of helping people with AIDS. It has a threefold mission: to push the government to increase services, to help those who are sick by providing services and counseling to them and their families, and to educate the public and prevent the further spread of HIV. There are 250 staff members and 1,400 volunteers. Support groups usually meet in the evenings.

Gay & Lesbian Switchboard of New York Project
212-989-0999. 10am–midnight.
A phone information service only. Callers who need legal help can be referred to lawyers, and there's information on bars, restaurants and hotels. The switchboard is especially good at giving peer counseling to people who have just come out or who may be considering suicide. There are also details on all sorts of other gay and lesbian organizations. Outside New York (but within the U.S.), callers can contact the switchboard's sister toll-free line, the Gay & Lesbian National Hotline at 888-THE-GLNH.

Lesbian & Gay Community Services Center
Permanent address: 208 W 13th St between Seventh and Eighth Aves (212-620-7310) www.gaycenter.org. Subway: F, 1, 2, 3, 9 to 14th St; L to Eighth Ave. Temporary location: 1 Little W 12th St at Hudson St. Subway: A, C, E, 1, 2, 3, 9 to 14th St; L to Eighth Ave. 9am–11pm.
Founded in 1983, the Center provides political, cultural, spiritual and emotional sustenance to the lesbian and gay community. While it principally offers programs and support for locals, there's plenty to interest the visitor, including a free information packet for tourists and those new to the city. You'll be amazed at the diversity of groups (around 300) that meet here. The Center also houses the National Museum and Archive of Lesbian and Gay History and the Vito Russo lending library. *Note:* Until its permanent space is reopened as planned in fall 2000, the Center is located at a temporary "swing space."

Lesbian Herstory Archive
P.O. Box 1258, New York, NY 10116 (718-768-3953; fax 718-768-4663). By appointment only.
Newly housed in the Park Slope area of Brooklyn (which is becoming known as "Dyke Slope" for its large and growing lesbian population), the Herstory Archives, started by Joan Nestle and Deb Edel in 1974, includes more than 10,000 books (theory, fiction, poetry, plays), 1,400 periodicals and many items of personal memorabilia. You too can donate a treasured possession and become part of Herstory.

Michael Callen–Audre Lorde Community Health Center
356 W 18th St between Eighth and Ninth Aves (212-271-7200) www.chp-health.org. Subway: A, C, E to 14th St; L to Eighth Ave. Mon–Thu 9am–8pm; Fri, Sat 9am–4pm.
Formerly known as Community Health Project, this is the country's largest (and New York's only) health center primarily serving the gay, lesbian, bisexual and transgender community. The center offers an exhaustive list of services, including comprehensive primary care, HIV treatment, free adolescent services, STD screening and treatment, mental health services, and peer counseling and education.

NYC Gay & Lesbian Anti-Violence Project
240 W 35th St between Seventh and Eighth Aves, suite 200 (212-714-1141). Subway: A, C, E, 1, 2, 3, 9 to 14th St; L to Eighth Ave. Mon–Thu 10am–8pm, Fri 10am–6pm; switchboard open 24 hours.
The project provides support for the victims of antigay and antilesbian attacks. Working with the police department's bias unit, the project provides advice on seeking police help. Short- and long-term counseling are available.

Fire Island

Over the years, Fire Island—a long, thin strip of land off the southern coast of Long Island—has become the favorite summer habitat for New York's gay men and a growing number of lesbians. Two particular island locales have become synonymous with sun- and sea-worshiping fags and dykes, flamboyant parties and general seasonal extravagance: the Pines (snotty, affluent and mostly gay) and Cherry Grove (tacky, suburban and mostly lesbian). The majority of the accommodations in both the Pines and the Grove are in private houses, which are rented out as shares for the summer season. Make friends with the right person and you could land yourself an invite. Otherwise you might have to settle for a day trip (as many New Yorkers do)—the very few hostel or hotel accommodations there are expensive and far from luxurious. For details, see *HX* or *HX for Her*.

GETTING THERE
By car or LIRR train from Penn Station to Sayville, then by passenger ferry. The station is about two miles from the ferry terminal, and cabs are always around. There are between 12 and 15 ferry departures a day, depending on the day and season. The ferry costs $11 round-trip (*see chapter* **Trips Out of Town**).

Long Island Railroad (LIRR)
718-217-5477 for schedules.

Sayville Ferry Company
516-589-0810 for schedules.

Boys' life

While the West Village has quaint historical gay sites such as the Stonewall (*see page 231*), friendly show-tune piano cabarets and unpretentious stores full of rainbow knickknacks and slogan T-shirts, the center of gay life has shifted slightly uptown to Chelsea, which flaunts a new attitude that can be daunting.

The neighborhood's main drag is Eighth Avenue between 16th and 23rd Streets, a strip lined with businesses catering to upwardly mobile gay men: gyms, sexy clothing and trendy home furnishing stores, tanning and grooming salons, galleries, cafés, bars, and midrange restaurants for brunch, business lunches and late dinners. Perfectly toned, youngish (25–40), mostly Caucasian men who might describe themselves as "straight-acting and appearing" are standard in Chelsea. If you're not one of them, be prepared to be snubbed or possibly ignored.

*Caped crusader: This **Gay Pride** reveler floats along a crowded Fifth Avenue.*

For open-air and open-market cruising, try the legendary trucker piers located at the end of Christopher Street along the Hudson River, or the Ramble in Central Park, located between the 79th Street Transverse and the Lake (but beware of police entrapment). And although the city has made every effort to clean up Times Square and turn it into an extension of Disney World, you can for the moment still find gay burlesque at the Gaiety, located right off Broadway on 46th Street (212-221-8868). This west-midtown area—once known as Hell's Kitchen but now known by the more appealing moniker Clinton—shows signs of being the next hot homo habitat. Just take a stroll up Ninth Avenue between 42nd and 57th Streets, and you'll see what we mean.

But if you're just an average T-shirt-and-jeans–type gay man, don't worry. Not only will you feel comfortable in almost any gay space, you'll be surprised at how much cruising happens on the streets while you're walking around town, and how easy it is to turn a glance into a conversation.

Most of Manhattan's dance clubs are a hop, skip and jump from Chelsea and feature a big gay house/techno night during the weekend, when you can spin and twirl with upwards of 500 half-naked men until the wee hours of the following day.

Somewhat in reaction to Chelsea, a counterculture scene of punk-rock-glitter-fashion boys and theatrical drag queens thrives in the East Village, centered on a handful of small, divey bars. The scene has an arty, bohemian vibe, and there are many equally lovely men to be found there, ranging from 1970s macho butches to Bowie-type androgynes. The scene tends to be even younger than the Chelsea version (although some men may appear to be younger than they are), and the crowd is more mixed, both racially and sexually. The bars also tend to feature terribly amusing live performances, which draw crowds in at midnight and spit them out by 4am.

Some habitués of Chelsea and the East Village do mix. Men of all ages, shapes and sizes frequent the city's leather/fetish bars and clubs, such as the Spike in Chelsea and the Lure in the West Village, an area known as the Meat Market—and not because of the gay life! (*see pages 230–231 for both*). If you're a devotee of the leather scene, you might want to plan your trip around either the New York Mr. Leather Contest, which takes place in the autumn, or the Black Party at Saint at Large—a special all-night leather- and S/M-themed circuit party that attracts thousands of people every March (*see page 231*).

Accommodations

Chelsea Mews Guest House
344 W 15th St between Eighth and Ninth Aves (212-255-9174). Subway: A, C, E to 14th St; L to Eighth Ave. Single $85, double $95–$165. No credit cards.
Built in 1840, this guest house has accommodations exclusively for gay men. The rooms are comfortable and well furnished and have semiprivate bathrooms. Smoking is not allowed.

Chelsea Pines Inn
317 W 14th St between Eighth and Ninth Aves (212-929-1023; fax 212-620-5646). Subway: A, C, E to 14th St; L to Eighth Ave. Doubles and triples $99–$129 (slightly higher during Gay Pride and holidays). AmEx, DC, Disc, MC, V.
This central location near the West Village and Chelsea welcomes gay male guests and lesbians as well. Vintage movie posters set the mood, and the 23 rooms are clean and comfortable; some have private bathrooms and all have radios, televisions and air-conditioning (essential in the summer months).

Colonial House Inn
318 W 22nd St between Eighth and Ninth Aves (212-243-9669, 800-689-3779). Subway: C, E to 23rd St. $80–$125 with shared bath; $125–$140 with private bath. Prices higher on the weekends. MC, V.
This beautifully renovated 1880s townhouse sits on a quiet street in the heart of Chelsea. It's run by, and primarily for, gay men. Colonial House is a great place to stay, even if some of the cheaper rooms are small. Major bonuses: free continental breakfast in the "Art Gallery Lounge" and a rooftop deck (nude sunbathing allowed!).

Incentra Village House
32 Eighth Ave between 12th and Jane Sts (212-206-0007). Subway: A, C, E to 14th St; L to Eighth Ave. $99–$239 ($20 more during Gay Pride and some holidays). AmEx, MC, V.
Two cute 1841 townhouses perfectly situated in the West Village make up this guest house run by gay men; lesbians and gay men are welcome. The rooms (singles, doubles and suites) are spacious, with private bathrooms and kitch-

enettes; some have working fireplaces. There's also a 1939 Steinway baby grand piano for show tune–spouting queens. While interestingly decorated, the rooms aren't always maintained at the height of cleanliness.

Bars

Most bars in New York offer theme nights, drink specials and happy hours, and the gay ones are no exception. Don't be shy, remember to tip the bartender, and carry plenty of business cards. *See chapters* **Cafés & Bars** *and* **Cabaret & Comedy.**

Chelsea

Barracuda
275 W 22nd St at Eighth Ave (212-645-8613).
Subway: C, E to 23rd St. 4pm–4am. No credit cards.
This Chelsea bar—which actually feels more like the East Village—continues to draw hordes of boys. More comfy and friendly than its neighborhood competition, the space is split in two, with a traditional bar area up-front and a frequently redecorated lounge in back, plus a pool table, pinball machine and nightly DJs. Theme nights include ferocious glamazon Mona Foot's Star Search on Thursdays. Boys on a budget, take note: There's never a cover.

g
223 W 19th St between Seventh and Eighth Aves (212-929-1085). Subway: 1, 9 to 18th St. 4pm–4am. No credit cards.
This classy lounge is the latest Chelsea sensation, attracting an A-list crowd of hunky men who are also fairly friendly. Don't miss the trendy juice/power-drink bar. (Can an in-house pedicurist be far behind?) One word of warning: Late in the evening, the space is often filled to capacity, while outside there's an intimidating line of unfortunates waiting to get in. Go early and avoid the scene.

The Spike
120 Eleventh Ave at 20th St (212-243-9688). Subway: C, E to 23rd St. 9pm–4am. No credit cards.
The Spike was once the quintessential late-'70s Levi's/leather gay bar. Today, however, it's pretty soft around the edges, since the new clones are all hanging out at the Lure (*see* **West Village**). Still, the Spike has taken on a newer and more varied generation of cruisers and preclubbers. Weekend evenings retain an easygoing and fairly traditional leather flavor.

East Village

Beige
B Bar, 40 E 4th St at Bowery (212-475-2220). Subway: B, D, F, Q to Broadway–Lafayette St; 6 to Bleecker St. Tue 10pm. AmEx, MC, V.
Fashions may come and go, but here it's the fashionable who come and go, sashaying through these stylish rooms with designs on the crowd of good-looking boys and a few extremely stylish girls. (Some of them are even dykes.) Dress to impress, or you'll feel out of place at this groovy fete.

Boiler Room
86 E 4th St between First and Second Aves (212-254-7536). Subway: F to Second Ave. 4pm–4am. No credit cards.
For most self-respecting East Village boys, a stop here on the weekends isn't just an option—it's a moral imperative. Probably the most intensely cruisey of East Village bars, this unassuming joint is busy on weeknights and absolutely

Bulk rate: Chelsea's **American Fitness Center** *helps serious circuit boys (and girls) beef up their bods.*

mobbed on Friday and Saturday nights. The jukebox features a varied selection of new hits and classics, and there are video-game machines for the easily bored.

The Cock
188 Avenue A at 12th St (212-777-6254). Subway: L to First Ave. 9:30pm–4am. No credit cards.
This lively, deliberately seedy haunt carries on the East Village raunch tradition with cheap drinks, spicy shows and a bevy of stylishly sexy boys (What? You thought the name referred to a rooster?) and even a few girls. The music ranges from campy '80s to full-bore rock & roll.

Wonder Bar
505 E 6th St at Ave A (212-777-9105). Subway: F to Second Ave. 6pm–4am. No credit cards.
At its best, this lounge hosts an impossibly, appealingly diverse mix of people—most shockingly, men and women—making it an ideal hangout. The only downside is that most nights the smoke is as thick as the crowd. DJs spin soul, trip-hop and classics.

West Village

hell
59 Gansevoort St between Greenwich Ave and Washington St (212-727-1666). Subway: A, C, E to 14th St; L to Eighth Ave. 7pm–4am. AmEx, MC, V.
Conveniently located near the club Mother and the late-night restaurant Florent, this newish bar sports the requisite red color scheme and celebrity photos with drawn-on devil horns. It's casual, chic and comfortable to boot.

The Lure
*409 W 13th St between Ninth and Tenth Aves
(212-741-3919). Subway: A, C, E to 14th St; L to Eighth
Ave. Mon–Sun 8pm–4am. No credit cards.*
This newfangled fetish bar attracts a broad, energetic, sometimes posey bunch. Wednesdays it hosts Pork, a raunchy
party for the younger set; you'll find men in uniforms, fetish
performances and more mystery than most NYC bars offer.
A strict (and very amusing) dress code is enforced: Wear
leather, rubber or uniforms, but don't dab on the cologne and
don't even think about wearing tennis shoes. (Wednesday
night is less strict.)

Stonewall
*53 Christopher St between Sixth and Seventh Aves
(212-463-0950). Subway: 1, 9 to Christopher
St–Sheridan Sq. 2:30pm–4am. No credit cards.*
This is a landmark bar, next door to the actual location of
the 1969 gay rebellion against police harassment. If you don't
already know it, ask the bartender to talk you through the
story. There's a good pool table and friendly customers, but
these days Stonewall is more a historical monument than an
exciting destination.

Uptown

The Works
*428 Columbus Ave between 80th and 81st Sts
(212-799-7365). Subway: B, C to 81st St. 2pm–4am.
No credit cards.*
The major hangout for young gay men on the Upper West
Side draws a decidedly yuppity thirtysomething crowd. On
Sunday evenings there's a popular beer blast: Between 6pm
and 1am you pay $5 to drink all the brew you can manage.
Part of the proceeds benefit the homebound AIDS patient
meal-delivery service God's Love We Deliver.

Clubs

Almost all New York clubs have gay nights; many
of those we list are one-nighters rather than permanent venues. There's also a large number of
fund-raising parties and other events worth looking out for. For more clubs, the majority of which
are gay-friendly, plus more information about
some of those below, *see chapter* **Clubs**.

Dance clubs

La Nueva Escuelita
*301 W 39th St at Eighth Ave (212-631-0588).
Subway: A, C, E to 42nd St–Times Sq. Thu–Sun
10pm–5am. MC, V.*
Extravagant, not-to-be-missed drag follies featuring a bevy
of Latin talents are staged nightly here. There's also sweaty
dancing to salsa, merengue and house. The predominantly
Latin crowd is friendly.

Mother
*432 W 14th St at Washington St (212-366-5680).
Subway: A, C, E to 14th St; L to Eighth Ave. Tue–Sun
10:30pm.*
This is one of the only vestiges of truly twisted New York
nightlife left. Queer (but not necessarily gay) revelers gather here every week for clever fetish, dress-up and perfor-
mance-oriented theme nights, such as Tuesday's legendary
Jackie 60 (which will have its final night the last Tuesday
of 1999); Saturday's **Click & Drag**, a cyber-fetish costume
parade (you must conform to the dress code, or at least wear
all black—call for info); and Friday night's women's party

Clit Club (*see* **Dyke Life**, *page 234*). There are also theatrical presentations earlier in the evening. Don't leave the
city without checking out this incredible institution.

Saint at Large
To get on the mailing list: 212-674-8541.
The now-mythical Saint, with its huge aluminum-domed
interior, was one of the first venues where New York's gay
men enjoyed dance-floor freedom. The club closed, but the
clientele keeps its memory alive with a series of four huge
circuit parties each year. These parties—the S/M-tinged
Black Party, the White Party (those names refer not to skin
color but to the mood of the events), Halloween and New
Year's Eve—attract legions of muscle-bound and image-con-
scious gay men from around the U.S.

Twilo
*530 W 27th St between Tenth and Eleventh Aves
(212-268-1600). Subway: C, E to 23rd St. Sat 10pm.*
Crowds of gay men flock to this futuristic fete every Saturday night to worship at the shrine of super-DJ Junior
Vasquez. Cavernous and always bursting at the seams, with
a sound system that keeps you shivering for days, this is a
sure bet for boogying boys.

Squeezebox
*Don Hill's, 511 Greenwich St at Spring St
(212-334-1390). Subway: 1, 9 to Houston St. Fri 10pm.*
Are you gay but sick and tired of disco? Join the all-ages,
pansexual, celebrity-studded crowd of twisted sisters and
queer headbangers at this unique punk-glitter-glam-rock
club. The crowd is about two-thirds gay, with a healthy
bunch of women. Excellent live bands and rock & roll drag
queens perform soul-shaking sets each week. Beware the
mosh pit!

Roxy
*515 W 18th St between Tenth and Eleventh Aves
(212-645-5156). Subway: A, C, E to 14th St; L to
Eighth Ave. 11pm.*
Hordes of muscle boys and club crawlers pack Saturday
nights at this venerable pleasure pit. The winning formula—the requisite go-go boys and carousing drag queens, and
DJs spinning happy house music—guarantees a satisfying
megaclub experience.

Sex clubs

Despite the city's crackdown on adult businesses,
a few bathhouses and sex clubs for men still exist.
Apart from the barlike **J's Hangout** (675 Hudson Street at 14th Street, 212-242-9292)—which is
less blatantly sexual and more of an after-hours
desperation cruise—there is the **West Side Club**
bathhouse (27 West 20th Street between Fifth and
Sixth Avenue, 212-691-2700) in Chelsea and its sister establishment, the **East Side Club** (227 East
56th Street at Second Avenue, 212-753-2222). For
more current details, consult *HX* magazine's Getting Off section.

Restaurants and cafés

Few New York restaurants would bat an eye at a
same-sex couple enjoying an intimate dinner. The
neighborhoods mentioned above have hundreds
of great eating places that are de facto gay restaurants, and many that are gay-owned and operat-

ed. Below are a few of the most obviously gay places in town. *See chapter* **Restaurants.**

Big Cup
228 Eighth Ave between 21st and 22nd Sts (212-206-0059). Subway: C, E to 23rd St. Mon–Thu 7am–1am; Fri 7am–2am; Sat 8am–2am; Sun 8am–1am. No credit cards.
A big, colorful, bustling coffee joint with a modest selection of sweets and sandwiches, Big Cup's charm lies in its mismatched chairs, quippy staff and friendly, flirtatious clientele. You can hang out for hours during the day, but at night the throng can be overwhelming. Summer months find the choked sidewalk outside a virtual meat market.

Eighteenth & Eighth
159 Eighth Ave at 18th St (212-242-5000). Subway: A, C, E to 14th St; L to Eighth Ave. Meals Mon–Thu, Sun 9am–midnight; Fri, Sat 9am–12:30am. Average main course: $12. MC, V.
Health-conscious, high-carbo food makes this small restaurant one of the great success stories of Chelsea. It's always full of cute, cruisey boys and girls, and the wait for a table is sometimes shockingly long.

Food Bar
149 Eighth Ave between 17th and 18th Sts (212-243-2020) Subway: A, C, E to 14th St; L to Eighth Ave; 1, 9 to 18th St. Daily lunch: 11am–4pm. Dinner: 5pm–midnight. Average main course: $13. Amex, MC, V.
Don't let the tan, buffed and beautiful boys who parade in and out of this stylish eatery dissuade you from checking it out. While its patrons may seem direct from Roxy, and more than a smattering of women would certainly be a welcome sight, Food Bar serves excellent grub; its weekend brunch menu is

particularly tasty. Just be sure to check your teeth before putting the make on any of your many muscular neighbors.

Lips
2 Bank St at Greenwich Ave (212-675-7710). Subway: 1, 2, 3, 9 to 14th St. Brunch: Sat, Sun noon–6pm. Dinner: Sun–Thu 5:30pm–midnight; Fri, Sat 5:30pm–1am. Average main course: $16. AmEx, DC, MC, V.
The attraction at this drag-theme eatery is not the food, and it's certainly not the service; it's the novelty of having a dish named for a drag queen delivered to your table by a drag queen who at any moment will let loose in an old-fashioned lip-sync. It's about as mainstream as drag gets, but the loud show tunes and camp classics playing on video monitors will satisfy queens who relish the overblown.

Lucky Cheng's
24 First Ave between 1st and 2nd Sts (212-473-0516). Subway: F to Second Ave. Sun–Thu 6pm–midnight (drag shows at 8, 9:30 and 11pm); Fri, Sat 6pm–1am (shows at 7:30 and 11pm). Average main course: $15. AmEx, DC, Disc, MC, V.
More drag dining. Cheng's was the first and does it better, though. The queens are raunchy and their performances are boisterous, if not exactly inspired. Still, the food is passable and the drinks strong. Straight people will probably dig it more than seasoned queers.

Townhouse Restaurant
206 E 58th St at Third Ave (212-826-6241). Subway: N, R to Lexington Ave; 4, 5, 6 to 59th St. Brunch Sun noon–4pm. Lunch: Mon–Sat noon–3:30pm. Dinner: Mon–Thu 5–11pm; Fri, Sat 5pm–11:30pm; Sun 6–11pm. Average brunch: $12.50. Dinner: $16.50–$30. AmEx, DC, MC, V.

Prints charming: A couple of ladies-in-waiting unwind at the East Village bar **Meow Mix.**

A very elegant uptown haunt for true (read: more mature) gentlemen and their gentlemen friends (most of them in suits). Very gay, very upscale and full of old-world discretion. The food is continental, decent and affordable.

Gyms

See chapter **Sports & Fitness** *for more fitness facilities, including YMCAs.*

American Fitness Center
128 Eighth Ave at 16th St (212-627-0065). Subway: A, C, E to 14th St; L to Eighth Ave; 1, 9 to 18th St. Mon–Fri 6am–midnight; Sat, Sun 8am–9pm. $15–$20 per day. AmEx, Disc, MC, V.
This fully equipped übergym is barbell-bunny heaven. It's vast and spotless, with 15,000 square feet (1,400 square meters) of free-weight space, acres of cardiovascular machines and endless aerobics classes.

David Barton
623 Broadway between Houston and Bleecker Sts (212-420-0507). Subway: B, D, F, Q to Broadway–Lafayette St; 6 to Bleecker St. Mon–Fri 6am–midnight; Sat, Sun 8am–8pm. $15 per day. AmEx, MC, V.
Barton, husband of party promoter Susanne Bartsch, mixes fitness with fashion and nightlife at his gyms. Sleek locker rooms, artfully lit weight rooms and pumping music may make you feel as if you should have a cocktail instead of another set of reps. Besides free weights, Barton offers the three essential *Cs*: classes, cardio equipment and cruising. There is another, less architecturally compelling location in Chelsea at 552 Sixth Ave between 15th and 16th Sts.

Dyke life

The most exciting aspect of lesbian life in Manhattan is that the women you'll see out and about in bars, clubs, restaurants, bookshops, community meetings and lesbian cabarets will truly defy all stereotypes. While lesbian culture is not as visible or as geographically concentrated as gay men's, it is also far less segregated (with some exceptions), either by age or race, and is far more friendly and welcoming.

If you're into community activism, you'll find plenty to spark your interest (although the glory days of outrageous civil disobedience have past): Just check in at the Lesbian & Gay Community Services Center (*see page 228*). The Center also offers a wide range of support groups and 12-step meetings for people in recovery. But if you're a dyke who's not into the activist or recovery scene and just wants to have some unbridled fun, New York City has plenty to offer.

Brooke Webster's full-time East Village lesbian bar Meow Mix (*see page 234*) is a welcome gathering spot for alternadykes. And the unflappable promoter Caroline Clone continues to offer women large-scale dance parties including Her/SheBar and WOW Bar. The idea that lesbians want more for their money has also given old, standard bars in the West Village a reason to try a little harder. Meanwhile, lesbian discos

are getting progressively larger and are no longer held only in funky, out-of-the-way dives. Unfortunately, the rising popularity of these clubs doesn't guarantee they'll be around for long, so check the lesbian bar guide *HX for Her* or *Time Out New York* for the most current information. As a rule, your male friends, even if they are gay, will not be welcome in most women's bars and clubs unless the venue or the night is specifically advertised as mixed.

Outside Manhattan, Park Slope in Brooklyn remains a sort of lesbian residential hub, but beyond visiting the Lesbian Herstory Archives or the Audre Lorde Project (*see page 227*) or just hanging out in Prospect Park, there isn't much to see.

If you're staying in Brooklyn and plan to travel into Manhattan to take advantage of dyke nightlife, take a taxi back. Though stories of how dangerous New York is at night are greatly exaggerated, it's still not a good idea to ride the subway alone late at night (*see* **Safety**, *page 234*).

Accommodations

See **Colonial House Inn** and **Incentra Village House**, *pages 229–230.*

East Village Bed & Breakfast
244 E 7th St at Ave C, apartment 6 (212-260-1865). Subway: F to Second Ave. Singles $60, doubles $85, breakfast included. No credit cards.
This small, friendly, women-only B&B, run by women and located deep in the bowels of the East Village, has only two rooms, so reservations are essential.

Markle Residence for Women
123 W 13th St between Sixth and Seventh Aves (212-242-2400). Subway: F, 1, 2, 3, 9 to 14th St; L to Sixth Ave. $128–$220 per week, including two meals (one-month minimum). MC, V.
Offering women-only Salvation Army accommodation in a pleasant Greenwich Village location, the Markle has clean, comfortable rooms, all of which have telephones and private bathrooms.

Bars and lounges

See **Beige** *and* **Wonder Bar**, *page 230.*

Crazy Nanny's
21 Seventh Ave South at Leroy St (212-366-6312). Subway: 1, 9 to Christopher St–Sheridan Sq. 4pm–4am.
An old faithful, Nanny's is a loud neon-decorated bar and disco with TV screens and a pool table downstairs; there's a DJ and a big-screen TV upstairs. Nanny's has also started staging theme nights; depending on who is DJing, the crowd might be predominantly black women or a mixed, trendy bunch of fags and dykes. It's a good place to hang out and have a frosty cold one, especially after a softball game on a weekend afternoon. Daily happy hour with two-for-one drinks 4–7pm.

Henrietta Hudson
438 Hudson St at Morton St (212-924-3347). Subway: 1, 9 to Christopher St–Sheridan Sq. Mon–Fri 3pm–4am; Sat, Sun 1pm–4am.

This is a watering hole for middle-class suburban girls with lots of hair. Women love it for cruising; it's laid out so you can eye everyone at once, then make your choice and make a move.

Julie's
204 E 58th St between Second and Third Aves (212-688-1294). Subway: E, F to Lexington Ave; 6 to 51st St. 5pm.
Julie's is an incredibly discreet, elegant bar for mature, professional, often closeted women in search of the same. It stays open as late as 4am if business is good. Hors d'oeuvres are served from 5 to 8pm.

Meow Mix
269 Houston St at Suffolk St (212-254-0688). Subway: F to Second Ave. Mon 5pm–4am; Tue–Fri, Sun 8pm–4am; Sat 3pm–4am.
Brooke Webster's alternative dyke bar appeals to youngish, edgy women and their men friends. There's a laid-back vibe even when the space plays host to raucous parties, go-go dancers, live bands (like Sexpod and the Lunachicks), readings and performances. Be on the lookout for slumming celebs.

Clubs

Great club nights are the holy grail of New York City—something that's fabulous one week sucks or is closed down the next, and so the search continues. These are the current lesbian hot spots, but don't panic if they're not around in a few months' time—there are bound to be new nights and venues blossoming in their places. Check *HX for Her* for current info.

Clit Club
Fridays at **Mother** *(see page 231 for listings). Fri 10pm–5am .*
The longest-running lesbian night (seven years and counting) is still going strong, with new weekly midnight performances ranging from sexy stripteases to obscure performance art. Quality DJs and bodacious go-go girls are still standard here. Renovations have transformed this once-dark dive into a larger, more user-friendly space. Under the auspices of Mother, the club no longer has a restrictive policy discouraging men, but the only males who come by are the Mother regulars: gays and cross-dressers who hang out here other nights of the week. Similarly, dykes are welcome at Mother any night.

Squeezebox
See page 231 for listings.
Squeezebox is New York's hippest, hottest drag/dyke rock & roll party. With great live bands and tattooed go-go boys and girls gyrating on the bar amid a super-mixed, celebrity-peppered crowd, you can count on seeing plenty of the hottest downtown dykes around.

Restaurants and cafés

Cowgirl Hall of Fame
519 Hudson St at 10th St (212-633-1133). Subway: 1, 9 to Christopher St–Sheridan Sq. Lunch: noon–4pm. Dinner: 5–11pm. Average main course: $20. MC, V.
In name and spirit, this is a great girl place, though everyone will enjoy it. With its Tex-Mex food, country music on the jukebox and cowgirl memorabilia all over the walls, the place is pure country kitsch. Women with kids come again and again because their high-chair and entertainment needs

are ably met by the sympathetic single-parent owner, Sherri. The preclub scene revs up on frozen margaritas at the steer horn–decorated bar; in the warmer months, the sidewalk tables are great for people-watching.

Rubyfruit
531 Hudson St at Charles St (212-929-3343). Subway: 1, 9 to Christopher St–Sheridan Sq. Mon–Thu 3pm–2am; Fri, Sat 3pm–4am; Sun 11:30am–2am. Average main course: $20. AmEx, DC, Disc, MC, V.
A warm and energetic band of women patronizes Rubyfruit, the only lesbian bar and restaurant in town. Though the food is solidly good, it's not the main selling point. The congenial customers and a varied program of cabaret and music make this a good place for fun-loving old-school dykes.

Safety

New York women are used to the brazenness with which they are stared at by men and develop a hardened or dismissive attitude toward it. If your unwelcome admirers ever get verbal or start following you, ignoring them is better than responding—unless you are confident about your acid-tongued retorts. Walking into the nearest shop is your best bet to get rid of really persistent offenders.

As for more serious safety issues, with a minimum of awareness and common sense you can reduce the chances of anything happening to you to almost zero. Take the usual big-city precautions: Stay in areas where there are people, don't carry or wear anything that could catch a thief's eye, and try not to look lost or vulnerable. Just act as if you know where you are going, and you will probably get there safely. Advice issued by the New York Police Department includes: Never carry anything you'd fight for, don't carry a separate wad of "mugger's money" but simply hand over all your cash (if you're found to have kept money back, you'll be in worse trouble), and never resist when a weapon is involved. For further safety advice, *see chapter* **Directory**. For the **NYC Gay & Lesbian Anti-Violence Project** *see page 228*.

Brooklyn Women's Martial Arts Center for Anti-Violence Education
421 Fifth Ave between 7th and 8th Sts, Park Slope, Brooklyn (718-788-1775). Subway: F, R to Fourth Ave–9th St. Mon–Fri 10am–6pm. No credit cards.
This is a center dedicated to martial-arts training for women and children. Its programs teach defensive techniques for real-life situations, including both physical and nonphysical methods of dealing with aggression or attack. Free child care is offered, and there are classes in the evenings and on weekends. Classes in karate and tai chi are offered.

Rape Hotline
Sex Crimes Report Line of the New York City Police Department (212-267-7273). 24 hours.
Reports of sex crimes are handled by a female detective from the Police Department, who will inform the appropriate precinct, send an ambulance if requested and provide counseling and medical referrals. A detective from the Sex Crimes Squad will interview the victim.

Kids' Stuff

***Growing up with cool parents amid oodles of culture,
New York City kids are more than all right***

New York is a noisy, nonstop, loudmouthed, horn-honking, in-your-face city where anything goes and everything seems possible—which could be why so many kids think it was made for them. It's the perfect environment for short attention spans and experience-hungry spirits: It's possibly the only city in the world where a child can wake up in the morning and make breakfast for animals in a zoo kitchen, practice an obscure Indian dance in the afternoon and go to a pajama-party storytime before bed. Kids don't get bored in New York. They get "overscheduled."

Since parents here scramble to get their tots into good nursery schools, educational value is the focus even of play. From September through May, museums and other institutions offer lots of hands-on learning. In summer, the emphasis shifts to unmitigated fun, though there's still plenty to inspire: free outdoor theater in parks and parking lots, Lincoln Center's wonderful Out-of-Doors festival, Central Park's SummerStage and much more.

There are also the unscheduled pleasures of the street. If you let them, kids will have a ball scal-

ing industrial loading bays, ogling street performers, swinging on subway poles or just wandering around taking it all in. Especially during the warm months, street life feeds all of a child's senses and will provide yours with endless stories to take home.

The weekly *Time Out New York* magazine and Friday's *New York Times* have good listings of children's activities. Also read the monthly *Parent Guide* distributed free in libraries, toy stores, play centers and other child-friendly places. Pick up a copy of *Events for Children* from any branch of the New York Public Library for extensive listings of free storytellings, puppet shows, films and workshops in libraries. The Donnell Library, home of the Central Children's Room, is the best place for events; it also houses the original Winnie the Pooh and other toys that belonged to Christopher Robin (*see chapter* **Museums**).

All Barnes & Noble and Borders megastores have regular free story-reading hours and other activities; pick up a calendar in any branch. You might also want to invest in a copy of Alfred Gingold and Helen Rogan's slim paperback, *The*

*Curiouser and curiouser: Kids in **Central Park** crawl over Alice, the caterpillar and his hookah.*

Cool Parents' Guide to All of New York (City Books). For a guide to restaurants that welcome children, check out Sam Freund and Elizabeth Carpenter's *Kids Eat New York* (The Little Bookroom). Sam was nine when he compiled this book with his mom. The New York CitySearch website (www.citysearchnyc.com) has well-organized family listings, and you can search by child's age, location or date.

Though there's no end of events and activities designed specifically for kids, don't pass by some of the cutting-edge stuff for adults; many zany Off-Broadway shows are sure hits with children, as are most "new media" art shows. For more ideas, *see section* **New York by Neighborhood** (*including* **Park places**, *pages 50–51, and* **Heaven central**, *pages 70–71), and chapters* **New York by Season**, **Trips Out of Town** *and* **Sports & Fitness**.

Baby-sitting

Babysitters' Guild

212-682-0227. 9am–9pm. No credit cards.
Long- or short-term baby-sitters cost $12–$20 an hour and speak 16 languages among them. If you tell the agency folk you'll need a sitter more than once during your stay, they'll do their best to book the same sitter for you each time.

Avalon Nurse Registry & Child Service

212-245-0250. Mon–Fri 8:30am–5:30pm; Sat, Sun 9am–8pm. No credit cards.
Avalon arranges full- or part-time nannies and baby-sitting. A sitter (four-hour minimum) costs $10 an hour, plus $2 for each additional child and travel expenses.

Pinch Sitters

212-260-6005. Mon–Fri 7am–5pm. No credit cards.
Pinch Sitters specializes in emergency child care, mainly by creative types moonlighting between engagements, and mainly for creative types with unpredictable schedules. The agency will try to get you a sitter within the hour. To be safe, call in the morning for an evening sitter or the previous afternoon for a daytime sitter. Charges are $12 an hour (four-hour minimum).

Amusement parks

Astroland

1000 Surf Ave at W 8th St, Coney Island, Brooklyn (718-372-0275). Subway: B, D, F, N to Stillwell Ave–Coney Island. Winter phone for details; summer noon–late (weather permitting). $1.75 single kiddie rides. No credit cards.
Coney Island's amusement park is rather run-down and tacky (to some), but a delight to children nonetheless. In summer, you can ride the frightening Cyclone roller coaster (younger kids will like the Tilt-a-Whirl), watch a snake charmer, get sticky cotton-candy fingers, bite into a Nathan's Famous hot dog and, if you navigate around the boom boxes, enjoy the sun and sand.

*Target practice: Boys take aim at **Astroland** amusement park in Coney Island.*

Circuses

Check the press for details of when the artsy, animal-free, French-Canadian Cirque du Soleil is in town (usually April). The music, costumes and staging are pure fantasy, though younger children might find the stylish clowns a little grotesque. Tickets are snapped up fast.

Big Apple Circus

Damrosch Park, Lincoln Center (212-268-2500; tickets from Centercharge 212-721-6500, Ticketmaster 212-307-4100). Subway: 1, 9 to 66th St–Lincoln Ctr. Prices vary.
New York's own traveling circus was founded 12 years ago as a traditional, one-act-at-a-time alternative to the Ringling Bros. three-things-at-once extravaganza. Big Apple prides itself on being a true family affair, with acts by the founder's two children and his equestrienne wife. The circus has a regular winter season (Oct–Jan) in Damrosch Park and, budget permitting, travels to other city parks in early spring.

Ringling Bros. and Barnum & Bailey Circus

Madison Square Garden, Seventh Ave at 32nd St (212-465-6741). Subway: A, C, E, 1, 2, 3, 9 to 34th St–Penn Station. Apr. $10.50–$42.50. AmEx,.DC, Disc, MC, V.
The original (and most famous) American circus, this has three rings, lots of glitz and plenty to keep you glued to your seat, as well as Barnum's famous sideshow of freaks, which was recently revived. It's extremely popular, so reserve seats well in advance.

UniverSoul Big Top Circus

Venue and performance schedule changes year to year (212-307-7171) $8–$40.
This African-American circus has all the requisite clowns, animal acts and hoopla. Owned and operated by the man who promoted the Commodores, UniverSoul is the result of a two-year nationwide search for black circus performers.

Museums and exhibitions

Most of these museums offer weekend workshops for children. See **Bring us your budding Picassos**, *pages 238–239*, for art museum info. See section **New York by Neighborhood** *and* chapter **Museums** for plenty more options, including the revamped dinosaur halls at the American Museum of Natural History, the Liberty Science Center (don't miss the Touch Tunnel), the New York Transit Museum and the Sea, Air and Space Museum, a collection of military and maritime paraphernalia housed on an aircraft carrier.

Brooklyn Children's Museum

145 Brooklyn Ave at St. Mark's Ave, Brooklyn (718-735-4400). Subway: 3 to Kingston Ave; B43, B45, B47, B65 bus. Weekends only, a free shuttle bus runs hourly from the Brooklyn Museum of Art and the Grand Army Plaza subway station. Winter Wed–Fri 2–5pm; Sat, Sun 10am–5pm; summer Mon, Wed, Fri–Sun 10am–5pm. Winter and spring school vacations 10am–5pm. Suggested donation $4. No credit cards.
Founded in 1899, this was the world's first museum designed specifically for children. Its focus today is on opening kids' eyes to world cultures—especially those represented by the city's immigrant population. You reach the exhibits via a walkway through a long, water-filled tunnel. In the music studio, children can play instruments from around the globe,

as well as synthesizers, and dance on the keys of a walk-on piano. A new gallery houses exhibitions from museums around the country. There are weekend performances and special workshops daily.

Children's Museum of the Arts

182 Lafayette St between Broome and Grand Sts (212-274-0986). Subway: N, R to Prince St; B, D, F, Q to Broadway–Lafayette St; 6 to Spring St. Wed–Sun noon–5pm. Mon–Fri $4, weekends $5. AmEx, MC, V.
A favorite hangout for the under-sevens, this is less a museum than an art playground, with a floor-to-ceiling chalkboard, art computers and vast stores of art supplies—perfect for young travelers pining for their crayons. Visual- and performing-arts workshops are scheduled regularly. Children must be accompanied by adults.

Children's Museum of Manhattan

212 W 83rd St between Broadway and Amsterdam Ave (212-721-1234). Subway: 1, 9 to 86th St. Tue–Sun 10am–5pm. $5. AmEx, Disc, MC, V.
The Children's Museum of Manhattan promotes literacy of every kind through its dynamic and playful hands-on exhibits. Currently, WordPlay lets toddlers discover the pleasures of language in a 1,900-square-foot play environment, Body Odyssey lets kids discover what's going on inside them, and Seuss! is a play environment based on Dr. Seuss's books. Bigger kids can head to the sound studio, equipped with keyboards and digital sound-editing equipment. Then there's the state-of-the-art media lab, where they operate the cameras, edit tape, play talk-show host and make their own TV shows. Workshops are scheduled on weekends and during school vacations.

Lower East Side Tenement Museum

*See chapter **Museums** for listings. Children's tours Sat, Sun noon, 1, 3pm. $8, children $6.*
Housed in an old tenement building that was home to successive families of new immigrants, this museum offers a weekly interactive children's tour of the Sephardic Confino family's former home. The tour is led by 13-year-old Victoria Confino (actually a staff member posing as her), who teaches visitors about New York in the early 1900s by dancing the fox-trot, playing games and answering questions—such as "Where does everyone sleep?" Recommended for ages 7 to 14.

New York Hall of Science

*See chapter **Museums** for listings.*
Located on the site of the 1964 World's Fair, flanked by prehistoric-looking rocket ships and housed in the mysterious former Space Pavilion, the Hall of Science offers curious minds some terrific adventures. In the most popular of its interactive exhibits, the immense outdoor Science Playground (open late spring through fall; ages six and up), youngsters engage in whole-body science exploration, discovering principles of balance, gravity, energy and sound as they play.

Socrates Sculpture Park

*Broadway at Vernon Blvd, Long Island City, Queens (718-956-1819). Subway: N to Broadway. 10am–sunset. Free. See chapter **Outer Boroughs**.*
Unlike most art institutions, this outdoor city-owned spread of large-scale contemporary sculpture is utterly devoid of snarling guards and DON'T TOUCH signs. Without even risking an adult's glare, children climb on, run through, sit astride and generally interact with works that seem to have been plopped haphazardly around the four-acre park.

Sony Wonder Technology Lab

550 Madison Ave between 55th and 56th Sts (212-833-8100). Subway: 6 to 51st St; E, F to Fifth Ave. Tue, Wed, Fri, Sat 10am–6pm; Thu 10am–9pm; Sun noon–6pm (school groups have priority Tue–Fri 10am–noon). Free.

Most children think this is the coolest place on earth. At six digital workstations, visitors can play at being medical diagnosticians, remix a Celine Dion song, design computer games, edit a music video or crisis-manage an earthquake. Best of all is the High Definition Interactive Theater, where the audience directs the action in an exciting video adventure. Get here early—by 2:30pm on weekends—or you might not get in.

Growing Up with Opera
John Jay Theater, 899 Tenth Ave at 59th St (212-769-7008). Subway: A, C, B, D, 1, 9 to 59th St–Columbus Circle. $15–$25. AmEx, MC, V.
Short operas, some especially for young audiences, are sung in English by the Metropolitan Opera Guild. The guild has recently added a participatory series for preschoolers (tickets $10), staged in smaller theaters around the city.

Jazz for Young People
Alice Tully Hall, Lincoln Center, 65th St at Columbus Ave (212-875-5599; tickets 212-721-6500). Subway: 1, 9 to 66th St–Lincoln Ctr. $10–$15. AmEx, MC, V.
These interactive concerts, led by trumpeter and jazz educator Wynton Marsalis, help children figure out answers to such questions as "What is jazz?"

Little Orchestra Society
Florence Gould Hall, 55 E 59th St between Madison and Park Aves (212-971-9500). Subway: 4, 5, 6 to 59th St; N, R to Lexington Ave. $32. AmEx, MC, V.
"Lolli-Pops" presents participatory orchestral concerts for children ages three to five, combining classical music with dance, puppetry, theater and mime. A spectacular *Amahl and the Night Visitors* with live sheep is done every Christmas. "Happy Concerts" for ages five and up are staged at Avery Fisher Hall.

New York Philharmonic Young People's Concerts
Avery Fisher Hall, Lincoln Center, 65th Street at Columbus Ave (212-875-5656). Subway: 1, 9 to 66th St–Lincoln Ctr. $6–$16. AmEx, MC, V.
Musicians address the audience directly in these legendary educational concerts, initiated by the late Leonard Bernstein. Each concert is preceded by an hour-long "Children's Promenade," during which kids can meet orchestra members and try out their instruments.

Brooklyn Botanic Garden
See chapter Outer Boroughs *for listings.*
In the indoor Discovery Center, children learn about plants and nature through some inventive exhibits. The garden's

Bring us your budding Picassos
At the city's best grown-up museums, art can often be child's play

With "arts in education" a buzz phrase around the city these days (and a powerful magnet for government and corporate support), museum education departments have been busily beefing up and expanding both school time and family programming. Sure, you could be your own child's tour guide, but wouldn't you rather someone else got to say, "Don't touch, don't run…"? Besides, museum educators truly know how to interest children in the art, how to encourage discussion and how to keep youngsters at the center of the museumgoing experience. Best of all, from a kid's point of view, is that all of this happens in the company of other kids: It's a social experience.

Brooklyn Museum of Art
See chapter Museums *for listings. Sat (plus weekdays during some school vacations) 11am, 2pm. Tour free with museum ticket.*
With its famous Egyptian collection, totem poles and masks and chairs of its African collection, the Brooklyn Museum of Art is naturally child-friendly. Arty Facts is the museum's lively drop-in program for four- to seven-year-olds, focusing on a different theme each month—for example, legs (teapot legs, chair legs, human legs). Children examine in depth three or four works in the museum's galleries, learn about the people who made them and the materials they used, and then go make their

own related art in a real art studio. Afterward, there's storytelling in the galleries (at 4pm).

Metropolitan Museum of Art
See chapter Museums *for listings. Tours Oct–May Sat 11am–12:30pm and 2–4:30pm; Sun 11am–12:30pm. Call for summer schedule. Tour free with museum ticket.*
Most kids will want to head straight for the Egyptian galleries for a look at mummies and the awesome Temple of Dendur. And then what? The Met's education department has it all planned out. Every week, groups of children ages 6 to 12 and their accompanying grown-ups are led to a specific area of the museum, where they go hunting for whatever relates to the theme of the day—it could be flowers in the arms-and-armor galleries or serpents in medieval art. There's plenty of discussion, and kids are encouraged to sketch what they see using the materials provided. Independent types can use the museum's self-guided children's tours ("art hunts"), designed with an unusually acute sense of what makes kids tick; themes range from mummies to colonial children. Instructions are in large type with very cool graphics, a simple floor map, step-by-step directions and playful questions and tidbits of information. A tour takes about an hour.

Museum of Modern Art
See chapter Museums *for listings. Gallery talks on selected Saturdays 10–11am. Family Films on selected Saturdays noon–1pm. "Tours for Tots" on selected Saturdays 10–10:45am. "Art Safari Tour" on selected Saturdays 10am–noon. Admission $5–$20 per family. Registration required.*

highlight, a 13,000-square-foot (1,200-square-meter) Discovery Garden, lets children play botanist, make toys out of natural materials, weave a wall and get their hands dirty.

New York Botanical Garden
See chapter **Outer Boroughs** *for listings. Children's Adventure Garden $3, students and seniors $2, children $1. Ask about Garden Passport, which includes grounds and Adventure Garden admission.*
The immense Children's Adventure Garden, opened in spring 1998, is an interactive "museum of the natural world" with "galleries" both indoors and out. Children can also run under Munchy, a giant topiary; poke around in a touch tank; and plant, weed, water and harvest in the Family Garden. Ask for a kid's guide to the Enid A. Haupt Conservatory (admission $3.50), the spectacular glass house.

Nelson Rockefeller Park
Hudson River at Chambers St (212-267-9700). Subway: A, C, 1, 2, 3, 9 to Chambers St. 10am–sunset. Free.
River breezes always keep this park several degrees cooler than most of the city, a big plus in the summer. There's plenty for kids to do here besides watch the boats. (Saturday's a good day for ocean liners.) They can play on Tom Otterness's quirky sculptures in the picnic area (near the Chambers Street entrance), enjoy one of New York's best playgrounds and participate in art, sports or street-game activities (Mon–Thu afternoons, May–Oct; call for locations). Other activities such as kite flying and fishing are planned throughout the summer. Two blocks north on Pier 25 is a minigolf course as well

A melting clock, a sleeping gypsy, bright drips and splashes, tiny buildings with tinier cars—the Museum of Modern Art has it all. Excellent guided gallery talks for families introduce children ages five to ten to the highlights of MoMA (before the museum opens to the public). A film series screening airtight shorts that relate to the day's theme follows at noon. "Tours for Tots" are whimsical walks around the museum for four-year-olds and their adult companions. *Art Safari,* a book by MoMA's education department inspired the "Art Safari Tour," which helps kids look carefully at eight animal-related artworks in the collection. Check out the related website at www.moma.org. The entrance for all tours is at the John Noble Education Center, 18 W 54th St.

Solomon R. Guggenheim Museum
See chapter **Museums** *for listings. Tours some Sundays 2–4pm. $10 per child plus adult museum admission.*
The cool museum with the spiral ramp you're not allowed to run down offers occasional tours of special exhibitions for children ages five to ten. Each tour is followed by an artist-led workshop—not your typical artsy-craftsy affair. Preregistration is essential for all Guggenheim programs.

Whitney Museum of American Art
See chapter **Museums** *for listings. Tours Sat 1pm; workshops Oct–May selected Saturdays 9–11am. Tour free with museum ticket, workshop $6 per family.*
The Whitney's "Look Out!" tours include discussion and sketching. Specially trained teenage docents lead the tours, telling young visitors about the artists and their work; as you might expect, young children listen in rapt attention to their slightly older peers. "Family Fun!" art-making workshops, for which you must register in advance (212-570-7710), are truly imaginative and interactive events: You look at the work of a single American artist and then try to get a sense of what went into the making of it—so kids might, for example, end up posing for and drawing one another.

as a sand-and-sprinkler area for overheated tots. The River Project (212-941-5901) on Pier 26 admits children on weekends; they can help set river traps, examine small creatures under microscopes and feed the aquarium fish.

Central Park

Manhattanites don't have gardens; they have parks (*see* **Park places,** *pages 50–51, and* **Heaven central** *pages 70–71).* The most popular (and populated) is Central Park, where there are plenty of places and programs specially for children. **Arts in the Park** (212-988-9093) organizes an extensive program of children's summer arts events in several parks throughout the city. Don't miss the beautiful **antique carousel** ($1 a ride) and the **Heckscher Playground,** which has handball courts, horseshoe pitches, several softball diamonds, a puppet theater, a wading pool and a crèche.

Charles A. Dana Discovery Center
See **Heaven central** *pages 70–71 for listings.*
Now that Harlem Meer has been restored and stocked, you can take the kids fishing there April through October. Poles and bait are given out (with a parent's ID) to children over five until 90 minutes before closing; staff is available to help. Other activities: bird watching and workshops such as kite making or sun printing (1–3pm most weekends).

Conservatory Water
Central Park at 74th St near Fifth Ave. Subway: 6 to 77th St. July–Aug Sun–Fri 11am–7pm; Sat 2–7pm; Spring, Fall Sat, Sun 2–7pm (weather permitting).
Known as Stuart Little's Pond after E.B. White's storybook mouse, this ornamental pond is the place to watch model yacht races. When the boatmaster is around, you can rent one of the remote-controlled vessels ($10/hour). Be warned—it's not as speedy as Nintendo. The large bronze statue of Alice in Wonderland nearby is excellent for climbing.

Henry Luce Nature Observatory
See **Heaven central** *pages 70–71 for listings.*
This is the newest children's hot spot in Central Park, with telescopes, microscopes and simple hands-on exhibits that teach about the plants and animals living (or hiding) in the surrounding area. Workshops are held on weekend afternoons, spring through fall (1–3pm). Kids (with a parent's ID) can borrow a discovery kit—a backpack containing binoculars, a bird-watching guide and various cool tools.

North Meadow Recreation Center
Central Park at 79th St (212-348-4867). Subway: A, C, B to 81st St.
Borrow (with ID) a fun-in-the-park kit bag containing a Frisbee, hula hoop, whiffle ball and bat, jump rope, kickball and other diversions.

Stories at the Hans Christian Andersen Statue
Central Park at Conservatory Water (212-929-6871, 212-340-0906). Jun–Sept Sat 11am; Jul Wed 11am. Free.
For generations, children have gathered at the foot of the statue for Saturday stories read by master storytellers from all over America—a real New York tradition, not to be missed. On Wednesdays, children's librarians from the branch libraries read their favorite stories.

NY Skateout
44 E 63rd St; classes meet at various places in Central Park (212-486-1919). Skate lessons Apr–Oct Sat 9am. $25 for a two-hour class. Call to reserve.

Classes are offered for beginners and more advanced skaters (ages seven and up). Once they get the hang of it, children skate in supervised groups around the park's loop road. NY Skateout is dedicated to skating safety: Don't even think of showing up without all the gear. Call for information on equipment rental.

Wildman's Edible Park Tours
Various city parks, including Central and Prospect Parks. Call for meeting place and instructions (718-291-6925). $10, children $5. No credit cards.
Irrepressible urban forager and naturalist "Wildman" Steve Brill was once arrested for munching Central Park's dandelions; now his eat-as-you-go foraging tours are sanctioned by the parks commissioner. His tours aren't meant specifically for kids, but he pays them special attention, and they delight in his joke-laden banter.

Play spaces

For older children itching to burn some energy, try Chelsea Piers, which has a gymnasium, roller rink and half-pipe for both in-line skating and skateboarding (*see* **No pier pressure here**, *page 274*).

Playspace
2473 Broadway at 92nd St (212-769-2300). Subway: 1, 2, 3, 9 to 96th St. Mon–Sat 9:30am–6pm, Sun 10am–6pm. $6.50. No credit cards.
In this play space with huge plate-glass windows, children ages six and under build in the immense sandbox, ride on toy trucks, dress up and climb on the jungle gym. Though this is not a drop-off center, the play is supervised; parents can relax—read, even—in a small café to the side. There are also drop-in games, art classes and storytimes. Admission is good for the day: You can leave and come back.

Rain or Shine
Call 212-0532-4420 for information.
This parent-accompanied play space, devoted to imaginative play for kids ages six months to six years, was between locations at press time. Call for its new address, which is likely to be in the East 20s.

Puppets

International Festival of Puppet Theater
212-439-7529, ext 2000. Sept 2000.
This biennial festival of puppet theater from several continents is produced by the Jim Henson Foundation. Although its central component is cutting-edge productions for adults, children will also enjoy the rich blend of offerings. Watch for other puppet activity piggybacking on the festival.

Los Kabayitos Puppet Theater
CSV Cultural Center, 107 Suffolk St between Delancey and Rivington Sts (212-260-4080, ext 12). Subway: F to Delancey St; J, M, Z to Essex St. $10, children $6. No credit cards.
New York's only scaled venue for puppetry is housed in a tiny, steeply raked auditorium decorated like the inside of a Victorian toy theater. You can see matinee children's shows here; your kids may also enjoy productions intended for adults, some of which are spectacular and fantastical enough to engage young audiences.

The Puppet Company
Mazur Theatre at Asphalt Green, 555 E 90th St at York Ave (212-539-3004). Subway: 4, 5, 6 to 86th St. Oct–May Sat, Sun 2:30pm. $8. No credit cards.
The company's hand-puppet host, the debonair Al E. Gator, introduces the play. Each show includes a humorous, inven-

tive puppet revue and a short puppet-making demonstration. Performances last about 50 minutes and are recommended for children three to seven.

Puppetworks
338 Sixth Ave at 4th St, Park Slope, Brooklyn (718-965-3391). Subway: M, N, R to Union St. Sat, Sun 12:30, 2:30pm. $7, ages 2–18 $5. No credit cards.
This company, established in 1938, offers two plays a season, alternating weekly. Usually performed with marionettes, the lavish productions are based on classic tales, such as *Beauty and the Beast* or *Alice in Wonderland*, and are always accompanied by classical music. Puppetworks performs occasional seasons in Greenwich Village, too; call the Brooklyn number for information.

Swedish Cottage Marionette Theater
Central Park at 81st St (212-988-9093). Subway: B, C to 81st St. Sept–May Tue–Fri 10:30am, noon; Sat 11am, 1, 3pm; Jun–Aug Mon–Fri 10:30am, noon. $5, ages 2–12 $4. No credit cards.
Run by New York's Department of Parks and Recreation, this intimate theater in an old Swedish schoolhouse was recently renovated. Reservations are essential.

Theaters

Several small theaters and repertory companies offer weekend matinee family performances. Most of these are musical productions of questionable value. Check magazine or newspaper listings for details (*see chapter* **Directory**). The following are the best of New York's family theaters, plus a theater festival for small hipsters.

New Amsterdam Theater
See chapter **Theater** *for listings.*
Disney laid claim to 42nd Street by renovating this splendid theater, an Art Deco masterpiece. Its inaugural show: *The Lion King*, directed by wizardly puppeteer Julie Taymor.

New York International Fringe Festival
Various venues in the East Village and Lower East Side. Call 888-FRINGE-NYC for a schedule. Three weeks in August. $11, children $7.
Fringe Jr, the kids' component of this downtown festival, grows bigger every year, along with the number of children living in the area. There's now a slew of shows just for kids, and several on the adult program that are recommended for older children. Fort Fringe Jr is a kind of clubhouse at the festival's main venue where youngsters can play, create and participate in workshops. Most exciting of all to many kids is AlFresco, the festival's free outdoor and store-window performance and installation component (watch out for human chess games and roving robots) which opens annually with a block-long street-theater performance. At press time, another downtown performance festival—this one organized by the hip performance space Todo con Nada—is scheduled to take place at the same time as the Fringe Festival. The Pure Pop Theater Festival promises family entertainment with a rock & roll sensibility—Niñapalooza. Look out for it.

New Victory Theater
209 W 42nd St between Broadway and Eighth Ave (212-382-4020; tickets Telecharge 212-239-6200). Subway: N, R, S, 1, 2, 3, 9 to 42nd St–Times Square; A, C, E to 42nd St. $10–$30. AmEx, MC, V.
New York's only year-round, full-scale children's theater (and the first of the New 42nd Street theaters to be reclaimed from porndom when it opened, fully renovated, in 1995), the New Victory is a gem that shows the very best in interna-

*Landing strip: Hundreds of butterflies fly free in the **Bronx Zoo**'s Butterfly Zone.*

tional theater and dance. During the summer, Theatreworks USA presents a season of free musical theater for kids.

TADA! Youth Ensemble

120 W 28th St between Sixth and Seventh Aves (212-627-1732). Subway: 1, 9 to 28th St. Dec, Jan, Mar, Jul, Aug; call for times. $12, under 17 $6. No credit cards.
This group presents musicals performed by and for children. The ensemble casts, ages eight and up, are drawn from open auditions. The shows are usually musical comedies—extremely well presented, high-spirited and very popular. Reservations are advised; call for details of weeklong vacation workshops.

West End Kids' Productions

West End Children's Theatre (212-877-6115), West End Cafe, 2911 Broadway at 113th St. Subway: 1, 9 to 110th St. Prices and schedules vary. AmEx, MC, V.
West End Kids' Productions programs a variety of acts which offer pre- or post-theater dining and performances that include puppetry, magic—and some acts that defy description. They are also responsible for Carolines Kids' Klub which has monthly stand-up comedy by kids as well as auditions and are held at the famous comedy venue (*see chapter* **Cabaret & Comedy** *for listings*). Call for reservations.

Zoos

Bronx Zoo/Wildlife Conservation Society

See chapter **Outer Boroughs** *for listings.*
Some 4,000 animals and 543 species live in reconstructed natural habitats here—one of the world's largest and most magnificent zoos. Inside is the Bronx Children's Zoo, scaled down for the very young, with lots of domesticated animals to pet, plus exhibits that show you the world from an animal's point of view. Camel and elephant rides are available from April to October. Don't miss the sea-lion feeding (daily at 3pm).

Central Park Wildlife Center

Fifth Ave and 64th St (212-861-6030). Subway: N, R to Fifth Ave. Mon–Fri 10am–5pm; Sat, Sun 10:30am–5:30pm. $3.50, ages 3–12 50¢, under 3 free, seniors $1.25. No credit cards.
This small zoo (with 130 species) is one of the highlights of the park. You can watch seals frolic above and below the waterline, crocodiles snap at swinging monkeys, and huge polar bears swim endless laps like true neurotic New Yorkers. The chilly penguin house is a favorite summer retreat for hot kids. The Tisch Children's Zoo has 27 more species of animals.

New York Aquarium for Wildlife Conservation

Surf Ave at W 8th St, Coney Island, Brooklyn (718-265-3405). Subway: D, F to W 8th St–NY Aquarium. Summer Mon–Sun 10am–6pm; winter Mon–Sun 10am–5pm. $8.75, children and seniors $4.50. No credit cards.
Although the aquarium is rather funky, kids enjoy seeing the famous Beluga whale family. There's also a re-creation of the Pacific coastline and an intriguing glimpse of the kinds of things that manage to live in the East River, plus the usual dolphin show and some truly awesome sharks. Watch the dolphins being fed daily at 11:30am and 3pm. Added bonus: Coney Island's Astroland is just a short stroll away.

Museums

Spanning vast treasure troves and dozens of specialized collections, New York is a mecca for museum lovers

New York's museums are superb. More than 60 institutions hold collections of everything from art and antiquities to dolls and Ukrainian folk costumes; others feature hands-on science exhibits. The buildings themselves are equally impressive and eclectic. The spiral uptown Guggenheim is a real jaw-dropper, and the granite cube of the Whitney Museum, with its cyclops-eye window and concrete moat, is a striking contrast to the surrounding architecture.

It is usually self-defeating to try to cram several museum visits into a single day, or even to try to see every exhibit at a major museum such as the Metropolitan Museum of Art or the American Museum of Natural History. Pace yourself: Some museums have excellent cafés or restaurants, so you can break for coffee or a complete meal. Sarabeth's at the Whitney, Sette MoMA at the Museum of Modern Art, the Museum Café in the Pierpont Morgan Library and the Jewish Museum's Café Weissman all provide excuses to take a break from the collections. Don't forget to *see chapters* **Downtown, Midtown, Uptown** *and* **Outer Boroughs** for ideas on other sights to see while in the neighborhood.

Though entry usually costs no more than the price of a movie ticket, museum admission prices may still come as a shock to visitors. This is because most New York museums are funded privately and not by government money, a reason that the New York Historical Society, the city's oldest museum, had to close for two years (it has now reopened). However, most of the city's major museums, including the Metropolitan, the Whitney, the Museum of Modern Art and the International Center for Photography (*see chapter* **Art Galleries**), offer the public at least one evening a week when admission is free or by voluntary donation.

Many of New York's best-known museums—such as the Frick Collection, the Pierpont Morgan Library, the Schomburg Center for Research in Black Culture, the Whitney and the Guggenheim—started out as private collections. The Cloisters, at the northern tip of Manhattan in Fort Tryon Park, was John D. Rockefeller's gift to the city. Its reconstructed Gothic monastery houses the Met's beautiful collection of medieval art. When the sun's shining and the sky's a deep blue, bring a picnic lunch, admire the red-tile roof and inhale the delicate scents of the garden. It's a treat.

Try not to miss the audio tour at the provocative Ellis Island Museum, the eye-opening exhibitions at the Museum of Jewish Heritage and the tour at the Lower East Side Tenement Museum. All give visitors insight into NYC's multicultural history. Across the river, New Jersey's Liberty Science Center, with its hands-on exhibits and rooftop terrace overlooking Manhattan and the Statue of Liberty, is an unexpected pleasure. If you go on the weekend, when the ferry service is operating, it doubles as a sightseeing trip.

Don't hesitate to visit any of the museums if you have kids in tow; most have special events for children if they aren't already kid-friendly (*see* **Bring us your budding Picassos**, *pages 238–239*).

The prize for most neglected museum has to go to the Brooklyn Museum of Art. Its size and grandeur come as a pleasant surprise as you emerge from the subway station just outside the Brooklyn Botanic Garden, but there's an even greater surprise inside: the excellent exhibits. Even though it's the second-largest museum in New York, it rarely draws the huge crowds that head for museums in Manhattan. And that's a shame, because its Egyptian collection rivals the Met's, and its recent temporary shows have been first-class.

One of the best features of NYC's museums is that they do not rest on their fantastic reputations and are constantly changing, expanding and enhancing themselves. One of the most dramatic examples of this is the American Museum of Natural History's construction of the Rose Center for Earth and Space, to be completed in 2000. This new facility will center around the technologically advanced Hayden Planetarium—a structure to be housed in an 87-foot sphere visible through a clear glass enclosure. Other additions include the Hall of the Universe and the Hall of Planet Earth.

The art museums are just as forward-thinking: The MoMA recently teamed with Queens's hot showcase for young talents, P.S. 1, and the Dia Center for the Arts has announced plans to build a satellite facility upstate (*see chapter* **Art Galleries**).

It might be traditional to save museums for a rainy day, but since most are air-conditioned, they also offer a glorious respite from summer heat.

Most of New York's museums are closed on New Year's Day, Presidents' Day, Memorial Day, Independence Day, Labor Day, Columbus Day,

*Barge in: Red Hook's **Waterfront Museum** is a ghost of Brooklyn's shipping past.*

*The people's court: Rest your museum-weary feet in the **Metropolitan**'s Englehard Court.*

Thanksgiving and Christmas Day. Some change their opening hours in the summer, so it's wise to check before setting out.

Major institutions

American Museum of Natural History

Central Park West at 79th St (212-769-5000, recorded information 212-769-5100). Subway: B, C to 81st St. Mon–Thu, Sun 10am–5:45pm; Fri, Sat 10am–8:45pm. Suggested donation $8; concessions $4–$5. AmEx, MC, V (gift shop only).

The fun begins right in the main rotunda, as a towering barosaur, rearing high on its hind legs, protects its young from an attacking allosaurus. It's an impressive welcome to the largest museum of its kind in the world, and a reminder to visit the dinosaur halls on the fourth floor. During their 1995–96 renovation (by the firm responsible for much of the excellent Ellis Island Museum), several specimens were remodeled in light of recent discoveries. The Tyrannosaurus rex, for instance, was once believed to have walked upright, Godzilla-style; now it stalks, head down, with tail parallel to the ground, and is altogether more menacing. The rest of the museum is equally dramatic. The newest part of the permanent collection, the Hall of Biodiversity, examines world ecosystems and environmental preservation. Renovation continues fast and furiously as the new Rose Center for Earth and Space is due to be completed in 2000. There's also a particularly good Native American section and an absolutely stunning collection of gems, including the obscenely large Star of India blue sapphire. An Imax theater shows bigger-than-life nature programs, and there are always innovative temporary exhibitions, in addition to an easily accessible research library with vast photo and print archives and a friendly, helpful staff.

Brooklyn Museum of Art

200 Eastern Pkwy at Washington Ave, Park Slope, Brooklyn (718-638-5000). Subway: 2, 3 to Eastern Pkwy. Wed–Fri 10am–5pm; Sat 11am–9pm; Sun 11am–6pm. Suggested donation $4, students $2, seniors $1.50; concessions $1–$10. AmEx, MC, V (gift shop only).

The Brooklyn Museum, founded 176 years ago, recently appended the word *Art* to its name as part of a campaign to draw wider attention to the world-class collections inside this gorgeous 19th-century Beaux Arts building. The African art and pre-Columbian textile galleries are especially impressive, and the Native American collection is outstanding. There are many works from the ancient Middle East and extensive holdings of American painting and sculpture by such masters as Winslow Homer, Thomas Eakins and John Singer Sargent. And don't miss the Egyptian galleries: The Rubin Gallery's gold-and-silver–gilded ibis coffin, for instance, is sublime. Two floors up, the Rodin sculpture court is surrounded by paintings by French contemporaries such as Monet and Degas. The 1999–2000 season includes a large show imported from London, "SENSATION: Young British Artists from the Saatchi Collection," which will include bad boy Damien Hirst's pickled pig and absolutely fabulous work by Mona Hatoum, Sarah Lucas, Chris Ofili and Rachel Whiteread. There's also an informal café (which closes at 4pm) and a children's museum.

The Cloisters

Fort Tryon Park, Fort Washington Ave at Margaret Corbin Plaza, Washington Heights (212-923-3700). Subway: A to 190th St. March–October Tue–Sun 9:30am–5:15pm; November–February Tue–Sun 9:30am–4:45pm. Suggested donation $10 (includes admission to the Metropolitan Museum of Art on the same day), under 12 free if accompanied by an adult; concessions $4. No credit cards.

The Cloisters houses the Met's medieval art and architecture collections in an unexpectedly tranquil, rural setting. The museum was constructed 60 years ago in authentic

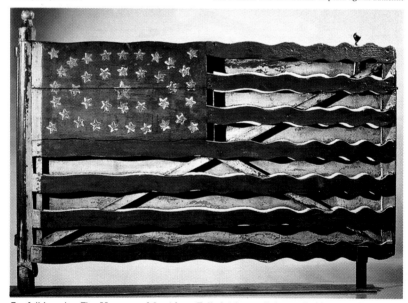

*For folk's sake: The **Museum of American Folk Art** is small, but well worth a visit.*

Middle Ages–style; the result is a convincing, red-tiled Romanesque structure overlooking the Hudson River. Don't miss the famous unicorn tapestries or the Annunciation Triptych by Robert Campin.

Cooper-Hewitt National Design Museum

2 E 91st St at Fifth Ave (212-849-8400). Subway: 4, 5, 6 to 86th St. Tue 10am–9pm; Wed–Sat 10am–5pm; Sun noon–5pm. $5, under 12 free, no admission charge Tue 5–9pm; concessions $1.50. No credit cards.
The Smithsonian's National Design Museum is worth a visit for both its content and its architecture—the turn-of-the-century building once belonged to Andrew Carnegie. Architects responded to his request for "the most modest, plainest and roomy house in New York" by designing a 64-room mansion in the style of a Georgian country house. This is the only museum in the U.S. devoted exclusively to historical and contemporary design; its changing exhibitions are always interesting. Sign language interpretation is available on request (212-849-8387).

Frick Collection

1 E 70th St at Fifth Ave (212-288-0700). Subway: 6 to 68th St. Tue–Sat 10am–6pm; Sun 1–6pm. $7, students and seniors $5, under 10 not admitted, ages 10–16 must be accompanied by an adult. No credit cards.
This private, predominantly Renaissance collection, housed in an opulent residence once owned by industrialist Henry Clay Frick, is more like a stately home than a museum. American architect Thomas Hastings designed the 1914 building in 18th-century European style. The paintings, sculptures and furniture on display are consistently world-class, among them works by Gainsborough, Rembrandt, Renoir, Vermeer, Whistler and the French cabinetmaker Jean-Henri Riesener. The indoor garden court and reflecting pool are especially lovely.

Solomon R. Guggenheim Museum

1071 Fifth Ave at 88th St (212-423-3500). Subway: 4, 5, 6 to 86th St. Sun–Wed 9am–6pm; Fri, Sat 9am–8pm. $12, students and seniors $7, under 12 free, voluntary donation Fri 6–8pm. AmEx, MC, V.
Designed by Frank Lloyd Wright, the Guggenheim itself is a stunning work of art. In addition to works by Kandinsky, Picasso, van Gogh, Degas and Manet, the museum owns Peggy Guggenheim's trove of Cubist, Surrealist and Abstract Expressionist works, and the Panza di Biumo collection of American Minimalist and Conceptual art from the 1960s and '70s. The photography collection began after a donation of more than 200 works by the Robert Mapplethorpe Foundation. In 1992, the museum reopened after a two-year renovation; a new ten-story tower increased the museum's space to include a sculpture gallery (with great views of Central Park) and a café. Since then, the Guggenheim has made news with its ambitious global expansion, its penchant for sweeping historical presentations (such as its elegant overview of 5,000 years of Chinese art) and its in-depth retrospectives of such major American artists as Robert Rauschenberg. Admission prices are among the highest in the city; and if you are willing to fork over $16 for a dual ticket, you're granted entry to the Guggenheim's Soho branch. Even if you don't want to pay to see the collection inside, visit the museum to admire the stunning white building coiled among the turn-of-the-century mansions on Fifth Avenue.
Other location: Guggenheim Museum Soho, *575 Broadway at Prince St (212-423-3500). Subway: N, R to Prince St. Wed–Fri, Sun 11am–6pm; Sat 11am–8pm. Dual-entrance fee for both locations $16, for Soho admission only adults $8, children and seniors $5.*
The downtown Guggenheim opened in 1992 to showcase selections from the permanent collection, as well as temporary exhibitions.

Buddha call: The **Japan Society** *features traditional and contemporary Asian art.*

Metropolitan Museum of Art

1000 Fifth Ave at 82nd St (212-535-7710) www.metmuseum.org. Subway: 4, 5, 6 to 86th St. Tue–Thu, Sun 9:30am–5:15pm; Fri, Sat 9:30am–8:45pm. Suggested donation $10, students and seniors $5, under 12 free if accompanied by an adult; concessions $4. No credit cards. No strollers on Sundays.
It could take several days, even weeks, to cover the Met's 1.5 million square feet (139,354.5 square meters) of exhibition space, so try to be selective. Egyptology fans should head straight for the Temple of Dendur. There's also an excellent Islamic art collection and more than 3,000 European paintings, including major works by Rembrandt, Raphael, Tiepolo and Vermeer. The Greek and Roman halls have gotten a face-lift, and the museum has also been adding to its galleries of 20th-century painting. Each year, a selection of contemporary sculptures is installed in the open-air roof garden (open between May and October); have a sandwich there while taking in the panorama of Central Park. On weekend evenings, enjoy the classical quintet performing on the mezzanine overlooking the Great Hall. And don't forget the Costume Institute or the new Howard Gilman photography gallery. Foreign-language tours are available (212-570-3711).

Museum of Modern Art

11 W 53rd St between Fifth and Sixth Aves (212-708-9400) www.moma.org. Subway: E, F to Fifth Ave. Sat–Tue, Thu 10:30am–5:45pm; Fri 10:30am–8:15pm. $9.50, students and seniors $6.50, under 16 free if accompanied by an adult, voluntary donation Fri 4:30–8:15pm. No credit cards.
The Museum of Modern Art, or MoMA for short, holds the finest and most comprehensive collection of 20th-century art

Rock on: Transcend the material at the **Isamu Noguchi Museum** in Queens.

in the world. The permanent collection is exceptionally strong on works by Matisse, Picasso, Miró and later Modernists. The photo collection has major holdings by just about every important figure in the medium. The film and video department is simply outstanding, with a collection of more than 14,000 films; it hosts more than 20 screenings per week in two plush theaters (advance ticket purchase recommended). The elegant Italian restaurant Sette MoMA (212-708-9710) overlooks the lovely Abby Aldrich Rockefeller Sculpture Garden; an informal café is on the ground floor. Free gallery talks begin at 1pm and 3pm daily (except Wednesday) and on Thursday and Friday evenings at 6pm and 7pm. A sculpture touch-tour is available to visually impaired visitors by appointment (212-708-9864).

Other locations: P.S. 1 Contemporary Art Center, *22–25 Jackson Ave at 46th Ave, Long Island City, Queens (718-784-2084). Subway: E, F to 23rd St–Ely Ave; G to 21st St–Van Alst; 7 to 45th Rd–Court House Sq. Wed–Sun noon–6pm. Suggested donation $4.* Known for its cutting-edge exhibitions and international studio program, this alternative contemporary art space was recently acquired by MoMA; now, anything and everything is possible.

National Museum of the American Indian

George Gustav Heye Center, U.S. Customs House, 1 Bowling Green between State and Whitehall Sts (212-668-6624). Subway: 1, 9 to South Ferry; N, R to Whitehall St. Fri–Wed 10am–5pm; Thu 10am–8pm. Free. The galleries, resource center and two workshop rooms of this museum, a branch of the Smithsonian Institute's sprawling organization of museums and research institutes, occupies two floors of the grand rotunda in the exquisite old U.S. Customs House. Located just around the corner from Battery Park and the Ellis Island ferry, it offers displays based on a permanent collection of documents and artifacts that offer valuable insights into the realities of Native American history. Exhibitions are thoughtfully explained, usually by Native Americans. Of special interest is "All Roads Are Good," which reflects the personal choices of storytellers, weavers, anthropologists and tribal leaders. Only 500 of the collection's one million objects are on display, which is one reason that, despite the building's lofty proportions, the museum seems surprisingly small. A main branch, on the Mall in Washington, D.C., will open in 2002.

New Museum of Contemporary Art

583 Broadway between Houston and Prince Sts (212-219-1222) www.newmuseum.org. Subway: B, D, F, Q to Broadway–Lafayette St; N, R to Prince St; 6 to Bleecker St. Wed, Sun noon–6pm; Thu–Sat noon–8pm. $5, under 18 free, no admission charge Thu 6–8pm; concessions $3. AmEx, DC, Disc, MC, V. Since its founding in 1977, this Soho institution has been the focus of controversy. It quickly became a lightning rod for its fusion of art, technology and the politically correct with major group shows that gravitated heavily toward the experimental, the conceptual and the latest in multimedia presentations. Even its window displays drew crowds. Now a $3-million renovation and expansion of its Victorian cast-iron building has given it a friendlier entrance, an airy second-floor exhibition space and an intimate downstairs bookshop and reading room visible from the street. Although it continues to mount important midcareer retrospectives for underrecognized artists, the museum has adopted a broader, more international outlook.

Pierpont Morgan Library

29 E 36th St between Madison and Park Aves (212-685-0008). Subway: 6 to 33rd St. Tue–Thu 10:30am–5pm; Fri 10:30am–8pm; Sat 10:30am–6pm; Sun noon–6pm. $7, seniors and students $5, under 12 free. Concessions. No credit cards.

This beautiful Italianate museum—also an extraordinary literary-research facility—was once the private library of financier J. Pierpont Morgan. Mostly gathered during Morgan's trips to Europe, the collection includes three Gutenberg Bibles, original Mahler manuscripts and the gorgeous silver, copper and cloisonné 12th-century Stavelot triptych. A subtly colorful marble rotunda with carved 16th-century Italian ceiling separates the three-tiered library from the rich red study. Guided tours are available Tuesday through Friday at noon. There's also a modern conservatory attached to the museum, with a tranquil courtyard café.

Whitney Museum of American Art

945 Madison Ave at 75th St (212-570-3600, 212-570-3676). Subway: 6 to 77th St. Wed, Fri–Sun 11am–6pm; Thu 1–8pm. $12.50, students and seniors $10.50, children under 12 and members free, Thu 6–8pm free. AmEx, MC, V.
Like the Guggenheim, the Whitney sets itself apart first with its unique architecture: a gray granite cube designed by Marcel Breuer. Inside, the Whitney is a world unto itself, one whose often controversial exhibitions not only measure the historical importance of American art but mirror the culture of the moment. When Gertrude Vanderbilt Whitney, a sculptor and art patron, opened the museum in 1931, she dedicated it to living American artists. Its first exhibition consisted of work by eight artists. Today, the Whitney holds approximately 12,000 pieces, the work of nearly 2,000 artists, including Edward Hopper (the museum owns his entire estate), Andrew Wyeth, Arshile Gorky, Georgia O'Keeffe, Jackson Pollock, Alexander Calder, Alice Neel, Louise Nevelson, Jasper Johns, Andy Warhol, Agnes Martin and Jean-Michel Basquiat. The museum is also perhaps the country's foremost showcase for American independent film and video artists. Over the past decade, it has vastly expanded its collection of contemporary photography as well. Still, the Whitney's reputation rests mainly on its temporary shows, particularly the show everyone loves to hate: the Biennial Exhibition. Held every odd-numbered year, it remains the most prestigious assessment of contemporary American art in the U.S. The next Biennial has been postponed until March 2000 to make way for "The American Century," a huge two-part exhibition on view through mid-February 2000. There are free guided tours daily; the expanded gift shop next door is now accessible through a lobby passage. Sarabeth's (212-570-3670), the museum café, is open daily till 4:30pm and offers a lively, up-from-below view of Madison Avenue and food that is pricey but excellent.

Whitney Museum of American Art at Philip Morris

120 Park Ave at 42nd St (212-878-2550). Subway: S, 4, 5, 6, 7 to 42nd St–Grand Central. Mon–Fri 11am–6pm; Thu 11am–7:30pm; sculpture court Mon–Sat 7:30am–9:30pm; Sun 11am–7pm. Free.
The Whitney's Midtown branch, located in a lobby gallery, is devoted to changing solo projects by contemporary artists.

Art and design

American Academy and Institute of Arts and Letters

Audubon Terrace, Broadway between 155th and 156th Sts (212-368-5900). Subway: 1, 9 to 157th St. Thu–Sun 1–4pm. Free.
This organization honors 250 American writers, composers, painters, sculptors and architects. Edith Wharton, Mark Twain and Henry James were once members; today's list includes Terrence McNally, John Guare, Kurt Vonnegut and Alison Lurie. It's not actually a museum, but there are annual exhibitions open to the public and a magnificent library

of original manuscripts and first editions, open to researchers by appointment only.

American Craft Museum

40 W 53rd St between Fifth and Sixth Aves (212-956-3535). Subway: E, F to Fifth Ave. Tue, Wed, Fri–Sun 10am–6pm; Thu 10am–8pm. $5; concessions $2.50. No credit cards.
This is the country's leading art museum for 20th-century crafts in clay, fiber, glass, metal and wood. There are temporary shows on the four bright and spacious floors, and one or two exhibitions from the permanent collection each year, concentrating on a specific medium. The shop, though small, sells some unusually stylish jewelry and ceramics.

Dahesh Museum

601 Fifth Ave at 48th St (212-759-0606). Subway: B, D, F, Q to 47th–50th Sts–Rockefeller Ctr. Tue–Sat 11am–6pm. Free.
This jewel-box museum houses the private collection of Sallim Moussa Achi, a Lebanese philosopher with a consuming passion for European Academic art. The collection focuses on Orientalism, landscapes, scenes of rural life, and historical or mythical images painted by 19th- and early-20th-century artists whose work you won't see in public collections anywhere else.

Forbes Magazine Galleries

62 Fifth Ave at 12th St (212-206-5548). Subway: L, N, R, 4, 5, 6 to 14th St–Union Sq. Tue, Wed, Fri, Sat 10am–4pm. Free; under 16 must be accompanied by an adult.
The late magazine publisher Malcolm Forbes assembled this wonderful private collection of treasures. Besides toy boats and soldiers, the galleries showcase historic presidential letters and—best of all—a dozen Fabergé eggs and other superbly intricate pieces by the famous Russian jeweler and goldsmith Peter Carl Fabergé. Gallery hours are subject to change, so call to check before visiting.

The Museum at FIT

Seventh Ave at 27th St (212-217-7999). Subway: 1, 9 to 28th St. Tue–Fri noon–8pm; Sat 10am–5pm. Free.
The Fashion Institute of Technology has the world's largest collection of costumes and textiles; only two galleries are open to the public. Recent exhibitions have been devoted to designers such as Cristobal Balenciaga and Norman Norell but have also included East Village streetwear and a history of shoes.

Museum of American Folk Art

2 Lincoln Sq, Columbus Ave between 65th and 66th Sts (212-977-7298). Subway: 1, 9 to 66th St–Lincoln Ctr. Tue–Sun 11:30am–7:30pm. Free.
The exhibits are exquisite. The range of decorative, practical and ceremonial folk art encompasses pottery, trade signs, delicately stitched log-cabin quilts and even windup toys. The craftsmanship is often breathtaking. There are occasional lectures, demonstrations and performances, and a museum shop next door.

National Academy of Design

1083 Fifth Ave at 89th St (212-369-4880). Subway: 4, 5, 6 to 86th St. Wed, Thu, Sat, Sun noon–5pm; Fri 10am–6pm. $8, under 5 free, no admission charge Fri 5–8pm; concessions $3.50. No credit cards.
Housed in an elegant Fifth Avenue townhouse, the Academy comprises the School of Fine Arts and a museum containing one of the world's foremost collections of 19th- and 20th-century American art (painting, sculpture, architecture and engraving). The permanent collection includes works by Mary Cassatt, John Singer Sargent and Frank Lloyd Wright. Temporary exhibitions are always impressive.

Isamu Noguchi Garden Museum

32-37 Vernon Blvd at 33rd Rd, Long Island City, Queens (recorded information 718-204-7088) www.noguchi.org. Subway: N to Broadway. Shuttle bus from the Asia Society, 725 Park Ave at 70th St, every hour on the half-hour 11:30am–3:30pm. Apr–Oct Wed–Fri 10am–5pm; Sat, Sun 11am–6pm. Suggested donation $4; concessions $2. No credit cards.

Sculptor Isamu Noguchi designed stage sets for Martha Graham and George Balanchine, as well as sculpture parks and immense works of great simplicity and beauty. Noguchi's studios are now a showcase for his pieces—in 12 small galleries and a sculpture garden. There's a guided tour at 2pm (call 718-721-1932), and films are shown throughout the day.

Queens Museum of Art

New York City Building, Flushing Meadows–Corona Park, Queens (718-592-9700). Subway: 7 to 111th St. Wed–Fri 10am–5pm; Sat, Sun noon–5pm. Suggested donation $4, students and seniors $2, children under 5 free. No credit cards.

Located on the site of the 1964–65 World's Fair, the Queens Museum recently saw a thorough $15-million renovation. In addition to the art collections and fine, site-specific temporary exhibitions, the museum offers a permanent miniature model of New York City. It's fun to try to find where you're staying—rent binoculars for $1 apiece. Dusk falls every 15 minutes, revealing tiny illuminated buildings and a fluorescent Central Park. The model is constantly updated; there had been some 60,000 changes at the last count.

Nicholas Roerich Museum

319 W 107th St at Riverside Dr (212-864-7752). Subway: 1, 9 to 110th St. Tue–Sun 2–5pm. Donation requested.

Nicholas Roerich was a Russian-born philosopher, artist, architect, explorer, pacifist and scenery painter who collaborated with Nijinsky, Stravinsky and Diaghilev. The Roerich Peace Pact of 1935, an international agreement on the protection of cultural treasures, earned him a Nobel Peace Prize nomination. Roerich's wife bought this charming townhouse specifically as a museum to house her late husband's possessions. Paintings are mostly from his Tibetan travels and display his interest in mysticism. It's a fascinating place, but Roerich's intriguing life story tends to overshadow the museum.

Studio Museum in Harlem

144 W 125th St between Seventh Ave and Malcolm X Blvd (212-864-4500). Subway: 2, 3 to 125th St. Wed–Fri 10am–5pm; Sat, Sun 1–6pm. $5, no admission charge first Saturday of each month; concessions $1–$3. No credit cards.

The Studio Museum started out in 1967 as a rented loft space. In the next 20 years, it expanded onto two floors of a 60,000-square-foot (5,500-square-meter) building—a gift from a New York bank—and became the first black fine-arts museum in the country. Today, it shows changing exhibitions by African-American, African and Caribbean artists and continues its prestigious artists-in-residence program.

Municipal Art Society

457 Madison Ave between 50th and 51st Sts (212-935-3960, tour information 212-439-1049). Subway: E, F to Fifth Ave; 6 to 51st St. Mon–Wed, Fri, Sat 11am–5pm. Free.

This center for urban design was founded in 1980. It functions as a gallery, bookshop, lecture forum and campaign office, with exhibitions on architecture, public art and community-based projects. The MAS is also headquarters of the Architectural League and the Parks Council. Its greatest attraction may be its location: inside the historic Villard Houses, opposite St. Patrick's Cathedral.

Arts and culture

Ethnic

Asia Society

725 Park Ave at 70th St (212-517-2742). Subway: 6 to 68th St. Tue, Wed, Fri, Sat 11am–6pm; Thu 11am–8pm; Sun noon–5pm. $4, under 12 free if accompanied by an adult, no admission charge Thu 6–8pm; concessions $1. No credit cards.

The stalwart eight-story headquarters of the Asia Society reflects its importance in promoting Asian-American relations. It sponsors study missions and conferences, and promotes public programs on both continents. Galleries show major art exhibitions from public and private collections, including the permanent Mr. and Mrs. John D. Rockefeller III collection of Asian art. Asian musicians and performers often play here; call for a schedule.

China Institute in America

125 E 65th St between Park and Lexington Aves (212-744-8181). Subway: 6 to 68th St. Mon, Wed, Fri, Sat 10am–5pm; Sun 1–5pm; Tue, Thu 10am–8pm. Suggested donation $3, children under 12 free; concessions $3. AmEx, MC, V.

With just two small gallery rooms, the China Institute is somewhat overshadowed by the Asia Society. But its exhibitions, ranging from works by Chinese women artists to selections from the Beijing Palace Museum, are impressive. The society also offers lectures and courses on such subjects as cooking, calligraphy and Confucianism.

French Institute–Alliance Française

55 E 59th St between Madison and Park Aves (212-355-6160). Subway: N, R to Lexington Ave; 4, 5, 6 to 59th St. Mon–Thu 9am–8pm; Fri 9am–6pm; Sat 9am–1:30pm. Free.

This is the New York home for all things French: The Institute (or the Alliance Française) holds the city's most extensive all-French library and offers numerous language classes and cultural seminars. There are also French film screenings and live dance, music and theater performances.

Garibaldi-Meucci Museum

420 Tompkins Ave between Chesnut Ave and Shaughnessy Ln, Staten Island (718-442-1608). Travel: Staten Island Ferry, then S52 bus. Tue–Sun 1–5pm. Suggested donation $3.

The 1840s Gothic revival home of Italian inventor Antonio Meucci, this museum is also the former refuge of Italian patriot Antonio Garibaldi.

Goethe-Institut/German Cultural Center

1014 Fifth Ave at 82nd St (212-439-8700). Subway: 4, 5, 6 to 86th St. Library: Tue, Thu noon–7pm; Wed, Sat noon–5pm. Gallery: Tue, Thu 10am–7pm; Wed 10am–5:30pm; Fri 10am–4pm; Sat noon–5pm. Free.

Goethe-Institut New York is just one branch of a German multinational cultural organization founded in 1951. Located across the street from the Metropolitan Museum in a landmark Fifth Avenue mansion, it mounts shows featuring German-born contemporary artists, as well as concerts, film screenings and lectures. A library offers books in German or English, German periodicals, videos and audiocassettes.

Hispanic Society of America

Audubon Terrace, Broadway between 155th and 156th Sts (212-926-2234). Subway: 1 to 157th St. Tue–Sat 10am–4:30pm; Sun 1–4pm. Library: Tue–Fri 1–4:30pm; Sat 10am–4:30pm. Free.

Two limestone lions flank the entrance to this majestic building in Hamilton Heights, a gentrified area of Harlem. Outside, an equestrian statue of El Cid, Spain's medieval hero, stands on the Beaux Arts terrace between the society's two

Mondo monographs: The **New Museum**'s bookstore stocks the latest art publications.

buildings. Inside, there's an ornate Spanish Renaissance court and an upper gallery lined with paintings by El Greco, Goya and Velázquez. The collection is dominated by religious artifacts, including a number of 16th-century tombs from the monastery of San Francisco in Cuéllar, Spain.

Japan Society
333 E 47th St between First and Second Aves (212-752-3015). Subway: E, F to Lexington Ave; 6 to 51st St. Tue–Sun 11am–6pm (during exhibitions only). Suggested donation $3. No credit cards.
The Japan Society promotes cultural exchange programs and special events plus exhibitions three or four times a year. The gallery shows both traditional and contemporary Japanese art. The society's film center is a major showcase for Japanese cinema in the U.S. There's also a library and language center in the lower lobby wing.

Jewish Museum
1109 Fifth Ave at 92nd St (212-423-3230). Subway: 4, 5, 6 to 86th St. Mon, Wed, Thu, Sun 11am–5:45pm; Tue 11am–8pm. $8, under 12 free, no admission charge Tue 5–8pm; concessions $5. No credit cards.
A fascinating collection of art, artifacts and media installations, the Jewish Museum is housed in the 1908 Warburg Mansion, which was renovated in 1993 to include the underground Café Weissman. The museum commissions a contemporary artist or group of artists to install a new show each year, and the results are always stellar. The permanent exhibition tracks the Jewish cultural experience through exhibits ranging from a 16th-century mosaic wall from a Persian synagogue and a filigree silver circumcision set to an interactive Talmud—there's even a Statue of Liberty Hanukkah lamp. Most of this eclectic collection was rescued from European synagogues before World War II.

El Museo del Barrio
1230 Fifth Ave between 104th and 105th Sts (212-831-7272). Subway: 6 to 103rd St. Wed–Sun 11am–5pm. Donation $4, under 12 free; concessions $2. AmEx, MC, V.

At the top of Museum Mile, not far from Spanish Harlem (the neighborhood from which it takes its name), El Museo del Barrio is dedicated to the work of Hispanic artists in the United States as well as that of Latin Americans. Typical exhibitions are contemporary and consciousness-raising; El Museo also sponsors community events like the festive annual celebration of the Mexican Day of the Dead (Nov 1).

Museum for African Art
593 Broadway between Houston and Prince Sts (212-966-1313). Subway: B, D, F, Q to Broadway–Lafayette St; N, R to Prince St; 6 to Bleecker St. Tue–Fri 10:30am–5:30pm; Sat, Sun noon–6pm. $5, under 2 free; concessions $2.50. MC, V (over $10).
This tranquil museum was designed by Maya Lin, who also created the stunningly simple Vietnam Veterans' Memorial in Washington, D.C. Exhibits change about twice a year; the quality of the works shown is high, and they often come from amazing private collections. There's an unusually good bookshop with a children's section.

Museum of Jewish Heritage: A Living Memorial to the Holocaust
18 First Pl at Battery Pl, Battery Park City (212-968-1800). Subway: 1, 9 to Rector St. Sun–Wed 9am–5pm; Thurs 9am–8pm; Fri and holiday eves 9am–2pm; closed Saturdays and Jewish holidays. $7, students and seniors $5, under 5 free. Advance ticket purchase recommended; call the museum or Ticketmaster (212-307-4007).
You don't have to be Jewish to appreciate the contents of this institution, built in a symbolic six-sided shape (recalling the Star of David) under a tiered roof. Opened in 1997, it offers people of all backgrounds one of the most moving cultural experiences in the city. The well-thought-out exhibits feature 2,000 photographs, hundreds of surviving cultural artifacts and plenty of archival films that vividly detail the crime against humanity that was the Holocaust. The exhibition continues beyond those dark times into days of renewal, ending in an upper gallery that is flooded with daylight and gives especially meaningful views of Lady

*If the shoe fits: The **Museum at FIT** collects everything from sandals to stilettos.*

Liberty in the harbor. It's an unforgettable experience. Closed-captioned video is available.

Tibetan Museum
338 Lighthouse Ave off Richmond Rd, Staten Island (recorded information 718-987-3500). Travel: 1,9 to South Ferry, then Staten Island Ferry and S78 bus. Apr–Nov Wed–Sun 1–5pm; Dec–March Wed–Fri 1–5pm. $3. No credit cards.
This mock Tibetan temple stands on a hilltop high above sea level. It contains a fascinating Buddhist altar and the largest collection of Tibetan art in the West, including religious objects, bronzes and paintings. There's a comprehensive English-language library containing books on Buddhism, as well as on Tibet and Asian art. The landscaped gardens house a zoo of stone animals (with birdhouses and wishing well) and offer good views.

Yeshiva University Museum
2520 Amsterdam Ave at 185th Street (212-960-5390). Subway: 1 to 181st St. Tue–Thu 10:30am–5pm; Sun noon–6pm. $3; concessions $2. No credit cards.
The museum usually hosts one major exhibition a year and several smaller ones, mainly on Jewish themes.

Historical

American Numismatic Society
Audubon Terrace between 155th and 156th Sts (212-234-3130). Subway: 1 to 157th St. Tue–Sat 9am–4:30pm; Sun 1–4pm. Free.
The collection covers 26 centuries of filthy lucre.

Brooklyn Historical Society
128 Pierrepont St at Clinton St, Brooklyn Heights, Brooklyn (718-624-0890). Subway: N, R to Court St; 2, 3, 4, 5 to Borough Hall. Mon, Thu–Sat noon–5pm. $2.50, no admission charge Mondays; concessions $1. No credit cards.
What do Woody Allen, Mae West, Isaac Asimov, Mel Brooks and Walt Whitman have in common? Answer: They were

all—along with Al Capone, Barry Manilow and Gypsy Rose Lee—born in Brooklyn. Thus they merit tributes in this tiny, recently refurbished museum dedicated to Brooklyn's past glories. There are displays on the borough's firefighters, its Navy Yard and its famous baseball team, the Dodgers, who won the World Series in 1955—only to break Brooklyn's heart by moving to Los Angeles two years later.

Fraunces Tavern Museum
54 Pearl St at Broad St, second and third floors (212-425-1778). Subway: 1, 9 to South Ferry. Mon–Fri 10am–4:45pm; Sat, Sun noon–4pm. $2.50, under 6 free; concessions $1. No credit cards.
This tavern used to be George Washington's watering hole and was a prominent meeting place for anti-British groups before the Revolution. The 18th-century building, which has been partly reconstructed, is unexpectedly quaint, considering its setting on the fringes of the financial district. Most of its artifacts are displayed in period rooms. The changing exhibitions are often interesting.

Hall of Fame for Great Americans
Hall of Fame Terrace, 181st St and University Ave, Bronx (718-289-5161). Subway: 4 to Burnside Ave. 10am–5pm. Free.
The Hall of Fame is a covered walkway lined with bronze busts of preeminent Americans, with sections devoted to scientists, authors, soldiers and statesmen. As the last two categories suggest, the tributees are mostly male, among them the Wright Brothers, Thomas Mann and Franklin D. Roosevelt. The Hall isn't very heavily visited—the subway ride is long, and then it's a 20-minute walk through the Bronx to its home behind Bronx Community College. On the other hand, it does sit on the highest natural summit of New York City—a getaway!

Lower East Side Tenement Museum
90 Orchard St at Broome St (212-431-0233). Subway: F to Delancey St; J, M, Z, to Essex St; B, D, Q to Grand St. Visitors' Center: Tue–Fri noon–5pm; Sat, Sun 11am–5pm. $8; concessions $6. AmEx, MC, V.
For a fascinating look at the history of immigration, visit this 19th-century tenement. The building, in the heart of what was once Little Germany, contains two reconstructed apartments belonging to a German Jewish dressmaker and a Sicilian Catholic family; tours are obligatory if you want to see the tenement itself; it's worth booking ahead, since they sell out. Tours are Tuesday through Friday every half hour 1 to 4pm; Thursday at 6 and 7pm; Saturday, Sunday every half hour 11am to 4:30pm. The museum also has a gallery, shop and video room, and organizes local-heritage walking tours.

Merchant's House Museum
29 E 4th St between Lafayette St and Bowery (212-777-1089). Subway: 6 to Astor Pl. Mon–Thu, Sun 1–4pm. $5, under 12 free if accompanied by an adult; concessions $2. No credit cards.
Seabury Tredwell was the merchant in question. He made his fortune selling hardware and bought this elegant Greek Revival house three years after it was built in 1832. The house has been virtually untouched since the 1860s; decoration is spare (except for the lavish canopied four-poster beds) and ornamentation tasteful. Guided tours are conducted on Sundays; call for details.

Museum of the City of New York
1220 Fifth Ave at 103rd St (212-534-1672) www.mcny.org. Subway: 6 to 103rd St. Wed–Sat 10am–5pm; Sun noon–5pm. Suggested donation $5; concessions $4. No credit cards.
Several ongoing exhibitions showcase the vast, fascinating history of New York City. Recent installations have examined George Washington's time in NYC, the 50th anniversary of *South Pacific's* Broadway premiere and the Astor Place Riots.

New York Historical Society
*2 W 77th St at Central Park West (212-873-3400).
Subway: B, C to 81st St. Tue–Sun 11am–5pm. Suggested
donation $5; concessions $3. No credit cards.*
The society, which had been closed for several years after running out of money, is back in business. Founded in 1804, it was one of America's first cultural-educational institutions and is New York's oldest museum. Exhibitions can include anything from Paul Robeson's diaries to a display about Pocahontas. The permanent collection includes such items as Tiffany lamps, lithographs and a lock of George Washington's hair.

Skyscraper Museum
*16 Wall St at Nassau St (212-968-1961). Subway: J, M,
Z to Broad St; 2, 3, 4, 5 to Wall St. Tue–Sat noon–6pm.*
This museum in lower Manhattan recently moved to a 1931 Art Deco banking hall designed by the same architects as the Empire State Building. Inside you'll find a lavish history of the world's tallest buildings—past, present and future—as told though photos, architectural drawings, contracts, builder's records and other artifacts.

Abigail Adams Smith Museum
*421 E 61st St at First Ave (212-838-6878). Subway: N, R
to Lexington Ave; 4, 5, 6 to 59th St. Tue–Sun 11am–
4pm. $3, under 5 free; concessions $2. No credit cards.*
This 18th-century coach house once belonged to the daughter of John Adams, the second president of the U.S. The house is filled with period articles and furniture (Abigail died in 1813), and there's an adjoining formal garden.

South Street Seaport Museum
*Herman Melville Gallery, 213 Water St at Beekman St
(212-748-8600). Subway: A, C to Broadway–Nassau St;
2, 3, 4, 5 to Fulton St. Wed–Mon 10am–6pm. $6;
concessions $3–$6. AmEx, MC, V.*
The museum sprawls across 11 blocks along the East River—an amalgam of galleries, historic ships, 19th-century buildings and a visitors' center. The staff (mostly volunteers) is friendly, and it's fun to wander around the rebuilt streets, popping in to see an exhibition on tattooing before climbing aboard the four-masted 1911 *Peking*. The Seaport itself is pretty touristy, but still a charming place to spend an afternoon. Near the Fulton Fish Market building, there are plenty of cafés to choose from.

The Statue of Liberty and Ellis Island Immigration Museum
*Travel: 4, 5 to Bowling Green, then ferry from Battery
Park to Liberty Island and Ellis Island (212-363-3200,
ferry information 212-269-5755). Ferries every half hour
daily 9:15am–3:30pm. $7; concessions $3–$5, including
admission. Ticket sales at Castle Clinton, Battery Park,
8:30am–3:30pm. No credit cards.*
There's an interesting museum devoted to the statue's history contained in the pedestal itself. On the way back to Manhattan, the tour boat takes you to the Immigration Museum on Ellis Island, where more than 12 million people entered the country. The exhibitions are an evocative and moving tribute to anyone who headed for America with dreams of a better life. The audio tour (available in five languages; $3.50, concessions $2.50–$3) is excellent.

Waterfront Museum
*290 Conover St, Red Hook Garden Pier, Red Hook,
Brooklyn (718-624-4719) www.myplanet.net/
waterfrontmuseum. Travel: M, N, R to Court St; A, C, F to
Jay St–Borough Hall; 2, 3, 4, 5 to Borough Hall. Then B61
bus toward Red Hook from either Jay and Willoughby Sts
or Atlantic and Court Sts to Beard St stop. Walk one block
west to Conover St. Barge is 2 blocks south. Garden Pier
open daily 24 hours; Barge open during special
events only. Call for schedule. Free.*

Documenting New York's history as a port, this museum is located on a 1914 Lehigh Valley Railroad Barge. Listed on the National Register of Historic Places, it's the only surviving wooden barge of its kind afloat today. See superb views of Manhattan and the working New York harbor.

Media

American Museum of the Moving Image
*35th Ave at 36th St, Astoria, Queens
(718-784-0077). Subway: G, R to Steinway St. Tue–Fri
noon–5pm; Sat, Sun 11am–6pm. $8.50; concessions
$4–$5. No credit cards.*
Only about a 15-minute subway ride from midtown Manhattan, AMMI is one of the city's most dynamic and entertaining institutions. Built within the restored complex that once housed the original Astoria studios (where commercial filmmaking got its start and continues today), it offers an extensive daily film and video program that should satisfy even the most demanding cinephile. If you're curious about the mechanics and history of movie and television production, the core exhibition, "Behind the Screen," will give you intensely interactive insight into every aspect of it—storyboarding, directing, editing, sound-mixing and marketing. You can even make your own short at a digital animation stand. The museum has a café, but there are other restaurant options nearby; as the largest Greek community outside Greece, Astoria boasts some terrific Greek restaurants.

Museum of Television and Radio
*25 W 52nd St between Fifth and Sixth Aves (212-621-
6600). Subway: E, F to Fifth Ave; B, D, F, Q to 47th–
50th Sts–Rockefeller Ctr. Tue, Wed, Fri–Sun noon–6pm;
Thu noon–8pm. $6; concessions $3–$4. No credit cards.*
This is a living, working archive of more than 60,000 radio and TV programs. Head to the fourth-floor library and use the computerized system to access a favorite *Star Trek* or *I Love Lucy* episode. The assigned console downstairs will play up to four of your choices within two hours. The radio listening room works the same way. There are also special public seminars and screenings. It's a must for TV and radio addicts.

Newseum/NY
*580 Madison Ave between 56th and 57th Sts
(212-317-7503, recorded information 212-317-7596)
www.mediastudies.org. Subway: E, F, N, R to Fifth
Ave. Mon–Sat 10am–5:30pm. Free.*
These are the branch galleries of a Washington, D.C. center for media studies, and the entrance through a pleasant, glassenclosed atrium of a midtown office tower hardly prepares visitors for the intensity of what lies ahead. Newseum/NY presents topical photography exhibitions that illuminate, with no small emotional impact, the work of prize-winning news photographers and correspondents the world over. Sponsored by the Freedom Forum, it also presents accompanying film and lecture series that encourage public discussion of First Amendment issues. Exhibitions change three or four times a year. Documentaries screen at 1pm every Monday and Friday and run about an hour; reservations are not necessary.

Military

Intrepid Sea, Air and Space Museum
*USS Intrepid, Pier 86, 46th St at the Hudson River
(212-245-2533, recorded information 212-245-0072).
Subway: A, C, E to 42nd St–Port Authority. Memorial
Day–Labor Day Mon–Sat 10am–5pm; Sun 10am–6pm;
Labor Day–Memorial Day Mon–Wed, Sun 10am–5pm.
$10; concessions $5–$7.50. AmEx, MC, V.*
This museum is located on the World War II aircraft carrier *Intrepid*, whose decks are crammed with space capsules and various aircraft. There are plenty of audiovisual shows and hands-on exhibits to appeal to children.

*Kenya touch it? No, but there's still a lot to admire at the **Museum for African Art**.*

New York Public Library

The multitentacled New York Public Library, founded in 1895, comprises four major research libraries and 82 local and specialist branches, making it the largest and most comprehensive library system in the world. The library grew from the combined collections of John Jacob Astor, Samuel Jones Tilden and James Lenox. Today, it holds a total of 50 million items, including nearly 18 million books, with around a million items added to the collection each year. Unless you're interested in a specific subject, your best bet is to visit the system's flagship building, officially called the Center for the Humanities. The newest branch, the Science, Industry and Business Library, opened in 1996.

Center for the Humanities

455 Fifth Ave at 42nd St (recorded information 212-869-8089) www.nypl.org. Subway: B, D, F, Q to 42nd St; 7 to Fifth Ave. Mon, Thu–Sat 10am–6pm; Tue, Wed 11am–6pm.
This landmark Beaux Arts building is what most people call the New York Public Library. The famous stone lions out front are wreathed with holly at Christmas; during the summer people sit on the steps or sip cool drinks at the outdoor tables beneath the arches. The free guided tours of the building at 11am and 2pm include the beautiful reading room (recently renovated); the first Gutenberg Bible brought to America; and a handwritten copy of George Washington's farewell address. The Bill Blass Public Catalogue Room was recently restored and renovated and now contains computers for surfing the Internet. Special exhibitions are frequent and always worthwhile, and lectures in the Celeste Bartos Forum are always well attended.

Donnell Library Center

20 W 53rd St between Fifth and Sixth Aves (212-621-0618). Subway: E, F to Fifth Ave. Mon, Wed, Fri 10am–6pm; Tue, Thu 10am–8pm; Sat 10am–5pm. Free.
This branch of the NYPL has an extensive collection of records, films and videotapes, with appropriate screening facilities. The Donnell specializes in foreign-language books—in more than 80 languages—and there's a children's section of more than 100,000 books, films, records and cassettes…and the original Winnie the Pooh dolls.

Library for the Performing Arts

Lincoln Center, 111 Amsterdam Ave between 65th and 66th Sts (212-870-1630). Subway: 1, 9 to 66th St–Lincoln Ctr. Free.
This facility with outstanding research and circulating collections covering music, drama, theater and dance is closed until late 2000 for renovations. For the circulation section, visit the Mid-Manhattan Library, 455 Fifth Ave; and for the research materials go to the Library Annex, 521 W 43rd St.

Science, Industry and Business Library

188 Madison Ave between 34th and 35th Sts (212-930-0747) www.nypl.org/research/sibl/index.html. Subway: 6 to 33rd St. Mon, Fri, Sat 10am–6pm; Tue–Thu 11am–7pm. Free.
The world's largest public information center devoted to science, technology, economics and business occupies the first floor and lower level of the old B. Altman department store. Opened in 1996 after a $100 million renovation, the new Gwathmey Siegel–designed branch of the NYPL has a circulating collection of 50,000 books and an open-shelf reference collection of 60,000 volumes. Aiming to help people in small businesses, the library also specializes in digital technologies and the Internet.

Schomburg Center for Research in Black Culture

515 Malcolm X Blvd at 135th St (212-491-2200) www.nypl.org/research/sc/sc.html. Subway: 2, 3 to 135th St. Mon–Wed noon–8pm; Thu–Sat 10am–6pm; Sun 1pm–5pm. Free. Tours by appointment.
This extraordinary trove of vintage literature and historical memorabilia relating to black culture and the African diaspora was founded by its first curator, Puerto Rico–born bibliophile Arthur Schomburg, who established the collection in 1926. The Schomburg also hosts live jazz concerts, films, lectures and tours (*see* **Black pride** *page 77*).

Science and technology

Liberty Science Center

Liberty State Park, 251 Phillip St, Jersey City, NJ (recorded information 201-200-1000). Travel: PATH train to Grove St, then connecting park bus; weekend ferry service (info 800-533-3779). Tue–Sun 9:30am–5:30pm. Exhibition halls $9.50, concessions $6.50–$8.50; halls and Omnimax cinema $7, concessions $9.50–$11.50. AmEx, Disc, MC, V.
This is an excellent museum with innovative exhibitions and America's largest and most spectacular Imax cinema. The observation tower provides great views of Manhattan and an unusual sideways look at the Statue of Liberty. The center's emphasis is on hands-on science, so get ready to elbow your way among the excited kids. It's pleasant to arrive by ferry on the weekend.

New York Hall of Science

47–01 111th St at 46th Ave, Flushing Meadows, Queens (718-699-0005) www.nyhallsci.org. Subway: 7 to 111th St. Group bookings Mon–Wed 9:30am–2pm; Thu–Sun 9:30am–5pm. $6; concessions $3. AmEx, MC, V.
Since its opening during the 1964–65 World's Fair, the New York Hall of Science has built the largest collection of hands-on science exhibits in the city; it's now considered one of the top science museums in the country. The emphasis here is on education, and the place is usually filled with schoolchildren, for whom it successfully demystifies science with stimulating interactive exhibits. The museum includes a 48-foot-high entrance rotunda, a new dining pavilion and a 300-seat auditorium.

Urban services

Fire Museum

278 Spring St at Varick St (212-691-1303). Subway: 1, 9 to Houston St. Tue–Sun 10am–4pm. Suggested donation $4; concessions $1–$2. AmEx, MC, V.
This small but cheerful museum is located in an old three-story firehouse whose pole still gleams next to a few vintage fire engines and several displays of fireman ephemera dating back 100 years. Two tours a day allow groups of up to 30.

New York Transit Museum

Schermerhorn St at Boerum Pl, Brooklyn Heights, Brooklyn (718-243-3060). Subway: M, N, R to Court St; G to Hoyt–Schermerhorn Sts; 2, 3, 4, 5 to Borough Hall. Tue, Thu, Fri 10am–4pm; Sat, Sun noon–5pm. $3; concessions $1.50. No credit cards.
Don't look for a building—the Transit Museum is housed underground in an old 1930s subway station. Its entrance, down a flight of stairs, is beneath the Board of Education building, opposite the black-and-white-striped New York City Transit Authority building. Nose around vintage subways with wicker seats and canvas straps, a selection of antique turnstiles and plenty of ads and public service announcements—including one explaining that spitting "is a violation of the sanitary code." So there!

Music

*Music lovers, get your ear plugs, your dancing shoes and
your ID, and head out into the wonderland*

Popular music

New Yorkers have always been spoiled when it comes to music: The mix of cultures and styles found in this city results in the most amazing permutations. Here, hip-hoppers can pick up guitars and saxes, punk rockers can play that funky music, and be-boppers can kick that Afro-Caribbean flavor. And it's *all* good.

New York nightlife, however, can be as specialized and categorized as the racks at Virgin Megastore. The days of barely legal venues stirring up untelevised revolutions are, for the moment, gone. These days, most clubs are as eager to comply with Mayor Giuliani's puritanical "Quality of Life" laws as they are to book grade-A music.

Which isn't to say the scene is totally dead. Wetlands Preserve has managed to become both

a home to crusty Phish wanna-bes and the Roots' live hip-hop jam sessions. Brownies, an East Village rock spot, recently installed a DJ booth for late-night dance parties. For some time now, the legendary CBGB club has hosted simultaneous punk extravaganzas and dub parties.

In a nutshell, knowing where to go in NYC is strictly a matter of taste. Want loud rock? Head to Coney Island High. Need a shot of reggae? Hop a cab to S.O.B.'s. Craving a bit of jazz? There's always the Village Vanguard. Following is a list of ideas for you music-hungry travelers. For more complete music listings, venues and information on upcoming shows, check *Time Out New York*. *The Village Voice* and *New York Press* also have listings; they're both free and are available in stores, in sidewalk vending boxes and at some newsstands. For more live music venues, *see chapters* **Clubs**, **Cabaret & Comedy** and **Gay & Lesbian**. If you want to drink alcohol

*Lady sings the blues: Abbey Lincoln is one of many jazz greats to play the legendary **Blue Note**.*

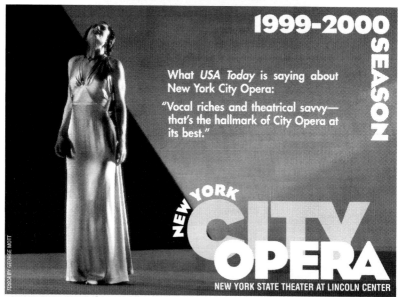

at any of these venues, bring a photo ID that indicates your age. Even if you are obviously 21 or older, you'll probably be asked to prove it. You can generally buy tickets at the door. However, for the larger venues, you should purchase them in advance (sometimes weeks ahead for popular artists), which can be done by phone. For more ticket info *see* **Classical & Opera,** *page 265.*

Arenas

Continental Airlines Arena
East Rutherford, NJ (201-935-3900). Travel: NJ Transit bus from Port Authority Bus Terminal (212-564-8484). From $22.50. No credit cards.
New Jersey's answer to Madison Square Garden is the Meadowlands Complex, and it's the place to see Jersey natives Bon Jovi and Bruce Springsteen, or perhaps a visiting Rage Against the Machine and Celine Dion.

Madison Square Garden
Seventh Ave at 32nd St (212-465-6741). Subway: A, C, E, 1, 2, 3, 9 to 34th St–Penn Station. $22.50–$75. No credit cards.
Awright, Noo Yawk! Are you ready to rock & roll? The acoustics here may be more suited to the crunch of hockey and the slap of basketball, but MSG is the most famous rock venue the world over. It packs them in for massive events by folks such as Kiss and Puff Daddy and the Family. Just don't be shocked at the ticket prices for the megastars.

Nassau Coliseum
1255 Hempstead Turnpike, Uniondale, NY (516-794-9303). Travel: LIRR to Hempstead, then N70, N71, N72 bus. From $22.50. No credit cards.
Nassau Coliseum is Long Island's answer to Continental Airlines Arena. As such, it doesn't have a lot of character, but that quality isn't usually required for enormdomes, is it? Many of the same shows that play MSG and the Continental Airlines Arena come here as well, although the Coliseum is probably the quintessential venue for viewing Billy Joel, the pride of Long Island.

Concert halls, theaters and ballrooms

92nd Street Y
See **Classical & Opera,** *page 266, for listings.*
The superstars who perform at this century-old bastion of cultural events are generally established poets and other tweedy types, but the Y's music program is surprisingly variegated. In addition to contemporary classical music, the schedule extends to gospel, various indigenous folkloric styles and jazz of the mainstream variety. Jazz in July, the program's centerpiece, entices both young and old swingers into the comfy surroundings.

Apollo Theatre
253 W 125th St between Malcolm X and Adam Clayton Powell Jr. Blvds (Lenox and Seventh Aves) (212-749-5838). Subway: A, C, B, D, 2, 3 to 125th St. $9–$30. AmEx, MC, V.
In its heyday, there was no place as atmospheric as this classic Harlem spot to see a hip-hop or R&B gig, as well as Wednesday's Amateur Night. Once a launching pad for stars such as Ella Fitzgerald and Michael Jackson, it is now full of black comedians and soul singers hitting as many notes as they can before they reach the right one. Taped for TV's *Showtime at the Apollo,* Amateur Night is a fun way to see the Apollo audience in all its glory. There's an obvious police

presence, especially for the big hip-hop events with the likes of Big Pun and Fat Joe—which means there's no need to worry about venturing into Harlem at night.

Beacon Theatre
2124 Broadway at 74th St (212-496-7070). Subway: 1, 2, 3, 9 to 72nd St. $30–$80. No credit cards.
The Beacon is almost like the legendary Fillmore East transplanted to the Upper West Side. What else can you say about the site of the Allman Brothers' annual monthlong residency? The odd Off Broadway show, like Kenny Rogers's annual holiday extravaganza, takes place here, but the name of the game here is music.

Brooklyn Academy of Music
See **Classical & Opera,** *page 265, for listings.*
Jazz and pop-based world music don't generally wander into this hallowed hall until the fall, when the Next Wave Festival of cutting-edge music, theater and dance sets up shop. *See chapters* **New York by Season, Dance** *and* **Theater.**

Carnegie Hall
See **Classical & Opera,** *page 265, for listings.*
Although a gig at Carnegie is still synonymous with hitting the big time, nowadays, many of the venue's showcases are simply a reminder that the hall's acoustics were designed for classical music—period. Of course, that doesn't stop the folk veterans in the Band from playing here annually, and it didn't stop Carnegie's honchos from launching a yearlong jazz program under the direction of superstar trumpeter Jon Faddis. In between, you might catch world-renowned pop stars such as Barry Manilow and João Gilberto.

Colden Center for the Performing Arts
See **Classical & Opera,** *page 265, for listings.*

Florence Gould Hall at the Alliance Française
See **Classical & Opera,** *page 265, for listings.*

Merkin Concert Hall
See **Classical & Opera,** *page 266, for listings.*
The Merkin Hall lies just across the street from Lincoln Center's performing arts complex. Its smaller, equally elegant digs provide an intimate setting for jazz and experimental music that isn't likely to get heard at Alice Tully or Avery Fisher Hall.

New Jersey Performing Arts Center
See **Classical & Opera,** *page 266, for listings.*

Radio City Music Hall
1260 Sixth Ave at 50th St (212-247-4777). Subway: B, D, F, Q to 47–50th St–Rockefeller Ctr. From $25. No credit cards.
The most awe-inspiring Art Deco hall in New York, if not the world, Radio City Music Hall is almost as exciting as its superstar performance roster. In addition to acts as varied as Erykah Badu and Elvis Costello playing with Burt Bacharach, this show palace is also home to the annual Christmas Spectacular (featuring the Rockettes!) and family fare like the *Rugrats* tour. *See chapter* **New York by Season.**

Symphony Space
2537 Broadway at 95th St (212-864-1414). Subway: 1, 2, 3, 9 to 96th St. $10–$25. AmEx, MC, V.
Although Symphony Space plays host to a plethora of music from pop to classical, the 1,000-seat hall is probably best known as the stronghold for the multiculti concerts presented by the World Music Institute. The crowds register as much enthusiasm for Malian soulstress Oumou Sangare and Gypsy revelers Haidouks as they do for the Cuban song-and-dance troupe Los Muñequitos de Matanzas. Almost without

fail, many local homesick nationals end up dancing onstage with the visiting stars by concert's end.

The Theater at Madison Square Garden

Seventh Ave at 32nd St (212-465-6741). Subway: A, C, E, 1, 2, 3, 9 to 34th St–Penn Station. Prices vary. No credit cards.
This is a smaller, classier version of Madison Square Garden—and since it's not an arena it sounds better. The Theater hosts both pop neophytes (Lauryn Hill) and old-timers (Luther Vandross), who probably could sell out the Garden anyway but want that intimate vibe .

Town Hall

123 W 43rd St between Sixth and Seventh Aves (212-840-2824). Subway: B, D, F, Q to 42nd St; N, R, S, 1, 2, 3, 9, 7 to 42nd St–Times Sq. $15–$25. V, MC, AmEx.
A venerable theater with ear-pleasing acoustics and seats for everyone, Town Hall was conceived as the people's auditorium, and its democratic bookings keep that spirit alive today. In addition to shows by folk stars such as Kate and Anna McGarrigle, you can also catch showcases by disco institutions like Martha Wash, French atmospherists Air and Fred Hersch, and plenty of Celtic and world-beat events.

Large and midsize venues

Bowery Ballroom

6 Delancey St between Bowery and Chrystie St (212-533-2111). Subway: 6 to Spring St; J, M to Bowery. $1–20. V, MC bar only.
In a remarkably short time since opening in May 1998, this roomy outpost of the Mercury Lounge has become the most coveted venue in town for rock acts (Patti Smith, R.E.M.) as well as for DJ sets by the likes of the Chemical Brothers and Fatboy Slim. Astute booking and splendid acoustics and sightlines are only half the story, as there are spacious bars downstairs and overlooking the stage. It's ideal for those "I loathe this band but still want to drink here" moments.

Hammerstein Ballroom

Manhattan Center, 311 W 34th St between Eighth and Ninth Aves (212-564-4882). Subway: A, C, E to 34th St. $10–$20. No credit cards.
Built inside the Moonie-owned Manhattan Center, the Hammerstein Ballroom is a multitiered space that is the favored venue for visiting electronicists like Underworld, the Orb and Massive Attack, as well as alterna-titans like Radiohead and Björk. Although an acoustic nightmare—the sound hardly seems loud enough—the stage visibility is pretty good.

Irving Plaza

17 Irving Pl at 15th St (212-777-6800). Subway: L, N, R, 4, 5, 6 to 14th St–Union Sq. $10–$30. No credit cards.
For quite some time, Irving Plaza was unique: a midsize venue that was very often the first stop to superstardom for aspiring national touring acts. Now, there's competition, but Irving is still nothing to sniff at. Elegant decor, an upstairs lounge and a giant screen playing videos and TV-footage collages from the Emergency Broadcast Network complement a sterling booking reputation. Baaba Maal, Lucinda Williams, the Residents, Kruder & Dorfmeister and loads of up-and-coming acts played here in the last year.

Roseland

239 W 52nd St between Broadway and Eighth Ave (212-245-5761, concert hot line 212-249-8870). Subway: B, D, E to Seventh Ave; C, 1, 9 to 50th St. From $15. No credit cards.
Once upon a time, going to Roseland was a dreadful experience, simply because the 1930s-era ballroom never seemed

able to cope well with sell-out rock crowds. But with the introduction of a new mezzanine, this next-step-before-arenadom is far more palatable. Once the natural preserve of grungesters like Soundgarden and Pearl Jam, these days, Roseland has widened its scope with the likes of Liz Phair and Blur.

The Supper Club

240 W 47th St between Eighth Ave and Broadway (212-921-1940). Subway: N, R, S, 1, 2, 3, 9, 7 to 42nd St–Times Sq. $12–$15. AmEx, MC, V.
The Supper Club is a gorgeous, ornate venue in the Theater District that has acoustics clean enough to please such particular artists as Belle and Sebastian, Rufus Wainwright and Beck. (*See chapter* **Cabaret & Comedy**.)

Bars and pubs

Arlene Grocery

95 Stanton St between Ludlow and Orchard Sts (212-358-1633). Subway: F to Second Ave; J, M, Z to Essex St. Free. No credit cards.
Irish-themed rock, hard-boiled folkies, indie fixtures and baby bands looking for a break abound at this crucial showcase spot, named for the actual Lower East Side market that it replaced. Unusual for a free venue, its sound system is top-notch.

Baby Jupiter

170 Orchard St at Stanton St (212-982-2229). Subway: F to Second Ave; J, M, Z to Essex St. Free–$3. MC, V.
This pleasant, spacious Lower East Side venue not only has food, drink and theater events, but it's becoming an increasingly important spot for secret hipster shows (by the likes of Silver Jews and Will Oldham), as well as being decent for hearing arty music by up-and-comers such as Ezster Balint. The sound system isn't great, but the comfy old couches and relaxed vibe more than make up for it.

Baggot Inn

82 W 3rd St between Thompson and Sullivan Sts (212-477-0622) www.citysearch.com/nyc/thebaggotinn. Subway: A, C, E, B, D, F, Q to W 4th St–Washington Sq. $5. AmEx, MC, V.
Formerly the Sun Mountain Café, the Baggot Inn refurbished its interior along with its booking policies: Good Irish rock can be heard, as well as typical horrid Bleecker Street fare.

Bitter End

147 Bleecker St at Thompson St (212-673-7030) www.bitterend.com. Subway: A, C, E, B, D, F, Q to W 4th St–Washington Sq. $5. AmEx, Disc, MC, V.
The ne plus ultra of Bleecker Street joints is now free of the looming lease troubles that plagued it for years. The Bitter End will forever feature singer-songwriters who are quite jazzed to perform where Dylan played all those years ago.

Bottom Line

15 W 4th St at Mercer St (212-228-6300). Subway: N, R to 8th St. $15–$25. No credit cards.
Words of warning: Catch the management on a bad night or attend a particularly crowded evening, and you'll find yourself a prisoner at the Riker's Island of rock. Even so, Allan Pepper's cabaret-style club has persisted for 25 years, longer than any similar venue. Roots music, singer-songwriter stylings, the occasional jazz or fusion gig and Buster-friggin'-Poindexter and His Spanish Rocket Ship all find a home here.

Brownies

169 Ave A between 10th and 11th Sts (212-420-8392). Subway: L to First Ave. $7–$10. AmEx, Disc, MC, V.
Brownies was *the* club of note during the alt-rock boom of the early '90s; as college rock and postpunk hit their peaks, this dingy bar was the joint where they all played. Since

the alt-bust, Brownies struggled, but it has recently undergone remodeling. Booths and a fresh coat of paint may move one to dub this "the Brownies Lounge," but it's far more comfortable than before. And the booking is getting better bit by bit.

CBGB
315 Bowery at Bleecker St (212-982-4052) www.cbgb.com. Subway: B, D, F, Q to Broadway–Lafayette St; 6 to Bleecker St. $3–$12. No credit cards.
Despite the declining quality of its bookings and soundpersons, this famed venue will forever be a tourist attraction, because it is, after all, the birthplace of punk. The brave staff still endures live auditions on Sundays and Mondays, but the usual programming includes local indie and punk bands, vintage big names such as Tom Tom Club, and hip traveling acts like Royal Trux.

CB's 313 Gallery
313 Bowery at Bleecker St (212-677-0455). Subway: B, D, F, Q to Broadway–Lafayette St; 6 to Bleecker St. $6–$10. AmEx, MC, V.
The Gallery is CBGB's more cultivated neighbor. It's just as long and narrow, but it's festooned with local artists' work instead of graffiti and layers of posters. Acoustic fare dominates.

Coney Island High
15 St. Marks Pl between Second and Third Aves (212-674-7959). Subway: N, R to 8th St; 6 to Astor Pl. $5–$10. No credit cards.
Smack in the center of the East Village's most garish strip is this three-floor glam/punk/metal stronghold, part-owned by D Generation's Jesse Malin. The downstairs main room hosts the big-name bills—the Fall, Queens of the Stoneage, Hellacopters and Nashville Pussy have played there, and a multitude of heavy-metal and hardcore blowouts take place regularly—whereas the upstairs room runs the gamut of small-fry outfits. CIH approaches CBGB levels of fetidness when it's packed, but it has shaped up as one of the best clubs around.

Continental
25 Third Ave at St. Marks Pl (212-529-6924). Subway: N, R to 8th St; 6 to Astor Pl. Free–$6. No credit cards.
The skies will rain blood, the earth will belch fire, the day of reckoning will come and the celebrated dive bar Continental will still be there, booking local grease-a-billy, hard-rock, punk and garage bands for little or no cover.

The Cooler
416 W 14th St between Ninth Ave and Washington St (212-229-0785) www.thecooler.com. Subway: A, C, E to 14th St; L to Eighth Ave. Free–$15. AmEx, MC, V.
This spacious former meat locker isn't always climate-controlled—especially in the dead of winter or at a crowded summer show. Mondays are free, and the bills are usually intriguing, mixing indie rock with the more avant-garde. This club also hosts a variety of electronic dance happenings from Brazilian junglist Amon Tobin to hip-hop founding father Afrika Bambaataa. And there are lots and lots of arty Sonic Youth–related side projects.

Don Hill's
511 Greenwich St at Spring St (212-334-1390). Subway: C, E to Spring St; 1, 9 to Houston St. $5–$12. AmEx, DC, MC, V.
This is the home of Squeezebox, the long-running punk-meets-drag summit. Don Hill's may be located in the far-west reaches of Soho, but its heart is clearly in the East Village as it hosts weekly parties and special events that cater to the glam side of the rock spectrum. The decor has the inexplicably bizarre yet comforting feel of an airport lounge.

Downtime
251 W 30th St between Seventh and Eighth Aves (212-695-2747). Subway: 1, 9 to 28th St. $5–$12. AmEx, MC, V.
During the week, run-of-the-mill rock bands play in this vertically spacious bar with an upstairs lounge and pool table. On Saturdays, there are retro-themed events for folks who can't get enough of the film *Swingers*.

Fez
Inside Time Café, 380 Lafayette St at Great Jones St (212-533-2680). Subway: B, D, F, Q to Broadway–Lafayette St; 6 to Bleecker St. $5–$18, plus two-drink minimum. AmEx, MC, V.
With its gold lamé and red velvet curtains, Fez is one of the city's finest venues for that glittering lounge/cabaret atmosphere. It books a variety of local events, including the popular Loser's Lounge tribute series. Every Thursday night, the Mingus Big Band introduces a new generation of listeners to the robust, sanctified jazz of the late bassist-composer-bandleader Charles Mingus. It's dinner-theater–style seating leaves little standing room, so make reservations and arrive early.

The Knitting Factory
74 Leonard St between Broadway and Church St (212-219-3055) www.knittingfactory.com. Subway: A, C, E to Canal St; 1, 9 to Franklin St. $5–$20. AmEx, MC, V.
In addition to being the city's avant-garde music mall, the Knitting Factory features a variety of basic indie bands (Neutral Milk Hotel, Smog) and local genre jumpers (Arto Lindsay, Vinicius Cantuária) in the main space, as well as smaller shows in the tiny Alterknit Theater. See **Jazz & Experimental**, *page 262.*

Lakeside Lounge
162 Ave B between 10th and 11th Sts (212-529-8463) www.lakeside.com. Subway: L to First Ave. Free. No credit cards.
This bar was opened to serve discerning urban country and roots jockeys, as well as self-styled beer drinkers and hellraisers. As such, the Lakeside is such a nice hang that it's almost a shame when the bands start playing and you can't hear your buddies. Nonetheless, bands booked here err on the side of rootsy and raw.

Le Bar Bat
311 W 57th St between Eighth and Ninth Aves (212-307-7228) www.lebarbat.com. Subway: A, C, B, D, 1, 9 to 59th St–Columbus Circle. $10–$20; free before 9pm (8:30pm Sat). AmEx, MC, V.
This is a bizarre bar venue set in an old cavelike recording studio. The bands here are usually happy party-time funk and soul providers and the crowd a jolly bunch of after-workers.

Lion's Den
214 Sullivan St between Bleecker and W 3rd Sts (212-477-2782). Subway: A, C, E, B, D, F, Q to W 4th St–Washington Sq. $5–$10. AmEx.
This cavernous dive cult caters to the tastes of Bleecker Street regulars and NYU students. Lion's Den books plenty of Deadhead-friendly jam bands, reggae, funk and rock.

The Living Room
84 Stanton St at Allen St (212-533-7235). Subway: F to Second Ave; J, M, Z to Essex St. Free. No credit cards.
The Living Room is another of the many young clubs/coffeehouses popping up in the Ludlow/Lower East Side hipster mecca.

Luna Lounge
171 Ludlow St between Houston and Stanton Sts (212-260-2323). Subway: F to Second Ave. Free. No credit cards.
This Ludlow Street venue is a nice alternative to the often-packed Max Fish across the street, and Luna has live music

Go with the flow: At Tribeca's **Wetlands**, the Roots host free-form hip-hop jams.

every night for free. The basic alt and indie bands play in the back room, which is as comfy and stuffy as your parents' basement, though probably a bit smokier.

Maxwell's
1039 Washington St, Hoboken, NJ (201-798 0406). Travel: PATH train from 33rd, 23rd, 14th, 9th or Christopher St to Hoboken or bus #126 from Port Authority Bus Terminal. $5–$12. AmEx, DC, MC, V.
Two years ago, it looked as if Maxwell's, without a doubt the most consistently forward-looking rock club in the metropolitan area for the past 15 years, would become one of the many frat-boy hangouts lining Washington Street in Hoboken. But in 1998, Maxwell's rich heritage was rescued by talent booker and now part-owner Todd Abramson. Since Maxwell's is in another state, many visiting acts play a date here as well as at the Bowery Ballroom, Knitting Factory, Tramps, etc. It can get a little close when it's crowded, but one should tolerate that sort of thing when one is at a landmark. Edible bar food is available in the front dining room. Music ranges from garage and punk to indie and roots.

Meow Mix
269 Houston St at Suffolk St (212-254-0688). Subway: F to Second Ave. $5. No credit cards.
It's the hippest lesbian establishment in Manhattan; it was featured prominently in *Chasing Amy* and Fran Drescher name-checked it on *The Tonight Show*. But Meow Mix is also a haven for individuals of all stripes—men are welcome. The atmosphere is your typical brew-fueled neighborhood watering hole; the music ranges from trashed-up glam to singer-songwriter fare and an anything-goes DJ aesthetic. Check out the popular tribute nights the last Sunday of every month, when a handful of downtown faves give it up for anybody from Kiss to the Monkees.

Mercury Lounge
217 E Houston St at Ave A (212-260-4700) www.mercurylounge.com. Subway: F to Second Ave. $6–$12. MC, V.
The small Mercury Lounge built its reputation on providing excellent sound for showcasing music, hence it became a first-choice for many artists. Let's hope that it stays that way, even though its staff seems to be focusing on its big sister club, the Bowery Ballroom. Still, the Merc has a nice atmosphere, a good beer selection and a quality program.

Nightingale Bar
213 Second Ave at 13th St (212-473-9398). Subway: L to First Ave. $5. No credit cards.
The stage at this noisy bar is about six inches off the ground, and the mirror behind the stage gives an illusion of space. But when seeing a band at Nightingale Bar, there's no way to avoid feeling as though you're right up there with them. This is the place that gave the world Blues Traveler and the Spin Doctors. And don't miss local garage rockers the Fleshtones when they do a series here.

Paddy Reilly's Music Bar
519 Second Ave at 29th St (212-686-1210) www.paddyreillys.com. Subway: 6 to 28th St. $5–$10. AmEx.
The premier local bar for Irish rock hosts the likes of Black 47 and a weekly *seisiun* (a traditional Irish jam session).

Rodeo Bar
375 Third Ave at 27th St (212-683-6500). Subway: 6 to 28th St. Free. AmEx, MC, V.
Rodeo Bar looks like any other midtown joint—and half of it is, actually. But the sawdust-strewn northern half books local roots outfits and occasional visiting country phenomenons, like Dale Watson and BR5-49.

Sidewalk
94 Ave A at 6th St (212-473-7373). Subway: F to Second Ave; 6 to Astor Pl. Free. AmEx, MC, V.
Behind the front room at this neighborhood café, you'll find the world capital of "antifolk." In other words, low-maintenance acoustic music rules, whether it's irreverent and ingenious (which describes antifolk guru Lach or perennials the Humans) or self-important folkie swill.

Tonic
107 Norfolk St between Delancey and Rivington Sts (212-358-7503). Subway: F to Delancey St; J, M, Z to Essex St. $10. No credit cards.
Tonic is a new, very downtown and very laid-back venue that books mostly jazz, experimental, klezmer and other more avant-garde genres. However, the Sunday-night series devoted to rock, pop and roots music, and recent gigs by Holiday Hootenanny, Martha Wainwright and Shackwacky shouldn't be overlooked. Tonic recently got its liquor license as well. *See* **Jazz & Experimental**, *pages 262–263.*

Tramps
51 W 21st St between Fifth and Sixth Aves (212-727-7788). Subway: F, N, R to 23rd St. $5–$20. No credit cards.
Somewhere between beer hall and pub club, Tramps features an excellent variety of music: Recent dates have included Yo La Tengo sharing a bill with free-jazz act Other Dimensions in Music, an underground hip-hop hoo-ha, weekly zydeco parties with dance lessons and Cajun food, Vanilla Ice and Merle Haggard. Tramps offers more all-ages concerts than most. Next door is the yummy Time Café, which serves southern-style grub.

Westbeth Theater Center Music Hall
151 Bank St between West and Washington Sts (212-741-0391) www.westbeththeater.com. Subway: A, C, E to 14th St; L to Eighth Ave. $8–$35. No credit cards.
The Westbeth is a 500-capacity space with decent sound that has seen shows from Pavement, Elliott Smith and Beth Orton. It has a nice extra bar area outside the main room in which to hang if you're not digging the opening act.

Wetlands Preserve
161 Hudson St at Laight St (212-966-4225) www.wetlands-preserve.org. Subway: A, C, E, 1, 9 to Canal St. Free–$15. AmEx, MC, V (drinks only).

Deadheads seeking to keep the vibe alive after Jerry Garcia's death flock here for Dead cover bands and musicians peripherally connected to the band. More than that, this club regularly books ska, funk, reggae, jungle, hip-hop and hardcore marathons—making it a veritable haven for urban sounds of all types. The Roots have been hosting a weekly hip-hop free-form jam that's proven to be very popular.

Windows on the World

1 World Trade Center, West St between Liberty and Vesey Sts (212-524-7000) www.windowsontheworld.com. Subway: A, C to Chambers St; E to World Trade Center; N, R, 1, 9 to Cortlandt St. $5. AmEx, MC, V (drinks only).
Windows is a romantic bar in which to sip very expensive drinks, sample dull food and dance to trendy DJs such as Lucien, Arling and Cameron, and Fantastic Plastic Machine, all atop the World Trade Center—on the 107th floor, actually. There are occasional live acts, from lounge-pop bonbons such as Combustible Edison and Beat Positive to jazz acts and near-electronica types. After a while, you might feel as though you're at an upscale wedding reception.

Jazz & Experimental

Birdland

315 W 44th St between Eighth and Ninth Aves (212-581-3080) www.birdlandjazz.com. Subway: A, C, E to 42nd St. $15–$25. AmEx, MC, V.
The flagship venue for the recent jazz resurgence in midtown, Birdland presents many of jazz's biggest names in the neon splendor of Times Square. The dining area's three-tiered floor plan allows for maximum visibility, so patrons can enjoy everyone from Pat Metheny and Jon Faddis to Chico O'Farrill while also enjoying pretty fine cuisine. To compete with the rest of the Monday-night big bands in residence elsewhere, the club has enlisted the Toshiko Akiyoshi Jazz Orchestra, featuring Lew Tabackin.

Blue Note

131 W 3rd St between MacDougal St and Sixth Ave (212-475-8592) www.bluenote.net. Subway: A, C, E, B, D, F, Q to W 4th St–Washington Sq. $10–$65, plus $5 minimum. AmEx, DC, Disc, MC, V.
"The jazz capital of the world" is how this famous club describes itself, and big names who play here are greeted as if they're visiting heads of state. Recent acts have included Dave Brubeck, David Sanborn, Ray Charles, Lionel Hampton and Grover Washington Jr. All this comes at a price: Dinner will cost you more than $25 a head.

Iridium

48 W 63rd St at Columbus Ave (212-582-2121) www.iridiumjazz.com. Subway: 1, 9 to 66th St–Lincoln Ctr. $25–$30, plus $10 minimum. AmEx, DC, Disc, JCB, MC, V.
This club's location—across the street from the venerable Lincoln Center—guarantees that its lineups are generally top-notch. Amid a decor that's a little bit Art Nouveau and a little bit Dr. Seuss, Iridium lures upscale crowds by booking a mix that's equally split between household names and jazz-savvy ones. Monday nights belong to the legendary guitarist, inventor and icon Les Paul, who often ends up sharing the stage with one of the guitar heroes who swear by his prize invention, the Gibson solid-body electric guitar.

The Jazz Standard

116 E 27th St between Park and Lexington Aves (212-576-2232) www.jazzstandard.com. Subway: 6 to 28th St. $10–$20, plus a $10 minumum at tables. V, MC, AmEx, DC.
The Jazz Standard's two-level floor plan makes it a club for all jazz tastes. Upstairs there's a restaurant/watering hole piping in the kind of cool sounds that enhance dinner and

conversation. Downstairs, where talented instrumentalists (Gary Bartz, Eliane Elias, David "Fathead" Newman) and singers (Wesla Whitfield, Vanessa Rubin) hold sway in the 130-plus–capacity music room, the fine acoustics and unobstructed sightlines will delight both the aficionado and the jazz rookie out for a little night music.

Knitting Factory/ AlterKnit Theater/Old Office

74 Leonard St between Broadway and Church St (212-219-3055) www.knitting factory.com. Subway: A, C, E to Canal St; 1, 9 to Franklin St. $5–$20. AmEx, MC, V ($15 minimum charge).
The Knitting Factory is recommended for those who like their music a little off the rails. New York's avant-garde music mall, it features an up-to-the-minute blend of experimental jazz (David S. Ware, Tim Berne, James "Blood" Ulmer, Lounge Lizards), rock (Jonathan Richman, Kristin Hersh, Vernon Reid, Trans Am), alternative cinema and poetry. The café and bar are open throughout the day, and the main room holds 250 people.

Lenox Lounge

288 Lenox Ave between 124th and 125th Sts (212-427-0253). Subway: 2, 3 to 125th St. $10. No credit cards.
They say Billie Holiday loved this Art Deco paradise. So did a small-time hustler named Malcolm—pre-X. Although the jazz here isn't always traditional, the hardbop outfits that jam here (Cecil Payne, James Spaulding, John Hicks) make no bones about carrying on an old tradition.

Roulette

228 West Broadway at White St (212-219-8242) www.roulette.org. Subway: C, E to Canal St; 1, 9 to Franklin St. $10. No credit cards.
Ever thought you might want live music in your living room? Well, improvising trombonist/Roulette proprietor Jim Staley has saved you the trouble. His friends represent an encyclopedia of world-renowned music experimentalists, so the atmosphere in his ten-year-old salon is relaxed and informal—until the music starts up. You're just as likely to run into computer-music pioneers such as David Behrman as you are to hear avant-jazzers like Dave Douglas.

Smalls

183 W 10th St at Seventh Ave (212-929-7565). Subway: 1, 9 to Christopher St–Sheridan Sq. $10. No credit cards.
The spot where jazz new jacks rub elbows with their college-student counterparts and Beat-era nostalgists, Smalls books both high-profile up-and-comers (Jason Lindner, Myron Walden, James Hurt) and established stars such as Lee Konitz. There's no liquor license, but you can bring your own or sample some of the juices at the bar.

St. Nick's Pub

773 St. Nicholas Ave at 149th St (212-769-8275). Subway: A, C, B, D to 145th St. $5. No credit cards.
St. Nick's may be the closest thing to an old-fashioned juke joint you're likely to find in the city: It's got live music six nights a week, a charmingly makeshift decor, and mature patrons who take their hedonistic impulses seriously. It's possible to hear every type of music here (except hip-hop), but Monday night's amazing jam session with Patience Higgins's Sugarhill Jazz Quartet is the draw.

Sweet Basil

88 Seventh Ave South between Bleecker and Grove Sts (212-242-1785) www.sweetbasil.com. Subway: 1, 9 to Christopher St–Sheridan Sq. $17.50–$20, plus $10 minimum. AmEx, MC, V.
Past players here have included Art Blakey and Abdullah Ibrahim; the club now showcases young players (Abraham

Burton, Mark Turner, Renee Rosnes, Marc Cary) as well as veterans. There's a jazz brunch on Saturdays and Sundays.

Tonic

107 Norfolk St between Delancey and Rivington Sts (212-358-7503). Subway: F to Delancey St; J, M, Z to Essex St. $10. No credit cards.
Don't think of Tonic as the little music venue that could. Consider it the downtown space that did. We suggest you abandon all expectations once you enter here, because Tonic has become known as the place where the avant-music scene's biggest names forge spine-tingling one-offs. You're just as likely to hear Marc Ribot and Big John Patton jamming with John Zorn as you are to see Arto Lindsay or Sonic Youth's Thurston Moore get onstage with just about anybody.

Village Vanguard

178 Seventh Ave South at Perry St (212-255-4037). Subway: A, C, E, 1, 2, 3, 9 to 14th St; L to Eighth Ave. $15–$20, plus $10 minimum. No credit cards.
This basement club is still going strong after 60 years. Its stage—a small but mighty step-up that has seen the likes of John Coltrane, Bill Evans and Miles Davis—still hosts the crème de la crème of mainstream jazz talent. The Monday-night regular is the 17-piece Vanguard Jazz Orchestra, which has now held the same slot (originally as the Thad Jones/Mel Lewis Jazz Orchestra) for more than 30 years.

Zinno

126 W 13th St between Sixth and Seventh Aves (212-924-5182). Subway: F, 1, 2, 3, 9 to 14th St; L to Sixth Ave. $10, plus $15 minimum. AmEx, MC, V.
A supper club for those who want more than mere polite background noise with their dinner, Zinno is where some of the mainstream's most accomplished jazzers (Hilton Ruiz, Michael Moore, Bucky Pizzarelli) get to perform in relaxed, intimate duos and trios. The cuisine isn't hard on the palate, either.

Reggae, World & Latin

Copacabana

617 W 57th St between 11th and 12th Aves (212-582-2672) www.copacabana.com. Subway: A, C, B, D, 1, 2, 3, 9 to 59th St–Columbus Circle. $3–$40. AmEx, MC, V (for table reservations only).
It's not for nothing that the Copacabana's reputation precedes it. For decades it has been the venue that introduced the superstars of Latin music to the tourist masses. The Copa can get pricey at times, but after an ecstatic night of dancing to, say, Cubanismo, you're not likely to leave disappointed.

Gonzalez y Gonzalez

625 Broadway between Bleecker and Houston Sts (212-473-8787) www.gonzalezygonzalez.com. Subway: B, D, F, Q to Broadway–Lafayette St; 6 to Bleecker St. Free. AmEx, MC, V.
From the front window, Gonzalez may seem like merely a tourist Tex-Mex restaurant, but walk past the palm trees and the bar and you'll find a Latin-music lover's paradise, complete with stage and cozy makeshift dance floor. Once there, you'll be compelled to find a partner and squeeze yourself in—especially on Wednesdays, when Johnny Almendra and Los Jovenes del Barrio hit you with a blast of flute- and violin-flavored Cuban *charanga*.

Latin Quarter

2551 Broadway at 96th St (212-864-7600). Subway: 1, 2, 3, 9 to 96th St. $10–$20. MC, V.
On the Latin-music scale, the Latin Quarter is to the cognoscenti what the Copacabana is to everybody else. Connoisseurs by the hundreds mob the place during the weekend, making the Quarter's giant dance floor seem like a

cozy corner. What the dancers come for is salsa (Tito Nieves, Conjunto Clasico, Jose "El Canario" Alberto) merengue (Kinito Mendez, Oro Solido) and hot Latin freestyle.

S.O.B.'s

204 Varick St at Houston St (212-243-4940) www.sobs.com. Subway: 1, 9 to Houston St. $10–$25. AmEx, DC, Disc, JCB, MC, V.
S.O.B.'s stands for Sounds of Brazil, but that's not the only kind of music you'll hear at the city's premier spot for musicians from south of the border. There's samba but also reggae (Sugar Minott, the Congos), other Caribbean stuff (Sweet Micky, Malavoi) and even Afropop (Kanda Bongo Man, Ricardo Lemvo and Makina Loca). Mondays belong to La Tropica Nights, devoted to the biggest names in salsa. Looking like the safari-style burger joint at Disneyland, S.O.B.'s will quench your thirst for all things percussive and exotic.

Zinc Bar

90 Houston St between La Guardia Pl and Thompson St (212-477-8337). Subway: A, C, E, B, D, F, Q to W 4th St–Washington Sq. $15, $5 minimum. No credit cards.
A cozy—and we mean cozy—subnook situated where Noho meets Soho, Zinc Bar is the place to catch up with the most die-hard night owls. It's got an after-hours feel that actually starts well before daybreak, and the atmosphere is enhanced by the astonishingly cool mix of jazz (Ron Affif), Latin (Juan Carlos Formell), Brazilian (Cidinho Texiera's Showfest), African (Leo Traversa) and flamenco bands that gig there nightly.

Blues, Folk & Country

Chicago B.L.U.E.S.

73 Eighth Ave between 13th and 14th Sts (212-924-9755). Subway: A, C, E to 14th St; L to Eighth Ave. Free–$20. AmEx, MC, V.
When Otis Rush or some other titan of the blues comes to town, he often settles in at this cozy West Village club. The opening acts can be startlingly bad, but the chance of seeing the likes of Johnnie Johnson at close range makes this a must-visit club. The open jams are also of note.

Louisiana Bar & Grill

622 Broadway between Bleecker and Houston Sts (212-460-9633). Subway: B, D, F, Q to Broadway–Lafayette St; 6 to Bleecker St. Free. AmEx, MC, V.
Apart from the fine Cajun cuisine available here, the Louisiana is known for booking top-shelf rockabilly, country and blues acts, including local legends the Harlem All-Stars.

Manny's Car Wash

1558 Third Ave between 87th and 88th Sts (212-369-2583) www.mannyscarwash.com. Subway: 4, 5, 6 to 86th St. Free–$15. AmEx, MC, V.
Every evening, nationally prominent and popular local blues acts blare from the tiny stage of this elongated nightspot on the city's Upper East Side. Patrons are generally locals and can be serious blues lovers or junior Wall Streeters ogling the single women (women get in free on Monday nights). A blues jam occurs on Sunday nights, when there's mostly standing room only.

Terra Blues

149 Bleecker St at Thompson St (212-777-7776) www.nytoday.com/terrablues. Subway: A, C, E, B, D, F, Q to W 4th St–Washington Sq. Free–$15. AmEx, MC, V.
Gracing the stage at this otherwise ordinary Bleecker Street bar is a wide range of blues-based artists, both local and imported—you'll hear authentic Chicago guitar pickers as well as NYC blues from the likes of duo Satan and Adam.

Nightclubs with live music

Life
158 Bleecker St at Thompson St (212-420-1999).
Subway: A, C, E, B, D, F, Q to W 4th St–Washington Sq.
$15–$20. AmEx, MC, V.
This nightclub has an erratic live-music schedule. If you
don't feel like dancing to run-of-the-mill DJ fodder—or hip-
hop maestro Funkmaster Flex, who spins here regularly—
come here for the "Lust for Life" parties on Wednesday
nights, when punked-up bands (Honky Toast, the Toilet
Boys) and thriving has-beens (Dee Snyder, Gene Loves
Jezebel) take over the place.

Nell's
246 W 14th St between Seventh and Eighth Aves
(212-675-1567) www.nells.com. Subway: A, C, E, 1, 2, 3,
9 to 14th St; L to Eighth Ave. $10–$15. AmEx, MC, V
(for drinks only).
With plush interiors modeled after a Victorian gentlemen's
club, this lushly appointed room was the place to be seen in
the late 1980s—if you could get in. The crowd has shifted
from the international jet set to the upscale hip-hop set (the
late Notorious B.I.G. shot a video here). On the ground floor
live jazz, blues and reggae acts hit the stage, while DJs pack
the dance floor in the basement.

Roxy
515 W 18th St between Tenth and Eleventh Aves
(212-645-5156) www.roxynyc.com. Subway: A, C, E to
14th St; L to Eighth Ave. $12–$20. No credit cards.
This is mainly a dance club, with a history stretching back
to when it was the epicenter of hip-hop. Live performances
don't happen regularly, but the Chemical Brothers, Everything but the Girl and Sick of It All have all taken bows at
this roller rink–sized space.

Shine
380 Canal St at West Broadway (212-941-0900).
www.shine.com. Subway: A, C, E, 1, 9 to Canal St.
$6–$15. V, MC, AmEx (for drinks only).
One of the hottest spots in Tribeca, Shine has a red velvety
interior that has been the location of many a Leonardo DiCaprio
spotting. Local bands of questionable repute often play, but
more impressive have been the erratic appearances by up-and-
comers like Rufus Wainright, New Radicals and Cornelius.

Webster Hall
125 E 11th St between Third and Fourth Aves
(212-353-1600). Subway: L, N, R, 4, 5, 6 to 14th
St–Union Sq. $20–$25. MC, V.
The lowest common denominator in NYC clubs, Webster Hall
doesn't so much revel in the rock and dance cutting-edge as
it does dull it down for those whose main objective is to get
drunk and, more importantly, laid. Coincidence or not, Mick
Jagger and Madonna have staged MTV specials here.

Outdoor summer venues

The Anchorage
Cadman Plaza West between Hicks and Old Fulton Sts,
Brooklyn. (212.206.6674). Subway: 2, 3 to Clark St; A,
C to High St. $7–$20. No credit cards.
There isn't a more evocative space to catch an avant-rock or
DJ event (think: John Zorn, Sonic Youth, Giant Step) than this
art cavern inside the base of the Brooklyn Bridge; it's so
roomy, you'll think you're outside.

Bryant Park
Sixth Ave between 41st and 42nd Sts (212-983-4142).
Subway: B, D, F, Q to 42nd St; N, R, S, 1, 2, 3, 7, 9 to
42nd St–Times Sq. Free.

Directly behind the Beaux Arts–beauty New York Public
Library, Bryant Park is a serene, attractive and distinctly
European-style park with a substantial free concert series.

Castle Clinton
Battery Park, Battery Pl at State St (212-835-2789).
Subway: C, E to World Trade Center; N, R, 1, 9 to
Cortlandt St; 2, 3 to Park Pl; 4, 5 to Bowling Green. Free.
Space is limited at this well-preserved fortress situated in the
heart of Battery Park, but its seats offer lucky summer-music
hounds a comfortable, unobstructed view of classic performers like Frank Sinatra Jr., John Mayall's Bluesbreakers
and John Zorn's Masada.

Central Park SummerStage
Rumsey Playfield, 830 Fifth Ave at 72nd St
(212-360-2777). Subway: B, C to 72nd St; 6 to 68th St.
Free, benefit concerts $15–$25. No credit cards.
During a humid summer weekend, SummerStage is one of
the great treasures available to New Yorkers. Although there
are always two or three shows with a substantial ticket price,
the majority of concerts at this amphitheater are free. Think
about it: Solomon Burke or Stereolab, Junior or James Brown,
under crystal-blue skies, for no charge, with beer!

Downing Stadium
Randall's Island (212-582-0228). Travel: 4, 5, 6 to 125th
St, then M35 bus to Stadium.
This former soccer stadium and adjoining field on an East
River island host such events as Lollapalooza, the Vans
Warped Tour, the Tibetan Freedom Concert and Reggae Sun-
splash. It is by no means lovely; it is by all means convenient.

Giants Stadium
Rte 3, East Rutherford, New Jersey (201-935-3900).
Travel: NJ Transit Bus from Port Authority Bus
Terminal. $20–$75. V, MC, AmEx.
Here's where you catch biggies like U2 and the Stones while
jet airliners heading to and from Newark Airport crowd the
sky. The band members look like ants holding instruments,
and you'll have to wait a long, long time for beer. But the hot
dogs aren't that bad, and because it's outdoors, it's the last
venue in the Meadowlands where you can actually smoke.

Jones Beach
Long Island (516-221-1000). Travel: LIRR from
Penn Station to Freeport, then Jones Beach bus. $18-$45.
No credit cards.
From July to September, a diverse group of performers—
perhaps Diana Ross, Oasis, Barry White, Blues Traveler or
PJ Harvey—performs under the setting sun at this beach-
side amphitheater.

Lincoln Center Plaza
10 Lincoln Center Plaza at W 62nd St (212-875-5400).
Subway: 1, 9 to 66th St–Lincoln Ctr. Free.
The home of Lincoln Center's summer Out-of-Doors and
Midsummer Night Swing festivals, Lincoln Center Plaza
hosts many of New York's sundry cultural communities.
Over the course of a week, it's possible to hear the world's
hottest Latin and African bands as well as a concert by tenor-
saxophone god Sonny Rollins. It all takes place in the splendor of the city's key center for the performing arts.

Prospect Park Bandshell
9th St at Prospect Park West, Park Slope, Brooklyn
(718-965-8969). Subway: F to Seventh Ave; 2, 3 to
Grand Army Plaza. Free.
Prospect Park Bandshell is to Brooklynites what Central
Park SummerStage is to Manhattan residents: the place to
hear great music in the great outdoors, at no cost. The shows
mirror the borough's great melting pot, so you're just as likely to hear Afropop or Caribbean music as jazz and blues.

Classical & Opera

A glance through the listings of a typical week in NYC will reveal more than a dozen classical-music events occurring in a single evening, probably more than anywhere except London. Carnegie Hall is still the place to play for visiting orchestras and soloists, and Lincoln Center on a busy night might simultaneously host two operas, an orchestral concert and a piano recital. The number of performances in the city's churches, schools, cultural centers and other spaces is also staggering. Frequently, the performers or commentators will offer preconcert lectures or panel discussions for free or for a small fee.

For information on concerts, times and locations, see *Time Out New York*'s classical-music listings or the Sunday *New York Times*. The Theater Development Fund (*see chapter* **Dance**) also provides information on all music events via its NYC/On Stage service.

Tickets

You can buy tickets directly from most venues. The Ticket Buyers Club of the New York Philharmonic provides orchestral tickets at considerable discounts. TKTS offers 25 to 50 percent discounts (with a service charge) for same-day tickets for most Lincoln Center events, including the New York Philharmonic, the Chamber Music Society, the Juilliard School and the New York City Opera (though not the Met).

CarnegieCharge
212-247-7800. 8am–8pm. AmEx, MC, V. Surcharge $4.50 per ticket.

Centercharge
212-721-6500. Mon–Sat 10am–8pm, Sun noon–8pm. AmEx, Disc, MC, V. Alice Tully Hall, Avery Fisher Hall and Lincoln Center Festival (which takes place in July) events only.

New York Philharmonic Ticket Buyers Club
212-875-5656. Mon–Fri 10am–5:30pm. AmEx, DC, MC, V.

Ticketmaster
212-307-4100. Mon–Sun 6:45am–11pm. AmEx, Disc, MC, V. For New York State Theater, Town Hall and BAM tickets. Surcharges vary.

TKTS
Duffy Square, W 47th St at Broadway (212-221-0013). Subway: N, R, S, 1, 2, 3, 9, 7 to 42nd St–Times Sq. Wed, Sat, Sun noon–2pm; daily 3–8pm. Also: 2 World Trade Center (mezzanine) between Church, Vesey, West and Liberty Sts (212-221-0013). Subway: C, E to World Trade Ctr; 1, 9 to Cortlandt St. 11:30am–5:30pm.

Backstage passes

It's possible to go behind the scenes at several of the city's major concert venues. See what the divas see: Backstage at the Met (212-769-7020) takes you around the famous opera house; Lincoln Center Tours (212-875-5350) escorts you inside all three of the center's major halls; Carnegie Hall (212-247-7800) shepherds you through what is perhaps the world's most famous concert hall. It's also possible to sit in on rehearsals of the New York Philharmonic, usually held on the Thursday before a concert. They generally cost $12.

Concert halls

For the New York State Theater, Avery Fisher Hall, Metropolitan Opera House and Alice Tully Hall, *see* **Houses of high culture,** *page 268.*

92nd Street Y
Kaufmann Concert Hall, 1395 Lexington Ave at 92nd St (212-415-5440). Subway: 4, 5, 6 to 86th St. $20–$40. AmEx, MC, V.
Back in the 1970s, the Y began to exercise the ear as well as the body by developing an extensive and imaginative series for its acoustically excellent Kaufmann Concert Hall. The programming got very adventurous a few years ago (evenings devoted to Luciano Berio, and Peter Sellars's stagings of Bach cantatas with costumes by Isaac Mizrahi), but nowadays, the emphasis is on more traditional orchestral, solo and chamber masterworks.

Brooklyn Academy of Music
30 Lafayette Ave between Flatbush Ave and Fulton St, Brooklyn (718-636-4100) www.bam.org. Subway: G to Fulton St; D, Q, 2, 3, 4, 5 to Atlantic Ave; B, N, R to Pacific St. $20–$75. AmEx, MC, V.
BAM stages music and dance in a beautiful house that is America's oldest academy for the performing arts. The programming is more East Village than Upper West Side: BAM helped launch the likes of Philip Glass and John Zorn. Current music director Robert Spano has made the resident Brooklyn Philharmonic Orchestra play together and sound good, though the group doesn't get the monetary support its Manhattan counterparts get. Every fall and winter, the Next Wave Festival of theater and music provides an overview of the more established avant-garde, while the spring BAM Opera season brings innovative European productions to downtown Brooklyn. See *chapters* **Dance** and **Theater.**

Carnegie Hall
154 W 57th St at Seventh Ave (212-247-7800) www.carnegiehall.org. Subway: A, C, B, D, 1, 9 to 59th St–Columbus Circle; N, R to 57th St. $20–$70. AmEx, DC, Disc, MC, V.
You don't have to practice, practice, practice to get there; you can take the subway. A varied roster of American and international stars regularly appears in the two auditoriums: Carnegie Hall itself and the smaller, lovely Weill Recital Hall.

Colden Center for the Performing Arts
LeFrak Concert Hall, Queens College, 65–30 Kissena Blvd, Flushing, Queens (718-793-8080). Travel: F to Parsons Blvd, then take the Q25 or Q34 bus to campus. $8–$25. AmEx, Disc, MC, V.
The home of the Queens Philharmonic, this multipurpose hall also stages concerts by international artists who are in town

for Manhattan performances. Due to the center's remote location, tickets are often half the price of those in Manhattan.

Florence Gould Hall
at the Alliance Française

55 E 59th St between Madison and Park Aves (212-355-6160). Subway: N, R to Fifth Ave; 4, 5, 6 to 59th St. $15–$35. AmEx, MC, V.
Brushing up on your French to attend the recitals and chamber works performed at this intimate space isn't imperative, but the programming does have a decidedly French accent, both in artists and repertoire.

Merkin Concert Hall

Abraham Goodman House, 129 W 67th St between Broadway and Amsterdam Ave (212-501-3330) www.elainekaufmancenter.org. Subway: 1, 9 to 66th St–Lincoln Ctr. $10–$25. AmEx, MC, V (for advance purchases only).
This unattractive theater with rather dry acoustics is shamefacedly tucked away on a side street in the shadow of Lincoln Center. But its mix of early music and avant-garde programming—heavy on recitals and chamber concerts—can make it a rewarding stop.

New Jersey Performing Arts Center

1 Center St at the waterfront, Newark, NJ (973-642-8989). Travel: PATH train to Newark, then the Loop shuttle bus two stops to the center. $10–$100. AmEx, DC, MC, V.
Designed by Los Angeles–based architect Barton Myers, NJPAC is the first major concert hall built on the East Coast in more than 30 years. The complex is impressive, featuring the oval-shaped, wooden 2,750-seat Prudential Hall and the more institutional-looking 514-seat Victoria Theater. It may sound far away, but, in fact, it takes only about 15 minutes to get to NJPAC from mid-Manhattan. It's a good place to catch big-name acts that may be sold out at stodgy Manhattan venues. In 1999–2000, the Boston Symphony Orchestra, the San Francisco Symphony, the Festival Orchestra of Poland and the Royal Philharmonic Orchestra are among the performers slated to appear.

Town Hall

123 W 43rd St between Sixth and Seventh Aves (212-840-2824). Subway: B, D, F, Q to 42nd St; N, R, S, 1, 2, 3, 9, 7 to 42nd St–Times Sq. Prices vary. AmEx, MC, V.
This recently renovated hall has a wonderful, intimate stage and excellent acoustics. Classical music often shares the programming lineup with New Age speakers, pop concerts and movie screenings.

Other venues

These are some of the more notable spaces. In addition, many museums, libraries and galleries offer chamber music.

Bargemusic

Fulton Ferry Landing, next to the Brooklyn Bridge, Brooklyn (718-624-4061). Subway: A, C to High St. $15–$23. No credit cards.

*Play that funky music: **EOS Orchestra** perform quirky, thoughtful and fun classical concerts.*

Two concerts a week (Thursday and Sunday) are held year-round on this barge, moored by the Brooklyn Navy Yard. It's a magical experience, with gorgeous views of the Manhattan skyline—but dress warmly in winter.

CAMI Hall
165 W 57th St between Sixth and Seventh Aves (212-397-6900). Subway: N, R to 57th St. Prices vary. No credit cards.
Located across the street from Carnegie Hall, this 200-seat recital hall is rented out for individual events, mostly by classical artists.

Continental Center
180 Maiden Ln at Front St (212-721-0965). Subway: A, C to Broadway–Nassau St; 2, 3, 4, 5 to Wall St.
The Juilliard Artists in Concert series offers free lunchtime student recitals in the center once a week; more frequently during the summer.

Hotel Wales
1295 Madison Ave at 92nd St (212-876-6000). Subway: 6 to 96th St. Free.
The Wales offers a great chance to see chamber music for free on Sundays.

The Kitchen
512 W 19th St between Tenth and Eleventh Aves (212-255-5793). Subway: C, E to 23rd St. $10–$20. AmEx, MC, V.
Occupying a 19th-century building that was once an icehouse, the Kitchen has been a meeting place for the avant-garde in music, dance and theater for more than 25 years.

Kosciuszko Foundation House
15 E 65th St at Fifth Ave (212-734-2130). Subway: N, R to Fifth Ave; 6 to 68th St. $10–$15. MC, V.
This renovated East Side townhouse accommodates a fine chamber-music series with a twist: Each program must feature at least one work by a Polish composer. That makes for a lot of Chopin, but there are unexpected treasures as well.

Metropolitan Museum of Art
See chapter **Museums** *for listings.*
Concerts are held in the Grace Rainey Rogers Auditorium, near the Egyptian galleries, or occasionally beside the Temple of Dendur. Since this is one of the city's best chamber-music venues, the concerts usually sell out quickly.

Miller Theater at Columbia University
Broadway at 116th St (212-854-7799). Subway: 1, 9 to 116th St. AmEx, MC, V. Prices vary.
Don't come expecting only student recitals. Columbia's acoustically excellent space attracts some international names and innovative, multidisciplinary programming. (When was the last time you saw a staged version of Jacques Offenbach's "A Trip to the Moon"?)

New York Public Library for the Performing Arts
40 Lincoln Center Plaza (212-870-1630). Subway: 1, 9 to 66th St–Lincoln Ctr. Free.
Bruno Walter Auditorium, which usually hosts recitals, solo performances and lectures, is undergoing renovation, but events are being held in other branches and venues.

Roulette
228 West Broadway at White St (212-219-8242). Subway: A, C, E to Canal St; 1, 9 to Franklin St. $10. No credit cards.
Roulette is the place to go for all sorts of experimental music in a Tribeca loft—very downtown.

Society for Ethical Culture
2 W 64th St at Central Park West (212-721-6500). Subway: 1, 9 to 66th St–Lincoln Ctr.
This quasi-religious cultural center often hosts concerts (the Eos Orchestra is based here) in an intimate, acoustically pleasing setting.

Theodore Roosevelt Birthplace
28 E 20th St between Broadway and Park Ave South (212-260-1616). Subway: N, R, 6 to 23rd St. $2. No credit cards.
Shortly after TR's death, New Yorkers pitched in to rebuild the childhood home of the only U.S. president born in Manhattan. On Saturday afternoons, there's a concert series in the house's small upstairs auditorium. For the price of entry, you can see a concert and get a tour. Often, the same person will take your money, escort you upstairs in the elevator, turn the pianist's pages and give you a house tour. Now *that's* service.

Sylvia & Danny Kaye Playhouse
Hunter College, 68th St between Park and Lexington Aves (212-772-4448). Subway: 6 to 68th St. $20–$45. AmEx, MC, V.
Across town from Lincoln Center, this refurbished theater has an eclectic program of professional music and dance.

Symphony Space
2537 Broadway at 95th St (212-864-5400). Subway: 1, 2, 3, 9 to 96th St. $17–$40. AmEx, MC, V.
The programming here is eclectic; best bets are the annual Wall to Wall marathons, which offer a full day of music featuring a given composer or theme.

John L. Tishman Auditorium
The New School, 66 W 12th St at Sixth Ave (212-229-5689). Subway: F, 1, 2, 3, 9 to 14th St. $10. AmEx, MC, V.
The New School offers the Schneider concerts, a modestly priced chamber-music series that runs from April to October and features up-and-coming young musicians, as well as more established artists who play here for a fraction of the price charged elsewhere.

World Financial Center
West St between Liberty and Vesey Sts (212-945-0505). Subway: N, R, 1, 9 to Cortlandt St. Free.
Logan's Run meets *Blade Runner* at the glassed-in Winter Garden (palm trees spring straight from the marble floor, and you can see the bright lights of the World Financial Center and the World Trade Center). The free concerts (timed to fit the schedule of the working day and usually amplified) range from chamber and choral music to Eno-esque installations for public spaces.

Churches

An enticing variety of music, both sacred and secular, is performed in New York's churches. Many of the resident choirs are excellent, while superb acoustics and serene surroundings make churches particularly attractive venues. A bonus: Some concerts are free or very cheap. The Gotham Early Music Foundation sponsors a terrific annual early-music series at churches around the city. For tickets and information, call 516-329-6166.

Cathedral of St. John the Divine
1047 Amsterdam Ave at 112th St (212-662-2133). Subway: 1, 9 to 110th St.
The 3,000-seat interior is an acoustical cavern, but the stunning Gothic surroundings provide a comfortable home to

Houses of high culture

From Beethoven to Bang on a Can, music at Lincoln Center is world-class

In the 1950s, the tenements and playgrounds that were the setting for Leonard Bernstein's *West Side Story* were demolished. The land, an area near the southwest corner of Central Park, was developed into Lincoln Center, a four-block complex of buildings and public spaces housing many of the city's most important musical institutions. The striking concrete-pillared 1960s architecture of Avery Fisher Hall, the New York State Theater and the Metropolitan Opera House surrounds a black marble fountain by Philip Johnson. There's also the Lincoln Center Theater building, containing the Vivian Beaumont and Mitzi E. Newhouse theaters, as well as Damrosch Park's Guggenheim Bandshell and the New York Public Library for the Performing Arts (*see page 267*). Restaurants at Lincoln Center include the overpriced but convenient Café Vienna, the Panevino Ristorante in Avery Fisher Hall (212-874-7000) and the Grand Tier at the Met (212-799-3400).

Lincoln Center has tended to rely on the tried-and-true: The Great Performers series (October–June) attracts the likes of Jessye Norman, Yo-Yo Ma and Daniel Barenboim (call 212-721-6500 for tickets). But recent additions, such as the Bang on a Can Festival and the Bard Music Festival, are a welcome change. More adventurous is the Lincoln Center Festival, the polar opposite of the center's long-running Mostly Mozart series.

Lincoln Center
65th St at Columbus Ave (212-875-5400, programs and information 800-LIN-COLN; www.lincolncenter.org). Subway: 1, 9 to 66th St–Lincoln Ctr. AmEx, MC, V.

Alice Tully Hall
212-875-5050. $25–$75.
Built to house the Chamber Music Society of Lincoln Center (212-875-5788), Alice Tully Hall somehow makes its 1,000 seats feel intimate. It has no central aisle; the rows have extra leg room to compensate. The hall accommodates both music and spoken text well; its vocal recital series is one of the most extensive in town.

Avery Fisher Hall
212-875-5030. $14–$73.
Originally called Philharmonic Hall, this 2,700-seat auditorium used to have unbearable acoustics. It took the largesse of electronics millionaire Avery Fisher, and several major renovations, to improve the sound quality. The venue is now both handsome and comfortable. This is the headquarters of the New York Philharmonic (212-875-5656), the country's oldest orchestra (founded in 1842) and one of the world's finest, now under the direction of Kurt Masur. Its evangelical philosophy has given rise to free concerts and regular open rehearsals. The hall also hosts performances by top international ensembles as part of the Great Performers series. Every summer, the famous Mostly Mozart series is held here.

Metropolitan Opera House
212-362-6000. $24–$200.
With enormous mystical paintings by Marc Chagall hanging inside its five geometric arches, the Met is the grandest of the Lincoln Center buildings and a spectacular place to see and hear opera. It's home to the Metropolitan Opera, and it's also where major visiting companies are most likely to appear. Met productions are lavish (though not necessarily tasteful), and casts are an international who's who of current stars. Under the baton of artistic director James Levine, the orchestra has become a true symphonic force. Audiences at the Met are knowledgeable and fiercely partisan—subscriptions stay in families for generations. Tickets are expensive, and unless you can afford good seats, the view won't be great. Still, standing-room tickets are available for less than $15, though you have to wait in line on Saturday mornings to buy them. The English-language subtitles that now appear on the backs of seats allow audiences to laugh in all the right places. While over-the-top Franco Zeffirelli productions still tend to be the norm, the Met has started commissioning productions by the likes of Robert Wilson—to mixed reception from conservative Met audiences. (Wilson was booed at the premiere of his production of *Lohengrin.*) The Met has programmed some daring productions recently, including Schoenberg's *Moses und Aron* and Carlisle Floyd's *Susannah*, but the classics remain the Met's bread and butter.

New York State Theater
212-870-5570. $20–$90.
Recently, the New York State Theatre board shocked the faithful when it considered raising funds by selling a Jasper Johns painting it had commissioned. (*The New York Times* in particular was outraged, but the scandal has blown over; the painting will stay). NYST houses the New York City Opera, which has tried to upgrade its second-best reputation by being defiantly popular and defiantly ambitious. This means hiring only American singers, performing many works in English, bringing American musicals into opera houses, giving a more theatrical spin to old favorites and developing supertitles for foreign-language productions. City Opera has championed modern opera—mixing Tan Dun's *Ghost Opera* with *Madama Butterfly*—with a few great successes and some noble failures. It's ultimately much cooler than its stodgier neighbor. Tickets are about half the price of the Met, and the theater is a gem.

Walter Reade Theater
212-875-5601. $15–$30.
Lincoln Center's newest concert hall is a glorified movie house: This is ground zero for the Film Society of Lincoln Center, and its acoustics are the driest in the complex. Yet the uniformly perfect sight lines make up for it. The Chamber Music Society uses the space for its Music of Our Time series, and the post-Minimalist Bang on a Can festival houses its resident ensemble here. A Sunday-morning concert series features pastries and hot drinks in the lobby.

such groups as the Ensemble for Early Music and the church's own heavenly choir.

Christ and St. Stephen's Church
120 W 69th St at Broadway (212-787-2755).
Subway: 1, 2, 3, 9 to 72nd St.
This West Side church offers one of the most diverse concert rosters in the city.

Church of the Heavenly Rest
2 E 90th St at Fifth Ave (212-289-3400). Subway:
4, 5, 6 to 86th St.
Heavenly Rest is home to the Canterbury Choral Society and the New York Pro Arte Chamber Orchestra.

Church of St. Ignatius Loyola
980 Park Ave at 84th St (212-288-2520). Subway:
4, 5, 6 to 86th St.
This church's Sacred Music in a Sacred Space series is a high point of Upper East Side musical life.

Corpus Christi Church
529 W 121st Street between Broadway and Amsterdam
Ave (212-666-9350). Subway: 1, 9 to 116th St.
Fans of early music can get their fix from Music Before 1800 (212-666-9266), a resident ensemble that has also presented the U.S. debuts of many prominent European groups.

Good Shepherd Presbyterian Church
152 W 66th St between Broadway and Amsterdam Ave
(212-799-1259). Subway: 1, 9 to 66th St–Lincoln Ctr.
Musically, Good Shepherd is best known for the twice-weekly recitals of the Jupiter Symphony, under music director Jens Nygaard. Other classical-music events are also presented here.

Riverside Church
490 Riverside Dr at 120th St (212-870-6700).
Subway: 1, 9 to 116th St.
With its active internal musical life (fine choir, fine organ) and visiting guests (the Orpheus Chamber Orchestra, among others), Riverside plays a large part in the city's musical life.

St. Bartholomew's Church
109 E 50th St between Park and Lexington Aves (212-
378-0248). Subway: E, F to Lexington Ave; 6 to 51st St.
Large-scale choral music and occasional chapel recitals fill the magnificent dome behind the church's facade, designed by Stanford White.

St. Paul's Chapel at Trinity Church
Broadway at Fulton St (212-602-0747). Subway: A, C, J,
M, Z to Broadway–Nassau St; N, R, 1, 9 to Rector St; 2,
3, 4, 5 to Wall St.
Historic Trinity, in the heart of the Financial District, offers individual concerts and the Noonday Concerts series.

St. Thomas Church Fifth Avenue
1 W 53rd St at Fifth Ave (212-757-7013). Subway:
B, D, F, Q to 47–50th Sts–Rockefeller Ctr.
Some of the finest choral music in the city can be heard here by the only fully accredited choir school for boys in the country. The church's annual *Messiah* is a must-see.

Schools

Juilliard, Mannes and the Manhattan School of Music are all renowned for their students, their faculty and their artists-in-residence, all of whom regularly perform for free or for minimal admission fees. Noteworthy music and innovative programming can be found at several other colleges and schools in the city.

*A night at the opera: The **Lincoln Center Festival** makes summer evenings classic.*

Brooklyn Center for the Performing Arts at Brooklyn College
Campus Rd at Hillel Pl, one block from the junction of
Flatbush and Nostrand Aves, Brooklyn (718-951-4543).
Subway: 2, 5 to Flatbush Ave–Brooklyn College. $20–$50.
AmEx, MC, V.
While it mostly hosts concerts by mass-appeal pop performers, this hall, smack in the middle of Flatbush, also serves as a destination for traveling opera troupes and soloists of international acclaim.

Greenwich House Music School
46 Barrow St between Bedford St and Seventh Ave
South (212-242-4770). Subway: 1, 9 to Christopher
St–Sheridan Sq. Prices vary. MC, V.
Greenwich House's Renee Weiler Concert Hall puts on a wide variety of chamber concerts by students, faculty and visiting guests. Student recitals are free.

Juilliard School of Music
Juilliard Theater, Morse Hall, Paul Recital Hall, 60
Lincoln Center Plaza (212-769-7406) www.juilliard.edu.
Subway: 1, 9 to 66th St–Lincoln Ctr. Mostly free.
New York's premier conservatory stages weekly concerts by student soloists, orchestras and chamber ensembles, as well as excellent student opera productions.

The best of the fests

Whatever the season, there's mucho music for your ears

The heartbeat of New York follows the rhythm of its music—so it's a good thing that there are several festivals every year to keep it pounding. Here's a few that have happened for at least several years running—but look for exact dates and schedules in *Time Out New York*.

Autumn Blues Festival

www.worldmusicinstitute.org.
New York is by no means a blues town comparable to Memphis or Chicago. But each year, in early November, the World Music Institute invites a passel of blues artists—whether wizened living links to a vanishing rural tradition or new jacks with worldly influences galore—to come and show how to connect the dots.

Bang on a Can Festival

Office: 222 E 9th St, 10003. (212-777-8442; fax 212-364-1727) www.bangonacan.org.
Think of Bang on a Can as the annual showcase for the rambunctious side of classical music. The composers, instrumentalists and improvisers who play the fest are as accomplished as any on the classical circuit, but in many cases, they gave up dreams of prime-time because it wouldn't embrace their late-20th-century need to kick out the jams. The highlight of every festival is the daylong BoaC Marathon, where you might catch art-music heads like Ben Neill or Fred Frith following a revamped interpretation of a Xenakis, Cage or Stockhausen piece performed by Sonic Youth's Thurston Moore or Lee Ranaldo.

Bell Atlantic New York Jazz Festival

Knitting Factory and various venues. (212-219-3006) www.jazzfest.com.

Michael Dorf used to call this decade-old fete the What Is Jazz? Festival, but no more. You never know what corporate heading Knitting Factory owner-impresario Dorf will be putting in front of his annual jazz fest—one year it was Texaco, before that Heineken—but the event is guaranteed to be the most sprawling of the year. Now, he spreads the biggest names in jazz (Joe Henderson, the Art Ensemble of Chicago, Dave Holland, McCoy Tyner) over the first half of June, and adds alterna-draws (P-Funk All-Stars, Jon Spencer Blues Explosion, Galactic) to further distinguish his fest from his rival/mentor George Wein's long-running JVC Jazz Festival.

CMJ Music Marathon, MusicFest, and FilmFest

Office: 11 Middle Neck Rd #400, Long Island, NY 11021-2301 (516-498-3150; fax 516-466-7161) www.cmj.com.
CMJ is an annual industry schmoozefest at which hundreds of bands play all over the city; there are also trade-show–type fairs and panel discussions at a large Manhattan hotel. It usually takes place in September or November, over a four-day period. CMJ stands for *College Music Journal*, which publishes trade and consumer mags that track college radio airplay, retail sales, etc. The festival traditionally books hip young things (i.e., college rock) in genres such as rock, indie rock, hip-hop, electronica, alternative country and so on. Other than South by Southwest in Austin, Texas, (in March) and the Winter Music Conference (in Florida), this is the most important industry confab for music-biz pros.

Digital Club Festival

www.digitalclubfestival.com

*Can-do spirit: The classical impulse heads downtown for the **Bang on a Can Festival**.*

This weeklong affair was previously called the MacFest and the IntelFest, and now it's the Digital Club Festival, which is organized by Knitting Factory mogul Michael Dorf and Andrew Rasjej. It takes place in the summertime, usually in July, and features hundreds of bands at more than 20 Manhattan venues. Traditionally, it hasn't featured very many exciting acts, but it might still be a chance for those visiting NYC to check out the local talent all at once.

Guinness Fleadh
Downing Stadium, Randall's Island (see **Outdoor summer venues**, *page 264, for listings).*
At this celebration of Irish and Irish American music, the Guinness flows, the bands rock and, since it always seems to rain in late June, the field gets very muddy. Past Fleadhs have featured Ireland natives like Sinéad O'Connor, Van Morrison and Shane MacGowan, as well as non-Irishmen (not even close) Lucinda Williams and Hootie & the Blowfish.

JVC Jazz Festival
Various venues (212-501-1390)
www.festivalproductions.net.
JVC Jazz Festival head George Wein developed the concept for this yearly event up in Newport, RI, some 40-plus years ago, so one might consider this the grandaddy of jazz events. Not only does JVC Jazz fill big-time halls like Carnegie, Avery Fisher and the Beacon Theater with a parade of music's biggest draws (James Brown, João Gilberto, Herbie Hancock, Cassandra Wilson, Dave Brubeck), it also spreads jazz throughout the city by offering gigs in Harlem (the Schomburg Center, the Studio Museum in Harlem) and half-price deals with downtown clubs like the Village Vanguard, Sweet Basil and Dharma. As if that wasn't enough, JVC also sponsors an old-school mini-swing fest at the Sylvia & Danny Kaye Playhouse and free concerts of more adventurous music (like Marc Ribot and James Carter) in the splendor of Bryant Park.

Museum of Modern Art Summergarden
See chapter **Museums** *for listings.*
Throughout the summer, 20th-century classical works are performed in the MoMA sculpture garden. You'll quite likely think you're in a Woody Allen movie, but bring your own neuroses.

Vision Festival
Venue changes annually. www.visionfest.org
Now that corporate sponsorship has moved the Knitting Factory's jazz fest closer to the mainstream, the Lower East Side–based Vision Festival is the only full-fledged avant-garde jazz event in town. Organized every May by Iron Man bassist William Parker and his wife, dancer Patricia Nicholson, the multimedia event brings together some of the biggest draws in free-jazz (Matthew Shipp, Peter Brøtzmann, Joseph Jarman, Tim Berne) with dancers, poets and visual artists. It's where DIY spirit and freewheeling music go hand in hand.

Washington Square Music Festival
Washington Sq Park, West Fourth St and La Guardia Pl (212-431-1088). Suway: A, C, E, B, D, F, Q to W 4th St–Washington Sq. Free.
This concert series, held in the heart of Greenwhich Village, features chamber-orchestra and ensemble works every Tuesday night in June and July.

Manhattan School of Music
120 Claremont Ave at 122nd St (212-749-2802). Subway: 1, 9 to 125th St. Mostly free.
MSM offers master classes, recitals and off-site concerts by its students, faculty and visiting pros. The opera program is one of the most adventurous in town.

Mannes College of Music
150 W 85th St between Amsterdam and Columbus Aves (212-496-8524) www.newschool.edu/academic/ mannes.htm. Subway: B, C, 1, 9 to 86th St. Free.
Long considered a weak link in the city's conservatory triumvirate that includes Julliard and Manhattan, Mannes has recently been raising its profile. Concerts are by a mix of student, faculty and professional ensembles-in-residence. See the Orion String Quartet at Lincoln Center for big bucks, or here for free.

Opera

The Metropolitan Opera and the New York City Opera may be the big guys (*see* **Houses of high culture,** *page 268*), but they're hardly the only ones in town. The following companies perform a varied repertory—both warhorses and works-in-progress—from Verdi's *Aida* to Wargo's *Chekhov Trilogy*. Call the individual organizations for ticket prices, schedules and venue details.

Amato Opera Theater
319 Bowery at 2nd St (212-228-8200). Subway: 6 to Bleecker St.
With a theater only 20 feet wide, Anthony and Sally Amato's charming, fully staged productions are like opera in someone's living room. Lots of well-known singers have sung here, but casting is sometimes inconsistent.

American Opera Projects
463 Broome St between Greene and Mercer Sts (212-431-8102). Subway: 6 to Canal St.
AOP is not so much an opera company as a living, breathing workshop for the art form. Productions are often a way to follow a work-in-progress.

Dicapo Opera Theater
184 E 76th St between Lexington and Third Aves (212-288-9438). Subway: 6 to 77th St.
This top-notch chamber-opera troupe benefits from City Opera–quality singers performing in intelligently designed small-scale sets. A real treat.

New York Gilbert & Sullivan Players
See **Symphony Space,** *page 269.*
Every January at Symphony Space, this troupe presents one of the Big Three (*HMS Pinafore, The Mikado* or *The Pirates of Penzance*) alongside another G&S work.

Opera Orchestra of New York
154 W 57th St at Seventh Ave (212-799-1982). Subway: A, C, B, D, 1, 9 to 59th St–Columbus Circle; N, R to 57th St.
The program organizers unearth forgotten operatic gems and showcase great new talent in semistaged concert performances at Carnegie Hall.

Regina Opera Company
Regina Hall, 65th St and Twelfth Ave, Bay Ridge, Brooklyn (718-232-3555). Subway: B, M to 62nd St; N to Ft. Hamilton Pkwy.
The only year-round opera company in Brooklyn, Regina offers full orchestras and fully staged productions.

Sports & Fitness

Whether you're a would-be pro or a professional fan, New York's got a court, field—or ticket—for you

When it comes to spectator sports, particularly the big four (baseball, basketball, football and hockey), New Yorkers believe they hold a special monopoly on wisdom. This is a place where every third person you meet is convinced that, given enough time and money, he or she could run the local team better than whoever is running it now. New Yorkers read the tabloids back to front, and arguments over half-remembered sports trivia can be far more heated than disputes about politics, sex or religion.

The New York metropolitan area has more professional teams than any other city in America: two basketball, three hockey, two baseball and two football, not to mention myriad pro and amateur soccer, lacrosse and rugby leagues. New Yorkers are passionately devoted to their local heroes; they may grouse about the players and condemn the owners, but when the home team is in contention for a championship, the city practically grinds to a halt during games. If the team wins, it's ticker-tape parades and pandemonium in the streets.

Baseball is very much a product of the five boroughs. The basic rules of the game were drawn up by a New York team in 1846, and the first professional leagues originated in the city during the 1870s. Babe Ruth and the Yankees' "Murderers' Row" of the 1920s cemented the game's hold on the popular imagination. Joe DiMaggio reinforced it in the 1930s. During the 1950s, three of New York's boroughs had great teams; there were endless debates over the relative merits of the Bronx-based Yankees' Mickey Mantle, the Manhattan-based Giants' Willie Mays and the Brooklyn Dodgers' Duke Snider. More recently, the Mets (who replaced the Dodgers and Giants after they moved west) and the Yankees have vied for New Yorkers' hearts, with a stellar Yankee team generally emerging triumphant.

For a time, when "Broadway Joe" Namath stood at the helm of the New York Jets, it seemed as though the football gridiron might supplant the baseball diamond in the hearts of New Yorkers. But it is basketball that grips the city now–the Knicks are perennial contenders for a championship (and perennial losers) and the up-and-coming New Jersey Nets excite fans across the river.

Spectator sports

All the daily papers carry massive amounts of sports analysis and give listings of the day's events and TV coverage—concentrating on the National Basketball Association, National Hockey League, National Football League and Major League Baseball. *The New York Times* may have the most literate reporting, but the tabloids—the *Daily News* and the *New York Post*—are best for hyperdetailed information and blunt, insistent opinions. Local cable and broadcast television is likewise inundated with sports—the Fox Sports and Madison Square Garden networks (channels 26 and 27 in Manhattan) provide 24-hour events and news. For information on special events, contact the New York Convention & Visitors Bureau (212-397-8222) or go to their website (www.nycvisit.com).

BOX-OFFICE TICKETS

Your first call for tickets should be to the team itself. You may be referred to Ticketmaster (212-307-7171), which sells the same tickets, with an added service charge. For many events, however—especially football and basketball—demand for tickets far outstrips supply. If you are certain that neither the team nor Ticketmaster can help, you have two options: scalpers or ticket brokers. If you're staying in a hotel, it's worth having a word with the concierge, as they often have excellent connections.

SCALPERS

If you buy from scalpers, you won't be able to get your money back if you're tricked—but if you're careful, this can be a reliable way of buying seats. Before you part with any cash, check that the ticket has the correct details, and make sure you know where your seats will be. Diagrams of stadium seating arrangements are printed in the front of the Yellow Pages. Sometimes scalpers will overestimate demand and, as game time nears, try to unload their tickets at bargain prices. The police have been cracking down on scalpers in recent years—particularly outside Madison Square Garden, home of the Knicks and Rangers—so be discreet.

TICKET BROKERS

Ticket brokers offer much the same service as scalpers, although their activities are more regulated. It's illegal in New York state to sell a ticket for more than its face value plus a service charge, so these companies operate from other states by phone. They can almost guarantee tickets for sold-

*Bomber away! Pinstripe pinup Derek Jeter of the **Yankees** waits for his pitch.*

No pier pressure here

Chelsea Piers offers a whole world of sports on the Hudson waterfront

When the Chelsea Piers first opened as New York's premier passenger ship terminal in 1910, *The New York Times* called it "the most remarkable urban design achievement" of its day. Almost 90 years later, after a long period of decline, neglect and decay, the Chelsea Piers reopened in 1996 as a 30-acre waterfront sports and entertainment complex. No longer merely remarkable, the *Times* says the new Chelsea Piers "represents a remarkably well-wrought balance of public and private priorities." The complex blends nature and narcissism most harmoniously and its expansiveness is a sight to behold, even if you didn't bring your running shoes.

If you choose not to take a spin around the indoor running track or scale the climbing wall, the Chelsea Piers offers plenty of options. There are park spaces to stroll through, sundecks to bathe on, a spa to unwind in and boats to embark on for a romantic moonlight cruise along the Hudson (*see chapter* **Tour New York**). The Chelsea Piers hosts a variety of special events so call for a schedule. And the sitcom *Spin City* is filmed in one of the studios there (*see chapter* **Film & TV**).

All activities are open to the public and priced individually; call (212-336-6262) to purchase a day "passport" for the Sports Center. The Gold Passport ($50, ages 16 and up) provides access to the Sports Center, Golf Club, Roller Rinks, Sky Rink and Field House. The Silver Passport ($35, ages 12 and up) provides access to the Golf Club, Roller Rinks, Sky Rink and Field House. Most equipment is available for rental or purchase on the premises.

This wheel's on fire: All skill levels get their turn at the skate park at **Chelsea Piers**.

Chelsea Piers
Piers 59–62. Enter at 23rd St at the West Side Hwy. Travel: C, E to 23rd Street then M23 bus to river.

Sports Center at Chelsea Piers
Pier 60 (212-336-6000). Day membership $35 ($50 on weekends). Weekdays 6am–11pm; weekends 8am–9pm. Must be at least 16 years old with proper ID to use facilities.
The Sports Center contains a quarter-mile indoor track, Olympic swimming pool, basketball courts, hard and sand volleyball courts, weight room and cardio machines, two studios of fitness classes, steam room, sauna, an indoor climbing wall and the Origins Feel-Good Spa.

Sky Rink
Pier 61 (212-336-6100). Adults $10.50, children and seniors $8, skate rental $5, helmet rental $3. Call rink for hours.
The Sky Rink is Manhattan's only year-round, indoor ice skating rink. It has several general skating, figure skating and ice hockey programs including lessons and performances. It often closes for a few hours in the early evening for cleaning.

Roller Rinks
Pier 62 (212-336-6200). General skating 10am–5pm (weather permitting). Adults $5, children $4. Skate Park 10am–10pm. Weekdays $8.50 all day, weekends $8.50 per session. Equipment rental (including protective gear) adults $13.50, children $8.
There are two outdoor, regulation-sized roller skating rinks for general skating. The Skate Park features an 11-1/2-foot vertical ramp, six-foot mini vert ramp, mini vert ramp with spine and a four-way fun box for in-line skating.

AMF Chelsea Bowl
Between Piers 59 and 60 (212-835-BOWL). Sun–Thu 9am–2am; Fri, Sat 9am–4am. $6 per person per game, $4 ball and shoe rental.
This mega-complex features 40 lanes, a huge arcade and bar, and glow-in-the-dark "disco" bowling every night.

Golf Club
Pier 59 (212-336-6400). Off-peak: weekdays 6am–5pm, 10pm–midnight. Minimum $15 (100 balls). Peak: weekdays 5pm–10pm, Sat–Sun 9am–12am. Minimum $15 (68 balls). Golf Academy (212-336-6444). Mon–Thu 9am–10pm; Fri–Sun 9am–5pm.
The Golf Club features 52 weather-protected and heated driving stalls (stacked four-stories high), a 1,000-sq-ft practice putting green, an automatic ball transport system, and a 200-yard artificial-turf fairway that extends along the pier.

Field House
Pier 62 (212-336-6500). Batting cages: 10 pitches per $1 token. Hours vary. Gym and climbing wall: ages 4–adult, $15 per person. Basketball and playing fields: one hour $7 per person. Toddler gym: $8 per session.
The 80,000-square-foot field house includes a gymnastics training center, a rock-climbing wall, basketball courts, turf fields, batting cages, a toddler gym, dance studios and locker rooms.

out events, and tend to deal in the better seats. Not surprisingly, this is a service you pay for. Good seats for the basketball playoffs run close to $1,000, and tickets for most Giants football games start at $100. Look under "Ticket Sales" in the Yellow Pages for brokers. Three of the more established are Prestige Entertainment (800-2GET-TIX), Ticket Window (800-SOLD-OUT) and Union Tickets (800-CITY-TIX).

Baseball

For a while, it looked as if the national pastime had passed its time in New York. The 1995 players' strike turned off fans nationwide, pro basketball was at the height of its popularity, and neither the Mets nor the Yankees were performing particularly well. That's all changed. Mark McGwire's 1998 home-run record brought fans back to the game in droves, as the American League Yankees developed into the best team in the sport—winning the 1996 and 1998 World Series—and the National League Mets are coming on strong in their own right. Tickets are available at the stadiums for most games from April to early October, but they're almost impossible to get for the postseason championship games—which in recent years have been a likely destination for the Yankees but not the Mets.

New York Mets
Shea Stadium, 123–01 Roosevelt Ave at 126th St, Flushing, Queens (718-507-8499). Subway: 7 to Willets Point–Shea Stadium. Information Mon–Fri 9am–5:30pm. $10–$30. AmEx, Disc, MC, V.

New York Yankees
Yankee Stadium, River Ave at 161st St, Bronx (718-293-4300, ticket office 718-293-6000). Subway: B, D, 4 to 161st St–Yankee Stadium. Information Mon–Fri 9am–5pm; Sat and during games 10am–3pm. $12–$27. AmEx, Disc, MC, V.

Basketball

The basketball scene is dominated by the two NBA teams, the New York Knicks and the New Jersey Nets, with the Knicks reigning supreme in most New Yorkers' hearts. Tickets for most games, however, range from expensive to unobtainable. If you miss out or can't afford pro tix, exciting basketball action can be seen at the local colleges (St. John's University in Queens has done well recently) or for free by watching the hustlers play pickup games on street courts *(see Hoops—there it is, page 276).*

New York Knickerbockers (Knicks)
Madison Square Garden, Seventh Ave at 32nd St (212-465-6741). Subway: A, C, E, 1, 2, 3, 9 to 34th St–Penn Station. Ticket office Mon–Fri 9am–6pm; Sat 10am–3pm. Official prices are fairly meaningless—ticket information is usually restricted to "This game is sold out."

New Jersey Nets
Continental Airlines Arena, East Rutherford, NJ (201-935-8888, tickets 201-935-3900). Travel: bus from Port Authority Bus Terminal, 42nd St and Eighth Ave, $3.25

each way (212-564-8484). Ticket office Mon–Fri 9am–6pm; Sat 10am–6pm; Sun noon–5pm. $30–$75. AmEx, MC, V.

St. John's University Red Storm
Madison Square Garden. Seventh Ave at 32nd St (212-465-6741). Subway: A, C, E, 1, 2, 3, 9 to 34th St–Penn Station. Season runs from November to March.

Boxing

Madison Square Garden
Seventh Ave at 32nd St (212-465-6741). Subway: A, C, E, 1, 2, 3, 9 to 34th St–Penn Station.
After several decades in which the biggest bouts were fought in Atlantic City or Las Vegas, boxing has been returning to the Garden, once considered a mecca for fans of the sport. There are usually a few major fights in the course of a year.

Golden Gloves Boxing Championships
The Theatre at Madison Square Garden. Seventh Ave at 32nd St (212-465-6741). Subway: A, C, E, 1, 2, 3, 9 to 34th St–Penn Station.
The Golden Gloves, a long-running New York tradition and amateur boxing's most prestigious competition, takes place every April.

Heavy Hands/Church Street Boxing Gym
25 Park Pl between Church St and Broadway (212-571-1333). Subway 4, 5, 6 to Brooklyn Bridge–City Hall.
This relatively new addition to the boxing scene functions as both workout gym and venue. Amateur fights (including women's bouts) are staged throughout the year, as well as professional kickboxing.

Cricket

The comedy of hearing an American attempt to explain cricket is rivaled only by a European doing the same for baseball. Nonetheless, thanks to its large populations of Indians, Pakistanis and West Indians, not to mention Brits, New York has more than 50 teams and at least two parks where the sound of leather on willow can be heard. The season runs from April to October.

Van Cortlandt Park
Van Cortlandt Park South and Bailey Ave, Bronx. Subway: 1, 9 to 242nd St. There are six or seven pitches here. The Commonwealth Cricket League, the largest league in the nation, plays on Sundays, May–September.
The New York Cricket League (201-343-4544) also arranges Sunday matches.

Walker Park
50 Bard Ave at Delafield Court, Staten Island. Travel: ferry to Staten Island, then S61 or S74 bus to Bard Ave.
The Staten Island Cricket Club (718-447-5442) plays here most weekends during the season.

Football

The combination of beer and machismo known as football culture may be more indigenous to the American heartland than to this metropolis, but New York is one of the only cities capable of supporting two professional teams. Of course, they both play in Giants Stadium, which is in New Jersey, but that's just a technicality. From August to

December every year—and longer if the playoffs are involved, which they increasingly are—New York is as fanatical a football town as any.

The Giants have a 20-year waiting list for season tickets, so the only way to see a game is to know someone with a season ticket or pay blood money to a broker. The Jets are slightly more accessible. The team has a waiting list of 11,000 but sells scattered single seats for $40 on a first-come, first-served, cash-only basis from the its main office in Hempstead, NY, and via Ticket-

master (*see page 272*). Even this limited opportunity may soon disappear if the Jets continue to improve as they have in recent years.

New York Giants
Giants Stadium, East Rutherford, NJ (201-935-8222). Travel: bus from Port Authority Bus Terminal, 42nd St at Eighth Ave, $3.25 each way (212-564-8484).

New York Jets
1000 Fulton Ave, Hempstead, NY (516-560-8200). The Jets play home games at the Giants Stadium, for directions, *see above.*

Hoops—there it is

From Coney Island's rough-and-tumble playgrounds to the Garden's celebrity glitz, basketball rules in New York City

They don't call basketball "the city game" for nothing. It may be the invention of a New England WASP, Dr. James Naismith, but it was black inner-city youths who perfected the sport. Basketball's minimal demand for space and equipment make it ideal for an urban environment, and the level of play on the street courts of the city today is good enough to draw the pros during their off-season. If you have the skills to ball with the best—or just want to see some high-quality hoops—check out any of the public courts below.

Dunkin', go nuts: Games abound in the city.

The hottest ticket in town today is courtside for New York Knicks games at Madison Square Garden, where scene-makers, corporate types and hardcore fans rub shoulders with celebrity fixtures like Spike Lee and Woody Allen. What draws them is a mix of pure athleticism, intuition, improvisation and individual expression not seen in any other sport—and the perpetual hope of a championship. If you can't find (or afford) tickets, get thee to a good sports bar and drink in the atmosphere.

The current Knicks team, which has had the misfortune to play in the same era as the sublime Michael Jordan and his Chicago Bulls, seems doomed to eternal bridesmaidhood. New York's also-ran status is a bitter pill for a town that not-so-secretly believes itself the navel of the world. The team today is like the city—richly talented and neurotically insecure. Both are slightly unsettling and incredibly exciting to watch. Meanwhile, across the river in New Jersey, the Nets are a rapidly maturing team that may be poised to eclipse the Knicks before long.

Hottest street games

Asphalt Green
90th St at East End Ave. Subway: 4, 5, 6 to 86th St.

The Battlegrounds
151st St at Amsterdam Ave. Subway: 1, 9 to 145th St.

Goat Park
99th St at Amsterdam Ave. Subway: 1, 2, 3, 9 to 96th St.

Marcus Garvey Park
121st St at Madison Ave. Subway: 4, 5, 6 to 125th St.

West 4th Street Courts (the Cage)
Sixth Ave at 4th St. Subway: A, C, E, B, D, F, Q to W 4th St–Washington Sq.

Hockey

A game of speed and skill with the perpetual threat of spectacular violence, hockey is popular in New York, but not prohibitively so. In recent years, the New Jersey Devils have far surpassed their colleagues, the New York Islanders and Rangers. While hard to get, tickets are available; they go on sale at the beginning of the season, which runs from October to April.

New Jersey Devils
Continental Airlines Arena, East Rutherford, NJ (Devils information 201-935-6050). Travel: bus from Port Authority Bus Terminal, 42nd St at Eighth Ave, $3.25 each way (212-564-8484). Ticket office 9am–5pm and during games. $20–$74. AmEx, MC, V.

New York Islanders
Nassau Memorial Coliseum, Hempstead Turnpike, Uniondale, Long Island (516-794-4100). Travel: Long Island Railroad (718-217-5477) from Penn Station, Seventh Ave at 32nd St, to Westbury Station. Ticket office 9am–7pm and during games. $19–$70. AmEx, MC, V.

New York Rangers
Madison Square Garden, Seventh Ave at 32nd St (212-465-6741). Subway: A, C, E, 1, 2, 3, 9 to 34th St–Penn Station. $22–$55. AmEx, DC, Disc, MC, V.

Horse racing

There are four major race tracks just outside Manhattan: Belmont, Aqueduct, the Meadowlands and Yonkers. If you don't want to trek out to Long Island or Jersey, head for an Off-Track Betting (OTB) outpost and catch the action and (reliably seedy) atmosphere there instead.

Aqueduct Racetrack
110th St at Rockaway Blvd, Ozone Park, Queens (718-641-4700). Subway: A to Aqueduct Racetrack. Oct–May. Clubhouse $3, grandstand $1. No credit cards. Thoroughbred races are held five days a week (Wed–Sun) during the season.

Belmont Park
2150 Hempstead Turnpike at Plainfield Ave, Elmont, Long Island (718-641-4700). Travel: Pony Express or Belmont Special from Penn Station to Belmont Park. May–Oct. Clubhouse $4, grandstand $2. No credit cards. Thoroughbred racing five days a week (Wed–Sun) in season. The Belmont Stakes, the third leg of the Triple Crown, is usually held on the second Saturday in June.

Meadowlands Racetrack
East Rutherford, NJ (201-935-8500). Travel: bus from Port Authority Bus Terminal, 42nd St at Eighth Ave, $3.25 each way (212-564-8484). Jan–Aug harness, Sept–Dec Thoroughbred. Clubhouse $3, grandstand $1, Pegasus Restaurant $5. No credit cards. Feb–Apr Wed–Sun; May–Aug Tue–Sat; Sept–Dec Wed–Sat.

Yonkers Raceway
Central Park Ave, Yonkers, NY (914-968-4200). Travel: 4 to Woodlawn, then #20 bus to the track. Mon, Tue, Thu–Sat 7:40–11:30pm. Evening tickets $2.25, daytime free. No credit cards.
Harness racing isn't as glamorous as Thoroughbred racing, but you can lose your money here all the same.

Soccer

Soccer is very popular in New York, especially in the outer boroughs, where you can catch matches every summer weekend in parks in the Polish, Italian and Latin American neighborhoods. A higher standard of play can be seen in the games of the New York/New Jersey MetroStars, part of the professional Major League Soccer that was established after America hosted the World Cup in 1994. The team plays at Giants Stadium in New Jersey, and the season runs from March to September. The MetroStars draw an international crowd and have attracted a devoted following.

New York/New Jersey MetroStars
Giants Stadium, East Rutherford, NJ (201-935-3900). Travel: bus from Port Authority Bus Terminal, 42nd St at Eighth Ave, $3.25 each way (212-564-8484). $15–$30. AmEx, MC, V.

Tennis

U.S. Open
USTA Tennis Center, Flushing, Queens (718-760-6200, tickets 888-673-6849). Subway: 7 to Willets Point–Shea Stadium. Late Aug–early Sept. $31–$66 day tickets. AmEx, DC, Disc, MC, V.
Tickets go on sale June 13, though seats tend to be snapped up by corporate sponsors.

Chase Championships
Madison Square Garden, Seventh Avenue at 32nd St (212-465-6500). Subway: A, C, E, 1, 2, 3, 9 to 34th St–Penn Station. Second and third weeks of Nov. $15–$75. AmEx, MC, V.
The top 16 women's singles players and top 32 doubles teams compete for megabucks in this premier indoor tournament. Tickets go on sale at the end of April.

Wrestling

Professional wrestling is more entertainment than sport—the Greco-Roman athletes of old would be dismayed to see what goes by the name "wrestling" these days. On the other hand, they might have a lot of fun. Local venues include: Madison Square Garden (212-465-6741), Nassau Memorial Coliseum, Uniondale, Long Island (516-794-9303) and Continental Airlines Arena, East Rutherford, NJ (201-935-3900). Call for dates and ticket information.

Active sports

New York also offers plenty for those who define "sports" as something a bit more active than watching others play. Central Park is an oasis for everybody from skaters to cricket players (*see* **Heaven central**, *pages 70–71*). Gyms have practically replaced bars as hip pickup spots (*see* **Fit to be tried**, *page 279*), and massive complexes such as Chelsea Piers have brought suburban space to the big city (*see* **No pier pressure here**, *page 274*).

Department of Parks & Recreation

Call 888-NY-PARKS for a list of scheduled events.

Women's Sports Foundation

Information and referral service 800-227-3988.
Mon–Fri 9am–5pm.
The staff here is happy to answer any queries you may have
about women's events, facilities and sporting history.

Biking

You can rent bikes at the Loeb Boathouse in Central Park, where the 7.2-mile (11.5 km) road loop
is closed to traffic on weekends (*see* **Heaven central**, *pages 70–71*). Also try **Metro Bicycles**
(1311 Lexington Avenue at 88th Street; 212-427-
4450; $7 per hour, $35 per eight-hour day. AmEx,
Disc, MC, V. Driver's license or credit card required
as security). If you want to rent a bike in Brooklyn, try **Sizzling Bicycle** (3100 Ocean Parkway
entrance on West Brighton Beach Avenue; 718-
372-8985; $6 per hour, $30 per day).

Bike New York

Hosteling International, 891 Amsterdam Ave at
103rd St (212-932-2300). Subway: 1, 9 to 103rd St.
Advice and classes on all aspects of cycling, from risking
death on the busy Manhattan streets to scenic mountain biking outside the city limits. The club also arranges the excellent Five-Borough Bike Tour every May.

Time's Up Club

212-802-8222.
This alternative-transportation advocacy group sponsors
rides throughout the year, including "Critical Mass," in
which hundreds of cyclists and skaters go tearing through
Greenwich Village on the first Thursday of every month.

Fast and Fabulous

212-567-7160.
This "queer and queer-friendly" riding group leads tours of
various lengths throughout the year, usually meeting in Central Park and heading out of the city.

Bowling

See **No pier pressure here**, *page 274.*

Bowlmor Lanes

110 University Pl between 12th and 13th Sts
(212-255-8188). Subway: L, N, R, 4, 5, 6 to 14th
St–Union Sq. Tue, Wed, Sun 10am–1am; Thu
10am–2am; Mon, Fri, Sat 10am–4am. $3.95 per
person per game before 5pm, $4.95 after, $5.95 on
weekends; $3 shoe rental. AmEx, MC, V.
A recent renovation of this historic Greenwich Village alley
(Richard Nixon bowled here!) has made it the bowling
equivalent of a hip downtown nightclub.

Leisure Time Recreation

625 Eighth Ave at 40th St, in the Port Authority Bus
Terminal (212-268-6909). Subway: A, C, E to 42nd St;
N, R, S, 1, 2, 3, 9, 7 to 42nd St–Times Sq. Sun–Thu
10am–11pm; Fri, Sat 10am–4am. $4.75 per person
per game; $3 shoe rental. MC, V.
Let fly a few strikes down one of 30 lanes while you're waiting for your bus. Or sink some shots at the bar.

Dance

See chapter **Dance**.

Golf

See **No pier pressure here**, *page 274.*

*The fast lane: Develop your inner alley cat at **Bowlmor Lanes**, in Greenwich Village.*

Kissena Park Golf Course
164–15 Booth Memorial Ave at 164th St, Flushing,
Queens (718-939-4594). Travel: 7 to Main St–Flushing,
then Q65 bus. Daily dawn–dusk. Green fees Mon–Fri
before 3pm $19, Sat $21.50, Mon–Sun $11 after 3pm;
club rental $10 per round. No credit cards.
The short "executive" course has great views of the Manhattan skyline. Pro lessons cost $35 for 30 minutes. Par 64.

Richard Metz Golf Studio
425 Madison Ave at 49th St, third floor
(212-759-6940). Subway: E, F to Lexington Ave; 6 to
51st St. Mon–Fri 9am–7pm; Sat 10am–6pm; Sun
11am–5pm. One 30-min lesson $60, five lessons $250,
ten lessons $400. AmEx, DC, Disc, JCB, MC, V.
Practice your swing into a teaching net and then analyze the movement on video. Lessons cater to all levels. There are three nets, several putting areas and a golf shop.

Silver Lake Park
915 Victory Blvd at Clove Rd, Staten Island
(718-447-5686). Travel: Ferry to Staten Island, then
S67 bus. Daily dawn–dusk. Green fees Mon–Fri $19
(after 1pm $17, at twilight $10); Sat, Sun $21.50;
booking fee $2. AmEx, MC, V.
The course is difficult, with narrow fairways and hills to negotiate. Console yourself with nature when your ball ends in the woods once again—it's a very picturesque setting. Par 68.

Van Cortlandt Golf Course
Van Cortlandt Park South at Bailey Ave, Bronx
(718-543-4595). Travel: 1, 9 to 242nd St; BXM3 bus.
Daily 30 minutes before sunrise–30 minutes after sunset.
Green fees weekdays $26, weekends $27; club rental from
$25 per round. AmEx, MC, V.
The oldest public course in the country, rich in history and easily the most "New York" of the city's 13 public courses. It's quite short but challenging—narrow with lots of trees and hilly in places. Par 70.

Horseback riding

Claremont Riding Academy
175 W 89th St between Amsterdam and Columbus Aves
(212-724-5100). Subway: 1, 9 to 86th St. Mon–Fri
6:30am–10pm; Sat, Sun 6:30am–5pm. Rental $35 per
hour; lessons $42 per 30 minutes; introductory package for
first 3.5 hours $100. AmEx, MC, V.
The academy teaches English-style (as opposed to Western-style) riding. Beginners use an indoor arena; experienced riders can also clop along the six miles (9.6km) of trails in Central Park.

Kensington Stables
51 Caton Pl, Windsor Terrace, Brooklyn (718-972-
4588). Subway: F to Fort Hamilton Parkway. 10am–
sundown. Guided trail ride $20 per hour; lessons $40
per hour. AmEx, V, MC.
The ring here is small, but there are miles of trails in lovely nearby Prospect Park (Brooklyn's answer to Central Park).

Ice skating

See **No pier pressure here,** *page 274.*

Rockefeller Center Ice Rink
1 Rockefeller Plaza, Fifth Ave between 49th and
50th Sts (recorded information 212-332-7654).
Subway: B, D, F, Q to 47–50th St–Rockefeller Ctr.
Oct–Apr Mon–Thu 9am–1pm, 1:30–5:30pm,
6–10:30pm; Fri, Sat 8:30–11am, 11:30am–2pm,
2:30–5pm, 5:30–8pm, 8:30pm–midnight; Sun
8:30–11am, 11:30am–2pm, 2:30–5pm, 5:30–10pm.

Fit to be tried

When you need a gym fix, single-day passes help you sweat it out

For some, the idea of going to a gym while on vacation is about as alluring as doing your taxes while having sex, yet other travelers find that they just don't feel right without their regular workout. For them, the following megagyms offer single-day memberships (some form of photo ID is usually required). Most have more than one branch: Call for more details, as well as information about opening times, classes and facilities. Towel and locker rental are usually available.

Asphalt Green
555 E 90th St between York and East End Aves
(212-369-8890). Subway: 4, 5, 6 to 86th St. Day
membership $15.
The fee gets you access to the pool, the gym or the aerobics classes. An additional $10 is required for each additional facility; free sauna access with the pool.

Equinox
2465 Broadway at 92nd St (212-799-1818).
Subway: 1, 2, 3, 9 to 96th St. Day membership $25
11am–5pm Mon–Fri; $35 all other times.
Other location: *897 Broadway at 19th St (212-*
780-9300).

New York Sports Club
151 E 86th St between Lexington and Third Aves
(212-860-8630). Subway: 4, 5, 6 to 86th St. Day
membership $25.
Day membership at New York Sports Club includes access to the weight room, aerobics classes, squash courts, cardio machines and studios, steam room and sauna. For a little extra, you can also get a massage.

World Gym of Greenwich Village
232 Mercer St between Bleecker and 3rd Sts
(212-780-7407). Subway: B, D, F, Q to
Broadway–Lafayette St; 6 to Bleecker St. Day
membership $20.
All the amenities of regular membership (except personal training) are available, including a weight room, aerobics classes and machines, a boxing gym, and steam rooms in both the men's and women's locker rooms.

Mon–Thu $7.50, children under 12 $6; Fri–Sun $9,
children under 12 $6.75; skate rental $4. No credit cards.
Rockefeller Center's famous outdoor rink, under the giant statue of Prometheus, is perfect for atmosphere but a little small. It's not to be missed however, when the giant Christmas tree is lit.

Wollman Memorial Rink
Midpark at 62nd St (212-396-1010). B, Q to 57th St;
N, R to Fifth Ave. Mon, Tue 11am–3pm; Wed, Thu
11am–9:30pm; Fri, Sat 11am–11pm; Sun 11am–9pm.
$7, children and seniors $3; skate rental $3.50. Open
mid-Oct–Mar 31.

In-line skating

A familiar sound on New York streets is the quiet skish-skish of in-line skaters. It's not unusual to see the more insane-on-wheels hurtling toward oncoming traffic at 30 miles per hour. A slightly more tame version can be found whirling around Central Park, either on the Park Drive loop (closed to traffic on weekends) or near the bandshell at 72nd Street. The "coneheads," or slalomers, strut their stuff at Central Park West and 67th Street, across from Tavern on the Green.

To give it a try yourself, visit Wollman Memorial Rink. If you don't want to be restricted to the rink, you can rent skates at the rink for $15 a day with a $100 deposit. Or try one of many shops close to the park, such as **Blades** (160 East 86th Street, 212-996-1644; and 120 West 72nd Street, 212-787-3911). Your safest bet is to stick with the pack and follow the flow of traffic. On weekends, there are plenty of people around to rescue you if you wipe out—there's even a volunteer force of skate patrollers (in red T-shirts with white crosses) who run free stopping clinics for beginners. You'll find them on Saturdays and Sundays from 12:30pm to 5:30pm at the 72nd Street entrance near the Rumsey Playfield. If you'd prefer to be indoors, head for the Chelsea Piers complex (*see* **No pier pressure here**, *page 274*).

Wollman Memorial Rink
Midpark at 62nd St (212-396-1010). Subway: B, Q to 57th St; N, R to Fifth Ave. Thu, Fri 11am–6pm; Sat, Sun 11am–8pm. $4, children and seniors $3; skate rental $6; pad and helmet rental $3.
In recent years, group skates—some mellow and social, others wild blitzkriegs on wheels—have become very popular in the city. Bring skates, helmets and a sense of adventure.

*A day at the races: Catch Thoroughbred action at **Aqueduct Racetrack** in Queens.*

Empire Skate Club of New York
P.O. Box 20070, London Terrace Station, New York, NY 10011 (212-774-1774) www.empireskate.org.
This club organizes frequent in-line and rollerskating events throughout the city, including island-hopping tours and moonlight rides.

Time's Up
212-802-8222.
See **Biking**, *above.*

Pool

Chelsea Billiards
54 W 21st St between Fifth and Sixth Aves (212-989-0096). Subway: F, N, R to 23rd St. 24 hours. 9am–5pm $4 per hour for first player, $8 for two or more players; Mon–Thu, Sun 5pm–9am $5 per hour for first player, $10 for two or more players; Fri, Sat 5pm–9am $6 per hour for first player, $14 for two players, $2 each additional player. AmEx, MC, V.
Cue up in this comfortable and welcoming pool hall (with full-size snooker tables, too). Beer and snacks are available.

Amsterdam Billiard Club
344 Amsterdam Ave at 77th St (212-496-8180). Subway: 1, 9 to 79th St. Sun–Thu 11am–3am; Fri, Sat 11am–4am. $7–$8 per player per hour. Group lessons $8 per person, private $35–$50 per hour.
This swanky club owned by comedian David Brenner was named No. 1 Billiard Club in the Country by *Billiards Digest* and features a fireplace and a full bar.
Other locations: *210 E 86th St (212-570-4545).*

Racquetball

Manhattan Plaza Racquet Club
450 W 43rd St between Ninth and Tenth Aves (212-594-0554). Subway: A, C, E to 42nd Street. 6am–midnight. $10–$28 per court per hour, plus $10 guest fee. AmEx, MC, V.
Rates vary according to time of day. The club also has five hard-surface tennis courts ($32–$50 per court per hour, plus $20 guest fee).

Running

Join the joggers in Central Park, Riverside Park or around Washington Square in the early morning or early evening. It's best, for women especially, to avoid jogging alone. And don't carry anything that's obviously valuable. For the New York City Marathon, *see chapter* **New York by Season.**

New York Road Runners Club
9 E 89th St between Fifth and Madison Aves (212-860-4455). Subway: 4, 5, 6 to 86th Street. Mon–Fri 10am–8pm; Sat 10am–5pm; Sun 10am–3pm. Membership from $30. AmEx, Disc, MC, V.
Hardly a weekend goes by without some sort of run or race sponsored by the NYRRC, the largest running club in the world. Most races take place in Central Park and are open to the public. The club also offers safety and training tips.

Squash

New York Sports Clubs
151 E 86th St at Lexington Ave (212-860-8630). Subway: 4, 5, 6 to 86th St. Nonmember fee $25.

This uptown branch of the NYSC chain, which has the greatest number of regulation international courts in the city, is the epicenter of the New York squash world. Its well-rounded coaching staff provides evening and weekend clinics and caters to any level of play. This venue also hosts a variety of tournaments and training weekends. It's the best place to see the stars in action and even join them on the court. American-style squash courts are also available at NYSC's branches on 62nd Street at Broadway and Fifth Avenue at 37th Street.

The Printing House Racquet and Fitness Club

421 Hudson Street between Leroy and Clarkson Sts (212-243-7600). Subway: 1, 9 to Houston St. $16.50 for round-robin Mon, Fri 6–8pm.
Although its four courts are just shy of regulation width, the Printing House offers the coolest game of squash in the city—even if you don't have access to the spectacular panoramic penthouse fitness facility. You *can* play in the happy-hour round robin (after which players hit a local bar) on Mondays and Fridays. Former top-20 star and pro-in-residence Brett Newton attracts a steady flow of international players.

Swimming

Municipal Pools

800-201-7275 (Parks Department).
An annual membership fee of $25, payable by money order only at any recreation center, entitles you to use all New York's municipal indoor pools for a year. You need proof of your name, an address in the New York City area and a passport-size photograph to register. Outdoor pools are free to all, and open from July to September. Some of the best and most beautifully maintained city-run pools are: Asser Levy Pool, 23rd Street at FDR Drive (212-447-2020); Carmine Street Recreation Center, Clarkson Street and Seventh Avenue South (212-242-5228); East 54th Street Pool, 348 E 54th Street at First Avenue (212-397-3154); West 59th Street Pool, 59th Street between Tenth and Eleventh Avenues (212-397-3159).

Sheraton Manhattan Hotel

790 Seventh Ave at 51st St (212-581-3300). Subway: B, D, E to Seventh Ave; N, R to 49th St. Open to nonguests Mon–Fri 6am–9:45pm; Sat, Sun 8am–7:45pm. $20 for nonguests. AmEx, DC, Disc, MC, V.
Pricier than the municipal pools but much less crowded, this is the place to come if you want to swim in peace.

Tennis

The city maintains excellent municipal courts throughout the city. Permits are available from the Department of Parks (212-360-8133), cost $50 ($20 for senior citizens, $10 for those under 18) and are valid for the season (April to November). *See also* Manhattan Plaza Racquet Club, *page 280.*

HRC Tennis

Pier 13 and 14 on the East River (212-422-9300). Subway: 2, 3, 4, 5 to Wall St. Open to nonmembers. Daily 6am–midnight. Court fees $50–$120 per hour. AmEx, MC, V.
This is part of the New York Health & Racquet Club. There are eight green clay courts under bubbles on twin piers in the river. Ten tennis pros are on hand to give lessons ($28 per hour plus court fees).

Midtown Tennis Club

341 Eighth Ave at 27th St (212-989-8572). Subway: 1, 9 to 28th St; C, E to 23rd St. Mon–Thu 7am–11pm; Fri

7am–8pm; Sat, Sun 8am–8pm. Court fees $36–$72 per hour. AmEx, MC, V.*
This club offers eight indoor hard courts and four outdoor ones when weather permits.

YMCAs

There are Ys throughout the five boroughs, all with a wide range of facilities. Three of the Manhattan sites offer day rates for visitors. Y membership in another country may get you discounts, and if you're already paying for accommodations, the sports facilities are free.

Harlem YMCA

180 W 135th St at Seventh Ave (212-281-4100). Subway: B, C to 135th St. Mon–Fri 6am–10pm; Sat 6am–6pm. Membership $10 per day, $75 per month, $537 per year. MC, V.
The main attractions here are a four-lane swimming pool, basketball court, full gym and sauna.

Vanderbilt YMCA

224 E 47th St between Second and Third Aves (212-756-9600). Subway: 6 to 51st St; 4, 5 to 42nd St–Grand Central. Mon–Fri 6am–11pm; Sat, Sun 7am–7pm. Membership $20 per day, $70 per month, $840 per year. AmEx, MC, V.
Members can use the two swimming pools, a running track, a sauna and a gym with basketball, handball and volleyball—plus yoga and aerobics classes.

West Side Branch YMCA

5 W 63rd St between Broadway and Central Park West (212-875-4100). Subway: A, C, B, D, 1, 9 to 59th St–Columbus Circle. Mon–Fri 6am–11pm; Sat, Sun 8am–8pm. Membership $15 per day, $60 per week, $100 per month. MC, V.
This Y has two pools and three gyms with all the equipment you could imagine, plus an indoor track, squash courts, and facilities for basketball, volleyball, handball, racquetball, boxing, aerobics and yoga. There is also a full range of classes. Day rate includes access to everything.

Yoga

Integral Yoga Institute

227 W 13th St between Seventh and Eighth Aves (212-929-0585). Subway: A, C, E, 1, 2, 3, 9 to 14th St; L to Eighth Ave. Mon–Fri 10am–8:30pm; Sat 8am–6pm; Sun 10am–2pm. Hatha III classes $12; all others $10.
Integral Yoga Institute offers classes for beginners as well as more advanced students. The schedule is flexible, so there's no need to book ahead, but do arrive 15 minutes before class begins.
Other locations: *200 W 72nd St at Broadway, fourth floor (212-721-4000).*

Yoga Zone

138 Fifth Ave between 18th and 19th Sts, fourth floor (212-647-YOGA). Subway: L, N, R, 4, 5, 6 to 14th St–Union Sq. Mon–Thu 7:30am–9pm; Fri 7:30am–7:30pm; Sat 9am–5:45pm; Sun 9am–6:30pm. $17 per class, $12 for early morning/lunchtime classes, introductory offer of three classes for $30. Hours vary.
You'll practically trip over all the models and actors, but that's beside the point. Classes here emphasize the less strenuous side of yoga and last at least an hour. Ample time is devoted to breathing, posture and stretching. Yoga Zone also offers Pilates classes.
Other locations: *160 E 56th St between Lexington and Third Aves, 12th floor (212-935-YOGA).*

Theater

Thanks to a vast choice of venues and a thrilling array of talent, New York is a great place to get stagestruck

The Big Apple is the big cheese when it comes to live theater. There are myriad venues throughout Manhattan—and more in the outer boroughs. New York's long tradition as an artists' proving ground still prevails: This is the only city in the States where superstars regularly tread the boards eight times a week. Big-name players who have recently stuck their necks out on the sometimes unforgiving NYC stages include Kevin Spacey, Natasha Richardson, Jennifer Jason Leigh—even filmmaker and stage novice Quentin Tarantino and singer-songwriter Paul Simon, both of whom were crucified by local critics. The stakes are high, but the gamble remains ever alluring.

Audiences eager to experience this ephemeral art form continue to pack the city's performance spaces, which range from the landmark palaces of the glittering (and recently sanitized) "Great White Way" of Broadway to more intimate houses along 42nd Street's Theater Row (technically Off Broadway) and the nooks and crannies of Off-Off Broadway. Unlike in Hollywood, the performer-fan relationship is up-close-and-personal in the New York theater world. Not only can you watch your favorite actors with only a bit of air separating you, but you can also grab autographs at the stage door and maybe even dine at the same restaurant afterward. Whatever your dramatic wishes may be, New York theater can and undoubtedly will satisfy you.

INFORMATION

The Sunday Arts and Leisure and Friday Weekend sections of *The New York Times* are reliable sources of information, as are the listings in *Time Out New York*, *In Theater*, *New York* magazine, *The New Yorker* and the free *Village Voice*. In addition, there are several phone lines offering everything from plot synopses and show times to agents ready to sell tickets (you'll need a Touch-Tone phone). The best is **NYC/On Stage** (212-768-

*Animal instinct: Julie Taymor transformed Disney's cuddly **Lion King** into a theatrical spectacle.*

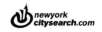

*The missing slink: Sexy, sultry **Cabaret** now seduces in the legendary disco Studio 54.*

1818), a service of the Theater Development Fund (*see chapter* **Dance**), which will tell you about performances on Broadway, Off Broadway and Off-Off Broadway, as well as classical music, dance and opera events. The **Broadway Line** (212-302-4111, outside New York 888-411-BWAY) gives similar information but is restricted to Broadway and Off Broadway shows, and you must know which show you are interested in before using it.

BUYING TICKETS

Provided you have a major credit card, buying Broadway tickets requires little more than picking up a telephone. Almost all Broadway and Off Broadway shows are served by one of the city's 24-hour booking agencies. The information lines (above) will refer you to ticket agents, often on the same call. **Telecharge** (212-239-6200) and **Ticketmaster** (212-307-4100) carve up the bulk of the shows between them, with the smaller **Ticket Central** (212-279-4200) specializing in Off Broadway and Off-Off Broadway shows. You'll have to pay a service charge to the agency, but since most theaters don't take telephone orders, you don't have much choice, unless you opt to buy tickets in person at the theater box office.

The cheapest full-price tickets on Broadway are for standing room and cost about $15, though not all theaters offer these. If a show is sold out, it's worth trying for standby tickets just before show time. Tickets are slightly cheaper for matinees and previews, and for students or groups of 20 or more. Keep an eye out for twofers—vouchers that allow you to buy two tickets for slightly more than the price of one. These generally promote long-running Broadway shows and occasionally the larger Off Broadway ones. Some sold-out shows offer good seats at reduced rates (usually $20) after 6pm on the day of performance; those in the know start lining up hours beforehand. The best way to obtain discount tickets, however, is to go to **TKTS** (*see chapter* **Music**), where you can get as much as 75 percent off the face value of some tickets. Arrive early to avoid the line, or come around 7pm, when most shows are about to start. You can also buy matinee tickets the day before the show at the TKTS booth in the World Trade Center. (One caveat: Avoid scam artists selling tickets to those waiting in line. Often the tickets are fake.)

NEW YORK SHAKESPEARE FESTIVAL

The Delacorte Theater in Central Park is the fair-weather sister of the Public Theater (*see page 287*). When not producing Shakespeare, the Public offers the Bard outdoors for free during the New York Shakespeare Festival (June to September). If you're in the city during the summer, you won't want to miss these innovative alfresco productions. Recent summer schedules have included *The Taming of the Shrew* and *Tartuffe*. Tickets are free and are distributed at 1pm on the day of the performance, at both the Delacorte and the Public.

The British are coming!

Well, actually, they've arrived—and they're taking over the Great White Way

So you're itching to see the latest West End hit but can't afford the trip to London? If the current trend continues, you'll have a second chance to see it—on Broadway.

Like a brightly lit strip of flypaper, the Great White Way continues to draw a slew of buzzworthy, nonmusical Brit hits. New York stages have a long-standing history of welcoming inter-

*Smoke signals: Rupert Graves and Natasha Richardson get a little **Closer**.*

national fare (especially in nonprofit theaters and Off Broadway institutions like the stellar Brooklyn Academy of Music, a.k.a. BAM), but import fever hit Broadway's commercial community a few years ago and shows little sign of cooling down.

The 1997–98 season saw transatlantic transfers of *The Judas Kiss*, Martin McDonagh's *The Beauty Queen of Leenane*, a fresh interpretation of *The Chairs* and the Tony winner *Art*. The 1998–99 season was dominated by English productions: David Hare weighed in three times (with *The Blue Room*, *Via Dolorosa* and *Amy's View*), American Kevin Spacey chilled out in *The Iceman Cometh*, Natasha Richardson headlined *Closer* and Irish yarn-spinner Conor McPherson introduced Americans to *The Weir*. And it looks as if the Union Jack will be waving over 2000 as well.

Box-office grosses are high and producers are pleased, but some patriotic diehards are grumbling that American playwrights are being ignored. In the musical arena, American composer Frank Wildhorn (*Jekyll & Hyde*, *The Scarlet Pimpernel* and *The Civil War*) has trumped the trend of British song spectacles, with all three of his tuners running concurrently. Perhaps the pendulum will swing, and straight plays will be singing a different, accent-free song. Only time—and revenues—will tell.

Normally, 11:30am is a safe time to get there, but when shows feature box-office giants, the line starts as early as 7am. Two tickets are allotted per person.

Delacorte Theater

A few minutes' walk inside Central Park. Enter the park from either Central Park West at 81st St or Fifth Ave at 79th St (212-539-8750). Subway: B, C to 81st St; 6 to 77th St. Then follow the signs in the park.

Broadway

Broadway is booming. In recent years, box-office receipts for newly opened shows have repeatedly broken records and, by putting movie stars in leading roles, Broadway now competes directly with Hollywood for its audiences. It hasn't hurt that the formerly seedy and sex-oriented Times Square has undergone an extensive cleanup. (Disney is a major investor in area real estate, and the neighborhood is becoming more and more like one of its theme parks.)

"Broadway," in theatrical terms, is the district around Times Square on either side of Broadway (the street), generally between 41st and 53rd Streets. This is where the grand theaters are clustered, most built in the first 30 years of the 20th century, several newly renovated. Officially, 37 of them are designated as being on Broadway, for which full-price tickets cost up to $100. The big shows are hard to ignore; newer blockbusters like *The Lion King, Chicago, Fosse* and *Cabaret* join long-running shows such as *Cats, Phantom of the Opera, Les Misérables, Miss Saigon* and *Rent*, all of which declare themselves on vast billboards. Still, there's more to Broadway than cartoon-based musicals and flashy Andrew Lloyd Webber spectacles. In recent years, provocative new dramas by such playwrights as Tony Kushner, Terrence McNally, Horton Foote and Wendy Wasserstein have been resounding successes, as have many revived classics and British imports (*see* **The British are coming!**, *above*).

Watch for the irrepressible **Roundabout Theater**, the critically acclaimed home of classics played by all-star casts (and the force behind *Cabaret*'s latest incarnation, to open its deluxe new Broadway space (the Selwyn Theatre, 229 W 42nd St, 212-719-1300) in January 2000. In the meantime, the Roundabout is producing plays in the smaller Gramercy Theatre (127 E 23rd St, 212-777-4900). You may subscribe to the Roundabout's full season or buy single tickets, if available.

Broadway District
Subways: A, C, E to 42nd St–Port Authority; N, R, S, 1, 2, 3, 9, 7 to 42nd St–Times Sq; B, D, F, Q to 42nd St; N, R to 49th St; 1, 9, to 50th St.

Off Broadway

Off Broadway theaters usually have fewer than 500 seats; earlier in the century, most were located in Greenwich Village. These days, Off Broadway theaters can be found on the Upper West Side, the Upper East Side and in midtown.

As Broadway increasingly becomes a place of spectacle sans substance, playwrights who would once have been granted a Broadway production now find themselves in the more audacious (and less financially demanding) Off Broadway houses, where they find audiences who want plays with something to say.

So if it's brain food and adventure you're after, dine Off or Off-Off Broadway—but be prepared for considerable variations in quality. Listed below are some of the most reliable theaters and repertory companies. Tickets cost about $10 to $45.

Atlantic Theater Company
336 W 20th St between Eighth and Ninth Aves (212-645-1242). Subway: C, E, 1, 9 to 23rd St.
Created 15 years ago as an offshoot of acting workshops taught by David Mamet and William H. Macy, this dynamic little theater (in a former church sanctuary on a lovely Chelsea street) has presented more than 80 plays. Productions have included Mamet's *Edmond*, the premieres of Howard Korder's *Boys' Life* and Craig Lucas's *Missing Persons*, and the American premiere of Martin McDonagh's *The Beauty Queen of Leenane*.

Brooklyn Academy of Music
30 Lafayette Ave between Flatbush Ave and Fulton St, Brooklyn (718-636-4100) www.bam.org. Subway: D, M, Q, 2, 3, 4, 5 to Atlantic Ave; B, N, R to Pacific St.
Brooklyn's grand old opera house—along with the Majestic Theater, one block away at 651 Fulton St—stages the famous Next Wave Festival during the last three months of each year. The festival is a program of theatrical, musical and dance pieces by American and international artists. Recent ventures have included a much-acclaimed pairing of Caryl Churchill one-acts and the Robert Wilson–Lou Reed collaboration *Time Rocker. See chapter* **Dance.**

Lincoln Center
65th St at Columbus Ave (212-362-7600, tickets 212-239-6200). Subway: 1, 9 to 66th St–Lincoln Ctr.
The Lincoln Center complex houses two amphitheater-shaped drama venues: the 1,040-seat Vivian Beaumont Theater (considered a Broadway house) and the 290-seat Mitzi

E. Newhouse Theater (considered Off Broadway). Expect polished productions of new and classic plays, with many a well-known actor.

La MaMa E.T.C.
74A E 4th St between Bowery and Second Ave (212-475-7710). Subway: 6 to Astor Pl; F to Second Ave.
This little gem is where Off Broadway began. When acclaimed producer Ellen Stewart opened La MaMa ("Mama" is her nickname) in 1962, it was New York's best-kept theater secret. (Did you know, for example, that Harvey Fierstein's *Torch Song Trilogy* started at La MaMa?) Now, with more than 50 Obie (Off Broadway) Awards to its name, it's a fixture in the city's dramatic life. But if you're looking for traditional theater, skip La MaMa. New ground is routinely broken here, and some of it is rather muddy.

Manhattan Theatre Club
City Center, 131 W 55th St between Sixth and Seventh Aves (212-581-1212). Subway: B, D, E to Seventh Ave.
Manhattan Theatre Club has a reputation for sending young playwrights on to Broadway. The club's two theaters, in the basement of City Center, are the 299-seat Mainstage Theater, which offers four plays each year by both new and established playwrights, and the Stage II Theater, an outlet for works-in-progress, workshops and staged readings. One of the Club's highlights is its Writers in Performance series. Guest speakers have included Isabel Allende, Eric Bogosian and Toni Morrison.

New York Theatre Workshop
79 E 4th St between Bowery and Second Ave (212-460-5475). Subway: 6 to Astor Pl; F to Second Ave.
Founded in 1979, this Off Broadway company produces new plays using young directors who are eager to harness challenging works. Besides initiating plays by the likes of David Rabe (*A Question of Mercy*) and Tony Kushner (*Slavs!*), it is most noted for the premiere of *Rent*, Jonathan Larson's Pulitzer Prize–winning musical, which continues to pack 'em in since transferring to Broadway. The Workshop also offers a home to upstart performance artists through its O Solo Mio festival.

Playwrights Horizons
416 W 42nd St between Ninth and Tenth Aves (212-564-1235). Subway: A, C, E to 42nd St–Port Authority.
This power-packed company boasts more than 300 premieres of important contemporary plays, including dramatic offerings like *The Substance of Fire, Driving Miss Daisy* and *The Heidi Chronicles*, and musicals such as *March of the Falsettos* and *Sunday in the Park with George*. More recently, the works of newcomers Adam Guettel (*Floyd Collins*) and Brian Crawkey (*Violet*) and the brilliant Christopher Durang (*Betty's Summer Vacation*) have been staged.

The Public Theater
425 Lafayette St between E 4th St and Astor Pl (212-539-8500). Subway: 6 to Astor Pl; N, R to 8th St.
This Astor Place landmark is one of the most consistently interesting theaters in the city. Founded by Joseph Papp (who bought the building from the city for $1) and dedicated to the work of new American playwrights and performers, the Public also presents new explorations of Shakespeare and the classics; there's a constant influx of short-run goodies. The building houses five stages and a new coffee bar, plus a cabaret space, Joe's Pub (*see chapters* **Cafés & Bars** *and* **Cabaret & Comedy**). The Public is now under the aegis of George C. Wolfe, who directed *Bring in 'da Noise, Bring in 'da Funk* and the first New York production of Tony Kushner's *Angels in America. See* **New York Shakespeare Festival,** *page 285.*

The Vineyard Theater

108 E 15th St at Union Sq East (212-353-3874)
www.vineyard.org. Subway: L, N, R, 4, 5, 6 to 14th
St–Union Sq.
This subscription theater in Union Square produces new plays and musicals, and also attempts to revitalize works that have failed in other arenas. The Vineyard has recently been on a streak of successes, including Paula Vogel's *How I Learned to Drive* and Edward Albee's *Three Tall Women*. This consistently excellent theater is also home to such playwrights as Craig Lucas and caustic wit Nicky Silver.

Off-Off Broadway

The technical definition of Off-Off Broadway is a show created by artists who may not be card-carrying pros, presented at a theater with fewer than 100 seats. It's here that the most innovative and daring writers and performers get the opportunity to experiment. Pieces often meld various media, including music, dance, mime, film, video and performance monologue—sometimes resulting in an all-too-indulgent combo of theater and psychotherapy.

But Off-Off Broadway is not restricted to experimental work. You can also see classical works and more traditional contemporary plays staged by companies such as the Jean Cocteau Repertory Company and at venues like the Second Stage Theater. Tickets at Off-Off Broadway venues cost roughly $10 to $25. *See chapters* **Dance** *and* **Cabaret & Comedy.**

Adobe Theater Company

453 W 16th St between Ninth and Tenth Aves (212-352-0441). Subway: A, C, E to 14th St; L to Eighth Ave.
Keep your eyes peeled for new work by this spry nonprofit company, which has mounted 24 shows in the past seven years. Its wacky works appeal to young, hip audiences that can appreciate a theatrical stew filled with pop-culture references. Recent productions have included *Notions in Motion*, a juicy update of Pirandello; *The Handless Maiden*, a modern fable; and *Duet!*, a romance for cynics.

Bouwerie Lane Theatre

330 Bowery at Bond St (212-677-0060). Subway:
F to Second Ave; 6 to Bleecker St.
Housed in the old cast-iron German Exchange Bank, this is the home theater of the Jean Cocteau Repertory Company, which is devoted to producing the classics in rep. Recent works include Joe Orton's *What the Butler Saw*, Tom Stoppard's *Rough Crossing* and Maxwell Anderson's *Winterset*.

Drama Dept.

212-541-8299.
This newish company leaped onto the scene with a couple of high-profile critical hits, including Douglas Carter Beane's *As Bees In Honey Drown* and a sparkling revival of *As Thousands Cheer*. Fueled by Hollywood money and a large company of heavy-hitting actors, writers and directors, Drama Dept. mounts lively and ambitious productions that are worth checking out.

Irish Repertory Theatre

132 W 22nd St between Sixth and Seventh Aves (212-727-2737). Subway: F, 1, 9 to 23rd St.
Dedicated to performing works by both veteran and contemporary Irish playwrights, this company in Chelsea has produced some interesting sold-out shows. Notable are the productions of Frank McCourt's *The Irish and How They Got That Way* and Hugh Leonard's *Da*. There's no blarney here.

The Kitchen

512 W 19th St between Tenth and Eleventh Aves (212-255-5793). Subway: A, C, E to 14th St; L to Eighth Ave.
This small, experimental theater—with a season running from September to May—recently celebrated its 25th anniversary. It presents an eclectic repertoire of theater, music, dance, video and performance art. The Kitchen is a reputable place to see edgy New York experimentation. Artists such as Laurie Anderson, David Byrne and Cindy Sherman began their careers here.

Pearl Theatre Company

80 St. Marks Pl between First and Second Aves (212-505-3401). Subway: 6 to Astor Pl; N, R to 8th St.
Housed on the punk promenade of the East Village, this troupe of resident players relies primarily on its actors' ability to present the classics clearly. Besides Shakespeare and the Greeks, Pearl has successfully produced the works of Ionesco, Sheridan, Molière and Shaw, plus lesser-known playwrights like Ostrofsky and Otway—all on a small, minimally dressed stage, with actors in the simplest of costumes.

Performance Space 122

150 First Ave at 9th St (212-477-5288). Subway: L to First Ave; 6 to Astor Pl; N, R to 8th St.
One of New York's most exciting venues, P.S. 122 (as it's casually known) is housed in an abandoned school in the East Village. It's a nonprofit arts center for experimental works with two theaters presenting dance, performance, music, film and video. Artists develop, practice and present their projects here; P.S. 122 has provided a platform for Eric Bogosian, Whoopi Goldberg, John Leguizamo and Philip Glass.

The Performing Garage

33 Wooster St between Broome and Grand Sts (212-966-3651). Subway: 1, 9 to Houston St; C, E to Spring St.
The Performing Garage features the works of the Wooster Group, whose members include Richard Foreman, Willem Dafoe, Elizabeth LeCompte and Spalding Gray. Gray developed his well-known monologues here, among them *Swimming to Cambodia*; Dafoe once played the lead in Eugene O'Neill's *The Hairy Ape* and appeared in a daring blackface version of *The Emperor Jones*. In addition to presenting deconstructed versions of theater classics, the company hosts a visiting artists series, dance performances and monthly readings.

Second Stage Theatre

307 W 43rd St at Eighth Ave (212-246-4422). Subway: A, C, E to 42nd St–Port Authority; N, R, S, 1, 2, 3, 7, 9 to 42nd St–Times Sq.
Created as a venue for American plays that didn't get the critical reception it was thought they deserved, Second Stage now also produces the works of new American playwrights. It staged the premieres of Tina Howe's *Painting Churches* and *Coastal Disturbances*, David Mamet's *The Woods*, and *Ricky Jay and His 52 Assistants*, directed by Mamet. In 1999, the company moved into a beautiful Rem Koolhaas–designed new space just off Times Square.

Signature Theatre Company

555 W 42nd St between Tenth and Eleventh Aves (212-244-7529). Subway: A, C, E to 42nd St–Port Authority.
Each season, this unique award-winning company focuses on the works of a single playwright in residence. (The 2000 scribe is Maria Irene Fornes.) Signature has in the past delved into the oeuvres of John Guare, Arthur Miller and Horton Foote, whose *The Young Man from Atlanta* originated here and went on to win the Pulitzer Prize.

*Basic training: **Grand Central Terminal** is the starting point for upstate excursions.*

Trips Out of Town

Trips Out of Town

If New York City sightseeing isn't enough for you, beaches, mountains and more are just a few hours away

Notice the traffic heading for the bridges and tunnels on Friday afternoons? New Yorkers will defend their city to the death—but come the week's end, they're lining up to get out. All kinds of getaways, from frenetic beaches to tranquil historical regions, are within a few hours' reach. Interested in nature? Central Park can't touch the roaring rapids and grassy trails of the Catskill and Adirondack mountains, havens for hiking, fishing and all-around bonding with the natural world. If you're looking for riskier business, scratch that itch with the many roller coasters and slot machines nearby. Of course, there are safer investments—you can return home with bundles of bargain-priced designer garb from regional outlet malls. And if the hassle of subway navigating and cab hailing has made you more tense than when you got to New York, there's a slew of spas and spiritual centers a stone's throw away. Just remember, wherever you go, one fact remains the same: On Fridays and Sundays, the traffic is crazy. Take advantage of your visitor status and plan your retreat midweek or during off-peak times.

GENERAL INFORMATION

Travel literature is abundant in New York City. Look for special packages if you're planning to spend a few days away. *The New York Times* publishes a travel section every Sunday, which carries advertisements for resorts and guest houses. *Time Out New York*'s Travel section and annual "Summer Getaways" issue (published in late May) can also help point you in the right direction.

GETTING THERE

For all the places listed, we've included information on how to get there from New York City. **Metro-North** and the **Long Island Rail Road** are the two main commuter rail systems. Both offer theme tours in the summer. **Amtrak** is the national rail service for intercity travel. Call **Port Authority Bus Terminal** for information on all bus transportation from the city. Car-rental rates in New York are exorbitant; you can save up to 50 percent by renting a car somewhere outside the city, even if it's from the same company. For more information on airports, trains, buses and car rentals, *see chapter* **Directory**.

Amtrak

212-582-6875, 800-USA-RAIL; www.amtrak.com.
Amtrak is the non-commuter line, so rates are a bit more.

Long Island Rail Road

718-217-LIRR, 516-822-LIRR; www.lirr.org.
Most trains run from Penn Station to Long Island; however, a few leave from Flatbush Ave in Brooklyn and all connect in Jamaica, Queens.

Metro-North

212-532-4900, 800-METRO-INFO; www.mta.nyc.ny.us.
Metro-North runs lines from Grand Central Terminal to upstate New York (on the east side of the Hudson river).

Port Authority Bus Terminal

212-564-8484.
Many different bus operators depart from Port Authority.

Beach life

You've heard it all before: Manhattan is surrounded by water, but there's nowhere to swim. Luckily, nearby beachfront towns have no shortage of rolling waves and glistening sands. Of course, it is possible to get to the coast without leaving the city limits—the candy-coated and frenzied Coney Island and Brighton Beach will make you feel as though you're back in Times Square (*see* **The antidote to urban overload**, *page 296*). But many urban natives prefer the isolated and serene beaches of Long Island and the New Jersey Shore. From Memorial Day (late May) to Labor Day (early September), New Yorkers scramble to get out to their beachside rentals in the Hamptons, Fire Island and Shelter Island. The beaches get more impressive the farther you travel from Manhattan.

The Hamptons

The Hamptons, a series of small towns along the south fork of eastern Long Island, are the ultimate retreat for New York's rich and famous. Socialites, artists and hangers-on drift from benefit bash to benefit bash throughout the summer season. For sightseers, it's tough to choose between the spectacular sun-drenched beachfront and the superstar estates. (Steven Spielberg's palace in East Hampton and Alec Baldwin and Kim Basinger's massive homestead in Amagansett—which housed a fund-raising benefit for Bill Clinton in '98—are but two examples.) For an up-to-date social calendar, pick up *Dan's Papers*, or two free local rags, *Hamptons Magazine* or *Country Magazine*; all are available at various retail stores.

Castle keep: Bet your life savings at one of **Atlantic City**'s 13 casino resorts.

After Memorial Day, the beautiful beaches of **East Hampton** attract celebs looking for a little rest and relaxation. Still, as you stroll along the ocean, don't be at all surprised by the pervasive presence of cell phones and laptops. The trends change more quickly than the winds on the beach, but **Della Femina Restaurant** and **Nick and Toni's** are old standbys that promise sophisticated contemporary food and at least one celebrity sighting per night. Also keep your eyes peeled for Billy Joel noshing on a doughnut at **Dreesen's** or John F. Kennedy Jr. blading along the town's tree-lined streets. **The Mill House Inn** is a comfortable bed-and-breakfast in town.

Known for its antiques shops and galleries, **Southampton** is coveted by New York's artistic community. Many great brushmen have kept studios here over the years, among them Willem de Kooning. If you're looking to buy, stop into the shops and galleries on Jobs Lane. While Southampton is generally quieter than East Hampton, all the premier dance clubs are located here. **The Tavern** and **Jet East** are beach-bound versions of Manhattan's clubbing scene, with VIP lounges, crowded dance floors, and lots of pretty faces.

Distant and remote, **Montauk**, on the very eastern tip of Long Island, is also the least commercialized town in the Hamptons. The **Montauk Point Lighthouse** is New York State's oldest (erected in 1795), and historical memorabilia is on display inside. The culture here is simple and unpretentious: The best dinner consists of a three-pound lobster at **Gosman's Dock**. Despite the rural feel, rental cottages and hotels can still empty your wallet in the height of the summer season. For the best rates, look for pre- and postseason deals. The **Royal Atlantic Beach Resort** has family-style cottages set on the water.

East Hampton Chamber of Commerce
79A Main St, East Hampton, NY 11937 (516-324-0362) www.easthamptonchamber.com.

Montauk Chamber of Commerce
P.O. Box 5029, Montauk, NY 11954 (516-668-2428) www.montaukchamber.com.

Southampton Chamber of Commerce
76 Main St, Southampton, NY 11968 (516-283-0402) www.southamptonchamber.com.

Della Femina Restaurant
99 N Main St, East Hampton, NY (516-329-6666). 6–11pm during the high season, 6–10pm off-season. Average main course: $26. AmEx, Disc, MC, V.

Dreesen's
33 Newtown Ln, East Hampton, NY (516-324-0465). Mon–Sat 8am–6pm. AmEx, Disc, MC, V.

Gosman's Dock
West Lake Dr, Montauk, NY (516-668-2549).

Jet East
North Sea Rd, Southampton, NY (516-283-0808).

The Mill House Inn
33 N Main St, East Hampton, NY (516-324-9766)
www.millhouseinn.com. Doubles $125–$425. MC, V.

Montauk Point Lighthouse
516-668-2544.

Nick and Toni's
136 N Main St, East Hampton, NY (516-324-3550).
Mon–Thu 6–11pm; Fri, Sat 6–11:30pm; Sun
11:30am–2:30pm, 6–11pm; limited hours in the off-
season. AmEx, MC, V.

Royal Atlantic Beach Resort
South Edgemere St, Montauk, NY (516-668-5103).
$200–$400. AmEx, Disc, MC, V.

The Tavern
125 Tuckahoe Ln, Southampton, NY (516-287-2125).

GETTING THERE
Take the Montauk line on the **LIRR** to East Hampton, Southampton or Montauk ($10.25–$15.25). The **Hampton Jitney** (212-936-0440, 516-283-4600, 800-936-0440; $22, Tue–Thu children and seniors $17) runs regular bus service between Manhattan and the Hamptons, and even provides complimentary newspapers and OJ on morning trips. By car, take the Long Island Expwy (I-495) east to Exit 70 (Country Rd 111) south. Continue for three miles to Sunrise Highway (Rte 27) eastbound.

Shelter Island

True to its name, **Shelter Island** is the perfect place to take shelter from the chaos of urban life. This tiny island is accessible only by ferry from Long Island (it makes a good day trip from the Hamptons), which keeps crowds to a minimum. There are a few gift shops and an ice-cream parlor but little else to distract you from sailing, cycling, fishing or just relaxing on the beach. About a third of the terrain is occupied by **Mashomack Preserve** (South Ferry Rd; 516-749-1001), an undisturbed wildlife preserve densely populated by ospreys (fish-eating hawks) and other waterfowl. The island is also a good source of early American historical paraphernalia. The town of Shelter Island was founded by merchants in the 17th century and later was used as a refuge by Quakers exiled from Boston. The current **Sylvester Manor** stands on the site of the town's first home, built in 1652. Other historic destinations are the **Quaker Cemetery, Manhasset Chapel Museum** and **Haven House** (contact the Chamber of Commerce for information). One of the few spots to bunk for the night is **Chequit Inn,** though the hippest place to stay would be the **Sunset Beach,** a hotel owned by Andre Balazs (he also has Manhattan's Mercer Hotel).

Shelter Island Chamber of Commerce
P.O. Box 598, Shelter Island, NY 11964 (516-749-0399)
www.onisland.com.

Mashomack Preserve
South Ferry Rd (516-749-1001).

Chequit Inn
23 Grand Ave (516-749-0018) www.shelterislandinns.com.
Doubles $80–$195. AmEx, MC, V.

Sunset Beach Hotel
35 Shore Rd (516-749-2001). Mon–Fri $150–$160; Fri–
Sun $275–$295 with two-night minimum. AmEx, MC, V.

GETTING THERE
Take the Greenport line on the **LIRR** to the end of the line ($10.25–$15.25) or the **Sunrise Express Bus Service** (516-477-1200, 800-527-7709. Round-trip $29, reservations required). By car, take the Midtown Tunnel to I-495 (the Long Island Expwy). Make a right at Exit 73 (Riverhead) onto Rte 58 (Old Country Rd). Rte 58 will become Rte 25; continue into Greenport and follow the signs for the North Ferry station. From Greenport, take the ferry (516-749-0139; Mon–Sun 5:40am–12midnight. One way $1, cars $7) to Shelter Island.

Fire Island

Running parallel to the southern coast of Long Island, **Fire Island** is a pencil-thin, 30-mile-long strip of land dividing the Great South Bay on one side and the Atlantic Ocean on the other. The most relaxing part of vacationing here is that cars are banned (i.e. relief from honking horns and roaring engines). But you will have to make do with walking a lot and getting sand in your shoes. Most short-term visitors to the island find themselves in or around the major towns of **Ocean Beach** and the **Pines**. If you really don't feel like walking, water taxis can be found at every public dock.

   Ocean Beach is a sanctuary for sunbathing, Frisbee-throwing, volleyball-playing families and twentysomethings. The town has neither the frills nor the conveniences of the Hamptons, but nothing will stop an Ocean Beacher from enjoying a day in the sand. Burgers and bar food are served at **Albatross** (Bay Walk; 516-583-5697), and anyone with a taste for butter cream–frosted cakes and gooey brownies ends up at **Rachel's Bakery** (325 Bay Walk; 516-583-9552. May–Oct 7am–4am) sooner or later. Sunset cocktails at the **Fair Harbor** dock on Saturday evening are a tradition in the area; throw a bottle of wine or a six-pack in your beach bag and follow the sand path known as the Burma Road to Fair Harbor, five towns and a 20-minute walk to the west. City slickers in Ocean Beach tend to share summer rentals with groups of friends or other families, cramming 26 people into a four-bedroom house. For something more roomy, try **Klegg's Hotel** (516-583-5399) or **Jerry's Accommodations** (516-583-5399).

   A mecca for the Chelsea boys and other members of New York's affluent gay male community, the **Pines** (also called the Fire Island Pines) is a world—and a half-hour water-taxi ride—away from Ocean Beach. Elaborate modern wood and glass houses with up to ten bedrooms line this community's carless streets. Pines residents keep a very tight social schedule: sunning in the morning, working out in the afternoon and then napping before cocktails at sunset. At 8pm, it's the "tea dance" (which involves neither tea nor dancing) outside the world-famous club the **Pavilion** (516-597-6131), followed by dinner at home (never before ten). Then it's back to the Pavilion at 2am for partying until dawn. Guest rooms are available at **Botel** (516-597-6500), an unattractive concrete structure that houses the Pines' heavily populated gym, and at the more quaint **Pines Place** (516-597-6131). Wherever you stay, make sure to get an invite for cocktails and dinner at one of the fabulous beach houses.

GETTING THERE

Ocean Beach: Take the Babylon line on the **LIRR** to Bay Shore ($6.50–$9.50), then walk or take a cab to the ferry station. Tommy's Taxi (516-665-4800. Mon–Sat $16, Sun and holidays $19) runs regular van service from various locations in Manhattan. By car, take the Long Island Expwy to Sagtikos Pkwy. Then take the Southern State Pkwy eastbound to Exit 42 south (Fifth Ave in Bay Shore); follow the signs for the ferry. From Bay Shore, take the Fire Island Ferry (99 Maple Ave, Bay Shore; 516-665-3600; www.ferryvision.com. Round-trip $11.50, children $5.50). **The Pines:** Take the Montauk line of the **LIRR** to Sayville ($6.50–$9.50), then walk or take a taxi to the ferry station. From May to October, **Islander's Horizon Buses** (212-477-0094, 516-654-2622; www.islanderstravel.com) run between Manhattan and the Sayville ferry station, Friday through Monday ($20 one way). By car, take the Long Island Expwy to Exit 59 south, then turn right onto Ocean Ave and continue for 6.5 miles. Turn left on Main St and follow the green-and-white signs to the ferry. From Sayville, take the Sayville Ferry (41 River Rd; 516-589-0810; round-trip $11, children under 12 $5) across the bay.

The Jersey Shore

The state of New Jersey is a prime target for many New Yorkers' scathing wit. But the state's hundred miles of Atlantic seafront include some splendid beaches (though erosion has taken its toll) and provide insight into classic American oceanside culture. The best beaches are often private (Long Beach and Ocean Beach); the public ones are usually choked with noisy crowds from northern Jersey's industrial cities.

Two hours south of NYC, **Wildwood** boasts enormous beaches and the kind of huge boardwalk that typifies New Jersey's shoreline. The wooden promenade is packed with fairground rides, sideshows and food stands. Try the frozen custard, pork rolls and elephant ears—all local delicacies. Ride on the roller coasters and the huge Ferris wheel, have an old-time photo taken, or just stroll along the 100-year-old boardwalk.

Along the same lines as Wildwood, **Ocean City** is a festival of pure kitsch. The immense boardwalk is lined with lights and squawking natives, but the lazy beach and neon-pink cotton candy make it easy to have some fun. If you're starving for some

high culture, stop in at the **Ocean City Arts Center**, which displays traditional arts and crafts as well as regional boardwalk art. **The Flanders Hotel** is a good place to crash for the night.

The Flanders Hotel
11th Street at the Boardwalk (609-399-1000) www.theflanders.com.

Ocean City Arts Center
1735 Simpson Ave (609-399-7628).

Ocean City Chamber of Commerce Information Center
P.O. Box 157, Ocean City, NJ 08226 (609-399-2629) www.oceancityvacation.com.

Wildwoods Convention & Civic Center
4500 Boardwalk, Wildwood, NJ 08260-0217 (609-729-9000).

Cape May

Cape May, 170 miles from New York City, and on the southernmost tip of New Jersey, is said to have been the nation's first seaside resort. The ticky-tacky boardwalk culture generally associated with the Jersey Shore is nowhere to be found here. Instead, Cape May has many beautifully restored gingerbread Victorian homes. Don't miss the **Pink House** (33 Perry Street by Carpenters' Lane), a rosy three-tiered Gothic-revival home with intricate lattice-trimmed porches. The best time to go is early September, when the crowds have thinned but the water is still warm enough to swim in. Rent a bike and pedal down to **Cape May Point,** where the Atlantic meets the Delaware Bay and visitors fervently sift through the sand for pieces of polished quartz, called "Cape May diamonds." Nearby **Cape May Point State Park** has a lovely bird sanctuary (609-884-2736). The Cape May Lighthouse is the oldest continuously operating lighthouse in the United States (call the **Mid-Atlantic Center for the Arts** for information).

If you want to stay overnight, note that in summer most hotels require a two- to four-night minimum stay. Try the venerable **Chalfonte Hotel,** a 19th-century building styled after an Italian villa. And eat at the **Mad Batter,** which provides upscale vacation chow.

Greater Cape May Chamber of Commerce
P.O. Box 556, Cape May, NJ 08204 (609-884-5508) www.capemaychamber.com.

Chalfonte Hotel
301 Howard St (609-884-8409) www.chalfonte.com. Doubles $103–$188 includes breakfast. AmEx, MC, V.

Mad Batter
In the Carroll Villa Hotel, 19 Jackson Street; 609-884-5970. Hours vary, call ahead. AmEx, Disc, MC, V.

Mid-Atlantic Center for the Arts
1048 Washington St, Cape May, NJ 08204 (609-884-5404, 800-275-4278) www.capemaymac.org.

GETTING THERE

NJ Transit buses (973-762-5100) leave from Port Authority Bus Terminal for Wildwood ($45.25 round-trip), Ocean City ($40 round-trip) and Cape May ($48.25 round-trip). By car, take the Garden State Parkway (from the Lincoln or Holland Tunnel) south to the last exit.

Outdoor excursions

Nearly half the population of the state of New York is crammed into the five boroughs of New York City. This leaves the other 47,000 square miles (122,000 square kilometers) relatively unpopulated. Hikers, climbers and skiers will be pleased to hear this area includes some of the most dramatic mountain scenery in the U.S. The Catskills, an offshoot of the Appalachian Mountains just 90 miles from the city, is New York's nearest major forest and park area. Farther north—about a five-hour trip— are the Adirondacks, the largest area of untouched beauty in the state. Closer to sea level, adventurers don't have to travel far to enjoy some water sports, pedal pushing and spelunking. These catch-all organizations can help you plan any wilderness trip.

Appalachian Mountain Club

New York–North Jersey Chapter, 5 Tudor City Pl, 41st St at First Ave (212-986-1430) www.amc-ny.org. Subway: 4, 5, 6, 7 to 42nd St–Grand Central. Tue and Fri 11am–6pm.
AMC is the New York area's authority on hiking, skiing and every outdoor pursuit in between. You have to be a member to participate in activities, but a four-month "guest card" can be purchased for only $15.

Hostelling International–American Youth Hostels

891 Amsterdam Ave between 103rd and 104th Sts (212-932-2300). Subway: 1, 9 to 103rd St.
HI-AYH's Bike, Hike, and Ski Clubs are open to everyone, regardless of whether you're a member or a student.

Boating

You can raft, canoe and kayak in several bodies of water outside New York City. On the deceptively named Lake Placid, daredevils can ride the roaring rapids with **Middle Earth Expeditions**; the day trips are generally $75 per person, two-day intensive trips range from $195–$375 per person. **Ausable Chasm** is a narrow (20 feet/6 meters) gorge in Adirondack Park's Lake Champlain where float rides run daily from mid-May through mid-October. **Kittatinny Canoes** offers the tamest option, renting canoes and kayaks for trips along the Delaware River for $25–$28 per person.

Ausable Chasm

518-834-7454, 800-537-1211; www.ausablechasm.com. $19, children under 12 $17, under 5 free.

Kittatinny Canoes

800-FLOAT-KC, 717-828-2338; www.kittatinny.com.

Middle Earth Expeditions

HCRO1, Box 37, Route 73, Lake Placid, NY (518-523-9572).

Camping

There are more than 500 public and privately owned campsites throughout New York State. Some are so remote that they can be reached only by boat; others are within close range of the five boroughs and accessible by public transportation. Reservations are recommended but not always necessary. Two of the more popular areas to camp are the vast Adirondack Park and, much closer to the city, the forests of the Catskills.

New York State Office of Parks, Recreation & Historic Preservation

Empire State Plaza, Albany, NY 12238 (518-474-0458).
This government organization provides information on all parks and park activities within the state.

New York State Campgrounds

800-456-CAMP.
Call to make campsite reservations.

Caving

Life underground isn't confined to the subway system. Cobleskill, New York, a few hours north of the city, harbors deep natural caverns with captivating grottoes and rock formations—and a large population of bats. The **Howe Caverns**, at 156 feet underground, can lay claim to the Venus Lake (traversable by boat) and even a subterranean bridal altar. The staff has plans in the works for a massive Y2K New Year's bash. When you ascend to ground-level you can stay the night at the **Howe Caverns Motel**. If the effortless elevator rides and paved brick walkways inside Howe are too soft-core for you, more adventurous spelunking excursions of less-explored caves can be arranged in advance through the **National Speleological Society**.

Howe Caverns / Howe Caverns Motel

RR1, Box 107, Howes Cave, NY (518-296-8900) www.howecaverns.com.
Call Howe Caverns directly to reserve a room (double $58–$78).

National Speleological Society

2813 Cave Ave, Huntsville, AL 35810 (256-852-1300) www.caves.org.

Climbing

The Shawangunks (or "Gunks"), in the Catskills, offer some of the best climbing in the country, with sheer rock cliffs more than 300 feet (95m) high. You need to buy a day pass from the **Mohonk Preserve**. Before you go, load up on supplies at **Tents & Trails**, a great store for climbing equipment in Manhattan. Upon arrival, stop in Ulster County's local climbing store, **Rock and Snow**—the staff is always happy to give advice. There's no better place to make camp than at the **Mohonk Mountain House Hotel**, a lavish castle on a secluded lake; the prices are steep but the lush grounds and rich food (full board for two is included in the room rate) justify the expense. A more economical option

Going batty: **Howe Caverns** *in upstate New York are filled with bats—and tourists.*

is the national landmark stone house at **Jingle Bell Farm**, full breakfast and use of the pool (in season) are included in the room rate.

Jingle Bell Farm

1 Forest Glen Rd, New Paltz (914-255-6588) www.jinglebellfarmbnb.com. Doubles $115–$130.

Mohonk Mountain House Hotel

1000 Mountain Rest Rd, New Paltz (914-255-1000, 800-772-6646). Doubles $145–$445. AmEx, Disc, MC, V.

Mohonk Preserve

3197 Rte 4455, Gardiner, NY (914-255-0919) www.mohonkpreserve.com. Day pass $5, weekends and holidays $7.

Rock and Snow

44 Main St, New Paltz (914-255-1311). April–Oct Mon–Thu 9am–6pm; Fri 9am–8pm; Sat 8am–8pm; Sun 8am–7pm. Nov–Mar Mon–Thu 10am–6pm; Fri 10am–7pm; Sat 9am–7pm; Sun 9am–6pm. AmEx, MC, V.

Tents & Trails

21 Park Pl between Church St and Broadway (212-227-1760). Subway: 4, 5, 6 to Brooklyn Bridge; 2, 3 to Park Pl; N, R to City Hall; A, C to Chambers St. Mon–Wed, Sat 9:30am–6pm; Thu, Fri 9:30am–7pm; Sun noon–6pm. AmEx, MC, V.

Cycling

The many rolling hills in New York's surrounding areas are a cyclist's dream. *City Cyclist* is a free cycling magazine available at bike shops; it provides helpful tips, as well as listings of upcoming biking events in the five boroughs and elsewhere.

To get rolling, try the Five Boro Bike Club (*see chapter* **New York by Season**), operated by Hostelling International. Its day trips, ranging from the "pancake flat" Grover's Mill, New Jersey, to the "moderate terrain" of New York's Orchard Beach, are free and leave directly from locations in Manhattan. The bike-rental rates are quite reasonable.

The more expensive **Brooks Country Cycling Tours** combines luxurious vacations with lower-body–workout bicycle trips of varying intensity. BCCT's tours include van transportation from NYC to rural destinations, as well as accommodations and some meals for overnight tours; rentals start at $30 per day. Consider taking your wheels on a day trip ($72) through the strawberry fields of eastern Long Island, or a longer trip to such scenic locales as Martha's Vineyard (four days, $744) and rural Vermont (three days, $564).

Bicycle Habitat

244 Lafayette St between Spring and Prince Sts (212-431-3315; www.bicylclehabitat.com). Subway: 6 to Spring St; N, R to Prince St. Mon–Thu 10am–7pm; Fri 10am–6:30pm; Sat, Sun 10am–6pm. AmEx, MC, V.
This shop is an excellent source of bike equipment and offers tune-ups for $35–$200.

Brooks Country Cycling Tours

140 W 83rd St between Columbus and Amsterdam Aves (212-874-5151) www.brookscountrycycling.com. Subway: 1, 9 to 72nd St. Disc, MC, V.

Fishing

With a license, you can fish in the state of New York's 70,000 miles (112,000 kilometers) of streams and rivers and 4,000 lakes and ponds. For freshwater destinations, you must be between the ages of 16 and 69 and purchase a license. New York rates are $14 resident, $35 nonresident for the season, three- and five-day passes available at most fishing-tackle stores. For information about licenses for New York, call 518-457-3521; for New Jersey, 609-292-2965; for Connecticut, 860-424-3105. To get a license by mail, or for other fishing information, contact the **Department of Environmental Conservation**.

The best way to zero in on prime catches is to hire an expert. **Tom Akstens** is a fly fisherman in the Adirondacks who gives private lessons in this artful sport. Two-day sessions cover basic fly-fishing technique ($200 for one person, $350 for two), while advanced six-hour clinics focus on line control and nymphing techniques for more experienced anglers ($150 for one person, $250 for two). Rest up from your long days on the water at the **Highwinds Inn**, a cozy guest house with five bedrooms and an impressive kitchen.

For more local fishing instruction, try Michael Padua of **Sweetwater Guide Service** in the Catskills. Padua can lead you to trout, shad, smallmouth bass and walleyes; he teaches both fly and regular fishing, and will also arrange local accommodations.

There are also plenty of coastal areas where ocean fishing is permitted. Resorts on Long Island and the Jersey Shore can hook you up with charter boats and equipment. These operators can usually take care of license requirements (saltwater fishing requires a different license from freshwater fishing).

Capitol Fishing
218 W 23rd St between Seventh and Eighth Aves (212-929-6132). Subway: C, E, 1, 9 to 23rd St. Mon–Wed, Fri 9am–6pm; Thu 9am–7pm; Sat 9am–5pm. AmEx, Disc, MC, V.
Both saltwater and freshwater equipment are sold here. It's also possible to rent equipment.

Department of Environmental Conservation (DEC)
50 Wolf Rd, Albany, NY 12233 (518-457-3521) www.dec.state.ny.us.

Highwinds Inn
Barton Mines Rd, North River, NY (518-251-3760, 800-241-1923) www.highwindsinn.com. Doubles $75–$92, breakfast and dinner included. Disc, MC, V.

Sweetwater Guide Service
399 Gables Rd, Narrowburg, NY (914-252-3439).

Tom Akstens
P.O. Box 111, Bakers Mills, NY 12811 (518-251-2217) akstens@aol.com. No credit cards.

Urban Angler
118 E 25th St between Lexington and Park Aves, third floor (212-979-7600). Subway: 6 to 23rd St. Mon, Tue, Thu, Fri 10am–6pm; Wed 10am–7pm; Sat 10am–5pm. AmEx, Disc, MC, V.
This is the best fly-fishing store in New York. Stop by for licenses, equipment and friendly advice on the top places to fish in the region—they've got info on both surf-casting (saltwater) and freshwater.

Hiking

Any wooded area makes suitable trekking terrain, but marked trails can keep you from going astray. The most famous, and popular, is the **Appalachian Trail**. Stretching from Maine to Georgia, this 2,159-mile (3,450km) trek is tackled by four million hikers annually (call the Appalachian Mountain Club, page 294, for more infor-

The antidote to urban overload
When Manhattan's too much, what a difference a day-trip can make

Bear Mountain
Upstate New York, Palisades Pkwy and Rte 9W (914-786-2701). Travel: Short Line Buses (212-736-4700) from Port Authority Bus Terminal.
In less than an hour, the bus will drop you off at an appalling visitors' center that has hundreds of families picnicking on fast food in the parking lot, but a ten-minute walk into the wilderness will take you away from it all. Explore the 66 miles of hiking, biking and cross-country ski trails or go for a swim in Hessian Lake.

The Cloisters
*Uptown Manhattan. See chapter **Museums** for listings.*
In Fort Tryon Park, near the northern tip of Manhattan, is this peaceful medieval setting for a romantic picnic.

Coney Island
*Brooklyn. See chapter **Outer Boroughs** for listings.*
A day at the beach here can bring you back to the 1950s. Take a ride on the Cyclone roller coaster or try the original Nathan's Hot Dogs. Subway: B, D, F, N to Coney Island–Stillwell Ave.

Dutchess Wine Trail
Upstate New York, Clinton Vineyards (call 914-266-5372 for travel information).
Hit three wineries in one day in the bucolic Hudson Valley. Clinton Vineyards organizes a comprehensive (and intoxicating) survey of the region's grapes, focusing on premier champagnes, red wines and white wines.

Jones Beach
*Long Island, (516-785-1600) See **Beach life**, page 290.*

New Yorkers take the crowds with them when they go on vacation—this hot spot for day-tripping city dwellers is the largest public beach in the world. Perfect for picnicking or sunbathing, Jones Beach is only 33 miles from Manhattan.

Masker Fruit Farms
Upstate New York, Ball Rd, Warwick, off Rte 17A (call 914-986-1058 for travel information). Sept–Nov.
Why go to the market when you can pick your own? This U-pick apple orchard gives you an empty bushel for a couple bucks and lets you go to work. The farm is only open during the harvest season, so the apples are always fresh and juicy.

Robert Moses State Park
Fire Island (516-852-5200). Travel: LIRR to Babylon, Long Island (one-way $5.75–$8.50, children and seniors $3–$4.25), then Suffolk Buses (late June–early Sept $1.50 each way).
This long stretch of white sand fronts the grassy dunes of Fire Island. If you walk far enough toward the lighthouse (516-661-4876; www.516web.com/museum/FILPS), you can strip down on a little-known nude beach. The park also allows cars.

William T. Davis Wildlife Refuge
Staten Island, Travis Ave between Victory Blvd and Richmond Ave (718-727-1135). Travel: Staten Island Ferry, then S44 or S62 bus.
Staten Island is the borough with the fewest skyscrapers and the most trees. The William T. Davis Wildlife Refuge in the heart of the island covers more than 260 acres and is home to a profusion of fauna. Make sure to bring a camera, since this is the place to snap pics of rare species of red-tailed hawks and northern harriers.

mation). The **Long Island Greenbelt Trail Conference** is a collection of five linked trails, spanning all of Long Island. The **Finger Lakes Trail System** is another massive network of hiking trails, covering 800 miles from Canada to the Catskills. Both the Greenbelt and the Finger Lakes trails are open to the public free of charge; maps are available for a low fee. Also keep in mind that many hiking trails are excellent for cross-country skiing in the winter.

Finger Lakes Trail System
P.O. Box 18048, Rochester, NY 14618 (716-288-7191).

Long Island Greenbelt Trail Conference
23 Deer Path Rd, Central Islip, NY 11722 (516-360-0753).

Skiing and snowboarding

Convenient winter-sports getaways include **Ski Windham** and **Hunter Mountain** in the Catskills or **Catamount** and **Jiminy Peak** in the Berkshires, located 110 miles north of New York City on the Massachusetts border. Sticklers for fresh powder and challenging slopes drive the extra few hours to get to **Killington** and the lesser-known **Mad River Glen** in Vermont. Sports superstores such as Blades and Paragon arrange all-inclusive trips by bus during the winter season.

Blades
659 Broadway at Bleecker St (212-477-7350, 888-55BLADES) www.blades.com. Subway: 6 to Bleecker St. Mon–Sat 11am–9pm; Sun 11am–7pm. AmEx, MC, V.
Blades draws a big snowboarding crowd; its trips usually consist of noisy busloads of young "shredders." The $55 Hunter Mountain package includes lift tickets and transportation, as well as complimentary movies and bagels on the bus. Rentals are available for an extra $20.

Paragon Sports
867 Broadway at 18th St (212-255-8036). Subway: L, N, R, 4, 5, 6 to 14th St–Union Sq. Mon–Sat 10am–8pm; Sun 11am–6:30pm. AmEx, Disc, MC, V.
Paragon's trips are slightly more adult than Blades', with an even blend of skiers and boarders. Fifty-eight dollars gets you transportation and a lift ticket for one day at Hunter Mountain. Rentals are also available.

Catamount
413-528-1262, 800-342-1840; www.catamountski.com. Full-day lift tickets $25–$39, children 7–13 and seniors 62 and over $20–$25, children under 6 free.

Hunter Mountain
518-263-4223; lodging 800-775-4641; weather conditions 800-FOR-SNOW; www.huntermtn.com. Full-day lift tickets $37–$44, students 13–18 $33–$39, children under 12 and seniors $22–$28.

Killington
802-422-3333, 800-621-6686; weather conditions 802-422-3261; www.killington.com. Full-day lift tickets $52, ages 13-18 $47, under 13 $33.

Jiminy Peak
413-738-5500; lodging 800-882-8898; www.jiminypeak.com. Full-day lift tickets $32–$42, students and seniors $26–$29.

Mad River Glen
802-496-3551; www.madriverglen.com. Full-day lift tickets $29–$36, students 6–15 and seniors $20–$24, children under 6 free.

Ski Windham
518-734-4300, 800-SKI-WINDHAM; for ski conditions 518-734-4SNO; www.skiwindham.com. Full-day lift tickets $33–$42, children 7–12 $29–$34.

Fun and games

If Lotto doesn't satisfy your gambling jones, you'll have to head for the state border. As in most of the country, casino gambling is illegal in New York, but you can hit the road to New Jersey or Connecticut and be hemorrhaging money on blackjack tables within a couple of hours. If you're under 21 years old, you'll have to skip the betting scene and get your thrills from a roller-coaster ride—the pure adrenaline rush is reason enough to head for one of the nearby theme parks.

Gambling

It's not exactly a class act, but **Atlantic City**, whose roulette wheels have been spinning for more than 20 years, is the oldest gaming town in the East. The most famous of the 13 casino resorts are **Trump Plaza** (800-677-7378); Donald Trump's **Taj Mahal** (800-825-8786); and **Caesar's Atlantic City** (800-524-2867), which just completed construction of its spanking new 26-story **Centurion Tower** hotel. The famous, brightly lit and constantly crowded **Boardwalk** runs parallel to the Atlantic Ocean, connects nearly every casino, and is going strong 24 hours a day, seven days a week. If you don't want to walk, the **Pacific Avenue Bus** can shuttle you from one gambling hall to another. Besides stomach-engorging all-you-can-eat buffets, overpriced bars and chintzy gift shops, there are floor shows and concerts. Sample the gooey offerings at **Original James Salt-Water Taffy**, and while you're strolling, stop in at **Ripley's Believe It or Not! Museum**. It displays, among other oddities, a roulette wheel made entirely of jelly beans. Another attraction is the annual Miss America Pageant, held in September at the Boardwalk Convention Hall.

The autonomous Native American nations in Southeastern Connecticut, not bound by state laws, are free to make their own rules for—and revenues from—games of chance. The Mashantucket Pequot tribe turns a very nice profit at the immense **Foxwoods Resort Casino**, located 145 miles northeast of New York in bucolic Mashantucket, Connecticut. With 6,000 slot machines, a 3,200-seat bingo hall, hundreds of gaming tables and a 75-table poker room, visitors have plenty of opportunities to squander their life savings. For lounge lizards, Foxwoods offers concerts by the likes of Ray Charles, Willie Nelson and Smokey Robinson. Accommodations at Foxwoods range from the thrifty **Two Trees Inn** (doubles from $80) to the high-rolling **Grand Pequot Tower** (doubles from $145). For reservations at both call 800-FOXWOOD. Ten miles to the east, in Uncasville, the Mohegan tribe operates the **Mohegan Sun**, whose circular gaming room is divided into four seasonal quadrants surrounding the "Wolf Den." Other ancient influences include wolf icons and creation-myth quilts hanging over baccarat, Spanish 21 and high-stakes bingo tables. There are no hotels on the Mohegan Sun property, but the casino provides information on available lodgings in nearby Norwich and Mystic, Connecticut. While the gaming goes on all night at the casinos, the partying doesn't—in accordance with Connecticut law, alcohol service stops at 1am.

Atlantic City Convention & Visitors Authority
2314 Pacific Ave, Atlantic City, NJ 08401 (888-228-4748, 609-348-7130) www.atlanticcitynj.com.

Foxwoods Resort Casino
860-312-3000, 800-PLAY-BIG; www.foxwoods.com.

Mohegan Sun
888-226-7711; www.mohegansun.com.

Original James Salt-Water Taffy
1519 Boardwalk (609-344-2408). $4.89 per pound.

Ripley's Believe It or Not! Museum
1441 New York Ave at the Boardwalk (609-347-2001). 10am–10pm. $8.95, children 5–12 $6.95, under 4 free.

GETTING THERE
Atlantic City: Greyhound bus from Port Authority Bus Terminal to various casinos; return bus picks you up at the Atlantic City Bus Terminal, two blocks from the Boardwalk at the corner of Atlantic and Michigan Aves. $24 round-trip. The trip to Atlantic City takes about two and a half hours.
Foxwoods: For information on public transportation rates and packages, call 888-BUS-2-FOX. By car, take I-95 north to Exit 92, then Rte 2 east.
Mohegan Sun: Academy Bus Tours (212-971-9054; Mon, Wed, Sat; $21-$25 round-trip) to the Mohegan Sun leave from Manhattan, Dream Lines runs from Brooklyn (718-232-3813; Thur; $20 round-trip) and Happy Time Charter (800-543-5461; Mon, Wed, Sun; $22 round-trip) leaves from the Bronx. By car, from I-95 north take Exit 76 to I-395 north. Then take Exit 79A (Rte 2A) east and continue for about one mile to Mohegan Sun Blvd.

Theme parks

Mountain Creek
Vernon, NJ, on Rte 94, 47 miles (72km) from Manhattan (973-827-2000) www.mountaincreek.com. Travel: By car, take I-80 west to Rte 23 north, then Rte 515 north and go one mile on Rte 94 south. Groups should call ext 319 for transportation discounts. Early June Sat, Sun 10am–7pm; mid-June–early Sept Mon–Sun 10am–7pm; call for fall schedule. Adults $28, children under four feet tall $15, under three feet free. Group discounts available. AmEx, MC, V.
An immense water park in the summer, Mountain Creek (formerly Action Park) caters to fun-loving families looking to splash away the summer heat. Under new ownership, the area has been revamped (de-cheesed) to better fit its rural mountain setting—200 acres of woods and hills.

Bring your swimming gear and enjoy high-action rides like Wild River or the more kid-friendly Lost Island. Since the 1998 season, Mountain Creek has also offered 47 trails for skiing and snowboarding in the colder months. Winter activities begin mid-Dec; call for more information.

Playland
Rye, NY (914-967-5230). Travel: By train, take Metro-North (New Haven line) from Grand Central Terminal to Rye, then connecting bus #76. By car, take I-95 north to Exit 19 and follow the signs to the park. Summer Tue–Thu, Sun noon–11pm; Fri, Sat noon–midnight; call for winter hours. Admission to park free, rides "cost" 3–5 tickets (24 tickets $14, 36 tickets $18). MC, V.
An old-fashioned amusement park set on the shore of Long Island Sound, this 72-year-old facility is popular for both its nostalgic attractions and its modern rides, including the Dragon Coaster, Chaos and the virtual-reality extravaganza, Morphis. Kiddyland offers Arctic Flume, Demolition Derby and even Slime Buckets for the little tykes. Other attractions include video arcades, miniature golf, picnic grounds, a pool and a beach on the sound. Ice-skating rinks and other frosty facilities are open in the winter months (call 914-925-2761 for information). A fireworks show is held on the Fourth of July, as well as every Wednesday and Friday night throughout July and August.

Six Flags Great Adventure & Wild Safari
Jackson, NJ, on Rte 537, 50 miles (80km) from Manhattan (732-928-1821) www.six.flags.com. Travel: By bus, NJ Transit (973-762-5100) from Port Authority Bus Terminal ($39 round-trip, incl. admission). By car, take Exit 7A off the New Jersey Tpke or Exit 98 off the Garden State Pkwy to I-195, Exit 16. May–Sept 10am–10pm (closing time variable), limited opening times in Oct. $35.99, children under four feet tall half price, seniors over 55 $21.98. AmEx, Disc, MC, V.
Six Flags entices Manhattanites with the slogan "Bigger than Disneyland and a whole lot closer." The park features a gargantuan drive-through safari park with 1,200 land animals, a mammoth offering of gut-churning rides and the obligatory fast food chains. Don't miss Six Flags' signature rides, the Great American Scream Machine, Batman and Robin, and the Chiller, where you can experience 0–70 mph acceleration forward and backward in four seconds.

History lessons

You can learn a lot about this region's people and life *and* see some beautiful country at the same time.

Hudson Valley

If you're keen on history or just enjoy scenery, the **Hudson Valley** in Westchester County, New York, will satisfy you. The breathtaking former summer residences of such famous New Yorkers as John D. Rockefeller Jr. and Franklin Roosevelt dot the river, and most are now open to the public for much of the year. The trip to and from the Hudson Valley can easily be made in a day, but if you have the time, don't deny yourself the pleasures of the area's cozy inns and lavish culinary offerings. Metro-North frequently offers discounted rates to the area, and **New York Waterway**, in conjunction with **Historic Hudson Valley**, runs cruises from Manhattan and New Jersey to several of the historic houses.

*Real estates: John D. Rockefeller's **Kykuit** and other historic homes line the Hudson Valley.*

Any time of the year, **Cold Spring** is a haven of peace and quiet, and the stunning view from the bank of the Hudson takes in the Shawangunk Mountains across the river. The town is only 50 miles (80km) from Manhattan, but light-years away culturally. The best place to crash is the **Hudson House**, a peaceful, convenient inn with an excellent contemporary American restaurant. From the inn, follow Main Street into the heart of town, where a number of narrow-frame houses with airy porches and shuttered windows sit alongside the four-story commercial buildings. The tiny town is chock-full of antiques shops, and the **Main Street Café** sells fresh-baked goods.

Just a mile away is the town of **Garrison**, home to the **Boscobel Restoration**, a Federal-style mansion built in 1804 by States Morris Dyckman, a wealthy British loyalist.

The town of **Rhinebeck** is cherished by history buffs in the New York area. **Wilderstein**, an 1852 Italianate villa, was rebuilt in Queen Anne style at the turn of the century. The town also boasts the oldest hotel in the nation, the **Beekman Arms**—which dates back as far as 1700. The Beekman may be historic, but the kitchen is nothing if not cutting-edge. Manhattan's celebrity chef Larry Forgione (An American Place) took over the inn's **Beekman 1766 Tavern** in 1991, updating the menu with such innovative dishes as Applewood Grilled Monkfish and Center Cut Pork Scaloppini (both $18.95). When you're done eating, check out the **Beekman Arms Antiques Market and Gallery**, in a converted barn just steps away. Rhinebeck hosts weekly air shows on Saturdays and Sundays from 2 to 4pm at the **Old Rhinebeck Aerodrome**.

The definitive Hudson Valley estate is a former home of Franklin and Eleanor Roosevelt, **Springwood**, in **Hyde Park**. Family photos, presidential documents and even FDR's boyhood pony cart fill the house with memories of the great New Dealer and his groundbreaking wife. Also located in Hyde Park is the **Culinary Institute of America**—of which Forgione is an alumnus—where chefs-in-training prepare French, American, Italian and spa cuisines in four different dining rooms. Characteristic of the region, Hyde Park has several antique shops—the **Village Antiques Center** and the **Hyde Park Antique Center** represent approximately 75 dealers between them. A good place to rest up after all these activities is **Fala House**, a private one-bedroom guest house with a pool—call ahead for reservations.

Dutchess County Tourism, Rhinebeck and Hyde Park
3 Neptune Rd, Poughkeepsie, NY 12601 (914-463-4000).

Historic Hudson Valley
150 White Plains Rd, Tarrytown, NY 10591 (914-631-8200) www.hudsonvalley.org.
This historical society maintains several mansions in the area, including John D. Rockefeller Jr.'s **Kykuit** (914-631-9491. Apr–Nov. $20, seniors $19, children $17) and Washington Irving's **Sunnyside** (914-591-8763. Mar–Dec. $8, seniors $7, children 6–17 $4), as well as **Philipsburg Manor** (914-631-3992. Mar–Dec. $8, seniors $7, children 6–17 $4), **Van Cortlandt Manor** (914-271-8981. Apr–Dec. $8, seniors $7, children 6–17 $4) and **Montgomery Place** (914-758-5461. Apr–Dec. $6, seniors $5, children 6–17 $3).

Beekman Arms
4 Mill St, Rhinebeck, NY (914-876-7077, 800-361-6517) www.beekmanarms.com. Doubles $85–$140. AmEx, Disc, MC, V.

Beekman Arms Antiques Market and Gallery
4 Mill St, Rhinebeck, NY (914-876-3477). Mon–Sun 11am–5pm. MC, V.

Beekman 1766 Tavern
4 Mill St, Rhinebeck, NY (914-871-1766). Mon–Thu 11:30am–3pm, 5:30–8:30pm; Fri–Sun 11:30am–3pm, 5:30–9:30pm. AmEx, Disc, MC, V.

Boscobel Restoration
1601 Rte 9D, Garrison, NY (914-265-3638)
www.boscobel.org. Apr–Oct Mon, Wed–Sun 9:30am–5pm;
Nov, Dec Wed–Sun 9:30am–4pm. $7, seniors $6, children
6–12 $4, children under six free. MC, V.

Culinary Institute of America
433 Albany Post Rd, Hyde Park, NY (914-471-6608)
www.ciachef.edu. AmEx, Disc, MC, V.
Reservations and appropriate attire required.

Fala House
East Market St, Hyde Park, NY (914-229-5937).
Mar–Nov. $85. No credit cards.

Hudson House
2 Main St, Cold Spring, NY (914-265-9355)
www.hudsonhouseinn.com. Doubles $140-$225.

Hudson River Heritage
P.O. Box 287, Rhinebeck, NY 12572 (914-876-2474).

Hyde Park Antique Center
544 Albany Post Rd, Hyde Park, NY (914-229-8200).
10am–5pm. AmEx, Disc, MC, V.

Main Street Café
129 Main St, Cold Spring, NY (914-265-4548).
7am–5pm. No credit cards.

Old Rhinebeck Aerodrome
44 Stone Church Rd off Rte 9, Rhinebeck, NY
(914-758-8610) www.oldrhinebeck.org. Jun–Oct. $10,
children $5. MC, V.

Putnam County Visitor's Office, Cold Spring
110 Old Route 6, building 3, Carmel, NY 10512
(914-225-0381, 800-470-4854) www.visitputnam.org.

Springwood
U.S. 9, Hyde Park, NY (914-229-2501). 9am–5pm. $10,
children under 17 free. MC, V.

Village Antiques Center
597 Albany Post Rd, Hyde Park, NY (914-229-6600).
Mon–Sun 10am–5pm. MC, V.

Wilderstein
64 Morton Rd, Rhinebeck, NY (914-876-4818). May–Oct
Thu–Sun noon–4pm; Thanksgiving weekend Fri–Sun
1–4pm; Dec Fri, Sat 1–4pm. $4.

GETTING THERE
Ask about special package rates from **New York Water-way** (800-53FERRY). **Metro-North** has trains to the Hudson Valley daily ($7.75–$10.25). **Short Line Buses** (212-736-4700, 800-631-8405; www.shortlinebus.com; $24.80 round-trip) also runs regular bus service to Rhinebeck and Hyde Park. By car, take the Saw Mill River Pkwy to the Taconic Pkwy north to I-84 west. For Cold Spring, take Rte 9 south to Rte 301 west. For Rhinebeck and Hyde Park, take Rte 9 north.

Newport, Rhode Island

Located in southeastern Rhode Island, historic Newport, once a thriving whaling town, became a popular summer retreat for the Rockefellers, Astors and Vanderbilts. The city's dozens of Gilded Age mansions, some with more than 70 rooms, can be found primarily on Ocean Drive and Belle-vue Avenue. The **Preservation Society** main-

tains seven of these estates as museums. The **Marble House**, originally occupied by William K. Vanderbilt, was designed with 5,000 square feet of marble amid the decor. The **Breakers**, built for Cornelius Vanderbilt, is a spectacular home constructed in the style of an Italian palace.

If all this wealth makes you hungry, you can continue your historical tour at the **White Horse Tavern**, the oldest pub in America. Newport doesn't just rest on its historical laurels, however. The **JVC Jazz Festival** (401-847-3700) alights here each August, featuring such legends as George Benson, Tito Puente and Herbie Hancock. If these blue notes are your style, book early—tickets for the summer festival invariably sell out months in advance. Or simply forgo the frenzied scene and stop in to hear jazz and blues year-round at **Christie's Restaurant** and the **Newport Blues Cafe**.

Whenever you go, make sure you see the harbor. While the many yachts docked here aren't quite as lavish as the Gilded Age summer homes of old, they're pretty close. Two places to take refuge for the night are the **Admiral Farragut**, a small inn in the center of town charmingly decorated with Shaker furniture and American folk art, and the **John Banister House**, a 1751 colonial home–turned–inn with antiques and a fireplace in every room. The *Pineapple Post* is a helpful newsletter available at the Visitor's Bureau and other tourist-friendly locations.

Newport Convention & Visitor's Bureau
23 America's Cup Ave, Newport, RI 02840
(401-845-9123, 800-976-5122; www.gonewport.com).
Mon–Sun 9am–5pm.

Admiral Farragut
31 Clark St, Newport, RI (401-846-4256, 800-343-2863)
www.admirals.com. $85–$175. AmEx, Disc, V.

Breakers
Ocre Point Ave, Newport, RI (401-847-2445). Mar–Nov
Mon–Sun 10am–5pm. $12, children 6–17 $4, under 6
free. AmEx, Disc, MC, V.

Christie's Restaurant
351 Thames St, Newport, RI (401-847-5400). AmEx,
Disc, MC, V.

John Banister House
56 Pelham St at Spring St, Newport, RI (401-846-0050)
www.johnbanisterinn.com. $95–$300, depending on the
season. No credit cards.

Marble House
Bellevue Ave, Newport, RI (401-874-6544). Mar–Nov
Mon–Sun 10am–5pm. $9, children 6–17 $3.50, under 6
free. AmEx, Disc, MC, V.

Newport Blues Cafe
286 Thames St, Newport, RI (401-841-5510). Cover
$3–$10. AmEx, Disc, MC, V.

Preservation Society
424 Bellevue Ave, Newport, RI (401-847-1000)
www.newportmansions.org. Mon–Fri 9am–5pm.

White Horse Tavern
26 Marlborough St at Farewell St, Newport, RI (401-849-3600). Mon–Wed 6–10pm; Thu–Sun noon–3pm, 6–10pm; closing times earlier in the off-season.

GETTING THERE
By train, take **Amtrak** to Providence, RI, then transfer to a **Bonanza** shuttle bus ($42 each way). By car, take I-95 east to Exit 3 in Rhode Island, then take Rte 138 east.

Lancaster, Pennsylvania

Wholesome types and insatiable romantics may want to explore Pennsylvania's charming **Dutch Country**, located 159 miles west of New York City. The area's Amish and less conservative Mennonite residents are Anabaptist sects—actually German, not Dutch, in origin—who settled here in the 17th century after escaping religious persecution in Europe. Among the farmlands of **Lancaster**, **Strasburg** and **Intercourse**, the Amish lead their startlingly old-fashioned lifestyle according to the "Old Order" of serving God through simple living and tilling the soil. The exclusionary nature of the Amish community conflicts with the burgeoning curiosity of tourists; visitors are often not welcome on family farms. The **Amish Farm and House** is a museum-style re-creation of an Amish home. A more authentic experience can be had by arranging a private visit or overnight stay with a willing Old Order family (a donation or fee is expected): call **Dee Dee Myers** (717-664-4888) or **Emanuel Fisher** (717-768-3091) directly.

Old-fashioned crafts, particularly quilt making, prevail in the area. Local craftwork is sold by small Amish businesses such as **Hannah Slotzfoos Quilts**. If you're not buying, you can browse through numerous examples at the **Quilt Museum** in the **People's Place**, a center for Pennsylvania Dutch arts and crafts in Intercourse. Lancaster also has a rich Revolutionary War history, highlighted by **Historic Lancaster Walking Tours**.

Groff's Farm Restaurant is not run by Amish, but it serves family-style plates of hearty fried chicken, mashed potatoes and shoo-fly pie, a sticky molasses-based concoction. The **Historic Strasburg Inn** offers modern guest rooms in a quaint colonial building.

Pennsylvania Dutch Convention and Visitors Bureau
501 Greenfield Rd, Lancaster, PA 17601 (717-299-8901, 800-735-2629).

Mennonite Information Center
2209 Millstream Rd, Lancaster, PA 17602 (717-299-0954).

Amish Farm and House
2395 Rte 30 east, Lancaster, PA (717-394-6185). www.amishfarmandhouse.com. Nov–Mar Mon–Sun 8:30am–4pm; Apr, May, Sept, Oct 8:30am–5pm; Jun–Aug 8:30am–6pm. $5.95, children 5–11 $3.50, under 5 free.

Groff's Farm Restaurant
Pinkerton Rd, Mount Joy, PA (717-653-2048). Tue–Sat 11:30am–1:30pm, 5–8pm. Disc, MC, V.

Hannah Slotzfoos Quilts
216 Witmer Rd, Lancaster, PA (no phone).

Historic Lancaster Walking Tours
100 South Queen St, Lancaster, PA (717-392-1776). Mon 1pm; Tue 10am, 1pm; Wed, Thu 1pm; Fri, Sat 10am, 1pm; Sun 1pm. $7, seniors $6, students $4.

Historic Strasburg Inn
1 Historic Dr, Strasburg, PA (717-687-7691) www.800padutch.com/strasinn.html. Doubles $89–$149. AmEx, Disc, MC, V.

Quilt Museum in the People's Place
3513 Philadelphia Pike, Intercourse, PA (717-768-7171). Mon–Sat 9:30am–5pm; summer Mon–Sat 9:30am–8pm. $4, children $2. MC, V.

GETTING THERE
Amtrak has direct service to Lancaster ($40 each way). By car, take the New Jersey Tpke to the Pennsylvania Tpke. Then take Rte 222 south to Rte 30 and continue into Lancaster.

Shopping sprees

Bitchy salespeople, an 8.25% sales tax and crowds from hell can make shopping in Gotham a regrettable experience. The price tags at designer boutiques could pay off your mortgage, and discount superstores like Century 21 and Syms have all the comfort and sophistication of used car dealerships. Don't despair: You can make it back to your hometown with armfuls of stuff without losing either your life savings or your self-respect. User-friendly outlet malls in nearby suburban towns stock past-season items from popular and high-end merchants at yard-sale prices.

Clinton Crossing
Clinton, CT (860-664-0700) www.chelseagca.com. Travel: By car, take I-95 north to exit 63 (Clinton), make two lefts, and Clinton Crossing is on the left. Jan–Mar Mon–Wed 10am–6pm, Thu–Sat 10am–9pm; Apr–June Mon–Sat 10am–9pm, Sun 10am–6pm; July, Aug Mon–Sat 10am–9pm, Sun 10am–8pm; Sept–Dec Mon–Sat 10am–9pm, Sun 10am–6pm.

An upscale shopping center on the Connecticut shoreline, Clinton Crossing is operated by Chelsea Premium Outlet Centers, which also runs Liberty Village and Woodbury Commons. Don't expect blinding fluorescent lights and mall Muzak—these shopping centers are modeled after country villages, complete with (albeit synthetic) shingled cottages and cobblestone streets. But the provincial look can be deceiving—Clinton Crossing keeps its urban edge with several designer shops and a Barneys New York Outlet, featuring contemporary couture fashions. Once you've been through all 35 clothing outlets here (including Brooks Brothers, Calvin Klein, Danskin, Fila and Malo), pick up half-priced high-society leather goods at Coach or houseware necessities at Crate & Barrel. For a complete pampering experience, special off-season packages are available for shoppers at the nearby Saybrook Point Inn & Spa (Old Saybrook, CT; 860-395-2000; www.saybrook.com). All Chelsea Premium Outlet Centers advertise discounts of 25 to 65 percent.

Liberty Village

Flemington, NJ (908-788-5729; www.chelseagca.com). Travel: By bus, take Trans-Bridge Bus Lines (800-962-9135; round-trip $23.30, children under 12 $11.60, seniors $10.80) from Port Authority Bus Terminal. By car, take the New Jersey Tpke south to exit 14, then take Rte 78 west to Rte 31 south, at the Flemington traffic circle take Rte 12 west for half a mile, Liberty Village is on the right. Mon–Sat 10am–6pm; Thu–Sat 10am–9pm; Sun 10am–6pm.

Liberty is only a modest collection of 60 stores, but customers wrestle with fewer crowds than they would at all-encompassing locations like Woodbury Commons. This quaint complex, erected in 1981, is the oldest outlet village in the nation. New Jersey does not charge sales tax on clothing and shoes, so you and your credit card can rampage through Donna Karan, Ellen Tracy, Perry Ellis, Cole-Haan and Joan & David factory stores guilt- and tax-free. Unfortunately, six-percent sales tax is charged on accessories, home furnishings and gift items. The trip from the city is only an hour, but if one day of shopping isn't enough, "Shop and Stay" packages are available at local bed-and-breakfasts (call Liberty Village for information).

Tanger Outlet Center

Riverhead, NY (800-407-4894) www.tangeroutlet.com. Travel: By bus, take Sunrise Coach Lines (800-527-7709; round-trip $29, children under five free) from midtown Manhattan to Tanger's entrance gate. By train, take the LIRR (round-trip $20.50–$30.50) from Penn Station to Riverhead. By car, take the Long Island Expwy (I-495) east to exit 73, turn right onto County Rd 58 (Old Country Rd), Tanger is on the right. Mon–Sat 10am–9pm; Sun 10am–7pm; call for holiday hours.

Some rest-stops on the way to the beach are a lot more exciting than roadside gas station minimarts. This Long Island shopping oasis, 60 miles from Manhattan, is the perfect detour from the road to the Hamptons (*see* **Beach life**, *page 290*). Tanger is actually two separate malls—Tanger I and Tanger II—serviced by a connecting trolley and constituting 160 stores between them. Tanger's array of department stores and thriving brands such as Levi's and BCBG provide enough merchandise to suit any discriminating shopper, and discounts here can be as high as 70 percent. Can't find a baby-sitter? Tanger's unusual family services include more than 20 children's apparel stores, a spacious playground, a fully-stocked Maternity Works outlet and convenient "Maternity Parking" for expecting moms.

Woodbury Commons

Central Valley, NY (914-928-4000; www.chelseagca.com). Travel: By bus, take Short Line Buses (800-631-8405, 212-736-4700; www.shortlinebus.com; round-trip $22.45, children $12.45, ask about special packages) from Port Authority Bus Terminal. By car, take the George Washington Bridge to the Palisades Interstate Pkwy north to exit 9W, the New York State Thruway (I-87 north), to exit 16, pay $3 toll and follow signs to Woodbury Commons. Jan–Mar Mon–Wed 10am–6pm, Thu–Sat 10am–9pm, Sun 10am–6pm; Apr–Dec Mon–Sat 10am–9pm, Sun 10am–8pm.

Near the peaceful towns and historic estates of the Hudson Valley (*see* **History lessons**, *page 298*), this massive outlet center provides a scandalously indulgent experience for discount-obsessed clotheshorses. The only Prada outlet on the East Coast is located here, which is reason enough to make the trip. Other havens for New York natives are the Giorgio Armani General Store, Gucci and Versace outlets, and a plush collection of cashmere sweaters from TSE. Discounted items from the Gap, Banana Republic, Adidas, Nike and Patagonia will appeal to traditional mall dwellers, while department store regulars can revel in Woodbury's Barneys New York, the Neiman Marcus "Last Call Clearance Center," and the 32,679-square-foot Off 5th–Saks Fifth Avenue Outlet.

Soul searching

If bustling New York City has you stressed out, these relaxing retreats in the nearby Catskill Mountains can help revive you.

New Age Health Spa

Neversink, NY 12765 (914-985-2571, 800-281-8838). Travel: Minivans are available between Manhattan and the spa for $40 one-way (800-682-4348). By car, take the George Washington Bridge to the Palisades Interstate Pkwy north to exit 9W, the New York State Thruway (I-87 north), continue to Exit 16 (Harriman), then take Rte 17 west to Exit 100A (Liberty). Make a right on Rte 55E, drive 8.5 miles to Neversink.

Surrounded by 160-acres of wilderness, the New Age Health Spa is low-key and low-intensity. Participants rise at 6am daily and rejuvenate their minds and bodies by engaging in weight-training, water aerobics and tai chi. The standard rate ($193–$227 per night) includes all meals and activities, consultation with staff nutritionists and a rustic but private room. Thriftier vacationers can share a room with friends or be assigned roommates (nightly rate in triple rooms can be as low as $114). Pampering opportunities include Hydro Colon Therapy (yep, it's what you think, $60) and Loofah Body Polishes ($70), which use almond lather to restore your tired skin. For less touchy-feely types, there are tennis courts and a pool.

The Siddha Yoga Meditation Ashram

371 Brickman Rd, Hurleyville, NY 12747 (914-985-7601) www.siddhayoga.org. For more information, contact the SYMA Foundation Information Center P.O. Box 600, South Fallsburg, NY 12779-0600 (914-434-2000, ext 2202). Mon–Fri 10am–noon, 3–5pm; Sat 10am–2pm.

Siddha Yoga is a Hindu spiritual center, led by Swami Chidvilasananda (also known as Gurumayi), who follows the teachings of ancient Indian sages. Guests (a few of whom have been Hollywood stars) follow a rigorous regime of chanting, selfless work and spiritual study. Interested in learning the wisdom of the ages? Special weekend packages are available, but the ashram does not advertise or publish rates. Siddha Yoga is not a Motel 6—drop-ins are not allowed. Call in advance and say you'd like to come for the weekend. If they're interested in having your company, they'll quote you a price.

Zen Mountain Monastery

P.O. Box 197PC, South Plank Rd, Mt. Tremper, NY 12457 (914-688-2228) www.zen-mtn.org/zmm. Travel: By bus, take Adirondack Trailways (800-858-8555) from Port Authority Bus Terminal to Mt. Tremper. By car, take the George Washington Bridge to the Palisades Interstate Pkwy north to exit 9W, the New York State Thruway (I-87 north), to Exit 19 (Kingston). At the traffic circle, take Rte 28 west for 20 miles to Rte 212 (on the right) for one-half mile and turn left at the four-way intersection. The monastery gate is on the right.

The ZMM headquarters, at the base of Tremper Mountain, is located in a century-old building, intricately constructed from white oak. Burned-out travelers can expect to find inner peace at Zen Mountain Monastery, but it's no walk in the park. Enrollees have to rise during the predawn hours and work through the "eight stages of Zen" daily. The monastery encourages three-month stays, but weekend retreats are available for the more time-conscious. The Introduction to Zen Training Weekend ($195) is recommended for beginners, teaching *zazen* (a form of meditation), liturgy, art and body practice. This is way beyond the lotus position—Abbott John Daido Loori and his staff offer training in psychotherapy, wilderness skills and Polaroid photography. Lodgings are dormitory-style and all meals are vegetarian.

*Notes from the underground: Four million New Yorkers ride the **subway** daily.*

Directory

Directory

These indispensable tips will help you conquer the Naked City

Getting to and from NYC

By air

Excellent fares may be found with a bit of looking. Read the papers, search the Web and consult a few agents before you buy.

Internet

Many sites claim to have the lowest fares and many airlines discount tickets bought over the Internet. A few to investigate are **www.airlinereservations.net**, **www.air-fare.com/lowest.htm**, and **www2.travelocity.com**.

Newspapers

The best place to get an idea of available fares is the travel section of your local paper. If that's no help, seek out a Sunday *New York Times*. The travel section is loaded with advertisements for discounted fares.

Travel agents

Agents are highly specialized, so find one who suits your needs. Do you want adventure? budget? consolidator? business? luxury? round the world? student? (if so, *see* **Student Travel**, *page 316*). Find an agent through word of mouth, newspapers, the Yellow Pages or the Internet. Knowledgeable travel agents can help you with far more than air tickets, and a good relationship with an agent can be invaluable, especially if you don't like to deal with sometimes tedious travel details.

By bus

Buses are usually an inexpensive (though sometimes uncomfortable) means of getting to and from New York City. They are particularly useful if you want to leave in a hurry, as many buses needn't be prebooked. Most out-of-town buses arrive and depart from Port Authority.

Bus lines

Greyhound Trailways

800-231-2222; www.greyhound.com. 24 hours. AmEx, Disc, MC, V.
Long-distance bus travel to destinations across North America.

New Jersey Transit

973-762-5100; www.njtransit.state. nj.us. 24 hours. AmEx, MC, V.
Bus service to most everywhere in the Garden State.

Peter Pan

800-343-9999; www.peterpan-bus.com. 24 hours. AmEx, Disc, MC, V.
Extensive service to cities across the Northeast.

Bus stations

George Washington Bridge Bus Station

Fort Washington Ave and Broadway between 178th and 179th (212-564-1114). Subway: A to 175th St; A, 1, 9 to 181st St.
A few bus lines serving New Jersey and Rockland County, New York, use this station from 5am to 1am.

Port Authority Bus Terminal

40th–42nd Sts between Eighth and Ninth Aves (212-564-8484). Subway: A, C, E to 42nd St.
Be warned that the area around the terminal is notoriously seedy—although, like Times Square, it is getting better. Many transportation companies serve New York City's commuter and long-distance bus travelers. Call for additional information.

By car

Driving to the city can be scenic and fun. The obstacles arise once you're there, or almost there. Don't forget that Manhattan is an island and you'll have to take a bridge or tunnel to get into the city.

Traffic can cause delays of ten to fifty minutes—plenty of time to get your money out for the toll (about $4).

Car rental

If you are interested in renting a car for a trip out of town, car rental is much cheaper on the city's outskirts and in New Jersey and Connecticut. Reserve ahead for weekends, and note that street parking is very restricted, especially in the summer (*see* **Getting around**, *page 305*). If you're coming from the U.K., most New York authorities will let you drive on a U.K. license for a limited time, though an international one is better. All car rental companies listed below add sales tax. They also offer a "loss damage waiver" (LDW). This is expensive— almost as much as the rental itself—but without it you are responsible for the cost of repairing even the slightest damage. If you pay with an AmEx card or a gold Visa or MasterCard, the LDW may be covered by the credit-card company; it might also be covered by a reciprocal agreement with an automotive organization. Personal liability insurance is optional but recommended (but check if your travel insurance or home policy covers it already). You will need a credit card (or a large cash deposit) to rent a car and usually have to be over 25 years of age. If you know you want to rent a car before you travel, ask your travel agent or airline if they can offer any good deals.

Avis
800-331-1212. 24 hours. Rates from $50 a day, unlimited mileage; special weekend rates. AmEx, DC, Disc, MC, V.

Budget Rent-a-Car
212-807-8700. In the city 6:30am–11pm, at the airports 5am–2am. Rates from $62 a day, unlimited mileage; special weekend rates. AmEx, DC, Disc, JCB, MC, V.

Enterprise
800-325-8007. Mon–Fri 7am–7pm, Sat 8am–2pm, Sun 9am–9pm. Rates from $35 a day outside Manhattan; around $60 a day on the island; unlimited mileage restricted to New York, New Jersey and Connecticut. AmEx, DC, Disc, MC, V.
We highly recommend this cheap and reliable service. The most accessible branches outside Manhattan are Hoboken (PATH train from 34th Street) and Greenwich (Metro-North from Grand Central). Agents will collect you from the station.

Parking

If you drive to NYC, find a garage, park your car and leave it there until you leave. Parking on the street is subject to endless restrictions (for information on alternate-side street parking, call 212-225-5368), ticketing is rampant and car theft is common. Garages are plentiful but expensive. If you want to park for less than $15 a day, try a garage outside Manhattan and take public transportation in. Listed below are the best deals in Manhattan. For other

options—and there are many—try the Yellow Pages.

GMC Park Plaza
407 E 61st St between First and York Aves (212-888-7400).
GMC has more than 50 locations in the city; this location is the cheapest, at $13 overnight including tax.

Kinney System Inc.
800-569-7275.
The city's largest parking company is accessible and reliable, though not the cheapest in town. Rates vary, so call for prices at your location of choice.

Mayor Parking
Pier 40, West St at West Houston St (800-494-7007). 24 hours.
Mayor Parking offers both indoor and outdoor parking at excellent rates. Call for information.

By rail

Thanks to the beloved automobile, passenger trains are not as common as in other parts of the world; American rails are used primarily for cargo. Most passenger trains from New York carry commuters. For longer hauls, call Amtrak. *See chapter* **Trips Out of Town**.

Train service

Amtrak
800-872-7245; www.amtrak.com.
Amtrak provides all long-distance train service throughout America. Train travel is more comfortable than bus service but it's more expensive (a sleeper can cost more than flying) and less flexible. All trains depart from Penn Station.

Long Island Rail Road
718-217-5477; www.mta.nyc.ny. us/lirr/index.html.
Rail service to Long Island from Penn Station.

Metro-North
212-532-4900 or 800-638-7646; www.mta.nyc.ny.us/mnr/index.html.
Trains to cities north of Manhattan from Grand Central.

New Jersey Transit
973-762-5100 or 800-722-2222; www.njtransit.state.nj.us.
Commuter service to New Jersey.

PATH Trains
800-234-7284; www.nj.com/ njtransit/path.html.
PATH (Port Authority Trans Hudson) trains run from six stations in Manhattan to various places across the river in New Jersey, including Hoboken, Jersey City and Newark. The system is fully automated and costs $1 for each trip. You need change or a crisp dollar bill to put in the machines. Trains run 24 hours a day, but you can face a very long wait outside rush hours. Manhattan PATH stations are marked on the subway map.

Train stations

Grand Central Terminal
42nd–44th Sts between Vanderbilt and Lexington Aves. Subway: S, 4, 5, 6, 7 to 42nd St–Grand Central.
Grand Central is home to Metro-North, which runs trains to more than 100 stations throughout New York State and Connecticut.

Penn Station
31st–33rd Sts between Seventh and Eighth Aves. Subway: A, C, E, 1, 2, 3, 9 to 34th St–Penn Station.
Long Island Rail Road, New Jersey Transit and Amtrak (long-distance) trains depart from this terminal.

Directory

Getting around

Despite its reputation, New York City is quite easy to navigate. What public transportation lacks in cleanliness it makes up in reach and reasonable efficiency. The Metropolitan Transportation Authority (MTA: 718-330-1234; www.mta.nyc.ny.us) runs the subways and buses, as well as a number of the commuter

services to points outside Manhattan. Otherwise, your best alternative is to hail a cab.

To and from the airport

For a full list of transportation services between New York City and its three airports call **800-AIR-RIDE** (800-247-

7433), a touch-tone menu of recorded information provided by the Port Authority. Though public transportation is the cheapest method, the routes are indirect and can be frustrating and time-consuming to use. Private bus services are usually the best budget option. Medallion (city-licensed) cabs from the New York airports line up at designated locations. Though it is not legal, many car-service drivers and non-licensed "gypsy cabs," solicit riders around the baggage-claim areas—avoid them.

Airports

John F. Kennedy International Airport

718-244-4444
There's a subway link from JFK (extremely cheap at $1.50), but it takes almost two hours. Wait for a yellow shuttle bus to the Howard Beach station and take the **A train** to Manhattan. For about $15, a private **bus service** is a more pleasant option (*see listings below*). A **medallion yellow cab** from JFK to Manhattan is a flat $30 fare plus toll and tip. From Manhattan back, the rate isn't set, but expect it to be about the same. Or try a **car service** for around $32 (*see* **Taxis and car services**, *page 307*).

La Guardia Airport

718-476-5000
Seasoned New Yorkers take a 20-minute ride on the **M60 bus** ($1.50), which runs between the airport and 106th Street at Broadway. The route crosses Manhattan at 125th Street in Harlem, where you can get off at the Lexington Avenue subway station for the 4, 5 and 6 trains or at Lenox Avenue for the 2 and 3. You can also disembark on Broadway at the 116th Street–Columbia University subway station, where you can take the 1 and 9 trains. Other options: Private bus lines cost around $14; taxis or car services charge about $25 plus toll and tip (*see* **Taxis and car services**, *page 307*).

Newark Airport

973-961-6000
Though a bit farther afield, Newark isn't difficult to get to or from. The best option is a **bus service** (*see listings below*). A **car service** will run about $32 and a **taxi** around $40 plus tolls and tip (*see* **Taxis and car services**, *page 307*) .

Bus services

Carey Bus

718-632-0500
This service operates to or from JFK and La Guardia airports between 6am and midnight, with stops near Grand Central Terminal (on the east side of Park Avenue between 41st and 42nd Streets), inside the Port Authority terminal (*see* **Bus stations**, *page 304*) and outside a host of midtown hotels.

Gray Line

212-757-6840 or 800-622-3427
A minibus service runs from each of the three area airports to any address in midtown (between 23rd and 63rd Streets) from 7am to midnight; the wait at the airport is never more than 20 minutes. On the outbound journey, Gray Line picks up at several hotels (you must book in advance).

Olympia Trails

212-964-6233
Olympia operates between Newark Airport and outside Penn Station, Grand Central Terminal or the World Trade Center, or inside Port Authority; the fare is $10 and buses leave every 15–20 minutes. Call for exact drop-off and pick-up locations.

Buses

Buses are fine if you aren't in a hurry. If your feet hurt from walking around, a bus is a good way of continuing your street-level sightseeing. They're white and blue with a route number and a digital destination sign. The fare is $1.50, payable either with a token or MetroCard (*see* **Subways**, *page 307*) in change (silver coins only, no bills accepted). Express buses operate on some routes; these cost $3. If you're traveling on a bus going uptown or downtown and want to continue your journey crosstown (or vice versa) ask the driver for a "transfer" when you get on—you'll be given a ticket for use on the second stage. MetroCards allow ticketless, automatic transfers from bus to bus and between buses and subways. You can rely on other passengers for advice, but bus maps are available from all subway stations and the New York Convention and Visitor's Bureau. Buses make only designated stops, about every two or three blocks going north or south and every block east or west; between 10pm and 5am you can ask the driver to stop anywhere along the route. All buses are equipped with wheelchair lifts. Contact the MTA (718-330-1234;

www.mta.nyc.ny.us) for further information.

Driving

A car is often useless in Manhattan. Drivers are fearless, and taking to the streets is not for the faint-hearted. Don't bother renting a car unless you are planning a trip out of town (*see* **Getting to and from NYC**, *page 304*). Otherwise restrict your driving to evening hours, when traffic is less heavy and on-street parking a bit more plentiful. Even then, keep your eyes on the road and be prepared for anything.

Breakdowns

AAA Emergency Road Service

212-757-2000 or 800-222-4357; 24 hours.

Citywide Towing

522 W 38th St between Tenth and Eleventh Aves (212-924-8104). 24 hours. No credit cards.
All types of repairs are done on foreign and domestic autos. Free towing is offered if the firm gets the repair job.

Parking

Don't ever park within 15 feet (5m) of a fire hydrant, and make sure you read the parking signs. Unless there are meters, most streets have "alternate side parking"—i.e., each side is off limits for certain hours on alternate days. The **New York City Department of Transportation** (212-442-7080) provides information on daily changes to parking regulations. If precautions fail, call 212-477-4430 for car towing/car impound information. *See* **Getting to and from NYC**, *page 304.*

24-hour gas stations

Amoco

610 Broadway at Houston St (212-473-5924). AmEx, DC, Disc, JCB, MC, V. No repairs.

Gulf

FDR Drive at 23rd St (212-686-4784). AmEx, Disc, Gulf, MC, V. Some repairs.

Hess
*Tenth Ave at 45th St
(212-245-6594). AmEx, Disc,
MC, V. No Repairs.*

Shell
*Amsterdam Ave at 181st St
(212-928-3100). AmEx, Disc, MC,
V. Repairs.*

Subways

Much maligned but actually
clean, efficient, heated/air-
conditioned and far safer than
its reputation would suggest,
the subway is easily the fastest
way to get around during the
day. It runs all night, but with
sparse service and fewer riders
so it's advisable (and usually
quicker) to take a cab after
10pm. Entry to the system
requires a MetroCard or a
token costing $1.50 (both also
work on buses), which you can
buy from a booth inside the
station entrance.

Once through the turnstile
you can travel anywhere on the
network. If you're planning to
use the subway a lot, it's worth
buying a MetroCard, which is
also available at some stores
and hotels. Only with a Metro-
Card can you transfer free
between subways and buses.
There are two types: pay-per-
use cards and unlimited ride
cards. Any number of pas-
sengers can use the pay-per-use
cards, which start at $3 for two
trips and run as high as $80. A
$15 card offers 11 trips for the
price of 10. The unlimited ride
MetroCard—an incredible
value if you plan to ride the
subway frequently—is available in three denominations: a
one-day Fun Pass ($4, *not*
available in stations), a seven-
day pass ($17) and a 30-day
pass ($63). These are good for
unlimited rides on the subway
or buses but can only be used
once every 18 minutes (so only
one person can use them at a
time). Contact the MTA (718-
330-1234; www.mta.nyc.ny.us)
for further information.

Trains are known by letters
or numbers and are color-
coded according to the line on
which they run. Stations are
named after the street they're
on. Entrances are marked with
a green globe (a red globe
marks an entrance that is not
always open). Many stations
(and most of the local stops)
have separate entrances to the
uptown and downtown plat-
forms—look before you pay.
"Express" trains run between
major stops; "local" trains stop
at every station. Check on the
map (posted in all stations and
reprinted on pages 343–346)
before you board.

To ensure safety, don't wear
flashy jewelry, hold your bag
with the opening facing you,
and board the train from the
off-peak waiting area marked
at the center of every platform.
This is monitored by cameras
and/or is where a conductor's
car will stop.

Taxis and car services

Once you start using cabs in
New York, you'll begin to wish
they were this cheap everywhere in the world. Yellow
cabs are hardly ever in short
supply, except in the rain and
at around 4 or 5pm, when rush
hour gets going and when
many cabbies—inexplicably—
change shifts. If the center light
on top of the cab is lit, it means
the cab is available and will
stop if you stick your arm out.
Jump in first and then tell the
driver where you're going (New
Yorkers give cross streets, not
building numbers). Cabs carry
up to four people for the same
price: $2 plus 30¢ per fifth of a
mile, with an extra 50¢ charge
after 8pm. This makes an
average fare for a three-mile
(4.5km) ride about $5 to $7,
depending on the traffic and
time of day. Unfortunately,
some cabbies know the city as
poorly as you do, so it helps if
you know where you're

going—and speak up. In
general, tip 15 percent. The cab
number and driver's number
are posted on the dashboard if
you have a problem. There's
also a meter number on the
receipt. If you want to complain
or trace lost property, call the
**Taxi and Limousine
Commission** at 212-302-8294
(Mon–Fri 9am–5pm). Late at
night, cabbies stick to fast-
flowing routes and reliably
lucrative areas. Try the
avenues and the key east/west
streets (Canal, Houston, 14th,
23rd, 42nd, 59th, 86th). Bridge
and tunnel exits are also good
for a steady flow from the
airports, and passengerless
cabbies will usually head for
nightclubs and big hotels.
Otherwise, try one of the
following:
Chinatown: Chatham Square,
where Mott St meets the Bowery, is
an unofficial taxi stand; or hail one
exiting the Manhattan Bridge at
Bowery and Canal St.
Financial District: Try the
Marriott World Trade Center or 1
World Trade Center; there may be a
line but there'll certainly be a cab.
Lincoln Center: The crowd
heads toward Columbus Circle for a
cab; those in the know go west to
Amsterdam Ave.
Lower East Side: Katz's Deli
(Houston St at Ludlow St) is a
cabbies' hangout; otherwise try
Delancey St, where cabs come in over
the Williamsburg Bridge.
Midtown: Penn Station and Grand
Central Terminal attract cabs
through the night, as do the Port
Authority (Eighth Ave between 40th
and 42nd Sts) and Times Square.
Soho: If you're west, try Sixth Ave;
east, the gas station on Houston St at
Broadway.
Tribeca: Cabs here (many arriving
from the Holland Tunnel) head up
Hudson St. Canal St is also a good bet.

Car services

The following companies will
pick you up anywhere in the city,
at any time of day or night for a
prearranged fare:

All City Taxis *718-402-2323*

Bell Radio Taxi *212-691-9191*

Sabra *212-777-7171*

Tel Aviv *212-777-7777*

Directory A–Z

Computers

There are hundreds of computer dealers in Manhattan, though if you are considering a purchase, you might want to buy out of state to avoid the hefty sales tax. Many out-of-state dealers advertise in New York papers and magazines.

Kinko's
24 E 12th St between University Pl and Fifth Ave (212-924-0802). Subway: L, N, R, 4, 5, 6 to 14th St–Union Sq. 24 hours. AmEx, Disc, MC, V.
This is a very efficient and friendly place to use computers and copiers. Most branches have several workstations and design stations, including IBM and Macintosh, plus all the major software. Color output is available. Check the phone book for other locations.

Fitch Graphics
130 Cedar St at Liberty St (212-619-3800). Subway: N, R, 1, 9 to Cortlandt St. Mon–Fri 8am–11pm (some services until 5pm only). AmEx, MC, V.
A full-service desktop-publishing firm, with color laser output and all pre-press facilities. Fitch works with both Mac and IBM platforms and has a bulletin board so customers can reach them online.
Other location: *5 W 45th St (call 212-840-3091 for hours).*

User-Friendly
139 W 72nd St between Columbus and Amsterdam Aves (212-580-4433). Subway: 1, 2, 3, 9 to 72nd Street. Mon–Thu 9am–10pm; Fri 9am–6pm; Sat 11am–7pm; Sun noon–8pm. AmEx, MC, V.
Rent Macs and PCs loaded with all the right software at User-Friendly's two locations.
Other location: *1065 Sixth Ave at 40th St (212-575-3536).*

USPC
360 W 31st St between Eighth and Ninth Aves (212-594-2222). Subway: A, C, E to 34th St–Penn Station. 9am–5pm Mon–Fri. AmEx, MC, V.
Rent by the day, week, month or year from a range of computers, systems and networks from IBM, Compaq, Macintosh and Hewlett-Packard. Delivery within one hour is possible.

Consulates

Check the phone book for a complete list of consulates and embassies.

Australia *212-408-8400*

Canada *212-596-1700*

Great Britain *212-745-0200*

Ireland *212-319-2555*

New Zealand *212-832-4038*

Consumer information

Better Business Bureau
212-533-6200; www.bbb.org. Mon–Fri 9am–5pm.
The BBB offers advice on consumer-related complaints: shopping, services, etc. Each inquiry costs $4.30 (including New York City tax).

New York City Department of Consumer Affairs
212-487-4444. Mon–Fri 9:30am–4:30pm.
File complaints on consumer-related matters.

Customs and immigration

Check with a U.S. embassy or consulate to see if you need a visa (*see **Visas**, page 319*). Standard immigration regulations apply to all visitors arriving from outside the United States, which means you may have to wait up to an hour when you arrive. During your flight, you will be handed an immigration form and a customs declaration form to be presented to an official when you land.

You may be expected to explain your visit, so be polite and be prepared. You will usually be granted an entry permit to cover the length of your stay. Work permits are hard to get, and you are not permitted to work without one (*see **Students**, page 316*).

U.S. Customs allows foreigners to bring in $100 worth of gifts ($400 for Americans) before paying duty. One carton of 200 cigarettes (or 100 cigars) and one liter of liquor (spirits) are allowed. No plants, fruit, meat or fresh produce can be taken through customs. If you carry more than $10,000 worth of currency, you will have to fill out a report.

If you must bring prescription drugs to the U.S., make sure the container is clearly marked and that you bring your doctor's statement or a prescription. Of course, marijuana, cocaine and most opiate derivatives and other chemicals are not permitted, and possession of them is punishable by stiff fines and/or imprisonment. Check with the U.S. Customs Service (800-697-3662 or 212-446-4547; travel.state.gov/visa_services.html) before you arrive if you have any questions about what you can bring. If you lose or need to renew your passport once in the U.S., contact your country's embassy (*see **Consulates**, above*).

Student immigration

Upon entering the U.S. as a student, you will need to show a passport, a special visa and proof of your plans to leave (a return airline ticket). Even if you have a student visa, you may be asked to show means of support during your stay (cash, credit cards, traveler's checks, etc.).

Before they can apply for a visa, non-nationals who want to study in the U.S. must obtain an I-20 Certificate of Eligibility from the school or university they plan to attend. If you are enrolling in an authorized exchange-visitor program, including a summer course or program, wait until you have been accepted by the course or program before worrying about immigration. You will be guided through the process by the school.

You are admitted as a student for the length of your course, in addition to a limited period of any associated (and approved) practical training, plus a 60-day grace period. After this you must leave the country or apply to change or extend your immigration status. Requests to extend a visa must be submitted 15 to 60 days before the initial departure date. The rules are strict, and you risk deportation if you break them.

Information on these and all other immigration matters is available from the **U.S. Immigration and Naturalization Service** (INS). Its New York office is in the Jacob Javits Federal Building, 26 Federal Plaza, New York, NY 10278. The hotline (212-206-6500) is a vast menu of recorded information in English and Spanish. It is available 24 hours and is clear and helpful. Advisors are available at 800-375-5283 from 8am to 5:30pm Monday through Friday. If you already know which forms you need, you can order them by calling 212-870-3676. You can visit the INS between 7:30am and 3:30pm Monday through Friday.

The **U.S. Embassy Visa Information** line (in the U.S. 202-663-1225; in the U.K. 0891-200-290) provides more information on obtaining student visas. Alternatively, you can write to the Visa Branch of the Embassy of the United States of America, 5 Upper Grosvenor Street, London W1A 2JB.

When you apply for your student visa, you will be expected to prove your ability to support yourself financially (including the payment of school fees), without working, for at least the first nine months of your course. After

the first nine months, you may be eligible to work part-time, though you must have specific permission to do so.

If you are a British student who wants to spend a summer vacation working in the States, contact **BUNAC** at 16 Bowling Green Lane, London EC1R 0BD (0171-251-3472), which can help arrange a temporary job and the requisite visa.

Disabled

New York is a challenging city for a disabled visitor, but there is support and guidance close by. The **Society for the Advancement of Travel for the Handicapped**, which promotes travel for the disabled worldwide, is based in New York City. This nonprofit group was founded in 1976 to educate people about travel facilities for the disabled. Membership is $45 a year ($30 for students and senior citizens) and includes access to an information service and a quarterly news-

letter. Write or call SATH, 347 Fifth Ave, suite 610, New York, NY 10016 (212-447-7284; fax 212-725-8253).

Another useful resource is the **Hospital Audiences, Inc.** guide to New York's cultural institutions, *Access for All* ($5). The book tells how accessible each place really is, including information on the height of telephones and water fountains, hearing- and visual aids, passenger loading zones, and alternative entrances.

HAI also has a service for the visually impaired that provides audio descriptions of theater performances. The program, called Describe! (212-575-7660), consists of prerecorded audiocassettes with a description of the theater, the sets, characters, costumes and special effects. It also offers live service during performances.

All Broadway theaters are equipped with devices for the hearing impaired; call **Sound Associates** (212-239-6200) for more information. There are a number of other stage-related resources for the disabled. Call

Weather or not

Rain or shine, New York City is mighty fine

Here is the average temperature and rain/snowfall for NYC by month—but, remember, there's always something to do indoors when it's too yucky to wander around outside.

	Temperature		Precipitation	
	°F	°C	inches	cm
Jan	32.0	0.0	3.2	8.1
Feb	33.4	0.8	3.1	7.9
Mar	41.3	5.2	4.2	10.7
Apr	52.0	11.2	3.8	9.7
May	62.6	17.0	3.8	9.7
June	71.0	21.9	3.2	8.1
July	77.0	25.0	3.8	9.7
Aug	75.2	24.0	4.0	10.2
Sept	70.0	21.0	3.7	9.4
Oct	57.5	14.2	3.4	8.6
Nov	47.0	8.3	3.9	10.4
Dec	36.5	2.6	3.8	9.7

Telecharge (212-239-6200) to reserve tickets for wheelchair seating in Broadway and Off Broadway venues. Theater Development Fund's **Theater Access Program** (TAP) arranges sign language interpretation for Broadway shows. Call 212-221-1103 or 212-719-4537. **Hands On** (212-627-4898) does the same for Off-Broadway performances. For more information on facilities for the disabled, *see* **About the Guide**, *page vii.*

In addition, the organization **Big Apple Greeter** (*see chapter* **Tour New York**) will help any person with disablities enjoy New York City.

Lighthouse Incorporated

111 E 59th St between Park and Lexington Aves (212-821-9200, 800-334-5497). Subway: 4, 5, 6 to 59th St; N, R to Lexington Ave. Mon–Fri 9am–5pm.
In addition to running a store selling handy items for sight-impaired people, this organization provides help and info for the blind dealing with life—or a holiday—in New York City.

Mayor's Office for People with Disabilities

52 Chambers St at Broadway, room 206 (212-788-2830). Subway: A, C, 1, 2, 3, 9 to Chambers St. Mon–Fri 9am–5pm.
The Mayor's office organizes services for disabled people.

New York Society for the Deaf

817 Broadway at 12th St (212-777-3900). Subway: L, N, R, 4, 5, 6, to 14th St–Union Sq. Mon–Thu 9am–5pm, Fri 9am–4pm.
Advice and information on facilities for the deaf.

Electricity

The U.S. uses a 110–120V, 60-cycle AC voltage, rather than the 220–240V, 50-cycle AC used in Europe and elsewhere. Except for dual-voltage, flat-pin plug shavers, you will need to run any foreign-bought appliances via an adaptor, available at airport shops and some pharmacies and department stores.

Emergencies

Ambulances

In an emergency, dial **911** for an ambulance or call the operator (dial 0). To complain about slow service or poor treatment, call the Department of Health: Emergency Medical Service (718-416-7000).

Fire

In an emergency, dial **911**.

Police

In an emergency, dial **911**. For the location of the nearest police precinct or for general information about police services, call **212-374-5000**.

Health and medical facilities

Clinics

Walk-in clinics offer treatment for minor ailments. Most require immediate payment, although some will send their bill directly to your insurance company. You will have to file a claim to recover the cost of prescription medicines.

D*O*C*S

55 E 34th St between Park and Madison Aves (212-252-6000). Subway: 4, 5, 6 to 33rd St. Open 7 days a week with extended hours. AmEx, MC, V.
These excellent primary-care facilities are affiliated with Beth Israel Medical Center. No appointment is necessary.
Other locations: *1555 Third Ave at 88th St (212-828-2300); 202 W 23rd St at Seventh Ave (212-352-2600).*

Doctors Walk-in

57 E 34th St between Madison and Park Aves (212-252-6000). Subway: 6 to 33rd St. Mon–Fri 8am–5:30pm; Sat 10am–1:30pm. Basic fee $75. AmEx, MC, V.
If you need X-rays or lab tests, go as early as possible—no later than 4pm Monday through Friday. No lab work is done on Saturday.

Dentists

Emergency Dental Associates

800-439-9299. 24 hours.

NYU College of Dentistry

212-998-9800. Mon–Thu 8:30am–8pm, Fri 9am–6pm. Base fee $65. MC, V.

If you need your teeth fixed on a budget, you can become a guinea pig for final-year students. They're slow but proficient, and an experienced dentist is always on hand to supervise.

Emergency rooms

You will have to pay for emergency treatment. Call your travel insurance company's emergency number before seeking treatment to find out which hospitals accept your insurance. Emergency rooms are always open at:

Cabrini Medical Center

227 E 19th St between Second and Third Aves (212-995-6120). Subway: L, N, R, 4, 5, 6 to 14th St–Union Sq.

Mount Sinai Hospital

Madison Ave at 100th St (212-241-7171). Subway: 4, 5, 6 to 96th St.

Roosevelt Hospital

428 W 59th St at Ninth Ave (212-523-4000). Subway: A, C, B, D, 1, 9, to 59th St–Columbus Circle.

St. Luke's Hospital

1111 Amsterdam Ave at 113th St (212-523-3335). Subway: 1, 9 to 116th St.

St. Vincent's Hospital

153 W 11th St at Seventh Ave (212-604-7998). Subway: 1, 2, 3, 9 to 14th St; L to Sixth Ave.

Gay and lesbian health

See chapter **Gay & Lesbian.**

Pharmacies

See chapter **Shopping & Services.**

Duane Reade

224 57th St at Broadway (212-541-9708) Subway: N, R, to 57th St. AmEx, MC, V.
This chain operates all over the city, and some stores offer 24-hour service. Check phone book for additional locations.
Other 24-hour locations: *2465 Broadway at 91st St (212-799-3172); 1279 Third Ave at 74th St (212-744-2668); 378 Sixth Ave at Waverly Pl (212-674-5357).*

Love Drug

209 E 86th St between Second and Third Aves (212-427-0954) Subway: 4, 5, 6 to 86th St. Mon–Sat 8am–midnight; Sun 9am–midnight.
This chain has pharmacies in its uptown locations but also runs

health- and beauty supply stores throughout the city. Check the phone book for additional locations.
Other location: *2330 Broadway between 84th and 85th Sts (212-362-6558).*

Women's health

Eastern Women's Center
44 E 30th St between Park and Madison Aves (212-686-6066). Subway: 6 to 33rd St. Tue–Sat 9am–5pm. AmEx, MC, V.
Pregnancy tests cost $20; counseling and gynecological tests are also available.

NYC Department of Health/Bureau of Maternity Services & Family Planning
2 Lafayette St at Reade St, 18th floor (212-442-1740). Subway: N, R to City Hall. Mon–Fri 8am–5pm.
Pick up leaflets and advice; call for an appointment. Contact the **Women's Health Line** (212-230-1111) on the 21st floor of the same building for contraceptive advice.

Planned Parenthood
Margaret Sanger Center, 26 Bleecker St at Mott St (212-274-7200). Subway: B, D, F, Q to Broadway–Lafayette St; 6 to Bleecker St. Mon–Fri 8am–8pm; Sat 8am–4pm.
No walk-ins. This is the main branch—newly relocated to a state-of-the-art facility—of the best-known, most reasonably priced network of family planning clinics in the U.S. Counseling and treatment are available for a full range of gynecological needs, including abortion, treatment of STDs, HIV testing and contraception. Phone for an appointment and more information about services.

AIDS and HIV

CDC National HIV & AIDS Hotline
800-342-2437; 24 hours.

Alcohol and drug abuse

Alcoholics Anonymous
212-647-1680. 24 hours.

Cocaine Anonymous
212-262-2463. 24-hour recorded info.

Drug Abuse Information Line
800-522-5353. 24 hours.
This program refers callers to statewide recovery programs.

Pills Anonymous
212-874-0700. 24-hour answering service.
You'll find information on drug-recovery programs for users of marijuana, cocaine, alcohol and other addictive substances, as well as referrals to Narcotics Anonymous meetings.

Child abuse

Childhelp's National Child Abuse Hotline
800-422-4453. 24 hours.
Trained psychologists provide general crisis counseling and can help in an emergency. Callers include abused children, runaways and parents having problems with children.

Gay and lesbian health

See chapter **Gay & Lesbian**.

Psychological services

Center for Inner Resource Development
212-734-5876. 24 hours.
Trained therapists will talk to you day or night, and deal with all kinds of emotional problems, including the consequences of rape.

Help Line
212-532-2400. 9am–10pm.
Trained volunteers will talk to anyone contemplating suicide, and can also help with other personal problems.

The Samaritans
212-673-3000. 24 hours.
People thinking of committing suicide or suffering from depression, grief, sexual anxiety or alcoholism can call this organization for advice.

Rape and sex crimes

St. Luke's/Roosevelt Hospital Rape Crisis Center
212-523-4728. Mon–Fri 9am–5pm, recorded referral message at other times.
The Rape Crisis Center provides a trained volunteer who will accompany you through all aspects of reporting a rape and getting emergency treatment.

Sex Crimes Report Line of the New York Police Department (NYPD)
212-267-7273. 24 hours.
Reports of sex crimes are handled by a female detective. She will inform the appropriate precinct, send an ambulance if requested and provide counseling and medical referrals. The detectives will make house calls. Other issues handled: violence against gays and lesbians, child victimization and referrals for the family and friends of victims.

Victim Services Agency
212-577-7777. 24 hours.
VSA offers telephone and one-on-one counseling for any victim of domestic violence, personal crime or rape, as well as practical help with court processes, compensation and legal aid.

For a list of public holidays observed in the United States, *see* **U.S. Holidays**, *page 12*. Banks and government offices are closed on these days (and sometimes others). Public transportation still operates, though usually with less service. Many stores and restaurants remain open on holidays except for Christmas—and even then a few will still not close their doors on December 25.

If you are not an American, it's advisable to take out comprehensive insurance before arriving; it's almost impossible to arrange in the U.S. Make sure that you have adequate health coverage, since medical expenses can be high. For a list of New York urgent-care facilities, *see* **Emergency rooms,** *page 310*.

Legal Aid Society
212-577-3300. Mon–Fri 9am–5pm.
Legal Aid gives free advice and referral on legal matters.

Legal Services for New York City
212-431-7200. Mon–Fri 9am–5pm.

This is a government-funded referral service that offers assistance to people with any kind of legal problem.

Sandback, Birnbaum & Michelen Criminal Law
212-517-3200, 800-766-5800. 24 hours.
This is the number to have in your head when the cops read you your rights in the middle of the night.

Locksmiths

The following emergency locksmiths are open 24 hours. Both require proof of residency or car ownership plus ID.

Champion Locksmiths
16 locations in Manhattan (212-362-7000). $15 service charge day or night plus minimum of $35 to fit a lock. AmEx, MC, V.

Elite Locksmiths
470 Third Ave between 32nd and 33rd Sts (212-685-1472). $35 during the day; $75–$90 at night. No credit cards.

Lost property

For property lost in the street, contact the police. For lost credit cards or traveler's checks, *see* **Money**, *below*.

Buses and subways
New York City Transit Authority, 34th St–Penn Station, near the A train platform (718-625-6200). Mon–Wed, Fri 8am–noon; Thu 11am–6:45pm.

Grand Central Terminal
212-532-4900. Call for items left on Metro-North trains.

JFK Airport
Contact your airline or call 718-244-4444.

La Guardia Airport
Contact your airline or call 718-476-5115.

Newark Airport
Contact your airline or call 973-961-6000.

Penn Station
212-630-7389. Call for items left on Amtrak, New Jersey Transit and the Long Island Rail Road.

Taxis
212-221-8294. Call this number if you leave anything in a taxi. (It worked for Wallace and Gromit!)

Luggage lockers

Luggage lockers appear to be a thing of the past, for security reasons. However, there are baggage rooms at Penn Station, Grand Central Terminal and the Port Authority Bus Terminal.

Messenger services

A to Z Couriers
65 W 36th St at Sixth Ave (212-633-2410).
Cheerful couriers deliver to all neighborhoods, including the Bronx, Brooklyn, Queens and Long Island.

Breakaway
43 Walker St at Church St (212-219-8500). Subway: A, C, E to Canal St. Mon–Fri 7am–9pm; by arrangement Sat, Sun. AmEx, Disc, MC, V.
Breakaway is a highly recommended citywide delivery service with 25 messengers who promise to pick up within 15 minutes of a request and deliver within the hour.

Jefron Messenger Service
141 Duane St between West Broadway and Church St (212-964-8441). Subway: 1, 2, 3, 9 to Chambers St. Mon–Fri 7am–6pm. No credit cards.
Jefron specializes in transporting import/export documents.

Money

The U.S. dollar ($) equals 100 cents (¢). Coins range from copper pennies (1¢) to silver nickels (5¢), dimes (10¢), quarters (25¢) and less common half-dollars (50¢). Occasionally you might get a silver dollar, a Susan B. Anthony dollar (about the size of a quarter) or a $2 note in change. These are rare and worth keeping.

Paper money is all the same size and color, so make sure you fork over the right bill. It comes in denominations of $1, $5, $10, $20, $50 and $100. The design of the $20, $50 and $100 dollar bills has been updated recently by the U.S. Treasury, though the old bills are still good and in circulation. Small shops will rarely break a $50 or $100 bill,

so it is best to limit your cash to smaller denominations.

ATMs

New York City is full of Automated Teller Machines (ATMs). Most accept Visa, MasterCard or American Express, among other cards, if they have an affiliated PIN number. There is a usage fee, although the convenience (and the superior exchange rate) often makes it worth the extra charge.

Call the following for ATM locations: **Cirrus** (800-424-7787); **Wells Fargo** (800-869-3557); **Plus Systems** (800-843-7587). If you've lost your number or have somehow demagnetized your card, most banks will give cash to card holders.

Banks and currency exchange

Banks are generally open from 9am to 3pm Monday through Friday, though some have longer hours. You need photo identification, such as a passport, to change traveler's checks. Many banks will not exchange foreign currency, and the *bureaux de changes*, limited to tourist-trap areas, close around 6 or 7pm. It's best to arrive with some dollars in cash but to pay mostly with traveler's checks (possible in most restaurants and larger stores—but ask first and be prepared to show ID). In an emergency, most big hotels offer 24-hour exchange facilities but charge high commissions and give atrocious rates.

American Express Travel Service
65 Broadway between Rector St and Exchange Pl (212-493-6500). Subway: N, R, 1 to Rector St. Mon–Fri 8:30am–5:30pm.
AmEx will change money and traveler's checks and offer other services such as poste restante. Call for the location of other branches.

Chequepoint USA
22 Central Park South between Fifth and Sixth Aves (212-750-2400). Subway: N, R to 59th St. 8am–9:30pm.
Foreign currency, traveler's checks and bank drafts are available here. **Other location:** *1568 Broadway at 47th St (212-869–6281).*

People's Foreign Exchange
19 W 44th St between Fifth and Sixth Aves, suite 306 (212-944-6780). Subway: B, D, F, Q to 42nd St. Mon–Fri 9am–6pm; Sat, Sun 10am–3pm.
Free foreign exchange on banknotes and traveler's checks.

Thomas Cook Currency Services
29 Broadway at Morris St (800-287-7362). Subway: 4, 5 to Bowling Green. Mon–Fri 9am–5pm.
Complete foreign exchange service is offered. **Other locations:** *JFK Airport, 7 branches all open 7:30am–10:30pm daily (718-656-8444); 1590 Broadway at 48th St; 511 Madison Ave at 53rd St (800-287-7362 for all locations).*

Credit cards
Bring plastic if you have it, or be prepared for a logistical nightmare. It's essential for things like renting cars and booking hotels and handy for buying tickets over the phone. The six major credit cards accepted in the U.S. are Visa, MasterCard, Discover, Diners Club, JCB and American Express. If cards are lost or stolen, contact:

American Express *800-992-6377*

Diners Club *800-234-6377*

Discover *800-347-2683*

JCB *800-366-4522*

MasterCard *800-826-2181*

Visa *800-336-8472*

Traveler's checks
Before your trip, it is wise to buy checks in U.S. currency from a widely recognized company. Traveler's checks are routinely accepted at banks, stores and restaurants

throughout the city. Bring your driver's license or passport along for identification. If checks are lost or stolen, contact:

American Express
800-221-7282

Thomas Cook *800-223-7373*

Visa *800-336-8472*

Wire services
If you run out of "greenbacks," don't expect your embassy or consulate to lend you money—they won't, although they may be persuaded to repatriate you. In an emergency, you can have money wired.

Western Union *800-325-6000*

MoneyGram *800-926-9400*

Newspapers and magazines
Dailies
Daily News
The *News* has drifted politically from the Neanderthal right in the 1950s and 1960s to a moderate but tough-minded stance under the ownership of real-estate mogul Mort Zuckerman. Pulitzer Prize–labor-friendly Hispanic pundit Juan Gonzalez has great street sense, and in 1997, the paper appointed its first female editor, Debby Krenek.

New York Post
The *Post* is the city's oldest surviving newspaper, founded in 1801 by Alexander Hamilton. After many decades as a standard-bearer for political liberalism, the *Post* has swerved sharply to the right under current owner Rupert Murdoch. The *Post* has more column-inches of gossip than any other local paper, and its headlines are usually the ones to beat. Many New Yorkers read the *News* and the *Post* from back to front.

The New York Times
Olympian as ever after almost 150 years, the *Times* remains the city's (and the nation's) paper of record. It has the broadest and deepest coverage of world and national events—as the masthead proclaims, it's "all the news that's fit to print." The mammoth Sunday *Times* weighs in at a full five pounds of newsprint, including magazine, book review,

sports, arts, finance, real estate and other sections.

Other dailies
One of the nation's oldest black newspapers, *Amsterdam News*, offers a left-of-center Afrocentric view. New York also supports two Spanish-language dailies, *El Diario* and *Noticias del Mundo. Newsday* is the Long Island–based daily with a tabloid format but a more sober news style. *USA Today,* also known as McPaper, specializes in polls and surveys, skin-deep capsules of news and a magazine-like treatment of world events.

Weeklies
The New Yorker
Known for its fine wit, elegant prose and sophisticated cartoon art, *The New Yorker* has been published since the 1920s. In the postwar era, it established itself as a venue for serious, long-form journalism. It usually makes for a lively, intelligent read.

New York
This magazine is part newsweekly, part lifestyle report and part listings. Founded 30 years ago by Clay Felker, *New York* was a pioneer of New Journalism, showcasing such talents as Aaron Latham, Gloria Steinem and Tom Wolfe.

The New York Observer
Published on the Upper East Side, the *Observer* is a full-size weekly newspaper on salmon-colored paper. It focuses on the doings of the "overclass," its term for the upper echelons of business, finance, media and politics, and it contains some of the most knowing observations to be had on New York's power elite.

Time Out New York
Of course, we think the best place to find out what's going on in town is *Time Out New York,* launched in 1995. Based on the tried-and-trusted format of its London parent, *TONY* is an indispensable guide to the life of the city. In 1998, it was nominated for a National Magazine Award for General Excellence.

Other weeklies
Downtown journalism is a battlefield pitting the neo-cons of the **New York Press** against the unreconstructed hippies of *The Village Voice.* The *Press* uses an all-column format; it has youth's energy and irreverence as well as its cynicism and self-absorption. *The Voice* is sometimes passionate and ironic, but just as often strident and predictable. Both papers are free. On the sidelines, found in a squadron of Manhattan street-corner newspaper

bins, are *Our Town* and the *Manhattan Spirit*, two sister publications that feature neighborhood news and local political gossip.

Monthlies

Interview

Andy Warhol's magazine is firmly New York–based, covering the world of fashion and entertainment with maximum style.

Paper

Paper covers the city's trend-conscious set with plenty of insider buzz on bars, clubs, downtown boutiques and the people you'll find in them.

Photocopying and printing

Dependable Printing

Flatiron Building, 175 Fifth Ave at 32nd St (212-533-7560). Subway: N, R to 23rd St. Mon–Fri 8:30am–6pm, Sat 10am–4pm. MC, V.
Dependable provides offset and color printing, large-size Xerox copies, color laser printing, binding, rubber stamps, typing, forms, labels, brochures, flyers, newsletters, manuscripts, fax service, transparencies and more.
Other location: *257 Park Ave South between 20th and 21st Sts (212-982-0353).*

Directional Printing Services

280 Madison Ave between 39th and 40th Sts (212-213-6700). Subway: S, 4, 5, 6, 7 to 42nd St–Grand Central. Mon–Fri 9:30am–5:30pm. No credit cards.
This company specializes in assisting international firms and offers foreign-language typesetting and printing, as well as graphic design, brochures and reports, and more.

Kinko's

See **Computers,** *page 308.*

Servco

130 Cedar St at Liberty St (212-285-9245). Subway: N, R, 1, 9 to Cortlandt St. 8:30am–5:30pm. No credit cards.
Photocopying, offset printing, blueprints and binding services.
Other location: *56 W 45th St (call 212-575-0991 for hours).*

Postal services

U.S. Postal Service

Stamps are available at all post offices and from vending machines in most drugstores (where they cost more). It costs 33¢ to send a 1 oz letter within the U.S. Each additional ounce costs 23¢. Postcards within the U.S. need 20¢ postage; international postcards require 50¢. Airmail letters to anywhere overseas cost 60¢ for the first 0.5oz (14g) and 40¢ each additional 0.5oz.

General Post Office

421 Eighth Ave at 33rd St (212-967-8585/24-hour postal information 800-725-2161). Subway: A, C, E to 34th St–Penn Station. Open 24 hours; midnight–6pm for money orders and registered mail.
This is the city's main post office; call for the local branch nearest you. There are 59 full-service post offices in New York; lines are long, but stamps are also available from self-service vending machines. Branches are usually open 9am to 5pm, Monday through Friday; Saturday hours vary from office to office. The 24-hour line provides extensive postal information.

Express Mail

Information: 212-967-8585.
You need to use special envelopes and fill out a form, which can be done either at a post office or by arranging a pickup. You are guaranteed 24-hour mail delivery to major U.S. cities. Letters—both domestic and international—must be sent before 5pm.

General Delivery/ Post Restante

390 Ninth Ave at 30th St (212-330-3099). Mon–Sat 10am–1pm.
Visitors without local addresses can receive their mail here; mail should be addressed to recipient's name, General Delivery, New York, NY, 10199. You will need to show some form of identification—a passport or ID card—when picking up letters.

Couriers

DHL Worldwide Express

2 World Trade Center, Liberty St between West and Church Sts (800-225-5345). Subway: E to World Trade Ctr. 8:30am–8:30pm. AmEx, DC, Disc, MC, V.
DHL will send a courier to pick up at any address in New York City, or you can deliver packages to its offices and drop-off points in person. No cash transactions are allowed. Along with its international services, DHL also operates a messenger service within New York.

Federal Express

Various locations throughout the city; call and give your zip code to find out the nearest office or get pickup at your door (800-247-4747). 24 hours. AmEx, DC, Disc, MC, V.
Federal Express rates (like those of its competitor United Parcel Service) are based on the distance shipped rather than a flat fee. An overnight letter to London costs about $25.50. You save $3 per package on the cost if you bring it to a Federal Express office. Packages headed overseas should be dropped off by 3pm, packages for most destinations in the U.S. by 8pm (some locations have a later time; call to check).

United Parcel Service

Various locations throughout the city; free pickup at your door (800-742-5877). 24 hours. AmEx, DC, MC, V.
Like DHL and FedEx, UPS will send a courier to pick up at any address in New York City, or you can deliver packages to its offices and drop-off points in person. UPS offers domestic and international service.

Private mail services

Mail Boxes Etc. USA

1173A Second Ave between 61st and 62nd Sts (212-832-1390). Subway: N, R to Lexington Ave; 4, 5, 6 to 59th St. Mon–Fri 9am–7pm; Sat 10am–5pm. AmEx, MC, V.
Mailbox rental, mail forwarding, overnight delivery, packaging and shipping are available. There's also a phone-message service, photocopying and faxing, telexing, typing services and business printing. There are more than 30 branches in Manhattan, many offering 24-hour access to mailboxes; check phone book for locations.

Telegrams

Western Union Telegrams

800-325-6000. 24 hours.
Telegrams to addresses worldwide are taken over the phone at any time of day or night, and charges are added to your phone bill. Service is not available from pay phones.

Radio

There are nearly 100 stations in the New York area, offering a huge range of sounds and styles. On the AM dial, you can find some intriguing talk radio and phone-in shows that attract everyone from priests to nutcases. There's plenty of news and sports as well. Although the Federal Communications Commission's recent deregulation of ownership rules has allowed such broadcast giants as Chancellor Media to buy up some of New York's most prominent commercial radio stations, many independent stations still thrive, offering everything from underground sounds to Celtic tunes. Radio highlights are printed weekly in *Time Out New York* and the Sunday *New York Times*, and daily in the *Daily News*.

News and talk

WINS-AM 1010, WABC-AM 770 and **WCBS-AM 880** offer news throughout the day, plus traffic and weather reports. Commercial-free public radio stations **WNYC-FM 93.9/AM 820** and **WBAI-FM 99.5** provide excellent news and current-affairs shows, including *All Things Considered* (weekdays AM: 4–6pm, 7:30–8pm; FM: 5–6:30pm, 7–8pm), and guest-driven talk shows, notably WNYC-AM's *New York and Company* (weekdays noon–2pm) and WNYC-FM's *Fresh Air* (weekdays 4–5pm). WNYC also airs Garrison Keillor's *A Prairie Home Companion* and Ira Glass's quirky *This American Life*. WBAI is one of the very few electronic media platforms for left-wing politics anywhere in the States.

The AM phone-in shows will take you from one extreme to the other. **WLIB-AM 1190** provides the voice of black New York, with news and talk from an Afrocentric perspective, interspersed with Caribbean music. Former Mayor Dinkins has a lunchtime dialogue show from noon to 1pm on Wednesdays. Neofascist Rush Limbaugh airs his scarily popular views on **WABC** (noon–3pm), where you can also get some therapy from Dr. Laura Schlessinger (weekdays 9–11:45am) and, in the evening, the heavily street-accented demagoguery of Guardian Angels founder Curtis Sliwa (weekdays 10pm–1am).

Two classical stations, **WQXR-FM 96.3** and **WNYC-FM 93.9**, serve a varied diet of music and opera, WNYC being slightly more progressive.

Jazz

WBGO-FM 88.3 "Jazz 88" plays phenomenal classic jazz. Here, Branford Marsalis broadcasts his weekly *JazzSet* program, which features many legendary artists. And there are special shows devoted to such categories as piano jazz and the blues. **WQCD-FM 101.9** is a soft jazz station and **WCWP-FM 88.1** plays jazz as well as hip-hop, gospel, and world music.

Dance and pop

American commercial radio is rigidly formatted, which makes most pop stations extremely tedious and repetitive during daylight hours. However, in the evenings and on weekends, you'll find more interesting programs. **WQHT-FM 97.1** "Hot 97" is New York's commercial hip-hop station, with big Steph Lova and former *Yo! MTV Raps* hosts Ed Lover cooking up a breakfast show for the homies; there's rap and R&B throughout the day. On Friday the station also has *Ladies Night* featuring women in hip-hop. **WKTU-FM 103.5** is the city's premier dance music station; RuPaul even hosts the morning-show from time to time.

WBLS-FM 107.5 is an "urban (meaning black) adult" station, playing classic and contemporary funk, soul and R&B. There's Chuck Mitchell's house and R&B mix overnight on Saturday, plus *Hal Jackson's Sunday Classics* (blues and soul). **WWRL-AM 1600** switched from its gospel format to R&B in 1997. **WRKS-FM 98.7** "Kiss FM" has an "adult" contemporary format, which translates as unremarkable American pop. The only legacy of its more soulful days is the Sunday-morning gospel show (6–9am).

WCBS-FM 101.1 is strictly oldies, while **WTJM-FM 105.1** "Jammin Oldies" plays a mix of the '60, '70s and '80s. **WPLJ-FM 95.5** and **WHTZ-FM 100.3** are Top 40 stations. **WLTW-FM 106.7** "Lite FM" plays the kind of background music you hear in elevators.

Rock

WAXQ-FM 104.3, WNEW-FM 102.7 and WXRK-FM 92.3 "K-Rock" offer a digest of classic and alternative rock. K-Rock also attracts the city's largest group of morning listeners, thanks to Howard Stern's controversial 6–11am weekday show. **WLIR-FM 92.7** offers "alternative" (indie and Gothic) sounds with a British bias. **WSOU-FM 89.5** is a college station devoted to heavy metal. At **WFMU-FM 91.1**, the term "free-form radio" still has some meaning: An eclectic mix of music and oddities like Joe Frank's

eerie stream-of-consciousness monologues (Thursdays at 7pm).

Other music

WQEW-AM 1560 "Radio Disney" has kids' programming. **WYNY-FM 107.1** plays country music. **WEVD-AM 1050** broadcasts wacky talk shows, sports games and music. It's the Lower East Side's pirate radio station.

College radio

College radio is innovative and free of commercials. However, smaller transmitters mean that reception is often compromised by Manhattan's high-rise geography. Try New York University's **WNYU-FM 89.1** and Columbia's **WKCR-FM 89.9** for varied programming across the musical spectrum. Fordham University's **WFUV-FM 90.7** is mostly a folk/Irish station, but also airs a variety of shows, including good old-fashioned radio drama on *Classic Radio* every Sunday evening.

Sports

WFAN-AM 660 covers games live. In the mornings, New York talk radio fixture, Don Imus, offers his take on sports and just about everything else going on in the world. **WWRU-AM 1660** Radio Unica covers the Metrostars's soccer scores.

Restrooms

Visitors to New York—like New Yorkers themselves—are always on the go. But in between all that go, go, go, sometimes you've really got to…*go*. Contrary to popular belief (and the general smell, especially in summer), the street is no place to drop trou. The real challenge lies in finding a (legal) public place to take care of your business.

Though they don't exactly have an open-door policy, the numerous **McDonald's** restaurants and **Barnes & Noble** bookstores all contain (usually clean) restrooms. Just don't announce that you're not a paying customer, and you should be all right. The same applies to most other fast-food joints (Au Bon Pain, Wendy's, etc.) that don't have a host or maître d' at the door. Here are some other options around town that can offer sweet relief (if you hold your breath).

Directory

Downtown

Kmart
770 Broadway at Astor Pl. Mon–Fri 9am–10pm; Sat, Sun 11am–8pm.

Tompkins Square Park
Ave A at 9th St. Mon–Thu 8am–7pm.

Wall City Toilet
Centre St at Chambers St. 6am–9pm.

Washington Square Park
Thompson St at Washington Square South. 6am–midnight.

Midtown

Bryant Park
42nd St between Fifth and Sixth Aves. Mon–Sat 8am–7pm and until 1am in the summer.

Penn Station
Seventh Ave between 30th and 32nd Sts. 24 hours.

Port Authority
Eighth Ave at 41st St. 6am–1am.

St. Clement's Church
423 W 46th St between Ninth and Tenth Aves. Mon–Fri 10am–6pm; Sat, Sun 9–11am.

School of Visual Arts
209 E 23rd St between Second and Third Aves. Mon–Fri 8am–10pm.

United Nations
First Ave between 44th and 45th Sts. 9am–5pm.

U.S. Social Security Office
38 E 29th St between Madison Ave and Park Ave South. Mon–Fri 9am–4:30pm.

Uptown

Barneys New York
660 Madison Ave at 61st St. Mon–Sat 10am–8pm; Sun 10am–6pm.

Central Park
Midpark at 81st St. 7am–sundown.

Avery Fisher Hall at Lincoln Center
Amsterdam Ave at 65th St. Mon–Sat 10am–6pm; Sun noon–6pm.

Safety

Statistics on New York's crime rate, particularly violent crime, have nose-dived in the past few years, though bad things still happen to good people. More than ever, most of it stays within specific ethnic groups, happening late at night in low-income neighborhoods. Don't arrive thinking you need an armed guard to accompany you wherever you go; it is highly unlikely that you will ever be bothered.

Still, a bit of common sense won't hurt. Do not flaunt your money and valuables. Avoid desolate and poorly lit streets, and if necessary walk facing the traffic so no one can drive up alongside you. On deserted sidewalks, walk close to the street; muggers prefer to hang back in doorways and shadows. If the worst happens and you find yourself threatened, hand over your wallet or camera at once (your attacker will be as anxious to get it over with as you are), then call the police as soon as you can (dial **911**, free from any cell or pay phone).

Beware of pickpockets and street hustlers—especially in busy tourist areas like Times Square —and don't be seduced by card sharks or other tricksters you may come across. A shrink-wrapped camcorder for 50 bucks could turn out to be a load of bricks or magazines when you open the box.

If you look comfortable rather than lost, you should deter troublemakers.

Smoking

New Yorkers are the target of some of the strictest antismoking laws on the planet (*see* **About the Guide,** *page vii*). Now could be the time to quit.

Students

Student life in NYC is unlike anywhere else in the world. With the city as teacher and playground, it offers an endless extracurricular education. For further guidance, check the *Time Out New York Student Guide*, available free on campuses in August.

Student identification

Foreign students should get themselves an International Student Identity Card (ISIC) as proof of student status and to secure discounts. These can be bought from your local student travel agent (ask at your students' union). If you buy the card in New York, you will also get basic accident insurance—a bargain. The New York branch of the **Council on International Educational Exchange** can supply one on the spot. It's at 205 East 42nd Street between Second and Third Avenues (212-822-2700), and is open from 9am to 6:45pm Monday through Friday. Note that a student identity card may not always be accepted as proof of age for drinking (you must be 21).

Student travel

Most agents offer discount fares for those under 26; specialists in student deals include:

Council Travel
205 E 42nd St between Second and Third Aves (212-822-2700) www.counciltravel.com. **Other locations:** *(800-226-8624).*

STA Travel
10 Downing St at Sixth Ave (212-627-3111) www.statravelgroup.com. **Other locations:** *(800-777-0112).*

Tax and tipping

You'd be hard pressed to find anything more expensive in New York than in most Western-world capitals, but you will still have to account for a few extras. Sales tax (8.25 percent) is added to the price of most purchases, but is not marked on price tags. In addition, there's a lot of tipping to do. Wait staff get 15 to 20 percent (as a rough guide, double the sales tax on your bill) and cabbies 15 percent (many New Yorkers round up to an even dollar amount on small fares). But don't forget to tip bartenders ($1 a round), hairdressers (10 to 15 percent), hotel doormen ($1 for hailing a cab), porters ($1 per bag) and maid service ($2 per day on departure). Remember that the person who delivers your Chinese food probably receives no salary at all ($2 is considered a good tip).

Telephones

As of October 1, 1999, all New York City telephone numbers require 11 digits (1 + area code + local number) for dialing, even if you're calling from the same area code. The area codes for Manhattan are 212 and 646; Brooklyn, Queens, Staten Island and the Bronx are 718 and 347; generally (but not always) 917 is reserved for cellular phones and pagers. The Long Island area code is 516 and 631, and the codes for New Jersey are 201, 732, 973, 609 and 908. Numbers preceded by 800, 877 and 888 are free of charge when dialed anywhere in the United States. When numbers are listed as letters (e.g. 800-AIR-RIDE) for easy recall, dial the corresponding numbers on the telephone keypad.

General information

The Yellow Pages and White Pages have a wealth of useful information in the front, including theater-seating diagrams and maps; the blue pages in the center of the White Pages list all government-affiliated numbers and addresses. Hotels will have copies; otherwise, try libraries or Bell Atlantic (the local phone company) payment centers.

Collect calls or credit card calls

Collect calls are also known as reverse charges. Dial 0 followed by the area code and number, or dial AT&T's 800-CALL-ATT, MCI's 800-COLLECT, Sprint's 800-ONE-DIME; for calls to the U.K., dial 800-445-5667.

Directory assistance

Dial 411 (free from pay phones). For long distance directory assistance, dial 1 + area code + 555-1212 (long-distance charges apply); Bell Atlantic also offers national 411 directory assitance but the charges can be high.

Emergency

Dial 911. All calls are free (including pay phones and cellular phones).

International calls

Dial 011 + country code (U.K. 44; New Zealand 64; Australia 61).

Operator assistance

Dial 0.

Toll-free directory

Dial 1 + 800 + 555-1212 (no charge).

Pagers/cellular phones

InTouch USA

212-391-8323, 800-872-7626. Mon–Fri 9am–5pm. AmEx, Disc, MC, V.
The city's largest cellular phone rental company, InTouch rents out equipment by the day, week or month. It also offers (and can deliver) satellite pagers (with nationwide coverage), portable faxes and walkie-talkies.

Public pay phones

Public pay phones are easy to find. Most of them work, but the Bell Atlantic ones are the most dependable: Those from other phone companies tend to be poorly maintained. If someone's left the receiver dangling, it's a sign that something's wrong. Phones take any combination of silver coins: Local calls usually cost 25¢ for three minutes. If you're not used to American phones, know that the ringing tone is long; the "engaged" tone, or busy signal, is short and higher pitched.

If you want to call long distance or make an

international call from a pay phone, you need to use one of the long-distance companies. In New York, most pay phones automatically use AT&T, but there are some that don't; phones in and around transportation centers usually use other long-distance carriers with charges that can be outrageous. Look in the Yellow Pages under Telephone Companies. Sprint and MCI are respected brand names *(see* **Collect calls or credit card calls***, above).*

Make the call either by dialing 0 for an operator or by dialing direct (cheaper). To find out how much a call will cost, dial the number and a voice will tell you how much money to deposit. You can pay for calls with your credit card. The best way to make calls, however, is with a phone card, available in various denominations from any post office branch or from large chain stores such as Duane Reade or Rite Aid. Delis and kiosks sell phone cards, such as *New York Exclusive*, with incredible international rates. Dialing instructions are on the card.

Recorded information phone lines

These 24-hour information lines add extra costs to your phone bill. An opening message should tell you how much per minute you are paying.

Sports scores *900-976-1313*

Stock market quotations *900-976-4141*

Time *900-976-1616*

Weather forecast *900-976-1212*

Telephone-answering service

Messages Plus

1317 Third Ave between 75th and 76th Sts (212-879-4144). Subway: 6 to 77th St. 24 hours. AmEx, MC, V.

Messages Plus provides telephone-answering services, with specialized (medical, bilingual, etc.) receptionists if required, and plenty of ways of delivering your messages. It also offers pay or toll-free incoming call services, which can include options such as call forwarding, periodic generation of database reports tracking the user's telephone activity and pager rental. Faxes and telexes can be sent and delivered.

Television

A visit to New York often includes at least a small dose of cathode radiation and, particularly for British visitors, American TV can inflict culture shock. Each moment of network programming is constructed to instill fatal curiosity for the next, with commercial breaks coming thick and fast.

The TV day is scheduled down to the second, beginning with news and gossipy breakfast magazine programs (beware Kathie Lee Gifford), leading into a lobotomizing cycle of soap operas, vintage reruns and game shows—unbroken until around 3pm. Then talk shows such as *Oprah* and *Jerry Springer* take over, broadcasting peoples' not-so-private problems, with subjects along the lines of "I married my mother's lesbian lover" or "Mad Cow Disease ruined my family."

At 5pm, there's showbiz chat and local news, followed by national and international news at 6:30pm. Early evening is the domain of popular reruns (*The Simpsons, Friends, Frasier*) and syndicated game shows such as *Jeopardy!* and *Wheel of Fortune*. Huge audiences tune in at prime time, when action series, sports, movies and sitcoms battle for ratings. Finally, as sedate viewers go to bed, out come the neon personalities of the various late-night talk shows.

The only broadcast alternative to consumerist programming is public television. These stations receive little money from the government and rely heavily on "membership" donations garnered during on-air fund drives. Public television has its own nightly news and a few local productions; its *Frontline* and *P.O.V.* documentaries are often incisive.

And then there is cable—that is, the 50 or so channels of basic cable, plus "premium" channels offering uninterrupted movies and sports coverage. Pay-per-view channels provide a menu of recent films, exclusive concerts and sports events at around $5 a pop. Cable is also home of paid "infomercials" and the public-access channels, an array of weirdos and soft-core porn.

If you're feeling nostalgic, the Museum of Television & Radio has a huge collection of classic and hard-to-find TV shows. *See chapter* **Museums**.

Time Out New York offers a rundown of weekly TV highlights. For full TV schedules, including broadcast and cable television, save the Sunday *New York Times* TV section or buy a daily paper; they all have 24-hour listings.

The networks

Six major networks broadcast nationwide. All offer ratings-led variations on a theme. **CBS** (Channel 2 in NYC) has the top investigative show, *60 Minutes*, on Sundays, and its programming overall is geared to a middle-aged demographic (*Diagnosis Murder, Touched by an Angel*). But check out *Everybody Loves Raymond* (Mondays at 8:30pm) and *The Late Show with David Letterman* (weeknights at 11:30pm) for some solid humor. The most popular network, **NBC** (4), is the home of the long-running sketch comedy series *Saturday Night Live* (Saturdays at 11:30pm) and some hugely popular sitcoms, such as *Friends, Frasier* and *Just Shoot Me*. **ABC** (7) is the king of daytime soaps and working-class sitcoms (*The Norm Show, The Drew Carey Show*), while **Fox** (5) is popular with younger audiences for

hip shows such as *Ally McBeal, King of the Hill* and *The X-Files*. The other two networks, **UPN** (9) and **WB** (11), don't attract huge audiences, but have some offbeat programming such as *Buffy the Vampire Slayer, Dawson's Creek, Felicity, Home Movies* and *Star Trek: Voyager*.

WWOR (9), an affiliate of UPN, and offers cheesy movies and popular lowbrow reruns (*Baywatch, Married With Children, The Cosby Show*); **WPIX** (11) is known for its repeats of *Seinfeld, Frasier* and *Friends,* as well as Mets baseball. Yankees fans can tune into **WNYW** (5). There are also two Spanish channels, **WXTV** (41) and **WNJU** (47). Offering Mexican dramas and titillating gameshows, these are also your best bet for soccer.

Public TV

You'll find public TV on channels 13, 21 and 25. Documentaries, arts shows and science series alternate with *Masterpiece Theatre* and reruns of British shows like *Inspector Morse* and *Poirot* (in *Mystery!*). Channel 21 broadcasts *ITN World News* daily at 7pm and 11pm.

Cable

(Note: All channel numbers listed are for Time Warner Cable in Manhattan. In other locations or for other cable systems—such as RCN and Cablevision—check listings.) For music videos, there is the old-standby **MTV** (Channel 20) and its more conservative sibling **VH1** (19). The latter airs the popular *Behind the Music* series, delving into the sad lives of artists like Vanilla Ice and Milli Vanilli. Sports fans have **ESPN** (28), **ESPN2** (29), **MSG** (Madison Square Garden, 27) and **Fox Sports** (26). **CNN** (10), **MSNBC** (43), **Fox News Channel** (46) and **NY1** (1) offer news all day, the last with a local focus. **C-SPAN** (38) broadcasts the floor proceedings of the U.S. House of Representatives and an array of public affairs seminars.

Comedy Central (45) is your stop for 24-hour laughs, with hits like the raunchy cartoon *South Park* (Wednesdays at 10pm), plus a glut of stand-up and nightly reruns of classic *Saturday Night Live* shows, starring the young Eddie Murphy, Mike Myers, et al. **TNT** (3), **TBS** (8), and **USA Network** (23) offer a potpourri of quality reruns (*ER*) and feature films. **E!** (24) is "Entertainment Television," a pop-culture mix of celebrities and movie news. This is where you'll find New York icon Howard Stern conducting hilariously intrusive interviews and such tabloid TV as *The Gossip Show* and the unmissable *E! True Hollywood Story,* which profiles the likes of *Mr. T* and the *Brat Pack.*

Bravo (64) shows the kind of arts programs public TV would air if it could afford them, including *Inside the Actors Studio* and a good number of quality art-house films. **A&E** (16) airs the shallow but popular *Biography* documentary series, and **Lifetime** (12) is "television for women." The **Discovery Channel** (18) and the **Learning Channel** (52) feature science and nature programs, and show gruesome surgical operations, while **Nickelodeon** (6) offers programming more suitable for the kids and nostalgic fans of shows like *The Brady Bunch* and *Happy Days.* **Court TV** (51) scores big ratings with hot trials. The **History Channel** (17), the **Weather Channel** (36) and **Sci-Fi Channel** (44) are self-explanatory.

Public Access TV is on channels 16, 34, 56 and 57—surefire sources of bizarre camcorder amusement. Late-night **Channel 35** is where you'll find *the Robin Byrd Show,* a forum for porn stars, riddled with ads for escort services and sex lines. Premium channels, often available for a fee in hotels, include **HBO** (Home Box Office), **Showtime, Cinemax, The Movie Channel** and **Disney Channel,** all of which show uninterrupted feature films and exclusive "specials."

Time and date

New York is on Eastern Standard Time, which extends from the Atlantic coast to the eastern side of Lake Michigan and south to the Gulf of Mexico: This is five hours behind Greenwich Mean Time. Clocks are set forward one hour in early April and back one hour at the end of October. Going from east to west, Eastern Time is one hour ahead of Central Time, two hours ahead of Mountain Time and three hours ahead of Pacific Time.

In the U.S., dates are written in the order of month, day, year; so 2/5/99 is February 5th, 1999, not the 2nd of May, 1999.

Tourist information

Hotels are usually full of maps, leaflets and free tourist

magazines that give advice about entertainment and events—but be aware the advice is not always impartial. Plenty of local magazines (including *Time Out New York*) offer opinionated info.

Traveler's Aid Society
212-944-0013

New York Convention & Visitors Bureau
810 Seventh Ave at 53rd St (800-692-8474) www.nycvisit.com. Subway: B, D, E to 7th Ave; N, R to 49th St.; 1, 9 to 50th St. Mon–Fri 8:30am–5:30pm; Sat, Sun 9am–5pm.
Leaflets on all manner of things plus free, helpful advice about accommodations and entertainment, coupons for discounts and free maps are available here. The phone number gives you access to either a multilingual human or a huge menu of recorded information.

Translation and language services

All Language Services
545 Fifth Ave at 45th St (212-986-1688; fax 212-986-3396). Subway: S, 4, 5, 6, 7 to 42nd St–Grand Central. 24 hours. MC, V.
ALS will type or translate documents in any of 59 languages and provide interpreters.

Visas

Under the Visa Waiver Program, citizens of Andorra, Argentina, Austria, Australia, Belgium, Brunei, Denmark, Finland, France, Germany, Iceland, Ireland, Italy, Japan, Liechtenstein, Luxembourg, Monaco, the Netherlands, New Zealand, Norway, San Marino, Slovenia, Spain, Sweden, Switzerland and the United Kingdom do not need a visa for stays shorter than 90 days (business or pleasure), as long as they have a passport that is valid for the full 90-day period and a return ticket. An open standby ticket is acceptable.

Canadians and Mexicans don't need visas but must have legal proof of their residency.

All other travelers must have visas. Full information and visa application forms can be obtained from your nearest U.S. embassy or consulate. In general, send in your application at least three weeks before you plan to travel. To apply for a visa on shorter notice, contact the travel agent booking your ticket.

For information on student visas, *see* **Customs and immigration,** *page 308.*

U.S. Embassy Visa Information
In the U.S. 202-663-1225; in the U.K. 0891-200-290; travel.state. gov/visa_service.html.

Websites

Websites come and go with unpredictable frequency; check timeout.com (*below*) for the latest.

www.timeoutny.com
For info on all the city has to offer see *Time Out New York's* site.

www.ci.nyc.ny.us
The "Official New York Web Site" is produced by the folks at City Hall.

www.citysearchnyc.com
Here's up-to-the minute information on events.

www.clubnyc.com
The latest news and grooves on the city's nocturnal scene.

www.echonyc.com
Arts reviews, events listings and a city guide.

www.nynetwork.com
A useful list of New York websites.

newyork.sidewalk.com
Microsoft Network's NYC entertainment guide.

www.timeout.com
The *Time Out* website includes a guide to NYC with listings, features and free classified ads.

www.villagevoice.com
Listings and features from *The Village Voice.*

www.whitehouse.gov
Your connection to the high and mighty in U.S. government.

Further Reading

In-depth guides

Trudy Bell: *Bicycling Around New York City.*
Eleanor Berman: *Away for the Weekend: New York.*
Trips within a 250-mile radius of New York.
Arthur S. Brown and Barbara Holmes: *Vegetarian Dining in New York City.* Includes vegan places.
Eve Claxton: *New York's 100 Best Little Places to Shop.*
William Corbett: *New York Literary Lights.* An encyclopedic collection of info about NYC's literary past.
Flashmaps: *New York.* Maps geared to the visitor.
Sam Freund and Elizabeth Carpenter: *Kids Eat New York.* A guide to child-friendly restaurants.
Alfred Gingold and Helen Rogan: *The Cool Parents Guide to All of New York City.*
Hagstrom: *New York City 5 Borough Pocket Atlas.* With this thorough street map, you won't get lost.
Ruth Leon: *Applause: New York's Guide to the Performing Arts.* Detailed directory of performance venues.
William Marden: *Marden's Guide to New York Booksellers.* Some 500 dealers and stores.
Bryan Miller: *New York Times Guide to Restaurants in New York City.* By the famous food critic.
Corky Pollan: *Shopping Manhattan: the Discriminating Buyer's Guide to Finding Almost Anything.*
Lyn Skreczko and Virginia Bell: *The Manhattan Health Pages.* Everything from aerobics to Zen.
Earl Steinbicker: *Daytrips from New York.*
Time Out New York: *Eating & Drinking 2000.* A comprehensive new guide to 2,000 places to eat and drink in the five boroughs. Written by food critics.
Zagat: *New York City Restaurants.* The popular opinion guide.

Architecture

Margot Gayle: *Cast Iron Architecture in New York.*
Karl Sabbagh: *Skyscraper.* How the tall ones are built.
Robert A.M. Stern: *New York 1930.* A massive coffee-table slab with stunning pictures.
Robert A.M. Stern: *New York 1960.* Another.
Elliot Willensky and Norval White: *American Institute of Architects Guide to New York City.* A comprehensive directory of important buildings.
Gerard R. Wolfe: *A Guide to the Metropolis.* Historical and architectural walking tours.

Culture and recollections

Candace Bushnell: *Sex in the City.* Smart woman, superficial New York.
George Chauncey: *Gay New York.* New York gay life from the 1890s on.
William Cole (ed): *Quotable New York.* Hundreds of hilarious quotes about the city.
Martha Cooper and Henry Chalfant: *Subway Art.*
Josh Alan Friedman: *Tales from Times Square.* Sleaze, scum, filth and depredation in Times Square.
Nelson George: *Hip-Hop America.* The history of hip-hop, from the Bronx to Puffy.
A.J. Liebling: *Back Where I Came From.* Personal recollections from the famous New Yorker columnist.
Andrés Torres: *Between Melting Pot and Mosaic.* African-American and Puerto Rican life in the city.

Andrea Wyatt Sexton (ed): *The Brooklyn Reader: Thirty Writers Celebrate America's Favorite Borough.*

Fiction

Kurt Andersen: *Turn of the Century.* NYC at Y2K.
Paul Auster: *The New York Trilogy.* A search for the madness behind the method of Manhattan's grid.
James Baldwin: *Another Country.* Racism under the bohemian veneer of the 1960s.
Caleb Carr: *The Alienist.* Hunting a serial killer in New York's turn-of-the-century demimonde.
Jim Carroll: *The Basketball Diaries.* Sex, drugs and coming of age on Manhattan's streets.
E.L. Doctorow: *The Waterworks.* A tale inspired by Edgar Allan Poe and set in late 19th-century New York.
Bret Easton Ellis: *American Psycho.* A serial killer is loose among the young and fabulous in 1980s New York.
Ralph Ellison: *Invisible Man.* Coming of age as a black man in 1950s New York.
Larry Kramer: *Faggots.* Hilarious gay New York.
Philip Lopate: *Writing New York.* An excellent eclectic anthology of short stories set in a New York.
Jay McInerney: *Bright Lights, Big City.* The dark side of Manhattan's glamourous life.
Toni Morrison: *Jazz.* Music and glamour of 1920s Harlem.
Hubert Selby Jr.: *Last Exit to Brooklyn.* Depicts 1960s Brooklyn dockland degradation.
Betty Smith: *A Tree Grows in Brooklyn.* An Irish girl in 1930s Brooklyn.
Edith Wharton: *Old New York.* Four novellas of 19th-century New York, by the author of *The Age of Innocence.*
Tom Wolfe: *Bonfire of the Vanities.* Rich/poor, black/white. An unmatched slice of 1980s New York.

History

Irving Lewis Allen: *The City in Slang.* How New York living has spawned hundreds of new words and phrases.
Federal Writers' Project: *The WPA Guide to New York City.* A wonderful snapshot of 1930s New York by the writers employed under FDR's New Deal.
Robert Fitch: *The Assassination of New York.* Essay on the economic death of New York in the 1980s.
Clifton Hood: *722 Miles: The Building of the Subways and How They Transformed New York.*
Kenneth T. Jackson: *The Encyclopedia of New York City.* The authoritative reference work on New York.
Rem Koolhaas: *Delirious New York.* New York as a terminal city. Urbanism and the culture of congestion.
David Levering Lewis: *When Harlem Was in Vogue.* A study of the 1920s Harlem renaissance.
Shaun O'Connell: *Remarkable, Unspeakable New York.* History of New York as literary inspiration.
Jacob Riis: *How the Other Half Lives.* Pioneering photojournalistic record of gruesome tenement life.
Roy Rosenzweig and Elizabeth Blackmar: *The Park and the People.* A lengthy history of Central Park.
Luc Sante: *Low Life.* Opium dens, brothels, tenements and suicide salons in 1840-1920s New York.
Bayrd Stilm: *Mirror for Gotham.* New York as seen by its inhabitants, from Dutch days to the present.
Mike Wallace: *Gotham: A History of New York City to 1898.* The first volume of a mammoth history of NYC.

Index

Advertisers' Index

'Scuse me while I kiss the sky: The Chrysler Building is the foxy lady of the NYC skyline.

Maps

Street Index

65th St Transverse
Rd - H2
79th St Transverse
Rd - H2
86th St Transverse
Rd - G2
97th St Transverse
Rd - G2

Academy St - A1
Adam Clayton Powell
Jr Blvd - D2, F2
Albany St - N2
Allen St - M3
Amsterdam Ave - C1-G1
Ann St - N2
Arden St - B1
Audubon Ave - B1
Audubon Terr - D1
Ave A - L3
Ave B - L3
Ave C - L3
Ave D - L3
Ave of the Americas
(Sixth Ave) - L2

Bank St - L1
Barclay St - N2
Barrow St - L1
Battery Pl - N2
Baxter St - M2
Beach St - M2
Bedford St - L2
Beekman St - N2
Bennett Ave - B1
Bethune St - L1
Bleecker St - L2
Bowery - L2, M2
Bridge St - N2
Broad St - N2
Bradhurst Ave - D1
Broadway - A1-H1
Broadway - K2-M2
Brooklyn Bridge - N3
Brooklyn-Battery
Tunnel - N2
Broome St - M2, 3

Cabrini Blvd - B1
Canal St - M2
Carmine St - M2
Catherine St - M3

Centre St - M2
Chambers St - M2
Charles St - L1
Charlton St - M2
Cherry St - M3
Chittenden Ave - B1
Christopher St - L1
Chrystie St - M3
Church St - M2
Claremont Ave - E1, F1
Clarkson St - M2
Clinton St - M3
Columbus Ave - F1
Convent Ave - E1
Cooper St - A1
Crosby St - M2

Delancey St - M3
Desbrosses St - M2
Dominick St - M2
Duane St - M2
Dyckman St - A1, B1

E 2nd St - L2, 3
E 4th St - L2, 3
E 6th St - L2, 3
E 8th St - L2, 3
E 10th St - L2, 3
E 12th St - L2, 3
E 14th St - L2, 3
E 16th St - L2
E 18th St - L2
E 20th St - L2
E 22nd St - K2
E 23rd St - K2, 3
E 26th St - K2
E 28th St - K2
E 30th St - K2, 3
E 32nd St - K2
E 34th St - K2, 3
E 36th St - K2, 3
E 38th St - K2, 3
E 40th St - K2
E 42nd St - J2, 3
E 44th St - J2, 3
E 46th St - J2, 3
E 48th St - J2, 3
E 50th St - J2, 3
E 52nd St - J2, 3
E 54th St - J2, 3
E 56th St - J2, 3

E 58th St - J2, 3
E 60th St - J2, 3
E 62nd St - J2, 3
E 64th St - H2, 3
E 66th St - H2, 3
E 68th St - H2, 3
E 70th St - H2, 3
E 72nd St - H2, 3
E 74th St - H2, 3
E 76th St - H2, 3
E 78th St - H2, 3
E 79th St - H2, 3
E 80th St - H2, 3
E 82nd St - H2, 3
E 84th St - G2, 3
E 86th St - G2, 3
E 88th St - G2, 3
E 90th St - G2, 3
E 92nd St - G2, 3
E 94th St - G2
E 96th St - G2
E 98th St - G2
E 100th St - G2, 3
E 102nd St - G2, 3
E 103rd St - F2
E 105th St - F2
E 107th St - F2
E 109th St - F2
E 110th St - F2
E 111th St - F2
E 113th St - F2
E 115th St - F2, 3
E 117th St - F2, 3
E 119th St - F2, 3
E 121st St - F2
E 123rd St - E2
E 125th St - E2
E 127th St - E2
E 129th St - E2
East Broadway - M3
East Drive - G2, H2
East End Ave - G3
East Houston St - L3
Edgecombe Ave - D1
Eighth Ave - J1, K1
Eldridge St - M3
Eleventh Ave - J1, K1
Elizabeth St - M2
Essex St - M3
Exchange Pl - N2
Exterior St - A1

Fifth Ave - E2-L2
First Ave - F3-K3
First Pl - N2
Forsyth St - M3
Fort Washington
Ave - B1, C1
Frankton St - N2
Franklin D Roosevelt
Dr - G3, K3, L3,
N2, 3
Franklin St - M2
Frederick Douglass
Blvd - D1, E1
Freedom Pl - H1
Front St - N2
Fulton St - N2

George Washington
Bridge - C1
Gold St - N2
Grand St - M2, 3
Greene St - M2
Greenwich Ave - L2
Greenwich St - L1,
M2, N2

Hamilton Place - E1
Harlem River Dr - C1,
D1, 2
Harrison St - M2
Haven Ave - C1
Henry Hudson
Pkwy - A1-H1
Henry St - M3
Hester St - M2
Horatio St - L1
Howard St - M2
Hubert St - M2
Hudson St - L1, 2, M2

Isham St - A1

Jackson St - M3
Jane St - L1
Joe DiMaggio Hwy
(West Side Hwy)
K1 - M2
John St - N2

Kenmare St - M2
King St - M2

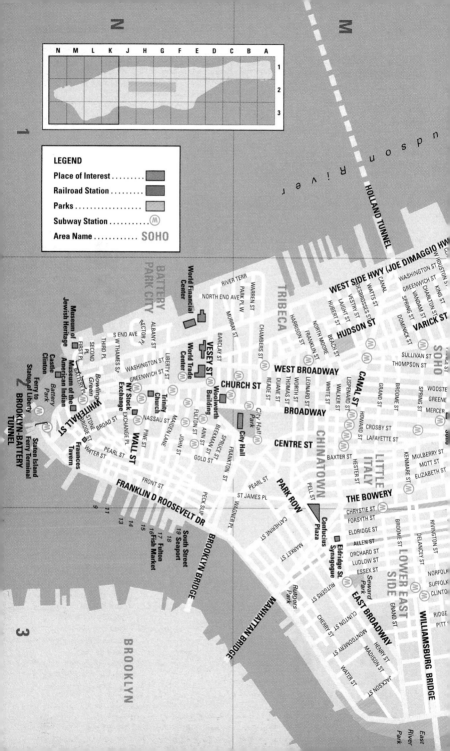

G

F

Soldiers' & Sailors' Monument

Riverside Church

W 88TH ST

Symphony Space

W 98TH ST
W 100TH ST
W 102ND ST
W 103RD ST

Barnard College

CLAREMON

WEST END AVE

W 115TH ST

W 98TH ST

Park

Riverside

Cathedral of St. John the Divine

W 121ST ST

BROADWAY

W 109TH ST

W 111TH ST
W 113TH ST

Columbia University

AMSTERDAM AVE

Cathedral Close

W 105TH ST
W 107TH ST

MORNINGSIDE DR

Morningside Park

UPPER WEST SIDE

W 96TH ST

COLUMBUS AVE

W 84TH ST
W 90TH ST
W 92ND ST
W 94TH ST

MANHATTAN AVE

W 86TH ST

FREDERICK Ⓜ **DOUGLASS BLVD**

WEST DRIVE

Central Park

9TH ST TRANSVERSE RD

The Pool

ADAM CLAYTON POWELL JR BLVD

86TH ST TRANSVERSE RD

WEST DRIVE

ST NICHOLAS AVE

Great Lawn

The Reservoir

Harlem Meer

LENOX AVE

EAST DRIVE

Conservatory Garden

Marcus Garvey Park

EAST DRIVE

Goethe

International Center of Photography

El Museo del Barrio

FIFTH AVE

E 86TH ST

Jewish Museum

E 96TH ST

Museum of the City of NY

SPANISH HARLEM

MADISON AVE

Cooper-Hewitt National Design Museum

E 105TH ST
E 107TH ST
E 109TH ST
E 111TH ST

PARK AVE

Guggenheim Museum

E 96TH ST

LEXINGTON AVE

YORKVILLE

E 113TH ST

E 121ST ST

E 84TH ST
E 88TH ST
E 90TH ST
E 92ND ST
E 94TH ST

E 100TH ST
E 102ND ST
E 103RD ST

E 115TH ST

THIRD AVE

SECOND AVE

E 117TH ST
E 119TH ST

FIRST AVE

Jefferson Park

FRANKLIN D ROOSEVELT DR

EAST END AVE

Carl Schurz Park

Gracie Mansion

N M L K J H G F E D C B A

1

2

3

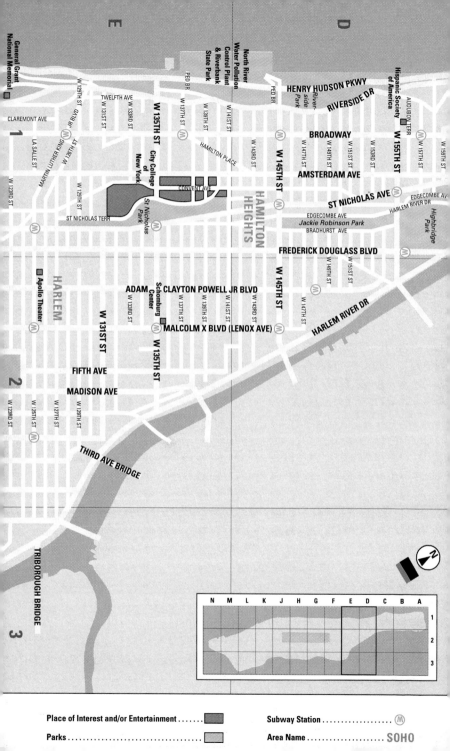

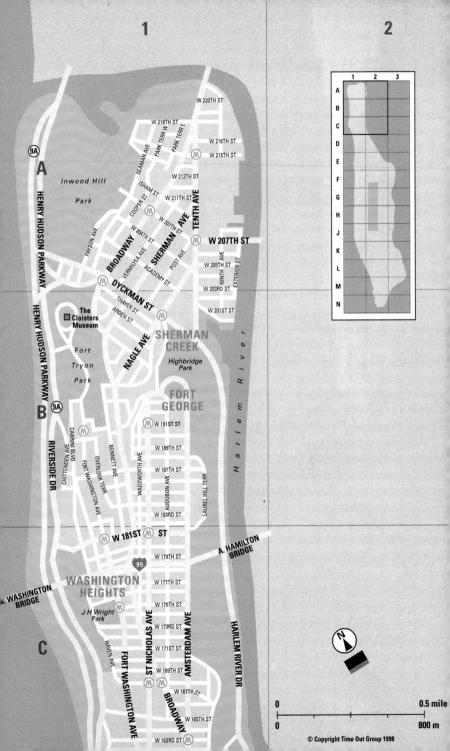

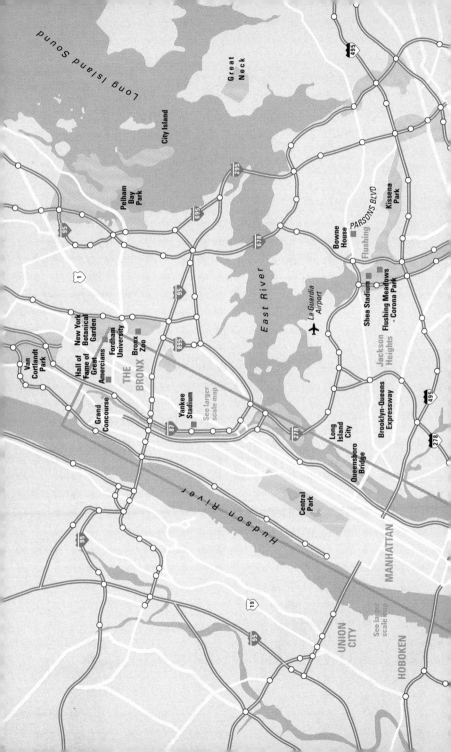

New York City

ATLANTIC OCEAN

QUEENS

BROOKLYN

Williamsburg

BUSHWICK AVENUE

LINDEN BOULEVARD

FLATBUSH AVENUE

OCEAN PARKWAY

4TH AVENUE

FORT HAMILTON PARKWAY

Bensonhurst

Bay Ridge

Brooklyn Bridge

Brooklyn Heights Promenade

Soldiers' & Sailors' Memorial Arch

Brooklyn Museum & Botanic Gardens

Prospect Park

Marine Park

Brighton Beach

Coney Island

JFK Airport

678

Jamaica Bay

Wildlife Refuge

Far Rockaway

Rockaway Inlet

Rockaway

Rockaway Point

Lower Bay

Upper Bay

Ellis Island

Liberty State Park

Liberty Island

JERSEY CITY

BAYONNE

Snug Harbor Cultural Center

STATEN ISLAND

278

278

78

5 km

3 miles

0

0

© Copyright Time Out Group 1998

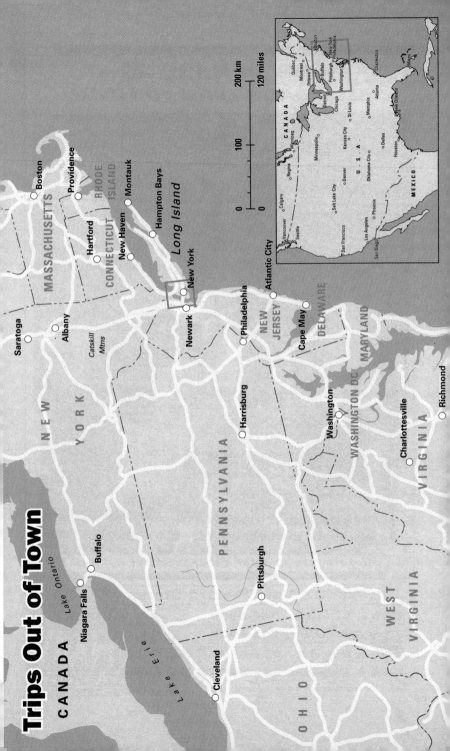

Trips Out of Town

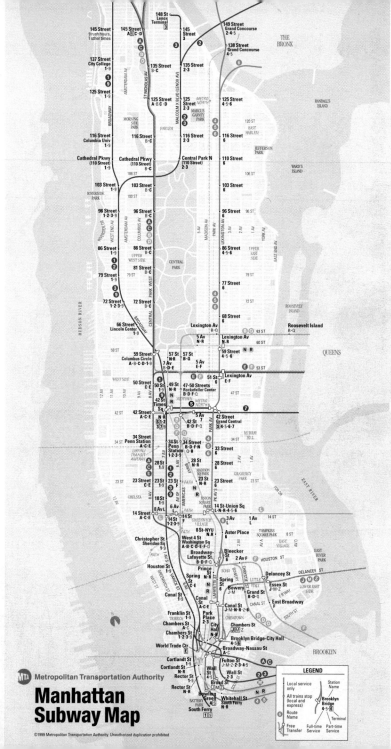

Manhattan
Subway Map

Metropolitan Transportation Authority

©1999 Metropolitan Transportation Authority Unauthorized duplication prohibited

LEGEND

Local service
only

All trains stop
(local and
express)

Route
Name

Free
Transfer

Station
Name

Brooklyn
Bridge
4·5·6

Terminal

Full-time
Service

Part-time
Service

MTA New York City Subway

Metropolitan Transportation Authority

Local service only

All trains stop
(local and express service)

Station served by
one of two lines

Free subway transfer

Rush hour service

Commuter rail service

Full time service

Part time service

Terminal

Local service

Express service

May 1999

© 1999 Metropolitan Transportation Authority
Design: Michael Hertz Associates, New York City

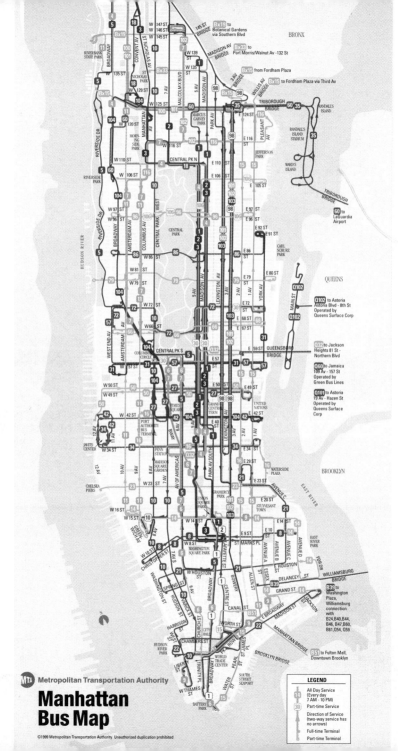

Metropolitan Transportation Authority

Manhattan
Bus Map

©1998 Metropolitan Transportation Authority Unauthorized duplication prohibited

TimeOut New York Guide — Please let us know what you think

About this guide...

1. How useful did you find the following sections? (19)

	Very	Fairly	Not very	
Welcome to New York	☐	☐	☐☐☐☐☐☐	(5)
New York by Neighborhood	☐	☐	☐☐☐☐☐☐	(6)
New York Necessities				(7)
Arts & Entertainment	☐	☐	☐☐☐☐☐☐	(8)
Trips Out of Town				(9)
Directory				(10)
Maps				(11)

2. Did you travel to New York? (17)

Alone? ☐   With partner? ☐☐☐
As part of group? ☐☐   With children? ☐☐☐
On business? ☐   I live here. ☐☐☐

3. How long was your trip to New York? (18)

Less than three days ☐☐☐☐
Three days to one week
One to two weeks
Over two weeks

4. Did you visit any other destinations in the USA? If so, which ones?

_____
_____
_____

5. Where did you get additional travel information from? (19)

Tourist Board ☐☐☐
Internet
Travel agents
Another guide book (please specify)

Other _____ (20/22)

6. Is there anything you'd like us to cover in greater depth?

_____

7. Are there any places that should/should not be included in the guide?

_____

8. How many other people have used this guide? (23)

none ☐ 1 ☐ 2 ☐ 3 ☐ 4 ☐ 5+ ☐

About other Time Out publications...

9. Have you ever bought/used Time Out magazine? (24)

Yes ☐   No ☐

10. Have you bought any other Time Out City Guides? (25)

Yes ☐   No ☐

If yes, which ones? (26/28)

11. Have you ever bought/used other Time Out publications? (29)

Yes ☐   No ☐

If yes, which ones? (30)

Film Guide ☐
Kids Out magazine
London Eating & Drinking Guide
London Pubs & Bars Guide
London Visitors' Guide
ici Londres
Paris Eating & Drinking Guide
Paris Free Guide
London Shopping Guide
Student Guide
Book of Country Walks
Book of London Walks
Book of Weekend Breaks (31)

Book of New York Short Stories ☐
Time Out New York magazine
Time Out New York Eating & Drinking Guide
Time Out Roma
Time Out Diary
www.timeout.com
www.timeoutny.com

About you...

12. First name: _____
Surname: _____
Address: _____

Postcode: _____ (32)

13. Year of birth _____

14. Sex: male ☐   female ☐ (43)

15. Are you: (44)

employed full-time
employed part-time
self-employed
unemployed
student
homemaker

16. At the moment do you earn: (45)

under £10,000 ☐☐☐☐☐☐
over £10,000 and up to £14,999
over £15,000 and up to £19,999
over £20,000 and up to £24,999
over £25,000 and up to £39,999
over £40,000 and up to £49,999
over £50,000 ☐☐☐☐☐☐☐

☐ Please tick here if you don't want to receive further information on related promotions or products.

Time Out Guides

FREEPOST 20 (WC3187)
LONDON
W1E 0DQ

City Guides are available from all good bookshops or through Penguin Direct.

Simply call 0181 899 4036 (9am-5pm) or fill out the form below, affix a stamp and return.

ISBN	title	retail price	quantity	total
0140273115	Time Out Guide to **Amsterdam**	£9.99		
0140273123	Time Out Guide to **Barcelona**	£9.99		
0140257187	Time Out Guide to **Berlin**	£9.99		
0140284052	Time Out Guide to **Boston**	£10.99		
0140273166	Time Out Guide to **Brussels**	£9.99		
014026745X	Time Out Guide to **Budapest**	£9.99		
0140266879	Time Out Guide to **Dublin**	£10.99		
0140266844	Time Out Guide to **Edinburgh**	£9.99		
0140266860	Time Out Guide to **Florence & Tuscany**	£10.99		
0140270620	Time Out Guide to **Las Vegas**	£9.99		
0140273158	Time Out Guide to **Lisbon**	£9.99		
0140274499	Time Out Guide to **London**	£9.99		
0140274456	Time Out Guide to **Los Angeles**	£9.99		
014027443X	Time Out Guide to **Madrid**	£9.99		
0140266852	Time Out Guide to **Miami**	£9.99		
014027314X	Time Out Guide to **Moscow**	£9.99		
0140274480	Time Out Guide to **New Orleans**	£9.99		
0140273107	Time Out Guide to **New York**	£9.99		
0140274510	Time Out Guide to **Paris**	£9.99		
0140274448	Time Out Guide to **Prague**	£9.99		
0140266887	Time Out Guide to **Rome**	£9.99		
0140267468	Time Out Guide to **San Francisco**	£9.99		
0140259732	Time Out Guide to **Sydney**	£9.99		
0140284060	Time Out Guide to **Venice**	£10.99		
		+ postage & packing		£1.50
		Total Payment		

(Please Use Block Capitals)

Cardholder's Name _____

Address _____

Town _____ Postcode _____

Daytime Telephone Number _____

Method of Payment (UK Credit cards only)

Barclaycard/Visa

☐☐☐☐ ☐☐☐☐ ☐☐☐☐ ☐☐☐☐

Access Card/Mastercard

☐☐☐☐ ☐☐☐☐ ☐☐☐☐ ☐☐☐☐

Signature (if paying by credit card) _____

Expiry date ☐☐ . ☐☐

Cheque

I enclose a cheque £ _____ made payable to Penguin Direct

Delivery will normally be within 14 working days. The availability and published prices quoted are correct at time of going to press but are subject to alteration without prior notice. Order form valid until May 2000. **Please note that this service is only available in the UK.** Please note your order may be delayed if payment details are incorrect.

Penguin Direct
Penguin Books Ltd
Bath Road
Harmondsworth
West Drayton
Middlesex
UB7 0DA